An Introduction to
SOCIAL PSYCHOLOGY

An Introduction to

RICHARD DEWEY, Ph.D.
Department of Sociology
University of New Hampshire

W. J. HUMBER, Ph.D.
Consulting Psychologist
Humber, Mundie & McClary
Milwaukee, Wisconsin

SOCIAL PSYCHOLOGY

The Macmillan Company
NEW YORK

Collier-Macmillan Limited
LONDON

9/16/74

Second Printing, 1966

Earlier edition, entitled
The Development of Human Behavior,
copyright 1951
by The Macmillan Company.

Library of Congress catalog card number: 66-18201

THE MACMILLAN COMPANY, NEW YORK
COLLIER-MACMILLAN CANADA, LTD., TORONTO, ONTARIO

Printed in the United States of America

PREFACE

The problems of social psychology are not of recent origin, nor are all of the facts and ideas about these problems new. This apparent platitude is a necessary part of any introduction to the field of social psychology. In a society afflicted with *neophilia*, where crazes, fads, and fashions render obsolete so many items once dear to us—automobiles, hats, evening gowns, architecture, tastes in music, and so on—one is very apt to regard as obsolete ideas that have been with us for more than a few years. A truth easily forgotten is that truth knows no temporal tests. Neither novelty nor hoary age is an adequate standard by which to measure the validity of an idea. The waxing or waning popularity of ideas, however lucidly explained sociologically or social-psychologically, can never be justified as reason for the adoption or rejection of these ideas. A social psychologist has recently drawn this fact to the attention of his readers:

> Fashions have their amusing and serious side. We can smile over the way bearded problems receive tonsorial transformation. Having tired of "suggestibility" we adopt the new hairdo known as "persuasibility." Modern ethology excites us, and we are not troubled by the recollection that a century ago John Stuart Mill staked down the term to designate the new science of human character. We like the neurological concept of "gaiting," conveniently forgetting that American functionalism always stood firm for the dominance of general mental sets over specific. Reinforcement appeals to us but not the age-long debate over hedonism. The problem of freedom we brush aside in favor of "choice points." We avoid the body-mind problem but are in fashion when we talk about "brain models." Old wine, we find, tastes better in new bottles.
>
> The serious side of the matter enters when we and our students forget that the wine is indeed old.[1]

From the sociological side P. A. Sorokin has called attention to this problem under his chapter entitled "Amnesia and the New Columbuses."[2]

It has been our intent to select those facts and to adopt those ideas that seem most clearly applicable to the study of human behavior and that are related, thus providing order in the frame of reference. Awareness of more recent publications on given topics is occasionally countered by

[1] G. W. Allport, "The Open System in Personality Theory," *Journal of Abnormal and Social Psychology, 61* (1961), 301.

[2] P. A. Sorokin, *Fads and Foibles in Modern Sociology and Related Sciences* (Chicago: Henry Regnery Company, 1956).

preference—we hope with good reason—for the earlier conceptual or factual statement. Thus, ideas utilized in this text are drawn from all ages with the conviction that the validity of ideas (concepts) is determined by their contribution to understanding rather than by their authorship or age.

The kinds of ideas and facts which we believe should be presented to the student who is beginning his study of social psychology are of a broad and general nature. We seek to provide those facts and concepts that will be of value to the educated adult as he encounters novel as well as familiar events in his tour of life, and do not pretend to provide him with the esoteric, vanguard ideas of the specialist in social psychology.

Finally, the text is written with undergraduates in mind, especially those who have not studied extensively in either psychology or sociology. It is in terms of the academic abilities and needs of such students that facts and concepts have been selected for this book. This approach is based upon the conviction that many, if not most, of the world's social problems exist because the populace does not possess elementary knowledge of the social sciences. This conviction is drawn from the authors' experiences of a quarter of a century of research, consulting, and teaching, the last having taken place in eleven different colleges and universities, ranging from small private schools to large, public universities.

R. D.
W. J. H.

CONTENTS

9. PERSONALITY TYPES: I. ROLE BEHAVIOR TYPES   328

Role behavior types: introverted-extraverted; inner-directed and other-directed; Thomas' and Znaniecki's social types; the homosexual.

10. PERSONALITY TYPES: II. POSITION OR STATUS TYPES, STEREO-TYPES, AND RESULTANT ROLE TYPES   356

The vicious circle and personality; prejudices and discrimination of dominant group; prejudice—sources of; discrimination as environmental influence; restricted social and economic life chances; reduced communication between majority and disadvantaged minority; Negro personality types; Jewish personality types; social stratification and personality types.

11. PERSONALITY IN RIOTS, MOBS, AND PANICS   421

Illustrations of riots, mob action, and panic group actions; social psychology of crowd and mob behavior: biological heritage—environment—acquired personal attributes; abstract and concrete crowds.

SOCIAL PSYCHOLOGY OF AGE GROUPS   PART III
                                                                    page 441

12. INFANCY AND PRESCHOOL YEARS   445

Interactive behavior in early months; fashions and fads in infant training practices; cross cultural comparisons of child training practices; biological maturation; socialization and enculturation—parent-child relationship; role learning in infancy; critical stages of learning; sibling relationship; development of selfhood and personality in the infant and preschool child; language and the self.

13. CHILDHOOD   488

Physiological development; relationship of physical features and self concept; child development and the cultural processes: role learning experiences; neighborhood and school relationships; character development and curriculum content; influence of the class structure on learning experiences; personality development in childhood.

ILLUSTRATIONS

TABLES

PART I

The Organism-Environment-Subject Frame of Reference

There are many social psychologies. Every person has his own set of social psychological concepts or ideas, with their accompanying labels, *with reference to which* he interprets his own and others' experiences, and *in terms of which* he thinks about his experiences, and expresses or communicates his thoughts and feelings. Each person's actions reflect his ideas about man's biological nature, the nature of human beliefs, attitudes, and motives, as well as the nature of all that constitutes the human environment. Most people have not had the opportunity to construct systematic, integrated conceptual systems of social psychology. Accordingly, the essence of a textbook in social psychology is the presentation of such a systematic framework of concepts, with appropriate symbols, that will enable the reader to think clearly about the nature of experiences and behavior, to perceive accurately the nature of human behavior, and to communicate his thoughts and feelings unambiguously.

The conceptual scheme that is employed in this text is drawn from numerous sources, among them the *Chicago school* of social psychology, which approach is usually associated with the varied works of L. Guy Brown, Charles Horton Cooley, John Dewey, Ellsworth Faris, George Herbert Mead, W. I. Thomas, and Florian Znaniecki. Rather than designate this conceptual system as a *symbolic-interactionist* or a *bio-social* framework, terms that may be familiar to the reader, we have chosen to call the approach employed here the *organism-environment-subject interactionist* frame of reference.

Although we recognize the very significant part played by language in human behavior, we do not emphasize it to the point that we would be warranted in calling our approach symbolic-interaction.

Symbolic systems are but one of several interactive variables, and cannot be given the status of independent variable. Too, although much of man's behavior is indeed bio-social in nature, it is more than that, and includes non-symbolic and non-social factors.

By its trinomial nature, the phrase *organism-environment-subject interaction* denotes that human behavior, and therefore personality, always involve three components, 1. man's biological or organic heritage, 2. his bio-social-physical environment, and 3. the subject's own knowledge, beliefs, feelings, and motives. For convenience, however, we shall henceforth use the simpler term *interaction*, or *interactionist*, to designate the tri-partite conceptual framework that is developed and applied in this book. In Part I the authors are analytical in their treatment of the three basic categories of personality components, but the analysis is carried out with a constant awareness that an item from any one category is meaningless except as it is related to appropriate items in the other two categories.

Perceptive men throughout the centuries have observed this need to study man with reference to his many relationships. Noteworthy is the familiar seventeenth century comment of John Donne:

> No man is an island, entire of himself; every man is a piece of the continent, a part of the main; if a clod be washed away by the sea, Europe is the less, as well as if a promontory were, as well as if a manor of thy friends or of thine own were; any man's death diminishes me because I am involved in mankind; and therefore never send to know for whom the bell tolls; it tolls for thee.

CHAPTER 1

DIMENSIONS OF SOCIAL PSYCHOLOGY

Social psychology . . . seeks to understand and account for those uniformities in feeling, belief, or volition—and hence in action—which are due to the interaction of human beings.
—*E. A. Ross. Social Psychology,* 1908, the first social psychology textbook

Social psychology is the study of the individual human being as he interacts, largely symbolically, with his environment. It studies the processes involved in this interaction between the individual and his world, and also a major result of this interaction, namely, personality. Even though social psychology as a separate discipline is of relatively recent origin, there is much agreement, if not general consensus, among social psychologists as to its field of inquiry.[1] However, even though current definitions of social psychology, as suggested by the foregoing footnote, make explicit or imply the interactional or relational nature of social psychology's data, they also usually restrict this relationship to *social* interaction. Careful study of the works noted reveals that social psychology's concern

---

[1] "With a few exceptions, social psychologists regard their discipline as *an attempt to understand and explain how the thought, feeling, and behavior of individuals are influenced by the actual, imagined, or implied presence of other human beings.*" Gordon Allport, "The Historical Background of Modern Social Psychology," in G. Lindzey (ed.) *Handbook of Social Psychology* (Cambridge: Addison-Wesley Press, 1954), p. 5. "Social Psychology may therefore be broadly viewed as the science of the behavior of the individual in society." David Krech, Richard S. Crutchfield, and Egerton L. Ballachey, *Individual in Society* (New York: McGraw-Hill Book Company, 1962) p. 4; Social psychology is concerned with ". . . explaining behavior of individuals as it is controlled, influenced or limited by the social environment." Alfred Lindesmith and Anselm Strauss, *Social Psychology* (New York: The Dryden Press, 1956) p. 3; "Social psychology is the scientific study of the experience and behavior of individuals in relation to social stimulus situations." M. Sherif and C. W. Sherif, *An Outline of Social Psychology,* rev. ed. (New York: Harper and Brothers, 1956) p. 4; "In short, social psychology is primarily focused upon those aspects of social behavior found when men interact with one another in manifest social relationships." E. L. Hartley and R. E. Hartley, *Fundamentals of Social Psychology* (New York: Alfred A. Knopf, 1959), p. 5; Attention of social psychology is ". . . focused only upon those regularities in human behavior that arise out of the fact that men are participants in social groups." T. Shibutani, *Society and Personality* (Englewood Cliffs, N.J.: Prentice Hall, 1961) p. 20; This list is not exhaustive, nor is it selected on the basis of judgments of quality concerning the books included; it is merely quantitatively representative of current thinking by both "psychological" social psychologists and "sociological" social psychologists.

3

is not purely social, and our experience has indicated the desirability of making this point explicit. Indeed, one of the sources quoted gives attention to this point.

> Restricting the definition of social psychology to the study of experience and behavior in relation to other people, leaving out their cultural products as stimulus situations, would amount to writing social psychology as though people were living in a pre-Stone Age (whatever that might have been).[2]

We could go even further, and suggest that a purely *social* psychology would amount to a study of angels, devoid of a world and its nonhuman objects.[3] As one reads through this or any other text, the great importance of man's relationships with nonhuman objects for the explanation of his personality becomes increasingly apparent. The concepts of wealth and property owe their significance mainly to this human-nonhuman relationship. Although the term *social psychology* is too well established in our current vocabulary to be abandoned now, it is reasonable to expect that in time a new term, perhaps *sociocultural psychology*, will become popular. The latter term denotes more accurately the nature of social psychological data.[4]

---

[2] M. Sherif and C. W. Sherif, *op. cit.*, p. 21. One social psychologist makes the nonsocial aspect of social psychology explicit: "Social psychology is the study of how human behavior is influenced by the presence, behavior, and *products* of other human beings, individually and collectively, past, present, and future." Joseph E. McGrath, *Social Psychology* (New York: Holt, Rinehart, and Winston, 1964) p. 1. Italics added.

[3] The word *object* denotes anything—tangible or intangible, material or non-material, human or nonhuman—the nature of which can be sensed, thought about, or known. Thus a book, an occupation, the self, an idea, a fear, a city, a disease, a theory, a sentence—are all objects of the senses or of the cognitive or mental processes. Even though an individual is an *object*, when he is the point of departure, the reference point, he becomes the subject and as such is contrasted with objects about which he has ideas, feelings, knowledge, and beliefs. Some psychologists, social psychologists, and sociologists prefer to use the terms *ego* and *alter* to denote the "self-and-other," or subject-object relationship.

[4] There are general problems involved in the current designations of academic disciplines. One student of human activity had this to say: "I feel the need to say that I much prefer the phrase, 'the social studies' to 'the social sciences'—not because I do not like physical scientists (on the contrary, I do, very much), but because the word 'science' has acquired great prestige and rather imprecise meaning. I do not feel any need to kidnap the prestige or to make the meaning even less precise by using it as a philosophical metaphor. Yet I suspect that if I wrote about 'the social studies,' readers would think only of high school civics, which of all fields of human learning is the one with which I most wish to avoid association. 'The Behavioral Sciences' is simply impossible; it was thought up, I suppose, as a propaganda device to get money for social research from Foundations and Congressmen who confuse 'social science' with 'socialism.' The best term would include history (and psychology, so far as it is concerned with human beings), and should be as non-controversial as possible, for we should argue *with* terms, not fight *over* them. Perhaps 'the human disciplines' would do." C. Wright Mills, *The Sociological Imagination* (New York: Grove Press, 1961), p. 18.

Psychology, especially physiological psychology, concerns itself with the human behavior potentials and seeks knowledge about the individual that is relatively free from social or cultural influences (knowledge about intelligence, emotions, learning, neurological capacities, unlearned impulses or drives, tension limits, and so on). The sociologist, on the other hand, studies customs and organizations, the patterned groupways and groupings involving persons, nonmaterial and material cultural products. Taking into account the data selected by both the psychologist and the sociologist, the social psychologist would focus, not upon the individual per se, nor upon the groups and institutions as such, but upon the way in which the individual and his environment interact. Thus social psychology is a field of study that is interstitial to psychology and sociology and holds the same relationship to these two fields as biophysics does to biology and physics. If one wishes to speak in terms of the *units* or *elements* of study, the psychologist's unit is the individual, the sociologist's unit is found in institutions and society itself, but the unit of study of the social psychologist is the interaction of individuals with other persons and with nonhuman objects. The social psychological unit of analysis is not the acting person, but at the very least, an *episode* that involves the person plus other objects.[5] This point will be developed further in Chapter 2.

The social psychologist's data are the behavior patterns, involving at least one individual and an object or objects, in which some change in the objects and/or some altered relationship occur. It may be a simple episode such as one person's influencing another to accompany him on a trip to a museum; it may be as involved as a person's being converted from one organized religion to another, or as a person murdering or marrying another. Whatever the action, it always involves interaction between an object and the subject in a sociocultural setting.[6]

As in other disciplines, it is important in social psychology to see *interrelationships* as a key concept. The social psychologist studies the processes involved in this interaction as well as the end product of these processes, namely, the personality which is itself a relationship involving, but not restricted to, the individual. This study includes the study of attitudes and behavior traits that all persons have in common, and the processes by which these attitudes and traits develop. The social psychologist inquires into the basic needs of man as a sociocultural being, and into the variety of ways in which these basic biogenic (innate,

[5] Nelson Foote, "Concept and Method in the Study of Human Development," in M. Sherif and M. O. Wilson (eds.), *Emerging Problems in Social Psychology*, The University of Oklahoma Lectures in Social Psychology; (published by the University Book Exchange Duplicating Service, 1957) p. 34.

[6] As will become clear in Chapter 2, the object may be a property of the subject himself, such as his body and parts thereof, or some attitude or idea of his, insofar as the interaction is a function of real or imputed attitudes of another human being.

unlearned) and sociogenic (acquired, learned) needs can be satisfied through interaction. He is interested in those features of social behavior that individuals in all cultures share in common. His datum is not the individual as such, nor is it the social group or institution, but the individual in action, the sociocultural interchange. Social psychology is a discipline in its own right, and is a branch of older fields of study only in the sense that each discipline is an abstraction, focusing on certain facets of the complex whole of sociocultural life.

THE DEVELOPMENT OF SOCIAL PSYCHOLOGY

Both the data and the attending problems with which we are concerned in this text existed many centuries before the term *social psychology* was born.[7] The serious literature of the ages, both fictional and nonfictional, has dealt at length and in depth with the interpersonal relationships which bulk large in today's social psychological writings. The heritage of philosophy from the ancient Greeks is filled with ideas and insights which we recognize today as being social psychological in nature. Their successors, from the immediate post-classical times to the present, sought answers to the same questions about human behavior. Social psychological theories and hypotheses are implicit in all writings about man's relationship to man, and are quite explicit in many. There is much concern with social psychological relationships throughout the Old Testament, and some of these relationships are also treated in the New Testament and the Koran, but with some novel departures. Toward the latter third of the nineteenth century, the confluence of several streams of thought set the stage for the appearance of what we know distinctively as social psychology. Philosophers were pursuing once again their quest for an understanding of man's actions, a quest that had been interrupted by the centuries-long practice of accepting only those ideas which were compatible with established (usually religious) dogma. The events of the fourteenth and fifteenth centuries, the Renaissance, broke the dike of custom which for so long had discouraged any departure from the narrowed channel of culture, and gave rise to a flood of questions, hypotheses and counter hypotheses, and many tentative new answers to millenia-old inquiries. Turning first to classical writings for answers in hitherto sacrosanct areas, and then to newer approaches, men began to question experience. Successes of biological and physical inquiries sponsored efforts to seek comparable rewards in the form of acceptable answers to the problems of social behavior that had plagued mankind for so long.

---

[7] Gordon W. Allport, "The Historical Background of Modern Social Psychology," in Gardner Lindzey (ed.) *Handbook of Social Psychology*, II (Cambridge, Mass.: Addison-Wesley, 1954), pp. 3–56.

Early efforts in psychology remained close to biology, and much was learned about the physiological potentialities of mankind at this level of inquiry. Gradually, however, some of the broader questions about human action came under the purview of psychologists and in the middle of the nineteenth century there arose in Germany a *folk psychology*[8] which inquired into the nature of man's relationships to his fellow man. Wilhelm Wundt (1832–1921) used the term *völkerpsychologie* but his interests were only indirectly related to those which characterize social psychology of today. However, he saw as the two main branches of "scientific psychology" experimental psychology and social psychology, the latter having as its data language, myth, and custom. Wundt perceived the need for a broader approach to the study of behavior but failed to escape an individualistic approach to the problems.[9]

The founder of sociology, Auguste Comte (1798–1857), did not include psychology as such in his well-known hierarchy of sciences, but claimed for sociology all phases except physiological psychology.

The first textbooks in social psychology appeared in 1908, one written by a psychologist and the other by a sociologist. Each based his book upon concepts that have since fallen into disuse or disrepute, but each illustrated the interest that the psychologist and the sociologist had in the area of social psychology.[10] The Ross book leaned heavily upon imitation as the key process in social behavior, and McDougall relied upon instincts for his motivational base. In 1913 Charles Ellwood wrote *Sociology in its Psychological Aspects* (New York: D. Appleton and Co.), in which he asserted that:

> The aim of social psychology is to give a psychological theory of social organization and evolution. It may be, therefore, best defined as the *psychological aspects of sociology*. A more accurate name for social psychology would be, then "psychological sociology."[11]

[8] One usually encounters the names of Moritz Lazarus (1824–1903) and Hermann Steinthal (1823–1899) in histories of psychology and social psychology. That these men were in the stream of events which led to modern social psychology is not to be denied, but a clear and direct relationship is not discernible. Their journal, *Zeitschrift fur Vokerpsychologie und Sprachwissenschaft*, first published in 1860, concerned itself primarily with philosophy and anthropology.

[9] *American Journal of Psychology*, 32 (1921), 166 ff. *See also* Fay B. Karpf, *American Social Psychology* (New York: McGraw-Hill Book Co., 1932) for treatment of Herbart, Lazarus, Steinthal, Wundt, and other contributors to the early development of social psychology. *See also* Lee J. Cronbach, "The Two Disciplines of Scientific Psychology," *American Psychologist*, 12 (1957), pp. 671–684.

[10] William McDougall, *An Introduction to Social Psychology* (London: Methuen & Co., Ltd., 1908); and E. A. Ross, *Social Psychology* (New York: The Macmillan Company, 1908).

[11] It is of some interest to note that in 1917 Ellwood apparently gave up his fight for "psychological sociology" and published *An Introduction to Social Psychology* (New York: D. Appleton & Co., 1917).

A counterclaim for psychology was made by Floyd Allport, who wrote that:

> Psychology in general and social psychology in particular, are thus foundation sciences of sociology. Social psychology has in fact grown up largely through the labors of the sociologists. It is a mistake, however, to suppose, as some have done, that it is a branch of sociology rather than of psychology.[12]

This particular tug-of-war between psychologists and sociologists involving social psychology was but one phase of a time-honored contest between these academic departments. Separate forms of particularistic explanations arose in the camps of these two intellectual protagonists which gave rise to futile controversies about heredity *versus* environment, instinct *versus* group mind, individual *versus* group, and so on. However, certain trends were under way that enabled both psychologists and sociologists to break through these parochial conceptions of human behavior and afforded them an opportunity to reconcile their apparent differences.

One of the first casualties was the demise of the *group mind* fallacy, which argued that there was some sort of intellect and will separate from the interacting individuals. Even though relatively few persons in the social sciences subscribed to this idea in its most extreme form, it did have its followers. This idea is not, however, as naïve as might at first appear. It arose as a function of the realization that man does, indeed, behave very differently in various kinds of groups than when he is alone. In the group mind we find another instance of a concept which, although demonstrably false, yields valuable insight. Its effectiveness ended for all intents and purposes in the mid-1920's, but it was still important enough to induce Floyd Allport to criticize it extensively in 1924.[13]

A much worthier opponent and a real barrier to the development of a truly social psychology among psychologists was the doctrine of instincts. As long as there seemed to be innate drives together with innate directives for the solution of the drives or impulses, there was little need for a social psychology with its social processes to explain human behavior. Instincts were used to explain wars, love-making, selection of occupations, criminal acts, mother love, self preservation, and so on. The instinct

---

[12] *Social Psychology* (Boston: Houghton Mifflin Co., 1924), p. 11. Allport was quite specific in his identification of social psychology. In his words: "There is no psychology of groups which is not essentially and entirely a psychology of individuals. Social psychology must not be placed in contra-distinction to the psychology of the individual; *it is part of the psychology of the individual*, whose behavior it studies in relation to that sector of his environment comprised by his fellows. His biological needs are the ends toward which his social behavior is a developed means. Within his organism are provided all the mechanisms by which social behavior is explained." p. 4. This was a common view of the time, but was modified for reasons which will be detailed later in this chapter. Italics in original.

[13] *Ibid.*, pp. 4–9.

hypothesis was generally accepted by social scientists during the latter part of the nineteenth century and the first two decades of the twentieth century. As late as 1922, it was observed that:

> Within recent years whole philosophies, social systems, economic structures have been erected with instincts as their foundation.[14]

Even so, the validity of this hypothesis began to be challenged by a variety of writers in psychology and sociology about the time of World War I. Writing in 1921 John Dewey anticipated the rejection of the instinct hypothesis by stating that:

> The use of the words instinct and impulse as practical equivalents is intentional, even though it may grieve critical readers. The word instinct is still too laden with the older notion that an instinct is always definitely organized and adapted—which for the most part is just what it is not in human beings. The word impulse suggests something primitive, yet loose, undirected, initial. Man can progress as beasts cannot, precisely because he has so many "instincts" that they cut across each other so that most serviceable actions must be *learned*.[15]

Although the thinking of psychologist Charles Josey had not at that time developed fully on this point, his *The Social Philosophy of Instinct* (written in 1922), must also be counted among the earliest works to raise many pertinent questions which challenged the instinct school. There were additional articles of this sort, but it remained for L. L. Bernard's *Instinct: A Study in Social Psychology* (1924) to apply the *coup de grace* to this approach and to end effectively this phase of individual psychology's history.[16] With the surrendering of the instinct hypothesis, suddenly and readily by some but gradually and reluctantly by others, both psychologists and sociologists sought elsewhere for explanations of the behavior of individuals.

At this time, moreover, there flourished another school of psychology which provided a second reason for the growing interest in social factors in psychological behavior. The *behavioristic* movement began to pervade several of the academic disciplines in the 1920's and in social psychology was especially evident in the writings of John Dewey and George Herbert Mead who were associated with the "Chicago school" of social psychology.

---

[14] Henry C. Link, "Instinct and Value," *American Journal of Psychology*, XXXIII (Jan., 1922), 1.

[15] John Dewey, *Human Nature and Conduct* (New York: Henry Holt & Co., 1921), fn. on p. 105. Italics in original. Other sources of criticism of the instinct hypothesis are Ellsworth Faris, "Are Instincts Data or Hypotheses?" *American Journal of Sociology*, XXVII (Sept. 1921), 188; Morris Ginsberg, *The Psychology of Society* (London: Methuen & Co., Ltd., 1921) p. 21.

[16] See Frank A. Beach, "The Descent of Instinct," in E. P. Hollander and R. G. Hunt (eds.) *Current Perspectives in Social Psychology* (New York: Oxford University Press, 1963), pp. 54–63.

This conceptual approach, contributed to by many but given its most popular treatment by John B. Watson, stressed the importance of focusing attention upon the actual, observable behavior of people. The behaviorists, viewing the original tendencies of the human being as highly modifiable (to untenable extremes at times), turned psychologists' attention to the influences of environments upon the overt behavior of the human organism. In time there occurred a confluence of ideas by psychologists and sociologists about the relationship of the individual and his surroundings. The view that the individual and the group are two aspects of the same thing, inextricably tied together by social processes (an idea given voice early by Charles Horton Cooley) became commonly accepted among social psychologists, whether psychologically or sociologically oriented. The behavioristic movement is generally thought of as a phase of individual psychology; but with certain modifications its concepts fit well into the later schools of social psychology which emphasize the interrelationship of the sociocultural and biological factors in the emergence of the behavioral aspects of human nature or personality.

Explanation of the nature of social psychology today would be incomplete without references to the tremendous impact upon all of the social sciences of Sigmund Freud (1865–1939). Though he has been variously interpreted, and his works have been perceived as supporting a number of schools of psychology and social psychology, an acquaintance with his writings reveals the importance he places upon experiences throughout life, but especially in the early years, in shaping the personality. Even with his emphasis upon innate tendencies which are instinctive in character, he stressed the interaction between these tendencies and the persons with whom the child was in contact during formative years. Many a social psychologist, and layman as well, has used variations on the Freudian theme, and often without being aware of the origin of the ideas. It was through the popularity of Freud's works and ideas that the importance of the unconscious aspects of the person's subjective life came to be recognized, although the concept of the unconscious did not originate with Freud. Thus this important influence in psychology helped shape the nature of social psychology's development.

A less important reason for the change in the direction of social psychological content in psychology is found in the confusion in the minds of the general public and college students between psychology in general and social psychology. For a number of years it was (in fact, it still is) common to hear students in introductory courses in psychology complain that they were studying physiology rather than psychology. They were, and are, often expecting to study social psychology and not psychology per se in the introductory course. That this external pressure has been of some significance in the development of social psychological courses in psychology departments seems likely. Some years ago one of the best sellers among introductory psychology texts was designed originally in response to the expressed desires of persons who were not psychologists, but who apparently identified psychology with social psychology.[17]

As a result of the pressures from both within and without the field, psychology has, over the last twoscore years, turned more and more to the subject matter and approach of social psychology. Introductory text books in psychology, (although including adequate coverage of maturation, sensory equipment, emotions, biogenic motives, learning, and conditioning), include discussions of social influences, class differences, personality, and other explicitly social materials.[18] That this would be the case was the prophecy of John Dewey in 1917, when he wrote; "I foresee, then, a great reflex wave from social psychology back into psychology."[19] Events since then certainly have shown his prophecy to be true.

Among today's introductory sociology textbooks, the one failing to devote one or more chapters to social psychological topics is rare indeed. That this inclusion of social psychological topics in introductory sociology texts is not of recent origin is evidenced by the statement in the first American textbook in sociology to the effect that:

> . . . all of the phenomena of society find their explanations in physical force. . . The student of society, therefore, must penetrate more outward manifestations, and seek to learn the nature of the influences which lie back of them. . . Without attempting at present to draw any hard and fast lines in the general field of social sciences, we would emphasize the peculiarly important character of the considerations involved in the psychical nature of society.[20]

[17] Dale Wolfle, "The First Course in Psychology," *Psychological Bulletin*, XXXIX (1942), 685–712.

[18] C. M. Loutitt, in a study of "Publication Trends in Psychology, 1894–1954" (*American Psychologist*, 12, Jan. 1957), reported that, whereas publications in general and physiological psychology declined during these years, explicitly social psychological articles showed an increase, as did other areas of psychology which have marked social psychological content, *e.g.* developmental, clinical, and educational psychology. The field of industrial psychology has added to this growing emphasis upon the interactional aspects of behavior.

[19] "The Need for Social Psychology," *Psychological Review*, XXIV (1917), 271. *See also* G. H. Mead, "Social Psychology as a Counterpart to Physiological Psychology," *Psychological Bulletin*, VI, pp. 401–408. That the "great reflex wave" predicted by John Dewey did not occur immediately is made clear by the American Psychological Association's President in his address in 1951. Dr. Robert Sears urged psychologists to abandon the "monadic" approach of studying the isolated person and turn attention to "diadic" approaches which always involve at least two actors.

[20] A. W. Small and G. E. Vincent, *Introduction to the Study of Society* (New York: American Book Company, 1894), pp. 305–306. Similar views appeared in other early sociology works, *Cp.* Franklin P. Giddings, *Elements of Sociology* (New York: The Macmillan Company, 1898), and R. E. Park and E. W. Burgess, in their widely influential book, *Introduction to the Science of Sociology* (Chicago: University of Chicago Press, 1921).

There is lack of a clear-cut division of labor among social psychologists, with social psychology courses (under a variety of names) showing up with great frequency in departments of psychology, sociology, education, philosophy, and anthropology. Consensus still eludes social psychologists; yet there is a continuing trend toward agreement among them, regardless of their academic home. The confusions and overlapping, and unfortunate isolation of scholars studying the same data, are as much functions of our system of college and university departments as they are of fundamental disagreement concerning the nature of the data or of the research techniques to be used. A large proportion of both psychologists and sociologists clearly indicate interests in social psychology in their membership designations in the American Psychological Association and the American Sociological Association, but very few are members of both organizations. Again, this is to be explained by the occupational labels, and the vested interest of each group in its respective department. The situation as it existed as recently as 1948, and which reflected the nature of the historical development of social psychology, was succinctly summed up by Professor T. M. Newcomb in the following paragraph:

> The history of social psychology may be likened to the digging of a tunnel. Sociologists did the first digging, starting from their own side of the mountain. Their information as to what lay on the psychological side of the mountain was necessarily limited and was mainly applied by way of speculation and analogy. The psychologists, who started burrowing somewhat later, had a vague sense of direction, but no map of the terrain where they needed to emerge. The two tunnels have been a-building for more than a half-century now, and they are still nowhere near meeting. They are not even going toward each other. The two teams of engineers scarcely bother to read each other's maps, though they have free access to them.[21]

Nevertheless, despite the fact that this picture is not entirely outmoded even today, the pressure of the logic of events and the continued fruitful exploitation of the concepts that involve more than the culture or the individual alone, have resulted in a growing consensus about the nature of social psychology, both in respect to data and approaches to the understanding of these data.

Despite continuing confusion and controversy over important concepts and preferred research orientations, there are convergencies in social psychology today which can best be referred to as over-all trends. On the whole, these trends are sufficiently general to transcend differences in preferred concepts and research topics. It should be noted, however,

---

[21] These remarks were made by Prof. Newcomb in his discussion of Talcott Parson's article, "The Position of Sociological Theory," in *American Sociological Review*, XIII, 6 (April 1948), 169–170.

they do not receive the same emphasis from all social psychologists. The emphasis of a given social psychologist may be on one or another of these trends, occasionally to the neglect of others. But it seems likely that every social psychologist has some concern and some part in all these trends and that social psychologists and social scientists have influenced one another.

Social psychologists of various persuasions seem to be concerned with the following trends:

1. A growing emphasis on studying social behavior within a framework of interacting influences, rather than concentrating exclusively either on internal influences (e.g., motives, effects of past experience, organismic states, etc.) or external factors (e.g., groups, culture, as supreme determinants).

2. Positive efforts through cross-cultural and inter-group comparisons to achieve a perspective necessary to guard against ethnocentrism in drawing conclusions.

3. Increased utilization of scientific methods and techniques.[22]

We are in general agreement not only with the judgment of the above statement concerning what is in fact the present trend of social psychology, but also with the conviction that this is largely as it ought to be. The interactionist approach won out over the other earlier approaches because within it can be fitted the many facts and concepts that have been developed and discovered during the past few decades. The interactionist idea was embryonic in the group mind concept, but could not break out under that concept. People certainly behaved differently when in groups, but the mystique of the group mind failed to help the student of collective and group behavior to understand the social influences. Instincts collapsed because they explained too much, and therefore too little. Behaviorism, in its opposition to instincts, sent its uncritical followers too far in the other direction and seemed to discount any limitations imposed by the biological heritage. Freud forced students of human behavior to think about the nature of man and his behavior but never quite escaped the charge that his approach was also a particularistic one, and therefore possessed limitations in its application. What emerged from the studies of these several conceptual schemes of human psychology was the realization that although one must of necessity consider the biological heritage of man, his environments, and his subjective attributes and variables, none of these by itself was sufficient to explain man's behavior. Each of these, viewed separately, is an abstraction from life's

[22] Muzafer Sherif, "Social Psychology: Problems and Trends in Interdisciplinary Relationships," in S. Koch *Psychology: A Study of a Science* (New York: McGraw-Hill Book Co., 1963), p. 67. *See also* Alex Inkeles, "Sociology and Psychology," *loc. cit.*, pp. 317–87. *See also* D. Cartwright, "A Decade of Social Psychology," *Current Trends in Psychological Theory* (Pittsburgh: University of Pittsburgh Press, 1961).

whole, and thus in some degree unreal. The true reality with reference to human behavior is now perceived as *human relations* which involve all three of the components noted above. This reality has come to be conceptualized in the phrase sociocultural interaction.

SUMMARY

There is a trend toward consensus among social psychologists concerning the subject matter of social psychology. Even though the definitions of this discipline explicitly restrict the field to *social* interaction, actually the texts take account of the nonhuman objects involved in individual behavior. Perhaps sometime in the future the field will be more accurately entitled *social cultural psychology.*

If one speaks of *units* of study for social psychology, those units are not individuals, but are *episodes of interaction,* simply "episodes involving the individual or subject and other objects." Those objects may be other persons or nonhuman objects.

The problems dealt with, and some of the ideas used by current social psychology, are of ancient age. The revival of intellectual inquiry which began in the fourteenth century bore fruit in subsequent centuries in the form of specific attention to social psychological data, and in the publication of the first texts in the early twentieth century.

The earlier efforts in social psychology sprang mainly from sociology, but psychologists soon entered the field and today are very prominent in every aspect of the discipline. Certain developments within and outside of psychology account for the confluence of interest of psychologists, anthropologists, and sociologists. However, their efforts were restricted mainly to the confines of their respective disciplines, and departmental allegiances and obligations continue to sponsor this academic segregation. Nevertheless, the attention given to the data selected for study, despite this departmental isolation, and the ". . . forest of distinctive terminology and research preferences,"[23] has lead to the consensus noted above, involving interactive theoretic frameworks, cross cultural comparisons, and application of scientific method and techniques. Sociocultural *interaction* has come to be the key concept in current social psychology.

SUGGESTED READINGS

ALLPORT, GORDON W. "The Historical Background of Modern Social Psychology," in G. Lindzey (ed.) *Handbook of Social Psychology* (Cambridge: Addison-Wesley Press, 1954).

BARNES, HARRY ELMER. *History of Sociology* (Chicago: University of Chicago Press, 1948).

[23] *Ibid.*

BERELSON, BERNARD (ed.). *The Behavioral Sciences Today* (New York: Basic Books, Inc., 1963).

BLUMER, HERBERT. "Social Psychology," in E. P. Schmidt (ed.) *Man and Society* (New York: Prentice-Hall, 1937).

CAMERON, NORMAN. *The Psychology of Behavior Disorders* (Boston: Houghton Mifflin Co., 1947).

CARTWRIGHT, D. "A Decade of Social Psychology," *Current Trends in Psychological Theory* (Pittsburgh: University of Pittsburgh Press, 1961).

COOLEY, CHARLES HORTON. *Human Nature and the Social Order* (New York: Charles Scribner's Sons, 1922).

COTTRELL, L. S., JR., and RUTH GALLAGHER. *Developments in Social Psychology—1930–1940* (New York: Beacon House, Inc., 1941).

DEWEY, JOHN. *Human Nature and Conduct* (New York: Henry Holt and Co., 1922).

FARNSWORTH, P. R., O. M. MCNEMAR, and T. MCNEMAR (eds.). *Annual Review of Psychology* (Palo Alto, Calif.: Annual Reviews, Inc.).

HOLLANDER, E. P., and R. G. HUNT (eds.). *Current Perspective in Social Psychology* (New York: Oxford University Press, 1963).

KARPF, FAY B. *American Social Psychology* (New York: McGraw-Hill Co., 1932).

KOCH, SIGMUND (ed.). *Psychology: A Study of a Science* (New York: McGraw-Hill Book Co., 1963) Vol. 5 and 6.

MEAD, GEORGE HERBERT. *Mind, Self and Society* (Chicago: The University of Chicago Press, 1934).

———, *Philosophy of the Act* (Chicago: The University of Chicago Press, 1938).

MURPHY, GARDNER. *An Historical Introduction to Modern Psychology* (New York: Harcourt, Brace and Company, 1949).

SHERIF, MUZAFER, and M. O. WILSON (eds.) *Emerging Problems in Social Psychology* (Published by University Book Exchange Duplicating Service, Oklahoma, 1957).

SULLIVAN, HARRY STACK. *Conceptions of Modern Psychiatry* (Washington, D. C.: The William Alanson White Psychiatric Foundation, 1947).

WATSON, JOHN B. *The Ways of Behaviorism* (New York: Harper and Brothers, 1928).

CHAPTER 2

THE INTERACTIONIST
FRAME OF REFERENCE

> A separate individual is an abstrac-
> tion unknown to experience, and so
> likewise is society, when regarded as
> something apart from individuals.
> —*Charles Horton Cooley*

Whether one calls it a theory, a conceptual frame of reference, or a theoretic orientation, each person develops a set of ideas with which he interprets his empirical, emotional, or mental experiences.[1] In this chapter are presented in broad outlines the frame of reference, or theory, which will be used throughout the book.

Some of the concepts employed in this particular theory will be familiar to the reader, and some will be new; some will be more familiar to sociologists, whereas others are drawn from a vocabulary better known to psychologists. This dual approach is necessary because of the interstitial nature of social psychology. Even though there is some evidence of convergence of interests among those persons working in social psychology, as noted in Chapter 1, many psychologists and sociologists are still, in the main, working from their respective sides of the mountain. This situation prompted the following statement which was deemed worthy of publication in a principal journal in 1961:

> But few would deny that to understand a person's behavior at a given point in time, it is necessary to have knowledge both of the person and of his environment at that time.
>
> While this premise is generally regarded as obvious, it is safe to say that in practice it is widely ignored. "Sociological" social psychologists stress the importance of group variables, while "psychological" social psychologists stress the importance of the individual variables. Imperialistic tendencies are common. Some sociologists would go so far as to

---

[1] Even though the term *empirical* is at times used as a synonym for experience, this is not semantically correct. As will be noted in greater detail in Chapter 6, empiricism and sensualism both have reference to the experiences of the several senses. Thinking and reasoning are equally experiential in nature. Even John Locke distinguished sensation from reflection in experience. See W. Windelband, *A History of Philosophy* (New York: The Macmillan Co., 1913), pp. 449–486, for a well-known exposition of this problem.

claim that most mental disease is a product of disturbed social conditions, while some psychologists would claim that wars are the direct result of aggressive tendencies of paranoid persons. . . . The field has suffered because of the tendency of its workers to "choose" sides rather than to work with the data of both sociology and psychology simultaneously. To account fully and accurately for more of the variance in social behavior, as well as to gain a better understanding of how the determinants interact, it is necessary to have a dual orientation rather than two orientations.[2]

This text, written by a psychologist and a sociologist in terms of formal education and training, attempts to provide such an integrated approach. The *interactionist* conceptual framework makes such an orientation mandatory. Rather than approaching the study of the data from an individualistic point of departure on the one hand or an environmental viewpoint on the other, the theoretic frame of reference presented here is constituted of three *interacting* categories of basic components. These are the *biological heritage,* including both that which is transmitted genetically and the modifications of this heritage through experience; the *environment* in its social, cultural, and geographical aspects; and the *acquired variables,* including the subjective and covert ideas, beliefs, knowledge, and feelings on the one hand and the overt, objectively observable factors on the other. Although all three of these component categories are both products of, and participants in, the *sociocultural processes,* this is especially true of the acquired variables. Further, because each is an abstraction when conceived by itself, the student of human behavior is presented with a dilemma when he begins to analyze his data. In the study and discussion of these interactive components, which should receive priority? Although there is some cogency to the argument that the three components should be detailed first, and only then should the processes which tie them together and give them meaning be given attention, we have chosen to present our discussion of the sociocultural processes before that of the acquired variables. The reason for this rests upon the fact that, for any given individual, the biological heritage and the environment are largely *givens* in that they exist prior to the development of the learned or acquired ideas, feelings, skills, and so on. The unreal nature of abstractions will be apparent in the inadvertent intrusion of these acquired attributes or variables into the discussion of the processes. This is unavoidable but not a barrier to the understanding of the interactive nature of reality. Abstractions, when recognized as such, are not only useful in human thinking, but necessary and inevitable. The accompanying figure (Figure 1) reveals at a glance the basic cate-

[2] Leo Meltzer, "The Need for a Dual Orientation in Social Psychology," *Journal of Social Psychology,* 55 (Oct. 1961), 43–47.

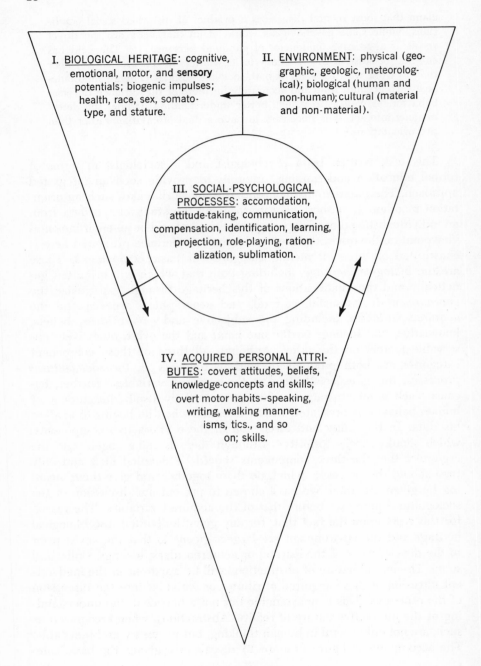

FIGURE 1. Interactionist frame of reference.

gories of interactive variables in the conceptual framework developed in this text.[3]

It is conceivable that one might infer from a superficial inspection of this model that anything and everything can influence human action, that human behavior is almost infinitely variable. The chapters that follow constitute an attempt to demonstrate the finitude of human behavior. Each of the three categories of interactive variables, some aspects of which are always involved in any given situation or episode, has finite characteristics which restrict the range of human behavior. Human behavior is complex, but complexity is not equivalent to infinite variability. *The complex behaviors with which the social psychologist deals are not amorphous interactions, with neither bounds nor patterns; in all of them there run universal human themes, plus numerous unique variations upon these themes.* The individual can be explained *only* in terms of his *relationships* with other persons, with himself, and with nonhuman objects. This is merely an extension of the scientific truism that nothing by itself has any meaning. A person can be friendly only if there is something, human or not, to befriend; without followers there can be no leaders and therefore no leadership qualities per se; guilt implies subjective attitudes as well as attitudes of others toward the subject; jealousy dissociated from others is unthinkable; humiliation implies a symbolic, cognitive, and emotional relationship with another person, real or imagined.

It is very easy to conceive of the "real" person as that which is encompassed by his skin; that is, the subcutaneous, covert, or subjective aspects of personality. Illustrative of a position based upon this view is the following:

> Human personality has a locus—within the skin. . . . But unless we rid ourselves of all definitions that place our personalities in *other* people's minds, we shall never have a secure enough locus for a theory of personality as a system. The biophysical view, unlike the biosocial, would hold that Robinson Crusoe in solitude has "as much" personality before as after the advent of his man Friday.[4]

It is not easy to keep in mind the fact that the knowledge, beliefs, feelings, traits, and habits which constitute these subjective aspects of personality (the personal modifications that have been learned) are meaningless by themselves. An attitude always implies an object. Fears

---

[3] Philosopher Elijah Jordan's terse statement: "A metaphysically distinct individual is the nearest possible logical definition of nothing," epitomizes the framework of concepts used here. *See Forms of Individuality* (Indianapolis: Progress Publishing Co., 1927), p. 63.

[4] G. W. Allport, *Personality and Social Encounter* (Boston: Beacon Press, 1960), pp. 20–21.

(except in the case of the psychotic paranoid with his "free-floating" fears) always are attached to some object, real or illusory; honesty, promptness, courtesy, sadism, possessiveness, and so on, whether in attitudinal or trait form, are relationship concepts and are devoid of meaning if taken in isolation. They do not constitute personality, as will be spelled out in detail in Chapter 8, but are only one of three categories of interactive variables that operate in the emergence of personality.

Environment as an isolated phenomenon is a fiction. Objects acquire the status of effective environment only when they are related to particular persons in some way, directly or indirectly. Custom and fashion mediate between and among peoples (direct noncultural interhuman contacts are almost nonexistent), and become environmental factors, sometimes in a most unobtrusive way. Even fighting is done in ways dictated by custom and fashion. On the other hand, mere physical proximity does not guarantee environmental status for any object—many a book in the college or university library lies well beyond the environmental limits of both student body and faculty. The mention of a book as environment implies a fact which was made explicit in Chapter 1, namely, that "social" sciences are of necessity more than social in nature. Those aspects of one's environment which one has learned to attach importance to, which one esteems, wishes to possess, to protect, to augment, or to enhance are called his *values*. We will have numerous occasions to employ this concept in both its environmental and personal aspects.

Chapters 3, 4, and 7 discuss in some detail the components of personality which are always interactive in human behavior. We have cautioned the reader against perceiving each of these categories of items as meaningful entities per se, rather than as the abstractions which in fact they are. However, there is another trap that awaits the student of human behavior who employs the interactionist approach, *viz.*, the tendency to see these processes of interaction as being independent of the interacting components. Interaction has no existence apart from things which interact. The authors have observed people writing and speaking as if the results of interaction described in subsequent pages would have been the same even if the components of the interactions had been baboons on the planet Mars. Any change in the nature of the interacting factors alters the nature of the processes of interaction; a different species, variations in environments, and different combinations of these will yield different processes. It is as much an error to fail to recognize the abstract nature of social processes per se as it is to so view the components described in Chapters 3, 4, and 7.

One of the social psychologists whose writings have long been influential in the field, especially in the tradition of the "Chicago school," points to some of the advantages of the interactionist approach, or, in more conventional terms, the interactionist *conceptual frame of reference.**

The idea of cause and effect is dropped from thinking in the frame of reference here presented. No element is seen as a causative factor, since there is not an element in life that has its meaning within itself; hence interaction becomes a chief concept in every explanation.

Heredity and environment, instead of being causative factors in human nature, are seen as interactive factors, having their meanings in terms of other elements. They function not as heredity and environment *per se* but as they are shaped in an interactive relationship. Any element in either the organic or the social heritage is an abstraction that becomes definite not in terms of its own nature alone but in terms of the interactive whole already in existence.

It is easy enough to see that this is true when an environmental factor is involved, but it is not quite so obvious to many when a physical factor is considered. This is because thinking is still colored by the old theory of organic motivation which came into existence under a doctrine of causation. This theory assumed that human nature and society became the outward consequences of biological forces, of native instincts and other organic units. Many have been reluctant to abandon this point of view, since it is so simple to use.

Had thinking been done in this frame of reference and in terms of interactive factors instead of cause and effect, the "individual-group controversy" would never have appeared and consumed so much time in the development of philosophy, social psychology, and sociology. "A separate individual is an abstraction unknown to experience, and so likewise is society, when regarded as something apart from individuals." (Charles H. Cooley, *Human Nature and the Social Order*; New York: Charles Scribner's Sons, 1922, p. 33). It is a waste of time to try to establish the individual or society as the unit through which all human nature can be explained when the two have no separate existence but are two interrelated aspects of a total situation. It was outside the frame of reference discussed above that the futile conflict over a basic science had its origin. There is no basic science in this frame of reference. In this frame of reference, thinking could not have achieved the ecclesiastical view of man that separated mind from body, nor would the early philosophizing and biological study have produced so many confusing dichotomies such as "structure and function," "heredity and environment," and the like.

Certain erroneous life philosophies that have affected the political, economic, religious and cultural lives of a whole population for generations have resulted from the thinking that has been done outside of the interactive relationships in this frame of reference. The philosophy of individualism is an important example. It has ignored the fact that there has never been and never will be an individualist who is not also a "collectivist." (The term is not used in its narrow political sense but in its broad connotative meaning). An individual cannot become human apart from a collectivity. Human nature is the phenomenon that ties the individual and his social heritage together; thus to be a human being is to be both a collectivist and an individualist. The nature of the collectivity determines the nature of the individualism and the character of the individualism determines the form of collectivism. After all, even the philosophy of individualism is a philosophy of a collectivity. If it were not, it could not exist. The "individualist" found the philosophy a widely accepted belief in the social heritage into which he was born. He is not even an individualist in the selection of his philosophy of individualism. It was passed on to him along with his language, his religion, his mode of dress, and other patterns.

In the same way there would not have been so much emphasis on "social determinants" if there had not been a search for cause and effect relationships. If the idea of interactive factors regulates the thinking, it is obvious that any social factor in a certain interactive relationship could be significant in either delinquency or nondelinquency, for instance, or in any other pathological behavior. Had there been an acceptance of the idea that nothing is important apart from interaction, the concept of free will would not have colored thinking for so long. "Will," to have importance, would necessarily be in interaction and would, therefore, not be free. Will, *per se*, is an abstraction. Like everything else, its nature is determined by the other interactive factors.[5]

Granting that any item of investigation short of the entire interactive complex involving *all* men and *all* cultural objects is an abstraction, it is important that the degree of abstraction from the whole be appropriate to the problems at hand. In the case of social psychological study, the abstraction must include more than the acting individual, or an environmental item. In other words, the attitudes, ideas, beliefs, and even the overt behavior or role of the person are too fragmentary to have significance for the social psychologist—such factors omit too much of the situation within which the behavior gains meaning.[6] In other words:

> "Role behavior" thus pertains to an individual's performance, but nonetheless it still remains abstracted from the reciprocal performances

[5] L. Guy Brown, *Social Pathology* (New York: F. S. Crofts and Co., 1945), pp. 9–11. This book, whose author in 1934 wrote a social psychological text with an interactionist frame of reference, is among the clearest statements of the theoretical and practical implications of the symbolic-interactionist approach. It has been, and still is, quoted by writers in social psychology. *See* the excerpts from his writings in J. Cuber and P. Harroff, *Readings in Sociology* (New York: Appleton-Century-Crofts, 1962) pp. 108–112.

[6] Later in the book the concepts *role*, *status*, and *position*, will be more fully discussed. Suffice it for the moment to indicate that by *role* or *role behavior* we mean the actual behavior of the person, and by *position* (sometimes *status*) we mean the assigned or expected behavior of a person. Thus a person may have the positions of husband and father, but may play the role of, or act like, an irresponsible adolescent.

of the other(s) which account for its concrete shape and appropriateness in the actual situation. One cannot predict very well from the early
portions of a "role behavior" what the later portions will be, unless
he can ascertain the concomitant responses and assertions of the
other(s).[7]

To which must be added that successful prediction requires that one
ascertain also the pertinent nonhuman factors of the stage setting in
question.

The merit of using such concepts as *situation, social act,* or *episode,* is
that they denote specifically the fact that more than the actor is involved.
They are terms that fit well into the interactionist approach to social
psychological data and act as safeguards against too narrow an abstraction from real life situations. It is all too easy to look at one phase of a
sociocultural episode or act, frequently that of one's own actions, and to
lose the true meaning of this action by overlooking the related actions of
others. However carefully one examines in isolation the behavior of an
individual, an understanding of this action will escape him if he does not
lift his eyes to view the broader scene of which the individual is a part.
This is in no way a derogation of individual psychologists, whose assignment is quite different from that of the social psychologist. Keeping in
mind the complex nature of our data, we should sensitize ourselves to the
following warning:

> Never will a social psychology be dug out of the depths of human
> nature as found in the psychological individual; *this is the construc-
> tionist fallacy, the assumption that a whole is explained by a descriptive
> summary of its parts.* . . . It is not the *detail* of fact, but the *entail* of
> fact, the meaning of fact in the large that is required.[8]

The quest for a simple approach to the understanding of human
nature in general and of personality in particular is enticing and is often
pursued. However, any simple explanation of things as complex as human
behavior is certain to be either incomplete or wrong. There is good advice
in the seemingly paradoxical admonition: "Keep the situation complicated or it will simplify into unreality."[9]

We have spoken of the basic, general characteristic of the interactionist frame of reference, namely, that none of the factors involved in

[7] Nelson Foote, "Concept and Method in the Study of Human Development," in
M. Sherif and M. O. Wilson (eds.) *Emerging Problems in Social Psychology,* The
University of Oklahoma Lectures in Social Psychology (published by the University
Book Exchange Duplicating Service, 1957), p. 34. The phrase *role behavior* is used
by, among others, Prof. T. M. Newcomb in an effort to indicate the dynamic referent
of the terms.

[8] E. Jordan, *Forms of Individuality* (Indianapolis: Progress Publishing Co., 1927)
pp. 73–74. Italics added.

[9] *Ibid.,* p. 73.

human behavior has meaning in isolation of the other factors. It is this basic principle which so often escapes our thinking, thus leading to so many needless and irrational arguments, quarrels, fights, wars, and other forms of social and personal disorganization or disorder. However, the reader may wonder just what the nature of this interaction process is. Chapters 5 and 6 detail the general characteristics of the interaction processes that are peculiar to the sociocultural relationships of man. Therefore the presentation of their characteristics here will be restricted to a few paagraphs which are designed to indicate the general direction in which the more explicit discussion of the processes will lead.

Processes are, of course, what happens when objects, of whatever nature, are so placed that they affect each other. Whereas it is possible to perceive purely physical processes of interaction that are devoid of either biological or social involvements, it is *not* possible to perceive biological processes that are not at the same time physical processes, nor is it possible to perceive social processes that are not also *both* physical and biological in nature. However, the structural characteristics of animals, especially those with well-developed spinal cords and brains, have implications for relationships with other objects that the strictly biological and physical conceptual categories no longer suffice. Reduction of all animal behavior to strictly physical or biological terms cannot provide an understanding of the observed behavior. Once the animals' structures are such as to introduce consciousness of sensory experiences, new conceptual categories are demanded, and we speak of psychological and social relationships. These man shares, as shown in Chapter 3, with a variety of other animals, and these we must understand if we are to comprehend what we perceive in the behavior of mankind. However, in addition to consciousness of objects, which man has in common with others of the animal kingdom, there are structural features in man's biological heritage that are unique to his species. Man's central and autonomic nervous systems are distinctive in a number of ways which will be detailed in Chapter 3. Suffice it for our immediate purposes to note the novel ingredients in man which make him the only *cultural* animal, and, moreover, an animal with particular *kinds* of cultures. These features which he shares with no other animal (at least not in significant degree) are both cognitive or intellectual *and* emotional in nature.

At the cognitive level, that which distinguishes man are his talents or abilities:

1. *To conceive of objects which he experiences, including himself, apart from their here-and-now relationships.*
2. *To label them.*
3. *To communicate orally and in writing with others of his kind.*

As one anthropologist has said, there is nothing about an ape's snout that prevents him from speaking, but there is something about the brain of an ape that precludes speech. In short, man's ability to abstract items from his experiences and to symbolize them permit him to escape the bounds of the present, to recall items from the past, combine them with things present, to think about them, to communicate about them to others, and thus to modify or anticipate the future.

At the emotional level, man's distinguishing features are:

1. *The generally undefined emotional potential (i.e., lack of instinctive feelings and motives) wherein the emotional relationship is unknown apart from interaction with the object in question.*

2. *Emotional needs for relationships with other persons and with nonhuman objects (e.g., desire for recognition and new experiences) which emerge through interaction with these objects.*

In summary, the unique psychological features of man are his highly flexible potential in terms of relationships with his object-world, which flexibility is a function of his unique talent for learning, his nonspecific emotional potential, and his ability to communicate with his fellow humans.

The interaction processes which are detailed in this text are constituted of modifications in the human being's knowledge and beliefs about himself, other human beings, and the nonhuman objects of his environment, of changes in his attitudes toward himself and toward other objects of his experiences, and of consequential changes in these other objects. Most, but not all, of these changes involve the direct influences of other human beings. In brief, the sociocultural processes of interaction are mostly social in nature but not exclusively so. One must grant that man could not be human apart from other humans, but the importance of relationships between man and his nonhuman environment must not be discounted. Differences in the behavior of man which are noted from place to place and from time to time must take into account the changed material and nonhuman biological environmental factors if the behavior is to be understood. Thus, the interactive processes are tri-dimensional and involve alterations in both man and his environment as they impinge upon each other. Changes in man's knowledge of, beliefs about, and attitudes toward his nonhuman environments change those environments, which changes in turn modify man's knowledge, beliefs, and feelings as these continue to shape his relationships to his world. The interaction involves man's thinking about himself and the world, looking at himself objectively and in terms of the imputed thoughts and feelings of others, and acting in terms of the consequent thoughts and attitudes insofar as environment permits. The interactive frame of reference takes into account all of these changes in the relationships, only one aspect of which is the integumented, under-the-skin complex of mental, emotional, sensory, and motor events. Once more, it is the *entail* of facts, not the *detail* of facts, which leads to understanding of the facts.

THE ANALOGY OF THE THEATER

The social sciences have resorted to a variety of analogies or models which have served as vehicles for research and for exposition. Physical models (Auguste Comte had planned on calling his study *social physics* but substituted *sociology* when he learned that another, Adolphe Quetelet, had already used the former term) have been popular, and several biological models have appeared—organic, functional, and evolutionary. Although the interactionist frame of reference that is used here is not an analogy or a model, throughout this book a model is used for purposes of illustration and clarification. This is the model of the theater,[10] and although it has not been exploited fully, it is a useful extension of George Herbert Mead's use of *role*—which he deliberately borrowed from the theater. This model is less subject to strain—requires fewer distortions than nonsocial models. If we expand Shakespeare's "All the world's a stage" to read "All the world's a theater," then the interactionist framework readily lends itself to description and analyses in theatrical terms. Life's drama, whatever and whenever its expression, has its stage and all of the wondrous stage props; its actors and actresses of all ages, sizes, and shapes, with its heroes and its villains, its beauties and its monsters. Some casts are large and some are small and this makes for significant differences in the quality of the performance. The audiences determine in large part how long the play shall last or run; culture provides the script but frequently it is pointless to attempt to discover its authors, and each real life drama has its own self-appointed critics as well as official ones. We shall see the applicability of this theatrical model or analogy system in succeeding chapters. It is important to keep in mind that we use the theater as an analogy or model *only*; its function is illustrative and pedagogical, not analytical. Its occasional use will prevent one slipping into meaningless abstractions, especially in taking the actor off the stage, away from the theater, and viewing him in a void. Omission of any part of the theater of life reduces the chance that the remaining parts will be understood.

SUMMARY

Theory, or conception, is essential as a means to understanding man's social behavior. The theoretical position, or conceptual frame of refer-

---

[10] The authors used the model of the theater in their earlier book, *The Development of Human Behavior* (New York: The Macmillan Co., 1951) in a limited way. Since then others have exploited it more fully. *Cf.* especially Erving Goffman, *The Presentation of Self in Everyday Life* (Garden City, New York: Doubleday and Co., 1959).

ence, used in this text is called an organism-environment-subject approach, or simply the *interactionist* frame of reference. It indicates the need for looking at the biological heritage of the individuals, the environmental factors, and the modified person factors as these three categories of variables interact in human behavior. To focus attention upon this fact of interconnectedness in social behavior, it is useful to employ such terms as *situation, social act,* or *episode* as the unit of study. This focus further stresses the fact that simple explanations of human behavior are rarely adequate. On occasion the interactive processes have been viewed as entities existing apart from the interactive attributes or variables. This is no less an error than failing to perceive the variables as abstractions.

SUGGESTED READINGS

BLUMER, HERBERT. "Science Without Concepts," *American Journal of Sociology*, XXXVI (Jan. 1931).

BROWN, L. GUY. *Social Pathology* (New York: F. S. Crofts and Co., 1945).

COOLEY, CHARLES HORTON. *Human Nature and the Social Order* (New York: Charles Scribner's Sons, 1922).

CUBER, JOHN F., and PEGGY B. HARROFF. *Readings in Sociology—Sources and Comment* (New York: Appleton-Century-Crofts, 1962).

JORDAN, ELIJAH. *Forms of Individuality* (Indianapolis: Progress Publishing Co., 1927).

MCGRATH, JOSEPH E. *Social Psychology: A Brief Introduction* (New York: Holt, Rinehart, and Winston, 1964).

PROSHANSKY, HAROLD, and BERNARD SEIDENBERG. *Basic Studies in Social Psychology* (New York: Holt, Rinehart and Winston, 1965).

STOODLEY, BARTLETT H. *Society and Self* (New York: The Free Press of Glencoe, 1962).

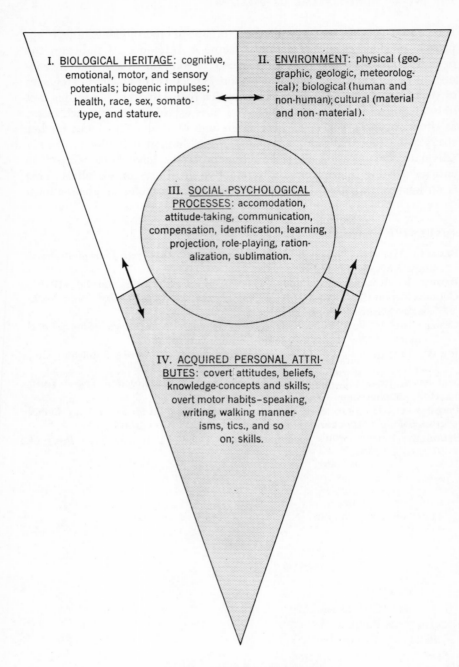

FIGURE 2. Interactionist frame of reference.

28

CHAPTER 3

BIOLOGICAL FOUNDATIONS OF PERSONALITY

A race of civilized beings descended from these great cats would have been rich in hermits and solitary thinkers. The recluse would not have been stigmatized as peculiar, as he is by us simians. They would not have been a credulous people, or easily religious. False prophets and swindlers would have found few dupes . . . Don't imagine them as a collection of tigers walking around on their hind legs. They would have only been like tigers in the sense that we men are like monkeys. Their development in appearance and character would have been quite transforming . . . They would have been courteous and sauve. No vulgar crowding would have occurred on the streets of their cities. No mobs. No ignominious subway jams . . . They would have been strong at slander . . . The super cat men would have rated cleanliness higher. Some of us primates have learned to keep ourselves clean, but it's no large proportion; and even the cleanest of us see no grandeur in soap manufacturing, and we don't look to manicures and plumbers for social prestige. A feline race would have honored such occupations . . . In a world of super cat men, I suppose there would have been fewer sailors; and people would have cared less for seaside resorts, or for swimming . . . Among them there would have been no anti-vivisection societies: No Young Cats Christian Associations or Red Cross Work: No vegetarians: No early closing laws: Much more hunting and trapping: No riding to hounds; that's pure simian . . . But the dominant characteristic of this fine race is cunning. And hence I think it would have been through their craftiness, chiefly, that they would have felt the impulse to study, and the wish to advance. Craft is a cat's delight: craft they never can have too much of. So it would have been from one triumph of cunning to another that they would have marched. That would have been the greatest driving force of their civilization.

—*Clarence Day, This Simian World*
Alfred A. Knopf, Inc.

But man is not descended from the big cats, and his sociocultural relationships are not as Mr. Day describes them in his imaginative book. Man acts like man because he cannot do otherwise. Any member of a given biological order is restricted in the things that it can do and cannot do, in what it wants to do and does not want to do, and in the way it can and does feel about life, by the very nature of its biological structure.

There is a biochemical organization characteristic of each kind of

plant and animal. This system gives to each type of organism its physiological uniqueness. Each organism achieves its characteristic structure
in terms of the chemical and physiological organization which is native
to it. In this connection William James has written:

> If I begin chopping the foot of a tree, its branches are unmoved by
> my act, and its leaves murmur as peacefully as ever in the wind. If, on
> the contrary, I do violence to the foot of a fellow man, the rest of
> his body instantly responds to the aggression by movements of alarm
> or defiance. The reason for this difference is that man has a nervous
> system whilst the tree has none . . .[1]

What activities an organism will engage in, what groups such organisms will form, what their interrelationships with the geographical,
biological, and social environment will be, in greater or lesser degree,
are related to the organism's structure. This in no way contradicts the
principle that biological structure per se, in isolation from other factors, counts for little. Human action always involves organism–plus–
geography–plus–culture.

Physiological structure remains one of the important variables in the
lives of all organisms. This is as true in the study of man as it is in the
study of forms of moss, of trees, of migratory fowl, or of the simpler
organic forms such as the paramecium. It is no less important for the
social psychologist to know the pertinent facts of man's physical structure than it is for the botanist to know the structure of bushes and trees
in his study of the relationships of plants to other objects. Penal systems,
belief in witches, fumbling attempts at education, futility in the treatment of the mentally ill, the subscription to instincts, failures in social
reform, dietary deficiencies, all involve ignorance of man's biological
heritage. Even today, we owe a significant proportion of our crime, delinquency, divorce, mental illness, feelings of guilt and shame, and school
failures to our inadequate knowledge of homo sapiens' biological nature.
In our ignorance, we ascribe to our fellow men and to ourselves an ability
to escape a biological heritage. Human behavior is always biosocial,
biocultural, or biogeographical.

Inasmuch as many of man's features are shared with other animals, it
is not necessary that the social psychologist concern himself directly with
all of man's biological heritage. He is not interested as a social psychologist in all of the physiochemical functions which are essential to keeping
man alive. Only those features that are more directly operative in the
sociocultural relationships of man are pertinent to our purposes. In this
chapter, we will concentrate not on human physiology, as such, but on
those aspects of man's biological capacities which enable him to develop

[1] William James, *Principles of Psychology*, I (New York: Henry Holt & Co.,
1890), 12.

in ways that are unique in phylogeny. The following brief classification is presented to locate man in the biological order, and to indicate his distinctive features which aid in the explanation of his social actions.

If we start with the broader categories, we do not find much that is of value to the social psychologist. For example, if we say that man is an animal we say little that is sociologically significant, because anything that lives and is capable of independent motion is classified as animal. In this category man finds himself listed with amoebae, insects, fishes, and bats. Even the next few steps in biological classification are of little significance to the social scientist. In Table I the reader can see some of

Table I
Biological Positions Which Man Shares with Other Animals

	Man	Fossil Man	Great Apes	Mon-key	Cow	Whale	Frog	Am-phi-oxus	In-sect
Kingdom: Animal	M	FM	GA	Mo	C	W	F	A	I
Phylum: Chordata	M	FM	GA	Mo	C	W	F	A	
Subphylum: Vertebrata	M	FM	GA	Mo	C	W	F		
Class: Mammal	M	FM	GA	Mo	C	W			
Sub-class: Eutheria	M	FM	GA	Mo	C				
Order: Primate	M	FM	GA	Mo					
Sub-order: Anthropoidea	M	FM	GA						
Family: Hominidae	M	FM							
Genus: Homo	M								
Species: Sapiens	M								

man's companions in each of the categories. Man's phylum is called *chordata* and indicates that he has an elongated bundle of nerves running the length of the organism, carrying impulses to and fro, and he is classed with a brainless, small, fish-like animal called amphioxus. To say that man is a member of the subphylum *vertebrata* merely classifies him with bullfrogs, snakes, and all animals with back bones, and distinguishes him from jellyfish, coral, insects, and shellfish. To know that man is *mammal* tells us only that, in common with horses, shrews, whales, porpoises, and tarsiers, man breathes air through lungs, and has a covering (more or less) of hair on his body, is warm blooded, and that the females give birth to and suckle the young. This distinguishes man from fish, amphibians, reptiles, and birds. Only the manner of giving birth has much significance for the social psychologist and the indirect relationship which this has for the family organization will be explored in a later chapter.

Man is of the order primate, as we know, yet even this relatively refined status in the zoological world provides only part of the explanation of man's sociocultural actions and structures. This status is defined in terms of a more erect posture, a well-developed clavicle (collarbone) which permits greater mobility of the forearms, prehensile (grasping) hands and/or feet, and opposability of thumbs and fingers. The great apes (gorilla, chimpanzee, gibbon, and orangutan) and monkeys are our equals in these items. In fact, in one of the special features of the primates, prehensility, the monkeys and apes outstrip man. The former have not only prehensile hands, but prehensile feet as well, not to mention the prehensile tails of the new world monkeys. The advantage of prehensile feet as well as hands in such occupations as tailoring, welding, cabinet making, and many others, is easily recognized. However, despite this structural physical advantage, monkeys and the great apes do not make good tailors, welders, or cabinet makers. Why this is so, and why the accomplishments of ape and man are so different cannot be answered by studying the skeletal physical structures of these two animals. If the structure of hands, feet, eyes, jaw, and of the muscular skeletal features of the body in general were the only differentiating features, the apes would drive cars, build machines, fly airplanes, build houses, and perform all of the other things that man can do. It is interesting to speculate what a wonderful steeple jack and construction worker the chimpanzee would make. Add to the prehensile feet the fact that the chimp is from two to two and one-half times as strong as man, pound for pound, and the structural superiority of the ape becomes obvious. Thus, if we would seek the structural features which distinguish man from other primates we would need to examine the next zoological category (homo sapiens) where the superior development of cortical structure (making possible symbolic behavior and complex learning) would readily become apparent.

In a textbook on social psychology the reader can expect that the focus of attention will be upon interpersonal relationships rather than upon the individual biological structures of people. Psychologists and psychiatrists have sometimes been inclined to concentrate upon the individual patient and his organism as the basic unit of attention. Even Sigmund Freud originally endeavored to explain his theories in terms of physiology and chemistry. There is a continuing interest on the part of some diligent researchers in finding a concrete and specific organic formula that will identify and make possible a chemical or surgical cure for criminality, mental illness, or various other types of aberrant behavior. At one time, insulin or electric shock was highly regarded as a possible answer. The more radical prefrontal lobotomy has fallen into disrepute as tranquilizing drugs offer better results with less gross threat to the patient. Perhaps some day a chemical formula or surgery will be helpful in this regard and no one should close his mind to this possibility. The focus of the attention of this book, however, (insofar as deviant behavior is concerned) is upon personality disorders as products of disturbances in interpersonal relations.

Adams describes mental illness in terms of maladaptive interpersonal behavior, often accompanied by feelings of subjective discomfort, unsatisfying human relationships, and social rejection.[2] The socially maladapted may also be described as people with disordered ways of communicating and inept ways of relating experiences. In this regard, we believe the tendency is for the contemporary psychiatrist and psychologist increasingly to become social scientists or more particularly social psychologists.

The social psychologist recognizes that men everywhere live in groups and that their behavior is shaped not only by biological needs, but also by the necessity of getting along with their neighbors. Men are animals, but they are the only animals that have attained culture and in so doing they have in many respects escaped the dominance of instincts and biological determinism. Sahlins speaks of this achievement as "The triumph of intellect over instinct—of altruism over individualism."[3]

BEHAVIORAL GENETICS

The science of genetics explains those elements of individual variability that are due to differences in organic inheritance. Heritability has been defined by Sutten as "the proportion of the variation in a trait which is attributable to genetic factors."[4] The members of the human species differ among themselves in many visible as well as covert ways. Variations in factors such as physique, eye color, facial features, skin pigmentation, and hair quality, largely result from the genetic heritage. Except for that person who has a monozygotic twin, everyone's genetic heritage is specifically unique.

There are many characteristics that may become physiological variables in human development, but which are not inherited through the germ plasm. Among these would be congenital disorders,[5] acquired traits, disease, malformations due to accidents and birth injuries; and these,

[2] We would not go so far as Adams who states that "Mental illness is a phenomenon involving interpersonal behavior, not a health or medical problem. Henry B. Adams, "Mental Illness or Interpersonal Behavior?," *American Psychologist*, 19, No. 3 (March 1964), 194. Our position would be closer to that of Meehl who recognizes that there may be an organic basis for some mental health problems (as in psychophrenia) but that the *content* of such behavior is certainly learned through association with other people. Paul E. Meehl, "Schizotaxia, Schizotypy, Schizophrenia," *American Psychologist*, 17, No. 12 (Dec. 1962), 837.

[3] M. D. Sahlins, "The Origin of Society," *Scientific American*, 203, No. 3 (1960), 76–86.

[4] H. Eldon Sutton, Elvira Gil De Lamario, and Marie B. Esterer, "Genetic Variation in Human Biochemical Traits," *Human Genetics*, 14, No. 3 (Sept. 1962), 51.

[5] Disorders present at birth that were acquired in embryo but which are not hereditary.

of course, are outside the province of genetics (except as they may become active environmental variables in the development of the growing organism).[6]

The heredity of an organism is fixed at the moment of fertilization. Nothing can ever be added to the heredity of a person after this time. Subsequent events can facilitate, select out which genes will be effective, which destroyed or ignored, but nothing more can be added. This statement assumes that the appearance of any particular behavior characteristic resulting from a specific genetic determinant will emerge only within a *specific environment*. Thus *both the genes as well as the environment* set limits to the development of the behavioral characteristic. Liverant argues that too often we assign a limiting role to heredity without also assigning the same limiting role to environment.

> Geneticists postulate that the appearance of any characteristic (behavioral or otherwise) depends upon the *interaction* of a *specific* genetics structure operating within a specific environment. In this sense genes set the limits within any given environment but those limits may vary as the environment varies. Without in any way arguing against the Wiseman-Morgan theory of the immutability of the germ plasm, it is no more logical to attribute a limited role to heredity than it is to assign the same role to environment. Perhaps the irrevocability of genetic determinants as compared to situational ones has contributed to this mode of thought, but it is one which contradicts the postulated interaction effect.[7]

The evolutionary development of man must be studied both genetically and culturally. There is a history of genetic systems and also a history of cultural systems and the interaction between these systems is essential in the development of man. Bruner states that, "The principal change in man over a long period of years—perhaps 500,000—has been alloplastic rather than autoplastic. That is to say, he has changed by linking himself with new, external implementation systems rather than by any conspicuous change in morphology."[8] Washburn and Howell pro-

---

[6] The reader will find the following sources adequate for a general knowledge of human genetics. James V. Neel and Wm. J. Schull, *Human Heredity* (Chicago: Univ. of Chicago Press, 1961); Gurt Stern, *Principles of Human Genetics* (San Francisco: W. H. Freeman and Co., 1960; John L. Fuller and W. Robert Thompson, *Behavior Genetics* (New York: John Wiley and Sons, 1960); and the serial reports of "The Hereditary Abilities Study," *The American Journal of Human Genetics*, 14 (1962); Warja Honnegger-Lavater and Hans Burla, *Genetics: Heredity, Environment and Personality* (New York: Dell Publishing Co., 1962). This last book, stressing nonverbal visual approach, provides an excellent brief introduction to genetics for the layman.

[7] Shephard Liverant, "Intelligence, A Concept in Need of Reexamination," *Journal of Consulting Psychology*, 24 (1960), 101–110.

[8] Jerome S. Bruner "The Course of Cognitive Growth," *American Psychologist*, 19, No. 1 (Jan. 1964), 1–15.

vide the following example of the necessary relationship between cultural stimulation and genetic determination.

> It would now appear . . . that the large size of the brain of certain hominids was a relatively late development and that the brain evolved due to new selection pressures *after* bipedalism and consequent upon the use of tools. The tool-using, ground-living, hunting way of life created the large human brain rather than a large brained man discovering certain new ways of life. (We) believe this conclusion is the most important result of the recent fossil hominid discoveries and is one which carries far-reaching implications for the interpretation of human behavior and its origins . . . The important point is that size of brain, insofar as it can be measured by cranial capacity, has increased some threefold subsequent to the use and manufacture of implements . . . The uniqueness of modern man is seen as the result of a technical-social life which tripled the size of the brain, reduced the face, and modified many other structures of the body.[9]

The evolutionary growth of man is modified from the inside out (genetically) but also from the outside in (culturally). To view the history of man solely as a result of genetic unfolding is no longer tenable. Because man is still evolving in human evolution, and because man more than ever is creating his own environment, it is of the greatest importance that in considering our evolutionary future we complement our understanding of genetic selection with a knowledge of the processes of social selection. This has led Hammond to make the following comment: "Man now evolves by selection for an environment that is largely of his own making. This creates problems: he may be changing his culture at a rate that surpasses his own evolutionary adaptation."[10] (*Cp.* this discussion of current adolescent problems in Chapter 14 as functions of this discrepancy between biological and cultural changes.)

Structure and Function

Man acts like man in part because he has inherited the physical structure of a man, and he does not act like an anthropoid or a tree because he has not inherited the physical attributes of those organisms. Man's structure is inherited through the germ plasm. Man does not through the germ plasm inherit moods, attitudes, character, or even habits. He may inherit these traits culturally but he does not gain them organically. Man inherits a body form and a biochemical system that

[9] S. L. Washburn and F. C. Howell, "Human Evolution and Culture," in S. Tax (ed.) *The Evolution of Man*, II (Chicago: The University of Chicago Press, 1960), p. 49.

[10] Peter B. Hammond (ed.) *Physical Anthropology and Archaeology* (New York: The Macmillan Co., 1964), p. 136. The reader's attention is called to the above quotation, from Washburn and Howell, which is to be understood in terms of Hammond's comments on the *selection* process in biological evolution.

enables him to modify and survive in his particular milieu. The structure that is inherited does not guarantee function. It only makes function possible and the latter is greatly influenced by cultural determinants acting in conjunction with the total organism's needs. Dubos has reported the remarkable instances of adaptation found among the aborigines of Central Australia who face unusual problems of survival due to the arid conditions of the region. Rainfall in this area is less than ten inches a year and temperatures reach 140° F.

> In addition to having developed an extraordinary instinct[11] for discovering water where white men would die of thirst, these aborigines exhibit physiological adaptations that permit them to survive with very small amounts of the precious fluid. They are able, for example, to use their stomachs as water bottles in which large volumes can be stored. Their enormously distended stomachs are the evidence of storage whenever they start for a trip across the desert from a place where water is available. A European, drinking large quantities of water, rapidly excretes the excess once his physiological requirements have been met. In contrast, the stomach in the aborigines is able to retain the water and let it out as needed, over many hours. Furthermore, their kidneys seem to be so efficient that they apparently require only half as much water to flush the same amount of waste products as would be the case for white men—thus reducing greatly their minimal requirements.[12]

In the course of both phylogeny and ontogeny it can be observed that structure precedes function. The anatomical substructure may mature in the evolutionary process long before function appears. In many instances subhumans have not yet developed far enough in the evolutionary scale to utilize the structures which they may already possess. For example, the parrot can imitate every syllable of human speech yet possesses no language of its own.

Lest we be accused of identifying man's behavior with his physical traits, let it be clearly recognized that we agree with Montagu when he says that "Function is, of course an aspect of structure, but as any elementary student of physiology should know, the functions of structure assume their particular character according to the environment in which they operate."[13]

A clear illustration of response to structure is found in the overt motor behavior of males and females which reflects the skeletal and musculature differences of the sexes. The preference of males for contact sports (foot-

[11] Presumably Dubos is using the word *instinct* at this point idiomatically, rather than literally. Men *learn* how to find water; they do not develop an *instinct* for this capability.

[12] R. Dubos, *Mirage of Health* (Garden City, N.Y.: Doubleday, 1961) p. 42.

[13] M. F. Ashley Montagu, "Our Changing Conception of Human Nature," *Import of Science on Society*, UNESCO (Winter 1952), 219–232.

ball, soccer, baseball, basketball, and so on) is only *in part* culturally determined. The female is ill-equipped to run, throw, tackle, or jump. Her shorter and knock-kneed legs ill prepare her for running and jumping. Her arms, which bend beyond the 180 degrees of the average male arm, are relatively poor throwing devices (although this enables her to avoid bruising them on her broad hips when she walks, as anthropologist W. W. Howells noted). Her smaller, sparer muscles and greater proportion of fat also restrict her relative to the male in activities requiring physical prowess based on strength. The occasional female athlete who is outstanding only emphasizes the sexual differences in structure. The well-known Babe Didrikson Zaharias did not possess an average female physique, but could be classified as an ectomorphic mesomorph. (See Figure 5.) Male high school athletes regularly break female world records in running, jumping, and throwing. To be sure, the structure of males restricts their participation in certain sports and occupations as surely as does the characteristic female structure.

Because of their physical structure women are admirably suited to care for and nurse children. If there are genetic reasons, other than appropriate structure, why women should be more devoted to children than are men, they have not been demonstrated.

If there are instincts which include the germinal transmission of function as well as structure, then such instincts are limited to more primitive forms of life than man. Biological heritage provides man with the structure with which he can interact with his environment, but this biological structure does no more than equip the actor with potentialities for playing multiple roles on the environmental stage.

BIOLOGICAL MOTIVATION IN SOCIAL BEHAVIOR

Any inquiry into the social behavior of man involves the question of motivation. Efforts to control and predict the behavior of human beings, including the behavior of one's self, of necessity take into consideration the question of the *why* of human actions. Innumerable failures in the field of social control and prediction can be attributed to inadequate understanding of the reasons which induce human beings to act as they do.

The term *motive* is derived from the Latin *movere* which means *to move*. In the simplest of terms, that which moves persons to activity is motivation. A motive may be simple or complex; it may be fully understood by the actor and those observing the action, or it may mystify both actor and spectators. Various words have come into being that enable one to discuss motivation in its different forms. Thus we speak of needs, drives, impulses, tensions, states of disequilibrium, and desires; all of these are, to be sure, forms of stimuli. Whereas, in the immature personality, these stimuli give rise to random, apparently inconsistent behavior, motivation implies a relatively stable relationship in the more mature personality. Habit assures us of this. The relationship may be between the personal variables and some part or function of the body, or it may involve interaction between these variables and some factor external to the body. In the past, such terms as stimulus-response and cause-effect have been popular in discussions of motivation, and within limits these concepts are of value in understanding human behavior, but their weakness lies in their limited scope where social behavior is concerned. The actions of the human being on the social level are much too complex to be adequately explained by the attention to a stimulus evoking a response, or a cause bringing about an effect. Almost all social action involves multiple stimuli and multiple responses and many interactive factors rather than a single cause-effect relationship. Even those who prefer to retain the stimulus-response approach to such problems have replaced the former symbols of S———R, by S———O———R, the "O" standing for the individual person. This change admits the importance of the individual with his multiple experiences as a modifier of both stimulus and response. Likewise, many who speak in terms of cause-effect do so with complete awareness that no single cause can be counted as adequate explanation of social action, as, for example, in investigating the causes of crime. Many interactive factors involving the biological heritage, the acquired personal variables, and the environment of the individual are investigated for an understanding of the criminal act, as they are for any human behavior.

We distinguish between three different categories to afford us an explanation of the *why* of human social behavior.

1. There are the many needs of the body which are satisfied largely by nonsocial activity, though one must be aware that even these relatively simple forms of motivation have important social implications. However, in general, we do not find them of signal importance in the explanation of social behavior of the human being. In this category falls the homeostatic needs including the need for optimum temperature range, for oxygen supply, for freedom of bodily movements, for sleep and rest, and for evacuation of bowels and bladder. The student should be cognizant of homeostasis, a concept first developed by Claude Bernard in the nineteenth century, who pointed out at that time that living organisms possess mechanisms that enable them to maintain a constancy of physiological condition in their internal milieu in spite of the fact that these conditions are subject to continuous variations in their environment. Walter B. Cannon, in the twentieth century, revived this concept, broadened the scope of its implications, and desig-

nated homeostasis as the mechanism that enables living organisms, including human beings, to maintain a constancy of conditions within their own systems. The homeostatic principle applies to mechanisms that are "built into" the organism as native and un-learned processes which automatically serve adjustment needs of the organism. A good example of the automatic nature of this principle is the ability of the organism to develop antibodies which effectively deal with an infection in the blood stream even when the organism has not previously been exposed to such infection. Whether or not the homeostatic principle applies to the preserva-tion of acquired statuses and social adjustments is a debatable question. Some researchers are exploring the idea that homeostasis may be basic to all human motivation.[14] To do so, they broaden the principle to include the preservation of self as well as organic equilibrium. It is the feeling of the writers of this volume that the homeostatic principle is primarily concerned with maintaining the inner equilibrium of the organism as it endeavors to preserve the primary statuses of the body and that its impact upon the socialization of the human organism is not sufficient to justify a longer treatment in a text in social psychology. Because the drives at this level do not appear to have important social psychological implication we will not proceed further to discuss them here.

2. There are the innate, unlearned, or primary motives; the hunger and thirst, sex, and random activity drives. These biogenic drives will be reviewed in the current chapter.

3. There are the acquired, learned, or secondary motives. These sociogenic motives will be dealt with in Chapter 7. We now turn our attention to the second of these categories of motives.

The Primary or Biogenic Drives

In contrast to the lower animals, many of whom are provided a bio-logical heritage that includes not only drives but also unlearned responses (instincts) which will meet these drives, man's biological heritage pro-vides him only the drives. The responses which are designed to fulfill the inborn demands for some form of behavior are learned by the individual through trial-and-error methods, and are already prepared for him in the form of customs and institutions of his culture, or are unconsciously acquired in the form of individual peculiarities of habit. How these processes operate in the development of human behavior is our present concern.

[14] Robert Roessler and Norman S. Greenfield, *Physiological Correlates of Psycho-logical Disorders* (Madison: The University of Wisconsin Press, 1962), p. 7.

THE HUNGER IMPULSE

Although the range of foods that can safely satisfy the hunger need is not without its limits, it is so wide that we can say, for practical purposes, that the hunger impulse is undefined at birth. Each individual learns to like certain foods; that is, learns that certain foods will be pleasant to consume in the process of satisfying the hunger impulse. In general, it can be said that, within the limits set by the variation in the distribution and amount of the taste buds on the tongue, biological nature does not predetermine what a given individual is going to prefer to eat.[15] The definition or canalization[16] of hunger and taste is largely a function of culture, as even a cursory examination of the cultural variation in food habits will reveal.[17]

> Despite the nutritional value of foods of animal origin, attitudes and customs restricting their use are widespread. In large areas of East and South Asia and of tropical Africa, for example, people refuse to drink milk, a practice as defiling in their eyes as drinking urine would be in ours. The most important restrictions derive from those religions, such as Buddhism and Hinduism, which preach vegetarianism, and which base their teachings on belief in the sanctity of life. Because many ancient scholars were involved in religious pursuits, they became staunch supporters of these beliefs, which have descended to their emancipated successors, as in western Europe.[18]

The world traveler soon learns that one man's meat is another man's emetic. The Hottentot's menu of ". . . mice, lizards, snails, caterpillars, beetles, locusts, ants, termites, and body lice," is not likely to tempt even hungry Europeans, Asians, or Americans. In fact, our Hottentot gourmet's selection is not only unappetizing but downright incredible to most

---

[15] There are still many unanswered questions concerning the nature of food selection in individual cases, such as the "clay eaters" of the southern highlands, the eating of plaster and ashes by children, and other so-called pathological conditions. Whether or not such activity reflects dietary deficiencies is not yet established, and even if this is true, we still have before us the problem of how the selection was made. In one recorded instance a young boy who was eating large quantities of salt was placed in a hospital, deprived of the abnormally large supply of salt, and soon died. Post mortem examination revealed a gross glandular deficiency which was in part compensated for by the huge salt intake. Reported in J. McV. Hunt (ed.) *Personality and Behavior Disorders*, I (New York: The Ronald Press Co., 1944), 602.

[16] *Canalize* and *canalization* are terms that refer to the learning process in which both biogenic and sociogenic impulses are given direction in a manner analogous to a canal giving direction to the flow of water. It is familiar to both psychologists and sociologists, but more commonly used by the former. The latter seem to prefer *channelize* or *define*.

[17] For discussions of cultural factors in diet see Margaret Mead, "Cultural Contexts of Nutritional Patterns," *Centennial* (Washington, D. C.: American Association for the Advancement of Science, 1950).

[18] Frederick J. Simoons, *Eat Not This Flesh* (Madison: The University of Wisconsin Press, 1961), p. 9.

of us. Nor need we leave our own culture for evidence of the nonspecific nature of the hunger drive. Sweetbreads, brains, kidneys, tongue, and chitlings are assiduously avoided by the majority. The variety of foods offered in any American or Canadian supermarket testifies to the varieties of means for hunger satisfactions in our culture.

Thus, the hunger drive does not require that a man eat a specific diet, but permits him to learn to enjoy a wide variety of foods and beverages. Of course, the nature of human tissues sets certain gross limits, but if these limits are not exceeded and the materials neither destroy the tissues nor fail to provide the body with adequate nourishment, they meet the requirements for satisfying the hunger need. As a matter of fact, certain items may fail to nourish the body or may even tend to destroy it, and still meet the hunger impulse. Man's sense of taste and his stomach often fail to distinguish adequate from inadequate diets. The relationships between the excessive consumption of sugar and tooth condition, between the consumption of polished rice and beriberi, and the seeming connection between cholesterol and coronary disease, are cases in point. A major danger in chronic alcoholism is dietary deficiency. An alcoholic may be sufficiently supplied with calories but be grossly deficient in other food components.

Enough has been said to emphasize the extreme range of food tastes in man, who is quite capable of learning to like to eat his enemy as he is pomegranates. The unique experiences which he has within the framework of a given culture or within certain groups determine his food tastes.

THE SEX IMPULSE AS MOTIVATION

Although there is considerable disagreement as to the period in life when the sex impulse makes itself felt for the first time, there is general agreement that such an impulse is a universal phenomenon. It is usually supposed that the onset of puberty is the period when maturation of the secondary sex characteristics is matched by the coming into being of the sex drive, but many contend that the drive is present prior to puberty. For our present purposes we need not enter into the complexities of this argument; it is enough to know that the drive exists, is of a generalized nature, and must be considered as one of the prime movers in the field of social behavior. The sex drive is defined or canalized usually in a manner which is spoken of as heterosexual, that is, the person is motivated to seek out members of the opposite sex in the solution of his sex impulses. Whether or not there is an innate tendency which predisposes a person to become heterosexually oriented is a question not yet answered, and one likely to plague investigators of social behavior for a long time to come. There may be other explanations for the fact that this is by far the most usual way in which the sex drive is canalized. The great variation from this way of defining the sex drive, which apparently occurs from place to place and from time to time, justifies one's conceiving of the sex drive as being highly modifiable through social experience. The sex drive may be, and often is, defined in a homosexual manner, wherein the sexual attraction usually found between sexes is confined to members of the same sex.[19] In addition, some persons have had experiences which have defined or canalized their sexual impulse or drive in such a way that they are attracted to both sexes, and they are said to be bisexual in nature. Although it is unusual behavior, some married persons do engage in homosexual behavior. Other persons, because of the particular way in which they have interacted with others, become autoerotic, that is, depend upon such behavior practices as masturbation for their sexual satisfaction. Still others may have become habituated to practices that are different from all of the above mentioned forms of behavior, and these we classify under the vague heading of sexual perversions, which may include such behavior as bestiality, exhibitionism, masochism, or sadism. Variation from heterosexual behavior is not, as some suppose, always a function of individual peculiarities. At certain times in history, and in certain localities in the world, the so-called abnormal forms of sexual behavior have assumed widespread proportions. Sometimes they come and go as short-lived fads, but sometimes they become established as institutional forms of behavior. The nature of the culture, rather than the biological impulse, determines the direction that the behavior will take as the persons in that culture attempt to meet their sex needs.

The institutions and organizations that arise in response to man's attempts to satisfy his sex urge are many in number and widely divergent in character.[20] In most societies the male is the initiator of any sex activity, whereas, in a few, the female takes the dominant role in such relations. Some societies permit their members to seek sex satisfaction as soon as they are biologically capable of so doing, whereas others postpone direct sex expression for five, ten, or more years beyond the attainment of puberty. In still other societies, such as our own, the established customs, institutions, and associations make no provision whatsoever for sex activity for certain adults, the unwed female being the most outstanding example. It is almost as if the spinster, widow, or divorcee is assumed to have no sex impulse, or at least to be able to sublimate it successfully upon

[19] Homosexuality will be discussed in Chapter 10. A. C. Kinsey, B. Pomeroy, and C. E. Martin, *Sexual Behavior in the Human Male* (Philadelphia: W. B. Saunders Company, 1948), and (with P. H. Gebhard), *Sexual Behavior in the Human Female* (Philadelphia: W. B. Saunders Company, 1953).

See also the older but excellent study by Lewis M. Terman and C. C. Miles, *Sex and Personality* (New York: McGraw-Hill, 1936), for extended discussion of sociosexual behavior in a large variety of cases.

[20] See Stuart A. Queen, Robert W. Habenstein & John B. Adams, *The Family in Various Cultures* (Chicago: J. B. Lippincott Co., 1961).

demand. Thus *how* a person will respond to the sex impulse is a function of his experience in interaction with the customs and rules of the society in which he lives, and not of the biological impulse itself. The latter is permissive, and not mandatory, with regard to the particular action to be followed.

THE RANDOM ACTIVITY IMPULSE

In every normal infant there appears to be a need to engage in some sort of random activity behavior that is not directly associated with either the specific drive of hunger or sex. The flailing of the arms and legs of the healthy infant, his vocalizations (other than crying), and probably his thinking are suggestive of this general urge to activity which has been called an impulse to random activity. It is definitely random, and becomes specific only as a result of experience and maturation.[21] It is to be emphasized that the definition of these impulses is not independent of the other drives and impulses of the personality, and to this matter we shall presently give attention. The point to be noted here is that these impulses, as in the case of the hunger and sex drives, are undefined at birth and can be turned in multiple directions, according to the unique experiences of the person concerned.

Whether a person will learn to stutter, to sing, to talk very fast or very slowly, to use the upper part of his vocal range or the lower, to speak Hindustani or English, to speak loudly or softly, is to be determined only partly by the biological equipment that is his. The directions that he will pursue in his definition or canalization of the random vocalization impulse are as much a function of the limits placed upon him by others in his culture as by those limits placed by the nature of the vocal cords, larynx, and the resonance chambers of the skull. As stressed in Chapter 2, it is in the interaction of the biological heritage, the environment, and the acquired personal variables that the definition comes about. These generalizations, of course, apply equally well to the impulse to mental activity, or the definition of the "intellectual processes" as L. Guy Brown calls them. Logical thinking or illogical thinking, rationally or irrationally directed study habits, the amount and nature of daydreaming, the substitution of mental imagery as compensation for overt social behavior, all are to be determined by the experiences which the person has. The

---

[21] L. Guy Brown analyzes this random activity impulse in terms of *random vocalizations* and *intellectual processes*. *Social Pathology* (New York: Appleton-Century-Crofts, 1945), Chap. 2, "The Organic Heritage." It seems preferable for our present purposes to use the more general term *random activity impulse* to comprehend both of these impulses as well as those involving the skeletal or voluntary muscles of the body. Some social psychologists prefer the term *drive* to denote ". . . an unlearned push from within—a push in no particular direction"; T. M. Newcomb, R. H. Turner, and P. E. Converse, *Social Psychology* (New York: Holt, Rinehart and Winston, 1965), p. 24.

mental endowment does not set the direction that the intellectual processes will take. Neither highly endowed mental equipment nor mental deficiency demands any specific behavioral adjustment. Neither all morons on the one hand, nor all mental giants on the other, pursue the same paths of behavior. Within these categories there is nearly as much variation in social behavior as there is in any random sample of persons within a given culture.

As in the cases of hunger and sex, it is the culture that indicates, in the vast majority of instances, just what the individual will do with his muscles, vocal equipment, and brain. In the United States people become violinists, sculptors, barbers, airplane pilots, elevator operators, or baseball players. The Eskimo does not do these things, but, of necessity, becomes a skilled hunter and fisherman. The Polynesian knows little or nothing about elevators, airplanes, or baseball, but much about outrigger canoes, spear fishing, and swimming. Just as the native of the Congo River basin of Africa or the Amazon region of West Brazil probably will not become a virtuoso of the violin, so the American urbanite will not learn how to trap and kill lions, pumas, and elephants, nor how to shrink human heads. Learned patterns of behavior (which are shared and passed from generation to generation by sociocultural means, and not by germ plasm) play leading roles in differentiating among the medicine man, the shaman, the brain surgeon, the priest, and the scientist.

Man, not guided by instincts, but possessing an agile mind, must learn his adjustments in the world. In this learning he frequently misjudges the nature of himself and the world, and perpetuates in custom his learned errors. Stuart Chase points out that through the misuse of words and other symbols, man, unlike other animals, frequently misinterprets the nature of his milieu. Mr. Chase reflects as follows as he watches his cat Hobie Baker:

> Hobie will never learn to talk. He can learn to respond to my talk, as he responds to other signs, sounds, smells, sights in his environment. He can utter cries indicating pain, pleasure, excitement. He can announce that he wants to go out of doors . . . But he cannot master words and language. This is in some respects fortunate for Hobie, for he will not suffer from hallucinations provoked by bad language. He will remain a realist all his life . . .[22]

> Generally speaking, animals tend to learn cumulatively through experience. The old elephant is the wisest of the herd. This selective process does not always operate in the case of human beings. The old are sometimes wise, but more often they are stuffed above the average with superstitions, misconceptions, and irrational dogmas . . . One may

[22] Stuart Chase, *The Tyranny of Words* (New York: Harcourt, Brace & Co., 1938), p. 49.

hazard the guess that erroneous identifications in human beings are
pickled and preserved in words, and so not subject to the constant
check of the environment, as in the case of cats and elephants . . .[23]

This human capacity for misjudgments and illogical action is unique
among the animals of the world—a fact that must be kept in mind if one
is to understand the culture of mankind. The mere existence of a custom—
even one centuries old—is no proof of its soundness.

Even this briefest of explanations of the problem enables us to see
that, although social behavior does reflect man's particular biological
make-up, no specific form of behavior is demanded by his biological
drives. Neither wars nor missionary efforts, scientific achievements nor
criminal enterprise, creative artistry nor an alley brawl, is attributable
directly to biological heritage. The latter is a necessary, but not a sufficient basis for social relationships and cultural growth.

The unlearned drives as we have described them are not ends in
themselves; drives by themselves are insufficient to explain behavior.
They are brought into this discussion because they can and do become
active and effective through interaction in developing human behavior.
The drive is but the first step in a cycle which seeks to restore the organism's status. The condition that will restore this status is sought after by
the organism which is in a state of readiness to be rewarded by the
achievement of this objective. This cycle begins, as we have already seen,
by a state of disequilibrium created by a particular tissue need or by a
complex of such needs. Tension continues until this need is more or less
satisfied by certain satisfactions appropriate to the need.

It should be pointed out that man enjoys many of his tensions. The
state of disequilibrium is not necessarily unpleasant nor is it something
that man would wish to permanently eradicate. Satiety is not man's ultimate goal. Disequilibrium is a more normal condition for man than
satiety. Schermerhorn argues that man's nature, especially his social psychological nature, is not one of balance and equilibrium, but is one of
being off balance, nonhomeostatic, of becoming.[24] It is in the process of
satisfying the tension need that man finds his satisfactions. A national
brewery is currently advertising the slogan "Have Fun with Your Thirst."
When man has satisfied the tension need he does not then avoid further
tension producing situations. If sexual tensions were really unpleasant
they could be eliminated through castration, a procedure which does not
seem to be favored by many. The enjoyment of food is one of the real
pleasures of living. Not being hungry at meal time is regarded as un-

[23] *Ibid.*, p. 51.
[24] Richard S. Schermerhorn, "Man the Unfinished," *Sociological Quarterly*, 4
(Winter 1963), 5–17.

fortunate. It is not unknown for weight conscious women who enjoy their food to regurgitate after a sumptious luncheon. In such instances equilibrium is not the goal.

It has been pointed out that organisms sometimes "deliberately raise tension in order to lower it."[25] George Homans is quoted as saying that ". . . there is a tendency for any group of men to complicate the conditions of their life, (and) to make the conditions more interesting . . . any circumstances interfering with the complication (are) felt emotionally as frustration."[26] Man probably could not survive without a certain amount of sensory stimulation and excitement. At McGill University and more recently at Princeton University it was discovered that if a human being's normal sensory lines are cut off or baffled, abnormal behavior, including hallucinations, frequently occurs. Subjects in the McGill study were isolated in quiet cubicles and were deprived of normal sensations. Hearing, vision, tactile and kinesthetic sensations were reduced to a minimum. Under these conditions, many subjects developed symptoms not unlike those of psychotics and if the experiments had been conducted longer more serious results might have occurred.[27] These studies in sensory deprivation underscore Langer's contention that man's brain is a symbol-making and retaining organ which requires interaction with other objects and persons to survive.[28]

The Relationship Between Biogenic and Learned Drives

It is essential that the biologically transmitted motives or drives be distinguished from those which emerge only after certain experiences. Even though this particular chapter is primarily concerned with the biogenic (unlearned) initiators of action, it is deemed advisable to note the relationship between these biogenic motives and the ways in which the organism attempts to satisfy them.

Figure 3 brings into focus four paired combinations of motives. In this figure, W refers to the *Why* (motive), H refers to the *How* (or the solution to the problem set by the motive), I refers to those motives which are believed to be innate, and L refers to motives which are socio-

[25] John Cumming and Elaine Cumming, *Ego and Milieu* (New York: Atherton Press, 1962), p. 15.

[26] *Ibid.*, p. 16. *See* Jerrold L. Wheaton, "Fact and Fancy in Sensory Deprivation Studies," *Aeromedical Reviews*, Review 5–59, School of Aviation Medicine USAF.

[27] W. H. Beston, Heron Woodburn, and T. H. Scott, "Effects of Decreased Variation in the Sensory Environment," *Canadian Journal of Psychology* (1954), 8, pp. 70–76. For a recent statement of the case against homeostasis as a motivational factor, *see* R. W. White, "Motivational Reconsidered," *Psychological Review*, 66 (1959), 297–333. White states that "There is no longer any compelling reason to identify either pleasure or reinforcement with drive reduction . . . [and that] . . . . raised tensions and even excitement seem to be cherished . . ." p. 328. We will again refer to the White article in the consideration of learned motives in Ch. 5.

[28] Susanne K. Langer, *Philosophy in a New Key* (Cambridge: Harvard University Press, 1951), p. 45.

W_I H_I	W_I H_L
W_L H_L	W_L H_I

W – "why" (impulse, motive)
H – "how" (how satisfied)
I – innate
L – learned

FIGURE 3. "A Paradigm of Psychologic Theories." [by William Bruce Cameron, *XV, 2 American Journal of Psychotherapy* (April 1961), pp. 205–11.]

genic or learned. Thus, the first cell in the figure is typical of behavior in which the motive and solution are both innate, as in simple instinct theory. Homeostasis would also be included here. Cell 2 postulates an innate source of energy (sex, hunger), but a solution which is learned. In cell 3, the *Why* is learned and the *How* is innate. This category poses some logical problems but the author of this paradigm suggests that an illustration is provided in the case of fear, which is learned, having as a consequence neurosis in the form of conversion hysteria. Fainting as a response to learned fear, grief, and so on, is also suggested by some, but the extent to which fainting is a learned response is still a mooted point. In any event, this category is of little value to the social psychologist.

The fourth cell categorizes those situations in which both the *Why* and the *How* are learned as in the desire for recognition and new experiences, the need for response and recognition. Reference to this figure may clarify our thinking and help avoid the error of explaining particular instances of behavior in terms of conflicting assumptions concerning human motivation.

THE NEUROLOGICAL SYSTEM

We have discussed some of the fundamental drives that energize behavior. The effectiveness with which these drives achieve their objectives is closely associated with the development and efficiency of the nervous system.

One-celled organisms like the paramecium and amoeba have no nervous system; their adaptation to the world is tropistic[29] and stereotyped.[30] As we go up the evolutionary scale, the complexity of the nervous system increases as does the number of things the organism can do. Nature has provided those organisms that are yet primitive in their nervous structure with tropisms, reflexes, and instincts, which enable them to operate on the basis of stereotyped behavior responses. These responses function satisfactorily for survival if the stereotyped habit is effective in the particular environment; but the organism may be seriously limited in its variability and adaptability. To a large extent, the human animal is not so restricted as are the lower organisms, because of his nervous system which enables him to make a greater variety of responses and to extensively modify his milieu.

The nervous system and its impact on human interaction and personality development may be considered under the following headings:

> The Receptors.
> The Effectors.
> The Central Nervous System.
> The Autonomic Nervous System.

The Receptors

The receptors (visual, auditory, tactile, olfactory, gustatory, kinesthesis, and equilibrium) are the only known means of communication the organism has with the outside world. Without them, the organism is incapable of being stimulated, irritated, or reached in any way. That there are wide individual differences in capacity to receive stimuli lays a foundation for the development of individual differences in style, taste, and interests. That all men vary in their capacities to receive sensation is readily apparent. The different shapes of eyeglasses required to permit adequate vision illustrate this point. The varying degrees of color-blindness further illustrate the presence of genetically determined differential response capacities. Some interesting research has been conducted on taste differentials since it was accidentally discovered in 1932 that a chemical compound—phenylthiocarbamide (PTC)—which was characterized as "bitter tasting" in chemical literature—did not taste bitter to

---

[29] A tropism is an involuntary response of an organism into a definite axial position with reference to the direction of a particular stimulating agent.

[30] It should also be pointed out that even the paramecium will, in an experimental situation, modify its stereotyped behavior in order to survive, i.e., turn somersaults to reverse its position, an action which is not natural to its behavior.

some laboratory staff members.[31] About 30 per cent of Americans are not sensitive to the bitter taste of a dilute solution of PTC. This differential taste sensation is not common to all bitter substances. However, there are other substances closely associated with PTC which provide similar results.[32] A recessive gene apparently accounts for these taste differences and, of course, is an inherited characteristic. Both racial and national differences occur in the ability to taste as "bitter" certain compounds. Blakeslee and Fox (1932),[33] and Blakeslee and Salmon (1935)[34] showed that the thresholds of a variety of substances, bitter, sweet, sour, and salty, varied unpredictably among individuals. Blakeslee comments that "we live in different taste worlds."

An interesting case involving a simple poison illustrates the wide variations which occur when human beings are tested in a systematic way. Williams reports an experiment by Percival in which the latter observed the differential skin reactions of people to the application of varying amounts of mercuric chloride.[35] Out of thirty-five subjects studied, one showed skin irritation when a solution of mercuric chloride of one part per 100,000 was applied, another responded to three parts per 100,-000, five more responded to ten parts, eleven more to thirty parts, thirteen more to one hundred parts, and four failed to respond to any of the concentrations tested. It is likely that similar native differences in capacity to respond to stimuli could be demonstrated for all the receptors. This has lead one scientist to comment, "A biologist must assert the absolute uniqueness of every human individual."[36]

These differences in native capacity for sensation may in part account for particular interests and adaptations. The differences in the mechanisms of sensation contribute to vocational choice, accident proneness, manner of dress, appreciation of music, recreational interests, and to some extent, the choice of a mate. The writers do not wish to suggest that all differences in perception can be accounted for by the receptors alone, however important their contribution may be. Most taste prefer-

[31] A. L. Fox, "The Relationship Between Chemical Constitution & Taste," *Proceedings of the National Academy of Science*, 18 (1932), 115–120.

[32] Lloyd M. Beidler, "Our Taste Receptors," *Scientific Monthly* (Dec. 1952), 343–349. Jozef Cohen and Donald P. Ogden, "Taste Blindness to Phenyl-thiocarbamide and Related Compounds," *Psychological Bulletin*, 46 (1949), 490–98; *and* Jozef Cohen, "Concerning Taste Blindness to PTC," *loc. cit.*, 48 (1951), 419–430.

[33] A. F. Blakeslee and A. L. Fox, "Our Different Taste Worlds," *J. Heredity*, 23 (1932), 96–110.

[34] A. F. Blakeslee and T. N. Salmon, "Genetics of Sensory Thresholds: Individual Taste Reactions for Different Substances," *Proc. of National Academy of Science*, 21 (1935), 84–90.

[35] R. J. Williams, *Biochemical Individuality* (New York: Wiley, 1956), p. 110.

[36] L. D. Dunn and T. Dobzhansky, *Heredity, Race and Society* (New York: Penguin, 1946), p. 46.

ences and interests are learned. Through experience we have learned to like some things and dislike others. The differences in taste sensations by themselves are hardly of sufficient magnitude to account for the various reactions to particular foods. Culture and training attach certain status and prestige value to some foods.

Whatever the cause, we do know that American advertising is set up to appeal to a wide variety of taste in American appetites and to stimulate status consciousness in dress, automobiles, homes, and so on. Some of this advertising is based on the different capacities of individuals to see, feel, hear, taste, and smell, that is, to *sense* the various stimuli presented to them. However, there are limits to persuasibility set by the human biological heritage beyond which persuasion is ineffective; many chemicals, gases, and sounds are obnoxious to *all* human beings, regardless of the setting, and therefore, in these instances, no amount or quality of advertising or persuasion could be effective.

The Effectors

The effectors are the organs of response. That is, they function only when they receive impulses from the receptors via the central nervous system. An effector cut off from the spinal cord is paralyzed and inoperative. The effectors in man may be divided into glands (endocrine or ductless, and duct glands), and muscles (striped or voluntary, and unstriped or involuntary).

The central nervous system does not directly control all these muscles and glands. Generally, it may be said that the striped or voluntary muscles and the duct glands are controlled centrally; but the smooth, unstriped or involuntary muscles and all the endocrine glands receive their stimulation directly from the autonomic system. The same variation of muscular and glandular efficiency among organisms is apparent here as was true in the matter of the receptors.[37]

Motor skills are also a function of these effectors. The reaction time of individuals varies greatly and makes for differences in athletic ability, certain aspects of musical talent,[38] accident proneness, and so on. However, judgment, insight, and motivation are important factors in how well the motor skills are utilized, so that good effectors do not guarantee efficient responses; they only make possible the capability of achieving such an adaptation.

THE ENDOCRINE GLANDS

One group of effectors which deserve special attention because of their close relationship to personality development are the endocrine

---

[37] R. J. Williams, *Biochemical Individuality* (New York: Wiley, 1956), p. 110.
[38] Paul R. Farnsworth, *The Social Psychology of Music* (New York: The Dryden Press, 1958).

glands (glands of internal secretion). Under the control of the autonomic nervous system, the endocrine glands supply the vital organs and the smooth muscles with their efferent innervation. The endocrine glands secrete hormones directly into the blood stream or lymphatic systems and these hormones exert a chemical effect which regulates various elements of growth, metabolism rate, and homeostasis. The endocrine glands represent a fertile field for speculation and research for those who like to find a chemical basis for personality development. Whereas significant strides have been made in medical therapy in the case of severe glandular deficiency (not many dwarfs or giants are to be seen today), the efforts to relate personality changes to endocrine imbalance have not yet resulted in clearly demonstrable conclusions. The fact that thus far nothing like a one-to-one relationship between personality traits and particular endocrine functions has been demonstrated should not surprise those who recognize the very interdependent nature of the endocrine system.

The endocrine system seems to be quite susceptible to at least partial domination by culture, climate, diet, and so on. For example, blood pressure and basal metabolism, on an average, are lower among people living in the Orient than in people living in America. Occidentals who have lived in the Orient a long time tend to develop lower blood pressure and lower basal metabolism, while Chinese coming to the United States, on the average, develop higher measures of these traits than they had when living in the Orient. Similarly, the age of menarche of girls living in Denmark is about fourteen years.[39] However, for Danish girls living in the United States the age of menarche is six months less.[40]

The endocrine glands can cause an upset in the nervous system of the organism, but the reverse can also happen. Murphy writes, "In the usual schematizations of the roles of the endocrines, emphasis has been placed upon their effects upon the nervous functions. Clinically, however, effects in the reverse direction have long been obvious. . . The nervous system can activate, and can therefore derange the endocrines. It is a common finding that a fright, a nervous shock, leaves an individual with a hyperthyroid condition. A neurochemical cycle is involved. We are dealing with no one way street from glands to external traits; excess thyroid activity may lead to apprehensiveness, but it may also arise from it."[41]

The lack of a simple and direct relationship between endocrine functioning and behavior should not minimize the importance of endocrinology for personality development. The problem will not be abandoned because of its complexity. It is likely that improved research techniques

[39] O. Klineberg, *Race Differences* (New York: Harper & Brothers, 1935).

[40] R. N. Franzblau, "Race Differences in Mental & Physical Traits," *Archives of Psychology*, XL (1935), No. 177.

[41] Gardner Murphy, *Personality—A Bio-Social Interpretation* (New York: Harper & Brothers, 1947), p. 98.

will in time isolate the specific influence of chemical activities in psychological and social development. The use of suppressant drugs with mental patients has already been successful in reducing patient anxiety to a point where the population of many mental hospitals is for the first time showing a modest decrease. These drugs have had the effect of opening up many closed wards, releasing some patients formerly regarded as unmanageable, and generally making possible a greater opportunity for utilizing the hospital wards more for treatment and less for custodial purposes. In spite of increasing admissions, there has been since 1956 a slight downward trend nationally in the number of resident patients in public mental hospitals at the end of each year.[42] Although improved therapy and pioneering experiments in out-patient programs must share the credit for this improvement, the major cause of this change is credited to the use of tranquilizing drugs. These drugs, it should be noted, do not ordinarily accomplish a cure in themselves. However, they have the effect on many patients of reducing anxiety to a point where the patient may engage in the kind of interpersonal experiences (group therapy) out of which appropriate and effective behavior may develop.

The Central Nervous System

The entire organism, including receptors, connectors, and effectors, is involved in behavior. There is, however, from the lower organisms to man, an increasing dependency upon the cerebral cortex for all complex neurological and psychological functions. Though the older portions of the brain, genetically speaking, retain some independent functions, conscious behavior in man is managed primarily by the cerebrum.[43] The

---

[42] *Planning of Facilities for Mental Health Service.* A report of the Surgeon General's Ad Hoc Committee on Planning for Mental Health Facilities, January 1961. Public Health Services Bulletin 808, U.S. Government Printing Office, 55 pages.

The spectacular effects of the drug known as LSD (lysergic acid diethylamide) illustrate the importance of perceiving the biological components of human personality in relationship to other non-biologic components. The discoverer of its psychological effects, Dr. Albert Hoffman, reported that he experienced ". . . a not unpleasant delirium which was marked by an extreme degree of fantasy . . . fantastic visions of extraordinary vividness accompanied by kaleidoscopic play of intense coloration continuously swirled about me." Reported by Sidney Cohen, M.D., "LSD and the Anguish of Dying," *Harper's Magazine*, 231 (September, 1965), 69. This reaction by a stable and mentally well person contrasts with the ". . . extended psychotic states, severe depressions, suicides, and prolonged paranoid reactions," which accompanied the indiscriminate use of the drug by unstable persons. Whether or not the drug's use leads to euphoric feeling states, or to the hospital emergency room, the psychotic ward, or the morgue is determined by the interaction of the drug with other phases of the personality, and not by the sheer bio-chemical processes.

[43] Not all psychologists view the brain as an active and directing force, preferring a motor theory of consciousness, *i.e.*, R. W. Perry, the noted physiological psychologist, regards the brain as a kind of transformer between the input of sensory information and the output of motor activity. The products of the brain, according to Perry, are not ideas and thought, but muscle actions. "The process is an adjustment to a

brain stem, and particularly the diencephalon,[44] represent the older and more primitive brain which managed the behavior of premammalian vertebrates. The development of the cortex in mammals and eventually in man was, in terms of evolutionary history, a fairly recent event.

. . . when in early man the instincts started to be screened at the level of consciousness, the dimensions of the cortex became enormous. In order to pack this huge expanse of cortical tissue into the smallest possible space, the surface of the hemisphere began to wrinkle at an early stage. The human cortex covers the hemispheres in deep and narrow folds. If the cortex were stretched smoothly over the hemispheres, a human brain would have to be the size of a beer barrel.

One of the most remarkable things about the growth of the cortex was the incredible acceleration of this process. While the earlier phases took tens of millions of years to evolve, the later phases were covered in a few hundred thousand years. It seems to be a general law of evolution that once a trend towards a single successful specialization has become firmly established, the speed with which this specialization develops gets faster and faster and may even develop of its own accord beyond the limits of usefulness.[45]

THE HUMAN BRAIN

The remarkable cerebral cortex of man is a highly complex organism which is able to produce organized behavior by means of sensory, motor, and association areas (in conjunction with the lower nerve centers). Although it has been possible to identify motor and sensory areas of the human brain, it has not been thus far conclusively demonstrated that there are localized areas for such faculties as memory, judgment, and reasoning.

Hebb has pointed out that:

. . . although the frontal lobe is the favorite place in which to localize the higher functions when one is speculating about these matters, it is still true that there is no proof that any single higher function depends on this part of the brain. At least as good a case might be made out for the parietal and temporal lobes as the seat of man's distinctive psychological characteristics—if these in fact depend on one part of the brain more than upon another.[46]

---

stimulus, not a reduplication or a representation of it." R. W. Perry, "Neurology and the Mind-Brain Problem," in Robert S. Daniel (ed.), *Contemporary Readings in General Psychology*. (Boston: Houghton Mifflin Co., 1959), pp. 247–261.

[44] The Diencephalon of the forebrain has three main parts: the hypothalamus; the subthalamus; the thalamus.

[45] A. T. W. Simeons, *Man's Presumptuous Brain* (New York: E. P. Dutton & Co., 1962), p. 36.

[46] D. O. Hebb, *The Organization of Behavior* (New York: John Wiley & Sons, 1949), p. 286. D. O. Hebb, "Intelligence, Brain Function and the Theory of Mind," *Brain*, LXXXII (1959), 260–275.

So adaptable is the brain that many human acts can be relearned following serious brain damage, providing the injury is outside the motor areas and is not bilateral. Intelligence test scores, in some instances, have not suffered as a result of lateral craniotomy.[47] Harlow speculates that eventually refined surgical techniques may make it possible to remove an entire neocortex with no defect resulting except transient motor impairment. Harlow facetiously comments, "At the very least it appears that Einstein was needlessly generous in bequeathing his entire brain to science."[48]

In spite of the evidence which indicates that some humans have survived major brain damage without severe or permanent loss to their mental capacities (as measured by intelligence tests), it is likely we have not yet heard the end of this story. It does not seem likely that human beings can suffer massive brain injury without experiencing a marked effect upon their mental capacity. Hebb postulates that the reason some individuals can obtain good scores on mental ability tests following the removal of parts of their frontal lobes may be a function of conceptual learning as distinguished from conditioned response or motor learning.

> The level of intelligence-test performance is a function of the concepts a patient has *already* developed. Once developed, a concept is retained, despite brain damage that, if it had occurred earlier, would have prevented the development. The patient with brain injury at maturity may continue to think and solve problems normally (in familiar fields), although his intelligence would have been far from normal if a similar injury had developed at birth. This explanation meets the clinical facts, and moreover, is supported by the way in which some intellectual capacities are retained in old age when others are disappearing.[49]

THE BRAIN AND MOTIVATION

It is obvious that man's relationships with the world of objects are largely shaped by the nature of man's nervous system, of which the brain is the distinctive human feature. Just how the brain operates in the determination of these relationships is less obvious. Nevertheless, we can perceive that, because of the finite character of man's brain, there are certain relationships that are possible if certain factors are present with which the central nervous system can interact, and that there are other relationships that are inevitable when man interacts with other objects. It is with the latter category of relationships that we are concerned at the moment. There are certain relationships between and among objects in general, and between the individual person and certain other objects, that man-

---

[47] *Ibid.*, p. 263.

[48] Harry F. Harlow and C. N. Woolsey, *Biological and Biochemical Basis of Behavior* (Madison: The Univ. of Wisconsin Press, 1958), p. 12.

[49] D. O. Hebb, *The Organization of Behavior* (New York: Wiley, 1949), p. 2.

kind is obliged to learn, that he cannot choose *not* to learn. Combinations of sensory experiences and mental processes force man, for example, to know that certain sharp objects injure human flesh, that fire burns, and that there is a difference between one's self and all other objects. Much of this kind of learning, which is imperative and nonoptional, involves the recognition of *signs* or *signals* that denote objects. Thus man learns that dark clouds in funnel form denote tornadic winds, and that weeping ordinarily means grief or unhappiness. If the appropriate combination of experiences occurs, learning takes place whether or not man wishes it. When we come to our discussion of learning we shall see that learning is not a function of the brain as a motivating factor, but is a function of interactive processes in which motivation per se is not directly involved. This type of learning is not, of course, unique to man.

ABSTRACTION AND SYMBOLIZATION AS FUNCTIONS OF MAN'S BRAIN

Two forms of mental experiences or processes that, in contrast to the associational learning just noted, occur only in man are: (1) the abstracting of objects—material and nonmaterial—from their existential contexts, and (2) the symbolizing, or attachment to these objects of names or symbols.

The former process, the conceiving of objects *as if* they had independent existence, of imagining them in various novel and complex combinations with other objects, sets man apart from all other animals.

N. L. Munn describes some of the differences in learning ability of various organisms depending upon the nature of their native endowment and upon the character of the teaching environment.

> Learning of all sorts of mazes by many different animals at various levels of evolution has demonstrated that practically all animals are modifiable to some degree. There is a fairly regular sequence of ability; as we go up the scale, we find the higher forms learning faster and mastering more complex mazes. The ant is rather far up the ladder.
>
> When we get to the mammals, the maze becomes an inadequate test of intelligence. The learning problem (making the proper turns in the proper sequence) is just too simple. In this sort of learning rats can beat college students, and have done so repeatedly. So it is apparent that at the rat level and above we must make our tests more subtle, because new mental abilities beyond sheer modifiability begin to emerge. The first of these is to think of something in its absence . . .[50]

[50] Norman L. Munn, "The Evolution of Mind," from *Contemporary Readings in General Psychology*, Robert S. Daniel, (ed.) (Boston: Houghton Mifflin Co., 1959), p. 171. Munn continues in this passage by adding ". . . that is, to represent or symbolize a stimulus which was present but is now gone. This capacity is usually examined by a delayed reaction test." This statement should not be interpreted to imply that the processes of abstraction and of symbolization are one and the same, for they are not.

Nonhuman animals are imprisoned within a temporal *present* with its highly specific existential combination of perceived objects, whereas man can escape the bounds of the present, of the *status quo*, by reaching into the past for items, by projecting them into the future in speculatively organized combinations and permutations hitherto unknown in actual existence. The kind of learning called *insight* is a function of this talent of the human nervous system, and always involves the brain. We see no point in attempting to refute the arguments that other animals seem to be able to engage in abstractions in a very limited degree. Even if one grants this, the differences of degree are so great between man and other animals that they amount to a difference in kind. The dreams of Walter Mitty are peculiarly human.

THINKING

Thinking is basically a mental trial-and-error process involving combining and recombining abstractions. To some extent man cannot help thinking, cannot help engaging in the process of speculating with abstractions; it is the nature of his brain, as it interacts with the sensory and autonomic nervous systems, to speculate and to abstract. In Chapter 5 this interaction process will be explored further. The answer to the question of why man thinks is that he cannot help doing so. As we shall see later, however, man is apparently able to learn to resist thinking rather successfully, and to be satisfied with a minimal amount of abstracting experiences. It appears that the process of clear thinking is better served by conceiving of it as a response to structural characteristics, akin to sensory processes, rather than as a motivational factor per se.

SYMBOLIZATION

Symbolization is another talent of the human brain and nervous system that augments the abstracting quality, but it is definitely not synonymous with it. This is the talent of attaching names, or symbols, to the articles abstracted. Anthropologist Joseph Bram reminds us that:

> We know, of course, that the word "symbols" means "things that stand for other things." The relationship between symbols and the "things" which they symbolize, however, is not a self-evident or natural one. . . . *Symbols* derive their specific function from group consensus or social convention, and have no effect whatever (outside of their rather trivial physical characteristics) on any person not acquainted with such consensus or convention.[51]

The human talent to develop and utilize symbols (rather than signs, as with subhumans) made possible the appearance of genuine speech and

---

[51] Joseph Bram, *Language and Society* (Garden City, New York: Doubleday & Co., 1955), p. 2.

language. The mental ability to communicate abstract thought in terms of symbols has made possible the sharing and accumulating of knowledge and experience that is the basis of culture.

The almost human apes can do many of the things of which man is capable including a degree of mental symbolization, but the apes fail to make a final step into the speech area. This, according to Munn, is due to a difference in the ape's brain capacity.

> The brain of a full grown chimpanzee weighs only about one pound,—one-third as much as ours. The ratio of its brain weight to its body weight is one to 150; in human beings it is about one to 50. That is to say, with a body as large and complex as our own, the chimpanzee has only one-third as much brain to manage it. Furthermore, in the ape's brain the frontal area, which is concerned with associations and symbolic functions, is much smaller in relation to the rest of the brain than ours.[52]

By contrast with all other creatures, mankind, however primitive, everywhere possesses the power of speech. Man's ability to conceive and manipulate objects, ideas, and relationships vicariously or internally, and not only through direct physical experience with them, has been tremendously enhanced by his talent for symbolizing. Critchley says:

> As substitute signs, symbols can refer to things out of sight and outside present experience. When an ape utters a cry of hunger, it can be looked upon as perhaps making a declaration, perhaps an imperative utterance, or even an exclamation of discomfort. No ape, however, has ever uttered the word "banana," for such a word is a concrete symbol, a tool of thought which only man can employ, and he can do so in a variety of ways, irrespective of the barriers of time and space. Man can refer to a banana in past or future tense, as well as the present. Man can talk about a banana in absentia. No animal can do these things. Likewise no monkey can emit a word meaning "hunger," for this term would constitute, or refer to, an abstract or universal idea.[53]

Langer regards man's capacity for symbolization as the key to his human destiny.

> Not higher sensitivity, not longer memory or even quicker association sets man so far above other animals that he can regard them as denizens of a lower world; no, it is the power of using symbols—the power of speech—that makes him lord of the earth. So our interest in the mind has shifted more and more from the acquisition of experience,

[52] Norman L. Munn, "The Evolution of Mind," from *Contemporary Readings in General Psychology*, Robert S. Daniel (ed.) (Boston: Houghton Mifflin Co., 1959), p. 173.

[53] Macdonald Critchley, "The Evolution of Man's Capacity for Language," *Physical Anthropology and Archaeology*, Peter B. Hammond (ed.) (New York: Collier & Macmillan Ltd., London, 1964), p. 52. Italics added.

the domain of sense, to the uses of sense-data, the realm of conception and expression . . . Symbol and meaning make man's word far more than sensation; Miss Helen Keller, bereft of sight and hearing, or even a person like the late Laura Bridgman, with the single sense of touch, is capable of living in a wider, a richer world than a dog or an ape with all his senses alert.[54]

Man's brain is instrumental in the formation of symbols which are attached to abstracted items of experience, but the brain does not operate as a motive, as some believe.[55] It is the position of the present authors that symbolization, insofar as the central nervous system is concerned, is a talent, a potential, and not an impulse. Inadvertently, in the pursuit of human goals, mankind develops symbols with which to manage abstracted aspects of experiences, in order to solve problems in his quest for satisfaction of innate and learned impulses to action. There is a uniformity in the motives of men in contrast to the very wide differences in the symbols which they learn, both in the quantitative and qualitative aspects of these symbols.

Thus, man's capacity for symbolic behavior and speech is due not only to a large brain capacity.[56] Critchley holds that man's early experiences in contact reactions were necessary in the genesis of symbolic behavior in man.

To convert man into a speaking animal, the factor of society is essential. He (Lord Monboddo) posed the question; which is the more important —language for the institution of society, or society for the invention of language? In his view, society came first and had existed perhaps for ages before language developed.[57]

[54] Susanne K. Langer, *Philosophy in a New Key* (New York: Mentor Books, The New American Library of World Literature, Inc., 1942, 1951), pp. 33–34.

[55] *Cf.* Susanne K. Langer, *Philosophy in a New Key* (New York: Mentor Books, the New American Library of World Literature, 1942, 1951). She argues that "The symbol-making function is one of man's primary activities, like eating, looking, or moving about. It is the fundamental process of his mind, and goes on all the time." (p. 45) If one accepts this statement as meaning merely that the brain is *instrumental* in the process, then we agree with it. If it connotes that the brain serves to motivate the process, then we disagree.

[56] Another view of man's brain is held by Bruner who states, ". . . In the history of evolution man's cranial structure is the *result* rather than the *cause* of his experiments with culture. Thus it is claimed that man's large brain resulted from his tool making and communal experiences rather than a large brained creature initiating these adaptations. Bruner, *op. cit.*, p. 15. Similarly, Steward and Shimking question the validity of assuming a causal relationship between genetics and culture. "A demonstration that genetic factors have shaped cultural patterns will require a rigorous scientific methodology that has not been developed." H. Hoagland and R. W. Burhoe (eds.) *Evolution and Man's Progress* (New York: Columbia University Press, 1962).

[57] Macdonald Critchley, "The Evolution of Man's Capacity for Language," in Sol Tax (ed.), *The Evolution of Man* (Chicago: University of Chicago Press, 1960), pp. 289–308.

Society predated and was a necessary prelude to the development of languages, and through these internalized experiences symbolic communication became possible. Just how language became internalized as a program for ordering experience is not yet clearly known. Jerome Bruner offers the following hypothesis which is consistent with social interaction theory: ". . . The process of internalization (of language) depends upon the interaction with others, upon the need to develop corresponding categories and transformations for communal action. It is the need for cognitive coin that can be exchanged with those on whom we depend. What Roger Brown has called the Original Word Game ends up by being the Human Thinking Game.[58]

Thus symbolization is a function of the human brain's talent for abstraction in combination with human motives operating on a social, problem solving level of action.

THE STRUCTURE OF INTELLIGENCE

The cognitive function is a significant personality variable that is in part dependent upon biological foundations. Most organisms are capable of learning, depending upon the complexity of their nervous systems and upon appropriate environmental stimulation. Both biological heritage and environment set limits beyond which mental ability may not develop, and we may assume that intelligence will rise to limits set by either, depending upon which is the lower. In an optimal environment, heredity will set the pace for mental development; but in a person with high mental endowment, environment will more likely be the principal determining factor.

Intelligence, as measured psychometrically, is not a simple unitary character. Individuals differ within themselves in terms of their capacities; for example, an individual may be very competent in solving problems in the areas of mathematical symbols, but be less adequate in working with verbal symbols.[59] Thus, in describing the intelligence scores of a person, it is necessary to specify both the cultural setting and the nature of the mental skill being measured. Although it cannot be measured directly, intelligence can be estimated or inferred by means of various tests which propose, by their own definition, to yield an index

[58] Bruner, *op. cit.*, p. 14. Piaget's work in linguistic theory and Miller's concept of the individual as an information processing system have called attention to the relationship between cognitive mental processes and the operation of computers. *See* James G. Miller, "Psychological Aspects of Communication Overloads," in R. W. Waggoner and D. J. Carek (eds.), *International Psychiatry Clinics: Communication in Clinical Practice* (Boston: Little, Brown & Co., 1964).

[59] Guilford writes, "The methods of multiple factor analysis . . . do not find a general psychological factor at the first order level and they find no second order factor that can properly lay claim to the title of intelligence." J. F. Guilford, "The Structure of Intelligence," *The Psychological Bulletin*, 53 (1956), 287–293.

or indexes of mental competency. In spite of all the criticism made of the Intelligence Quotient and the work of Binet and Terman, the contributions of these men have made possible a working definition of intelligence which is empirical and operational.

> The establishment of the intelligence quotient as an index of the general level of mental ability was a great scientific achievement—with far reaching practical effects in education, psychiatry, law, etc., because it made it possible to distinguish lack of ability from lack of interest, mental illness, or restricted education. The amazing success of this concept was perhaps partly due to the fact that it was an overly simple one. Wide variations in mental abilities can, and do, exist within any single individual.[60]

In the years since Binet, we have learned a great deal more about the structures of intelligence. Today, Guilford estimates that there may be as many as 120 separate mental abilities, and as of this date, fifty-five are known.[61] Binet and Terman's work has stood up as well as it has because, fortunately, they sampled a broad base of many kinds of mental skills, thus yielding a conglomerate but diversified and global score.

INTELLIGENCE AND CULTURE

If we accept the biological basis of mental potential, we must also specify the environmental conditions that will nurture this endowment. Even Binet assumed that mental capacity would evidence itself only under circumstances of adequate nurture. Much more is involved in experiencing cultural stimulation and proximity than simply possessing adequate genetic capacity.[62] The idea persists in some quarters that intelligence unfolds automatically in terms of maturation of structure. Liverant has pointed out that the interaction thesis concerning heredity and environment makes invalid the concept of innate capacity unless the latter term assumes the operations of an appropriate environment.

> Perhaps the most pronounced conceptual weakness of the present (intellectual) model lies in its inability to cope with environmental specificity. The position that individual differences in problem solving are a function of heredity given a relatively constant "demographic" environment (e.g., similar cultural opportunities or similar family life) grossly oversimplifies the specific and still unknown effects of the "psychological" environment on the hereditary potential.[63]

[60] Shephard Liverant, "Intelligence, A Concept in Need of Re-examination," *Journal of Consulting Psychology*, 24 (1960), 101–110.

[61] Guilford, *op. cit.*, p. 289.

[62] J. McV. Hunt, *Intelligence and Experience* (New York: The Ronald Press, 1961), p. 7.

[63] *Ibid.*, p. 109.

The crucial role of interpersonal relationships in developing mental capacity has been cited in the research of Stone,[64] Kellmer-Pringle,[65] and others.[66] Such research has lead Liverant to comment that ". . . Much more is involved in a child's inability to profit from the most 'well conducted' training procedures than lack of the proper genetic constituents."[67] Stone has shown that humans reared in an impoverished perceptual and social milieu may suffer irreversible damage in terms of problem solving capacities. Kellmer-Pringle has reported a series of studies relating to the learning problems of environmentally and emotionally deprived children.[68] In one of these studies two groups of preschool children (one institutionalized, the other not) were matched for age, sex, intelligence scores, and family background. Data were obtained on vocabulary and sentence structure under controlled and spontaneous conditions on the children's ability to understand and express themselves on simple sentences and on verbal expression in social intercourse. The institutionalized children in comparison with the nursery school children were found to be seriously handicapped in the use of these language skills.

While the most deprived child is often the most handicapped in terms of retardation, this is not necessarily the case. Kellmer-Pringle, in order to study the dynamics of deprivation and its effect on human development, studied intensively two groups of institutionalized children, members of *both* groups having been separated from their parents for the first time before they were five years of age. All children in both groups had lived in institutional residence for more than half their lives. The major difference which characterized the two groups was that one group was rated as "severely maladjusted" and the other was rated as "notably stable." The "unstable" group was very "backward" in language development and reading comprehension whereas the "stable" group achieved average mean scores on both these factors. The author concludes that:

> . . . Physical separation and prolonged institutionalization by themselves do not necessarily lead to emotional or learning difficulties. Susceptibility to maladjustment and resilience to the shock of separation and environmental deprivation appear to be determined by the quality

[64] L. J. Stone, "A Critique of Studies of Infant Isolation," *Child Development*, 25 (1954), 9–20.

[65] Mia L. Kellmer-Pringle, "Learning Difficulties of Deprived Children," in *Proceedings of the 16th International Congress of Psychology* (Bonn: North Holland Pub. Co., 1960), 392–394.

[66] Lotte Schenk-Danzinger, "Problems of Social Adaptation of Children Deprived of Maternal Care in Earliest Childhood," in *Proceedings of the 16th International Congress of Psychology* (Bonn: North Holland Pub. Co., 1960), 394–397.

[67] Liverant, *op. cit.*, p. 104.

[68] Kellmer-Pringle, *op. cit.*, p. 392.

of human relationships available to the child during critical periods of growth. It is the child who is rejected by his family and fails to find a substitute parent figure who is likely to become insecure, maladjusted and educationally backward.[69]

In the instances just cited it becomes clear that normal maturation of neurological structure does not by itself guarantee the achievement of effective behavior. Children do not ordinarily acquire their distinctly human behavior patterns until they have had an opportunity to interact with people who behave like human beings. Furthermore, it would appear that this reciprocal relationship between innate structure and environmental stimulation is sometimes specific to certain critical periods which, if missed, may be irreversible in their effect.

INTELLIGENCE AND CREATIVITY

The concept of intelligence and its measurement has often been used to describe individual differences in cognition as if the concept included all of the human mind and imagination. Scholars in recent years have questioned the validity of including creativity under the IQ metric. Thurstone, who has contributed his share to the building of psychometric devices, makes this point:

> To be extremely intelligent is not the same as to be gifted in creative work. This may be taken as a hypothesis. It is a common observation in the universities that those students who have high intelligence, judged by available criteria, are not necessarily the ones who produce the most original ideas. All of us probably know a few men who are both creative and highly intelligent, but this combination is not the rule.
> The confusion between intelligence and creative talent is common. For example, Quiz Kids are often referred to as geniuses. They would undoubtedly score high in memory functions, including incidental memory and rote memory. But it is doubtful whether they are also fluent in producing original ideas.[70]

Intelligence tests have been very useful as a primary device for selection, classification, and promotion in schools, employment situations, and in government responsibilities. Such testing has succeeded in identifying and "screening in" talent which might otherwise be overlooked. However, intelligence testing, if utilized as the sole criterion, may also "screen out" some unusual talent.

One of the best designed investigations of the relationship of intelligence and creativity was conducted by Getzels and Jackson.[71] The authors

---

[69] *Ibid.*, p. 394.

[70] L. L. Thurstone, *Applications of Psychology* (New York: Harper Brothers, 1952), p. 20.

[71] Jacob W. Jackson and Philip W. Getzels, *Creativity and Intelligence* (New York: John Wiley and Sons, 1962).

set for themselves the task of making a systematic inquiry into high creative ability in high school students and its relationship to high intelligence. They selected for their investigation two groups of adolescents
matched by age and sex. One group was composed of children who
were judged to be high in creativity but not concomitantly as high in
intelligence, and a comparative group of children who were high in
intelligence but not concomitantly as high in creativity. All were students
in an urban midwestern private school. The results of this extensive and
thoughtful investigation are rich in provocative ideas for the student of
human behavior, but for our purposes we are primarily interested in the
more conspicuous conclusions concerning the relationship of intelligence
and creativity.

The results of this study clearly indicated that both groups were able
to achieve similar academic results even though the high creative group
was twenty-three IQ points lower than the high intelligence group. Furthermore, the correlation between certain of the creativity tests and school
achievement was equal to and in some cases exceeded the correlation
between IQ and school achievement. The authors are quick to point out
that they do not minimize the predictive value of intelligence testing in
academic achievement, but add the following reservation:

> If we believe—as seems reasonable—that present measurements of
> intellectual functioning sample only a small portion of a person's intel-
> lectual resources then the discovery that those who possess cognitive
> ability not included in the I.Q. also do well in school achievement
> loses some of its mystery and recourse to some all-explanatory extraneous
> principles [such as over-achievement] becomes less necessary. The
> variance in the relationship between intelligence and learning left
> unexplained by the customary correlation of .50 is now most often
> attributed exclusively to emotional factors [including motivation]. On
> the basis of the present data, preliminary as it is, we would raise the
> general question whether part of this unexplored variance may not be
> attributable to cognitive factors of the type sampled in our creativity
> battery but not included in the I.Q. metric.[72]

E. Paul Torrance in another study modeled after the Getzels and
Jackson investigation also found that despite a sizable difference in intelligence quotient, the two groups which he studied (one highly creative,
the other highly intelligent) were equally superior in achievement to
the school population from which they were drawn.[73]

These studies show that over the whole range of creative endeavor
there is a small positive relationship between the intelligence quotient

---

[72] *Ibid.*, p. 28.
[73] E. P. Torrance, "Educational Achievement of the Highly Intelligent and the
Highly Creative," *Research Memorandum BER 60–18*, Bureau of Educational Research, Univ. of Minnesota (Sept. 1960).

and the various measures of creativity. However, the relationship is minimal and signifies only that a certain amount of intelligence is required for creativity but that creativity and intelligence are not synonymous.

THE MODIFIABILITY OF INTELLIGENCE TEST SCORES

For purposes of clarification it is important that we distinguish between intelligence as (A) a genetic component involving an inherited capacity for learning potential, or (B) an operationally defined characteristic as measured by so-called intelligence tests. Much of the criticism of intelligence evaluation has developed out of the confusion of these two definitions of intelligence. If intelligence B is fully dependent upon intelligence A, then intelligence is simply a function of heredity and maturation. But if we assume that intelligence B is an independent variable and not completely dependent upon intelligence A, then we would have to agree that intelligence B can be influenced by experience. In any discussion of intelligence it is important to clarify which definition of intelligence is under consideration.[74]

Many intelligence tests are merely measures of competency in a particular cultural environment. (Definition B.) If the score on such an intelligence test is used as a measure of such achievement, for purposes of comparing individuals in terms of knowledge or learning skills, this is sound reasoning. But if such measures are used to explain *why* (Definition A) one person is more successful than another in school or on the job, it is assuming the presence of a general native capacity which is inferred but which is not necessarily present, at least not on the basis of the test measure alone.

Innumerable investigations have been made to demonstrate that mental quotients can be changed. Volumes have been written on the possibility and extent of change in measured intelligence as a result of various environmental and pharmaceutical manipulations. Although the results of these investigations do not agree as to the extent of the modification, there is consensus that scores on mental tests can be improved by various means. Some of this improvement in measured test scores is due to the increased motivation resulting from the attention and recognition given the experimental subjects involved in the investigation. However, the fact that scores on intelligence tests can be modified by various environmental exposures, diet, or chemicals, is not the same as demonstrating a real change in mental capacity. It has not yet been convincingly demonstrated (except as a result of health correction) that a person's mental capacity (intelligence A) can be changed any more than can his height or eye color.

Consider a stoop-shouldered boy who at the time of induction into

---

[74] For a fuller discussion of this concept *see* Hebb, *op. cit.*, pp. 275–303.

military service is measured at five feet, ten inches. His measured height is less than his actual potential height as determined by the genes he inherited. After three years in service he is measured again. This time he measures six feet even. Has the Army increased his natural height? No, but it has taught him to stand up straight. He measures two inches taller and impresses others as being taller than when he went into service. Yet there is no basic change in his physical structure. It is not straining an analogy to point out that human beings who are functioning below their natural capacities can be stimulated, by an improved environment, good health, encouragement, and good teaching, to act more intelligently and to live closer to their potential. Such persons' basic intelligence has not been increased but they have learned to use their capacities more effectively.

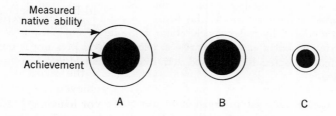

FIGURE 4. Diagrammatic representation of differences between measured native ability and achievement. (Adapted from Ruth Strang. *An Introduction to Child Study*, New York: The Macmillan Company, 1951.)

Figure 4 illustrates the scores made by three students in the same class on an individual intelligence test. The outer circumference line indicates the native mental ability of the individual as the test tries to measure it. This is, of course, an approximation only and may be influenced by many extraneous factors which the skilled psychometrician will check. The solid section within the circle may indicate the individual's actual performance, or the extent to which he is using his native endowment. In this illustration, achievement may be represented by grades made in school. Boy A made a higher mental age score than boys B or C. But B gets better grades than A. The tests help the teacher in this instance to know that A has the capacity to do better if she can find out what is holding him back. On the other hand, C has little natural facility for learning; and if the test score is supported by other evidence, the teacher should not become discouraged if the boy does not readily learn his lessons. This last boy probably could be encouraged by a good teacher to utilize his limited talents in areas where they would be effective. The teacher would probably do this by encouragement, individual attention, and adjusting the curriculum to suit the student's capacities.

The Autonomic Nervous System

We have seen how the central nervous system enables the organism to adjust to the external environment. This orientation is achieved with the cooperation of the energy and support of the autonomic nervous system, which makes possible the internal adjustments necessary to the smooth functioning of the entire organism. The autonomic system does not function independently or intermittently. The autonomic system constantly (more at times of emergency than others) strives to maintain a constant internal environment or homeostasis. Fulton cites the following example of the homeostatic functioning of the autonomic system:

A warm external environment initiates reflex sweating and peripheral vasodilation, with consequent increase in heat loss, but any tendency of the body temperature to fall will bring about shivering (heat production) and peripheral vasoconstriction (reduction in heat loss). The increased venous return to the heart caused by muscular exercise is accommodated by reflex acceleration of the heart and peripheral vasoconstriction, but a consequent rise in general blood pressure is immediately counteracted by increased activity of the aortic and carotid sinus reflexes.[75]

The autonomic system consists of motor nerves which extend to most of the smooth muscles and glands of internal secretion. Together with the endocrine glands, it constitutes a neurohumoral system which very largely controls the main organic functions of the body, such as the digestive, circulatory, respiratory.

EMOTION AS MOTIVATION

Our concern here is with those aspects of the autonomic nervous system which can become interactive in the social processes. This brings us directly to the subject of emotions which are commonly associated with certain functions of the autonomic system. Earlier, we discussed the organic drives as one of the factors which motivate behavior. When these drives are thwarted, the organism is likely to respond in a manner that we commonly term emotional. Depending upon the importance of the frustration, as interpreted by the individual, the tension may be resolved calmly or it may result in explosive behavior. There are those who would restrict the use of the term emotion to the latter explosive type of response but this seems too arbitrary. Emotion as herein conceived is an attitudinal relationship between the organism and some aspects of environment (including the organism itself) which can become of social value to the person concerned. Emotions, from the viewpoint of physiology, involve

---

[75] J. F. Fulton, *Physiology of the Nervous System* (New York: Oxford University Press, 1943), p. 463.

the total organism to a greater degree than, for example, the cold, intellectual orientation one may have toward some routine or objective task.

Even though the term *emotion* has a long history of wide usage, it is not yet sufficiently restricted in its denotative meaning to be thoroughly satisfactory as a scientific concept. Although careful investigations of the physiological referents of what is generally assumed to be emotion have helped narrow the scope of the concept, there are still many unanswered questions. As one psychologist has said, "At best the definition of emotion presents a difficult problem. No single definition has proved acceptable to all psychologists. The difficulty seems to be that no single criterion has been found which clearly differentiates emotional from nonemotional states."[76] Taking into consideration the various interpretations and the many unanswered questions concerning the nature of emotion, we will refer to the concept of emotion in this text as follows:

1. *In this book we shall employ the term primarily as an adjective, rather than as a noun.* We shall attach the term *emotional* to those activities of the human organism, which as best we can judge, involve primarily the autonomic nervous system and the visceral vascular system of the organism. Desirable as it might be to reserve the term for only the motivational aspects of experience, what generally comes under the rubric of *feeling* or *feeling-tone* so clearly involves the visceral vascular components of the organism that it must be accorded a place in the emotional category.

2. *Emotional activity is not deliberate, conscious behavior, but is activity that precedes or follows deliberate action; it is usually either motive on the one hand, or feeling-tone on the other.*[77]

[76] P. T. Young, *Motivation and Emotions* (New York: John Wiley and Sons, 1961), pp. 250–251. Evidence of the confusion in thinking regarding the nature of emotions is found by contrasting the view taken by some psychologists, that emotion is characterized by the disruption or disorganization of behavior (*Ibid.*, p. 457), with the view, that the concept is to be applied only to the secondary drives of the personality. *See* O. H. Mowrer, "On the Dual-Nature of Learning—A Re-Interpretation of 'Conditioning and Problem-Solving,'" *The Harvard Educational Review*, XVII (Spring 1947), pp. 122–123, footnote. In the former view, such diverse phenomena as resentment, laughter, fear, pain, sadness, envy, pride, and humiliation are designated as emotions, whereas according to the latter view, emotion must be restricted to drives and must not be accorded to the states which follow drive reduction or satisfaction. In the author's words, ". . . it is hardly sensible to speak of a *reduction* in emotion as 'emotion.'" (*Ibid.*). More recently a psychologist has written that: "Since no one has yet proposed any criterion which is generally applicable and which meaningfully differentiates between the traditional categories of emotional behavior and motivated behavior, we shall recognize no distinction between the phenomenon assigned to the two categories." Dalbir Bindra, *Motivation* (New York: The Ronald Press, 1959), p. 29.

[77] We say *usually* because, although emotional responses are rarely conscious behavior, the response may be of such a nature that it is not clearly recognizable as either motive or feeling-tone. Such instances are those wherein the organism loses sphincter control, faints, vomits, or exhibits hysteria in various forms. What seems to happen is that a crisis situation, either because of its sudden appearance, its ex-

To illustrate, a person may learn through interactional processes to hate another person; this fact establishes a given relationship between these two persons, an emotional relationship. If we are to understand social behavior clearly, we must stress the different nature of this emotional relationship in contrast to the action or social behavior taken in response to this emotional attitude. In this instance let us suppose that the first named individual, in response to his own anger, strikes or shoots the object of his hostility. This *behavior*, although motivated by an emotional orientation, is *not* emotional. Similar action or behavior could take place without any emotional component, for instance, the lifeguard's knocking out an hysterical individual or the coldly calculated behavior of the hired assassin. The feeling-tone which follows our "hero's" striking the person he hated may well be emotional in nature. The glow of satisfaction, or the remorse, which follows is surely emotional. This feeling-tone may, in turn, stimulate the individual to further action, that is, may become a motive.

3. In keeping with the tri-dimensional, interactionist frame of reference, it is important to note that *every person has as part of his biological heritage an emotional capacity*: (a function of the autonomic nervous system); *that is, he can learn to become emotional about objects, persons, or situations.*

However, with this physiological capacity come few or no directives that determine with which of myriad things and situations an emotional attachment will be made. What things one will fear, love, or define as repulsive or as sex objects are determined by the unique way in which the organism interacts with its environment. Few, if any, objects, persons, or situations evoke the same fear, repulsion, love, anger, elation, or depression in all persons. Everyday experiences afford many examples of the nonspecific nature of emotional responses. The writhing reptile that terrorizes so many persons, causing them to panic, is eagerly sought as a pet by others. The little boy who is adored by his parents may be regarded with dismay by the neighbors. The same political speech will excite no response in some, elation in others, and revulsion in still others, depending upon the cognitive interpretation the organism makes of the situation. The reader can supply countless instances to illustrate the fact that *one must learn which things will be effective in evoking an emotional response.*

---

treme nature, or its novel character, is not reduced by appropriate mental and muscular behavior as controlled by the central nervous system. The situation is one in which the emotional demand for action becomes so great that it takes over the organism; purposive behavior is reduced to a minimum or is absent entirely, and we say that the person is, for the moment, "all drive and no solution." It is much like an automobile with all motor but no steering wheel or brakes. Such emotional responses are, to be sure, the results of what has been learned or *not* learned from one's past experience.

In terms of evolutionary history, the autonomic nervous system, and particularly the sympathetic division, is an ancient structure which functions to aid the survival of organisms in an environment that is at times hostile and dangerous, requiring quick mobilization of energy for attack or escape. This theory, known as the *emergency theory of emotion*, was evolved from research performed by Walter B. Cannon.[78] The original function and value of these early affective responses is diminished in today's civilization, though a vestige of it may be noted in the quip of a famous manager of a professional baseball team, *viz.*, "Nice guys finish last!" Yet the impact of these physiological resources in the human body upon man's adaptations remains significant and must be reckoned with in much of his social behavior. His primitive capacity for aggressiveness, which served him well in an age dominated by muscle and claw, continues to influence his behavior today. The whole complex field of psychosomatic medicine evidences this fact. There seems to be growing evidence that many of the diseases that appear on the surface to be clearly biotic in nature involve as essential ingredients the operations of the autonomic nervous system.

Psychosomatic disorders arise, according to Simeons, because of the struggle between man's ancient drives and his human goals.

> . . . about half a million years ago, at the dawn of culture, our human ancestors began to use this unique human brain to overcome their physical limitations. They then rapidly refined abstract thought and built themselves an artificial environment to make up for their biological shortcomings. It was this trend towards an ever greater control over the world around him that led man into the appalling complexity of today's metropolitan life and into the psychosomatic diseases that are now threatening him with self-destruction.[79]

Psychosomatic ailments, according to Simeons, account for the bulk of urban man's ill-health and are the most frequent cause of his death. "Man shares this kind of affliction with no other living creature. . . . A disorder strictly comparable to psychosomatic disease never occurs in any wild animal."[80]

Some social scientists would not agree that cognitive functions are in conflict with man's primitive needs. Montagu states that ". . . all the available evidence gathered by competent investigators indicate that man is born without any aggressiveness within him whatsoever."[81] Maslow writes,

[78] Walter B. Cannon, *Bodily Changes in Pain, Hunger, Fear and Rage* (New York: Appleton-Century-Crofts, Inc., 1929).

[79] Simeons, *op. cit.*, p. 4.

[80]*Ibid.*, p. 2.

[81] Montagu, *op. cit.*, p. 311.

Those human impulses which have seemed throughout our history to be deepest, to be most instinctive and unchangeable, to be most widely spread among mankind, i.e., the impulse to hate, to be jealous, to be hostile, to be greedy, to be egoistic and selfish, are now being discovered more and more clearly to be acquired and not instinctive. They are almost certainly neurotic and sick reactions to bad situations, more specifically to frustrations of our truly basic and instinct-like needs and impulses.[82]

Montagu believes that man is not only nonviolent in his primitive nature but that in fact he is probably born with the need to love and be loved. Aggressive behavior, on the other hand, according to Montagu, is regarded as a learned response to frustration or the blocking of expected satisfactions. The point of view of these writers concerning the nature of man's innate needs is indeed more optimistic and hopeful for the future of civilization than the more traditional view would seem to justify. An open and inquiring attitude toward further evidence in this regard is in order.

EMOTION AS THE "GREAT EQUALIZER"

Someone once described a Hopi or Navaho Indian family as consisting of two parents, one or more grandparents, three children, and an anthropologist. With a degree of accuracy at least as great, families in certain urban and suburban settings might be described as consisting of two parents, two children, and one psychiatrist. The increasing use of clinical psychologists, psychiatric social workers, counselors of many kinds, and psychiatrists (plus all of the books, pamphlets, magazine and journal articles, and newspaper columns) gives ample evidence of the emotional distress that confronts and confounds thousands of people of nearly all ages and occupations, largely regardless of their material wealth, state of health, schooling, or intelligence. Emotional problems are no respecters of class, clan, group affiliation, or biological endowment variables. They plague the beautiful and the ugly, the young, those in the middle years, and the old, the gifted and the mentally retarded, the rich and the poor, the urbanite and the rural dweller. Wealth, health, intelligence, and habitat differentiate, whereas emotional needs are the common nature of mankind. Somatotypes vary greatly, and there is a wide range of individual differences in native intelligence and in motor capacities. Both relatively and absolutely, the emotional needs of man are much more homogeneous than such items as intelligence or body type. The needs for sexual expression, for affection, for recognition, for security, are common to all men. The giant and the dwarf, the genius and the

[82] A. H. Maslow, "Our Maligned Animal Nature," *Journal of Psychology*, 28 (1949), 273–278.

moron, can love or hate the same objects with apparently the same intensity.

Autobiographies and biographies in all languages are replete with instances of famous, wealthy, powerful, and gifted men and women behaving in response to emotional needs or desires that are identical (physiologically and psychologically) with the behavior of those held in low esteem, the impoverished (mentally and materially), and others in the unknown multitude. Michelangelo, Rembrandt, and Beethoven are examples and are described by Beckman as being "enigmatic, distrustful and misanthropic—all were in continuous conflict with the world and, at times, they certainly crossed the borderline of madness."[83] General Georges Boulanger might have become master of France in 1889 if cognition alone had determined the choice.

On election night, as the ballots were being counted, the streets of Paris were jammed. The President of the Republic sat in the Elysée Palace and awaited the roar that would greet the appearance of Boulanger as he walked in to take over. The Republican guard posted about the building to defend his office ostentatiously read Boulangist literature, wore Boulangist buttons. The crowds in the streets, poor as well as rich, female as well as male, chanted Boulangist songs. Cries of "Boulanger, Boulanger!" and "To the Elysée!" were continuous. Boulanger himself chose to receive the returns at the strategically located Restaurant Durant on the Rue Royale. It was only a short walk from there to the Elysée.

But while the President sat in the Elysée, Marguerite may have sat in Boulanger's apartment. She had contracted tuberculosis and the winter night's air was dangerous for her. Marguerite was no old fool's folly. The General, at the perilous summit of a man's life in his earliest fifties, was estranged from his wife. She had not been able to endure his vanity, she said. After that he had had a series of trivial, even vulgar affairs. Marguerite, a delicate soul, young and cultured, was the first to fall in love with him rather than with what he had to offer.

A woman at whose house the couple met said of her: "A queen on her throne could not be more majestic in her beauty. She will make of him what she wants him to be. If she loves him more than she loves herself, she will make him great. If not, he will be lost."

What thoughts went through Boulanger's mind as he sat in the Restaurant Durant that night can only be guessed. But he knew of Marguerite's consumption and that only a few more years of life were left to her. He knew, too, that if he staged a coup d'etat, he could not spend these years with her. He would have to spend them in the crowd at work.

The news came. Boulanger had won the election. A fever of ex-

[83] Harry Beckman, "Chemistry, Pharmacology and Mode of Action of Meprobomate," *Annals of New York Academy of Science*, 67, Art. 10 (1957), 673.

pectation swept the streets. The mobs clamored exultantly for action. Walk, begged Boulanger's aides, walk. It is only a few steps. Now or never, pleaded Rochefort. It cannot be tomorrow. Dramatically he took out his watch and held it in his hand. He counted out the quarter hours as they passed. The Day would end at midnight. It would never come again, he assured Boulanger.

At night the streets began slowly to empty. The Restaurant Durant emptied. The lights in the Elysée were turned out. Boulanger had gone to his apartment and to Marguerite, and did not emerge . . .

Meanwhile, in the aftermath of Boulanger's defection, a new Government had come into power, composed of men who agreed on only one thing—republicanism—and were determined to make a firm stand. Plans were made to arrest and prosecute Boulanger and his chief advisers, Déroulède and Rochefort, for an attempt to overthrow the Government by force and violence—a crime that came under the jurisdiction of the Senate.

But a police official slipped the news to Marguerite de Bonnemains. Fearing that he would be separated from his beloved, Boulanger fled with her to Belgium. He did not even risk waiting for confirmation of the news. The police watched over their flight. Frontier guards were ordered to permit the couple to pass without incident.

On April 1 the general's followers were shocked by the news in the press that their leader had fled rather than fight with them against a legal prosecution. Nevertheless, in the general elections in September, held while he was still in Belgium, a Paris constituency returned him to the Chamber. Forty-four other Boulangists were elected deputies.

But Boulanger refused to leave Brussels. He would not risk trial. After all, a trial, even if it resulted in acquittal, would have meant embracing what he had turned his back on the night of January 27. Marguerite was mortally sick. He did not leave her bedside.

The young woman died two years later, in 1891, in Brussels. Boulanger mourned her for two months. Then he went to her grave and killed himself on it. In his last will he asked that one tombstone be placed over the two graves inscribed with these words: "How did I survive for two months without thee?"[84]

This is another example from history of the leveling effect of man's emotional system. The occupation of a nation's top position, with all of the implications that this had for millions of Frenchmen, was weighed against Boulanger's relationship with a single person and was found wanting. Set apart from other Frenchmen by his energy, effective leadership, and political acumen, Boulanger became simply another undifferentiated Frenchman because of his autonomic nervous system.

Extensive learning at the cognitive or central nervous system level does not obviate the effectiveness of the impulses to action which emerge from the autonomic nervous system, either as innate undefined impulses,

[84] Nicholas Halasz, *Captain Dreyfus* (New York: Grove Press, 1957), pp. 88–91.

or as learned desires for affection, social approval, new experiences, or security.

One of America's most famous philosophers, whose knowledge included mathematics and physics as well as philosophy, acknowledged his inability to "exercise proper moral control" and of him, philosopher William James wrote:

> The poor cuss sees no chance of getting a professorship anywhere . . .
> It seems a great pity that as original a man as he is, who is willing
> and able to devote the powers of his life to logic and metaphysics,
> should be starved out of a career, when there are lots of professorships
> of the sort to be given in the country to "safe" orthodox men.[85]

BIOLOGICAL CHARACTERISTICS CULTURALLY EVALUATED

Certain biological features of man gain social psychological significance because of the way in which men look at them, and not because there is any necessary relationship between them and specific social action. Thus, it has been said facetiously that if Cleopatra's nose had been a half inch longer the course of history might have been changed. All biological features of man can, to be sure, become sociocultural objects; that is, can acquire meaning and values that affect sociocultural relationships. Variations in such items as height, weight, body form, cosmetic features, baldness, myopia, bowleggedness, are of concern to the social psychologist because of the values which various cultures may assign to specific physiological features.

For example, in some communities in southeastern Europe, cross-eyedness in girls is regarded as sexually attractive, and not as a physical handicap. Children in the United States or Canada whose eyes are crossed are regarded as disadvantaged and the problem is corrected whenever possible. Another example of this cultural definition of a specific biological feature as a social object is found in left-handedness. In some cultures this feature is of either neutral or negative value, but in ours it acquires a positive value in the game of baseball. The reason for this has nothing to do with left-handedness per se, but is found in the relationship of this biological feature to the rules of baseball. It so happens that Abner Doubleday, generally credited with being the founder of the national pastime, decided that the batter, after hitting the ball, would run toward the right, or to first base as it is now located. This rule gives the left-handed batter at least a full stride advantage over the right-handed batter, who upon the completion of his swing at the ball is facing left, or third base, and must turn approximately ninety degrees before he begins his dash toward first base. Had Doubleday seen fit to place first base

---

[85] James Feibleman, *An Introduction to Peirce's Philosophy* (New York: Harper and Brothers, 1946), p. 16.

where third now rests, the advantage would have been with the right-handed batter and not the left-handed one. This decision of baseball's founder has enhanced the fame and fortune of left-handed players ever since.

Any real or imagined organic feature can gain significance as a cultural object. Among the most conspicuous examples of this phenomenon are to be found in race relations and again in somatotyping.

Biological Aspects of Race

Among the men of this earth there are certain perceivable variations in nonfunctional, anatomical features. These differences in structure are not items which differ with each individual, but are structural items which are shared by groups, some relatively small, but many very large. They are structural items which would be less significant social-psychologically, perhaps even insignificant, were it not for the fact that long centuries of isolation have resulted in a rough correlation, *but only a rough correlation*, between these anatomical features and certain geographical areas of the world, and with such cultural items as language, dress, habits, diet, economics, and moral standards. Groups distinguishable because of these features are called *races*.

Few other subjects in the social sciences have been discussed as extensively during the past two decades as that of race. Despite this fact, however, much confusion still surrounds the concept *race*. The first assignment in the study of race is to secure a clear picture of the objective physical facts of race, and only after this is done is one free to discuss some of the social psychological implications of these racial characteristics.

Race in physical anthropology is becoming an increasingly narrow concept. In recent years there has been some agitation to abandon the concept of race entirely because of the misconceptions which have arisen concerning its nature. Livingstone recently stated that, ". . . There are excellent arguments for abandoning the concept of race with reference to the living populations of *Homo sapiens*."[86] This position is not meant to imply that there are no biological variations among the populations which comprise a species, but simply that this variability does not always conform to the discrete labels sometimes used to define races. However, to abandon a given concept or term in order thereby to remove ambiguities and misconceptions from a language has merit *only* if there is no objective reality to which such concepts or terms refer. Racial characteristics, as our society is presently constituted, would be just as real under any other name. The removal of all reference to the term *race*, from both

[86] Frank B. Livingstone, "On the Non-existence of Human Races," *Current Anthropology*, 3 (1962), 279.

written and spoken communications, would not improve the lot of say, the Negroes in South Africa or in the United States. The caste system would remain and the attendant barriers to the Negroes' social mobility would persist just as surely without the term *race* as with it. Social reality is not removed by changing names, and attempts to do so must be recognized as an evidence of belief in word magic. We will use the word *race* in this discussion in its popular sense, recognizing that all ethnic groups come from mixed origins and that there are no known specific physical characteristics or behavioral traits that are unique to any one race.

Despite the extensive publication of racial information stemming from equally extensive research into the nature of race, there are still widespread misconceptions regarding the subject. It requires no large amount of study to learn that the human species is not alike in physical appearance, that there are groups identifiable on the basis of skin, eye, and hair color; on shapes of noses, lips, and general facial contours; and on difference in stature. The abridged summary of the three major racial groups given in Table II, is adequate for our purposes in this text.

Table II
Characteristics of the Three Major Racial Groups

	Caucasian	Negro	Mongolian
Head	Varied—long (dolichocephalic) & broad (brachycephalic)	Dolichocephalic	Brachycephalic
Eye	Nothing distinctive except for occasional "Nordic fold" (skin fold on exterior side of eye)	Nothing distinctive	Heavy upper eye lids sometimes horizontal across entire eye, more often on inside of eye, giving slanting appearance
Eyebrow (supra-orbital) ridges	Varied, but more with heavy ridges than other two groups	Slight to absent	Moderate
Forehead	Varied, but more slanting foreheads than other two groups	Rounded foreheads	Moderate
Cheek Bones	Low and slanting	Low and slanting	High and angular

Table II (Continued)

Characteristics of the Three Major Racial Groups

	Caucasian	Negro	Mongolian
Nose	Most prominent of all— high, narrow convex nose, a Caucasian feature. Also great variety of nose shapes	Characteristically broad with low bridge and root	Smallest of all— low and relatively narrow
Prognathism (Protrusion of area between nose and chin; not chin as such)	None to moderate	Marked	Moderate
Lip	Varied from thin (slightly everted) to thick (markedly everted); former distinctive feature	Markedly everted	Moderately everted
Female Breast	Characteristically hemispheric	Characteristically conical	Characteristically disc shaped (adhering closer to rib cage)
Hair (Amount)	Most hairy (hirsute)	Least hirsute on head and body, moderate on face	Ample head hair, sparse on face and body
Hair (Form)	Straight (round in cross section) to wavy (oval in cross section) with some kinky mutations	Almost uniformly kinky (flat in cross section)	Almost uniformly straight
Pigmentation (Skin)	Dark brown (certain Asians) to very light or blond	Brown to black	Light to medium brown and reddish brown
Pigmentation (Hair)	Dark brown to very light	Black	Dark brown to black
Stature	Medium to tall (tallest average of three groups)	Medium	Medium to short

The question is sometimes raised as to why such features as baldness, obesity, myopia, mental deficiency are not included among items used to designate race. The answer seems to lie in the fact that these are universal features among mankind; they do not align themselves with geographic regions nor are they restricted to any culturally distinguishable groups. The attitudes, habits, and traits of man are not to be explained in terms of racial characteristics. There is nothing about the shape of skulls or eyes that will determine a man's attitudes toward his neighbors, toward classical music, or toward money, and certainly nothing about the color of his skin or hair, that enables one to predict his behavior as a citizen, soldier, or scholar. It may be of interest to note that of the several racial features, no one race is more "ape-like." The ape has a broad head, heavy brow-ridges and slanting forehead, strong prognathism, thin (slightly everted) lips, usually dark skin, abundant brown hair, and short stature. The reader can add up the score for himself.

Each of the three major groups (Table II) has identifiable subgroups, e.g., Alpine, Mediterranean, Nordic, Dinaric, East Baltic (Caucasian); Congo, Nilotic, Melanesians (Negro); American Indian, Indonesian, Eskimo (Mongolian). In addition there are miscellaneous groups such as the Pygmies, Australian Aborigines, Ainu, and Polynesians. These features are anatomical and structural, not physiological or functional. Except for certain minor items (such as the sickle cell)[87] there seem to be very few functional characteristics distinguishing one race from another.

Research has been able to reveal no valid evidence of significant racial differences in intellectual, emotional, digestive, or reproductive processes that are genetic in origin. It should also be kept in mind that differences between individuals on these variables are much more impressive than are mean differences between racial groups.[88]

Insofar as racial differences in intelligence test scores are concerned, we have already noted that such tests operate within cultural contexts and do not measure intelligence directly. The concept of intelligence is meaningful only as it is related to culture. It is not yet possible to measure intelligence apart from cultural symbols. In general, it is true that Caucasians make higher test scores than Negroes in the United States, but when northern Negroes are compared with the general population of the country they show up favorably. In the United States, Mongolians score highest (Japanese Americans) and lowest (American Indians). Jews in general score higher than non-Jews but the differences are reduced or eliminated when the scores of Jews and other Americans of northwest European origin are compared.

[87] James V. Neel, "Diabetes Mellitus: A 'Thrifty' Genotype Rendered Detrimental by Progress," *American Journal of Human Genetics*, 14 (1962), 353–362.

[88] *Race and Science* (New York: Columbia University Press, 1961), Copyright UNESCO.

Tead has indicated that in order to obtain a fair picture of differential intelligence as measured by tests, it is necessary to compare the results of tests taken in the same environment. Tead reports the following experience from New York City:

> When the education authorities of that city decided to set up a special school for promising children, 500 gifted children were selected on the basis of intelligence tests given in elementary schools throughout the city. When these 500 children were examined as to race, religious and national backgrounds, it appeared that the distribution was approximately the same as that of the population of New York City as a whole; that is, about 10 per cent of the 500 were Negro children, corresponding to the 10 per cent Negro population at large. The same proportions were true for Jews and for some national groups.[89]

In short, cultural rather than genetic factors appear to explain racial IQ differences. Anastasia, in a comprehensive review of the literature concerning racial differences in intellectual and personality development, concluded that it is improbable that such differences can be explained solely by genetic factors.[90] With more refined research techniques (including culture free tests), it may one day be possible to discover that there are significant differences in intelligence, emotion, and so on, among the races. However, to date evidence denies us the knowledge of which, if any, racial group will be deemed superior.[91]

At this point, we must hasten to add that the cultural evaluation of racial characteristics, either by the persons possessing these features or by others, often provides us with a basis for predicting social actions. This evaluation, which has varied widely over the years and from place to place, has played a large part in world history. Behavior between and among races has from time to time become institutionalized, and taken as natural, that is, as given, and therefore, as unchanging. This attachment of cultural values to races is called *racism* and will be discussed elsewhere in this text. The present struggle for and against the breakdown of time-honored behavior patterns between the Negro and Caucasian peoples in the United States is a case in point. The problem arises,

[89] Diana Tead, "Race and Intelligence," *Contemporary Readings in Psychology,* Leonard Carmichael (ed.) (Boston: Houghton Mifflin Co., 1959), pp. 130–132. This study could be questioned because the groups comprising the study may be atypical even though the environment was constant.

[90] A. Anastasia, *Differential Psychology* (New York: The Macmillan Co., 1961).

[91] Useful sources on race are: H. Hoagland and R. W. Burhal (eds.), *Evolution and Man's Progress* (New York: Columbia University Press, 1962); W. W. Howells, *Mankind in the Making* (Garden City, N.Y.: Doubleday and Co., 1959); G. E. Simpson and J. M. Yinger, *Racial and Cultural Minorities* (New York: Harper and Row, 1964). The reader may be aware of recent interest in blood types (and other minor genotypic items) as bases for racial classification, but for social psychological purposes such covert criteria are nonoperative.

not because of any socially given or instinctive division among racial groups, but from the cultural inventions of man in years gone by.

Physiological Anatomical Types

Just as we have found it useful to describe racial physiological differences in terms of their cultural evaluation, so will it be worthwhile to become acquainted with somatotyping and the cultural values sometimes assigned to various definitions of body types. The subject of somatotyping is introduced in this chapter because the student should be aware of the useful descriptive semantics involved and also because, in some quarters, the relationship of body types and temperament is still a lively subject. For our part, we believe any discussion of body types is important not so much because of any possible organic implications for personality and temperament but because individuals with particular body physiques may respond to an awareness of their own physique by accommodating to the expected temperamental stereotype. Young people, highly sensitive to any comparison of their physique with their peers, may take toward themselves attitudes and evaluations which are inappropriate and maladaptive. Whether or not people believe that body types yield particular temperaments may be finally important only to the extent that people believe this to be true. We will have occasion in this text to refer frequently to W. I. Thomas' principle, which states that if people define a situation as real, its consequences for them *are* real.

Too often the classification of the variety of human physiques is subjective and inconsistent. An objective working classification of physiological anatomical types will make it easier to discuss more consistently and meaningfully the variety of human physiques. Kretschmer, and later Sheldon, have provided us with physiological anatomical classifications which will make our discussion of this subject more meaningful.

Kretschmer's physical types are perhaps the best known.[92] There are, says Kretschmer, three clear-cut types and one left-over category. The aesthenic type is the long, lean physique that features thin muscles, narrow shoulders, narrow and flat chest, and delicate bone structure. The pyknic type, in contrast to the aesthenic, or leptosomatic type, is characterized by ". . . pronounced peripheral development of the body cavities (head, breast, and stomach), and a tendency to a distribution of fat about the trunk, with a more graceful construction of the motor apparatus (shoulders and extremities) . . . middle height, rounded figure, a soft broad face . . . the magnificent paunch protrudes from the deep vaulted chest which broadens out towards the lower part of the body.[93]

[92]Ernst Kretschmer, *Physique and Character* (New York: Harcourt, Brace and Co., 1925).
[93] *Ibid.*, p. 29.

The limbs of such persons are soft and round with little or no muscle relief, and the hands are soft, short, fat, and wide.

The athletic type is just what one would guess it to be from its title. The heavy, broad chest, the wide shoulders and the relatively narrow hips, the muscles that show in bold relief, the large bones, big hands, firm but elastic skin, the dearth of fat, and tall stature sharply distinguish this body structure from the others. The physiques which do not fit into these three categories or combinations thereof, are called either dysplastic or asymmetrical types.

Sheldon's somatotypes are strongly influenced by the works of Kretschmer. William H. Sheldon, an American student of medicine and psychology, developed the main three types of physiques to a much more refined degree than has been done heretofore. Deriving these types from three components of the body that are already manifest in the embryo of the species, Sheldon and his associates present some seventy varieties of body build, or somatotypes, as they are called.[94] The basic forms are refined counterparts of the Kretschmer system; the aesthenic or leptosomatic becomes the *ectomorph*; the athletic type of Kretschmer is the *mesomorph* according to Sheldon; and the pyknic is the *endomorph*. The same general characteristics are found in the corresponding types, but in the Sheldon system more precise measurement distinguishes them and the newer terms avoid the evaluative connotations of Kretschmer's type names. The three types of Sheldon are not claimed by him to be mutually exclusive, but are continuous variables which are found in some degree in all persons. However, the degree of concentration or dominance of each of these types is rated on a scale from one to seven; the higher the number, the greater the dominance in the particular configuration of endomorphy, mesomorphy, or ectomorphy. Any body build can be described by assigning three numbers to it, each number indicating the degree of endomorphy, mesomorphy, or ectomorphy. To date Sheldon has been able to note seventy-nine of the theoretically possible 343 types. The extreme endomorph is indicated by the combination 7–1–1, extreme mesomorph by 1–7–1, extreme ectomorph by 1–1–7, and the balanced build by 4–4–4. Sheldon also uses the dysplastic category of Kretschmer, but is better able to define it with his more precise system of differentiation of the types. Whatever the future may hold for such typing of the human physique, it does appear to be true for the present that the types do represent significantly different (but not discrete) body structures. The photographs in Figure 5 show clearly the three basic types, plus the combined type which approximates the most commonly found configuration of the three components.

[94] W. H. Sheldon, S. S. Stevens, and W. B. Tucker, *The Varieties of Human Physique* (New York: Harper and Brothers, 1940).

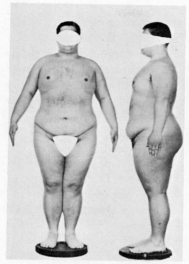

Extreme endomorph (with secondary
mesomorphy and minimal ectomorphy)

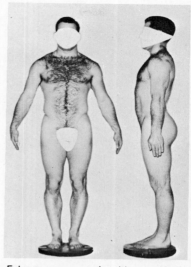

Extreme mesomorph (with secondary
endormorphy and minimal ectomorphy)

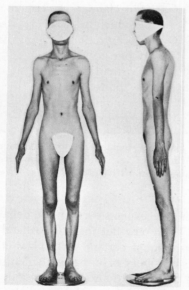

Extreme ectomorph (with secondary
mesomorphy and minimal endormorphy)

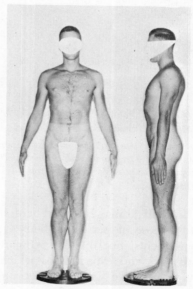

Average (balance in the three
basic components)

FIGURE 5. Representative Somatotypes.

FIGURE 6. "Norma," the average American girl (Age eighteen years). (Photograph courtesy of *The American Museum of Natural History*, New York. Figure modeled by Abram Belskie under the direction of Dr. Robert Latou Dickinson, *Cleveland Health Museum*.)

Briefly, it may be noted here, that culture expects certain role behavior from those of particular body types. These are not institutionalized requirements, but they nevertheless represent a certain crystallization of attitudes and expectations which the members of a particular cultural stage associate with those occupying these positions. Each actor is expected to perform certain prescribed roles in keeping with his somatotype. Subtle but persistent pressures will be exerted upon him (by himself as well as others) to satisfy these expectations. Thus the endomorphic clergyman or the ectomorphic butcher do not fulfill the role expectations

FIGURE 7. "Norman," the average American male (Age eighteen years). (Photograph courtesy of *The American Museum of Natural History*, New York. Figure modeled by Abram Belskie under direction of Dr. Robert Latou Dickinson, *Cleveland Health Museum*.)

of the positions they occupy and they are likely to be pointed out as interesting anomalies. The endomorphic girl who aspires to a place on the tennis team may become the object of amusement or the mesomorphic boy who enjoys esthetics may be seen as violating the expectations of the peer culture. The person who resists these expectations is likely to be a rather strong willed person or one who perhaps enjoys the attention he receives by being a nonconformist.

Of course it should be emphasized at this point that a person's own body becomes meaningful to him not only in terms of the culture's stereotyped role expectations of his body type, but also in terms of the attitudes he sees expressed towards his organism by all his significant others. It is in the process of social interaction with other people, with other objects, and with himself that a person's physique (as all personal variables) gains meaning and significance for him.

There are those who believe there is an organic relationship between body types and temperament. Sheldon's original claim for such a high coassociation has not been supported by subsequent studies although some investigators have reported a moderate relationship.[95]

We have discussed the variations in body form and it might be interesting to observe what normality in physical structure is in the United States. The composite statues in Figures 6 and 7 were constructed from the measurements of thousands of Americans, and represent the type of average for young men and young women. Undoubtedly many contrasting measures are covered up in the averaging process, yet the figures probably do represent a close approximation of the average American. It is to be noted that these figures do not represent the ideal, despite the fact that no handicap in social mobility is represented by these composite figures. The American and Canadian cultures do not attach high esteem to the many Normas and Normans among us. The ideal young woman is taller and more slender than Norma who would not satisfy the expectations of Hollywood or Broadway scouts, nor of modeling agencies. The ideal female model is apt to average near the normal male's height, and is selected for her long legs and broad shoulders.[96] Be that as it may, persons who hover near the measurements represented by Norma and Norman, will find the world built to fit them in most instances. They will find that they are of the majority. They are the 4–4–4's in Sheldon's terms.

SUMMARY

In this chapter we have considered some of the physiological structures which can become effective in human behavior. We found that it is not possible to identify behavior with particular biological structures. We have compared man's anatomy with those of other creatures in describing how man's behavior is in part a function of his unique structure. We also considered how environmental variables and stimuli are essential for the development of these organic potentials. Man, alone among all the creatures, has achieved culture, including the capacity for speech and symbolic behavior. These achievements have resulted at least in part from man's unique cortical structure, which has made it possible for him to accomplish many things not available to less well-endowed subhumans.

---

[95] S. Diamond, *Personality and Temperament* (New York: Harper and Co., 1957).

[96] *Cf.*, Harry L. Shapiro, *Americans Yesterday, Today, and Tomorrow*, Science Guide No. 126 of the American Museum of Natural History.

We also pointed out that some authorities contend that man's brain capacity is at least a partial result of his communal activities. Man has evolved as man because he has been a tool making and communal being with a brain capacity suitable to the task. We have also considered man's emotional needs. Man is a thinking animal but he is also a feeling creature. Man's cognitive achievements may have outgrown his emotional capacities. Finally, we have considered how man's organic characteristics can become cultural objects. As examples we have considered both race relations and somatotyping as cultural objects.

The student who plans a career in the area of social psychology should be encouraged to expand his knowledge of man's biological potential. Too often this aspect of man's interactive being is overlooked or accepted as an obvious *given*. We hope that this chapter may have encouraged renewed respect for the nature of man's organic potential and its significance for man's future as a communal being.

SUGGESTED READINGS

ANASTASIA, A. *Differential Psychology* (New York: The Macmillan Co., 1961).

BRUNER, JEROME S. "The Course of Cognitive Growth," *American Psychologist*, 19, No. 1, 1–15.

COON, CARLETON. *The Origin of Races* (New York: Alfred A. Knopf, 1963).

FULLER, JOHN L. and W. ROBERT THOMPSON. *Behavior Genetics* (New York: John Wiley and Sons, 1960).

HAMMOND, PETER B. (ed.) *Physical Anthropology and Archaeology: Selected Readings* (New York: The Macmillan Co., 1964).

HARLOW, HARRY F. and C. N. WOOLSEY. *Biological and Biochemical Basis of Behavior* (Madison: The University of Wisconsin Press, 1958).

HOAGLAND, H. and R. W. BURHAL (eds.). *Evolution and Man's Progress* (New York: Columbia University Press, 1962).

HOWELLS, WILLIAM W. *Mankind in the Making* (Garden City, N.Y.: Doubleday 1959).

HUNT, J. Mc V. *Intelligence & Experience* (New York: The Ronald Press Co., 1961).

MONTAGU, M. F. ASHLEY. "Our Changing Conception of Human Nature," *Import of Science on Society*, UNESCO (Winter 1952), pp. 219–232.

NEEL, JAMES V. and WILLIAM J. SCHULL. *Human Heredity* (Chicago: University of Chicago Press, 1961).

Race and Science. (New York: Columbia University Press, 1961) Copyright UNESCO.

ROESSLER, ROBERT and NORMAN S. GREENFIELD. *Physiological Correlates of Psychological Disorders* (Madison: The University of Wisconsin Press, 1962).

SCHERMERHORN, RICHARD S. "Man the Unfinished," *Sociological Quarterly*, 4 (Winter 1963), 5–17.

SIMEONS, A. T. W. *Man's Presumptuous Brain* (New York: E. P. Dutton, 1962).

SIMPSON, G. E. and J. M. YINGER. *Racial and Cultural Minorities* (New York: Harper and Brothers, 1958).

TAX, SOL (ed.). *The Evolution of Man* (Chicago: University of Chicago Press, 1960).

WILLIAMS, R. J. *Biochemical Individuality* (New York: John Wiley and Sons, 1956).

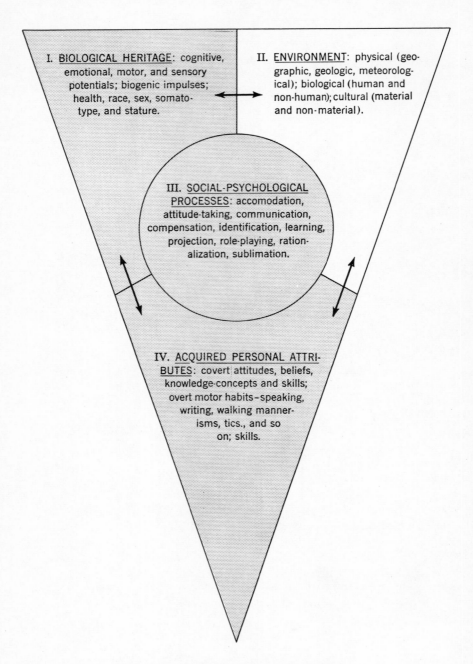

I. BIOLOGICAL HERITAGE: cognitive, emotional, motor, and sensory potentials; biogenic impulses; health, race, sex, somatotype, and stature.

II. ENVIRONMENT: physical (geographic, geologic, meteorological); biological (human and non-human); cultural (material and non-material).

III. SOCIAL-PSYCHOLOGICAL PROCESSES: accomodation, attitude-taking, communication, compensation, identification, learning, projection, role-playing, rationalization, sublimation.

IV. ACQUIRED PERSONAL ATTRIBUTES: covert attitudes, beliefs, knowledge-concepts and skills; overt motor habits–speaking, writing, walking mannerisms, tics., and so on; skills.

FIGURE 8. Interactionist frame of reference.

CHAPTER 4

BEHAVIORAL
ENVIRONMENTS

"All the world's a stage . . ."

It was noted in Chapter 3 that human behavior does not exist apart from protoplasm. Neither does it exist apart from other human beings and from the nonhuman objects which constitute man's environment. The social psychologist is interested in the total environment of mankind, which includes the accumulated knowledge, the groupways, the technical skills and the physical products of such skills be they bombs, stilettos, antibiotics, or Stradivarius violins. It includes the mountains, seas, deserts, herbs, minerals, soils, poisons, wind, rain, and snow. It also is made up in large part of what one might call the biosphere—all living things from microscopic life forms to elephants, including, of course, man himself. We cannot escape this environment, but we can modify it, and are in turn modified by it. Once again, neither the individual nor the environmental factor has any meaning by itself, but only as they become related through the interactive processes.

It is important to emphasize the truth that mere juxtaposition of a person or persons with some object, material or nonmaterial, is not sufficient to make that object part of his or their environment. Unless a person is modified in some way, in thought, feeling, or action, by the object—or it is modified by him—it is not part of his environment regardless of its nature or scope. Those who would discount the influences of environment are wont to point to instances of persons escaping this or that environment, say a slum or an unsavory family situation. Careful studies reveal that the grosser environment is selectively experienced by individuals who seem to be in it. The unique combinations of biological heritage, environmental factors, and previously acquired attitudes, knowledge, explain the differential behavior.[1]

---

[1] See Clifford Shaw, *Brothers in Crime* (Chicago: University of Chicago Press, 1938), for a well-known case study of a family of five slum dwelling brothers, one of whom never became delinquent. Some readers may prefer to speak of *actual* or *practical* environment as the equivalent of "environment" as used here, and *potential* environment as denoting those objects which, although in existence, are not significantly related to the persons in question. Another phrase, which some readers may prefer, is "life space," which denotes the limitations placed upon one's mobility by social factors as well as by physical objects such as houses, rooms, and mountains.

One frequently encounters the idea that although the persons living in simple, nonindustrial cultures are unsophisticated in things of the urbanized industrialized world, they are highly informed about the fauna and flora that surround them. However, this is often not true. A study of several isolated groups of people in the highland regions of eastern United States, revealed that the people were quite ill-informed about the complex plant and animal life in their midst. When asked the name of different flowers, a frequent reply was, "Oh, it's jest a posey."[2] The following quotations by a well known American sociologist provide us with an excellent introductory statement about the nature of environment and its relationships to man.

Animals are not attached to the soil like plants, but they are no less dependent on, and responsive to, environment. Human beings are usually capable of passing from one environment to another as well as of changing the conditions of a given environment to suit their own purposes. But they are not on that account more independent of the kind of environment in which they live. The environment is not simply the outside world, thought of as something that surrounds or "environs" us. If we think of it in that way, we underestimate its role. In truth, the relation of life and environment is extremely intimate. The organism itself, the life structure, is the product of past life and past environment. Environment is present from the very beginning of life, even in the germ cells. We think of our organisms as ourselves, and environment as that which lies outside us. But the capacities and attributes of the organism are relative to the whole environment in which they manifest themselves. The environment is more than a "conditioning" factor of a life that can be conceived of apart from it. Imagine, for example, that we were suddenly transported to a much larger planet. Our bodies would instantly become much heavier, and that fact alone would involve a myriad of other differences. We would no longer know ourselves, we would no longer, assuming we could exist at all, *be* ourselves. We never know life except in an appropriate environment, an environment to which it is already adjusted. Life and environment are, in fact, correlates.

So closely interwoven are the two that every variety of life, every species, in fact, every individual living thing has its own particular environment, in some degree different from that of others. Environment is not one but *infinitely various*. . . .

Furthermore, every change in a living creature involves some change in its relation to environment; and every change in the environment, some change in the response of the organic being. In its totality, as relative to any group (and ultimately to any individual), it is thus a factor of great complexity. Every difference of environment means a difference in our habits, our ways of living. On the other hand, our

[2] *See* Mandel Sherman, *Hollow Folk* (New York: The Thomas Y. Crowell Company, 1933) for a clear exposition of this situation.

habits, our ways of living, in so far as they differ, create for us a different environment selection within it, and a different accommodation to it.[3]

In emphasizing the importance of environment in the shaping of human behavior, one must guard against attributing too much influence to it. There have been numerous attempts to interpret life as a function of this or that particular environmental factor, but "environmental determinists" are not in good standing today.[4]

We can think of the total environment as a great theater, made up of: (1) *the stage*—on stage and back stage—with all of its props—mountains, seas, and innumerable artifices; (2) *the script*—the non-material aspects of culture, written largely in the past but modified by each performance or episode of life's drama; consisting of norms, group-ways, and sanctions; (3) *the actors and audiences* whose varied parts or roles determine in large measure the roles which any single actor can play. We now turn to a consideration of these three aspects of the universal theater that constitutes man's environment, within which the human drama unfolds.

THE STAGE

The theatrical analogy is appropriate for the study of man's behavior if it is not pressed too far. The stage's characteristics and its location set the limits to which the actors can go, whether it be the stage of the legitimate theater or the larger stage upon which society acts out its roles. Our concern here is with those nonsocial objects with which mankind establishes relationships that help to shape his personality. If we underestimate the importance of these physical aspects of man's experience, we run the risk of attempting to study human behavior in a void. Although the social influences are almost always involved in any given episode, such influences are shaped and limited by the nature of the nonhuman, nonsocial characteristics of the stage upon which the action occurs. It is to these props that we now turn attention.

The physical environment of man—the world's stage together with its props—can be classified into four major categories.

[3] R. M. MacIver and Charles H. Page, *Society* (New York: Rinehart and Co., 1949), pp. 73–74. This is MacIver's statement, reprinted from his earlier text.

[4] The writings of the late Ellsworth Huntington provide us with examples of geographic determinism. *See* his *Mainsprings of Civilization* (New York: John Wiley and Sons, 1945) as representative of this sort of environmental determinism. His works depended upon statistical correlation for much of the "proof" of climate's influence upon man's behavior. Earlier supporters of this sort of explanation of civilization are found in Edwin G. Dexter's *Conduct and the Weather* (New York: The Macmillan Co., 1899) and H. T. Buckle, *History of Civilization in England* (London: Longmans, Roberts and Green, 1872). Another form of environmental determinism is found in the writings of Karl Marx who viewed the economy as the independent factor in cultural change and individual behavior.

1. *Geographical—geological—meteorological.* The formation of personality inevitably is in some degree a function of where a person lives on or in the earth (or sometime in the future in space). We will detail in later chapters the influence of topography, minerals, moisture, temperature, and storms upon human behavior.

2. *Dwelling space—quantity and quality.* The complexity which we call human behavior is not untouched by his dwelling. It makes a difference whether the latter is an Iroquois long house, a single room home of a Mexican peasant, a multiroomed, palatial "cottage" in Newport, Rhode Island, a crowded tenement in East Harlem or South Boston, a dirt floor shack in the subtropical region of the United States, a penthouse on Telegraph Hill in San Francisco, a prison cell, or a flophouse on skid row.

It makes a difference whether a dwelling unit has two or more baths (as some nearly five million American households do) or has only a shared bathroom or none at all (as more than nine million American dwelling units do). Living space also affects social action. Nearly thirty-five million American households hold an average of .75 persons per room. Interpersonal relationships under these conditions can be very different from those surrounding the approximately two million households wherein there are 1.5 persons per room. The former "stage setting" would pemit six persons for eight rooms, whereas the latter would see six persons in only four rooms.[5]

Forty-three million dwelling units are structurally sound, and have full plumbing, but nearly six million units are either in a dilapidated state or are deterioriated and lack plumbing facilities. Over seven million household units have only cold water piped into the house or none at all.[6] The importance of these conditions is not difficult to see.

3. *Material wealth.* The contents of the dwelling and other forms of material wealth can, and usually do, gain meaning for the persons concerned. The vast majority of Americans own both radio and television sets, 92 per cent and 87 per cent, respectively.[7] Most Americans have automobiles, more than eleven million households report having two or more cars, and approximately the same have no cars.[8] Only 18 per cent have home freezers and 12 per cent have air conditioners, but 79 per cent have telephones. Slightly less than two million have no heating unit. These "props" enter into personality in many ways, as the reader knows, and will be discussed later.

4. *On stage and Backstage.* Whether at work or play, in the shop or office, a restaurant or at home, it makes a difference if a person has a

---

[5]*Census of Housing*—1960, 1, Part 1, p. XXVIII and XXIX. There are approximately fifty-eight million household units in the U.S.

[6] *Ibid.*, p. XXXVI.

[7] *Ibid.*, p. XL.

[8] *Ibid.*, p. XL.

"backstage" where he cannot be seen by strangers, clients, customers, or even by friends. Rare indeed is the person whose environment does not include these two quite distinct areas of action. One writer employs the concept *region* to denote these parts of the sociocultural stage, defining region as ". . . any place that is bounded to some degree by barriers to perception."[9] The backstage of the theater has its real-life counterparts in the waiters' kitchen retreat, the judges chambers, and the bath and bedrooms of dwelling units.

There will be occasions in later chapters to point out more specifically the relationships enforced and/or permitted by these variations in stage settings.

THE SCRIPT

A newborn babe does not select his environment any more than he selects his parents. To a very significant degree, what the child becomes as a personality is determined by the culture into which he is born, and by the established roles of those, both his elders and contemporaries, who will fashion the role which he is to play. In a real sense, the social heritage is the script for the drama which unfolds in a given society. This script prescribes the roles; it tells how a hero should behave, what constitutes villainous behavior, just what lines the females and children shall speak and when they shall speak them. Customs vary from stage to stage; in some the cast members have nothing to say regarding the play or drama, whereas in others they can even discharge the director if they believe him to be incompetent. On each stage the plays are apt to be deemed successes and have "long runs," changing so gradually or so little that the audience and players are not aware of any significant alteration. Sometimes a sudden change in plot and direction occurs (revolution) but this is not the rule.[10]

That there will be innovation is not only possible, but inevitable; however, the change is always in terms of what has gone before, and any individual in the process of building and changing the script ". . . is like the coral insect, always working on a mountain made up of the crystallized remains of dead predecessors."[11]

Culture as script also tells what rewards and penalties are appropriate and what functionaries shall apply these sanctions. On some stages all the actors use the same script, and harmony—or at least homogeneity—

[9] Erving Goffman, *Presentation of Self in Everyday Life* (Garden City, N.Y.: Doubleday and Co., 1959), p. 106. The reader will find this book an interesting description of human behavior in terms of theatrical concepts, although some may view it as a too literal analogy between the deliberate play-acting of the theater and the less self-conscious roles of everyday life.

[10] R. Dewey and W. J. Humber, *The Development of Human Behavior* (New York: The Macmillan Co., 1951), p. 94.

[11] Charles Horton Cooley, *Social Organization* (New York: Charles Scribner's Sons, 1909), pp. 321–322.

characterizes the "play," whereas on other stages many different scripts are followed and *cultural pluralism* is quite evident. Sometimes this pluralism makes for stimulating orchestrated variations on the cultural theme, and sometimes it results in conflict and cacophony.

The culture into which the child of today is born is the product of myriad years of effort, both rational and irrational, on the part of our ancestors. It is made up of both wisdom and folly, of verifiable fact, of myths, and of superstitions. The total cultural heritage of the world is extremely heterogeneous, a fact not so obvious as one at first might assume. Geographic and social isolation have combined to present a mosaic of differentiated fashions, customs, and institutions. A most important aspect of cultural heritage is the language which each of these cultural groups uses in communication, and this is a factor which further isolates these cultures one from the other. Those who speak a language unlike one's own often differ in food tastes, dress styles, ideas of what is correct or incorrect behavior, often bring up their children to believe things which are foreign to the outsider, and laugh at things which the stranger considers not at all funny.

In every culture there are *culture forms* which range from crazes and fads to the rigorously enforced customs which nearly all persons conform to with minimal external coercion. The terms used to denote these ways of acting, given below, are arranged on a continuum from left to right in order of increasing prevalence, permanence, obligatoriness, and organization. The obligatoriness is, to be sure, not always in terms of formal social controls. In primary or personal relationships, the controls involved in the groupways at the left in Table III are at times more stringent than

Table III
Group Ways or Culture Forms*

Craze	Fads	Fashions	Folkways	Mores
			Customs	

* *See* William Graham Sumner, *Folkways* (New York: Ginn and Co., 1940), one of the most widely read and influential books in sociology. Sumner's definition of folkways and mores is still accepted (p. 38). Sumner selected the Latin word *mores* as a name for the folkways with connotations of right and truth in respect to welfare embedded in them. (p. 38).

formal controls at the right end of the scale. Nevertheless, in terms of the total culture's demands, the forms of behavior on the left of the scale tend to be largely optional and the individual person usually may, if he wishes, act with great latitude without undue interference from others in his environment. Here we find such behavior items as peculiarities in speech, diction, and pronunciation; faddish or fashionable clothing preferences, hair styles, food preferences; forms of recreation; church preferences (in some cultures), and so on. As one moves from the behavior designated by the concepts on the left to those on the right, it becomes less true that he can act as he wishes, but must take into consideration the attitudes of those about him. Even in the case of folkways, which are defined as "expedient ways of doing things," departure from the usual or the customary is not made with impunity. Note the social cost of refusing to conform to such things as dress at formal functions, to have one's hair combed and cut in accordance with the customs of the given culture, to adhere to standards of cleanliness and etiquette.

Figure 9 illustrates the influence of culture in shaping attitudes and social values. While a man or woman will not be prosecuted by the courts of law for failure to conform to these behavior norms, each may be penalized by loss of economic opportunities, and social ostracism. In fact, minor infractions of the law may result in less cost to the individual than violations of courtesy and of the rules for eating and dressing. This is particularly true in an urban setting.

The mores are the ways of behaving which the persons with power, (whether the few in a feudal society or the many in a democratic one), believe to be essential to the welfare of the community. These reflect the musts and the must-nots of a culture. In primitive groups, particularly the preliterate ones, these rules are implicit and the whole group learns them and rarely violates them. In the urban, secular groups, the heterogeneity and size of the population make it necessary to back up these ways of acting with formal statutes or laws, with provision for enforcement of the laws by special groups created for this purpose. Thus in such a culture it is not easy to distinguish between the influences of informal sanctions and of laws, but it is still true that the majority of persons within the urban culture are controlled in their actions more by habitual attitudes (e.g., conscience), than by the explicitly formulated norms (e.g., laws). The removal of the laws and formal sanctions against homicide would not result in the wholesale slaughter of the populace by friends, associates, or even rivals and enemies in the social, political, or economic fields. Laws for the most part are important in restraining the small minority of persons who are not controlled by the implicit psychological bases for conformity. However, in all societies, even the most secular ones, there are certain customs, (mores), which need not be backed up with formal laws. In the United States, for instance, we have no need for explicit rules against cannibalism. Nevertheless, as pointed out above, it becomes increasingly important as the population becomes larger and more urban in nature to establish explicit rules of behavior covering a wide range of behavior, these rules being enforced by impersonal third-party groups.

The main point of these classifications is to emphasize the heteroge-

FIGURE 9.   Cultural heritage versus Biological heritage.

neity of the ways of doing things in our present culture and, therefore, to emphasize the inevitability of each person experiencing different configurations of behavior by combining, distorting, and otherwise incorporating them into his own unique patterns of acting. We stress once more the fact that, because the social experience of the individual is always a three-way interaction involving the biological heritage, the modifications of this heritage, and the environment, no two persons ever have identical experiences and each person's total environment is, therefore, unique. The meaning which the environmental factors have for the individual person is always in terms of the other components of his personality. To repeat, no two persons ever can be said to have the same total environment.

Norms and Sanctions

Mankind's groupways or culture forms do not just happen but are defined by other phases of the cultural environment, namely the *norms*, which are explicit or implicit statements defining what behavior is desirable, necessary, and encouraged, or undesirable, harmful, and forbidden. Synonyms for norms are rules, codes, standards, ordinances, and laws. The adjective *normative* carries the same ethical denotation.[12]

Norms per se are not effective in modifying or effecting behavior, *e.g.*, the groupways. They must be implemented by *sanctions*, which on the one hand are penalties, ranging from violent physical means (torture, imprisonment, or capital punishment) through heavy fines or ostracism, to verbal reprimands and other forms of social or self censorship. On the other hand are the rewards ranging from the freedom from force or coercion, through monetary gains, medals (Phi Beta Kappa or Congressional Medal of Honor), to simple approbation for conformity. The agencies or instruments of sanctions include such things as secret police, law courts, parents, teachers, gossiping neighbors, honorary associations, and conscience. The reader familiar with sociology will recognize the process of applying these rewards and penalties under the caption of *social control*.

American Ethos

The particular patterns of customs, fashions, shared attitudes, and values, and rates of culture change which distinguish one society from another are called *ethos*. Because of the many similarities among the

---

[12] It is to be noted that social scientists use the terms normal and abnormal, normality and abnormality to denote *quantitative* and not qualitative or ethical phenomena. With the increased use of statistics this is logical. The normal curve is a descriptive item, not a normative one, etymology to the contrary notwithstanding. Thus abnormal behavior may be normatively acceptable and normal behavior reprehensible. Thus extreme altruism is abnormal and racial prejudice is normal in our culture.

many cultures of the world, and the slight variations on basic cultural themes, the ethos of any peculiar society may be difficult to identify. Even in the so-called simple societies, the patterns of culture are complex. Even so, attempts to spell out cultural differences which distinguish one society from another are relatively common. It has been a favorite pastime of European writers to point out to the world the peculiarities of the United States. Mrs. Frances Trollope's caustic remarks revealed some of the less admirable features of nineteenth century Americans, especially of certain local areas in the Midwest. Somewhat later Charles Dickens failed to see much to acclaim during his lecture tour of the country. The well known appraisal by Alexis de Tocqueville judged American culture with a cogency which was matched by an ambivalence of attitudes. In the mid-twentieth century, English anthropologist Geoffrey Gorer wrote about certain aspects of the American ethos with indifferent success.[13] His view that the popularity of milkshakes (frappes, cabinets, or frosties, depending upon the section of the country) stems from our overly zealous avoidance of female nudity, may bring into question other judgments which he presents to his readers. Even Europeans who do not write about us have definite views of what our culture is noted for.[14]

Being fully cognizant of the pitfalls awaiting those who attempt the task, we believe it worth while to bring to the reader's awareness some features of the United States' cultural heritage which are relevant to personality development. With no pretense of its being exhaustive, we present the following list taken from the ethos of this country.[15] The degree to which these are unique to the United States is variable, and several may apply, for example, to neighboring Canada.

1. A penchant for self criticism.
2. The "American Creed."
3. An abiding faith in the effectiveness of formal schooling.
4. A neophilia for gadgets, clothes, recreation.
5. An emphasis upon the values of youth.

[13] Geoffrey Gorer, *The American People* (New York: W. W. Norton, 1948).

[14] *See* Magne Lundseth, Jr., "That European Arrogance," *Atlas*, 4 (Aug. 1962), 132–134. The author points out some misconceptions which Europeans entertain about the U.S., but adds a critique of his own. The *Atlas* magazine, devoted to foreign press comments on world affairs, is occasionally helpful in providing views of America by outsiders.

[15] *See* Robin Williams, *American Society* (New York: Alfred A. Knopf, 1958). "Major Value-Orientations in America," pp. 388–442, for a discussion of such items as "success," "activity," "humanitarian mores," "progress," and so on. A number of these are elaborations of items subsumed under the heading "American Creed," noted below. The reader will find stimulating Francis L. K. Hsu's "American Core Value and National Character," in F.L.K. Hsu (ed.) *Psychological Anthropology* (Homewood, Illinois: The Dorsey Press, 1961), pp. 209–230. Hsu is critical of the generally approbative nature of William's presentation of values in the United States. *See also* Jules Henry, *Culture Against Man* (New York: Random House, 1963).

6. Elusive and relative standards of success.

7. A faith in the ability of the physical and biological sciences to solve problems.

8. Sanction of aggression and violence.

A PENCHANT FOR SELF-CRITICISM

This tendency will be manifest in subsequent pages. In addition to the municipal, state, and federal reports of great variety, the social problem articles and textbooks of the social scientists, the fiction of the United States reveals a willingness to look critically at our cultural foibles. Such varied writers as Mark Twain, Sinclair Lewis, Upton Sinclair, Ernest Hemingway, John Steinbeck, Budd Schulberg, and Richard Wright have taken their turns in this self criticism.[16] In general, this is viewed as a healthy part of our culture, though European and African students in American universities note that their criticisms in the same vein are met with a defensive attitude on the part of American students.

The discrepancies between the letter and spirit of the "American Creed" are made explicit by certain newspapers, magazines, and journals. The existence of racial and credal prejudices are not swept under the rug except in the more provincial products of the press.

THE "AMERICAN CREED"

The "American Creed" is a phrase taken from Gunnar Myrdal's An American Dilemma,[17] and refers to the idealism which is incorporated (1) in the first ten amendments to the Constitution (the Bill of Rights); (2) in the Declaration of Independence's phrase "We hold these truths to be self-evident, that all men are created equal, that they were endowed by their Creator with certain unalienable Rights, that among these are Life, Liberty and the Pursuit of Happiness"; (3) in the teachings of the Judeao-Christian religious tradition; and, (4) in the English common law. Though the behavior of some Americans is not in accord with these ideals, rare is the American who will openly attest to his disavowal of them. We do not, as a group, pay only lip service to the American Creed as we do to the ideal of hard physical labor. The creed is part of the value system that constitutes our conscience, and when we or others violate it, we feel either guilty, ashamed, unhappy, or angry about the violation. If we maltreat an individual or a group, we find it necessary to rationalize our action in order to ease the proddings of our conscience. If

[16] Lundseth, op. cit., calls attention to two European writers, Georges Duhamel of France (Scenes de la vie future) and D. Oberndorfer (Von der Einsamkeit des Menschen in der Amerikanischen Gesellschaft), who have noted and written about American self criticism. The bestseller, The Ugly American, by W. J. Lederer and E. Burdick (New York: W. W. Norton, 1958), is a well-known example of this American characteristic.

[17] (New York: Harper and Bros., 1944).

we did not subscribe to an ethic such as that found in the American Creed, there would be no need for rationalizing or explaining many of our actions.

It is true that, once having pointed with pride to the opening lines of the Declaration of Independence and in other ways making clear their faith in democracy, Americans fall short of the democratic ideal. The franchise has been gradually but surely extended, and lower class background is not necessarily an insurmountable handicap to success as variously measured. However, democracy is not infrequently restricted to the political level, and individual aspirations for exclusive and restricted statuses of a large minority of Americans belie any wholehearted subscription to the democratic ideal insofar as this implies equal opportunity. The interest manifested in the vestiges of European royalty is incompatible with explicit democratic ideals—Queen Elizabeth of England and Princess Grace of Monaco excite a most undemocratic interest in the United States and Canada, especially among young women. Exclusive country clubs, debutante parties, the *Social Register*, private schools, and restricted neighborhoods, apartment houses, and hotels are hardly the trappings of democracy. Nevertheless, United States Governmental agencies spend hundreds of thousands of dollars to assure a young man the right to attend his own state university, and new laws seek to guarantee equal employment opportunities and the right to stay in hotels and inns of one's choice.

AN ABIDING FAITH IN THE EFFECTIVENESS OF FORMAL SCHOOLING

Few societies have spent as much of their wealth on schooling the masses of people. From the early New England public schools which sought to thwart the Devil, the "Old Deluder," through literacy and Bible reading, to the huge state university systems of the current day, Americans have voluntarily taxed themselves and gone into debt to assure their children of at least minimal schooling. Illiteracy has been reduced to 2.2 per cent of the population, twenty five years old and older,[18] and the average number of school years completed by persons above the age of twenty-five approximates the twelve-year mark.

Despite this, however, there exists an ambivalence in attitudes toward the product of these schools. The following quotation by a sharp critic of "educationists" makes the point clear:

Americans have unbounded faith in schools, but they seem to distrust the results of schooling. We send, at public expense, an ever-increasing proportion of the population to school and college, yet we are sus-

[18] *Statistical Abstracts* (1962), p. 120. For the age groups 14–24, 25–34, and 34–44, the rates of illiteracy are, respectively, 1.0, 1.4, and 2.1.

picious of the highly educated man who offers to make some return by devoting his special training to the public service. At graduation we are proud to see our sons and daughters march forward in cap and gown, but in the morning newspapers we recognize the very same cap and gown as the cartoonist's accepted symbol for folly and ineffectiveness.[19]

Further evidence of this ambivalence is found in a recent survey about attitudes toward science and scientists. Although 92 per cent of the persons interviewed thought that, "Science is making our lives healthier, easier, and more comfortable," and 87 per cent believed that science was the main reason for man's rapid progress, 40 per cent thought that "scientists are apt to be odd and peculiar people," and 25 per cent believed that "scientists always seem to be prying into things they really ought to stay out of."[20] Furthermore, colleges and universities, not trusting the students to select a well-rounded program, still believe it necessary to require certain basic liberal arts courses.

It is a known fact to all college and university teachers that a very significant proportion of persons enrolled are really more interested in a college degree than in a college education. One professor has remarked, with some cynicism and with at least an equal amount of realism, that slot machines placed at strategic points on a campus which would give credits toward graduation with the correct combination of lemons, cherries, and so on, would do much to erase the colleges' financial worries.

NEOPHILIA

The love of the new, manifested by the frequency with which the words *new* and *different*, or their synonyms, are employed in advertising scripts, separates American culture from more traditional ones. That this is in part a function of an economic system which thrives on fads and fashions cannot be denied, yet this desire for novelty extends beyond the purchase of new clothes and other commercial gadgets. The hair stylist makes as much money setting old as new styles, yet the latter come and go in fairly swift succession, and one hardly need dwell on the kaleidoscopic changes in dance and music forms among the younger set.

EMPHASIS UPON THE VALUES OF YOUTH

One need look no further than the income awarded the manufacturers and purveyors of cosmetics designed to postpone the evidence of time's

---

[19] Arthur Bestor, *Educational Wastelands* (Urbana, Illinois: The University of Illinois Press, 1953), p. 1. Even though this may be more open to question today than when it was written, it is still characteristic of many people.

[20] Stephen B. Whitney, "Public Opinion About Science and Scientists," *Public Opinion Quarterly* (Summer 1960), 387–388. It is of interest to note that only 46 per cent agreed that science will solve social problems such as crime and mental illness.

passage to perceive the validity of this asserted aspect of the American scene. Although it is true in many societies that "everyone wants to live a long time but no one wants to grow old," Americans disesteem age to a degree not known to some peoples. Again, this may reflect the youthfulness of the country itself, but whatever its source, the plaudits of the masses are usually reserved for the things that the young can do rather than for the values accessible principally to those who have lived a long time.

ELUSIVE AND RELATIVE STANDARDS OF SUCCESS

We have become a nation with standards of success that are beyond the reach of most persons. In the arts and sciences success is spelled by solid and objectively measured achievement—the physician, research scientist, and a few others achieve a status acknowledged by others and by the individual himself as satisfactory. However, this is not the case for the vast majority. The measures of success are not always objective in nature, but are comparative. Not knowledge per se, nor service to the community, but such relative criteria as wealth and power and popularity are the bases for judgment. Thorstein Veblen's well-known concepts of *conspicuous consumption* and *pecuniary emulation* are still descriptive of much in our efforts to live successfully. We hear that "it's no disgrace to be poor," but we see evidence about us that makes the statement less than credible. However, when is one right? When has he arrived? Don't the phrases *get ahead* and *get on top* indicate that one's goal is never quite reached? How many must one get ahead of? How many must one get on top of to succeed? Our society seems to be broken into innumerable pyramids, and within each, only those at the top are considered to be successes. Authors of a recent college textbook have this to say concerning the elusiveness of goals which spell success in our culture:

> When status-expectations are based on characteristics that only some possess, but to which all are expected to conform, some people either conform to the standards only at a cost of severe strain or cannot meet the standards and must experience a sense of defeat and failure. . . .
> This situation may apply to the many as well as to the few. It may be that the conformity required of the people in order to entitle them to self respect and the approval of others is set so high that most people, by definition, cannot conform. If, for example, the students who get admired or the businessmen who get praised or the professors who get recognition are the ones in the top 10 percent of their fields, then 90 percent of the people in those statuses are by definition failures, in a relative sense, at least. If, in other words, the social structure is such that the most people aspire to the better than most people, most people have to be frustrated; and the sense of failure they experience can be

as painful as the guilty conscience of Oedipus or the role of conflict of Hamlet.[21]

People strive for economic security in order to achieve a certain standard of living, but they also strive for economic reward as a symbol of success. Consider, for example, the motivation of the man who is told that he will receive a $100 increase in his monthly pay check beginning the first of the month. The man presumably will be jubilant. He will thank his boss, praise his company to his family, and feel more financially secure and important in himself. Suppose that a week later when he is driving home with a colleague who is doing about the same kind of work, he mentions his $100 raise. The friend says that he has also received a raise but that his amounted to $105. Now, how is the first man going to feel about his boss, his company, his success? The difference of $5 is not going to make much change in his economic security, but the $5 differential makes all the difference in the world to his feelings of self-worth. "One-upmanship" seems to have replaced "keeping up with the Jones" as an axiomatic guide. Fictional treatment of this kind of success criterion is seen in the novels *Kitty Foyle, Executive Suite,* and *Point of No Return.* The implications for social psychology of such a system of success criteria are important. The absence of objective measures of success, incorporating values which do not depend upon comparison, renders it difficult for individuals to know when they have succeeded. This lack of predictability, as will be argued in later chapters, spells insecurity for the people involved.

FAITH IN PHYSICAL AND BIOLOGICAL SCIENCES
TO SOLVE HUMAN PROBLEMS

Metals are more malleable than men. Whatever truth there is in this statement has appealed to Americans. Despite the fact that the creation of the thermonuclear bombs evidences the great need for knowledge about men who might use this means of destruction, relatively little is being done to overcome the lag between success in the physical and biological sciences, on the one hand, and the social sciences on the other. In one state university, there was a 100:4 discrepancy between the monies spent for research in the physical and biological sciences, and in the social sciences and humanities. In another state university, all of the physical and biological departments had money for research assistants and fellowships but none of the social sciences was so equipped. The reply to a big bomb is a bigger one. The answer to fast getaway cars for

[21] H. C. Bredemeier and R. M. Stephenson, *The Analysis of Social Systems* (New York: Holt, Rinehart and Winston, 1962), p. 130.

criminals is faster cars for the police. The quest for happiness is in more material gadgets; when Americans and Canadians will be willing to go as deeply into debt for education and art objects as we are now for cars and household appliances, certain problems now facing us will be less formidable.

SANCTION OF AGGRESSION AND VIOLENCE

The value incorporated in the "Don't tread on me!" theme is intrinsic to the American value system. It is against this background that the value system of the Mennonites, Amish, Quakers, and other pacifists and supporters of nonviolence stands out so remarkably. The "turn the other cheek" admonition is rarely listened to by Americans, and the man who does so is looked upon as a "sucker," if not a coward. The popular vote for the television and movie themes which incorporate no small amount of violence reflects the high value placed upon violence as a means of resolving problems. The "two-fisted, quick-tempered, gun-slinging" person, far from being despised as a throwback to a primitive culture, is more apt to be glorified and placed upon a hero's pedestal. The toys in the shops are further reflections of this violence theme. A culture which supports pugilism can hardly be said to oppose violence, and in such athletic contests as hockey, it is not the nonviolent players who receive the crowd's plaudits. The quip that "nice guys finish last in the American League" is a function of the same value theme. In introducing a popular university football player at a post-season banquet, the coach remarked "The nicest thing that I can say about this guy, is that he is the *meanest* player I have ever known." The remarkably histrionic, but none the less violent, performances of the professional wrestlers are hardly fare for those who abhor violence. The adolescent or adult male who responds to verbal insults in kind frequently loses stature; the "rock 'em-sock 'em" male holds higher rank among his age peers than does the peace-loving "sissy." Whether or not this is as it should be is another question; the fact is that this esteem for violence is part and parcel of our ethos.

THE ACTORS AND THE AUDIENCE

How many actors are there? How large is the audience? Where are they? What are they like? Answers to these questions must be known if we are to understand the behavior of any individual who is associated with the actors or audience in question. In brief, the social environment, constituted by other actors and the audience, must be understood if we are to understand the individual's actions.

Obviously, the total world's population of some three billion people does not exert an undifferentiated, blob-like influence upon any given individual. In any episode in a person's life, the number of actors involved, their location at the time, and their characteristics all have bearing upon the actor.[22] There is an interactive, selective process going on from the very beginning of life which determines which individuals will, and which will not, influence significantly the parts one is to play on life's stage. Although the human being is relatively helpless in his early life, he soon begins, insofar as he is able, to select his social environment in terms of his own likes and dislikes, needs and wishes. Under the heading of *significant* or *affective other*, we will discuss first this aspect of his social environment. However, each person becomes a member of social groups wherein his own attitudes and opinions may or may not have played a part in the social statuses or positions which he occupies in the community. This phase of the social environment is discussed under the heading of groups *as environment*.

The Significant or Affective Other[23]

In the day by day living, the individual develops attachments to some persons, becomes repulsed by others, and has a neutral relationship to many others. (Again, the exception is in those rural situations wherein the total group is a primary group.) He is positively attached to some, with varying degrees of affection, from the pleasant neighbor to the husband, wife, child, sibling, or parent. Some he dislikes, but perceives them as competitors or rivals, and uses them as bases for measuring his successes or failures. He is related to others in a secondary manner, based upon their position or status, and he must be cognizant of their attitudes and actions. Among such persons are his employers, policemen, or other persons upon whom one's life chances depend in some degree. Still others are those with whom he shares values simply because he is a rational, feeling human being—including the person or persons whom he encounters casually and infrequently.

This very heterogeneous group of people—real, imaginary, alive, or dead—whose actions, thoughts, and feelings—real or imputed—influence our own behavior, thoughts, and feelings, is called the affective or significant other.[24] Everyone alive has a *significant* or *affective other*, and consciously or unconsciously directs his actions, shapes his thoughts, and finds himself reacting emotionally with reference to these persons, sometimes as groups and at other times as individuals. A comparable concept is that of *reference group*, which some prefer to the more denotative concepts of significant or affective other. Reference group is an apt term,

[22] The actor's attitudes and knowledge, of course, enter the picture. These are dealt with more specifically in chapter 5, 6, and 7.

[23] For denotative reasons, the authors prefer (and use in their classes), *affective other* to *significant other*, but accept the fact that the latter has greater currency and therefore is used here in many instances. The two terms are synonyms.

[24] The important social psychological process of taking the attitude of others toward us, *role taking* as George Herbert Mead usually called it, will be discussed in detail in Chapter 5.

"This dress may not look like $200 to you,
but it will to J. B.'s wife!"

FIGURE 10.   Influence of significant other.

indicating that there are persons with reference to whom one's behavior, overt and covert, is modified. It has a shortcoming inasmuch as the term *group* is taken too literally by some persons, whereas the referent item in question at any given time may be a specific individual and not a group, or may be all persons involved, whether members of an identifiable group or not. Furthermore, as used in current social psychological literature, reference group has two meanings. In its first meaning it denotes a ". . . group in which the individual is motivated to gain or maintain acceptance," by seeking to respond to ". . . what he perceives to be the consensus among the group members."[25] In brief, he tries to fulfill the expectations of the group, of which he may or may not be a member. In this meaning of the term, it is approximately the same as the positive aspects of significant or affective other.

In its second meaning, reference group is used to denote any group against which the individual is measured. As has been pointed out, a person may acquire a comparison reference group ". . . because *other*

[25] Harold H. Kelley, "Two Functions of Reference Groups," in G. E. Swanson, T. M. Newcomb, and E. L. Hartley, *Readings in Social Psychology* (New York: Henry Holt and Co., 1952), p. 411. In this meaning, it is closely akin to significant or affective other. *See also* Ralph H. Turner, "Role-taking, Role Standpoint, and Reference Group Behavior," *American Journal of Sociology*, LXI (Jan. 1956), 316–328.

persons compare the individual with it."[26] Thus, if a person applies for a teacher's or electrical engineer's position, the group properly designated as the reference group is the one with which the applicant will be compared. He need not take the attitudes of these other persons toward him. In short, the members of this second kind of reference group need not be members of his significant other.

The important thing, however, is that the reader adopt some terms that will be useful in denoting for him the large, heterogeneous number of persons whose attitudes he takes toward himself and who therefore are important in the development of the individual's behavior and attitudinal patterns. Thus one's *significant other* constitutes one of the most important aspects of his environment, the purely social phases of that environment. In Chapter 7, different kinds of significant or affective others will be discussed, among them the more familiar *generalized other* of George Herbert Mead. For some persons, the affective other consists of only one or two persons, whereas others attempt to include in their significant other almost everyone with whom they associate. The significant other's importance for understanding any given personality cannot be over-emphasized, and will be incorporated in subsequent chapters of this text. Figure 11 illustrates the fact that all persons are not included in one's significant or affective other.

Groups As Environment

Although other actors as individuals are found in one's affective other, much of one's social environment is comprised of categories of people who are designated as "social groups."[27] We define *social group as two or more persons sharing the same status or position in a social system*. A group, social psychologically, exists because its members are similarly related to objects in the environment.[28]

This definition differs from the one usually found in social science literature. Typical of such definitions is the following: "A group, then, may be defined as a plurality of individuals who are in contact with one another, who take one another into account, and who are aware of some significant commonality."

However, we believe this restriction of the term *social group* to a special kind of group, usually small and primary, is untenable. In actual practice, almost all social scientists use the term as we do here, applying

---

[26] *Ibid.*, p. 412.

[27] *Cf.* discussion of reality of groups in D. Cartwright and A. Zander, *Group Dynamics* (Evanston, Ill.: Row Peterson, 1962), pp. 17–22; also Charles Warriner, "Groups Are Real," *American Sociological Review*, 21 (Oct.), 549–554.

[28] Michael S. Olmstead, *The Small Group* (New York: Random House, 1959), p. 21.

it in such phrases as reference groups, in-groups, out-groups, professional groups, alumni groups, political parties, minority groups, majority groups, ethnic groups, racial groups, and so on. However, the reader may prefer to use the term *category* rather than group for the nonprimary groups, and we believe that this preference will not prevent his understanding the following discussion of social groupings.

Our use of the term in its most general sense does not imply that a person's relationships to and within groups are undifferentiated, for this indeed is not the case. Subsequent pages in this chapter include discussions of the several categories of groups and some of the implications which they have for individual behavior. Groups, of whatever kind, are explainable in terms of the biocultural processes which are the inevitable accompaniment of human interaction. The "group maker" is not a simple factor, but is the whole complex of social processes which occur wherever human beings interact with each other and with countless nonhuman objects.[29] We shall, in this text, give more attention to the factors which constitute the "group maker" than to the groups per se. This is not to argue that groups are unimportant, but that they are functions of more pervasive processes and interactive components. They must be dealt with, but not necessarily as basic concepts from which to initiate the study of social psychology.[30]

Social Groups—Universal and Voluntary

An immediate prerequisite for any discussion of human groups is the distinction between those groupings that are mandatory and universal wherever mankind exists, and those groups that are functions of a particular culture or of personal social experiences of individuals. Our purpose is served here if attention is called to these groups as factors in the environment. Their functions in personality formation will be detailed in subsequent chapters.

UNIVERSAL SOCIAL GROUPS

Universal social groups are basically functions of the ascribed position or status—innate or acquired. Man is given no option in the forma-

---

[29] The phrase "group maker" is one of long standing. See E. A. Ross' discussion of it in his *Principles of Sociology* (New York: Appleton-Century-Crofts, 1930).

[30] A well-known student of group behavior makes this point. "Accordingly, my subject is often called the study of small groups. I have called it so myself, but I am now persuaded that the name is misleading. *Small groups are not what we study but where we study it.*" George C. Homans, *Social Behavior: Its Elementary Forms* (New York: Harcourt, Brace and World, 1961), p. 7. Italics added. *See also* Allan W. Eister, "Basic Continuities in the Study of Small Groups," in Howard Becker and Alvin Boskoff (eds.) *Modern Sociological Theory* (New York: Holt, Rinehart and Winston, 1957).

tion of these groups—he must relate himself to other persons and to the nonhuman object world in terms of these attributes and variables. Each of these groups demands social relations of rather specific nature. No society is without these groups—they are a constant feature in the heritage of the species, and are reflected in man's social organization. Examples of universal social groups include the following:

1. Age groups.
2. The mentally and physically ill.
3. Persons sharing common somatotypes.
4. Groups based upon sex structure and function.

Groups (or categories, as some prefer to call them) based upon these characteristics are, as has been stated, mandatory. These are the *givens* in the environment with which man in all societies must contend—they cannot be ignored in interpersonal activity. In Chapters 12 through 16 we will take into account one category of such universal groups, the age groups. If society is to survive, man is given no choice in the care of young children—he must develop institutions and customs to deal with them. The adolescent must cope with the sex impulse, and this is never left to pure trial and error. Even if it were, groups would still be formed as consequences of this universal impulse. The infirmities which accompany old age are not to be ignored, nor are they in any known society.

The realities of mental and physical ill health provide us with other groups that demand some appropriate social organization. Intelligence variations, especially those marked deviations in the deficient direction, force upon us certain kinds of social relationships. The impossibility of the extremely mentally deficient person relating himself to the world in a normal manner is obvious. A somewhat less apparent relationship is found in the way in which the different somatotypes demand differential social organization. These body types, discussed in some detail in Chapter 3, are functional in the formation of groups in every culture. Less specific in the demands they make, the endomorphic, mesomorphic, and ectomorphic components become selective factors in the formation of relationships with persons or nonhuman objects. The differential structures set limits to the relationships which can be formed in any given cultural setting. The forms of recreation and other avocations especially are apt to select groupings on the basis of somatotypes. Whether the recreation is wrestling alligators, mountain climbing, tumbling, football, dancing, or playing a musical instrument, the appropriateness of body structure to the activity will manifest itself. The 1–1–7 ectomorph does not go in for football, or weightlifting; nor does the ponderous 6–7–1 endomorphic mesomorph find much satisfaction in ballet, in high-wire circus performances, or in any craft which requires delicacy of movement or manipulation. It is hardly possible for a man to emerge as a great violinist when one of his fingers often covers positions on the finger board which, the notes indicate, two fingers should occupy. Similarly, the dwarf will find it quite beyond his anatomical ability to master the piano.

The most obvious differences between the sexes that are significant for group formation are the greater muscular strength of the male and the differential reproductive functions. To these may be added the skeletal differences already noted. These structural differences set limits to the kinds of relationships which can be developed. The straighter and longer legs of the male give him a fleetness that cannot be matched by the female (albeit certain females can outrun certain males because of atypical body structure). The straighter arm of the male is a more efficient throwing instrument, which permits certain activity denied the female. The division of labor among primitive hunters reflects these differences, as among the Australian Aborigines who assign to the men the pursuit of the larger, stronger, and more elusive game, whereas the women do the hunting and gathering of the herbs and more accessible animal life.

Lest we carry too far the demands of the bisexual nature of man, we take note of the fact that a study of history and anthropology attests to the principle that the further culture moves from the cave-dwelling existence to civilizations based upon intelligence rather than brawn, the less significant becomes bisexuality. The double standard reflects the bigger biceps of the male and the irrefutable evidence of sexual relations manifested by the female. The Pauline dogma that, "Neither was the man created for the woman, but woman for man," wanes before a system of justice based upon reason rather than muscle.

The ancedote is told of the husband and citizen of ancient Athens who, embarrassed at being informed by his male associates of his halitosis, berated his wife for not having told him of this offensive condition. Her answer was, "But, I thought that all men smelled this way!" This reply reveals the special groupings of women in the women's quarters of the ancient Greek home. The groupings, which were functions of the custom reflected in Menander's view that "the house door is the bound of the free woman," were not born of universal human characteristics but of the mores of that hoary period of history.

Further, what is woman's work and man's work becomes less clear as the industrialization and automation processes accelerate. In a push-button society, the females can do as well, and often better, than their heavy fingered brothers. Even in war, the greater stature and strength of the male loses its advantage, and often proves to be a handicap. Giants are not welcomed as pilots, tank operators, or submarine crew members. Thus culture and biological heritage cooperate to create groups based upon sexual differences at one time and to dissolve them at another, suggesting the instrumental nature of groups.

VOLUNTARY SOCIAL GROUPS

The groups based on ascribed biological and psychological statuses provide man with *givens*, in terms of which he must order his efforts to meet life's needs. The larger number of social groups, by far, are those which man invents to meet the problems posed by these groups and by other human requirements. It is to a consideration of these multifarious voluntary social groups that we now turn our attention.

In the strictest meaning of the word, such groups are abstractions, and as such omit too much from the picture to be of more than incidental value in the pursuit of knowledge about the nature of human behavior. The hope that one can isolate a group from the world which surrounds it and, by giving careful and intensive attention to it, be led to discoveries about the general characteristics of mankind, is a vain hope, and is illustrative of the constructionist fallacy. Groups are not essences which constitute either the larger society or the dynamic network of interacting processes out of which emerges personality. Moreover, although groups are inevitable and necessary, *there is no particular voluntary social group that is always and everywhere indispensable to the existence of mankind.* It is not in terms of groups that we understand the behavior of man, but in terms of the ways in which man is related to his fellow man and to the other objects of his environment.

Any attempt to classify human beings forces one to return to the generalizations about human beings. Looking at the problems of classification of people into groups from the perspective of the interactionist frame of reference, one is forced to consider more than the subjective factors of the individuals involved. It would be as egregious an error to build social classifications on subjective awareness as it would be to do so solely on the basis of biological factors.

Many human beings do not consider themselves animals, but this belief has nothing to do with their actual biological status. Similarly, many persons are in sociocultural groupings without being aware of their membership. Surely there is no American Association of Amalgamated Bores, yet the concept *bore* has genuine referents which cannot be denied, either by the bores themselves or by others. Further, to deny the category social group to the bores violates our understanding of the words *social* and *group*. The same point of logic is involved in such groups as the mentally ill. Accordingly, any classification of groups that takes into account the interactionist theoretic framework will, perforce, exceed the bounds of subjectivity and will take into account those aspects of the individuals' biological heritage, environment, and personal variables which are observed to be operative in the situation under surveillance.

What groups or categories *can* exist, *do* exist, or *must* exist among human beings are functions of the biological nature of man, the particular aspects of the total human environment with which any particular plurality of persons comes into contact, and the previous modification of the biological heritage in the forms of attitudes, knowledge, beliefs, and other subjective personal characteristics.

What groups man will form are functions of his total being operating in a multitude of environments. These voluntary groups reflect his knowledge, beliefs, and feelings. They come into being, persist, and disappear as functions of his foibles as well as his more rational thinking and acting. They are products of his unreasonableness, his prejudices, his unwarranted fears, and his laziness and inertia. Some groups give evidence of his ingenuity, altruism, and general objective understanding of himself and the world. Other groups give equally clear evidence that he is capable of egocentric, ethnocentric, neurotic, and even psychotic thinking, feeling, and acting. People form groups, join groups, remain in groups, or leave them because they believe, correctly or no, that their basic human needs and their acquired wishes will be met by such action. Any understanding of groupings among human beings demands a clear comprehension of the differences between the learning processes of the central and autonomic nervous systems, as discussed in Chapters 3 and 5. In brief, groups are to be perceived in terms of the total interactive sociocultural processes of mankind, and not as separate entities. Their nature is to be deduced from the broader psychological, social psychological, and sociological principles and facts. They are immediates, not ultimates; secondary, not fundamental.[31]

Additional Groups

In addition to the groups already alluded to in this chapter, the reader could provide us with a welter of group names which would exceed the demands of anyone. For every status or position occupied by man there is a group, and the combinations of position, status, and roles provide limitless groupings. It will hardly serve our purposes to create group names merely for the sake of demonstrating taxonomic virtuosity. Certain concepts, and accompanying labels, will facilitate communication and thinking. It is to this task of noting significant sociopsychological group names that we now turn.

INSTITUTIONAL GROUPS

Out of the millenia of man's trial and error efforts to discover ways of meeting his basic needs—ranging from the felt need to remain alive, to

---

[31] For a discussion of the problems involved in classification of groups on the basis of several variables, see H. C. Selvin and W. O. Hagstrom, "The Empirical Classification of Formal Groups," *American Sociological Review*, 28 (June 1963), 399–411. The factor analysis technique, rendered feasible by electronic computers, enables one to sort out significant differentiating items, but is still subject to the limitations that the end product cannot improve upon the judgment of the investigator in selecting the item to be included in the matrix.

recreational requirements—has come the realization that there are five major areas of life that cannot be left to hit-or-miss efforts. All successful societies have learned, by dint of their own efforts or by borrowing ideas from neighbors, that man's survival demands customary ways of:

1. Creating and allocating wealth (economy).
2. Creating, preserving, and transmitting knowledge (education).
3. Providing for the protection, affection, and socialization of the young (marriage).
4. Assuring strong emotional support of the essential values (religion).
5. Providing rules and regulations upon which the successful functioning of the other four customs depend (government).

No society survives without these deliberately maintained customs, which are called *institutions*.

Each institution requires agencies or instruments for its successful operation, and chief among such agencies are the assigned or voluntarily assumed statuses with the attending roles. Persons occupying the same positions on the one hand (*e.g.*, clergymen, unemployed, or school-age children), and those occupying complementary positions on the other (e.g., bureau members, families, court officials, or police force), constitute groups. Thus each institution operates with groups as instruments that are essential to the institution's proper action. However, as a knowledge of ethnology enables one to observe, the agencies or instruments of institutions (*e.g.*, groups) do not possess the universality that is characteristic of the institutions themselves. This is clearly illustrated by contrasting the social organization of a small, isolated, rural, agricultural society with a large, accessible, urban, industrial society. In the former, the family constitutes the sole institutional group. It is usually an extended or consanguine family, made up of several generations of people, with all of the children, cousins, grandchildren living in proximity to each other. It alone is responsible for the proper function of the institutions; it alone serves to maintain its mores and folkways by reminding its members of the norms or rules, and by applying both positive and negative sanctions.

In sharp contrast is the organizational pattern in the large, urbanized, industrialized society. Here the family is usually small, consisting of parents and their children, and is called a conjugal family. Its functions are essentially those of the marriage institution of providing affection, protecting the young from themselves, and socializing them. Each of the other institutions has its own institutional groups. The *state*, with its many bureaus and other groups, performs the governmental tasks; the *school, press, libraries, institutes, research associations, lectureships, radio,* and *television*[32] supplement each other's efforts to discover, preserve, and transmit knowledge; *churches, temples, synagogues*, and other ethically oriented associations serve to emphasize the need for emotional support of values deemed basic, (sometimes subjective in nature, and sometimes objective); and the *corporations, public and private bureaus, labor unions, employers' associations*, facilitate the creation and allocation of wealth that is essential to living.

In the institutional groups, as elsewhere, groups are prerequisites to successful operation of the institutions, but no single group is indispensable. Even the family, the most durable and universal of all groups, can be supplemented and actually supplanted by crèches, orphanages, boarding schools, preparatory schools, baby-sitters, and so on. Although it appears unlikely at the moment, it may come to pass that the future will see some other group take the place of the family as we know it. In the kibbutzim of present day Israel the family plays a much reduced role in the socialization and enculturation of the child. The children are cared for during most of their waking hours by specialists, in the company of other children, and the parents see them for only a short time at day's end. Almost all of the feeding and discipline assignments common in the families of the world are performed by persons especially trained for these tasks. Man, in the centuries ahead, will have to decide whether or not our own preference for the family as the institutional group for marriage is an ethnocentric one.[33]

PRIMARY, SECONDARY, AND TERTIARY GROUPS

There is need for terms that denote personal or intimate relationships as well as impersonal or formal relationships. The terms *primary* and *secondary* have become established in the vocabulary of social psychology for the purposes of indicating the nature of the groups. However, connotations have arisen in connection with these words and it is important that the reader think through the implications of their use. The following paragraphs are intended to assist in this process.

Primary Groups: The term *primary group* was coined by Charles Horton Cooley (1864–1929), a pioneer American social psychologist. He pictured the primary group in this manner:

> By primary groups I mean those characterized by intimate face-to-face association and cooperation. They are primary in several senses, but

---

[32] That each of these groups can, and often does, lend itself to other than educational efforts, *e.g.*, indoctrination and propaganda, is readily perceived. Some schools, in fact, owe their existence to the desire of their founders to thwart the educational processes.

[33] *Cf.* Milford E. Spiro, *Kibbutz; Venture in Utopia* (New York: Schocken Books, 1963); B. Bettelheim, "Does Communal Education Work?", *Commentary*, 33 (Feb. 1962). 117–125.

chiefly in that they are fundamental in forming the social nature and ideals of the individual. . . . Primary groups are primary in the sense that they give the individual his earliest and completest experience of social unity, and also in the sense that they do not change in the same degree as more elaborate relations, but form a comparatively permanent source out of which the latter are ever springing . . .[34]

Cooley lists the family and neighborhood groups among the most important of primary groups, and comments that ". . . the fact that . . . [they] are ascendant in the open and plastic time of childhood makes them even now incomparably more influential than all the rest."[35]

Even though Cooley noted the strong "we-group" feeling of primary groups, the above passages indicate that for him they were primary in an ordinal as well as a cardinal sense.

Since his presentation of the concept appeared, much has been written about the nature of the primary group, and even more has been both implied and inferred by its widespread use in social psychological literature.[36] Survival criteria include such items as a high degree of solidarity, informality of relationships, spontaneity of behavior, mutual acceptance of members, intimate knowledge of each other, smallness in size, long duration, frequency of interaction, homogeneity of membership, and predispositions ". . . to enter into a wide range of activitives . . . associated with a predominance of positive affect." If one were to classify groups in terms of all of these items, the resulting category would be very restricted, and would relegate to some other category many groups now accepted as primary by a large number of social psychologists.

Not only is it true, as Cooley wrote, that, "It is not to be supposed that the unity of the primary group is one of mere harmony and love,"[37] it is also a fact that in many primary groups enmity and outright hostility are enduring features of the relationships therein. This situation occurs whenever the conditions in the larger world weld the group together out of sheer necessity. The isolated pioneer family has no choice but to remain as an economic and social unit, however much its members would prefer

[34] *Social Organization* (New York: Charles Scribner's Sons, 1925), pp. 23, 26. *See,* for an elaboration of Cooley's several contributions to social psychology, R. Dewey, "Charles Horton Cooley: Pioneer in Psycho-sociology," in Harry Elmer Barnes (ed.) *An Introduction to the History of Sociology* (Chicago: University of Chicago Press, 1948), pp. 833–852.

[35] *Op. cit.,* p. 26.

[36] *Cf.* Ellsworth Faris, "The Primary Group: Essence or Accident," *American Journal of Sociology,* 38 (July 1932), 41–50; E. A. Shils, "The Study of the Primary Group," in D. Lerner and H. D. Lasswell (eds.) *The Policy Sciences* (Stanford: Stanford University Press, 1951); H. Blumer, "Psychological Import of the Human Group," in M. Sherif and M. O. Wilson (eds.) *Group Relations at the Crossroads* (New York: Harper and Brothers, 1953); A. P. Bates and N. Babchuk, "The Primary Group; A Reappraisal," *Sociological Quarterly,* 2 (July 1961).

[37] *Op. cit.,* p. 23.

not to do so, other things being equal. Prior to the cultural changes that sanctioned separation and divorce, many a family remained intact as a group, though mutual acceptance and positive identification had long since fled the scene. A gross misconception of the nature of the village and neighborhood life persists in the minds of many, who nostalgically view the "good old days" as the ideal. Oliver Goldsmith's *Deserted Village* is often taken as the prototype of this kind of lament for the ideal village and primary group life of days gone by, and as a protest against industrialization and urbanization. Goldsmith did write very effectively about the positive characteristics of village life as he recalled them, but one telling passage reveals the main reason for his chagrin at the passing of "Sweet Auburn, fairest village of the plain."[38] He seems vexed at being denied the opportunity to return to the village to display to the stay-at-homes his knowledge of the larger world, rather than mourning any intrinsic virtue of the village primary group that prompted his poem.[39] Had he written as eloquently of his reasons for leaving the village in the first place, we might today have a clearer picture of "Sweet Auburn" and of the primary groups which it represented. Further evidence that the primary relations of villages left something to be desired was the disruptive effect of the automobile. Early in the twentieth century the hitherto tight in-group character of small town social life changed drastically as the automobile progressed beyond the toy stage. Had the small towns' social life been as idyllic as some believe, the auto's centrifugal influence would have been significantly less. The criteria of mutual acceptance and "predominance of positive affect" hardly appear to be universal features of the groupings that we have come to recognize as primary.

At any time in history when there are gross discrepancies between the demands of custom, on the one hand, and the nature of human impulses on the other, repression of expression of the latter is a daily necessity. Under these conditions, certain attitudes may be kept under wraps for a lifetime, whereas under less repressive cultural conditions, much more intimate attitudes may be revealed after limited acquaintance. The well-known tendency of total strangers, such as fortuitous travel companions, to reveal quite intimate details of their lives, is illustrative of the primary group relationships which do not depend upon long-term acquaintance of group membership. Lovers, husbands, and wives learn

---

[38] R. Dewey, "The Neighborhood, Urban Ecology, and City Planners," *American Sociological Review*, 15 (Aug. 1950), 505–506.

[39] "In all my wand'rings round this world of care, In all my griefs—and God has given my share—I still had hopes my latest hours to crown, Amidst these humble bowers to lay me down; To husband out life's taper at the close, And keep the flame from wasting by repose. I still had hopes, for pride attends us still, Around my fire an evening group to draw, And tell of all I felt and all I saw; And, as a hare, whom hounds and horns pursue, Pants to the place from whence at first she flew, I still had hopes, my long vexations passed, Here to return—and die at home at last."

things about each other that parents and siblings never suspected. Although intimacy of knowledge about members is one general feature of primary groups, especially in terms of the overt behavior of members, duration of relationship will not guarantee this intimate knowledge, nor will a relatively brief acquaintance preclude it.

What, then, is the primary group relationship which distinguishes it from other kinds of social relationships? Intimate knowledge has been alluded to as a sound criterion. In the primary group, the persons are well aware of the "on stage" and "backstage" behavior of their fellow members. However, intimacy is a necessary but not sufficient aspect in the definition of the primary group. Erstwhile husbands and wives also know much about their former mates, but they hardly constitute a primary group. Closeness of contact, most often face-to-face in nature but at times maintained at a distance by forms of communication which enable members to overcome or breach distance, is essential. Some emotional relationship is a further essential item in the constitution of any primary group, though this may be affection or disaffection. Furthermore, it becomes apparent that these criteria set limits as to the size of the group and assure that it will always be small. One final function of the nature of the primary group relations is the fact that substitution of a nonmember changes or destroys the relationship. As one writer has put it:

> In the primary group, substitution of one person for another is difficult and often impossible. Husband, father, and friend are unique; they cannot be replaced.[40]

In a sense, it is not *what* you are, but *who* you are that counts in the primary group. Stated differently, primary contacts are personal, not impersonal, and what have come to be known as formal behavior patterns are quite inappropriate among primary group members. Thus, *the primary group is constituted of intra-group social relationships which are functions of the members' intimate knowledge of each other and of their unique emotional relationships with each other.*

Secondary Groups: In secondary groups, the answers to the question "What is he?" count for more than information as to *who* he is. Such relations are defined in terms of position and status, and the particular occupant of the position or status in question is relatively unimportant. The qualifications are in terms of performance, and many personal variables become inconsequential. The substitution of one person for another as bank teller, gas station attendant, anesthetist, short-stop, auditor, assembly line worker, or barber, providing that the skills are comparable, does not alter the relationships. Except in those areas wherein community

[40] Francis E. Merrill, *Society and Culture* (Englewood Cliffs, N.J.: Prentice-Hall, 1957), p. 79.

and primary groups are synonymous, these secondary or impersonal relations constitute an important part of one's life.

In larger urban industrial centers, it is possible for one to live with no primary group contacts whatsover, but one cannot avoid secondary contacts. The procurement of food, the attention to the traffic policeman, the receiving of wages, pensions, or dividends, or the payment of rent, taxes, and utility fees guarantee secondary contacts. The rooming house districts of cities provide us with the environment conducive to this diminution of primary group contacts. Secondary groups, such as corporations, may outlast any primary group. *Length of life of the group is no criterion upon which to differentiate primary from secondary group.*

The limits of secondary groups have not been yet successfully defined. That a bank is a secondary group, with its several complementary positions and statuses, none of which is geared to any particular person, is readily agreed upon. Are the teller and the depositor members of the same secondary group? If so, then the concept has very broad coverage indeed, including in the group all of the bank functionaries and customers, which would include the depositors but more, the state, federal, and private agencies with whom the bank has increasing relationships. It is difficult at the moment to perceive the value to be gained by attempting this coverage of such complex and heterogeneous relationships. The term then becomes so broad that it approaches being unwieldly and meaningless. This problem again brings up the fact that groups are functions of larger inter-relationships.

Tertiary Group: All of our associations are not included in the primary and secondary relationships. There is a residual category of people (except where one's life is restricted to small communities) who influence indirectly the lives of others. In the large city, the tertiary group consists of all those people whom we do not know intimately or with whom we have no special positional or status relationships. The tertiary group makes it possible to have a subway system but also may thwart your chances of getting a seat. These are the crowds at sales, the masses of people whom we rarely encounter in any but a most superficial and limited manner. Nevertheless, its existence influences the behavior of individuals for whom it is an environmental factor. It is a principal difference between rural and urban environments.

GROUPS AS ENDS IN THEMSELVES?

It is sometimes argued that the primary groups are ends in themselves whereas the secondary groups are merely means to some ulterior goal. This distinction does not appear to be a tenable one. The individual will abandon the primary group when it no longer provides him with the fulfillment of his needs for response as surely as he will his secondary con-

tacts if they fail to fulfill his economic, recreational, or legal requirements. Response is the goal, not the individuals concerned, and the world
of fiction and nonfictional writings are filled with instances wherein the
pursuit of the end will lead one into some primary relations and out of
others. Divorces, broken engagements, broken friendships, and other
separations of persons hitherto bound by primary relationships evidence
the fact that persons are not ends in themselves, but are means to the
goals of friendship, love, recognition, and emotional security. These values
are just as real as any item that may come from secondary relationships.
Here again the instrumental nature of groups is made clear, and warrants
one's arguing that understanding of human behavior is usually served
better by thinking in terms of primary and secondary relationships rather
than in terms of primary and secondary groups per se.

Proximity and Group Formation

Physical proximity assumes a dominant role in the formation of primary relationships when (1) the number of persons available is restricted;
(2) when the social environment is homogeneous; and (3) when prior
intense intimate relationships have not been established with relatives or
friends.

When the numbers are restricted, it is very much a part of human
nature to seek social contacts. The lonely army post, communities at the
extreme rural end of the rural-urban continuum, a ship's crew, are situations in which the need for human contact avails itself of whatever person or persons one can find. In each postwar period, tragedies are acted
out when the primary group relationships established in wartime, often
under relatively restricted opportunities for social contacts, are broken
up when the returnee is provided with a wider choice of persons with
whom he can fulfill his basic needs for affection, recognition, and so on.
The wife who seemed so satisfactory in one social setting proves to be
unacceptable "back home" with the renewal of contacts with a previously
established affective other, and the attending ruptured primary relations
are all too common in the wake of wars. The submarine crew, tight knit
and very primary under conditions of isolation from normal contacts and
under the stress of the war environment, cannot withstand the pressure
from the larger community once peace comes and the heterogeneity of
the crew's personalities is given full expression. The restricted affective
other of the submarine and its equally restricted nonsocial environment
provide a corresponding restriction of social choice, and the relationships
forced under these conditions often are rent by the expanded environment of the larger peacetime world of jobs, neighborhoods, formal organization, and relatives. The following case is illustrative of exigencies
operating in group formations.

Here started a series of beach landings, mostly unopposed, which would land us we knew not where. Here I was given my first real responsibility. I was given a squad of men and as a noncom I was supposed to see that the men were properly taken care of before I worried about my own welfare. There was no legitimate liquor on the island but all the men, me included, found something to drink, mostly grain alcohol. We used this effectively as an escape mechanism.

Friendships became deeper. People became more intimate. To a normal U. S. citizen we would have appeared homosexual in our actions and speech toward each other. Out there it was normal. By now we had been away from organized society for more than a month and it was beginning to tell. My orientation to this time had been toward a normal life and even the first days in the army had been normal to the extent that there were frequent meals, a warm barrack, bed, and shelter. This all changed. I learned the meaning of privation and sharing. Cold greasy rations, no bed, no mail, knee-deep in mud, and continual cold, fog, and rain. All of these things came to change my concept of life. I found that life was much more simple than people made it. Society only complicated life. We had our ethics which frowned on stealing and in most cases it worked better than did the laws back home. We shared everything, including secrets.

For a month or so after each landing there was more than enough to keep us busy. But after the beach was solid there was time to burn. Everyone dreamed. Especially of home and girls. Everyone drank the grain alcohol as a means of escape. Most fellows found that they could go only two to three weeks before they would get so disgruntled that they would turn to the oblivion that alcohol could bring. This would relieve and relax them. Almost every man on the island was suffering from the complete isolation. One day I met a very nice fellow who turned out to be a homosexual. The inhibitions that had once existed in me about such people had now ceased to be a barrier. My sex drive overpowered my inhibition.

HOMOGENEOUS SOCIAL ENVIRONMENTS

In a very interesting study of students at the Massachusetts Institute of Technology, it was shown that even such minor items as the location of the door on the converted barracks apartments determined the primary groups formations. However, these subjects were remarkably homogeneous in nature; all were veterans and approximately equal in age, intelligence, levels of educational aspiration, and all newly wedded. Proximity became a foremost factor in the selection of persons among whom developed abiding intimate relationships.[41] Study of some of the suburban "bedroom towns" which mushroomed immediately after the end of World War II seemed to indicate that the same proximity factor was

[41] Leon Festinger, S. Schachter, and K. Back, *Social Pressures in Informal Groups: A Study of Human Factors in Housing* (New York: Harper and Brothers, 1950).

operative in the formation of primary groups.[42] However, this may have been a function of the recency of the establishment of the suburb. Subsequent research in the same suburb indicated that proximity was effective only in those instances wherein other factors were shared in common by the neighbors. For some time it has been shown that the best neighbors are the children, for whom the neighborhood is the larger world, followed by the wives who do not work outside of the home, with the bread-winning husband, who spends most of his waking hours out of the home, the least neighborly of all. The nonsocial interests, manifested in differential occupations, forms of recreation (bridge, golf, boating, music, ham radio), supplant physical proximity as the group makers. These multiple extra-neighborhood factors take up so much of the time available that the good neighbor is frequently defined as one who is friendly but who, in general, "minds his own damned business."

PRIOR PRIMARY GROUP COMMITMENTS AND NEIGHBORING

With increasing mobility of the population, there is increasing likelihood that primary bonds have been established prior to one's movement into a particular neighborhood. A recent study has shown that in those families with relatives accessible to them in the larger community, there are fewer neighborhood contacts, with less integration, than among the neighbors who are not within easy visiting distance of relatives or other previously established primary group members.[43] If the family and relative relationships, being prior in time to the neighborhood ones, meet the primary social needs there is a reduced need for neighborhood contacts.[44]

Cultural Groups in the United States

In the discussion of the American ethos we have pointed out some of the attitudes that are dominant in American culture. There are other aspects of the culture than those that concern the manner in which man may think or feel about a situation; what he will do about it is limited by the objective reality of the situation. One's social situation is based only in part on attitude. The happenstance of birth, the inadvertent consequences of one's unique experience, and the attending circumstances over which the individual may have little or no control, often operate to assign a person to a particular group or status despite, rather than because of, his attitudes.

[42] William H. Whyte, *The Organization Man* (New York: Simon & Schuster, 1956). Robert Corley, unpublished research on Park Forest, Ill.

[43] Phillip Fellin and Eugene Litwak, "Neighborhood Cohesion Under Conditions of Mobility," *American Sociological Review*, 28 (June 1963), 375.

[44] *See also* Herbert Gans, "Park Forest: The Birth of a Jewish Community," *Commentary*, 11 (April 1951).

These positions or group memberships are maintained as part of the social heritage of the United States by a variety of forces, among them personal preference, society's rules and laws, tradition's "heavy hand," and an array of cultural influences. These forces often seem to the individual to be beyond man's purposive control. All of these add up to a complex patterning of social relationships which must be considered in any attempt to understand the nature of personality, or the sociocultural aspects of human nature, as it exists in the United States. In the following items, the majority and minority aspects of the culture can be easily noted.

SIZE OF COMMUNITY

Such epithets as "country bumpkin" and "city slicker" are of long standing and suggest personality stereotypes associated with rural and urban living. Often the behavior observed in the small community has nothing to do with the community size per se, but much to do with the kind of culture that has developed there. Community size determines what things are possible, and what things are not possible, and what things one is likely to do. The ruralite is becoming relatively scarce on the American and Canadian scene, reflecting an urbanization trend that has been apparent since the first United States census in 1790, when only 5 per cent could claim urban residence. Today 70 per cent of the American people are classified as urban, and only 7.5 per cent are farm residents. This urbanization has important ramifications for social psychology. Whatever the small town's and farm's influences may be upon personality formation, they are of waning importance. The reader can place himself according to community size in Figure 11.

NATIVITY OF THE UNITED STATES POPULATION

With the passage of the restrictive immigration legislation of the early 1920's, the flow of immigrants from abroad was reduced drastically. In contrast to the millions that once disembarked on this country's shores, laws restrict the incoming group from quota countries to approximately one hundred and sixty thousand annually. Whereas it was once possible to "go around the world" merely by visiting the foreign quarters of our large cities, the foreign born have been reduced to a mere five per cent of the total white population. Another 14 per cent of Americans have one or both parents who were born abroad. The majority of Americans living in the United States in 1920 were from north and western Europe, and it was upon this population base that the immigration laws of this time were preferentially based. Until the 1965 revision of the immigration laws, nearly 80 per cent of the quota for immigrants was assigned to the British Isles and northwestern Europe. It is not to be wondered at that the cultural values of the country reflect this fact.

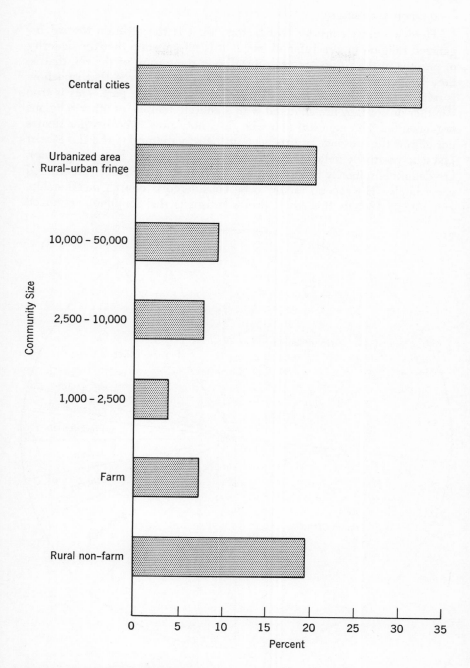

FIGURE 11. Population distribution in U.S. according to community size. (*Source*: U.S. Population—1960; *Characteristics of Population* Vol. I, Table 5.)

CHURCH MEMBERSHIP

Here we must consider two factors. First is the attitude toward organized religion in general, and in this it is safe to state that the majority of persons in the United States subscribe to some form of theism, that is, they believe in some Supreme Being or Beings or Force that somehow is related to the natural world of which the person is a part. This is true whether or not they are affiliated with a church, temple, or other religious organization. The agnostic (he who does not know, who neither denies nor affirms the presence or existence of the supernatural), and the atheist (he who positively believes that there is no supernatural being or power), are definitely minority group members, and their life chances are limited accordingly. The second factor to be considered is church membership, and Figure 12 tells this story. Protestantism is the dominant organized

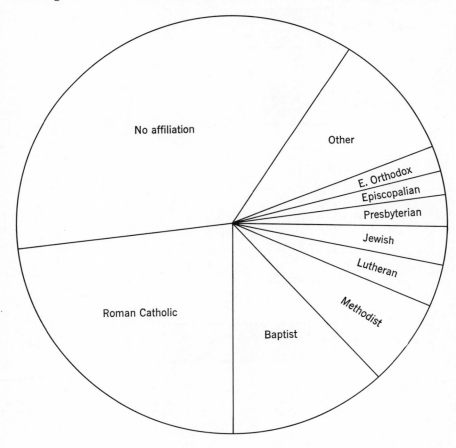

FIGURE 12. Distribution of U.S. population according to religious-group affiliation. [*Source: Encyclopaedia Britannica Book of the Year* (1964).]

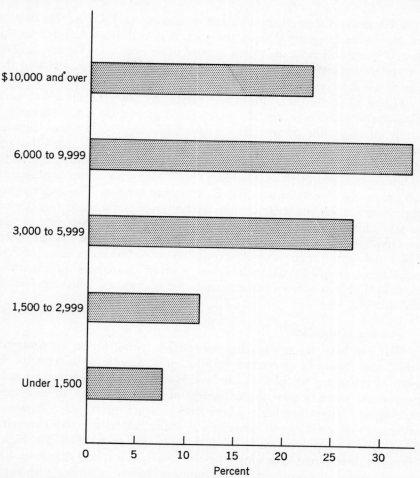

FIGURE 13. Distribution of U.S. employed population according to family income (1965). (*Source: Current Population Reports*, U.S. Bureau of the Census, Series P-60, N. 47, Sept. 24, 1965.)

religion, and its dominance over the cultural values of the country is a significant factor in the development of personalities, whether they be of the majority or of a minority religion in their beliefs. Non-Protestant groups are definitely minorities in the country at large, even though they constitute majorities in certain urban and suburban areas.

ECONOMIC STATUS

The income level into which a person is born and in which he lives greatly influences many of his attitudes and actions. This is true despite the fact that we in the United States have what is called an open class system; that is, persons can and do move from one class to another within their lifetimes. Although the chances of moving very far in this respect are somewhat less now than in the past, it is still more common in the United States and in Canada than in most other countries. Economic class determines not only the material goods that one can possess, but also the way of life associated with wealth.

Figure 13 shows that, although America has many families that have adequate wealth, there are also many families who do not. The median family income at the present time is approximately $6,600. If one chooses to use the income for all persons who are employed and above the age of fourteen, rather than the family income figure, the median is $4,647. (These figures represent cash income only.) Many American families still fall below the threshold of a barely adequate income. The implications of poverty for personality formation are both real and apparent, and must be taken into consideration if we are to understand the behavior of persons living in the lower income brackets. Their desire for material wealth, which they share with other Americans in more fortunate economic circumstances, coupled with their actual poverty, can create and maintain tensions that have serious consequences for patterns of behavior, feeling, and thought.

FORMAL SCHOOLING

The emphasis upon schooling was noted in the section on American ethos, and Figure 14 shows the distribution of Americans in terms of the years of schooling completed. The average for persons above the age of twenty-five years is now approximately eleven years, and an increasing number are attending high school and colleges each year. However, attendance at a college or university is still a minority group characteristic, with a disproportionate number of persons qualified for higher education being unable or unwilling to actually enroll and graduate. In a country which places so much importance on formal schooling, the implications for personality development and for interpersonal relationships are clear.

OCCUPATIONAL DISTRIBUTION

Closely correlated with income and schooling is occupational distribution of the population. The trend for the last few decades has been that of a reduction in the proportion of persons engaged in unskilled labor and other blue-collar work in comparison with white-collar workers. Automation, together with a marked drop in the proportion of agriculture workers (itself being a function of mechanization of farm life), and a corresponding demand for services associated with urban living have accounted for this shift. However, those still within the ranks of the blue-collar workers, many of whom may enjoy a high standard of living, do not share the same status in society accorded those in the white-collar

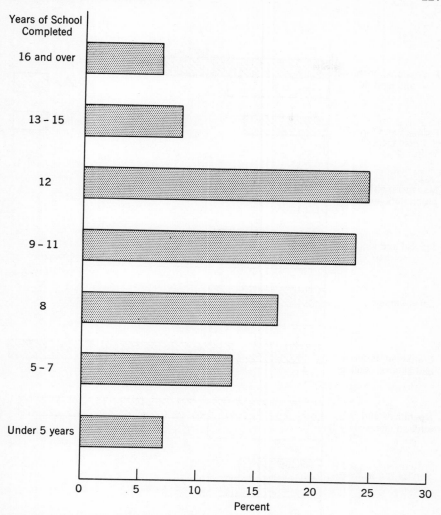

FIGURE 14. Years of school completed for persons in U.S. over 25 years of age (1960).
[*Source*: U.S. Census of Population (1960), I *Characteristics of Population*, Table 173.]

occupations. We may honor Abe Lincoln for his rise from rail splitter to president, but we respect him not because he was a rail splitter but because he fulfilled the American dream of achieving maximum upward mobility.

In Figure 15 one can see at a glance that the most desirable occupations are still filled by a small minority of persons. This would be even more apparent if the two top categories were divided into the really prestigious positions and the others. The juxtaposition of surgeons and

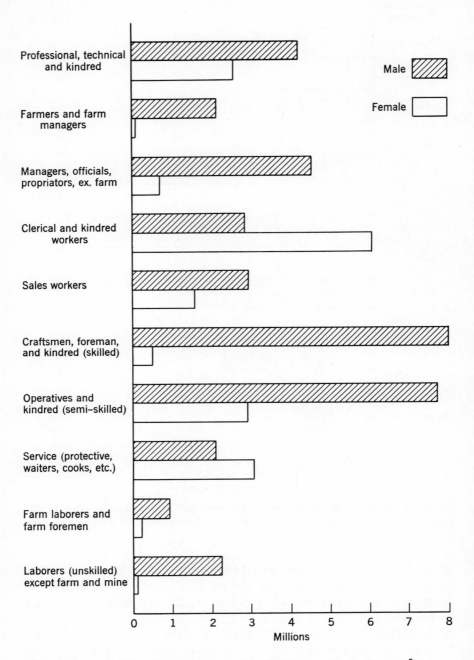

FIGURE 15. Occupational distribution of employed U.S. population, by sex. [*Source*: U.S. Census of Population (1960), **I** *Characteristics of Population*, Table 88.]

embalmers in the same category illustrates this point. Because the occupational statuses are more often than not the key statuses, as E. T. Hiller has pointed out, a knowledge of a country's occupational distributions is important.

MARITAL STATUS

The person who maintains his or her single status as he or she moves from late adolescence to adulthood, moves from the majority into the minority, and the longer the single status is maintained, the smaller becomes the minority. This figure shows the changing relationships of married and single persons as the age levels change. Within a few short years a person may become a minority group member. The social behavior and the life chances of the single person who is over thirty, particularly the female, are definitely altered. The adult social life of our culture is attuned to the married couple, and the single person has his or her social mobility curtailed in various ways.

In contrast to the proportions shown in Figure 16, in 1890, 44 per cent of the males and 34 per cent of the females were single, and as recently as 1940, 35 and 28 per cent of the males and females, respectively, were still unmarried. Under present day circumstances the single adult plays a role different from that ascribed to him or voluntarily assumed in the days when there were traditional roles for the "unclaimed treasure" and the bachelor uncle. More will be said about this point in Chapter 15.

RACIAL COMPOSITION

Although the United States is primarily a nation of Caucasoids, the fact of race cannot be ignored. The nonwhite population now constitutes something over 11 per cent of the total population, and this will probably increase for the next several decades. However, it may not reach the proportions at the time of the Civil War, about 15 per cent. Of the 11 per cent nonwhites, Negroes make up the great majority. Other nonwhites constitute about 1,600,000, distributed as shown in Table IV.

Table IV
Non–White Population of U.S.*

Negro	19,600,000
American Indian	523,600
Japanese	464,300
Chinese	237,290
Filipino	176,300
Other Non-White	218,000

* U.S. Bureau of Census, *Social and Economic Characteristics*, 1960.

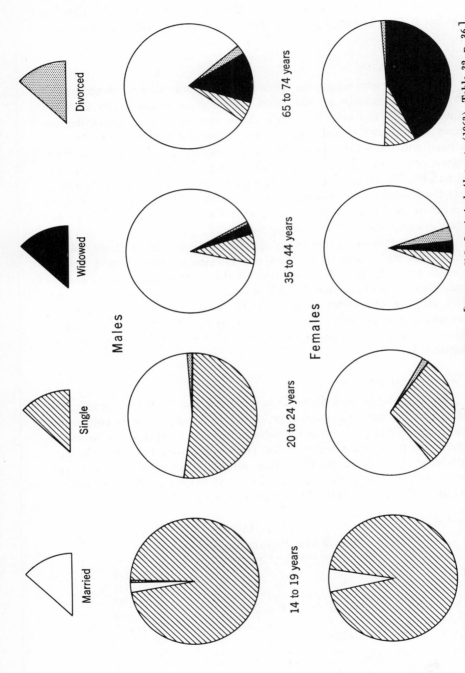

FIGURE 16. Marital status of selected age groups in U.S. (1963). [*Source: U.S. Statistical Abstracts* (1963), Table 32, p. 36.]

Three Contrasting Environments

Not only do different societies manifest varying cultural heritages, sub-groups within a society or nation also reveal markedly different cultural ethos. To emphasize the importance of environmental influences, we present here three vignettes of culture that differ radically. The first is taken from a very primitive way of life of Indians in the northern Mato Grosso area of Brazil; the second from lower class urban Americans whose heritage of slavery is still reflected in their customs (actual behavior), norms (the way they believe they *should* act), and sanctions (the rewards or penalties involved); the third is a way of life more familiar to the reader.

In each, the stage setting is different; the on stage and back stage regions are more sharply delineated in one than in the others. Each script is unlike the others in its norms, sanctions, and customs. The size and composition of the audiences—the affective other and reference groups—also vary in size and quality.

The social psychological significance of these three groupways will be more clearly perceived if the reader speculates about the implications for personality development of the children and adolescents growing up under these varying circumstances.

THE NAMBICUARA

Owning to the fact that they use no hammocks but sleep on the ground, they are always covered with dirt. On cold nights they remove the fires and sleep in the warm ashes. The Waklítisu [a subgroup of the Nambicuara] wear clothes only when they are given by the missionaries, who ask that they be worn. Their distaste for bathing permits not only a covering of dust and ashes to accumulate on their skin and hair but also particles of decayed meat and fish, which, combined with stale sweat, makes proximity to them rather distasteful. . . . On several occasions when a number of them had crowded into the small room we used for working we had to cease work in order to air the room.

Although the Nambicuara practice a shifting agriculture, their dependence upon the wild animal and plant life of the region is so extensive that they might well be classed as nomadic hunters and collectors. The semiarid plateau provides little in the way of agricultural land, game, or fish. What little farming is practiced is carried on in the narrow "galeria" forests of the headwater streams. The deep clear streams make fishing with timbo [a poison which stupefies the fish] difficult. Game in the forests and on the plain is scarce. Yet by exploiting all the resources of the area the Nambicuara are able to survive.

The dry season extends from May to September. Except for occasional south winds, which bring a cold drizzling rain for a day or two, the season is clear, cool, and dry, the daily temperature ranging from 60° to 80° F. During this period the grass withers, the livestock of the white men having to subsist on shrubs and what fodder the owners can provide. Horses and mules, particularly, suffer during these months. In August the Indians burn off the dry grass so that with the first showers new grass can grow out and attract the deer, which the Indians can then hunt.

The dry season, which the Nambicuara call kwenkisu, is the most difficult. By the end of June they have consumed the manioc, maize, beans, and other crops which they have planted. During July and August they subsist on palm nuts, cobaru beans, fruta de lobo, snakes, insects, fish, and whatever animals they can kill on the plateau or in the forest.

As the Nambicuara do not use hammocks, beds, or seats, there is not much in the way of furniture in their shelters. Utensils are restricted to a few gourd vessels, tin cans, burden baskets, and small flat baskets, fire fans, bows and arrows, and tools used by men. When they move, these articles are placed in burden baskets which are carried by the women. The Waklítisu do not make pottery, but they sometimes acquire pots from the Paressi in exchange for game or fish.

Except when the men go hunting such large game as the jaguar, tapir, and peccary, the acquisitive unit is the family. Every morning while Julio's band was camped in Utiarity a family or two could be seen going out, the husband walking in front armed with bow and arrows, the wife following and carrying a burden basket on her back and a baby strapped on her hip, an older child following her. As they move slowly along they collect fruits, nuts, insects, snakes, ants, lizards, rats, wild honey, and a great variety of grubs or larvae. When they come to a pond they wade around with small baskets in their hands and scoop out small fish. On one of these trips I observed them catching fish that were only two inches in length. They were later thrown on hot coals and eaten without being cleaned. Small birds no larger than a sparrow are shot if the man can get near enough to use his bow and arrow. If they come to a byrutu stalk of the right size they will cut it down, put it into the burden basket, and take it to camp. On their way home they will usually pick up dry firewood.

In late August, when the cicada begins to sing and the first thunder is heard, the Nambicuara return to undertake their planting activities. At a given signal, men with lighted bunches of dry grass set fire to dry trees and bushes all around the edges of the field. The rest of the people are concentrated at the river's edge at the bottom of the slope, and as animals, such as rats, lizards, and snakes, flee toward the water they kill them. After the fires have died down the people go through the field collecting grubs, insects, and whatever else that is edible.

The material equipment of the Eastern Nambicuara is extremely simple. Many items, such as the conical trap for catching fish, the floats for crossing rivers, the loom for weaving arm bands, and the mortar and pestle for crushing food products are made for the occasion and are discarded when the task is completed or when the people move. The small grater and the few gourd vessels, small baskets, and twine, the woman carries in her burden basket, whereas the modern axes, knives, and other tools, along with his ornaments, the man carries in a similar basket, or he straps this basket on the back of a boy while he walks in front of the file carrying his bow and arrows or gun ready to shoot whatever game is met along the way. Whenever they kill some animal or catch a few fish and feel hungry they stop and prepare a meal. During the dry season they are at home anywhere in their band territory, moving only when hunger spurs them on.[45]

BRONZEVILLE'S LOWER CLASS

When he arrived at the building, the squad car was at the door. He and the police went in together. Dr. Maguire pushed his way through the ragged group of children and their excited elders who jammed the hall of the dilapidated building.

"Right this way, Doc," someone called.

"What is it?" he asked jauntily. "Shooting or cutting?"

"She stabbed him," volunteered a little girl.

"Boy, she shore put that blade in him too!" A teen-age boy spoke with obvious admiration, while a murmur of corroboration rippled through the crowd fascinated by tragedy. For a moment, Dr. Maguire felt sick at his stomach. "Are these my people?" he thought. "What in the hell do I have in common with them?" . . . Then he forgot everything—squalor, race prejudice, his own little tricks of psychological adjustment. He was a doctor treating a patient, swiftly, competently, and with composure. Anger and doubt were swallowed up in pride. His glow of satisfaction didn't last long, however, for the woman who had cut the man was now blubbering hysterically. He barked at her, "Shut up. Get a pan of water, quick! He isn't dead, but he will be if you don't help me." He prepared a hypodermic, gave the shot, and dressed the wound.

"How'dja like to have to give him that needle, honey?" A teen-age girl shivered and squeezed her boy friend's hand, as she asked the question.

"Me? I ain't no doc. But, girl, he flipped that ol' needle in his shoulder sweet. Just like Baby Chile did when she put that blade in Mr. Ben. You gotta have education to be a doc. Lots of it, too." . . .

"The old man will be all right, now." Dr. Maguire was closing his bag. "Just let him lie quiet all day tomorrow and send him down to the Provident Hospital clinic the day after Christmas. The visit is five dollars."

. . . Baby Chile crawled into the bed with Mr. Ben. She cried and cried and stroked the bulky dressing on his shoulder. "Honey, I didn't mean to do that. I love you! I do! I do!"

Mr. Ben didn't say a word. The needle was wearing off and his

[45] Kalervo Oberg, *Indian Tribes of Northern Mato Grosso, Brazil*, Smithsonian Institution, Institute of Social Anthropology, Pub. No. 15, (Washington, D.C.: U. S. Government Printing Office, 1953) "The Nambicuara," pp. 84–95.

shoulder hurt. But he wasn't gonna let no woman know she'd hurt him.
He bit his lip and tried to sleep. He pushed her hand away from
his shoulder. He cursed her.

"Hush up, dammit, shet up!" he growled. "I wanna sleep." Baby
Chile kept moaning, "Why'd I do it? Why'd I do it?" "Shet up, you
bitch," Mr. Ben bawled. "I wisht they'da let them creepers take you to
the station! Cain't you let me sleep?"

Baby Chile didn't say another word. She just lay there a-thinking
and a-thinking. She was trying to remember how it happened. Step by
step she reconstructed the event in her mind as though the rehearsal
would assuage her feeling of guilt.

She'd been living with Mr. Ben six months now. Of course he
was old and he hadn't ever got the country outa him yet. But he
had a good job s'long as he kept the furnace fired and the halls swept
out. And he got his room free, bein' janitor. She had a relief check
coming in reg'lar for herself and her little girl. They could make it all
right as long as the case-worker didn't crack down on 'em. But Mr. Ben
was so suspicious. He was always watching her and signifyin' she was
turning tricks with Slick who helped him with the furnace and slept
in the basement. She wouldn't turn no tricks with Slick. He had bad
blood and wouldn't take his shots reg'lar. But you couldn't convince old
Mr. Ben. Ben didn't treat her little girl right, either. Course, it wasn't
his child. But he oughta act right. She cooked for him and slept with
him and never held her relief check back on him. He could treat her
child right. That was the cause of it all, anyhow.

Baby Chile had come home near dark after a day of imbibing
Christmas cheer. She must have been a little slug-happy. All she
remembered was chasing her little girl outa Mamie's kitchenette next
door, telling her to stay outa that whorehouse. . . . Then she remembered stretching out on the bed. Just before she lay down she'd asked
her daughter, "What Ben get you for Christmas, chile?"

"Nothin', Mother Dear."

"Nothin'?"

"No, ma'am."

Her eyes fell on the sideboard covered with new, shiny bottles
of whiskey and beer and wine—plenty of "Christmas cheer." A turkey
was cooking in the stove. "An' that no-'count bastard didn't get *you*
nothin'?" She remembered throwing herself on the bed in a rage. The
radio was playing Christmas carols—the kind that always made her cry
because it sounded like church back down in Mississippi. She lay there
half drunk, carols ringing in her ears from the radio, boogie-woogie
assailing them from the juke-box across the hall, the smell of turkey
emanating from the kitchen, and her little girl whimpering in the corner.

She recalled the "accident" vividly. She was dozing on her bed in
the one large room which along with the kitchen made up their home.
She woke up when Ben came into the room. She didn't know how long
she'd been sleeping. Whiskey and beer don't mix anyhow, and when you

been in and outa taverns all day Christmas Eve you get enough to lay you out cold.

When Mr. Ben opened the door near midnight she was almost sober, but mad as hell. Her head ached, she was so mad. Ben grunted, walked into the kitchen, and started to baste the turkey. She challenged him:

"You buy Fanny May a present?"

"Naw," he grunted. "I spent my money for the turkey and the drinks. Tomorrow's Christmas, ain't it? What you do with yore relief check? Drink it up? Why'n you get her a present? She's yore chile, ain't she?"

Ben wouldn't have been so gruff, but he was tired and peeved. That damn furnace hadn't been acting right and everybody was stayin' up all night to see Christmas in, and pestering him for more heat. And all the time he was trying to get the turkey cooked, too. Baby Chile oughta been doing it—she had been sashayin' roun' all day drinking other men's liquor. How'd anybody expect him to think about a present for Fanny May? That girl didn't like him and respect him, nohow— always walling her eyes at him, but polite as hell to "Mother Dear." Crap! Mr. Ben didn't say any of this out very loud. He just mumbled it to himself as he bent over the stove basting the turkey.

"Baby Chile stood up and stared at him. She felt her hell arising. She didn't say a word. She walked deliberately to the kitchen table and took up a paring knife, studied it for a moment, and then—with every ounce of energy that anger and frustration could pump into her muscles—she sank it between his shoulders and fled screaming into the hall. "Oh, I've killed Mr. Ben. I've killed my old man! I've killed him!"[46]

MIDDLE CLASS AMERICA

Mrs. Howard heard the school bus stop and realized that the children were coming sooner than she had planned. Apparently she had talked on the phone about the current practice of letting the Junior high pupils attend high school dances longer than she realized. She hurried to the kitchen door just in time to yell, "Take off your shoes! I have just waxed the kitchen floor and I am not going to have you track it up with dirt and sand from the drive-way." Joanne mumbled something to the effect that she might as well live in Japan, the way she was not permitted to wear shoes in the house.

"And another thing," Mrs. Howard continued, "I do not want to see again your bed and closet in the condition you left them in this morning. There is no excuse for not hanging up your clothes and making that bed. It was bad enough to see your pajamas on the floor, but how could you treat your new skirt and blouse that way? One would think

[46] St. Clair Drake and Horace R. Cayton, *Black Metropolis, A Study of Negro Life in a Northern City* (New York: Harcourt Brace and World, 1945), pp. 565–570.

that you had never been taught to care for your things. I hope that when you have to buy your own clothes that you will take better care of them. You're getting almost as bad as your brother. I hung them up this time, but the next time I am going to throw them out the window."

That evening at the table the report cards were the main topic of conversation, and even though the children, all three of them, had brought home cards with at least average grades, they were lectured about the need to do better. Alden had only one year to go before college, and how was he going to get in if he did not do better? No more hockey if the next report did not show an improvement. They went through the "what will people think" routine both about the published honor roll, and about the kind of college that the children could get into. Threats of "no more television, not even on week-ends," were repeated in the effort to motivate the three to work harder. Excuses in the form of "dumb teachers" and "favoritism" were proffered by the two girls, while Alden ate his meal in sullen silence. He was still resentful about having the privilege of using the family car withdrawn after his parents had learned about his participation in a beer-drinking episode on one of the side roads after a school dance. He has been declared "out of bounds" for his date of that evening by her parents, much to the embarrassment of Alden's folks. Alden's argument that "Well, you drink, why can't we?", did not impress them. He and his father were unable to discuss things of this sort calmly, and, as a matter of fact, rarely did they talk directly to each other even about routine matters. Mr. Howard told Alden once more the warnings that had been heard so often during the past few years. "You are too young to make all decisions for yourself." "You must have respect for the girls you take out, and treat them as you want others to treat the girl you will someday marry!" "Until you are ready to assume responsibility for your action you cannot expect to be given the privileges that come with such responsibility," and so on.

The Howards' values were much the same as those of their neighbors in this suburban community. They felt an overriding sense of responsibility for preparing their children for successful adult living, but admitted that there were times and situations which tried their ingenuity and resources. Corporal punishment was used rarely, and then only while the child was young, but lectures and other verbal approaches were used consistently and emphatically. One thing was insisted upon, that each child always let the parents know their whereabouts at all times. This irked the two older children considerably, as did the fact that there was always one parent up when they came home from the basketball games, parties, or dances. This was hardly a democratically run family—the parents were definitely the rule makers.

Environment, then, is not some passive set of objects against which man leans, nor is it an unrelenting mold which shapes man's actions. Viewed from the vantage point of interactionist social psychology, environment is part of personality, and gains its meanings from the particular ways in which it is related to the human organism involved. Writing nearly a half-century ago, John Dewey said it well in these words:

> Human nature exists and operates in an environment. And it is not "in" that environment as coins are in a box, but as a plant is in the sunlight and soil. It is of them, continuous with their energies, dependent upon their support, capable of increase only as it utilizes them, and as it gradually rebuilds from their crude indifference an environment genially civilized.[47]

SUMMARY

The behavioral environment is constituted of those objects—human and non-human—with which the person experiences cognitive or affective relations. Mere physical juxtaposition of man and object is not sufficient for the latter to become environmental to the person.

If the analogy is not taken too literally, it may be helpful to think of the human environment as being constituted of many theaters of varying sizes, with real-life counterparts of (1) *on stage* and *back stage*—with all of the appropriate geographical and artificial props; (2) the *scripts*—the non-material culture in the forms of norms, sanctions, and customs, inherited from the past in large part, but also modified slightly or radically by episodes of the present; and (3) the *actors* and *audiences*—ranging in size from single persons through primary groups and secondary groups to tertiary groups of huge proportions which may be of international character. All persons whose attitudes, beliefs, and actions socially affect the individual are said to constitute his *significant* or *affective other*. Among the audiences which constitute his social environment, i.e., his affective other, are his community—small or large; nationality groups; church, school, and occupational groups; and racial groups. Although it is often popular to define groups in a manner that restricts them to primary status, we prefer to broaden the concept in keeping with actual use, and to consider all persons sharing the same positions or statuses as constituting groups. Illustrative of sharply contrasting theaters are the Nambicuara of rural Brazil, a lower-class, non-white, urban slum, and a middle-class suburban setting.

SUGGESTED READINGS

BARNOUW, VICTOR. *Culture and Personality* (Homewood, Ill.: The Dorsey Press, 1963).

BENEDICT, RUTH. *Patterns of Culture* (New York: Houghton Mifflin, 1934).

CARTWRIGHT, D. and A. ZANDER. *Group Dynamics* (Evanston, Ill.: Row, Peterson, 1962).

[47] John Dewey, *Human Nature and Conduct* (New York: Henry Holt and Co., 1922), p. 296.

COOLEY, C. H. *Social Organization* (New York: Charles Scribner's Sons, 1925).

HARE, A. PAUL. *Handbook of Small Group Research* (New York: Free Press of Glencoe, 1962).

HENRY, JULES. *Culture Against Man* (New York: Random House, 1963).

HUS, FRANCIS L. K. *Psychological Anthropology* (Homewood, Ill.: The Dorsey Press, 1961).

HUNTINGTON, ELLSWORTH. *Mainsprings of Civilization* (New York: John Wiley and Sons, 1945).

KAPLAN, B. (ed.). *Studying Personality Cross Culturally* (Evanston, Ill.: Row, Peterson, 1961).

LEWIS, OSCAR. *Five Families* (New York: John Wiley & Sons, 1962).

OLMSTEAD, M. *The Small Group* (New York: Random House, 1959).

SHAW, CLIFFORD. *Brothers in Crime* (Chicago: University of Chicago Press, 1938).

SHERIF, M. and M. O. WILSON (eds.). *Group Relations at the Crossroads* (Oklahoma City: University of Oklahoma Press, 1953).

SIMS, NEWELL L. *The Problem of Social Change* (New York: Thomas Y. Crowell, 1939).

TOYNBEE, ARNOLD. *A Study of History, II* (London: Oxford University Press, 1934).

WILLIAMS, ROBIN. *American Society* (New York: Alfred A. Knopf, 1958).

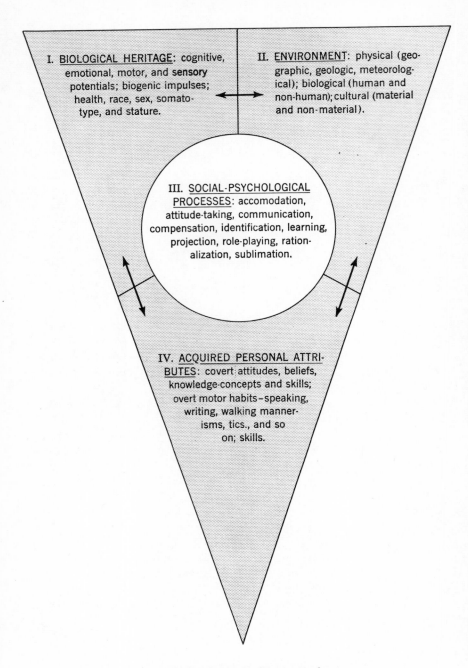

I. <u>BIOLOGICAL HERITAGE</u>: cognitive, emotional, motor, and **sensory** potentials; biogenic impulses; health, race, sex, somato-type, and stature.

II. <u>ENVIRONMENT</u>: physical (geo-graphic, geologic, meteorolog-ical); biological (human and non-human); cultural (material and non-material).

III. <u>SOCIAL-PSYCHOLOGICAL PROCESSES</u>: accomodation, attitude-taking, communication, compensation, identification, learning, projection, role-playing, ration-alization, sublimation.

IV. <u>ACQUIRED PERSONAL ATTRI-BUTES</u>: covert attitudes, beliefs, knowledge-concepts and skills; overt motor habits—speaking, writing, walking manner-isms, tics., and so on; skills.

FIGURE 17. Interactionist frame of reference.

CHAPTER 5

SOCIAL PROCESSES:
I. Learning and
Social Psychology

The social psychologist . . . describes the process through which the individual becomes a human being by bringing the human nature potentialities of his organic and social heritage into a life organization.

—*L. Guy Brown*

In Chapters 3 and 4 we have discussed in some detail two categories of factors that are indispensable to the development of human personality and which are therefore involved in all human behavior. Viewed social psychologically, the "heredity versus environment" argument is fruitless, inasmuch as personality cannot exist unless both are present. Walking involves both legs and something to walk on, talking involves both larynx and something to say. Furthermore, we must be constantly aware that neither of these categories has any meaning by itself, that *personality is not a birthright but an achievement,* and that many things must happen before that achievement becomes fact. This essential interaction is not a simple, unitary process, but is made up of several processes. These processes are what goes on when the "givens," the biological heritage and the environment, are brought together, producing the private attitudes, beliefs, and knowledge which immediately become interactive with the "givens."

There are, of course, different ways in which this complex of interactive processes can be analyzed, and varying emphasis may be given to this or that process. Our concern is with the sociocultural processes that are universal in scope and that occur wherever and whenever human beings are within interacting distance of one another. Attention will be given to (1) learning in its intellectual (or cognitive) and emotional aspects, involving the relationships of sensations, concepts, and perception; (2) symbolic communication; (3) adjustment processes or *mechanisms,* e.g., socialization and enculturation, role taking and role playing; compensation, identification, projection, rationalization, repression, and sublimation.

Inasmuch as the interactionist frame of reference is founded on learning, its comprehension demands an understanding of pertinent learn-

ing principles. Whether one focuses his attention upon a happy family—
exchanging items of interest and friendly jibes at dinner—or a distraught
couple contesting in a divorce court for the custody of the children, he is
observing learned behavior. The skilled clinical psychologist, psychiatrist,
or social case worker on the one hand, and the bungling, inept bore or
the neurotic or psychotic person on the other, are the products of learning. All that we know, whether skills or facts, and all that we believe and
feel result from learning experiences. What, then, of this important biosocial process does the social psychologist need to know? What need the
layman know about learning that he may live an ordered and reasonable
life?

There is no want for careful observational and experimental research
in learning, but much of it has been concerned with animals other than
humans, and therefore the research has necessarily been of a subvocal,
or at least of a sublingual, order. Because of the important role played in
human interaction by language, many of these learning studies are of
very limited value for social psychology.[1] It is, therefore, of relatively little
use to explore all of the learning theories, categories, and facts in depth.
Accordingly, we will restrict ourselves to those phases that seem to be
most helpful in the understanding of human behavior.

Clearly, then, learning is no simple process. Even the definition of
learning is not an easy task, but for our purposes in social psychology we
can accept the very broad definition of E. R. Guthrie: "Learning is
defined as the alteration in behavior that results from experience."[2]
Accepting this definition of learning, we can readily see that personality
development is largely a learning process. The alterations in the biological heritage that are revealed as cognitions, attitudes, habits, and so on,
in a person as a result of his myriad experiences, constitute much of the
subjective aspect of his personality; but more of this later. For the moment, it is important that we see learning as a process which establishes
relationships among many stimuli, *both internal and external to the
organism*, and the person. The learning process involves changes in the
ways in which the organism (*i.e.*, the individual person) will act with
regard to stimulus situations. It cannot be overstressed that *learning in
its biosocial aspects involves the establishing, reinforcing, or weakening
of relationships between the person and his environment*. The biological
changes that occur are important in the way in which they modify the

---

[1] Arthur W. Melton, "Taxonomy of Human Learning: Overview," in A. W.
Melton (ed.) *Categories of Human Learning* (New York: Academic Press, 1964)
p. 333.

[2] Some may believe that this definition is improved by Hilgard's qualification,
i.e. ". . . provided that the characteristics of the change in activity cannot be explained on the basis of native response tendencies, maturation, or temporary states
of the organism (*e.g.*, fatigue, drugs, *etc.*)." E. R. Hilgard, *Theories of Learning*
(2nd ed.) (New York: Appleton-Century-Crofts, 1956), p. 2.

relationship between the individual and other persons or other aspects of the physical universe. In this respect biosocial learning is not to be distinguished from learning in general; psychologists have pointed out that a complete picture of learning always includes the three factors of situation, organism, and response. In terms of the frame of reference used in this book, these three factors become environment, biological heritage, and subjective characteristics.

This is true not only of learning about laws, language, and customs, but also of such learning as that involved in sphincter control (toilet training). Although the latter concerns the establishing of a response to internal stimuli, the three factors are operative. Certainly learning sphincter control is mediated by the attitudes and overt actions of other persons, usually parents or other elders. How well a child learns it, when he learns it, and the importance of learning it can be known only when the pertinent items of all three of the interactive categories are known. In this, and in all other instances where learning operates, the social psychologist focuses his attention upon the processes as they operate to relate the individual human being to other aspects of the social order. At birth, the human organism has few relationships already established with other aspects of the natural order. In a sense, he must acquire a world in which to live. He is acted upon by members of his primary group and by certain inorganic conditions such as the weather, but his reactions must, except for the unlearned reflexes, be established through experience. This process of alteration of the organism, and therefore of its behavior, through the interaction with the world about him, begins very soon after birth, or, as indicated in Chapter 3, perhaps even before birth. One of the earliest relationships is that established with the mother, or the mother surrogate. Because of the pleasant feeling associated with this person, namely, the removal of unpleasant, generalized distress which he later comes to recognize as hunger, the infant responds positively to the voice and other signals of the mother's presence. This response was not present at birth, so something must have happened to the organism. Some alteration has occurred which places the organism in special relationship to the mother person. Just exactly what happens to the organism is not clearly known, but we do know that it involves the transmission of stimuli by way of neurons to some portion or portions of the nervous systems. We know that destruction of portions of the brain destroys the established relationships between the individual and the outside world. More we need not know for our present purposes. Whether it be a chemical change, an electrical modification, or some other physical alteration, or a combination of these, that which happens we identify as learning. As one psychologist puts it:

> In view of the lack of knowledge of what actually does take place inside the organism when learning occurs, it is preferable not to include

hypothetical neural processes in the definition of learning. We know that learning takes place. We should therefore be able to define what we are talking about without reference to any speculation whatever. This position does not deny that what we are calling learning may be a function of nervous tissue. It asserts only that it is not necessary to know anything about the neural correlates of learning in order to know that learning occurs.[3]

It may be helpful for the reader to keep in mind that learning is but a biological instance of the modification of a given aspect of the physical order, which modification helps to determine how that aspect will operate with reference to other aspects of nature. It has much in common, say, with the process that goes on when one rubs an amber rod with a piece of fur, which rod is then modified in such a way that it repulses negatively charged objects and attracts positively charged ones. We do not say that the rod "learned" to attract the one and repulse the other, but the situation is analogous to the changes which we call learning that takes place in human beings. The degree and manner in which any aspect of the universe can be modified depend upon the nature of the object, to be sure, but the process of altering the given object is basically the same. We rub the rod to obtain a certain relationship between it and other aspects of the universe, and we act upon the human organism, say by spanking a child, in order to establish a certain relationship between the organism and some aspect of the world about us, for instance fire or a heavily traveled street. We say that the electrical charges are rearranged in the amber rod; at that level of analysis we know little of what happens when a child is spanked for running into the street, so we label the result as "learning not to run into the street." The thing that both processes have in common is the establishing of a new relationship between two aspects of the natural universe. It is especially important that the social psychologist be aware of this naturalistic *relationship establishing* aspect of the learning process. It enables him to escape the danger of viewing the development of personality as something isolated from the environment of the given individual. Personality is a relationship, and not an independent entity, but of this point of view we shall learn more in Chapter 7. Let us turn for the moment to some specific aspects of the learning process.

THE CONDITIONED RESPONSE

The terms *conditioning* and *conditioned* are used frequently enough by social scientists and by laymen to warrant taking time to indicate what the referents are, and also what they are not. Conditioning is a special kind of learning pattern which involves the substitution of one stimulus

---

[3] Ernest R. Hilgard, *op. cit.*, p. 5.

for another. In such situations, a stimulus that is originally neutral or only mildly effective becomes, by association with another very effective stimulus (*e.g.*, negative in the form of electric shock or positive as in form of food), effective in bringing about a response that appears to be the same as that ordinarily elicited only by the latter kind of stimulus. The concept of conditioning or conditioned response serves this need well. This, as we shall presently see, extends the meaning beyond the simple conditioned reflex, but still gives it a specificity that avoids ambiguity. Because of the role that conditioned response studies have played in the clarification of learning theory, the following abbreviated description of the conditioning process is presented.

The process of establishing a conditioned response is as follows: some stimulus object or situation, such as an electric shock (called the unconditioned stimulus), that elicits a specific response is presented to the organism at the same time or shortly after the presentation of a second stimulus with neutral stimulus value, such as the sound of a buzzer or bell, or the blinking of a light.

The buzzer or light by itself is relatively ineffective in eliciting any overt behavior. After a number of trials in which both the unconditioned and neutral stimuli are presented in the manner indicated above, a response originally elicited by only the unconditioned stimulus (or a very similar response) is elicited by the previously neutral stimulus which is now called the conditioned stimulus.[4] It is to be noted that the response R_1, is the *same* response, according to this older (Pavlovian) theory, of the conditioned response. The process of substitution of one stimulus for another may be shown diagrammatically as in Figure 18, page 146 More extended discussion of this process can be found in any introductory textbook in psychology or educational psychology.[5]

Thus we see that the originally ineffective, incidental, or neutral stimulus of the buzzer becomes effective as a substitute stimulus in eliciting the quick movement from shocking objects.[6] It should be clear that the term *conditioned response* at once suggests the prior existence of a response that was *not* conditioned, but elicited by a specific stimulus or by stimuli. It may be an unlearned response or a learned one. In its clearest, most unambiguous sense, the conditioned response is a conditioned *reflex*. The unconditioned reflex is defined as *a relatively simple unlearned reaction to stimuli*. There is no difficulty finding consensus

[4] As E. R. Guthrie has pointed out, *prior* to its association with the effective or unconditioned stimulus, the buzzer, bell ringing cannot be called a "conditioned stimulus" (CS). "Association by Contiguity," in S. Koch, *Psychology: The Study of a Science*, 2 (New York: McGraw-Hill, 1960).

[5] *Cf.* Kimble, *op. cit.*, especially Ch. 2: "Conditioning in Historical Perspective."

[6] See Gregory A. Kimble, *Hilgard and Marquis Conditioning and Learning*, rev. ed. (New York: Appleton-Century-Crofts, 1961), Ch. I for discussion of classical and instrumental or operant conditioning.

I. Prior to association of S_1
and some previously neutral
sensory experience (e.g. Electric buzzer)

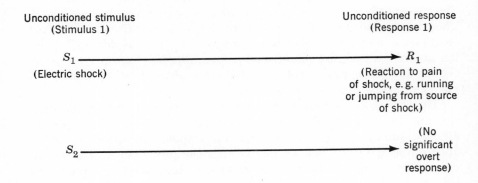

II. Following association of S_1 and S_2

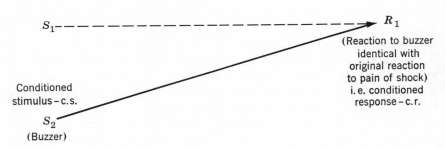

FIGURE 18. Traditional diagrammatic representation of classical conditioning.

among students of learning that the altered reactions of such reflexes as the knee jerk, pupillary contraction or expansion, salivary or sweat gland activity, or vomiting which are brought about by the association process diagrammed above are instances of conditioning. However, once one leaves the reflexes and gives attention to the broader phases of learning, the term *conditioning* loses its specificity.

Two-Phase Learning Theory

Throughout the history of experimentation in conditioning there have occurred responses to the conditioned stimuli that were not the same as the responses to the unconditioned stimuli. Some observers labeled these as "experimental errors" or otherwise dismissed them as irrelevant and unimportant. Such differences in response, however, perturbed some researchers to the extent that they sought further explanations. O. H. Mowrer, a psychologist, was among the first to perceive that there was more to the situation than the simple substitution of one stimulus for another, with the resulting old response being elicited. In brief, Mowrer suggested that there was an intervening or mediating factor that was not empirically accessible because of the rapidity with which the animal acted, seemingly, in response to the substitute or conditioned stimulus. What happened, according to Mowrer, was that the animal's first response was a covert, emotional one, R_2, usually fear of the anticipated shock and desire to escape it, and not an overt and observable act. This fear of anticipated pain and the wish to avoid it in turn became the stimulus for the animal, in response to which he sought to avoid the anticipated shock. Figure 19, page 148, indicates the two-phase nature (as conceived by Mowrer)[7] of the seemingly one-phase conditioning process.

R_2 = fear induced by perception that S_2 (C.S.) signifies forthcoming pain. This in turn becomes S_3 which motivates subject to action that permits escape from or avoidance of anticipated painful experience. The response may be the same as the original response, but it need not be. Any solution of the problem of avoiding the anticipated shock will suffice.

Mowrer's formulation of what happens in conditioning retains the items which are valuable for the social psychologist. In his words,

> Obviously, the classical conception of conditioning is much too simple to account adequately for the observed facts [i.e., the heterogeneous responses to the substitute stimuli]. As elsewhere indicated (Mowrer, *Learning Theory and Behavior*, 1960), it is not overt behavioral responses themselves that get "conditioned" but rather certain emotional (autonomic) reactions, notably those of hope and fear, which then in turn goad, guide, and correct behavior so as to make it move along sensible and biologically useful lines.[8]

[7] *Learning Theory and the Symbolic Process* (New York: John Wiley & Sons, 1960), pp. 14–15. Of this work, one reviewer has written: "The most interesting offshoot of the main line of American behavior theory has been Mowrer's revised two-factor theory, ... Stimuli, according to this theory, acquire the power to evoke affective states through classical contiguity conditioning. Instrumental [problem solving] responses occur because the feed-back stimuli consequent on them evoke positive states (hope or relief)." "Emotional Aspects of Learning," *Annual Review of Psychology*, 15 (Palo Alto, Calif.: Annual Review, Inc., 1964), p. 121. Although the "dual nature of learning" no longer denotes, as Mowrer formerly believed, association or sign learning and effect learning, the duality still exists in emphasizing the necessary distinction of cognitive and emotional learning.

[8] *Learning Theory and the Symbolic Process* (New York: John Wiley and Sons, 1960), p. 37. In keeping with Mowrer's own position and the one to be outlined immediately below, one would accept the verb *goad* as a function of the hopes and fears, but would argue that *guide* and *correct* are cognitive functions.

I. Prior to association of
S_1 and some previously neutral
sensory item (e. g. Electric buzzer, S_2)

Unconditioned stimulus   Unconditioned response
(Stimulus 1)   (Response 1)

$S_1 \longrightarrow R_1$

(Reaction to pain
of shock, e. g. jumping,
running from source
of shock)

II. Following association of S_1 and S_2

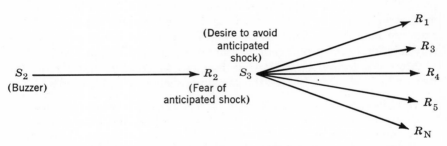

(Desire to avoid
anticipated
shock) R_1

                                                                    R_3

$S_2 \longrightarrow R_2 \quad S_3$ R_4
(Buzzer)   (Fear of
            anticipated shock) R_5

                                                                    R_N

FIGURE 19. Diagrammatic representation of conditioning according to Mowrer.

The importance of Mowrer's conceptualization of the processes involved in the conditioned response lies in its application to the innumerable instances of association learning among humans, wherein it is important to distinguish learning at the affect or emotional level from cognitive
learning.[9] Even though they are much more complicated, the learning
experiences of humans involve the same distinction between learning

---

[9] The scope of conditioned response has been expanded beyond its original meaning, which implied not only a substitute stimulus but also "experimental extinction,"
i.e., the extinction of the effectiveness of the conditioned, or substitute, stimulus
when it was not reinforced periodically by the unconditioned stimuli. B. F. Skinner
uses the term *operant conditioning* to denote the learning involved in, say, a rat push-
ing a lever to get a pellet of food. *See* his *Science and Human Behavior* (New York:
The Macmillan Co., 1953). We prefer to use the term *conditioning* to denote the
more restricted learning situation. Skinner's *operant conditioning* can be handled
semantically very well by simple association learning concepts.

problems (developing attitudes and sociogenic motives as detailed in Chapter 7), and instrumental or problem solving learning. The former is a function of the autonomic nervous system whereas the latter a function of the central nervous system.

Mowrer's formulation also helps to distinguish between learning and acting, i.e., between feeling and knowing, on the one hand, and behaving, on the other. Failure to make this distinction led, in the past, to the assumption that rewards and penalties aided or hindered learning, especially at the cognitive or intellectual level.[10] It was believed that the S–R bonds were strengthened if what was learned was pleasant, and weakened if unpleasant. Even though the picture is still unclear in all aspects, an increasing number of psychologists believe that learning takes place through contiguity of stimulus and response, or stimulus and stimulus, with relatively little influence by either reward or punishment. Fears are learned as readily as hopes, and the reinforcement operates to influence the instrumental, or problem solving, *behavior*. As one writer comments (concerning the theory of K. W. Spence, *Behavior Theory and Learning*), "The growth of habit strength is no longer assumed to depend upon reinforcement in the sense of "reward." The influence of motivational factors is now confined to performance."[11]

In the past, what is learned has been confused with the behavior that is a function of that learning. Whether it is rats running mazes, or boys and girls learning to dance, to solve arithmetic problems, or learning to cope with hunger, sex, and other innate impulses, rewards and penalties do not appear to have any *direct* role in learning or in inhibiting learning. It is well to keep in mind that no matter how strongly motivated one is

[10] This view is called the "law of effect" and is associated with the name of E. L. Thorndike, a pioneer American psychologist. *See Hilgard*, op. cit., Ch. 2, "Thorndike's Connectionism." The long-time exponent of the "law of association" in learning theory is E. R. Guthrie. His position is that association is the essential and sufficient experience in learning. However, he notes that sometimes "the stimuli did not always stimulate" and he is cognizant of the fact that experience must reach the perceptual level if learning is to take place at the higher levels in man. He states that "It is not enough that they be available in the physical situation, nor is it enough that the organism's attention orients sense organs to receive them; it is further necessary that they have meaning for the responding organism." "Association by Contiguity" in S. Koch, *Psychology: The Study of a Science*, 2 (New York: McGraw-Hill, 1960), p. 165. The reader will recognize the relationship of Guthrie's statement to the nature of knowledge as discussed later in this chapter.

[11] Berlyne, *op. cit.*, p. 121. More recently two psychologists noted that: ". . . what appears to have happened to reinforcement over the past several decades is this: *It has gradually lost much of its original attractiveness as an explanatory concept.* Guthrie and Tolman never subscribed to reinforcement in the formulation of their systems, and Skinner accepts reinforcement only in the sense of a descriptive principle, and not in terms of drive reduction or need reduction." J. P. Chaplin, T. S. Krawiec, *Systems and Theories of Psychology* (New York: Holt, Rinehart and Winston, 1963), p. 267. Italics in original.

to learn a problem's solution, *no learning takes place unless some action (mental or motor) is involved.*[12] What happens here, is that the motivation, in the form of anticipated reward or punishment (Mowrer's hope or fear) sets the stage for learning by inducing the subject to perform the action which is the *sine qua non* of learning.[13] Thus the principle is that the motivated subject performs those acts that are essential to learning, but that the reward and punishment are not directly involved in the learning process. Thus subjects, rats or men, learn which problems will be theirs because of their unique associational experiences, and learn (or fail to learn) how to solve these problems because they perform (or fail to perform) the essential acts requisite to instrumental learning.

The conditioned response is actually relatively unimportant in human learning. Involving, as it does, a substitute stimulus, it occurs but rarely in everyday life. However, on occasion the term is useful.

Operant Conditioning

Psychologist B. F. Skinner has given the name *operant conditioning* to a category of learning that some persons perceive as a special kind of conditioning, and others as a special type of associational contiguity learning. The present authors favor the latter view, but believe it important to bring this currently popular term to the reader's attention.

With his now-famous *Skinner box*, Skinner was able to demonstrate how rats and pigeons would perform certain tasks for appropriate rewards (*reinforcement* is the term preferred by psychologists), and would cease such behavior if punishment (*negative reinforcement*) or simply lack of reinforcement accompanied it. Thus the experimental environment enabled the animal to learn that if he pressed a bar, he was rewarded with food. If, later, he was shocked upon pressing the bar, he tended not to press it.

The ramifications and implications of Skinner's *operant conditioning* extend well beyond the pale of social psychology, and our remarks here are restricted to those areas pertinent to social psychology.[14] The difference between *operant conditioning* and classical (or *respondent* in Skinner's term) conditioning are clearly qualitative and, in the writers'

---

[12] This is not in conflict with Mowrer's statement (*op. cit.*, p. 12). Surely both man and other animals transfer knowledge to novel problem situations, and solve them without first experiencing the specific problem solving.

[13] *Cf.* Hilgard, *op. cit.*, for descriptions of the various learning theories.

[14] *Cf.* his early presentation of his work in *The Behavior of Organisms* (New York: Appleton-Century-Crofts, 1938). It is of some interest to note that, although the term *operant conditioning* is well known among psychological social psychologists today, more than a decade passed between its introduction in book form and its use in article titles in the *American Journal of Psychology*. In his *Science and Human Behavior*, (New York: The Macmillan Co., 1953), Skinner brought the concept to bear upon the broader sociocultural aspects of human behavior.

Now, as I see it, we have this human trained to produce food pellets when we depress the lever under the triangle symbol. But, can we generalize from this to an hypothesis about rat behavior?

FIGURE 20.   Operant "Conditioning."

opinion, so marked that it seems illogical to place them both in the same category of learning.[15]

The first of two important differences is that classical conditioning always involves at least one substitute (or "conditioned") stimulus.[16] This kind of learning is, as noted above, relatively unimportant and in the understanding of human behavior. This fact suggests the second signal difference between classical (respondent) conditioning and operant or instrumental conditioning, *viz.*, the wide applicability of the latter to human behavior.

Is there a difference between operant conditioning and other forms

[15] With regard to categories of learning, the remarks of one psychologist are of interest: "The most certain conclusions that one can reach about the traditional categories is that they are not the proper categories for use in understanding human learning even though they may serve a useful denotative function." Arthur W. Melton, "The Taxonomy of Human Learning Overview" in A. W. Melton (ed.) *Categories of Human Learning* (New York: The Academic Press, 1964), p. 333. One reason for this condition, if this be a valid observation, may be the overwhelming attention given to nonhuman animals by the students of learning theory.

[16] A less significant difference has been called to attention by psychologist G. Razran (*American Journal of Psychology* (Nov. 1955), 489–490). He notes that a study of one hundred instances of classical conditioning from Pavlov's laboratories showed extinction (loss of affectiveness of conditioned stimulus) to occur after, at most, only a few dozen nonreinforced trials, whereas hundreds, even thousands, of nonreinforced trials are noted in operant or instrumental conditioning.

of learning and/or behavior? In view of the recent disaffection for the "law of effect" in learning theory, it does not appear that the learning principles involved here are different from the currently interpreted association contiguity principles.

Skinner makes no claim that his studies of reinforcement have any bearing upon learning nor does he believe it desirable to interpret reinforcement as reduction of drive.[17]

What is reinforced or rewarded is, of course, behavior that is a function of contiguity learning and not the learning bond itself. Also, operant conditioning provides experimental evidence, if such be needed, for the validity of the pleasure-pain principle of behavior. With reference to learning spoken symbols, Skinner has this to say:

> If we wish to make a response of given form highly probable, we arrange for the effective reinforcement of many instances. If we wish to eliminate it from a verbal repertoire, we arrange that reinforcement shall no longer follow.[18]

The probability of the occurrence of all behavior, verbal or otherwise, is thus explained, though not necessarily by social, external reinforcement. Except in those episodes involving neurotic or psychotic obsessive-compulsive states, all behavior is operant in Skinner's terms, *insofar as human beings are concerned*, and, therefore, the phrase *operant conditioning* fails to add conceptual value as a social psychological instrument.[19]

It is true that *conditioning* has become a part of the layman's vocabulary, and we occasionally hear it said that such and such a person has become conditioned to a situation, meaning that he has learned to adjust to or live with some condition. However, this is not the psychologist's use of the term—at least not with reference to classical or respondent conditioning, and the fact that the terms *conditioning* and *learning* are fre-

---

[17] *Cf.* J. P. Chaplin and T. S. Krawiec, *op. cit.*, p. 242.

[18] *Verbal Behavior* (New York: Appleton-Century-Crofts, 1957), p. 29. For a criticism of some of the implications of too literal interpretation of reinforcement in language learning, see Joseph Church, *Language and the Discovery of Reality* (New York: Random House, 1961), pp. 80 ff. In agreement with the views expressed in the present text, Church comments: "Needless to say, parents are inclined to greet their children's first words, and spontaneous use of words, with delight and so to reinforce them; but the actual word comes first, indicating that it has already been learned, and the [social] reinforcement comes after." *Ibid.*, pp. 82–83. We also agree with Church in his comments about reinforcement and extinction of behavior in operant conditioning, *viz.* "Perhaps some of the difficulty comes about because learning theorists do not distinguish enough between behavior and the learning—specifically, the schematization—that underlies behavior." *Ibid.*, p. 84.

[19] One writer has this to say on this point: "When one searches for human experiments that fit the classificatory scheme for the simple instrumental [operant] conditioning experiments . . . , the result is a complete failure." David Grant, "Classical and Operant Conditioning," in A. W. Melton, *op. cit.*, p. 26.

quently used as synonyms is unfortunate for purposes of unambiguous communication and thinking. A careful construction of learning theory and the attendant terminology demands that the term be given more careful definition. One psychologist has written that to equate conditioning and learning is ". . . more of an insult than a theory."[20]

In attempting to restrict the term to certain phases of learning, some have used it to apply to those learning situations, wherein two previously unrelated factors become related in behavior as stimulus and response in such a manner that the response is automatic. However, this too seems to be too broad a use of the concept and confuses it with learning as such. If the word is to become a significant symbol and permit true communication, it must be restricted even further in its meaning. As one writer has pointed out, we have no need for another synonym for learning, nor for association (contiguity learning), but we do have need for a term to designate those learning situations wherein a substitute stimulus is involved.[21]

ATTITUDE LEARNING

Although the functioning of the two nervous systems, the central and the autonomic, cannot in actuality be *separated* as they operate in human behavior, it would be difficult to overemphasize the importance of the point that their functions can be *distinguished*. This recognition of different kinds of learning is especially significant for the social psychologist, and failure to take note of these differences can lead to much confusion and to ensuing failure in the attempts at understanding human behavior. The uncritical ease with which we interchange the expressions "I feel," "I think," and "I believe," is indicative of careless semantics and reflects inadequate thinking. Believing and feeling are quite different processes, neurologically and psychologically.

In the conditioning experiments, we see a very simple illustration of the relationship between emotional learning and cognitive learning. The fear of the anticipated shock or other noxious stimuli sets the problem, and herein lies the functioning of the autonomic nervous system. The problem of what to do behaviorally about the anticipated shock falls in the province of the central nervous system, especially the so-called higher aspects of it. Broadly speaking, man learns to fear (pain, deprivation of food, and so on) and to want (affection, recognition) by way of the autonomic nervous system. For the most part these fears and hopes are learned unconsciously, gradually, and without deliberation. What a man learns to fear or want is selected, to be sure, largely in terms of what he

[20] Norman L. Munn, *Psychology* (Boston: Houghton Mifflin, 1946), p. 101.
[21] Donald O. Gowgill, "Variant Meaning of the Terms Conditioning and Conditioned Response," *Journal of Social Psychology*, XXVIII (1948), 254. This article discusses in detail the contradictory meanings of the term as it is now used.

has learned empirically and rationally, but sensing and comprehending, although necessary, are not sufficient for this kind of learning. Even though its precise operation is poorly understood, learning at the emotional level is distinguishable from cognitive learning, and the important thing to understand for social psychology is that *emotional learning and relearning must of necessity involve emotional experiences.*

Evidence to support this proposition is in full supply. The following instances of attitude change, and lack of change, are selected because they illustrate the conditions under which emotional learning takes place.

WEEK END IN HARLEM

The first step in this experiment was to administer to 354 students in six classes at Columbia University's Teachers College a test of attitudes toward the Negro. An experimental group of forty-six students was then selected by invitation through mail. This group was found to have been made up of ten students from the southern states, twenty from the Middle Western states, four from the Far West, eleven from the East, and one from Canada.[22] The fact that twenty-one of the group fell below the mean score (of the test scores made by the total 453) indicated that the group was not made up of persons of either extreme anti- or pro-Negro feelings.

The essence of the experiment lay in a four-day seminar in the Negro area of Harlem, in New York City. Beginning with a brief historical description of Harlem, the changing social situation there, and other pertinent facts, the group was taken on a tour of Harlem by Negro hosts who pointed out some of the better parts of the area. This was followed by a series of dinners, lectures on various subjects, visits to both Protestant and Roman Catholic churches, musical entertainments, and visits to homes of Negroes. In the words of the experimenter, "It [the experiment] consisted in direct personal exposure to the complex influences exerted by middle-class Negro individuals and social groups—to their personalities, opinions, ideas, problems, worries, talents, achievements, and participation in community life."[23] In short, this experiment provided the students with experiences at the emotional level, and the learning process had important unconscious aspects. This is quite different from learning from a textbook that there are no significant differences between Negroes and whites, or being told that it is un-American to have aversions to other groups, or reading about the contributions of Negro scientists to culture. These latter experiences have their places in the attitude chang-

---

[22] F. Tredwell Smith, *An Experiment in Modifying Attitudes Toward the Negro*, Teachers College, Columbia University Contributions to Education No. 887 (New York: Columbia University, 1943), pp. 26 and 34.

[23] *Ibid.*, p. 45.

ing process, but they can never become adequate substitutes for the emotional experiences at the primary group level.

The effectiveness of the experiment is revealed in the fact that, when carefully tested against control groups who did not attend the four-day seminar, the changes in attitude were highly significant. At the end of ten months the groups were retested and the gains were maintained in most cases. For the group as a whole there was some perceptible decline in the effect of the experiment, but the differences from the initial test were still marked.[24] That this type of experience should show such results is not to be wondered at in light of what we know about learning theory. It is hardly logical to contrast the gains made here with those reported from lectures or courses dealing with Negro-white relations. It would be as logical to expect swimming to be learned through the lecture method as to expect fundamental emotional attitudes to be so altered.

However, lest one think that primary group experiences are all that are needed to alter attitudes from prejudice to acceptance, we point out that the personality of the individual involved and the social setting are always to be considered. Evidence of this need to consider all of the interactive factors is provided by the following experiment or observation.

ADOPTING SOUTHERN ATTITUDES

In this study, the problem was to discover the influence of attendance in a southern university upon attitudes toward Negroes of students from the northern states.[25] Tests revealed that whereas the scores (on tests revealing racial attitudes) of freshmen in the southern university who had come from the northern states approximated those made by the students in the northern university, the seniors (northerners) in the southern university approximated the scores of the native southerners. Although their attitudes did not become identical with the southerners, a change occurred in a less favorable direction. This change appears to be attributable to contact with prejudiced southern whites and with Negroes that were quite different from those encountered by the Columbia University students in their Harlem seminar.

THE ARMY AND ATTITUDES TOWARD THE NEGRO

The third study to be reported here concerns the attitudes of the white American soldier toward the Negro. The answers were given in response to the following question: "Some Army divisions have companies which include Negro platoons and white platoons. How would you feel about it if your outfit were set up something like this?"

[24] *Ibid.*, p. 96.
[25] V. M. Sims and J. R. Patrick, "Attitude toward the Negro of Northern and Southern College Students," *Journal of Social Psychology*, VII (1936).

A moment's glance at the table will show the influence of primary group contacts with the Negro groups. Those who had the experience of having a Negro platoon within their company were the most receptive to this setup, whereas those who had had no opportunity to observe such an arrangement were the most opposed to it.

Table V
Differential Association and Racial Attitudes*

	Would Like It	Just As Soon Have It As Any Other Set-Up	Rather Not, But It Would Not Matter Too Much	Would Dislike It Very Much
Infantrymen in a company which has a Negro platoon (80)	32%	28%	33%	7%
Infantrymen in other companies in the same regiment (68)	18%	33%	29%	20%
Field Artillery, Anti-Tank, and HQ units in the same division (112)	9%	29%	38%	24%
Cross section of other Field Force units which do not have Negro platoons in white companies (1450)	2%	9%	27%	62%

* The President's Commission on Civil Rights, *To Secure These Rights* (New York: Simon and Schuster, 1947), p. 86.

HOUSING AND NEGRO-WHITE ATTITUDES

One of the greatest sources of friction in our large cities is the relationship of racial groups in residential areas. Two studies provide us with objective illustrations of the nature of relationships in housing projects.[26] In a housing project identified by the author as "Hilltown," the tenants were asked how they thought the two races would get along. The results were these: of the persons who had previous experience in a biracial neighborhood, 9 per cent were optimistic ("We'll get along fine"); 72 per cent felt that they could accommodate with no trouble; and only 19 per cent were fearful of serious trouble and riots. On the other hand, of those who had no previous experience with a biracial neighborhood, 5 per cent were optimistic; 39 per cent thought that they could accommodate without trouble; but 56 per cent were fearful of serious trouble.[27]

[26] Robert K. Merton, "The Social Psychology of Housing," in *Current Trends in Social Psychology* (Pittsburgh: University of Pittsburgh Press, 1948).
[27] *Ibid.*, p. 212.

Here is further evidence of the nature of the experiences that are required to alter emotional attitudes.

A comparable study involved four housing projects in the New York metropolitan area. It contrasted the relationships between Negro and white tenants in two segregated and two integrated housing projects. The segregated projects were those in which separate buildings or separate parts of the project were set aside for the different races, whereas the integrated projects were those in which assignment to apartments was made without respect to race. The contrast between the interracial relations of the two types of projects is marked, and the differences are statistically significant. The social contacts with members of the other race are much more frequent in the integrated than in the segregated projects, and a positive change in attitude toward the Negro on the part of many of the occupants occurred in the integrated projects. The contrast with the segregated groups both as to attitude and overt behavior is marked.[28]

A more recent study reveals the same general process of attitude development and change. In a study of attitudes involving New Zealand children of European ancestry and of Maori (Polynesian) ancestry, using TAT (Thematic Apperception Test) cards depicting identical situations except for Caucasian or Maori facial features on one of the several subjects pictured, eight-, twelve-, and sixteen-year old children were asked to suggest what they believed the pictured situations might be. Subjects were separated into groups that had considerable contact with Maoris and those with little contact. Prejudice increased from the years eight to twelve for both groups, but continued to increase between the years twelve to sixteen for those with little contact. The authors conclude that the change in attitude between twelve and sixteen ". . . supports the suggestion that prejudice may be reduced by *equal* status contact."[29]

The importance of *equal status* contacts in reducing prejudice must not be overlooked. It most certainly would not conduce to prejudice reduction to place middle-class whites of whatever age in a Negro slum ghetto. It was observed, during World War II, that whites, previously of only average anti-Negro prejudice, who were placed in contact with Negro Americans with low intelligence test scores and little schooling, increased their prejudices significantly. However, it was also observed that whites whose contacts were restricted to carefully selected, well edu-

[28] Morton Deutsch and Mary Evans Collins, *Intergroup Relations in Interracial Housing: A Study in the Socio-Psychological Effects of Occupancy Pattern* (New York: Research Center for Human Relations, New York University, mimeographed, not dated), p. 13.

[29] G. M. Vaughan and R. H. T. Thomson, "New Zealand Children's Attitude Toward Maoris," *Journal of Abnormal and Social Psychology*, 62 (1961), pp. 704 (Italics added). This suggestion was central to G. W. Allport's *The Nature of Prejudice* (Cambridge, Mass.: Addison-Wesley Press, 1954).

cated, and highly intelligent Negro groups developed favorable biases toward the Negro. One of the present authors observed an impasse which developed in the attitudes toward Negroes between two World War II veterans. One had been in charge of a disciplinary barracks populated principally by illiterate, rural, southern Negroes, whereas the other (a bomber pilot) had developed a high esteem for the skills and courage of an all-Negro fighter squadron. Each had been exposed to unrepresentative samples of Negro Americans.

Thus we are provided with information concerning the nature of the influences which operate to change attitudes. These studies help to verify the theory of social psychology that is presented in this and other social psychology textbooks and research publications.

In each of these cases, it was the actual, daily, primary relationships which effected the altered attitudes, and not merely the cognitive aspects of the experiences. In other kinds of episodes the close relationship between what is known and what is felt is more apparent, as the following instance evidences:

> One day, while working in the glass-walled building which housed plants and certain of the college's collection of animals, a butter-fingered lab assistant dropped a piece of equipment on one of the glass display cases and took off in high gear. I soon learned the reason for his speedy departure as two snakes from the case spilled onto the floor between me and the only exit from the house. I am an English major, and have no truck with reptiles if I can avoid it, but I do know something about which snakes are poisonous and which are not. I saw what I thought were African vipers heading my way, and my heart began to pound, and I nearly panicked. However, a closer look at the snakes revealed that they were a harmless, if ugly, species. Although still a little shaken, I was no longer afraid, my pulse had returned to normal, and I stepped over the snakes to report to the lab director what had happened.[30]

In this case, the inseparable nature of the two kinds of learning is evidenced, but equally well demonstrated is the fact that there *are* two kinds of learning. It is to the second kind, the cognitive or intellectual, that we now turn our attention.

COGNITIVE OR INTELLECTUAL LEARNING

Philosophic problems that some people believe to have been solved once and for all many centuries ago have a way of intruding into the contemporary scene. One such problem involves two words that are very much in evidence today, explicitly or otherwise. The words *empiricism* and *rationalism* are aspects of an intellectual argument that began more than

---

[30] It is this kind of learned reaction which is frequently erroneously identified as a conditioned response.

two thousand years ago and which is not yet ended. The ancient Greeks, whose queries involved so many items that are still of interest and importance today, took sides on the question as to whether or not sensory experiences on the one hand, or thinking and reasoning on the other, were the real sources of knowledge. The Stoics were of one mind and supported the sensual or empirical experiences as the more important. They used the analogy of a blank tablet, a *tabula rasa* for the mind or soul upon which sensory experiences with the outer world are imprinted or impressed. Plato was a strong exponent of the reasoning power of mankind as the more significant means to learning.

Even more sharply divided on this same issue were the thinkers of the seventeenth and eighteenth century in England and Europe. There grew up in England a group of thinkers and writers who became known as the "British empiricists" who, despite differences among themselves, agreed upon the greater importance and priority of sensory experience as the source of knowledge. The names of John Locke (1632–1704) and David Hume (1711–1776) are frequently brought to mind when psychological empiricism is discussed. Representing the opposite side of the controversy were René Descartes (1596–1650) and Gottfried Leibnitz (1646–1716). The former school of thought again used the Stoic's analogy of the *tabula rasa*. The *rationalists*, as those opposing this approach were called, argued for the innate nature of knowledge, for the idea that knowledge was learned by the internal process of reasoning. If only one would think long and carefully enough, they argued, the truth would reveal itself. Truth is known by the certitude with which one perceived it as a result of his thinking or reasoning process. Descartes wrote: "And therefore it seems to me that I can already establish as a general principle that everything which we conceive very clearly and very distinctly is wholly true."[31]

On the other hand, the empiricists argued that the most certain of all knowledge was found in those things which were accessible to the senses. This is the highest and clearest knowledge, said the empiricists.

Our highest degree of knowledge is intuitive, without reasoning. Some of the ideas that are in the mind, are so there, that they can be by themselves immediately compared one with another; and in these the mind is able to perceive that they agree or disagree as clearly as that it has them . . . In this consists the evidence of all those maxims which nobody has any doubt about, but every man (does not, as is said, only

[31] René Descartes, *Meditations* (New York: Liberal Arts Press, 1951), p. 31. The only exceptions, according to Descartes, were *sensory* experiences which seemed clear but were deceiving. It is of interest that the Epicureans of Ancient Greece argued for the validity of sensory experiences as criteria of truth on the same basis of subjective certitude. Lest the reader underestimate the appeal of this metaphysical point, be it noted that a well-known American philosopher reasserted it in a public lecture given February 19, 1964.

assent to, but) knows to be true, as soon as ever they are proposed to his understanding. In the discovery of assent to these truths, there is no use of the discursive faculty, no need of reasoning, but they are known by a superior and higher degree of evidence.[32]

One might wonder whether these justly famous thinkers could argue that knowledge was attained (*i.e.*, learning took place) solely through sensory experiences *or* by use of concepts alone. If one reads their works carefully he will know that each group, whether called empiricists or rationalists, was well aware of both sensory experience *and* of thinking and reasoning processes, and took them into account. Locke, for instance, wrote that there is "very much need for reason," . . . [and that] . . . the greatest part of our ideas are such, that we cannot discern their agreement or disagreement by an immediate comparing of them. And in all these we have need of reasoning, and must by discourse and inference, make our discoveries."[33] Descartes, even though he noted (as all of us have at one time or another) ". . . . that these senses sometimes deceive me . . .," nevertheless took them into account.[34] It was the empiricists' overly strong insistence that learning resulted principally from sensory experiences with the external world, and the rationalists' no less vigorous argument for reasoning as the primary means of acquiring knowledge, that distinguished the two schools of thought, rather than their insistence upon either source as the *sole* one. On today's stage the protagonists of the two schools of thought are much closer together, and it is not often that one identifies writers or teachers in such terms. However, despite some evidence of an opposite trend over the last few decades, there still remains a general esteem for facts and a disesteem for thinking and theory as a means to problem solution or to knowledge.

This is true generally among laymen and for a significant proportion of academicians. The popularity of such phrases as *empirical research, empirical verification,* which are sprinkled throughout the learned journals, attests to the high value given empiricism in today's literature of the social sciences. Although there is disagreement on this issue, the present authors' experience and observations over the last quarter of a century have led them to the firm conviction that pursuit of empirical facts is associated with the scientist whereas theorizing is associated with the philosopher, the latter term occasionally being employed as an epithet by others. For a significant number of social scientists, empiricism has an evaluative connotation of rigorous mental discipline whereas theorizing suggests unchanneled mental meanderings. The term *brain trust,* which was attached to the advisers to Franklin Delano Roosevelt during the

[32] *The Philosophic Works of John Locke,* II (London: George Bell and Sons, 1899), p. 298.
[33] *Ibid.,* p. 298.
[34] *Op. cit.,* p. 16.

New Deal years, had derogatory implications. Several social science departments in well-known American universities show clear preference for research which is empirically oriented.

Nevertheless, the emphasis upon empiricism in recent decades is understandable in the light of the history of the social sciences. Too often in the past, subjective biases and prejudices served as the bases for writings in psychology, social psychology, and sociology. Current writers and teachers, rather than seeking to make a fetish of the term *empirical,* are attempting only to support objective analyses of research data, and stressing the need for perceptual evidence to complement the concepts that are brought to the problem. Few indeed fail to recognize that knowledge is constituted of more than pure empiricism.

Knowledge As a Function of Both Sense and Reason

Immanuel Kant, the famous eighteenth century German philosopher, came very close to summing up the present-day position regarding the source of knowledge: "Conception without perception is empty, perception without conception is blind." However, Kant's terms, as translated, do not quite tell the story. In current terminology, Kant's statement would be more accurate if sensation were substituted for perception. But even this correction would be incomplete, because cognition is a tripartite process, including *sensation, perception,* and *conception.*

Sensation is an unlearned biophysical process involving the sensory receptors (organs of taste, touch, hearing, smelling, seeing) and appropriate stimuli (chemical, pressure, sounds, certain gases, reflected light waves). Thus one "hears" if sound waves impinge upon the inner ear, regardless of the nature of the sound, be it words in his own or a strange language, sound made by musical instruments, or the explosion of gases in an internal combustion engine. Similarly, one "sees" if light rays (waves or particles) strike first an object and then the rods and cones of the retina, whether the objects reflecting the light be familiar or completely novel in nature, an old friend's face, or any photo of an unknown object— and so it is with the other senses; biophysical experiences (*empirical* experiences) occur, but have no meaning for the subject. The illiterate, with 20-20 vision, will see no meaning in a printed page, however long and carefully he may scrutinize it, because he has not acquired the concepts of signs and symbols, nor will the literate person note the symptoms of paranoia unless his ideas include an understanding of mental illness. Only through the acquisition of concepts by thinking can meaning be brought to sensory experiences.

From the very beginning of life the individual adds thinking to his empirical experiences, and thereby brings meaning to them. We have already noted this process in Chapter 3 in discussing the cognitive-sensory processes of sign recognition, abstraction, and symbolization, and pointed out that man's brain is such that he cannot help making certain perceptual relationships among his mental, emotional, motor, and empirical experiences. These ways of looking at and thinking about experiences are called *concepts*. The sign-learning talent, which man shares with other animals, is involved in thinking about self-evident relationships wherein the sign indicates, in an imperative manner, certain other objects, such as in the dark-cloud-approaching-rain sequence. Although signs or signals are important for human behavior, they are of secondary importance in thinking and, as we shall see in Chapter 6, in communication. Of far greater significance are the processes of abstraction and symbolization. In her well-known book, *Philosophy in a New Key*, Susanne K. Langer says that signs indicate things whereas words, or "substitute signs," are used to talk about things and as such are symbols.[35] Philip Wheelwright in his careful study, *The Burning Fountain*, says, concerning the symbol, "As distinguished from a signal it invites consideration rather than overt action."[36]

Even though we have argued that it is important to distinguish the processes of abstraction from those of symbolization, we agree in general with the importance attached to symbols as the distinguishing feature of man's cognitive processes. The innate capacity to symbolize objects sets man apart from other animals, permits him to consider things not in one's presence, events that have taken place in the past, and to speculate about events yet to come. Social behaviorist George Herbert Mead states that thinking is an internal conversation of gestures. In Mead's words:

> If a person retires to a secluded spot and sits down to think, he talks to himself. He asks and answers questions. He develops his ideas and arranges and organizes those ideas as he might do in conversation

[35] (New York: Penguin Books, 1942), p. 24.

[36] (Indiana University Press, 1954), p. 23. Professor Charles Morris in his book *Sign, Language, and Behavior* (New York: Prentice-Hall, 1946) defines a sign as "Something which controls behavior towards a goal in a way similar to (but not necessarily identical with) the way some other things would . . ." We can see here that Morris uses sign in a manner very similar to symbol as used by other people. O. H. Mowrer, a clinical psychology and learning theorist, subscribing to Ernst Cassirer's distinction between *propositional language* and *emotional language* [See Ernst Cassirer (1874–1945), *An Essay on Man* (Garden City, N.Y.: Doubleday, 1944), pp. 44 and 48] as the significant difference between man and infrahumans, notes that only the propositional involves true symbols. He illustrates by saying "a symbol is not distinguished from an ordinary sign in terms of *form*; it is only when the motivation behind its usage is taken into account that the difference clearly emerges. When a thirsty child cries, 'Water, water,' he is using a sign, in much the same way that lower animals do; but, when not thirsty himself but instead questioned by a playmate, he says, 'Water is in the pitcher,' he is using a symbol." *Learning Theory and the Symbolic Processes* (New York: John Wiley and Sons, 1960), p. 161. The reader will find much of interest in this source, especially Chapters 3 and 4.

with somebody else. He is a more appreciative audience, perhaps . . .
He takes different roles. He asks questions and meets them; presents
arguments and refutes them.[37]

In this manner man, by the private use of symbols, gains knowledge about
the world of objects about him. Without names for the almost innumerable items which enter one's experience, the thought processes are overly
simple or jumbled. Thinking, to the extent that it is an "internal conversation of gestures," is sharply delineated by the adequacy of the symbol
system. An historic example is that of the cultures in which the numerical
systems did not contain the concept, and therefore the symbol, of zero.

Despite the close relationship between them, it is important that one
keep separate the *symbol* and the concept or idea for which it stands.
Each can exist apart from the other, a fact which becomes important in
the discussion of communication in Chapter 6. Every school child can
testify that he knows many words and other symbols which he can recognize, reproduce, but the meaning of which has escaped him. The
difference between the average high school student and the great mathe-
maticians is not at the symbol level, but at the concept level. Learning the
Latin names for diseases and drugs does not make one a physician, no
more than the learning of the Greek alphabet by fraternity and sorority
pledges makes them Greek scholars. Thus symbolization is a necessary,
but not sufficient, process in the much more complex process of thinking
or reasoning.

Concepts are functions of man's quest for answers to puzzling conditions or situations. Everyone is more or less familiar with this process of
searching for meanings or explanations of perplexing experiences which
cannot be understood through sensory channels alone. As laymen we
speculate as to why a friend failed to keep a date, why we fail to achieve
certain goals, why certain persons drink or eat too much, or why failures
show up in the "very best" of families, and so on. The scientist does essentially the same thing in his quest for answers to his problems which cannot be answered merely by looking at or listening to them.[38] Both scientist
and layman develop *concepts*. The difference between the concepts developed by the layman and those of the scientist lies in the rigor with
which the latter tests his concepts, and his attention to their logical

[37] *Movements of Thought in the Nineteenth Century* (Chicago: The University
of Chicago Press), p. 401. *See also* H. H. Gerth and C. Wright Mills, *Character and
Social Structure* (New York: Harcourt Brace and World, 1953).

[38] The reader is urged to study Herbert Blumer's excellent statement on the nature of the concept in his article, "Science Without Concepts," *American Journal of
Sociology*, XXXVI (Jan. 1931). Blumer works with only two terms, perception and
conception, not dealing with the strictly sensory phase of cognition. Despite this fact,
the authors believe that this article is superior to any on the subject that have
appeared since its publication.

relationship with other concepts. Whereas the layman accepts rather uncritically many of the concepts that his cultural heritage has given to him, the scientist must test the consistency of his concepts if he is to develop a systematic theoretical system that is both valid and reliable. As one writer has stated it:

> To my mind, the chief difference is that the abstraction embodied in the common-sense concept is just accepted and is not made the subject of special analysis and study. Consequently, abstraction is soon arrested and not pushed to the length that is true in the case of scientific concepts. . . . With such a background it is to be expected that "common sense," as the term strongly suggests, refers to what is sensed [uncritically perceived, in our meaning of the term] instead of to what is acutely analyzed. This seems to be true in the case of common-sense concepts in much greater measure than in the case of scientific concepts; they are more a matter of feeling than of logical discernment. It seems that it is for this reason that an ordinary individual is puzzled when you ask him to define some common-sense term.
>
> There is another difference between common-sense concepts and scientific concepts which strikes me as important. Common-sense concepts are detached and disparate; scientific concepts show "a strain toward consistency." The abstraction embodied in a common-sense concept tends, I think, to have an absolutistic, independent existence; the abstractions within scientific concepts are always being related to one another. It is no accident that the concepts in a given science hang together in a system, nor that by doing so they make possible the structure of science.[39]

In the same vein of thought is this statement:

> "Common sense" is content with a miscellaneous collection of information. As a consequence, the propositions it asserts are frequently vague, the range of their application is unknown, and their mutual compatibility is generally very questionable. The advantages of discovering a system among facts is therefore obvious. . . . Moreover, inconsistencies between propositions asserted become eliminated gradually because propositions which are part of a system must support and correct one another.[40]

The application of concepts, scientific or otherwise, to empirical experiences gives rise to the third phase of the cognition process, namely, *perceptions*, or simply *percepts*. A perception is an experience (sensory, emotional, or cognitive) that has acquired meaning. The marks on this page are, to anyone with eyesight, at first merely sensory experiences with no meaning whatsoever. Add to these empirical experiences the

---

[39] *Ibid.*, pp. 522–525.

[40] Morris R. Cohen and Ernest Nagel, *An Introduction to Logic and the Scientific Method* (New York: Harcourt, Brace and Co., 1934), p. 396.

concepts of language, letters, words, grammar, syntax, and these markings acquire meanings and our experiences become perceptions. What we perceive, however, can become puzzles in turn and lead to further speculation, or concept formation, *e.g.*, new concepts can yield understanding of relationships among previously acquired perceptions. The concepts formed may lead to perception or to misperceptions; they may serve as blinders which restrict what we see, as well as windows which permit wider vision.

Perhaps an illustration of the way in which current concepts serve to "explain" a common situation will clarify the functions of concepts or theory. If we take for our purposes the case of a criminal who has committed an act that violates the laws of a society, we soon discover that not all persons explain the criminal's action in the same way. Equipped with different concepts, they come out with different perceptions of the reasons for what was done. The orthodox Marxist, for example, would be apt to interpret the criminal action as a function of the capitalistic economic system which forces the common man to criminal behavior because it deprives him of economic goods and services. The orthodox Freudian would disagree. With his concepts, a disciple of Sigmund Freud might see the criminal as a person whose sex drive became perverted because of its repression. He might interpret the crime as resulting from an unresolved Oedipus complex, or as a "death wish" transformed into external aggression. Another explanation is provided by the orthodox religionist, the Christian for example. For him the criminal is a person who "chose" not to exercise his God-given power to know right from wrong and act accordingly. Others may blame the action upon an urban environment, a rural environment, upon parents who smoke and drink, upon criminal instincts, or home discipline that was too harsh or too lax. These various interpretations of a single phenomenon suggest the old legend of the blind men of India, who, examining separate parts of an elephant and generalizing as to its nature, asserted it to be like a wall, a snake, a tree, a leaf, and so on. Some of these explanations may have a bit of truth to offer, but the factor which most of them have in common is that these concepts have not been challenged in the minds of the users. Even among the scientists there are differences in concepts, but each is willing to abandon his particular concepts or to modify them in terms of evidence submitted within the scientific framework.

In arriving at the explanations of crime the scientist does not derive his concept by the investigation of one or a few cases of crime. The procedure is to study and analyze many cases of acts that are called crime, to classify or categorize them, and to seek the element or elements that are common to all crime. He may discover that the category is too broad and cannot be explained by any given concept, but must be recategorized before any meaningful theory can be derived. The scientist is satisfied with nothing less than a knowledge of the items which characterize or are common to *all* crime and *all* criminals.

This process, simplified here to be sure, of arriving at conceptual explanations of conditions that do not yield to sensory or perceptual examination is the same for all sciences. For example, the quests for an explanation of cancer and coronary diseases are proceeding in this manner, *i.e.*, the medical scientists are attempting to identify and isolate those factors that are common to all cases of these diseases. Each of the concepts used in the frame of reference in this book was developed likewise by scholars studying human behavior from the scientific point of view. No concepts are presented as absolute truths, but only as the best explanations that honest, intelligent men have been able to provide to date. When and if better explanations, or concepts, are discovered, the scientists will accept them in place of the ones currently employed.

> Science is thus always ready to abandon a theory when the facts so demand. *But the facts must really demand it.* It is not unusual for a theory to be modified so that it may be retained in substance even though "facts" contradicted an earlier formulation of it. . . . When, as frequently happens, a science abandons one theory for another, it is a mistake to suppose that science has become "bankrupt" and that it is incapable of discovering the structure of the subject-matter it studies. Such changes indicate rather that the science is progressively realizing its ideal. For such changes arise from correcting previous observations or reasoning, and such correction means that we are in possession of more reliable facts.[41]

A case in point is the theory of instinct as applied to man. This theory was abandoned because it failed to provide understanding of human behavior, whereas the concepts of learned behavior and of unconscious motivation have been retained because they give us better explanations of certain aspects of human action than any competing concepts.

Thus in the cognition process there is a constant and circular interplay among sensation, perception, and conception. Each phase is tested by relating it to the others. As a person matures, the interplay is more and more restricted to perception and conception, with purely sensory experiences becoming rare if not almost impossible. With the growth of experiences, most of what one senses has some relevance, some bit of meaning even though the idea related to it may be erroneous. As one psychologist has said:

> Pure empiricism is a delusion. A theory-like process is inevitably involved in drawing boundaries around certain parts of the flux of experience to define observable events and in the selection of events that

[41] *Ibid.*, pp. 394–395. Italics added.

are observed." . . . Scientists are forced to make a drastic selection [of events], either unconsciously on the basis of perceptual habits and the folklore and linguistic categories of the culture, or consciously on the basis of explicitly formulated theory.[42]

Emotions and Cognitive Learning

My findings indicate that in the normal perceptions of self-actualizing people and in the more occasional peak experiences of average people, *perception can be relatively ego-transcending, self-forgetful, egoless.* It can be unmotivated, impersonal, desireless, unselfish, not needed, detached. It can be organized around the object as a centering point rather than being based upon the ego.[43]

One can agree with this statement, and more; it is very probable that everyone can achieve some degree of objectivity. Yet it is also apparent that misperception, abetted by attitudes, is very common. What one perceives and misperceives is often influenced by what he *wants* to see, a fact that has long been known. Shakespeare wrote, in King Henry IV, that "Thy wish was father, Harry, to that thought," and Francis Bacon observed that "Men's thoughts are much according to their inclination. . ." The relation of emotion to cognitive learning is indirect. Rather than influence the learning process directly by strengthening or weakening the bonds between stimulus and response, between object and subject, emotion guides the subject into or away from the situation or episode which is essential to learning. If a person wishes to learn, whether mathematics, abstract concepts, or skill at tennis or skiing, he sets the stage props that are appropriate to the learning. He attends to those things that are prerequisite to the learning of the concepts—the precepts. He seeks, sometimes through wasteful trial and error efforts and sometimes through more careful preparatory reasoning which reduces the errors to a minimum, to gain the insights that are necessary to the learning. If it is a skill he seeks, he acquires the knowledge available concerning the proper use of the skeletal muscles in the development of the skill. In a learning episode there is logic in the relationship between the desire to attain a goal and the means selected to reach the goal. Extraneous feelings, thoughts, and actions are excluded. Successful learning depends, as has been stressed, upon more than mere wishing.

Similarly, if one is not motivated to learn, he will not, voluntarily, involve himself in the episodic relationships that are required in learning. He does not concentrate upon the task at hand, but "closes his mind,"

[42] Neale E. Miller, "Liberalization of Basic S-R Concepts: Extensions to Conflict Behavior, Motivation, and Social Learning," *Psychology: A Study of a Science*, 2 (ed. Sigmund Koch) (New York: McGraw-Hill, 1959), pp. 196–292.

[43] A. H. Maslow, "Cognition of Being in the Peak Experiences," *Journal Genetic Psychology*, 94 (1959), 48–49.

permits his thoughts to wander, or otherwise frustrates the learning process. He avoids the environmental factors that would set the stage for the
learning experience. If one is in the "I don't know and I don't want to
know" emotional state (we are wont to say, incorrectly, "frame of mind")
the likelihood that learning will take place is reduced. Here we see the
operation of *prejudice* as opposed to bias, as these terms are discussed in
Chapter 7. A biased person may feel strongly about a given object, but
may also be willing to study it from a different viewpoint, whereas the
prejudiced person is unlikely to permit himself to look at the emotionally
laden situation objectively, to see the evidence accessible to his sensory
equipment. As a matter of fact, it is probably true that one cannot force
learning at the conceptual level if the subject is firmly set against it. The
person who could prove this statement false would be the world's greatest
teacher and would be sought out by millions of harassed teachers of unwilling pupils. In the case of the schoolboy ". . . creeping like a snail
unwillingly to school," the boy possesses ambivalent attitudes, and thus
there is *some* motivation to avoid punishment, to please the teacher or
parent, or to beat out a competitor, and so the child reluctantly permits
the appropriate associations to be established between subject and object
to the end that learning takes place. Unwilling to a degree, and whining,
the schoolboy "creeps to school" nevertheless, and thereby sets the stage
where learning may occur.

Evidence which seems to support this theoretic position is provided
by a study of students from the United States enrolled in a six weeks
summer school course in French at McGill University in Montreal. The
conclusion was reached that favorable attitudes toward France and a
willingness to identify with French people were correlated with success
in learning the French language.[44] These attitudes set the stage for the
experiences which were prerequisite to learning.

The explanation for the superior academic attainments of such minority groups in the United States as the American students of Jewish,
Scottish, and Japanese heritage is *not* that they performed the same acts as
other Americans but enjoyed them more, thereby reinforcing neural bonds.
The cold fact is that these highly motivated groups have behaviorial experiences which differentiate them from others, and these cognitive and
manipulative experiences account for the differential results. The world
famous violinist Jascha Heifitz estimates that he has practiced in excess
of 60,000 hours. Even though millions of persons hypothetically could
match this effort without achieving comparable results, it is most reasonable to assume that there are a significant number of human beings with
faculties equal to those of Heifitz, who, given the motivation, time, teach-

[44] W. E. Lambert, R. C. Gardner, H. C. Barik, and K. Turnstall, "Attitudinal
and Cognitive Aspects of Intensive Study of a Second Language," *Journal of Abnormal and Social Psychology,* 66 (1963), 362.

ing, and violin, could equal the remarkable performances of Heifitz. To be certain, even 90,000 hours of practice, if indifferent, inept, and error-ridden, will avail the subject little by way of competence on the violin.

CULTURAL VS. PERSONAL-SOCIAL LEARNING

Most of what the individual learns is determined by the customs and fashions of his society. He speaks the language, eats the foods, wears the clothes, thinks the thoughts, and accepts the attitudes that are prepared for him by his associates and ancestors. However, were this the only source of learning, progress and change would be unknown, and man would be in the cultural stage of the earliest of his progenitors. Obviously man discovers and invents things that were not known to him or his fellows previously. The need for conformity never is complete, and there is always, even in the most primitive and conservative society, room for change. The learning that results from individual innovation has been distinguished from cultural learning by calling it *personal-social*, a term invented by Kimball Young, one of the pioneers in the field of social psychology. Clearly, such learning must take place in a cultural setting, but it departs from the lines set down by tradition. Custom demands that clothing be worn in most cultures, but just what kind and amount is frequently left to the preferences and imagination of the individual. The difficulty of getting a high instep into a traditional shoe led to the blucher cut which permitted easier fitting; and the story of the Earl of Sandwich's (1718–1792) desire to eat without interrupting his gaming activity, and thereby inventing the "sandwich," is well known. Changes stem from differential perception that, in turn, is a function of whims, boredom, insight into old problems, and so on. Most changes, whether in architecture, foods, languages, child-rearing practices, religious beliefs and practices, are functions of personal-social learning. This means that learning itself is too gross a term to permit the denotative accuracy necessary to understanding interpersonal influence. Recognition of this extra-cultural learning process prevents the implication, or inference, of cultural determinism in personality formation. A social psychologist has commented that if it is assumed that culture determines behavior, ". . . we have only to compare cultures in order to understand behavior."[45] The truth in the maxim, *cultura ex cultura*, must not overshadow the part played by unique, personal-social learning.

SUMMARY

Personality is an achievement and not a birth right, and only through the operation of social processes does an individual become fully human. The

---

[45] M. Sherif and C. W. Sherif, *Reference Groups* (New York: Harper and Row, 1964), p. 74.

basic process of learning has been studied extensively, but mostly in non-human animals.

Learning is defined, in its biosocial aspects, as the establishing, reinforcing, or weakening of relationship between the person and his environment. It always involves as interactive variables or attributes the biological heritage, environmental factors, and the previously learned attitudes, ideas, and skills.

The conditioned response, a special case of associational or contiguity learning. Current literature differentiates *classical conditioning* from *operant* conditioning. The former is of relatively little importance for social psychology. This contrasts with the great importance of general associational learning (of which operant "conditioning" is a part) that is involved in both cognitive or intellectual learning and emotional learning. These two phases of learning are not separable in man's behavior, but the understanding of human behavior requires that their functions be distinguished conceptually and perceptually.

Evidence seems to support the view that reward or reinforcement does not directly facilitate learning (as was asserted in the *law of effect*), but does modify behavior that is a consequence of learning. No learning occurs at the mental, motor, or emotional level, regardless of the strength of the desires or fears, unless some actual mental, motor, or emotional behavior occurs. Learning will occur if the appropriate connections are experienced, at times even in the face of negative attitudes toward learning.

Evidence provided by both contrived and unplanned experiments strongly support the contiguity conception of learning and demonstrate the dual (cognitive and emotional) nature of learning.

Current emphasis upon *empirical research* has historical roots in the *empiricism* (sometimes called *sensualism*) versus *rationalism* debate as it pertained to learning theory in the eighteenth century. This debate has been largely resolved by the current recognition that learning, and therefore knowledge, is a function of both sense and reason. This becomes clear when one is able to recognize and to distinguish the three categories which we designate by the symbols *sensation*, *conception*, and *perception*.

Some knowledge is merely the acquired customs or fashions of one's times; some is an individual departure from tradition because of unique learning experiences. The phrases *cultural learning* versus *personal-social learning* are used to distinguish these two kinds of learning.

SUGGESTED READINGS

BLUMER, HERBERT. "Science Without Concepts," *American Journal of Sociology*, XXXVI (Jan. 1931).

CHAPIN, J. P., and T. S. KRAWIEC. *Systems and Theories of Psychology* (New York: Holt, Rinehart and Winston, 1963).

COWGILL, DONALD O. "Variant Meaning of the Terms Conditioning and Conditioned Response," *Journal of Social Psychology*, XXVIII (1948).

HILGARD, E. R. *Theories of Learning* 2nd ed. (New York: Appleton-Century-Crofts, 1956).

KIMBLE, GREGORY A. *Hilgard and Marquis Conditioning and Learning*. Rev. ed. (New York: Appleton-Century-Crofts, 1961).

KOCH, S. (ed.). *Psychology: The Study of Science*. Vol. 2 (New York: McGraw-Hill, 1960).

MCGEOCH, J. A., and ARTHUR L. IRION. *The Psychology of Human Learning* (New York: David McKay, 1961).

MEAD, GEORGE HERBERT. *Mind, Self and Society* (Chicago: The University of Chicago Press, 1934).

MELTON, A. W. *Categories of Human Learning* (New York: The Academic Press, 1964).

MOWRER, O. H. *Learning Theory and the Symbolic Process* (New York: John Wiley and Sons, 1960).

ROSE, ARNOLD (ed.). *Human Behavior and Social Processes* (Boston: Houghton Mifflin, 1962).

SKINNER, B. F. *Science and Human Behavior* (New York: The Macmillan Co., 1953).

CHAPTER 6

SOCIAL PROCESSES:
II. Communication and
Processes of Adjustment

Humpty Dumpty: "And only *one* for birthday presents, you know. There's glory for you."

"I don't know what you mean by 'glory'." Alice said.

Humpty Dumpty smiled temptuously: "Of course you don't—till I tell you. I meant 'there's a nice knock-down argument for you'."

"But 'glory' doesn't mean 'a nice knock-down argument'," Alice objected.

"When *I* use a word," Humpty Dumpty said, in rather a scornful tone, "it means just what I choose it to mean—neither more nor less."

"The question is," said Alice, "whether you *can* make words mean so many different things."

—*Lewis Carroll*

THE SIGNIFICANT SYMBOL

We have discussed the nature and importance of symbols in thinking, but symbols that are adequate for thinking may prove quite inadequate for communication. Completely unique symbolic systems could, and probably have, functioned quite satisfactorily for subjective ruminations and reasoning, but the essence of communication is the ascription of identical meanings to gestures or symbols by two or more interested people. Not all of our actions, as we have noted before, are social in nature but may involve interaction between persons and nonhuman objects. The latter kind of interaction is not communication and does not necessarily involve language, which has been defined as ". . . a structured system of arbitrary vocal symbols by means of which members of a social group interact."[1]

We need not waste time arguing whether the chemical compound H_2O is *really* water, eau, wasser, aqua, woda, or vatten. The university

---

[1] Joseph Bram, *Language and Society* (New York: Doubleday, 1955), p. 2. Edward Sapir warns against exaggerating the purely communicative aspect of language and reminds us of the autistic speech of children to support his warning. He goes on to say that "It is best to admit that language is primarily a vocal actualization of the tendency to see reality symbolically, that it is precisely this quality which renders it a fit instrument for communication. . . ." *Encyclopaedia of the Social Sciences*, IX (New York: The Macmillan Co., 1933), p. 159. Thinking, as discussed by G. H. Mead, also indicates the extra-communication function of language.

and college student rarely misunderstands this phase of language—he readily acknowledges the logical proposition that the particular symbols designed to denote an object are almost always arbitrary in nature. Consensus about which symbols are to be attached to which objects is sufficient for language purposes—*i.e.*, communication and reasoning about the objects in question.

We would agree with Alice that "The question is, whether you *can* make words mean so many different things." The hard fact is that, in general, agreement does exist upon the way in which words are used, and this agreement cannot be ignored if language is to be preserved. There may be instances of words having been, to use John Dewey's phrase, "cluttered up with the debris of man's past experiences" to the point where we must abandon them and invent new labels for our concepts, facts, and other objects. However, we often merely redefine them and agree upon the symbolic meaning.

> Symbols, regardless of their meaning or of their emotional change, do have a kind of persistency in them which excuses people for treating them as the object of knowledge. They happen to be the vehicle of knowledge, the shell of the mollusca, the case of the cicada, the husk not the kernel. It is they which are transmitted from person to person, from generation to generation. The "life" has gone out of them though each person and each generation puts new life into them.[2]

The life of a symbol is, of course, its meaning with reference to other symbols, but it is more than this when considered from the point of social life. In the definition of language given above, we see once more the need for sharing objects in common, in this instance the meaning of gestures and symbols. Without such commonly held meanings, gestures and symbols are obviously useless for purposes of communication. Some of the clearest writing about the nature of gestures and communication has been done by the philosopher and social psychologist, George Herbert Mead (1863–1929). In his words:

> What is essential to communication is that the symbol should arouse in one's self what it arouses in the other individual. It must have that sort of universality to any person who finds himself in the same situation. There is a possibility of language wherever a stimulus can affect the individual as it affects the other. With a blind person such as Helen Keller, it is a contact experience that could be given to another as it is given to herself. It is out of that sort of language that the mind of Helen Keller was built. As she recognized, it was not until she could get into communication with other persons through symbols which could

---

[2] George Boas, "Symbols and History," in R. N. Anshen, *Language: An Enquiry into its Meaning and Function* (New York: Harpers & Brothers, 1957), p. 119.

arouse in herself the responses they arouse in other people that she could get what we term a mental content, or a self.[3]

Mead further emphasizes this point in these words:

Gestures become significant symbols when they implicitly arouse in an individual making them the same responses which they explicitly arouse, or are supposed to arouse, in other individuals, the individuals to whom they are addressed; . . .[4]

Without this common meaning, gestures cannot be significant for all concerned, and no communication is possible. Anyone who has been frustrated in his attempt to communicate with very young children, mentally deficient or mentally ill persons, with deaf persons, or with persons who do not speak one's language, need not be told of the importance of significant symbols for communication.

That significant symbols do indeed call out in the person making the gesture the responses ". . . which they explicitly arouse, or are supposed to arouse . . ." in the individuals addressed is often demonstrated in our daily lives. The mother who calls "Stop!" to her young child who is headed for the street, frequently responds to her own vocal gesture by stopping herself. Young children at play often carry into action their voiced or unvoiced gestures toward other children, and not a few altercations stem from this very human tendency to respond to our own gestures as we expect others to respond.

Equally convincing of the validity of Mead's position is the failure to achieve unambiguous communication when the symbols are ill-defined. Among other problems which social scientists have to solve is that of symbolic ambiguities. Such terms as science, sociology, psychology, religion, democracy, role, status, position, institution, group, free-will, determinism, and so on, have yet to attain the status of significant symbols for all who use them. As long as such haphazard semantics exist, just so long will there be difficulty in communication and in thinking. Of the latter process, Mead has emphasized that "Only in terms of gestures as significant symbols is the existence of mind or intelligence possible; for only in terms of gestures which are significant symbols can thinking—which is simply an internalized or implicit conversation of the individual with himself by means of such gestures—take place."[5]

---

[3] *Mind, Self, and Society* (Chicago: Univ. of Chicago Press, 1934), p. 149. The dramatic moment when Miss Keller's teacher succeeded in carrying to her the idea that things have names is probably known to the reader. The realization that all things have names made communication possible.

[4] *Ibid.*, p. 47.

[5] *Ibid.*, p. 47. C. Wright Mills continues this line of thought as follows: "We can view language functionally as a system of social control. A symbol, a recurrent language form, gains its status as a symbol, an event with meaning, because it produces a similar response from both the utterer and the hearer. Communication must set

Language and Culture

It has been noted frequently that people take their language for granted much as they do the air they breathe, and are unaware of, or unconcerned with, the implications that it may have for other phases of life. Whereas the majority of people view language merely as a means of expressing their thoughts and feelings, there is a highly vocal minority which perceives language as playing a dynamic role in shaping the thoughts, actions, and feelings of its users. Any excursion into the language–culture problem will bring one into contact with what has come to be known as the *Sapir-Whorf hypothesis*. Edward Sapir (1884–1939) was an anthropologist-linguist who did much to initiate modern interest in the language–culture problem, and Benjamin Lee Whorf (1897–1941) was a highly successful chemical engineer and businessman who turned to linguistics as an avocation. Of the former, Whorf had this to say:

> Sapir has done more than any other person to inaugurate the linguistic approach to thinking and make it of scientific consequence, and moreover to demonstrate the importance of linguistics to anthropology and psychology.[6]

Both Sapir and Whorf, but especially the latter, are known by students of language as "linguistic relativists," a term denoting those persons who see language as playing a larger part in the shaping of nonlinguistic aspects of culture than is ordinarily assumed to be the case. In Whorf's words:

> When linguists became able to examine critically and scientifically a large number of languages of widely different patterns, their base of reference was expanded; they experienced an interruption of phenomena hitherto held universal, and a whole new order of significancies came into their ken. It was found that the background linguistic system (in other words, the grammar) of each language is not merely a reproducing instrument for voicing ideas but rather is itself the shaper of ideas, the program and guide for the individual's mental activity, for his analysis of impressions, for his synthesis of his mental stock in trade. Formulation of ideas is not an independent process, strictly rational in the old sense, but is part of a particular grammar, and differs, from

---

up common modes of response in order to be communication; the meaning of language is the common social behavior evoked by it. Symbols are the 'directing pivots' of social behaviors. They are also the indispensable condition of human mentality. The meanings of words are formed and sustained by the interactions of human collectivities, and thought is the manipulation of such meanings. Mind is the interplay of the organism with social situations mediated by symbols." "Language, Logic, and Culture," *American Sociological Review*, 4 (1939), 677.

[6] Benjamin Lee Whorf in John B. Carroll's (ed.) *Language, Thought, and Reality* (New York: John Wiley and Sons, 1956), p. 78.

slightly to greatly between different grammars. *We dissect nature along lines laid down by our native languages* . . . the world is presented in a kaleidoscopic flux of impressions which has to be organized by our minds—and this means largely by the linguistic systems in our minds. We cut nature up, organize it into concepts, and ascribe significances as we do, largely because we are parties to an agreement to organize it in this way—an agreement that holds throughout our speech community and is codified in the patterns of our language.[7]

Thus according to this view, what one knows, and *can* know, is largely a function of the grammar to which he has been exposed. Whorf argued that ". . . users of markedly different grammars . . . must arrive at somewhat different views of the world."[8] Much of Whorf's attempts to verify this interesting hypothesis involved the language of the Hopi Indians which he selected in part because of its sharp contrast with the more familiar Indo-European languages.[9] Illustrative of the linguistic relativists' ideas is the assertion that the Bororos in Brazil are incapable of noting the features which are common to all kinds of parrots for the reason that the Bororo language has names only for individual species and not for parrots in general.[10] The implications in the Sapir-Whorf hypothesis for conceptualization and communication are important and even a little frightening. If the hypothesis is valid then it follows that ". . . to the extent that languages differ markedly from each other, so should we expect to find significant and formidable barriers to cross-cultural communication and understanding."[11]

A psychologist echoes this judgment concerning the Sapir-Whorf hypothesis in stating that, "This is not only a theory of cognition; it is a theory of cognition which asserts that the cognitive processes themselves are determined in such a manner as to create almost insurmountable barriers to cross-cultural comparisons."[12]

---

[7] "Science and Linguistics," reprinted in J. B. Carroll (ed.), *op. cit.*, pp. 212–213. Italics added.

[8] Quoted by Franklin Fearing in "An Examination of the Conceptions of Benjamin Whorf in the Light of Theories of Perception and Conception" in Harry Hoijer (ed.), *Language in Culture* (Chicago: University of Chicago Press, 1954), p. 48.

[9] Whorf notes that the Hopi have no words for time and space as we know them, but that they can describe the universe satisfactorily without them, which probably seems strange to anyone accustomed to think in such terms. How could one work in the realm of physics without such concepts? According to Whorf and others, the Hopi, as well as other so-called primitive groups, are quite well prepared to deal with any and all phenomena of physics were the need to arise.

[10] Harry Hoijer, "Relations of Language to Culture," in Kroeber *et al.*, *Anthropology Today* (1953), pp. 560–561. In general American writers have usually repudiated this extreme type of determinism.

[11] Harry Hoijer, "The Sapir-Whorf Hypothesis," in Harry Hoijer (ed.), *Language in Culture* (University of Chicago Press, 1954), p. 94.

[12] Fearing, *op. cit.*, p. 54.

If the Sapir-Whorf hypothesis has validity, then the United Nations should give top priority to the establishment of a universal language. However, before we lend every effort to this immediate end, we should carefully consider certain weaknesses in the evidence supporting the Sapir-Whorf hypothesis.

Serious students of the problem raised by the linguistic relativists have attempted to test the Whorf hypothesis by carefully controlled experiments. A psychologist and an anthropologist sought to investigate the way in which language determines how various items would be matched or put together in terms of common characteristics.[13]

They investigated the influence upon perception of the grammatical rule in the Navaho language that it is obligatory to use special verbs in asking for certain shaped objects. For example a long, flexible object (such as a piece of string), or a long rigid object (such as a stick), or a flat flexible object (such as a paper or cloth) must be designated by using different verb forms.[14] On the basis of this linguistic characteristic of the Navaho-speaking people in contrast to our general verb of "to hand," it was postulated that in matching different colored objects, e.g., string or sticks, the Navaho children would be more apt to do it on the basis of form rather than color. This was borne out when a series of two pairs of objects were presented, one object of each pair to be matched with a third object. The Navahos who predominately spoke Navaho language significantly more often selected the *form* likeness as the basis for matching the objects whereas the Navahos who spoke English predominately selected *color*.

To make the situation complicated, however, a number of white children living in the Boston area when presented with the same sets gave responses which were much more similar to the Navaho dominant group than they were to the English dominant Navahos. It is significant that the experimenters gave a cultural explanation to this apparent contradiction. We are informed that:

The white children today, however, can hardly be considered a fair control group for the Indian children, for the cultural background of experience in the forms and colors is enormously different. Early and continued practice with toys of the form board varieties likely to impress the white children with the importance of form and size is contrasted with the "secondary" quality of color. Furthermore, social class is known to be correlated with the tendency to choose form over color,

[13] John B. Carroll and Joseph B. Casagrande, "The Function of Language Classifications and Behavior," E. Maccoby, T. M. Newcomb and E. E. Hartley, *Readings in Social Psychology* (New York: Henry Holt and Co., 1958).

[14] *Ibid.*, p. 27.

and our white American children tended to be from the upper-middle class.[15]

The difficulty of establishing the influence of language on these relatively simple perceptual situations indicates the problem which anyone must face in investigating linguistic relativism. The experimenters in this case were able to conclude only that this area of investigation is "a fruitful area for further study."

A volume consisting of seven papers, and nine round table discussions of these papers, by a philosopher, an historian-sinologist, a psychologist, a psychologist-linguist, a philosopher-anthropologist, two linguists, four anthropologists, and seven linguists-anthropologists, reveals the reason why the Sapir-Whorf idea has not progressed beyond the hypothesis state.[16] This study is an essential item in the bibliography of all who are seriously interested in investigating the Sapir-Whorf ideas concerning grammatical influences upon thought and behavior.

Lest we do Whorf and Sapir an injustice and attribute to them naïvete concerning linguistic determinism, it is well that we take note of some qualifications they placed upon the hypothesis. After asserting that many preliterate societies ". . . far from being subrational, may show the human mind functioning at a higher and more complex plane of rationality than any civilized," Whorf acknowledges their primitive cultural status and attributes it to a lack of philosophers, ". . . the existence of whom may depend on an economic prosperity that few cultures in the course of history have reached."[17] Thus he recognizes the economy as a determining factor with which grammar must share the cultural stage.

Sapir is more specific. He notes that:

> The importance of language as a whole for the definition, expression and transmission of culture is undoubted. The relevance of linguistic tales, in both content and form for the profounder understanding of culture is also clear. It does not follow, however, that there is a simple correspondence between the form of a language and the form of the culture of those who speak it. The tendency to see linguistic categories as directly expressive of overt cultural outlines which seems to have come into fashion among certain sociologists and anthropologists, should be resisted as in no way warranted by the actual facts. There is no general correlation between culture type and linguistic structure. As far as

---

[15] *Ibid.*, p. 31. *See also* Roger W. Brown and Eric H. Lenneberg, "Studies in Linguistic Relativity," in Maccoby, Newcomb, and Hartley, *op. cit.*, for another attempt to investigate the relationship between behavior and grammatic construction. This latter study is as much an investigation of the reaction to phonology as it is to the semantics involved in the situation. *See also* Brown's *Words and Things* (Glencoe, Ill.: The Free Press, 1958).

[16] Hoijer (ed.), *op. cit.*

[17] Whorf, *op. cit.*, p. 81. *See* Victor Barnow, "The Sapir-Whorf Hypothesis," *Culture and Personality* (Homewood, Ill.: The Dorsey Press, 1963), pp. 95–99.

can be seen, isolating or agglutinative or inflective types of speech are possible on any level of civilization. Nor does the presence or absence of grammatical gender, for example, seem to have any relevance for the understanding of the social organization of religion or folklore of the associated people. *If there were any such parallelism as has sometimes been maintained, it would be quite impossible to understand the rapidity with which culture diffuses in spite of profound linguistic differences between the borrowing and the giving communities.* The cultural significance of linguistic form, in other words, lies in a much more submerged level than on the overt one of definite culture pattern.[18]

Sooner or later in this problem of language and culture one is forced back to the problem of the relationship between sensations, conceptions, and perceptions. If, as Herbert Blumer has stated, it is true that concepts arise primarily when we are puzzled about certain sensory or perceptual experiences that we encounter, then the grammar per se plays a minor role. Where motivation enters the picture is not made clear in the Sapir-Whorf hypothesis. There is as much, and perhaps a great deal more, evidence that perceptions and the word labels with which one deals with concepts, arise from a thinking process that involves, but is not governed by, previously arbitrarily agreed upon idea labels. In order to think or to communicate, the concepts must be given labels. Without these "handles" we cannot maintain conceptual order. Unless there are concepts behind the words, the latter remain in the category of nonsense syllables. In attempting to explain culture mainly on the basis of language, the linguistic relativists have set for themselves the same problem that for so long has faced the biological, cultural, and geographical determinists.

The roles of motivation and values in language development are of importance on this point. Man seems to be able to think about, and communicate, the things in which he is interested. When classes of college students are asked to name as many colors, and as many parts of an automobile, as possible, the females exceed the males in naming the colors by approximately 50 per cent, whereas the same percentage in differences is noted for the automobile parts labels, but with a reversed sex ratio. When, and if, males begin to wear suits, shirts, and shoes of mauve, periwinkle, chartreuse, coral, Caribbean pink, and magenta, they, too, will learn words for such colors and will perceive them. Likewise, the number of females who recognize such items as tachometer, odometer, pinion gear, valve lifters, and wrist pins, is growing as more women buy and drive automobiles and pay for automobile repairs.

Another view of the effect of culture upon language is given by a history of philosophy professor who writes that:

---

[18] *Encyclopaedia of the Social Sciences*, 9, p. 165. Italics added.

In fact, the cultural revolution, which seems to have begun in the sixteenth century, shifted men's attention from anatomy to physiology, from structure to function, from geometry to algebra, from the static to the dynamic, and introduced a great emphasis on history, biology, and even music. The older interest of course has never died out and the revolution will perhaps never be complete, but in metaphysics—and indeed physics—the metaphor of growth, which is biological, has begun to replace the metaphor of the *thing*.[19]

As speed becomes more and more a part of our daily lives, our vocabulary grows as a function of this speed. When explosion-like noises occur and windows rattle and sometimes shatter, the demand for symbols with which to discuss this new phenomenon appears and housewives talk of broken "sound barriers." Such words and phrases as *hot rod, peeling off, laying rubber, drag, pick up,* accompany the achievement of newer speeds. The whole gamut of psychoanalytic terms reflects the dynamic aspects of Freud's social psychology and the host of today's *isms*—socialism, behaviorism, interactionism, capitalism, dynamism, and psychologism —are consequences of the shift from a static to a dynamic emphasis.

> Philologists and others who specialize in the study of language forms are occupationally inclined to consider language, the use of which is the major kind of symbolic behavior, the determinant of nonlinguistic conduct; semanticists have raised this view into a philosophical doctrine; and psychotherapists, including the Freudian variety, place great reliance on the magic of words . . . For the most part, then, the function of any language is to communicate, and what is thereby communicated depends upon the nonlinguistic content of the culture. If people have words for and talk about ghosts; if their language includes such words as "automobile," "radio," and "airplane," it is because they have these devices; they do not have the devices simply because they invented or otherwise obtained the words representing them.[20]

Thus, although acknowledging the indispensability of symbols in the life of mankind, especially in the interactive processes, we believe it important to perceive the symbolic process as a function of the things symbolized insofar as any given symbolic system is concerned. Logically, symbols are arbitrarily assigned only with the invention and application

---

[19] George Boas, in Ashen *op. cit.*, p. 111.

[20] R. T. LaPiere, *A Theory of Social Control* (New York: McGraw-Hill, 1954), p. 251. Similar is the comment of psychologist Joseph Church: "Finally, if language binds us as completely as Whorf seems to imply, it is hard to see how anybody ever says anything new or different." *Language and the Discovery of Language* (New York: Random House, 1961), pp. 135–136. *See also* R. W. Brown and E. H. Lenneberg, "A Study in Language and Cognition," *Journal of Abnormal and Social Psychology*, 49 (July 1954), 454–462, for interesting information on perception of colors and symbols. A factor of "codability" is suggested as a universal item in perceptual differentiation of colors.

of the first symbol. With each succeeding symbol's attachment to a given object, the arbitrariness is reduced. What other social psychologists have written about a symbolization as it relates to a special problem in social psychology (the development of interpersonal competence) is applicable to the interactionist framework as it is developed in this textbook:

> It is more than possible that inquiries into the abstract realism of symbolic processes will produce findings more potent in the development of interpersonal competence than the more proximate behavioral hypotheses ventured in the next chapter. It takes wings of greater breadth than the authors' however to fly in such thin air. We applaud those who will make the attempt while sticking closer to earth ourselves.[21]

Role Taking and Self-perception

The principles of learning and communication discussed above enable us to understand how it is that the individual escapes the egocentricity of the early years and learns to perceive himself as an object among other objects. This interactive process of learning about one's body, one's voice and mannerisms, one's ideas and attitudes, and other subjective characteristics has two distinct phases. In one way it is very much like learning about any object in which there are definite and objective means of knowing about one's self, and insofar as this is true, we have little need here to give much attention to it. However, when this process involves self-perception as a function of the thoughts, actions, and attitudes of other persons, a significantly different dimension is introduced. This process has been labeled by George Herbert Mead as *role taking*, and is of cardinal importance in social psychology.[22] This process of perceiving, or attempting to perceive ourselves as others see us, is a time-honored task, as the well-known lines of Robert Burns remind us:

> Oh wad some power the giftie gie us
> To see oursels as others see us!
> It wad fraw monie a blunder free us, . . .

No power short of learning can grant man this gift, and to some extent all men succeed in this quest. Life demands it.

---

[21] Nelson N. Foote and Leonard S. Cottrell, Jr., *Identity and Interpersonal Competence* (Chicago: The University of Chicago Press, 1955), p. 41.

[22] Mead meant to use the term only as an analogy, recognizing that "The latter phrase is a little unfortunate because it suggests an actor's attitude which is actually more sophisticated than that which is involved in our own experience." *Op. cit.*, p. 161. Although the term means "taking the expected behavior," and not "taking the actual behavior" of the other, it is too well established, especially among those of the "Chicago school," to warrant trying to coin a substitute, such as "attitude taking" or "perceptions taking." It is a significant symbol despite its denotative shortcomings.

In a less poetic fashion, one of the early writers in the field of social psychology elaborates upon the process of taking toward ourselves the attitudes of other persons:

> In a very large and interesting class of cases the social reference takes the form of a somewhat definite imagination of how one's self—that is an idea he appropriates—appears in a particular mind, and the kind of self-feeling one has is determined by the attitude toward this attributed to that other mind. A social self of this sort might be called the reflected or looking-glass self:
>
> > 'Each to each a looking-glass
> > Reflects the other that doth pass.'
>
> As we see our face, figure, and dress in the glass, and are interested in them because they are ours, and pleased or otherwise with them according as they do or do not answer to what we should like them to be; so in imagination we perceive in another's mind some thought of our appearance, manners, aims, deeds, character, friends, and so on, and are variously affected by it.
>
> A self-idea of this sort seems to have three principal elements: the imagination of our appearance to the other person; the imagination of his judgment of that appearance, and some sort of self-feeling, such as pride or mortification.
>
> The comparison with a looking-glass hardly suggests the second element, the imagined judgment, which is quite essential. The thing that moves us to pride or shame is not the mere mechanical reflection of ourselves, but an imputed sentiment, the imagined effect of this reflection upon another's mind. This is evident from the fact that the character and weight of that other, in whose mind we see ourselves, makes all the difference with our feeling . . . We always imagine, and in imagining share, the judgments of the other mind. A man will boast to one person of another's action—say some sharp transaction in trade —which he would be ashamed to own to another.[23]

This analogy helps us to understand the fact that one knows what he is like, in part, by accurately interpreting the reflected attitudes and actions of those about him. Man is highly dependent upon his fellow man for the satisfaction of most of his needs and desires; for this reason he

[23] This concept of the "looking-glass self" is the invention of Charles Horton Cooley, one of the most productive of the early American social psychologists. Although a pioneer in the field of social psychology, Cooley lived until 1929, a fact which again stresses the youthfulness of the discipline. The concept is discussed in his *Human Nature and the Social Order* (Charles Scribner's Sons, 1902), pp. 151–153. There are, to be sure, important exceptions to the statement that men attempt to behave in accordance with the expectations of those about them, and full cognizance of this will be taken in the further discussion of the social role which follows.

becomes aware of these reflected attitudes, and usually attempts to satisfy them by his behavior. He is able to do this only if he can correctly infer the attitudes of his associates, can accurately interpret the way in which they act toward him, be they friend or foe. The indispensability of significant gestures in one's interpretation of the expectations and evaluations of his significant other can be readily seen.

Cooley's description of the process is accurate in that it calls attention to the fact that the role-taking process often involves both the cognitive "taking the perception" of the other person toward one's self, and the emotional or affective "taking the attitude" of the other. It involves what the other thinks or believes about us as well as, usually, what he feels about us. It is quite possible for one to be aware of another's perception *and* attitude toward him without being affected by either perception or attitude. If the other is not part of his significant or affective other, the other's views are not influential.[24]

Some writers in the field of social psychology have stressed the importance of the fact that each individual, early in life begins to differentiate between himself and those aspects of his environment which are not himself. The very small child, of course, does not do this, but looks at his toes with the same attitude as upon any external aspect of the universe. The persistent use of the third person by the small child in referring to himself is suggestive of this. The "Johnny no do it," rather than "I no do it," is common among small children. When the individual becomes an object to himself, he then is said to have acquired a "self," and can take attitudes toward himself and make appropriate responses to such atti-

[24] Perhaps it is because we have not developed, in English, a word which denotes the dual processes indicated by the "looking-glass self" analogy that Mead's denotatively inaccurate phrase "taking the role of the other" has remained in use by social psychologists. The problem of differentiating the several emotional processes involved in social psychological interaction has not gone unrecognized, but attempts to give them identity and appropriate labels have not been conspicuously successful. Max Scheler's thoughtful considerations do not, in the authors' opinion, carry us much beyond the point of recognizing the complexities of the emotional processes which occur in social interaction. The following German terms, with translations into French and English, illustrate both the logic and the problems involved in one sociologist's comment that ". . . the social psychologist of the future will regard, with mingled amusement and amazement, that quaint historical epoch when "sympathy" was talked about as if it were a homogeneous entity." H. Becker, in his review of Scheler's *Wesen und Formen der Sympathic* (3rd ed.) (Bonn: Verlag von Friedrich Cohen, 1926) in *American Journal of Sociology*, XXXIII (Jan. 1928), 67. *Miteinanderfuhlen*: solidarity affective; compathy—mutual feeling. *Mitgefuhl*: participation affective; sympathy, fellow–feeling. *Nachfuhlen (gefuhl)*: imitative affective; mimpathy; vication–feeling. *Gefuhlsansteckung*: contagion affective; transpathy—emotional infection. *Einfuhlung*: intuition affective—empathy. *Einsfuhlung (-gefuhl)*: union (or fusion) affective; unipathy; identification; ideopathic unipathy; alter (other) absorbed by ego; heteropathic unipathy; ego absorbed by alter. *Cf.* translation by Peter Heath, *The Nature of Sympathy* (New Haven: Yale University Press, 1954).

tudes.[25] Were it not for this the sense of shame, humiliation, guilt, honor, and other forms of self-feeling, would not be possible. This concept is valuable in the study of human behavior, and the relatively little space accorded it here is not to be interpreted as a low esteem of its importance. A clear understanding of the concept is essential to the adequate discussion of the behavior of the individual in social action.

This process of role taking, of perceiving and evaluating ourselves and other objects in terms of the subjective variables of our associates (as we interpret such attitudes and percepts), is one of the inevitabilities of living on the human, social level. This lifelong attempt to judge and perceive objects (including ourselves) as others do, is essential to successful social participation, and is never finished because of the changes in one's significant other. When a person fails to perceive himself accurately, society labels him a bore, a criminal, or mentally ill; it avoids him, penalizes him, or locks him up. Even though one never comes to know completely the attitudes toward him held by his associates—even by one's closest friends and relatives—he must strive to approximate the evaluation and perception of himself held by others as he pictures his role in society. To do otherwise is to increase greatly the likelihood of one's playing, or attempting to play, a social role which the other members of the cast do not approve, thus becoming a misfit, a socially maladjusted person. The following case illustrates the point:

> Walter Z. conceives of himself as a witty, entertaining, sophisticated person. The difficulty is that this view of himself is not shared by the rest of the employees of the company where he works. The discrepancy in the evaluation of the part he is to play shows most clearly at the social gatherings of the employees, at which events Walter proceeds to tell his stories (most of which are quite inappropriate for the occasion), display his tricks, such as using two spoons as castanets, and to intrude into every small circle of people he sees. There is no indication that he senses the disinterest in his tricks, the distaste for his stories, or the dislike for his intruding into intimate groups or discussions. Occasionally he confides to others that he cannot understand why

[25] Such early writers as William James and James Mark Baldwin were aware of the value of the concept, but it remained for George Herbert Mead to bring the concept to its present stature. *Cf.* William James, *Principles of Psychology* (New York: Henry Holt and Company, 1890), pp. 290 ff. James writes that the individual person has ". . . as many different social selves as there are distinct *groups* of persons about whose opinion he cares," *Ibid.*, p. 294. His use of the term closely approximates the current concept of *social role*, and the implications that it has for the "generalized other" concept of Mead, which will be discussed presently, are clear. The Swiss psychologist, Piaget called attention to the behavior of the young child who has not acquired self-perception. He used the term "egocentricity" to denote this stage of development. Illustrative of this egocentricity, this oblivion of self, is seen in the young child who draws his stool or chair close to the television screen, thus blocking the view of all others. More will be said of this in the chapter on the preschool child.

he is not invited to the homes of the employees, or why he cannot "date" some of the office girls. The answer lies in the contrasting evaluations of him by himself and by the other employees. In contrast to his apparent unawareness of the attitudes and opinions of his fellow employees, the latter picture him as a crude, tactless, blundering dolt.

The significance of these perceptions and attitudes which one takes toward himself is clearly shown by the changes which occur when one is isolated from other persons for long periods of time. One of America's well-known explorers, Admiral Richard E. Byrd, provides us with an excellent picture of the changes brought about when such social influences are not present to control one's behavior. If the reader will keep in mind that Admiral Byrd's training as a member of an old and upper-class Virginia family, and as an officer in the United States Navy stressed "manners" far more than the experiences of most Americans, the departures from convention that Admiral Byrd reports become more significant. During his stay at "Advanced Base" in Antarctica, 80° 08' South Latitude, where he isolated himself for several months to make observations of weather conditions, he noted some of his behavior that was induced by this social isolation. The following is an entry in his diary for May 11, 1934:

Ten PM Solitude is an excellent laboratory in which to observe the extent to which manners and habits are conditioned by others. My table manners are atrocious—in this respect I've slipped back hundreds of years; in fact, I have no manners whatsoever. If I feel like it, I eat with my fingers, or out of a can, or standing up—in other words, whichever is easiest. What's left over, I just heave into the slop pail, close to my feet. Come to think of it, no reason why I shouldn't. It's rather a convenient way to eat; I seem to remember reading in Epicurus that a man living alone lives the life of a wolf.

A life alone makes the need for external demonstration almost disappear. Now I seldom cuss, although at first I was quick to open fire at everything that tried my patience. Attending to the electrical circuit on the anemometer pole is no less cold than it was in the beginning; but I work in soundless torment, knowing that the night is vast and profanity can shock no one but myself.

My sense of humor remains, but the only sources of it are my books and myself, and, after all, my time to read is limited. Earlier today, when I came into the hut with my water bucket in one hand and the lantern in the other, I put the lantern on the stove and hung up the bucket. I laughed at this; but, now when I laugh, I laugh inside; for I seem to have forgotten how to do it out loud. This leads me to think that audible laughter is principally a mechanism for sharing pleasure. . . . My hair hasn't been cut in months. I've let it grow because it comes down around my neck and keeps it warm. I still shave once a week—and that only because I have found that a beard is an infernal nuisance outside on account of its tendency to ice up from the breath and freeze the face. Looking in the mirror this morning I decided that a man without women around him is a man without vanity; my cheeks are blistered and my nose is red and bulbous from a hundred frostbites. How I look is no longer of the least importance; all that matters is how I feel. However, I have kept clean, as clean as I would keep myself at home. But cleanliness has nothing to do with etiquette or coquetry. It is comfort. My senses enjoy the evening bath and are uncomfortable at the touch of underwear that is too dirty.

I've been trying to analyze the effect of isolation on a man. As I said, it is difficult for me to put this into words. I can only feel the absence of certain things, the exaggeration of others. In civilization my necessarily gregarious life with its countless distractions and diversions had blinded me to how vitally important a role they really did play. I find that their sudden removal has been much more of a wrench than I had anticipated. As much as anything, I miss being insulted every now and then, which is probably the Virginian in me.[26]

This excerpt from an explorer's diary dramatizes for us the importance of the role played by the attitudes which others take toward us. It demonstrates the close relationship between self-control and social control. Similar responses were recorded by a novelist.

A number of years ago I had some experience with being alone. For two succeeding years I was alone each winter for eight months at a stretch in the Sierra Nevada mountains on Lake Tahoe. I was a caretaker on a summer estate during the winter months when it was snowed in. And I made some observations then. As the time went on I found that my reactions thickened. Ordinarily I am a whistler. I stopped whistling. I stopped conversing with my dogs, and I believe that subtleties of feeling began to disappear until finally I was on a pleasure-pain basis. Then it occurred to me that the delicate shades of feeling, of reaction, are the result of communication, and without such communication they tend to disappear. A man with nothing to say has no words. Can its reverse be true—a man who has no one to say anything to has no words as he has no need for words?[27]

This role taking process does not, to be sure, exhaust the influence that others exercise upon us. We see not only ourselves, but other objects, through the perceptions and attitudes of other people. This becomes evident in the following pages, first in the discussion of the process of learning to play roles in keeping with the social positions or statuses one occupies, and later in the discussion of solipsism and the experiments

[26] Richard E. Byrd, *Alone* (New York: G. P. Putnam's Sons, 1938) Copyright 1938, by Richard E. Byrd, p. 140.
[27] John Steinbeck, *Travels with Charley* (New York: The Viking Press, 1962), pp. 123–124.

that reveal the effectiveness of social pressures even when such pressures run counter to one's own judgments.

Role Playing

Closely related to self-perception, and in part dependent upon it, is the process of learning to do those things which we need to do, want to do, and which others expect us to do.[28] By attitude taking we learn (with varying degrees of success) what other persons expect of us by way of behavior. However, what a person actually does may not fulfill the expectations of others, and, furthermore, what a person does may be of no concern to others. Therefore, we need a word that will denote the part a person actually does play in the human drama because of, and sometimes in spite of, what others wish or expect him to do. *Role* is the word used for this purpose (some prefer *role behavior*), and we speak of a person playing this or that role in relationship to some person or object, and with some reference to his position or status in the community or society.

Even though each person's behavior is, inevitably, unique in certain ways, there are limits to which this uniqueness can be carried. In order to fit into society one must play definite and predictable roles. This ability to play constant roles must be learned, and the careful observer sees clearly the difficulty with which this role playing is achieved on the part of children. Infants and young children respond to stimuli from other persons and objects in very random fashion, and flit from one role to another in unpredictable manner. In the words of G. H. Mead:

> . . . there is a simple succession of one role after another, a situation which is, of course, characteristic of the child's own personality. The child is one thing at one time and another at another, and what he is at one moment does not determine what he is at another. That is both the charm of childhood as well as its inadequacy. You cannot count on the child; you cannot assume that all the things he does are going to determine what he will do at any moment. He is not organized into a whole. The child has no definite character, no definite personality.[29]

Parents, and others as well, will readily testify to the truth of the foregoing observation. Inconsistency is one of the outstanding characteristics of childhood, for the child finds it difficult to focus his attention

[28] The writers' dependence upon the works of George Herbert Mead, particularly his *Mind, Self and Society* (Chicago: The University of Chicago Press, 1934), is apparent. *See also* Anselm Strauss, *The Social Psychology of George Herbert Mead* (Chicago: The University of Chicago Press, 1956). Role is not simply a synonym for behavior, but is a special kind of behavior which is associated with status or position (expected behavior). Elaboration of these concepts will be found in Ch. 8, "Personality."

[29] George Herbert Mead, *Mind, Self and Society*, Copyright 1934, by University of Chicago Press, p. 159.

on any one aspect of his growing universe for more than a short period of time. Even as youngsters undertake conscious roles in playing "store," or playing at being parents, or firemen, or policemen, each child is observed to be reluctant to play one of these roles consistently, and prefers to change from one to the other in relatively rapid succession. There is too much that is completely novel in the expanding environment of the young child, and the pursuit of new experiences keeps him jumping from role to role. Such is the early play life of the child.

As the child grows older, certain factors enter the situation to alter this random role playing, not the least of which is the introduction of games into the play life. In these games a new relationship among the participants is brought into the picture, namely, organization. In all cultures such games exist, and to participate in them the child must learn the *rules*, that is, he must learn what is expected of all of the other players. That is, he must learn the roles which are appropriate to the given status. These rules are, of course, the *sine qua non* of the game. Anyone who has observed children of kindergarten and first grade ages in their attempts to play organized games will recall the reluctance with which many restrain themselves from trying to play all of the roles or positions. On the other hand, those children who have learned to play the game are intolerant of the newcomer who wishes to introduce novelty into the established procedure of the game, and for this reason the younger children are shunted aside despite protests from elders to "let Johnny play with you!"

Again in Mead's words:

> The game has a logic, so that such an organization of the self is rendered possible; there is a definite end to be obtained; the actions of the different individuals are related to each other with the reference to that end so that they do not conflict; one is not in conflict with himself in the attitude of another man on the team. If one has the attitude of the person throwing the ball he can also have the response of catching the ball. The two are related so that they further the purpose of the game itself. They are interrelated in a unitary, organic fashion. There is a definite unity, then, which is introduced into the organization of other selves when we reach such a stage as that of the game . . .[30]

In other words, each member of the social group, *i.e.*, the team, knows what is expected of him and he acts accordingly. The individual takes not only the attitude of each player toward himself and his expected role, but also the attitudes of each team player to the total situation. The importance of game playing in developing a maturity of personality should be clear.

[30] *Ibid.*, pp. 158–159.

The game is then an illustration of the situation out of which an organized personality arises. Insofar as the child does take the attitude of the other and allows that attitude of the other to determine the thing he is going to do with reference to a common end, he is becoming an organic member of society. He is taking over the morale of that society and becoming an essential member of it. He belongs to it in so far as he does allow the attitude of the other that he takes to control his own immediate expression. What is involved here is some sort of an organized process. . . . What goes on in the game goes on in the life of the child all the time. He is continually taking the attitudes of those about him, *especially the roles of those who in some sense control him and on whom he depends.* . . . Such is the process by which a personality arises.[31]

In a book, popular among social scientists, with the dramatic title, *The Presentation of Self in Everyday Life,*[32] a sociologist has made the most explicit use of the current terminology of the theater in the analysis of human behavior. Confining his observations largely to what have been called "microsociological" situations, Goffman presents lively descriptions and illustrations of the many ways in which people seek to manage the situation, or event, to the end that the others, *i.e.,* the audience, will perceive the intended impression.[33] In his words, "I will be concerned only with the participants' dramaturgical problems of presenting the activity before others."[34]

He uses well the language of the theater to illustrate the problems of maintaining successful social relations in a world of divergent and conflicting value systems. He acknowledges the necessity of having the audience go along with the definition of the situation that the performer is striving to project. Even though the author tells us, at the book's end, that "This report is not concerned with aspects of the theater that creep into everyday life,"[35] one easily gains the impression from reading the book that role playing in everyday life is much closer to deliberate, conscious stage performance than G. H. Mead had perceived it to be.[36] Goffman observes that we are all members of teams, or sets "of individuals whose intimate cooperation is required if a given projected definition of the situation is to be maintained,"[37] and therefore ". . . must carry within ourselves something of the sweet guilt of conspirators," and that ". . . if

[31] *Ibid.,* pp. 159–160. Italics added. This is the process, of course, which gives rise to the affective other, as these relationships were discussed in Chapter 4.

[32] Erving Goffman (Garden City, N.Y.: Doubleday, 1959).

[33] *Ibid.,* Preface XI. He sees his approach as especially applicable to "social life that is organized within the physical building or plant."

[34] *Ibid.,* p. 15.

[35] *Ibid.,* p. 254.

[36] *Ibid.,* p. 106.

[37] *Ibid.,* p. 104.

a performance is to be effective it will be likely that the extent and character of the cooperation that makes this possible will be concealed and kept secret."[38] He provides illustrations of the wide discrepancies between backstage behavior and on stage performances in hospitals, repair shops, stores, hotels, sororities, restaurants, and private homes. It is made very clear that in-group cooperation and loyalty is requisite to a successful definition of the situation that is to be projected. In contrasting the culture of the year 'round residents of a resort area with that of the guests, Goffman describes the following backstage or "back region":

> Within the hotel kitchen, where the guests' food was prepared and where the staff ate and spent their day, crofters' culture tended to prevail. It will be useful to suggest some of the details of this culture here.
>
> In the kitchen, crofter employer-employee relations prevailed. Reciprocal first-naming was employed, although the scullery boy was fourteen and the male owner over thirty. The owning couple and employees ate together, participating with relative equality in mealtime small talk and gossip. When the owners held informal kitchen parties for friends and extended kin, the hotel workers participated. This pattern of intimacy and equality between management and employees was inconsistent with the appearance both elements of the staff gave when guests were present, as it was inconsistent with the guests' notions of the social distance which ought to obtain between the official with whom they corresponded when arranging for their stay, and the porters and maids who carried luggage upstairs, polished the guests' shoes each night, and emptied their chamber pots.
>
> Similarly, in the hotel kitchen, island eating patterns were employed. Meat, when available, tended to be boiled. Fish, often eaten, tended to be boiled or salted. Potatoes, an inevitable item in the day's one big meal, were almost always boiled in their jackets and eaten in the island manner: each eater selects a potato by hand from the central bowl, then pierces it with his fork and skins it with his knife, keeping the peels in a neat pile alongside his place, to be scooped in with his knife after the meal is finished. Oilcloth was used as a cover for the table. Almost every meal was preceded by a bowl of soup, and soup bowls, instead of plates, tended to be used for the courses that came after.[39]

That such backstages exist is well known to the reader. Equally well known is the fact that many lives involve a minimum of deliberate "performances" and conspiracies to manage an impression which is, at best, an act. Nevertheless, Goffman's book succeeds in making clear the rela-

---

[38] *Ibid.*
[39] From *The Presentation of Self in Everyday Life* by Erving Goffman. Copyright © 1959 by Erving Goffman. Reprinted by permission of Doubleday & Company, Inc., pp. 116–117.

tionships involving role taking, role playing, and a significant other among whom values are not coincidental.

The Solipsistic Argument

Thus far in our discussion of social processes, we have implied that man can attain objectivity in his perception of his world. Occasionally in the history of man's thinking about language, communication, and knowledge, there appears the argument that one cannot know the object world as it actually is. This idea was first presented by the ancient Greeks during the time of the Sophists, those erstwhile teachers who came to view as their major function in life the teaching of the use of language to the end that any proposition, however logical, could be shown to be false. Among other ideas bandied about at the time was the one that the only thing that a person could know was his own experiences in his "stream of consciousness," as some people have chosen to call it. This view is called "subjective idealism," or in its extreme form, "solipsism." The solipsist argues that "We cannot know things-in-themselves: they exist for us only in our cognition of them, through the medium of sense given data."[40] F. H. Bradley (1846–1924) puts it this way: "I cannot transcend experience, and experience must be *my* experience. From this it follows that nothing beyond myself exists; for what is experience is its [the self's] states."[41] This position has a fascination for human beings but is demonstrably untenable. The basis of the argument involves the idea that two people cannot possibly know the same things since their own knowledge, beliefs, and feelings are private. That the latter is true no one can doubt. Your own knowledge is yours and no one else's. Your own feelings and beliefs are yours and are not those of another. However, if this is unqualifiedly true, the question which follows, and which frequently has been raised over the centuries, is, "How is it that people agree about the nature of the world if all experiences are private experiences?"

To this question, philosopher Bernard Bosanquet replies as follows:

The answer is, that they *correspond*. It is this conception from which we must start in Logic. We must learn to regard our separate words of knowledge as something constructed by definite processes, and corresponding to each other in *consequence of the common nature of these processes*. We know that we begin apart. We begin, in fact, though not conscious of our limits, with feelings and fancies and unorganized experiences which give us little or no common ground and power of cooperation with other people. But as the constructive process advances, the correspondence between our worlds is widened and deepened, and the greater proportion of what we are obliged to think

[40] *Encyclopaedia Britannica* (11th Ed.), 25, p. 361.
[41] *Appearance and Reality* (Oxford: The Clarendon Press, 1930), p. 218.

is in harmony with what other people are obliged to think. Now of course this would not be so unless reality, the whole actual system in which we find ourselves, were self-consistent.[42]

This view of how man's experience with the object world yields commonly held judgments is quite in keeping with the current interactionist conception of behavior. The interaction of man's common and comparable biological heritage with other persons and with nonhuman objects of necessity leads to comparable results in the form of attitudes, beliefs, and behavior. In Bosanquet's words, man is *obliged* to see the world in ways which are comparable to his fellows' because of the interaction of comparable objects, the individual subject himself among others.

To be sure, concave and convex lenses, hearing aids, and other devices demonstrate clearly that all sensory experiences are not identical. However, Bosanquet's generalization, namely, that the interaction of comparable items will give rise to comparable results is still valid. Furthermore, through observation of everyday situations, it can be demonstrated that a person's perception of his world can be identical to another's insofar as we understand the meaning of that word. There is no lack of empiric evidence to support this generalization.

This is no more, and no less, than the general principle of all science that when certain specific objects interact with each other, there are certain results which necessarily follow. If the processes are repeated an infinite number of times, the same results will manifest themselves. However, the perception of the world in comparable or identical ways depends upon the identity or comparability of the interacting factors. We see clearly that man is obliged to note that iron is harder than one's head, that fire burns, that injury to the body affects its operation, or that human infants are helpless. When we look to more complex aspects of life and the world, the obligation appears to be something less than obvious. We note that the racial problems are perceived differently by different groups and individuals. We note that ethical and aesthetic judgments frequently fall short of consensus. Does this mean that it is only within the compass of the simple relationships that the private worlds of each individual do not conflict or contradict each other? Not at all, but one must resort to the interactionist conception of human behavior to comprehend the facts.

Keeping in mind that each episode of human action involves the biological heritage, *and* the environment, *and* the knowledge, beliefs, feelings, and traits of the persons involved, we are obliged to perceive the degree to which persons' thoughts, feelings, and actions correspond. Once again, evidence abounds which demonstrates the validity of this statement. The ethnocentrism that characterizes almost every cultural group

[42] Bernard Bosanquet, *Essentials of Logic* (London: Macmillan & Co., Ltd., 1955), pp. 17–18. Italics added.

reflects the comparability of the basic components of human personality and behavior.[43] The botanist is obliged to see not only that oak wood is harder than basswood, but also that mosses are different structurally from ferns and shrubs. Likewise, the social psychologist is obliged to perceive not only that nonwhites in the United States are more apt to be illiterate and to have prison records than whites, but also that this behavior does not reflect any known innate predispositions to illiteracy or to crime. The traffic pattern of any large city would not be possible were it not for this correspondence of experiences that yield like perceptions of traffic signals, pedestrians, and intentions. Thus, the perception of the world in the same or corresponding ways is a function of comparable experiences involving comparable objects and *not* a function of the complexity or simplicity of the factors in question, be they physical, biological, or sociocultural.

The reader can, through a minute or two of careful reflection, demonstrate to himself the inevitability of the development of mutually understandable symbols or gestures. We speak to a person and he gives us an answer that we would expect him to give. We open a door for someone, he passes through, and thanks us, but even if he does not thank us we are convinced nonetheless that he understands and perceives the door the same way that we do. We go to a store to make a purchase, we ask the price, we get an answer, we pay the money, we get the expected amount of change. Each of those events is a demonstration that we perceive the world as our fellow man does. Our perceptions are verified, *i.e.*, reinforced or rewarded, continually, and indeed must be if we are to engage in ordered interaction with our world's objects. When this is not so, we begin to doubt either the mental health of ourselves or of others.

The impracticability of the solipsistic argument, and the necessity of viewing the object world as real is well stated in the following quotation:

> Whatever may be our philosophical viewpoint, we behave as if reality exists. When the landlady knocks on the door, a tenant pays the rent even if he believes in subjective idealism. Nor does he ask her to prove that she really exists before he pays her the rent. Moreover, the subjective idealist can make a decision as to whether or not it is his landlady who is at the door or merely something existing only in his "mind." In crossing the street, even an individual with a strong solipsistic orientation usually would jump out of the path of apparent danger if someone shouts "Lookout! a truck is coming!" He does not dismiss the truck as existing only in the shouter's mind nor does he dismiss the voice he hears as only a figment of his own "mind". . . . Without some methods of gauging the reality and veracity of our perceptions, it be-

---

[43] *Ethnocentrism*, as noted earlier, is that tendency of human beings to perceive their own customs and groupways to be the right and proper ones, and to judge other customs and groupways to be good or bad to the extent that they correspond or contrast with those of the subject's group.

comes impossible to get along in this world, at least outside of an institution.[44]

When one encounters episodes in which certain aspects are, in Max Weber's term, "specifically senseless," and that appear to be ". . . atypical, causally indeterminate, and arbitrary in occurrence, without a relevant history or future . . . , or moral necessity,"[45] some phase of social order is destroyed. When such "specifically senseless" actions occur on the part of others, the most extreme consequence is total inaction on the subject's part, but even when action does occur, ". . . one should encounter the behaviors of bewilderment, uncertainty, internal conflict, massive incongruity, psychosocial isolation, acute general anxiety, loss of identity, and various symptoms of depersonalization."[46]

Were one sadistically oriented, he probably could, with the cooperation of others, raise doubts in the mind of almost any person in the world concerning the latter's sanity by deliberately giving inappropriate responses to the gestures of the other person. Suppose that, in response to a person's comments or inquiries, he were to be confronted by conspiring associates, whose watches agreed on a time that was different from his, all of whom insisted that he had missed a day, that this was now Thursday rather than Wednesday as he thought it was, who insisted that he had resigned from his job (though he does not recall having done so), and who insisted that the reason for his resignation was that he had suffered some sort of mental breakdown with consequent behavior aberrations that led to his being considered incapable of continuing on the job. Were a group of conspirators to do this, it is very probable that the individual against whom they had conspired would develop serious doubts about his own ability to perceive the world correctly. It would be a rare person who would react otherwise, as indicated by certain experiments.

The prototype of experiments involving the influence of social pressure in the form of misperceptions of objects was performed by the social psychologist Muzafer Sherif.[47] The experiment involved the autokinetic effect, a visual illusion that a stationary pinpoint of light moves as one

[44] Abraham S. Luchins, "The Problem of Truth in the Study of Perception," *Psychological Record*, 13 (1963), p. 215.

[45] Harold Garfinkel, "A Conception of, and Experiment with, 'Trust' as a Condition of Stable Concerted Actions," in O. J. Harvey (ed.) *Motivations and Social Interaction* (New York: Ronald Press Co., 1963), p. 189. This article employs experiments to illustrate the mutual attitude taking (in Mead's terms "role taking") as detailed by George Herbert Mead in his discussion of the game as a socializing process. *See* Mead's *Mind, Self and Society* (Chicago: University of Chicago Press, 1933). One also sees in the Garfinkel article elaboration of Cooley's "looking-glass self."

[46] Garfinkel, *op. cit.*, p. 189.

[47] "A Study of Some Social Factors in Perception," *Archives of Psychology*, 27 (1935), No. 187.

watches it. The experiments were carried on in a darkened room where a subject was observed first in isolation, his judgment of the "movements" was recorded, and subsequently he was observed in a group wherein confederates of the experimenter made oral judgments. The subject tended to change his judgment to conform to that of the group average, and also to retain this judgment when once again, in isolation from others, he was asked to judge the "movements" of the pinpoint of light. This has been taken by some to indicate the unconscious process of internalization of group norms that the individual carries with him into novel situations. Other experimenters have since duplicated the tests and findings. In one study of autokinesis, the experimenters discovered that those persons with authoritarian characteristics yielded more to group pressure than did the others.[48]

Another technique for studying the social influence upon visual perception was used by psychologist Solomon E. Asch.[49] He was able to demonstrate that peoples' confidence in their judgments of relatively simple perceptual problems could be shaken, and their judgments reversed, if the subjects were confronted with contradictory judgments by other persons. Asch's experiment involved the use of several (usually six to eight) confederates coached to report erroneous judgments, and one naïve subject. The group was asked to judge which of the three black lines on one card was most nearly the same length as a single line on another card, the subject being last to report. One of the lines on the first card was equal to the line on the second card, but the other two were "substantially different." When, during the first two trials, all confederates agreed with the subject, the latter did not hesitate in making the correct judgment. However, on twelve of eighteen subsequent trials the confederates reported erroneous judgments. On such trials, especially when "opposed by a unanimous and arbitrary majority," Asch reported that the subject ". . . looks surprised, indeed incredulous, about the disagreement. . . . The dissenter becomes more and more worried and hesitates as the disagreement continues in succeeding trials; he may smile in an embarrassed way."[50] What the subject did not know, of course, was that all others in the group were instructed to give a wrong answer, so that he found himself "opposed by a unanimous and arbitrary majority."[51] The subjects' correct judgments in the face of this disagreement never exceeded 80 per cent, and on one occasion dropped below fifty per cent.

It is interesting to note that when, in other trials, the subject was opposed by a single confederate, his judgment was rarely incorrect, but

[48] Ray R. Canning and J. M. Baker, "Effect of the Group on Authoritarian and Non-Authoritarian Persons," *American Journal of Sociology*, 64 (1959), 579–581.
[49] "Opinions and Social Pressure," *Scientific American*, 193 (Nov. 1955), 32.
[50] *Ibid.*, p. 32.
[51] *Ibid.*, p. 34.

when presented with two partners who disagreed, 13.6 per cent of the subjects yielded, and the percentage jumped to 31.8 when three divergent judges confronted the subjects.[52] Further, when, in the larger groups, a single supporter appeared, the subject's wrong answers were reduced to one quarter of the number recorded when unanimously opposed.

It should be noted that some subjects became suspicious of the experiment and were excused. Certitude of perception probably played a role in their suspicions.

In still another study employing similar techniques on 106 male and ninety-nine female college students, social influences induced persons to make distorted judgments of stimuli that included clearly sensory items, factual statements, and statements of opinion.[53] The experimenter reported that ". . . some people will report personal judgments which are fantastically inaccurate, provided they are informed that others are making the same judgments."[54] A variation on this experiment involves younger children's reaction to suggestions from another child.[55] A series of twelve drawings, ranging from a clear picture of a bottle through a series of complex drawings in which the bottle becomes less and less discernible, was presented to pairs of children of equal age and intelligence. One of each pair of subjects was coached to say that he saw a bottle, a face, or a battleship. The influence took the form of shaping perception and not of inducing uncritical and blind reiteration of the coached suggestion. When subjects agreed with their partner's suggestion, they could point out the object in question. Apparently there was less actual misperception in this group than in the adult group noted above.[56]

At the conclusion of his study of social pressures on perceptual judgments, Asch asked, among other questions, "In what ways is independence related to sociological and cultural conditions?" A study which sought to throw some light upon this problem involved groups of Norwegians and Frenchmen.[57]

Using much the same technique of group pressure on a subject by way of disagreement as to which of two acoustical tones was the longer, (the subject was last of six judges to voice his opinion), the experimenter was able to show evidence that strongly suggests cultural (national)

[52] *Ibid.*, p. 34.

[53] R. D. Tuddenham, "The Influence of a Distorted Group Norm upon Individual Judgment," *Journal of Psychology,* 46 (1958), pp. 227–241.

[54] *Ibid.*, p. 237.

[55] A. S. Luchins, "Social Influence on Perception of Complex Drawings," *Journal of Social Psychology,* 21 (1945), 257–273.

[56] The reader is urged to see A. Paul Hare, *Handbook of Small Group Research* (New York: The Free Press of Glencoe, 1962), Ch. 2, "Norms and Social Control," for further elaboration of the numerous experiments on social influence upon behavior.

[57] Stanley Milgram, "Nationality and Conformity," *Scientific American,* 205 (Dec. 1961), 45–51.

differences. The subject came into the laboratory, saw several coats hanging, entered one of six booths, and was presented with earphones and a microphone. The deception here involves not only five confederates (who purposely gave wrong answers in sixteen of each thirty trials) but also a "synthetic group," i.e., the voices of the conspirators were taped, thus, as the author notes, eliminating the cost of paying the laboratory assistants by the hour.

Table VI
Per Cent Conforming to Group Pressure on Critical Trials (When Opposed by Others) *

	Norwegian	French
Experiment #1	62%	50%
Experiment #2 (told results to be used in aircraft safety signals)	56%	48%
Experiment #3 (permitted to write on paper)	50%	34%
Experiment #4 (involved sanctions, snickers, and accusations of showing off)	75%	59%
Experiment #5 (offered chance to hear tones repeated)	69%	58%

* Ibid., pp. 47–50.

Twenty subjects were used in each of the experiments, with the native language used in each instance.[58] Regardless of the inducements or negative sanctions involved, the French were consistently more independent and less conforming to group pressures. Whereas 12 per cent of the Norwegians conformed in all sixteen critical trials, only 1 per cent of the French did. Among the French, 41 per cent showed "strong independence" but only 25 per cent of the Norwegians did. However, both the Norwegian and French groups displayed the full range of responses from complete conformity to complete independence.

It is not easy to perceive the cultural factors that explain these national differences. Author Milgram suggests a greater cohesiveness among the Norwegians and a greater acceptance of diversity with the French. It

[58.] Ibid., p. 47.

is interesting to note that, upon being criticized for making divergent judgments, the men of Norway passively accepted it whereas 50 per cent of the Frenchmen retorted, some quite strongly. This last difference appears to fit the stereotyped picture of the stolid Norseman and the effervescent Frenchman.

Another experimenter used apparent, and deliberate, misinterpretation of significant symbols (which he chose to call "breaching the congruency of relevances") to show dependence of social order upon significant symbols. Two cases illustrate the point.

Case 4. During a conversation (with the male E's fiancée) the E questioned the meaning of various words used by the subject. For the first minute and a half the subject responded to the questions as if they were legitimate inquiries. Then she responded with "Why are you asking me these questions?" and repeated this two or three times after each question. She became nervous and jittery, her face and hand movements . . . uncontrolled. She appeared bewildered and complained that I was making her nervous and demanded that I "Stop it!" . . . The subject picked up a magazine and covered her face. She put it down and pretended to be engrossed. When asked why she was looking at the magazine, she closed her mouth and refused any further remarks.

Case 8. Apparently as a casual afterthought, my husband mentioned Friday night, "Did you remember to drop off my shirts today?"

Taking nothing for granted, I replied, "I remember that you said something about it this morning. What shirts did you mean, and what did you mean by having them 'dropped' off?" He looked puzzled, as though I must have answered some other question than the one asked.

Instead of making the explanation he seemed to be waiting for, I persisted, "I thought your shirts were all in pretty good shape; why not keep them a little longer?" I had the uncomfortable feeling I had overplayed the part.

He no longer looked puzzled, but indignant. He repeated, "A little longer! What do you mean, and what have you done with my shirts?"

I acted indignant too. I asked, "What shirts? You have sport shirts, plain shirts, wool shirts, regular shirts, and dirty shirts. I'm no mind reader. What exactly did you want?"

My husband looked confused, as though he was trying to justify my behavior. He seemed simultaneously to be on the defensive and offensive. He assumed a very patient, tolerant air, and said, "Now, let's start all over again. Did you drop off my shirts today?"

I replied, "I heard you before. It's your meaning I wish was more clear. As far as I am concerned dropping off your shirts—whichever shirts you mean—could mean giving them to the Goodwill, leaving them at the cleaners, at the laundermat, or throwing them out. I never know what you mean with those vague statements."

He reflected on what I said, then changed the entire perspective by acting as though we were playing a game, that it was all a joke. He seemed to enjoy the joke. He ruined my approach by assuming the role I thought was mine. He then said, "Well, let's take this step by step 'yes' or 'no' answers: Did you see the dirty shirts I left on the kitchenette, yes or no?"

I could see no way to complicate his question, so felt forced to answer "yes." In the same fashion, he asked if I picked up the shirts; if I put them in the car; if I left them at the laundry; and if I did all these things that day, Friday. My answers were "yes."

The experiment, it seemed to me, had been cut short by his reducing all the parts of his previous question to their simplest terms, which were given to me as if I were a child unable to handle any complex questions, problems, or situations.[59]

In another experiment—similar to the Asch and Milgram studies, twenty-eight premedical students listened to a faked interview between a "medical school interviewer" and an "applicant." The applicant acted, quite clearly, in a boorish, bragging, and evasive manner; he was rude, contradicted the interviewer, made derogatory remarks about other schools and professions, spoke ungrammatically and vulgarly, and pressed the interviewer for an on-the-spot evaluation of his [the applicant's] performance in the interview.

The students assessed the applicant as would be expected—identifying his weaknesses and reporting pervasive negative evaluations. The subjects were then given "objective information" from the "official record" of the applicant. The information was deliberately contrived to contradict the principal points in the students' assessment. The subjects' judgments that the applicant was ignorant, of lower class status, boorish and socially inept, were contradicted by the "facts" that the applicant received top grades in pre-medical courses, excelled in courses in Milton and Shakespeare, secured large sums of money from wealthy people for a hospital fund, and came from a wealthy, upper class family.[60]

Furthermore, the subjects were informed that the medical school interviewer, "Dr. Gardner," six psychiatric members of the admissions committee, and all but two of the other pre-med subjects rated the applicant highly. They were also told that the applicant had been admitted and was doing well, as had been predicted.

As would be expected, when confronted with overwhelming evidence of subjective error, of having misperceived the quality of the applicant, doubts concerning their own judgments were immediately raised in the minds of all but six of the twenty-eight subjects. Three of the six were certain enough of their judgments to express them and were excused, whereas the other three, convinced that it was an experiment, remained

[59] Harold Garfinkel, "A Conception of, and Experiments with, 'Trust' as a condition of Stable Concerted Actions" in *Motivation and Social Interaction—Cognitive Determinants*, edited by O. J. Harvey. Copyright © 1963 The Ronald Press Company, pp. 221–222.
[60] *Ibid.*, p. 229.

silent about their convictions. Five others changed their judgment as to the technical qualifications of the "applicant" but remained convinced of his boorish characteristics.[61]

When attempting to explain their failure to agree with the supposed judgments of almost all of the others, subjects made such remarks as:

> "That's rather shocking. It makes me have doubts about my own thinking. Perhaps my values in life are all wrong. I don't know."
> "They didn't mention any of the things I mentioned and so I feel like a complete failure."
> "I—I don't understand how I could have been so wrong. Maybe my ideas—my evaluations of people are—just twisted."
> "Unless you got 36 unusual people. [subject was told that 36 of 37 subjects disagreed with him] I can't understand it. Maybe it's my personality. . . . Now I'm more confused than I was at the beginning of the entire interview. I think I ought to go home and look in the mirror and talk to myself."[62]

Here again we see evidence that judgments must, and do, correspond if social order is to exist and if personal security and identity are to be established and maintained.

The following comments about the kinds of research reported in the preceding pages are compatible with our interactionist frame of reference. "The subject's final choice is the resultant of numerous and complexly interacting variables, among them being the nature and clarity of the task, the structure of the present social situation, the qualities attributed to those who compose it, previous experience with and expectations about the physical reality, and such basic variables of the subject's own personality as his value system, his intelligence, and his self-confidence."[63]

One has to guard against the temptation of generalizing from single studies, however carefully planned and executed they appear. That they be suggestive and illustrative is all that one can hope in the initial stage of small group research.

In the excellent studies reported above, a shift in one or another of the variables concerned would have altered the conclusions reached. Even though a study of certain researches on small groups appears to warrant the conclusions that group opinion is more apt to be effective if (1) the object judged is ambiguous, (2) if the judgment is made public, (3) if the majority holding the opinion is large, and (4) if the group making the judgment is a friendly one, these principles appear to fail if the judgments made are based upon strong religious convictions. Certainly history is replete with small groups and even individuals holding

---

[61] *Ibid.*, pp. 233–234.
[62] *Ibid.*, pp. 233–234.
[63] R. D. Tuddenham, *op. cit.*, p. 239.

tenaciously to judgments of ambiguous objects of religious faith in open defiance of both the larger public and smaller primary groups. For some-time to come, the small-group researchers' strongest contributions will probably lie in the solution of problems delineated by time and place, where specificity of the problem is matched by the specificity of the solution. These solutions to real, if temporary, problems are not to be demeaned.

At this moment we turn attention to two major social psychological processes which are functions of man's ability to learn, to communicate, to take the attitudes of others toward himself and other objects, and to know the world objectively.

PROCESSES OF ADJUSTMENT

In Chapter 5 and in the preceding pages of Chapter 6, we have presented the interactive processes of learning, communicating, role taking, role playing, and a discussion of the inevitability that, through these processes, man is obliged to acquire common perceptions of himself and the world, and that these common perceptions are essential to the explanation of social order. We now turn to processes of adjustment that incorporate the processes just mentioned. The following pages are given to the dis-cussion of the two major adjustment processes of socialization and encul-turation, and the minor processes of accommodation, compensation, identification, projection, rationalization, repression, and sublimation.

The reader can perceive readily how the processes of learning, com-munication, role taking, and role playing are involved in the processes to be discussed in the remaining pages of this chapter. Each of the adjustment processes is shaped by the interaction of the biological herit-age, the simple or complex environmental possibilities, and the acquired knowledge, beliefs, and attitudes that the person brings to each episode or act in terms of which an adjustment is attempted. Both the variables and attributes held in common by mankind, as well as the distinctive cultural variations, become, inevitably, involved in these adjustment processes.[64]

Socialization

Our concern here is with the ways in which the individual can be, and should be, related to his fellow man, directly and indirectly. In short, we are concerned with the problem of his learning how to act like a human being, regardless of where or when he lives. It is immediately recognized that learning the essentials of social living, which is called

---

[64] Cf. Erving Goffman, Stigma (Englewood Cliffs, N.J.: Prentice-Hall, 1963) and Anselm Strauss, Mirrors and Masks (New York: Free Press of Glencoe, 1959) for further elaboration of the interactive nature of these adjustment processes.

socialization, is dependent upon the attitude-taking process and the ability to perceive one's self as an object among other objects.

Among other things, this learning to be human involves the knowledge that life is a compromise of competing impulses, motives, or needs. The child must learn that various motives, whether they are biogenic or sociogenic, cannot be satisfied impulsively and exclusively. Nature is such that compromise is demanded for the preservation of life itself, and at the higher levels of human behavior, the fulfillment of the desire for affection or recognition demands that one check his impulses on many occasions. The pursuit of satisfaction of the hunger, sex, or recognition impulse, to the exclusion, or even neglect, of the other human impulses, will prove very costly in terms of socio-psychological penalties. One phase of this socialization process involves what Sigmund Freud has called the "pleasure principle" and the "reality principle." The impulsive, immature, childish actions which result from the person's doing whatever is immediately satisfying without regard for the consequences, is called the "pleasure principle." The child who finds a pound of candy on the table when he arrives home from school, and eats the whole pound with no regard for the gastronomic and social penalty which awaits him, is acting on the pleasure principle. Victims of the pleasure principle are the young couple who yield to the sex impulse for its immediate satisfaction, with no regard for consequences that may take the form of a forced and premature marriage, with all of the unhappy ramifications of such situations. On the other hand, the child who finds the candy, and eats a few pieces, receives the commendation of the parent for his restraint, has no stomach ache, and also has candy to eat during subsequent days. This child is operating on the reality principle. The reader can supply his own illustrations of both principles from his own experiences. The learning of the reality principle is not only desirable, it is absolutely essential for the preservation of human life. The fable of the frivolous grasshopper and the industrious, farsighted ant illustrates the two principles.

The process of learning to postpone immediate satisfaction (called by some "immediate reward," ImR) in order to attain greater satisfaction in the future ("delayed reward," DelR) has been studied with reference to other personal variables. One such study revealed that persons who value high achievement are more apt to have acted in terms of DelR than are persons who are prone to acquiesce to social influences. The latter variable is correlated with tendencies to seek ImR.[65] It seems reasonable to perceive both the tendency to seek delayed rewards and the need for achievement as functions of socialization.

Socialization, then, is the process of learning to see one's self objec-

[65] Walter Mischel, "Delay of Gratification, Need for Achievement; and Acquiescence in Another Culture," *Journal of Abnormal and Social Psychology,* 62 (1961), 543–552. *See* this source for a bibliography dealing with ImR and DelR.

tively as one value in a world of many values, and learning to behave in a manner which takes into account the nature of one's own needs and desires, but which also considers the needs and desires of others. Some form of the "golden rule" is of necessity involved—no society in which this phase of socialization is not developed can hope to survive. In short, it is learning to live with, to accept, and to adjust to the social environment in terms of the objective nature of that environment.

Enculturation

The discussed process of socialization is universal in its content, one which involves learning behavior that is common to all mankind, regardless of the nature of the culture in which the individual lives and to which he is accustomed. There is a kindred learning process, universal in application but not in content, which involves items of value which are bound by space and by time. This is *enculturation*, the learning of the particular cultural variations upon the universal human theme.[66] Learning to speak and to communicate is universal, whereas speaking Italian or Yiddish is culture bound behavior, and is a function of enculturation. To learn respect for others is universal, but the exact ways in which the respect is shown is culturally dictated and is a phase of enculturation. To show religious respect in the Temple or Synagogues, the heads of males must be covered, whereas in the Christian churches females must cover their heads but it is obligatory that males uncover theirs. A hissing audience in some countries reflects approval, but in America it means quite the opposite. The reader is probably familiar with the story, perhaps apocryphal, about the American spy who was detected in Europe because he forgot not to shift his fork from his left to his right hand after cutting his food. Britishers drive on the left hand side of the road, whereas the French and Germans use the right side. We find enculturation a useful term because of the tendency of persons to develop what have been called by sociologists *ethnocentric* attitudes with regard to their cultures, and to assume that the unique features of their own group are the universal, "natural," and proper ones. Enculturation is applied to either the learning

[66] Our use of the term here is similar to, but not identical with Herskovits'. It is agreed that "The socialization of man is understandably more complex than that of animals because human social institutions, as expressions of man's culture building ability, take on such varied and changing forms. This means, moreover, that the process of socialization is only a part of the process by means of which men adjust themselves to their fellows in working with the total body of traditions—economic, social, technological, religious, aesthetic, linguistic—to which they fall heir. . . . The aspects of the learning experience which mark off man from other creatures, and by means of which, initially, and in later life, he achieves competence in his culture, may be called *enculturation.*" This term was coined by anthropologist Melville J. Herskovits, *Man and His Works* (New York: Alfred A. Knopf, 1948), p. 39. Other uses which Herskovits makes of the term we do not agree with, or perhaps do not wholly understand. *Cf. Ibid.,* p. 640.

by a child of the particular folkways or mores (customs) of his own country, or, later in life, learning those of another country. It involves learning *content* for the universal culture forms, which content has both its cognitive and emotional aspects. Enculturation explains language accents, degrees of knowledge, but also explains why an agnostic scholar gains pleasure from attending a religious service. When subjected to multiple cultural demands, the process of enculturation can induce certain unpleasant and insecure feelings. The following selection from the *Tea House of the August Moon* illustrates the problem:

> World filled with delightful imagination.
> Illustration.
> In Okinawa . . . no locks on doors.
> Bad manners not to trust neighbors.
> In America . . . lock and key big industry.
> Conclusion?
> Bad manners good business.
> In Okinawa . . . wash self in public bath with nude lady
>   quite proper.
> Picture of nude lady in private home . . . quite improper.
> In America statute of nude lady in park win prize.
> But nude lady in flesh in park win penalty.
> Conclusion?
> Pornography question of geography.
> But Okinawans most eager to be educated by conquerors.
> Deep desire to improve friction.
> Not easy to learn.
> Sometimes painful.
>
> *Act I, Scene I*

Both young and old, native and foreigner, throughout the world would agree, even without the handicap of foreign conquerors, that enculturation is:

> Not easy to learn.
> Sometimes painful.

Subordinate Processes of Adjustment

Man often fails in the pursuit of material objects and sociocultural relationships that will satisfy his biogenic and sociogenic motivations. Even the most successful person experiences numerous failures in his lifelong quest for need and wish fulfillment; and sociopsychological health is denied him who cannot cope with failure. There exist compensatory processes which enable man to fail and yet to continue to play his roles in society. These are normal processes, not to be perceived as pathological crutches of psychological weaklings. Except in extreme and bizarre forms, they are part of the repertoire of every normal, healthy person. It has been cogently argued that mental illness is often the result of the inability to compensate, or rationalize failures. We shall briefly characterize several processes of adjustment or, as some social psychologists choose to call them, "ego defenses."

ACCOMMODATION

Among individuals acting separately, and among groups of persons, conflicts arise which are only rarely resolved by the complete annihilation of one or the other of the conflicting parties. Some *modus vivendi*, or way of life, is worked out so that the parties can return to the pursuit of life's goals. The adjustments may take several forms, with varying degrees of satisfaction for the previously conflicting persons.

Superordination-Subordination. In superordination-subordination, the unequal antagonists assume relationships in which one accepts a position inferior to the other, usually with resignation, rather than with willingness. At one time in the development of formally organized medical practice, the statuses of the physician and surgeon with reference to that of the nurse were not clearly established, and open conflict resulted. Today's medical practice leaves no doubt as to who is the superior in making decisions or assigning responsibilities. Even though the relationship is not completely satisfactory, especially for the nurses, and may someday be altered, the situation has become stabilized to a marked degree by the acceptance of a subordinate position by the nurse. Inasmuch as most nurses are females and most physicians male, this acceptance is made easier by another accommodation of very long standing, that is, the subordination of females to males. Although the females have been whittling away at the discrepancy between the prerogatives and duties of men and women for centuries, and have gained suffrage rights, property rights, and legal equality in several cultures, the female is still in a subordinate status on many counts.

Compromise. This form of accommodation involves parties who are nearly equal in bargaining power. In this process each party yields on more things than he wishes to, but accepts the mutual give-and-take as being preferable to the costs paid by continued conflict. The periodic strikes and post-strike settlements between management and labor illustrate this kind of accommodation. These may be short-term or long-term adjustments, each side biding its time to better its position for when the next process for a new compromise begins. Some strain always exists under this sort of relationship.

Tolerance. Akin to compromise is the less formally established relationship of tolerance. This is a putting up with situations, episodes, people, things, or events, rather than an acceptance of them. Illustrative of this kind of accommodation is the relationship which exists among the various racial and religious groups in our pluralistic society. Almost every religious group would prefer to have its creed and organization the dominant one, but to effect this at the moment would require either more power than it has at its command, or the use of this power would violate a basic ethical tenet of the group. Each tolerates the other, with each hoping that the situation will improve in its favor in the future with no sacrifice of its other values. This variety of accommodation exists, of course, between and among individuals as well as among groups.

Conversion. Values may be altered or reassembled in ways that will effect a more or less permanent adjustment to the previously existing conflict, and the person or group is said to have converted to the opponents' value system. Here persuasion and teaching substitute for force in the accommodating process. Conversion as a process is summed up in the old political adage, "If you can't beat 'em, join 'em." Examples of this form of accommodation are seen in the results of the successful religious missionary, and in some urban Democrats becoming Republicans upon moving to the suburbs.

COMPENSATION

Compensation is a very general term that is useful in designating those ways of behaving which are brought into play when a person finds himself in a social situation in which his basic needs and desires are not satisfactorily fulfilled. It takes several forms of expression, and cannot be taken as a narrowly homogeneous category of behavior. Although the term is used most frequently as an adjunct to the concepts of inferiority complex and the feeling of insecurity, its realistic application is on a much wider scale. It is not only in terms of the need to feel superior that one feels the need to compensate, or make up for felt deficiencies. These deficiencies may occur in the environment, the biological heritage of the person, or in his personality. Under environmental deficiencies we note these: inadequate material wealth, a cultural setting that does not esteem the abilities of the individual person in question, or a geographical environment within which the person cannot display his special abilities (for instance, the expert skater or skier who finds himself in a flat, hot country). Deficiencies in biological heritage (always in terms of the current social values, to be sure) are found in below average intelligence, short stature, giantism, "ugly" facial features, ill health, obesity, sexual impotence, or poor physical coordination. Subjective deficiencies may be the inability to correctly interpret the wishes of associates, inadequate learning of the social graces, lack of education, lack of vocational training, and so on. The felt deficiencies in each of these three determinants of human nature are, it must be remembered, relative to each other, and it is difficult to say that this or that factor is the independent item in the maladjustment. The individual case must be examined to discover which of the three factors can be altered to provide an improvement in adjustment.

Also, the compensatory behavior may be rational or irrational, and is apt to reflect the degree of rationality in the general behavior of the person concerned. In general, it can be said that the more rational the total behavior of the person, the less need there is for compensation in any form.

One of the most common forms of compensation is *substitution*. Because of previous experience, perhaps because of irrational behavior, a person may have attempted to secure recognition by athletic achievements. Proving inept in competitive sports, he may substitute dramatic, musical, or scholarly success. The degree to which this shift in effort is successful depends upon the multiple factors operating in the case; it may range all the way from extreme satisfaction with the newly found recognition to a lingering desire to be the football hero that plagues the person throughout his life. The so-called "hell-raiser" in the classroom substitutes this attention-getting action because of his failure to secure recognition by other more acceptable (on the teacher's part) means. The person who cannot, for a variety of reasons, satisfactorily meet his sexual wants in the usual culturally approved manner, may substitute autoeroticism, homosexuality, or sexual fantasies.

Daydreaming is normal, and often used to compensate for felt deficiencies in the world of reality. It becomes abnormal only when the person begins to confuse the world of his daydreams with the real world, or prefers to live in the dream world to the exclusion of reality. However, it often happens that the world of reality is so unsatisfactory that one can keep functioning as a normal person only in the hope that the daydreams, however impossible they may appear to others, can someday, somehow, be realized. Such apparently unrealizable dreams or hopes maintained the morale of many prison camp inmates. This situation contrasts with the Walter Mitty personality who substitutes fictional exploits to compensate for the unsatisfactory role which he actually plays.

Another common form of compensation is that which, for want of a better term, might be called bluffing. This characterizes the person whose behavior belies his actual feeling, who puts up a good front, but does so to hide his feelings of inadequacy, or attitudes that he believes would not be socially sanctioned. We provide here a good description of the type of personality that is covered up by bluffing:

> It is interesting to observe the remarkable change in the behavior of these subjects when the hard, bright exterior has been reached by the probings of the psychologist in the interview, and the subject has confessed to feelings of inferiority, uncertainty, and weakness. The burdensome cloak of defense is cast aside with a (literal) sigh of relief. The hitherto loud defiant voice becomes low and hesitant, blushes are frequent, some embarrassment and shame is evident at the beginning. There is little of the raucous, forced laughter that has charac-

terized the subject hitherto; the blocking, the sparring, the deliberate misunderstanding of the interviewer's questions, the convenient forgetting, the flip, superior, sometimes disdainful attitude, all of these disappear, to be replaced by a somewhat muted sincerity, honesty and straightforwardness. The interviewer loses his feeling that the subject is on guard and deliberately hiding himself.[67]

Thus we see that compensation is not a term which relates to a simple, singular way of making up for felt deficiencies. It may be pathological or normal, desirable or undesirable, depending upon the way in which it is used in the adjustment process. That which may be pathological for one person in a given situation may well be the only possible realistic solution to the problems besetting another person in a different situation.

IDENTIFICATION

When we see our friends in embarrassing situations, we suffer embarrassment; when we see our enemies meet with reverses, we sometimes experience a glow of satisfaction. Whenever we place ourselves emotionally in the value system of another person, we are said to be *identified* with that person. When their pains and their hopes are ours, and their successes are sources of pleasure for us, then we identify with them in a *positive way.* Positive identification is an important ingredient in love, and its presence or absence from a relationship between people helps to distinguish between genuine affection and a weird combination of pride of ownership and concupiscence that often passes for affection. *Negative identification*, (actually a semantic misnomer and contradiction), denotes that situation in which one person feels chagrin at the pleasures of another, and is elated at the latter's misfortunes.

A study, which reveals the influence of both positive and negative identification, was made of student perceptions of a Dartmouth-Princeton football game.[68] It was the last game of the season for both teams, and soon after the kickoff it became apparent that it was going to be a rough game. A star Princeton back, with national reputation, left the game with a broken nose in the second quarter, and in the third quarter a Dartmouth player's leg was broken. The newspaper reports of the game revealed the preferential attitudes of the respective writers.

Students of the two schools were queried both before and after seeing movies of the game, but the response appeared to be little affected by

---

[67] A. H. Maslow, quoted in Gardner Murphy, Lois B. Murphy, and T. M. Newcomb, *Experimental Social Psychology* (New York: Harper and Brothers, 1937), p. 439.

[68] A. H. Hastrof and H. Cantril, "They Saw a Game," *Journal of Abnormal and Social Psychology*, 49 (1960), 129–134. Princeton won the game.

Table VII
Differential Perception at a Football Game
(Numbers of Affirmative Answers to Specific Questions)

	Dartmouth	Princeton
Was the game played clean and fair?	13	0
Was it rough and dirty?	42	93
Was it rough and fair?	39	3
Did the Darthmouth players start the trouble?	36	86
Did Princeton?	2	0
Did both?	53	11

A. H. Hastrof and H. Cantril, "They Saw a Game," *Journal of Abnormal and Social Psychology*, 49 (1954), 131.

seeing either the game or the film.[69] The preceding tabular summary of some of the results reveals the operation of the process of identification.

Identification made for significant differences in the perception of actual rule infractions as the students watched the film.[70] Here we find one more instance of the influence of autonomic-nervous system learning upon central nervous system behavior.

PROJECTION

In some ways, projection is the reverse of positive identification. In projection, instead of accepting the value system of others as our own, we attribute to others our ideas and attitudes. The Old Testament admonition to cast out the beam in one's own eye before criticizing the mote in another's is testimony to the hoary character of man's awareness of the projection process. The dishonest man is distrustful of others; fearful individuals attribute cowardice to others; persons who like and enjoy social contacts assume that others do also.

A clergyman in a Midwestern city strongly opposed dancing, especially for young people. His sermons and daily efforts frequently expressed this opposition. When pressed by one of his parishioners for the basis of his vehement opposition, he replied with some astonishment at the naïvete of the inquirer, "You can't tell me that any male can dance with a female without wanting immediately to make love to her!" The clergyman was convinced that his own feelings were common to all people.

[69] *Ibid.*, p. 131.
[70] *Ibid.*

Another form of projection involves wish-fulfillment. Many a thwarted parent has sought to enjoy vicariously careers and other experiences through their children. This is often an unconscious process. Others wish their offspring to follow their footsteps. The following case illustrates the former aspect of the process.

I come from a country in west Africa where there is much diversity in the various geographic regions as one goes from east to west, north to south and vice versa. Not only are there many tribes and numerous dialects and various social norms but there is a significant difference between the coastal area with its cities and western influences and the hinterland which until recently was still very African.

The demands are very numerous especially on the younger generation. We are expected to keep family ties and yet gain more freedom from this unit in order to make a more substantial contribution to the society as a whole. We can no longer play the roles demanded in the traditional society of a few years ago. We have to redefine our values and change ourselves so that we can move faster.

Our parents or families recognize these problems. They also realize that certain changes in the society must occur if we are to cope with the other nations on all levels. Their solution to the problem lies in reorientating the minds and desires of the younger generations. They want us to act and think "western." So they anxiously set goals for us on the basis of what the society needs, how much prestige and money will be gained and how much the family name will be enhanced. This means that any indication of scholastic ability or show of any talents will be exaggerated. It will have to be utilized to the maximum. I must add that most families prefer the professions and other pedantic careers.

By my second year I was getting top grades. When I reached the seventh grade and received even better grades, everyone in the family began questioning me about what I was considering as a career. I had never thought about this matter before in any serious way but I had quite a few interests at that time. Upon the advice of our head mistress at school, I wrote my first letter home and towards the end of that letter, I mentioned I wanted to become a doctor, a scientist or a diplomat. Frankly, I had no sound idea what it entailed to pursue any of the fields I had selected.

By a process of elimination my family decided that medicine would suit my temperament and bring the best long run fruits. Why not? At that stage of my life, I showed a keen interest in human needs and sufferings and always asked questions about such things. I got along very well at school with almost everybody. I enjoyed reading books of adult standards which to them indicated I was more of an introvert with unusual insight and abilities which a doctor really had to be. Most important, I kept a collection of small animals which I watched grow up, recording their behavior patterns and other facts. Such hobbies are unusual for children back home so it made a great impact on my parents especially when they learned I sometimes cut up animals I found and the dead ones of my collections. There was little doubt that I was destined to become a doctor. For a few years I thought so too, though I enjoyed the social sciences much more. Then during my junior year in high school I realized my feelings for people did not mean I had to become a doctor. I found out that I enjoyed interaction with people when we were organizing activities and doing a variety of things.

Though I had always been fascinated by politics, I never read so much on the topic until my junior year. My best grades continued to be in history and related fields. However, I realized that in countries like ours, one would be at a great disadvantage if he or she simply studied politics. Besides, the needs of our country were too great to consider only politics unless one wanted to teach. I did not. Therefore, for the first time in my life, I was confused and mixed up. I tried to find a solution by applying various methods but did not. However, one thing I did find out, I did not want to become a doctor.

Finally I told my parents. They really blew up! They did not spare me a word in letting me know how I was disappointing the family. The constant question was: "Why don't you want to make anything of your life?" I was mad, frustrated and puzzled and did not completely change from medicine then but instead I developed a resentment for all courses related to medicine. I only did well in them in order to get honor grades so that I could take part in school activities I desired. Most of them required good grades or honor grades if one wanted to obtain most of the top leadership positions.

A year or so after my first announcement that I had changed my mind about medicine, I tried to get my idea across again. No one would understand. I never tried again to persuade them. However, this time I decided to find reasons why I wanted to become a doctor. I thought if I said I wanted to become a doctor enough times and applied my time with physical sciences, I would eventually believe I wanted to become a doctor and even enjoy the idea.

After completion of secondary school, I had the privilege of going abroad. I was very inspired as I observed and studied various countries and their people. I was also happy because I had some time alone in which I could decide what I really wanted to do in the future.

When I returned home, the differences with my family intensified and became more numerous. However, we agreed on one point: "The people in our country had to be motivated to desire accepting more responsibilities and thus make a greater contribution to their society which needed a lot of help." Our biggest point of disagreement was that I did not want to return to school immediately but perferred working for a youth group. Finally, after we could come to no compromise, I applied for a scholarship. I qualified for it by filling in some forms, passing a comprehensive examination and meeting the requirements of the board of examiners who interviewed me. This scholarship was to last for four years. My family was very proud and happy. It was decided that the older members of the family would finance me through medical school. In addition they were happy that I had finally decided to study in the U.S.A. where they always wanted me to study. I was very keen about visiting the U.S. but was not excited about coming to school here.

Coming here with no great scholastic motivation and almost an aversion for my field of study despite my rationalizations, I did minimum work right from the start. Finally during my junior year, it occurred to me that I was wasting my time and not doing justice to the scholarship foundation. I therefore resolved to make a stand to my family and no matter what they would say, I would not change my mind.

However, first I would have to decide what I really wanted to do. I also had to assume more responsibilities which I had neglected for so long. After an introspection, I was almost alarmed at the new person I saw. I had really retrogressed in many ways becoming worse in some instances. Despite my feelings of almost complete hopelessness, I made up my mind to get myself out of the big mess. I made several changes in my personal life and constantly searched for a career. Finally I came upon one, not until after mistakenly choosing one or two wrong ones. However, I was learning a lesson and I was growing.

Then, in order to free myself of feelings of guilt, I had to tell the members of my family about my new plans. As I had expected, they were quite disappointed and in some instances displeased and expressed great feelings of uncertainty about my future. I had prepared myself for all these reactions so I stood my ground. Now I feel free and relaxed and hope to make better use of the years ahead realizing that I am an individual having the feelings and drives of my people but I have to find my own way as my personality and potentialities will permit.

Not all cases of projection are as explicit as this one. It is a wise parent who scrutinizes the plans which he makes for his children; it is also a wise child who distinguishes between his genuine interests and those he pursues to please his parents.

A clear means of demonstrating the nature and variability of attitudes and perceptions in the subject-object relationship is to employ what have come to be called projective techniques of research. The word *projection* itself has a particular meaning in social psychology. It refers to the capacity or tendency of a person to see in another object or person certain feelings or attitudes which are part of the former's subjective make-up.

In the Thematic Apperception Test, a series of pictures is presented, one at a time, to the subject, and he is invited to make up a story using the material in the picture as stimulus and subject matter. The subject thus has an opportunity to project his own value systems into the stimulus situation and reveal them by his ascription of intentions, feelings, and so on, to the people in the pictures. This phenomenon is illustrated by the following well known conversation:

Hamlet. Do you see yonder cloud that's almost in shape of a camel?
Polonius. By the mass, and 'tis like a camel, indeed.
Hamlet. Methinks it is like a weasel.
Polonius. It is backed like a weasel.
Hamlet. Or like a whale.
Polonius. Very like a whale.

In this instance Hamlet brings to the unstructured object (the cloud) his own attitudes and feelings and clearly reveals his own anxieties, ineptness, and vacillations to Polonius.

Hermann Rorschach (1884–1922) introduced the use of ink blots (rather than clouds) to accomplish personality assessment. The Rorschach ink blots (some of them multicolored) are presented successively to the subject who is invited to respond to these stimuli. Since the ink blots on the cards are the same for all subjects (standardized), the independent variable becomes the subject himself.[71] The subject approaches each Rorschach card with whatever resources he is able to bring to this unstructured situation. The psychologist observing the behavior of the patient is interested not only in what the latter sees in each stimulus situation but also in what he does not see or does not choose to admit he sees. The psychologist is interested in the content of the subject's responses, and also the behavior that characterizes his performance as he manages this unstructured situation. The subject's approach to the problem, his management of his time, his ability to organize his responses, and his capacity for the management of his feelings as they are aroused by what he sees, are all material for evaluation. His behavior reveals his subjective, personal variables.

Projective testing techniques are useful for purposes of research, diagnoses, and therapy. However, for our purpose, we should note that every human being is always projecting attitudes and feelings in every situation, whether it be in reading a book or in a social encounter. Psychologist Hadley Cantril has said that we are constantly seeing things not as *they* are but as *we* are. Dreams are themselves a form of projection, the dreamer being the author, the actor, and the audience. The analysis of dreams is of course a well known procedure in psychoanalysis.

There are many ready-made illustrations of the differential perceptions that are attitude-based.[72] Strongly committed Republicans and

---

[71] The cognitive influences will be taken into account later in this chapter and in Ch. 7.

[72] *See* Mary Henle, "Some Effects of Motivational Processes on Cognition," *Psychological Review*, 62 (1955), 423ff., for a discussion of studies that show this attitude-perception relationship.

Democrats perceive the virtues and liabilities of political candidates more clearly if they know beforehand the candidates' party affiliation. The ability to perceive one's own children objectively is seriously restricted by the favorable attitudes which most parents have toward their own family members. A home run is a good thing or a bad thing, depending largely upon the attitude one has toward the team on which the home-run hitter is playing. Whether a person is a "dirty, sneaking spy" or a "brilliant espionage agent" is not determined solely by the objective nature of the person involved, but by the viewer's national loyalties. The relationship of attitudes to cognition and behavior are examined in Chapter 7, but an example may help the reader see the relationship.

A study was made of subjects who varied in the degree of their racial prejudice with regard to their perception of the likenesses or differences between themselves and strangers, white and colored. It was reported that ". . . high prejudiced subjects assumed greater dissimilarity between selves and a Negro stranger than between selves and a white stranger on such topics as undegraduate marriages, existence of God, political party, musical comedies, drinking, a Catholic president, premarital intercourse, etc."[73]

RATIONALIZATION

A universal human characteristic is the desire to appear rational in the eyes of our fellows—friends and foes alike. When, in the pursuit of the compromises among the several desires which goad us throughout life, we engage in behavior which, either to ourselves or in the imputed judgments of our associates, appears something less than reasonable, we are prone to reach for explanations which we believe will make the action *appear* to be the act of a rational being.

One kind of situation which elicits rationalization is illustrated by the famous fable about the fox and the grapes that he desired but that were beyond his reach, and which he dismissed in an afterthought as being sour anyway. It is the rare person who has not been caught in one or more "sour grapes" situations, and to give himself peace of mind, or to maintain his status with those about him, has sought for and has found explanations that assure him that the desired object was not worth seeking anyway. The "sweet lemon" philosophy in which a person convinces himself that his misfortune is really a blessing in disguise is equally effective in facilitating a type of adjustment.

Another illustration of the use of rationalization to justify our actions is that of the occasional extravagance with which we sometimes indulge

---

[73] D. Byrne and T. J. Wong, "Racial Prejudice, Interpersonal Attraction, and Assumed Dissimilarity of Attitudes," *Journal of Abnormal and Social Psychology*, 65 (1962), 247.

ourselves. Thus a man on a tight budget might yield to the effective pressures to purchase a new car and find it necessary to justify this conspicuous purchase to himself, to his family and to his neighbors. His argument with himself might run like this: "My car was two years old and needed a new set of tires. The new car has safety features that were not part of the old automobile and I feel much more confident driving in it on the freeways. Besides, I haven't taken an out of town vacation for three years and the family deserves something fresh and new. Furthermore, it is good for the economy—see how many dollars it puts into the pockets of other Americans." Thus the new car owner may rationalize his indiscreet purchase and feel reasonably comfortable about his guilt.

It is well to recognize that rationalization does not always involve faulty reasoning, or self-deception. In those many instances in which the original goal was not a rational one, either partly or entirely, there are sound explanations why this was so, and why the alternative path chosen was the wise one. The following case makes the point:

> I had won the state contest for Miss America and had participated in the finals at Atlantic City. The whole thing was exciting, and I met many very interesting people. The contest was not easy, and I can say that I learned something of value from the experience. However, were I to have the chance, I do not think that I would do it over again, and it is better for me that I did not win the national contest. The kind of life one must lead under these circumstances is an unusual one, and hardly conducive to establishing a normal life. I had a sample of what the winner must face after my return to college. It was not possible for me to act in a way to please many people. If I tried to be a little reserved, I was branded as a snob; if I tried to be friendly, the charge was that I was being a phony, trying to prove how "democratic" I was. It was a very unpleasant year, so much so that I transferred to another school. I am glad that I am not known here as a "Miss America" candidate. Anonymity has its real assets.

Merely because the young lady failed to achieve the goal for which she had earlier strived does not mean that any and all explanations of why she is better off having failed are false reasons. In terms of her over-all life chances for happiness and sound adjustment, her rationalizations may indeed be quite rational. Afterthoughts, reconsiderations of long term plans, and weighing of competing values may well lead one to conclude, logically, that his or her prior plans were faulty, and that the whole thing has turned out for the better, despite some keen disappointments along the way. One student of mental health has suggested that the person who cannot rationalize is more apt to become mentally disturbed than the normal person who frequently turns to rationalization in one form or another, and deals now with minor frustrations and at other times with major problems of unrequited desires. The test of rational reasoning has no necessary temporal dimension; that is, the fact that it occurs in the wake of disappointments does not mean that it is therefore irrational.

REPRESSION

Perhaps no adjustment or defense mechanism is as important in Freudian psychology as repression. This is the unconscious forgetting of certain memories or desires. These repressed desires, or memories, are presumed to evidence themselves in our dreams; but dreams do not always mean what they appear to mean. The force which repressed the thought or desire in the first place, Freud held, does not relinquish its hold completely even when sleep comes. It does permit one to dream symbolically, that is, to dream of things which stand in the place of the repressed thing. This representation is called the manifest content of the dream, the real or latent content being hidden to the dreamer. The role of the analyst is to help the dreamer discover the actual object, the memory of which has been repressed.

Despite the controversial nature of this Freudian concept, there is widespread acceptance of the validity of the concept, and few who have studied human behavior at the social psychological level have failed to perceive evidence for it. Even the tendency to remember pleasant episodes and to forget unpleasant ones is a form of repression. One need not subscribe to the complex of Freudian symbolism in order to perceive the existence of repression as a process.

SUBLIMATION

Unless one subscribes to a narrow interpretation of Freudian psychology, all substitutive behavior does not replace frustrated sexual impulses. The compensation mechanism noted above *may* involve sexual desires and behavior, but it more often is related to some other of the several biogenic or sociogenic impulses. In those instances where the substituted action replaces sexual functions, *sublimation* is the term used to denote the behavior. The difficulty of delineating clear-cut instances of sublimation is the same sort of problem one faces in any application of Freudian hypotheses. That persons do find substitutes for direct expression of broad creative impulses seems plausible at least, and the spinster's lifetime devotion to the nursery school may well be such an instance. The niece or nephew upon whom the doting aunt can lavish affection and attention are, perhaps, the objects of the sublimation mechanism or they may merely be the means of a person's receiving the satisfaction of certain sociogenic motives. Even less certain is the interpretation of architectural endeavors as sublimated parental impulses and sex drives. In any event, sublimation is a generally accepted term that applies to those compensatory behavior patterns which are believed to involve the diversion of sex impulses, however narrowly or broadly such impulses may be defined. There is a tendency on the part of certain writers to use the terms compensation and sublimation synonymously. This seems to be unwarranted.

SUMMARY

Communication is possible only when the gestures—verbal or otherwise—have the same meaning for the person making them that they do for the person to whom the gestures are directed. Gestures which have acquired this mutual meaning are called *significant symbols*. The extent to which persons who speak different languages can acquire and share significant symbols is debatable, the one side holding that symbols arise as functions of the interaction of man with his object world, whereas the other side—called *linguistic relativists*—argues that the grammatical base of a language is itself a determiner of what man will and can perceive. The burden of proof appears to lie with the latter group.

A major process of adjustment is that of self-perception wherein one learns to see himself as object, often but not always as a result of seeing himself through the eyes of others. Cooley's *looking glass self* is a useful analogy in permitting one to understand the nature of this self-perceiving process which G. H. Mead has called *role taking*. The process by means of which one learns to act out the part assigned to him because of the social positions which he occupies is called *role playing*.

Throughout history there has recurred the idea that the only reality is one's sense impressions, and that objectivity is not possible. This philosophic position, called *solipsism*, is deemed untenable. There is ample evidence that man can and does perceive the objects about him in comparable, if not identical, ways. Experiments which are designed to show that people yield in their judgments to social pressures, even to the extent of gross perceptual distortion, merely verify the fact that man does perceive the world objectively, but that he learns to rely upon others' objectivity for reinforcement of his perceptual judgments.

As functions of the more pervasive processes of learning and communicating there arise the adjustment processes, sometimes called adjustment mechanisms, of accommodation, compensation, identification, enculturation, projection, rationalization, repression, socialization, and sublimation.

SUGGESTED READINGS

ANSHEN, R. N. *Language: An Inquiry into its Meaning and Function* (New York: Harper & Brothers, 1957).

BOSANQUET, BERNARD. *Essentials of Logic* (London: Macmillan and Co., Ltd., 1955).

BRAM, JOSEPH. *Language and Society* (Garden City, N.Y.: Doubleday, 1955).

BROWN, ROGER W. *Words and Things* (Glencoe, Ill.: The Free Press, 1958).

CHURCH, JOSEPH. *Language and the Discovery of Language* (New York: Random House, 1961).

GOFFMAN, ERVING. *The Presentation of Self in Everyday Life* (Garden City, N.Y.: Doubleday, 1959).

HARVEY, O. J. (ed.). *Motivation and Social Interaction* (New York: The Ronald Press Company, 1963).

HILGARD, E. R. *Theories of Learning*, 2nd ed. (New York: Appleton-Century-Crofts, 1956).

HOIJER, HARRY. *Language in Culture* (Chicago: University of Chicago Press, 1954).

KIMBLE, G. A. *Hilgard Marquis Conditioning and Learning* Rev. ed. (New York: Appleton-Century-Crofts, 1961).

KOCH, S. *Psychology: A Study of a Science*, 2 (New York: McGraw-Hill, 1960).

MACCOBY, E. E., T. M. NEWCOMB, and E. E. HARTLEY. *Readings in Social Psychology* (New York: Henry Holt and Company, 1958).

MEAD, GEORGE HERBERT. *Mind, Self and Society* (Chicago: University of Chicago Press, 1934).

MOWRER, O. H. *Learning Theory and the Symbolic Process* (New York: John Wiley and Sons, 1960).

PFUETZE, PAUL. *Self, Society, Existence* (New York: Harper and Brothers, 1954).

WHORF, BENJAMIN LEE. *Language, Thought, and Reality*, ed. by John B. Carroll (New York: John Wiley and Sons, 1956).

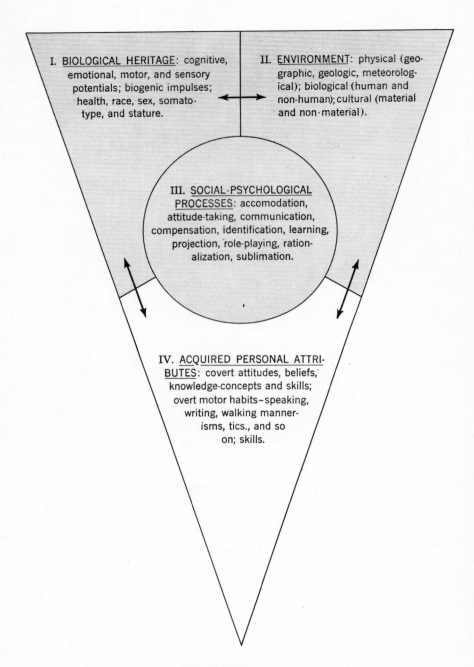

FIGURE 21. Interactionist frame of reference.

CHAPTER 7

ACQUIRED PERSONAL ATTRIBUTES

Humanization calls for both intellectual and emotional education. It is impossible to produce it without dealing with both its intellectual and emotional aspects. Even in order to deal with its intellectual aspect, both have to be taken into account.
—*Ralph Borsodi*

Although modification of the biological heritage occurs in some degree prior to birth, the major changes begin abruptly upon the infant's being thrust at birth into a new, larger, colder, and less protective environment.[1] It is with these changes that this chapter is concerned. Not being equipped with instincts that endow his biogenic drives with direction, the human infant must learn how he is to be related to his fellows and to the nonhuman world. The kind of body the child inherits, and his environmental opportunities make major contributions to this relationship, but of equal importance are the ways in which his mental, motor, and emotional potentialities become defined by his unique experiences as an individual. We will be concerned with the learned characteristics that mankind holds in common, as well as with the unique definitions given by the individual to all objects in life. We are immediately concerned with the ways in which man learns to relate himself to objects through his knowledge, his beliefs, his feelings, and his learned motor skills. Together, these constitute the subjective side of the total personality configuration. These are the acquired characteristics that the individual brings to each episode in his life, and that are modified (altered or reinforced) in some degree by each episode. These are the things that, for the most part, go on under the skin of the person, the things which *he* thinks, feels, or does, often through habit.

It is easy to think of these important *aspects* of personality as being equivalent to *total* personality. Each of these, however, acquires meaning only when seen in relationship to the other phases of life—the biological

[1] How significant the prenatal influences are for later personality development is a moot point, and a difficult one to investigate. Among others, M. F. Ashley Montagu believes such experiences to be quite important. *See* discussion of prenatal life in *The Direction of Human Development* (New York: Harper & Brothers, 1955), pp. 90–94. For additional research on prenatal development see Ch. 10.

heritage and the surrounding geographical, cultural, biological, and social factors which constitute life's stage. These subjective items are neither more nor less important than the other categories of the interactionist system. They are tied to the other factors of personality by the various social processes, described in Chapters 5 and 6. The learned or acquired attributes and variables are the products of, and participants in, these processes; they are brought by the person to each social episode or situation in which he participates.

These are the subjective factors that man acquires or learns at both intellectual and emotional levels—the feelings and motives which constitute attitudes, knowledge, beliefs, and ideas.

ATTITUDES

One American social psychologist has estimated that perhaps as many as ten thousand articles have been written in recent decades on the subject of attitudes. Another tells us that more has been written and published about attitudes during the past forty years ". . . than on any other topic."[2] That it is a much used term can be attested to by anyone, including the reader. However, as in the case of so many words which must serve both the specialist in social science and the layman, the word *attitude* is not free from ambiguity of meaning. We will not take the time and space required to discuss or even to list the multiple meanings attached to the word; others have done this job well. Despite its application to widely different forms of behavior, it has become so deeply entrenched in the vocabularies of both social scientists and laymen that it would defeat our attempts at communication were we to abandon it. Whether or not it will be eliminated from either or both of these vocabularies in the future is a moot question and not of importance to us at this time.[3]

When we ask what the attitude of a particular person is toward another person, his job, his employer, the tax system, reading, going to church, football, or classical music, we are told that the attitude is one of dislike, affection, hostility, preference, love, distrust, fear, repulsion, grief, or perhaps of indifference. In short, we are told about the evaluations of certain objects (tangible or not).[4]

---

[2] Muzafer Sherif and Carolyn W. Sherif, *An Outline of Social Psychology* (New York: Harper and Brothers, 1956), p. 488.

[3] On this point, one writer has this to say: "The personal guess of the writer is that the demise of attitude in the far future will be a happy day for social science, since this event will signify the emergence of a more integrated and scientific system of human behavior." L. W. Doob, "The Behavior of Attitudes," *Psychological Review*, LIV (May 1947), 145.

[4] Investigation of articles which contained the word *attitude*, published in a one-year period in four journals concerned with psychological and social psychological data, revealed that seventy-seven per cent used the word in simply an evaluative (feeling) sense, whereas the other twenty-three per cent incorporated cognitive elements (*e.g.*, belief), as well as feeling.

It seems that the purposes of clear thinking and communicating would be best served if the term attitude were reserved to denote those relatively stable judgments of value, the *feelings* which one possesses for certain objects of his experience. Even though one hears and finds useful such phrases as *scientific attitude*, or *objective attitude*, careful attention to the referents of such terms will enable one to perceive the emotional content thereof. The words *scientific attitude* denote the fact that the person with such an attitude will value highly an objective approach to the understanding of the world, and thus the essence of the relationship is still emotional in nature. It is preferable for clarity's sake to use the terms *concept* or *percept* (more commonly, *perception*) to denote the cognitive predispositions which constitute a major part of everyone's subjective makeup. This point will be developed later in this chapter. As the concept or percept can be spoken of as a "mind set," so an attitude can be perceived as an "emotional set," each term indicating the preparatory or predispositional nature of attitudes and concepts.

Attitudes, then, are the subjective aspects of a subject-object relationship at the emotional level. The relationship nature of attitudes is made clear by the following:

> Forming an attitude toward a group, an institution, a social issue is not an idle matter. It means one is no longer neutral to them; they are *value* laden for him in a positive or negative way. An attitude determines a certain expectation, standard, or goal, as the case may be. Events in line with it bring about satisfaction; events and things that are contrary to the attitude-determined expectations arouse dismay or dissatisfaction proportional to the place of that attitude in the individual's scheme of things. . . . Thus, we see that a social attitude important in the person's scheme has the essential earmark of a motive. Such an attitude sets the person for or against things; defines what is preferred, expected, and desired; marks off what is undesirable, what is to be avoided. In terms of its consequences in the person's behavior, an attitude is goal directed. We can, therefore, legitimately refer to social attitudes as sociogenic motives.[5]

However, to say that attitudes are motivational in nature does not indicate that they are always active. They are, for the most part, latent or abstract rather than manifest or concrete. Whether or not they are active or latent depends upon matters other than the attitudes themselves, and as in the case of other phases of the interactionist framework, attitudes

---

[5] Sherif and Sherif, *op. cit.*, p. 489. Italics added. Of similar content is the definition of Francis J. DiVesta and Jack C. Merwin, "An attitude was thus defined as a relatively stable tendency to respond with a positive or negative affect to a specific referent," *Journal of Abnormal and Social Psychology*, 60 (1960), p. 81. Nevertheless, because of their established vocabularies, some social psychologists may use quite consistently and successfully the concepts of "mental attitude" and "emotional attitude."

gain meaning only in terms of the episode in question. Attempted prediction of behavior on the basis of attitudes alone is a precarious process,
and often will prove to be in error, despite the stability of many of the
person's attitudes. Knowledge of all attitudes as well as the other personal
and nonpersonal items of the subject and his significant other must be in
hand before surety of prediction is probable or even possible.

In the quotation concerning attitudes, it was noted that once one
forms attitudes toward some objects, these objects are ". . . value laden
for him. . ." It is because of this that such objects are designated as
values, as indicated in Chapter 2. These are the objective aspects of the
relationship of which the attitudes are the subjective aspects. Values are
those items, material or nonmaterial, in one's experiences that one feels
and/or believes are important to him in his quest for satisfaction of his
needs and desires. Values include both experiential ends or goals, and
the means which are essential to the attainment of one's goals. Books
and guarantees of intellectual freedom are values for the scholar, just as
censorship and restrictions on free inquiry are values for those who would
institute subjective relationships which cannot withstand the light of
free inquiry. Concerts, music libraries, and high quality record players or
tape recorders are values for music lovers, but the freedom of movement
and distance from such places and events are values for the person who
cannot tolerate music. Thus values include those items in the object world
which one can exploit in the pursuit of the fulfillment or satisfaction of
his innate and acquired needs and desires. Some values are, of course,
learned; they are essentially functions of one's feelings, as well as of
one's knowledge of the relationship between means and ends, and the
accuracy of his self perception, which is, in turn, a function of taking
the attitudes of others toward him.

Prejudice and Bias As Attitudes

Despite the volumes which have been written about it, the term
prejudice is not yet an unambiguous concept.[6] Basically, prejudice is an
attitude toward some value, and is defined by Webster as "preconceived
judgment or leaning adverse to anything without just grounds or before

---

[6] *See* these representative writings: G. W. Allport and Bernard M. Kramer, "Some
Roots of Prejudice," *Journal of Psychology*, XXII (1946), 9–39; Leonard W. Doob,
"The Behavior of Attitudes," *Psychological Review*, LIV (1947), 135–156; Arnold
and Caroline Rose, *op. cit.*, Ch. X; Richard Schermerhorn, *These Our People* (Boston:
D. C. Heath and Co., 1949); and M. Janowitz, *Dynamics of Prejudice* (New York:
Harper & Brothers, 1950). Writing in 1963, one writer tells his readers that "Current
research [on prejudice] does not . . . bring any major modifications to the concepts
and data presented in Allport's authoritative work," S. Moscovici, "Attitudes and
Opinions," *Annual Review of Psychology, 1963* (Palo Alto, Calif.: Annual Review,
Inc., 1963), p. 235.

sufficient knowledge." This meaning of the term is close to the one that we employ here.

The directive role played by the cortical phases of the brain is revealed in prejudice, which is a misdirected emotional relationship. Prejudice is a function of ignorance about an object to which either a positive or a negative, an attractive or a repulsive, relationship has been established. In brief, the attachment is something different from one directed by reason. Prejudice may be attached to a type of cloth, a type of personality, a make of car, or styles of architecture as well as to racial or cultural groups and groupways. We distinguish between this term and that of *bias*, which Webster defines as "temperamental [emotional] inclination." If, after due examination of the facts at hand, and after direct and adequate opportunity to learn about a category of objects at both the cognitive and the emotional level, one still prefers a given object, he is then said to be biased. All men are, inescapably, biased, but prejudice is an expendable item, albeit complete absence of prejudice presupposes omniscience. Bias can be a function of knowledge (*e.g.*, years of musical study induce a preference or bias for certain kinds of music and an intolerance of others), whereas prejudice is reduced or destroyed by appropriate learning experiences at central and autonomic nervous system levels. Prejudice is more susceptible to removal or modification than bias because the bases for prejudices are often at odds with the total value and knowledge system of the person, whereas the biases may be supported by one's system of attitudes and knowledge. Thus the man who is prejudiced against a given member of an out-group on the grounds of alleged innate inferiority may also subscribe to the scientific ideal. If he encounters facts which challenge the allegation on scientific grounds, he is likely to recognize the dissonances which exist among his attitudes and beliefs. This recognition may pave the way for relinquishing the nonscientific belief, and subsequently the loss of the prejudice as well. He may, however, get no further than recognizing his prejudice for what it is, ceasing to act overtly in response to it, if his experiences remain on the cognitive and symbolic level.

Guilt and Shame As Attitudes

There is need in social psychology for terms which denote the feeling of remorse, an emotionally painful state which is a function of one's having violated his *own* moral values as dictated by his conscience. There is also need for a word which refers to the feeling which results from one's having failed to live up to the expectations of his significant or affective other, as this was described in Chapter 4. Both of these states are emotional in nature, but the objects of the attitudes are different, the one being the moral code subjectively subscribed to and the other the

more strictly social object, that is, the attitudes of others toward his behavior to which the subject may or may not be responsive. The words
shame and *guilt* are used to indicate the difference between these attitudes, but there is no consensus as to which is the proper one for each
of the two attitudes. The unabridged dictionaries are equivocal in their
decisions, and certain anthropologists and psychologists prefer to use
shame to designate the failure to fulfill social expectations and guilt to
mean the violation of inner values.[7] A significant minority sees the meanings as reversed, and the authors of this text believe that this minority
view is more in keeping with common usage and is logically more consistent.[8] When, for instance, one approaches another with the question,
"Aren't you ashamed of yourself?", he does not mean, "Aren't you sorry
you got caught violating one of *my* values?" Even more clearly is the
meaning implied by the statement, "You ought to be ashamed of yourself!" The referent of shame is a value subscribed to by the subject or at
least imputed to him. As one sociologist has noted, "The exposure of
oneself is at the heart of shame."[9] This writer comments further that
shame "Involves acting in terms of the pervasive qualitative demands of
oneself, more rigorous than external codes. . . . Surmounting guilt leads
to righteousness [whereas] transcending of shame may lead to sense of
identity, freedom."[10]

Consensus does exist that the word *guilt* is applicable to the act of
having violated a norm, whether one's own or that of others. Thus, the
distinctions between the *state* of guilt and *feeling* of guilt are separable,
and the one may exist without the other. Thus, a person may in fact be
guilty of manslaughter for having killed a pedestrian while driving a car
under the influence of alcohol without knowledge of having done so.
Or, conversely, one may feel guilty because of the misperception of a
situation in which he erroneously believes he was involved. The feeling
of guilt, however, may not carry with it any feeling of remorse or shame.
The espionage agent may reveal his guilt of being a spy by certain in-

---

[7] See Ruth Benedict, *The Chrysanthemum and the Sword* (Boston: Houghton
Mifflin Co., 1946), and Geoffrey Gorer, *The American People; A Study in National
Character* (New York: W. W. Norton, 1948); *Cf.* David Ausubel, "Relationships
between Shame and Guilt in the Socializing Process," *Psychological Review*, 62
(1955), 378–390, for a clear discussion of the relation between these two attitudes.
He indicates clearly the danger of ethnocentrism in cross-cultural studies blinding the
researcher to cultural variations of universal phenomena; *see also* Helen Merrill Lynd,
On Shame and the Search for Identity (New York: Harcourt, Brace and Co., 1958),
pp. 20–28, for instances of definitions different from the one espoused in this text.

[8] Magda Arnold, *Emotion and Personality* (New York: Columbia University Press,
1960), II, pp. 293ff.

[9] H. M. Lynd, *On Shame and the Search for Identity*, p. 32.

[10] *Ibid.*, pp. 208–209. See these pages for a 14-point contrast of "guilt axis" and
"shame axis."

advertent clues of autonomic nervous system origin, but he is ashamed
of neither his spy status nor his spying activity. Indeed, he is probably
quite proud of them. A case in point is Nathan Hale's famous statement
that "I regret that I have but one life to give for my country," which he
is said to have made just prior to his being hanged as a spy. His knowledge that the British disapproved of his action was sufficient to engender
guilt, but feeling of wrongdoing is essential to shame. Feelings of guilt
involve the failure to fulfill the expectations of others, whereas shame
involves the violation of one's own value system.

The complexity of the situations to which these concepts refer becomes clear in such episodes as the following. Subject A values the
friendship of certain members of his affective other, and feels that he
should fulfill their expectations with regard to his actions. However, even
though their friendship and positive attitudes are things which he values
highly and which he wishes to retain, he also subscribes to other values
which he and they do not hold in common and which would offend or
dismay his associates should they learn of his deviant attitudes. A finds
himself with ambivalent attitudes, which involve conflicting values. The
spy may often find himself in such a situation. During a long and successful espionage assignment in one country, a spy may develop (even contrary to his intentions) strong affectional bonds with individuals from
whom he is obliged by his assignment to extract information. If he is
apprehended, he will be guilty in fact of spying, will feel ashamed of
having exploited his friends to attain goals inimical to the values of these
friends, but will not be ashamed of his spying per se. The emotion associated with guilt is fear of the consequences, not remorse for what one
has done. Thus, the psychopath is capable of feelings of guilt, but not of
shame. There is a great difference between regretting that one has been
apprehended and the feelings of remorse and self-censure that accompany
shame. The guilty person may regret his action, but only because of the
costs he must pay because he was caught.

Shame and guilt coincide if, and only if, the value systems of the individual *and* of his friends and associates (significant other) are identical.
Under these circumstances, the person apprehended in violation of the
value system shared with others is in *fact* guilty, *feels* guilty, and is
ashamed of his acts.[11] To further complicate the problem, one must recognize that numerous occasions occur wherein the individual is not able
to distinguish clearly between feelings of shame and guilt. Ambiguities
and ambivalences are known to all persons at one time or another. Be this
as it may, these two attitudes, whatever we call them, remain important

[11] The concept *embarrassment* is necessary to augment *guilt* and *shame*, and denotes one's discomfiture at having revealed a relationship in which there is a dissonance between role behavior and social position. *Cf.* discussion in Ch. 8.

parts of the person's subjective repertoire that he brings to each new episode of life.

Conscience—a Function of Attitudes

Conscience, a commonly used word, has a complex meaning. Etymologically, it denotes a "knowing together" of what is right or wrong, being taken from the Latin *con* (with) and *scire* (to know). Although the cognitive-sensory factors are of necessity involved in conscience, its distinguishing features are emotional in nature. Conscience is made up of those several attitudes, mostly social but not exclusively so, that relate to the things that the individual himself *feels* to be of such sufficient value that they should, or should not, be violated or destroyed. Conscience incorporates emotional attitudes toward the ways in which one should be related to certain objects, be they human or not. It incorporates not only what one perceives to be proper action, but also what one *feels* should be the right behavior. In brief, conscience is constituted principally of attitudes.

The conscience is a function of taking the attitudes of others that one respects or introjects, and of values that the individual has discovered or invented for himself. In keeping with the discussion above, one has a "guilty conscience" if and when he fails to fulfill the expectations of his affective or significant other, that is, when his actions violate their normative standards insofar as his *self* is concerned. Shame accompanies the violation of one's own system of values, when one fails to listen to the purely subjective aspects of conscience.

Pleasure-Pain Principle

The infant does not have to learn that a pin sticking into him is painful, nor that prolonged deprivation of food results in a painful state.[12] He does have to learn which of many other kinds of experiences yield pleasure or pain. He has to learn which of innumerable objects he likes or dislikes, fears, and so on; that is, he must learn almost all of his attitudes. Some of those attitudes will have motivational value, as those which involve experience of pleasure and pain. Even though it is true that "In no mode of study of human life, in any of its manifold aspects, can we progress very far before encountering the concepts of pain and pleasure,"[13] it is sometimes overlooked in the explanation of the "why" of social behavior. It is one of those readily observable principles which, up to the present at least, has not prompted attempts at experimental verification. Careful observation of the behavior of others, as well as in-

---

[12] He must, of course, learn the nature of these pains, learn names for them, and learn their meaning by relating them to other experiences.

[13] T. S. Szasz, *Pain and Pleasure: A Study of Bodily Feelings* (New York: Basic Books, Inc., 1957), p. 9. Although the pleasure–pain principle involves certain biogenic factors, it is better, in the authors' judgment, to discuss it at this point.

trospection, will evidence the truth of the statement that we never do anything that we do not want to do, at least in the sense that what we do is less unpleasant than suffering the consequences of not doing it. Let us illustrate. Few persons like to arise early in the morning, whether it is to administer to the needs of the sick, to go to work, or to attend an early class. However, millions prefer getting out of bed at relatively early hours to staying in bed and suffering the loss of friends, jobs, the right to attend school, and so on. What a person does reflects his value systems, that is, the things which he has learned to esteem as valuable, such as material goods, the approval of his associates and friends, or the attainment of a status that meets his ideal. This is as true of the selfish person as it is of the person we call the altruist. With no intent to be cynical, one can recognize that the motives of the altruist are as much a function of subjective attitudes as are those of the person we usually label "selfish." The true distinction between the egoist and altruist is not to be sought in terms of self-interest, but in terms of the consequences of varying kinds of self-satisfying behavior. Some forms accrue only to the advantage of the individual (egoism or selfishness), whereas other forms contribute to the welfare of others (altruism or unselfishness). The altruist would be just as unhappy were he not permitted to help others as the egoist would be if he were not permitted to seek his own interest fulfillment without regard for others. We esteem the former and frown upon the latter in most cultures, but the explanation of the two types of social behavior is on the same level with regard to the pleasure-pain principle. The mother who sacrifices everything for her children would be miserable if she were forced to clothe and feed herself while her children were in dire need. Social planners or "social engineers" are ill-advised to attempt the elimination of pleasure-seeking as human motivation; such a program is unrealistic and impossible. The more fruitful approach is to see to it that the things that give pleasure to people are also the things that aid others, *i.e.*, are functional for the larger society. There is no other way inasmuch as we all do what we find most pleasurable in the given situation. That is, all mentally well persons act according to the pleasure-pain principle; when it becomes obvious that a person is *not* acting according to this principle, we say that the person is neurotic or psychotic, categorize the action as obsessive-compulsive, and label the person a masochist.

Another aspect of the pleasure-pain principle has been dramatized by the extreme statement of philosopher Schopenhauer, *viz.*, ". . . that pleasure is only the negation of pain, and that pain is the positive element in life."[14] ". . . to *live happily* only means to *live less unhappily*—to live a

[14] *The Essays of Arthur Schopenhauer*, translated by T. Bailey Saunders (New York: Willey Book Company, 1937), "Counsels and Maxims," p. 1.

tolerable life"[15] "Thus the satisfaction or the pleasing can never be more than the deliverance from a pain, from a want . . ."[16] which must be followed either by a new pain, or by languor, empty longing, or ennui; . . ."[17]

At first blush many would tend to reject this appraisal of pleasure as being devoid of any merit. However, a moment's reflection will indicate the realistic nature of the observation if one does not attempt to categorize *all* pleasure as negative in nature. What is pleasurable for a person depends to a great extent upon the situation in which the person finds himself. Illustrative of this point is the situation involving a glowing fire in the fireplace, a comfortable chair, a good book or some music to one's taste, a quiet house, and perhaps something to eat and drink. To the person who has been in this situation all day because of nothing else to do or because of illness, this picture spells boredom and discontent, but to the person who has worked hard all day in the cold, has not eaten for many hours, or who has been harassed by crowds of co-workers or customers, the quietude and comforts of fireplace, book, and food can be among life's greatest rewards.

In psychology, the pleasure-pain principle has often been treated under other headings. From Chapter 5 the reader will recall the discussion of respondent and operant conditioning. In both of these areas of learning-behavior investigation, the rewards and punishments (reinforcements) are perceivable as functions of the pleasure-pain principle. The chief proponent of the operant conditioning (which some see as associative-contiguity learning and not conditioning in the traditional meaning), concludes that the presence or absence of rewards (positive reinforcement) and penalties (negative reinforcement) makes certain behavior highly probable or improbable. He notes that the language learning aspect of the pleasure-pain principle is ". . . most conspicuous when verbal behavior is first acquired. The parents set up a repertoire of responses in the child by reinforcing [i.e. giving responses which are deemed pleasurable by the child] many instances of response."[18]

Schopenhauer's perception of pleasure as merely the reduction of pain finds its learning-theory counterpart in Clark L. Hull's views. This well known psychologist saw motive as a function of need reduction,

[15] *Ibid.*, p. 2.

[16] Arthur Schopenhauer, *The World of Will and Idea* (London: Routledge and Kegan Paul Ltd., 1948), p. 412.

[17] *Ibid.*, p. 413. It is of interest to note that Schopenhauer appears to suggest the positive nature of pleasure elsewhere in his works. He states that the highly intelligent and educated man is capable of ". . . leading an existence rich in thought and full of life and meaning, occupied by worthy and interesting objects . . . bearing in himself a source of noblest pleasure." T. B. Saunders (translator) *op. cit.*, "The Wisdom of Life," p. 43.

[18] B. F. Skinner, *Verbal Behavior* (New York: Appleton-Century-Crofts, 1957), p. 29.

whether the *need* is to avoid anticipated pain in the form of an electric shock, or the reduction of hunger or the sex impulse.

SOCIOGENIC MOTIVES

". . . there is a widespread discontent with theories of motivation built upon primary [biogenic] drives. Signs of this discontent are found in realms as far apart as animal psychology and psychoanalytic ego psychology."[19] One cannot explain satisfactorily the complex behavior of man with recourse only to the biogenic motives described in Chapter 3. Once the human infant begins to interact with the sociocultural world about him in response to the primary, biogenic impulses, there occur alterations in the biological heritage that in turn become forces of motivation. These appear slowly and gradually as the individual acquires concepts with which to interpret his sensations. He learns to perceive which relationships are enjoyable and those which he dislikes. He learns to desire certain kinds of experiences with both human and nonhuman objects, and these desires do not have any direct connection with specific tissue needs as in the instances of hunger, sex, and random activity drives or impulses.[20] This failure to identify specific organic bases for the sociogenic impulses has been interpreted by some as sufficient evidence for doubting their validity or universality. Nevertheless, every system of motivational theory, short of out-and-out instinct theory, includes some variation of sociogenic or learned motives. Each system has something in common with others, and among some there are many overlapping concepts.[21] Doubt does not exist concerning the actuality of such motives; the problem rests upon the discovery of the real categories. The categories of sociogenic or learned motives that are used in this text are essentially those taken from the works of W. I. Thomas and Florian Znaniecki and generally are known as "Thomas' Four Wishes." Thomas believed that the wide range of human wishes could be classified into four categories as follows:

1. The desire for new experience.
2. The desire for response.

[19] R. W. White, "Motivation Reconsidered," *Psychological Review*, 66 (1959), 328. White points out that ". . . many of the earlier tenets of primary drive theory have been discredited by recent experimental work." (*Ibid.*)

[20] Sherif and Sherif (*op. cit.*, pp. 407–408), note that attitudes are formed "which are not and never could be directly relevant goals or motives originating in the physiological functioning of the organism." M. Sherif was among the very first to use the terms *biogenic* and *sociogenic*. It also should be noted that these learned motives are attitudes, but that not all attitudes are motives, *i.e.*, induce action. However, this point must not be pushed to the extreme that one would argue that these sociogenic motives are independent of the zoological nature of mankind.

[21] Magda Arnold, for example, *op. cit.*, presents an interesting list of motives, among them "desire to know," "union with others," "empathy," "love of beauty," "joy of doing and making," "religious [supernatural] emotion," pp. 309–330.

3. The desire for recognition.
4. The desire for security.[22]

The fact that these wishes, or their counterparts, are ignored or referred to in a cursory manner by some textbook writers in the field of social psychology may be explained more by the absence of any integration of concepts into a system of social psychology than by the shortcomings of the concepts themselves. That some different ordering of desires may supplant them in the future is, of course, always a possibility as far as we know at the present, but until such an event occurs we will continue to employ the "four wishes" as valuable concepts in the explanation of human social behavior.[23]

It is of interest to note how closely the components of motivation as set forth by A. H. Maslow approximate those of W. I. Thomas. The latter's desire for security is matched by Maslow's "safety needs," the need for "a predictable, orderly world; and avoidance of the "new, unfamiliar, strange, and unmanageable"; the Thomas-Znaniecki "desire for response" has its counterpart in Maslow's "love and affection and belongingness needs"; the more familiar *desire for recognition* of Thomas becomes the "esteem needs" in Maslow's scheme of motivation, and of this he writes: "All people in our society (with few pathological exceptions) have a need or desire for a stable, firmly based, (usually) high evaluation of themselves, for self-respect, and self-esteem, and for the esteem of others." Less obviously related are the desire for new experience of Thomas and "the need for self-actualization" of the Maslow system, but of this latter he writes that if all of the other needs are met

[22] W. I. Thomas, *The Unadjusted Girl* (Boston: Little, Brown & Co., 1923), p. 4. It is of interest to note that an earlier version of these basic desires was presented in "Methodological Note," I, *The Polish Peasant in Europe and America*, which he wrote with Florian Znaniecki as co-author. In this version of the wishes they include "sexual response and general social appreciation" under *recognition*, and list as the fourth wish the *desire for mastery* or the "will to power," p. 73. It seems to the present authors that the later version is more adequate, and is less given to overlapping. In our present use of the four wishes, we will depart in some significant measure from the exact wording and conceptions used by Thomas and Znaniecki in their earlier works which were necessarily products of the theories of the time and therefore given to outmoded terminology and viewpoints. Also, because of the broader scope of the concept of *security*, we have chosen to treat it last rather than in the order suggested by Thomas and Znaniecki.

[23] *See* A. H. Maslow, "A Theory of Human Motivation," *Psychological Review* (1943), 376–382, and his expanded discussion in *Motivation and Personality* (New York: Harper & Brothers, 1954), pp. 84 ff. *See also* Robert R. Sears, "Dependency Motivation," in *Nebraska Symposium on Motivation—1963*, M. R. Jones (ed.) (Lincoln: University of Nebraska Press, 1963), pp. 25–64, for items which seem clearly to fall under Thomas' and Znaniecki's desires for security, recognition, and response, or under Maslow's safety, love, or esteem needs. Experimental correlates of these needs in children are analyzed by Sears.

". . . we may still often (if not always) expect that a new discontent and restlessness will soon develop, unless the individual is doing what he is fitted for." In the opinion of the present writers, this latter need is the most nebulous of the components of Professor Maslow's theory and the most difficult to demonstrate in human social activity. What a man is "fitted for" is not always easily discernible and does not appear to be independent of the desires for recognition, response, and the variety of new experiences which ward off boredom. The same can be said of Maslow's "desire to know and understand," which, it seems clear, is subordinate to other needs or desires.

We also agree with the following statements made some thirty years ago with reference to the four basic wishes:

> It is necessary to guard against a misconception of the nature and purpose of these wish categories, not as conscious and concrete wishes; the experienced desires are to be treated as expressions of and to be classified under, these generalized forms. In the second place, it is equally necessary to see that the four categories taken together are to be understood as inclusive; they comprehend all the positive wishes of the person. No concrete wish [in the sense of wishes acquired and operative on the social-cultural level of interaction] is ever experienced that does not fall within one or more of the categories. In the third place, the four categories must be understood as mutually exclusive; a satisfaction of one type cannot be substituted for satisfaction of another. The wish for new experience, for example, cannot be satisfied by more security; recognition does not satisfy the need for response; affection is not a substitute for fame. Every person to be a wholesome and adjusted personality must realize more or less adequate satisfaction of each type of wish. This has been termed by some students the fundamental law of wishes. Finally, the categories are to be understood as universally applicable. They are [among] the fundamental and permanent facts that unconsciously motivate the behavior of all persons.[24]

It is important for the reader to keep in mind the fact that the wishes that fall under these four categories are satisfied in many different ways. Their definition or satisfaction is a function of the interaction of the individual with other objects in his life space. The ways of behaving that the anthropologist Ralph Linton has classified as universals, alternatives,

---

[24]E. B. Reuter and C. W. Hart, *Introduction to Sociology* (New York: McGraw-Hill, 1933). It may be of interest to the reader that Professor Florian Znaniecki, who with Thomas was instrumental in setting forth these basic wishes in the first place, concluded that they are not simply heuristic devices to facilitate the study of certain aspects of individual social behavior. After having held them in rather low esteem for some twenty years, Professor Znaniecki later held that they referred to real categories of human behavior. *See* his *Origin and Development of Cultural Sciences* (Champaign, Ill.: University of Illinois Press, 1951).

specialities, and individual peculiarities show the wide variation in conformance that characterizes man's attempt to meet these fundamental desires.[25] Nevertheless, the finite nature of man's biological heritage and his life space is reflected in the limited number of ways of fulfilling his sociogenic needs. Nor need the wishes be developed in every person in equal degree; indeed, they cannot be. Marked variations are observable from individual to individual and from culture to culture. Reference to Chapter 4 will enable one to see the illustrations of the different ways in which the wishes can be met successfully, and we shall suggest additional ways in subsequent pages of this chapter.

The Desire for New Experience

The desire for new experience is the positive aspect of man's capacity for boredom. The human organism is of such a nature that it is capable of becoming satiated or bored with almost any experience if presented with it repeatedly and without respite. This applies to cognitive, sensory, motor, and emotional experiences. The positive phases of this motivational category are:

1. *Cognitive*: the desire to know, to understand, to learn what things mean. *Curiosity* is another term which calls attention to this learned motive.

2. *Sensory*: the desire to see, hear, taste, feel, smell something new.

3. *Motor*: the desire to learn new controls over the striated muscles—to walk, to climb, to swim, and so on.

4. *Emotional*: the desire to experience new feelings or a variety of feelings.

The last subcategory is close to, but not identical with, the sensory subcategory. The emotional thrill, or "kick," adds something to the experience of seeing, hearing, tasting, or "feeling" (e.g., being aware of kinesthetic movement or of stimulation of the various receptors). The experiences of being in love, riding a roller coaster, having an orgasm, being intoxicated, liking music, are something more than awareness of receptor stimulation. The finest foods, literature, or music in the world may become intolerable if no variety is permitted, and so it is with many of the social values as they are related to the personality in question.

It hardly seems necessary to set up experiments to verify this statement. Anyone who has worked with groups who face monotonous daily routines—as in prisons, some hospitals and schools—knows the importance of the maxim "variety is the spice of life." A psychologist has pointed out that the abandonment of the felt need to tie motivation to tissue need ". . . opens the way for consideration in their own right those

---

[25] *The Study of Man* (New York: Appleton-Century-Crofts, 1936), pp. 272–275.

aspects of animal and human behavior in which stimulation and contact with the environment seems to be sought and welcomed . . . and in which novelty and variety seem to be enjoyed for their own sake."[26] Those in charge of food service for prisoners, patients, and inmates need not be told of the importance of adding variety to quality if satisfaction is to be secured.

The impulse to motor and mental activity is rarely satisfied by narrowly defined activity. The "little" song which amuses performer and audience alike when first sung soon becomes a bore. The hit in popular music is soon played to death and is shelved in favor of a new arrival; today's hit is tomorrow's "corn." In challenging the validity of the "new experience" wish, one social psychologist has asked about the persistent appeal of such items as J. S. Bach's music, Mark Twain's writings, and the song "Silent Night." It is the great complexity of Bach's composition that defies man's capacity for boredom. A case in point is that of a college choir on tour whose members preferred a Bach motet least of all at the tour's beginning, but found it the only selection they could tolerate at the end of the tour. Even here a constant hearing of any *one* of Bach's Brandenberg Concerti would find most, if not all, listeners crying for relief. Twain's writings are complex enough but hardly challenging by themselves to satisfy many readers. Too, if "Silent Night" were sung daily throughout the year, it is unlikely that many would enjoy hearing it. Many readers probably can testify to a satiation for certain pieces of music after being exposed by public address systems to repetitive musical programs during the weeks between Thanksgiving and Christmas. Following the frequent playing of Beethoven's Fifth Symphony during World War II, many persons found that their former interest in it not only had waned, but had been replaced by irritation.

The desire for new experience, as with the other wishes, can lead to activity which is normal or abnormal, to behavior which will result in great benefit to mankind or to its near destruction. The unique experience of the individual, plus the social heritage in which the experience took place, will determine whether the desire for novelty leads to a new mathematical system, a new invention, or to a "hop" party where the participant begins a long and anxiety ridden career as a drug addict. As will be discussed later in greater detail, one of the strongest cases for the liberal arts education can be built upon the need for new experience.

---

[26] R. W. White, *op. cit.*, p. 328. White perceives this form of sociogenic motive as an effectance motive (which produces a "feeling of efficacy") and which ". . . leads the organism to find out how the environment can be changed and what consequences flow from these changes." *Ibid.*, p. 329. Elsewhere he comments that ". . . the exploratory drive appears to bear no relation whatever to a tissue need or deficit external to the nervous system." *Ibid.*, p. 301.

The person with a broad education is capable of satisfying his felt needs in a variety of socially approved ways, whereas the person of meager experience is forced to push relatively simple, narrow impulses to patho-logical ends in order to satisfy his jaded appetite for novelty.

Learning, it goes without saying, is a new experience in and of itself. Thus, the quest for knowledge, as illustrated by Maslow's "desire to know and understand," and his "aesthetic needs," is explainable in part as a function of man's quest for new experience. Maslow makes this explicit in observing that the ". . . needs to know and understand are seen in late infancy and childhood, perhaps even more strongly than in adulthood."[27]

J. McV. Hunt has made the observation that there seems to be ". . . the empirical principle that the more an infant has seen and heard, the more he wants to see and hear. . . . Once interest in novelty appears, it is an important source of motivation for cognitive learning. Perhaps it is the chief source of motivation for cognitive learning. Interest in novelty appears to motivate the improvement of locomotor skills, for the novel "needing" examination or manipulation are typically out of reach. It appears to motivate imitation of unfamiliar verbal phones and unfamiliar gestures and even fairly complex actions."[28] Hunt calls to the reader's attention the remarkable success which Maria Montessori had in teach-ing ungraded children between the ages of three and six years by taking advantage of this desire for novelty of new experience.[29] He also com-ments that the lack of interest in the Montessori method after the inter-ruption of World War I may be attributed to the fact that its assumptions clashed with the growing conviction of fixed intelligence which charac-terized the 1920's. However, the desire for new experience was implicitly accepted by the "progressive" schools of education. He then comments that "children do not have to be taught to be curious."[30] Plato has observed that learning is satisfying both as a means to certain desired ends, and as an end in its own right. It is especially in the latter aspect of learning that the value of novelty is most clearly manifested. The very words "the news" indicate the universality of this impulse.

After periods of enforced inactivity, stimuli of all sorts appear to have enhanced value. Illustrative of this point is a study of twenty-four naval cadets who were deprived of all social contacts for approximately eight hours. When tested for susceptibility to suggestion after the isolation, they were reported to be significantly more suggestible than the control

27 A. H. Maslow, *Motivation and Personality*, p. 96.

28 "The Epigenesis of Intrinsic Motivation and the Stimulation of Early Cognitive Learning," Paper prepared for the symposium on the stimulation of early cognitive learning, at APA meeting, Philadelphia, August 30, 1963, pp. 8, 10.

29 *The Montessori Method* (New York: Frederick A. Stokes, 1912).

30 *Ibid.*

group. The experimenters ruled out muscular inactivity as a possible causal item.[31]

Another aspect of the new experience motive is that the strength of the wish can be enhanced by withholding from individuals the opportunity to experience a particular phase of behavior. This may be the basis for the time honored view that the forbidden fruit is sweeter. Certainly it is true that the behavior forms designated as "sinful" hold a fascination for the uninitiated that they do not for those who have tasted them. The tremendous interest in sex among adolescents in America is not explainable in terms of the innate sex drive alone, but may be attributable in part to the curiosity about such experiences. If it were possible for one to deny young people the privilege of inspecting the motors under the hoods, or "bonnets," of cars, and if adults' conversation about such motors were restricted to adult company, with adults' immediately changing the subject as youth entered their presence, and replying to the youngsters' queries by saying they would have to wait until they were older, or that nice boys and girls weren't interested in such dirty things, would it be long before the young would be stealing out at night, flashlights in hand, to find out just what goes on under those hoods? The sacred churinga stones of the Australian aborigine provide us with an actual case in point. These objects (sometimes wooden), supposedly of supernatural origin, are hidden in secret and sacred places, and are not supposed to be seen by women or uninitiated boys. Death of the women and children was believed to be the consequence of violating this taboo.[32]

That tradition lays a heavy hand on primitive, preliterate societies is hardly to be denied, but it is an error to believe that these people are satisfied with a monotonous, humdrum existence. Some means of breaking daily routine exist in all cultures—some of the events unplanned and spontaneous but others institutionalized and highly stylized. The hunt, precipitated by news or rumor of a highly prized quarry, such as a seal or walrus in the Eskimo's Arctic abode, or a kangaroo in Australian

---

[31] M. B. Jones and J. E. Goodson, "The Effect of Boredom in Suggestibility," *Aerospace Medicine*, 30 (1959), 716–721. This study seems to provide support for the common observation that mob actions, riots, and so on, are made possible by the existence of a pool of persons who are more or less bored with their current status and are thus predisposed to accept any suggestion which promises some excitement. Rioting groups, large or small, do not usually attract persons who are engaged in stimulating debate, making love to desirable companions, working at hobbies, voluntarily fulfilling an obligation to a friend, or otherwise occupied in manners deemed valuable and pleasurable. For further experimental and observational evidence of man's basic need for variety of stimulation, *see* J. H. Wheaton, *Fact and Fancy in Sensory Deprivation Studies* (Brooks Air Force Base, Tex.: School of Aviation Medicine, 1959).

[32] H. R. Hays, *From Ape to Angel* (New York: Alfred A. Knopf, 1958), p. 95, and Hutton Webster, *Taboo* (Stanford: Stanford University Press, 1942), p. 286.

aborigine country, provides excitement for the moment and bases for tales to be told for weeks afterward.

The *Kula*, an involved, ceremonious exchange of objects that have no monetary value, helps to fulfill the sociogenic needs of the Trobriand Islanders. Over hundreds of miles of sea routes, a limited number of men from every village move the *soulava* (long necklaces of red shell) in a clockwise direction, and *mwali* (bracelets of white shell) in a counterclockwise direction.[33] Each participant (who is "once in the Kula, always in the Kula") retains each article for a short time and then passes it on to one of his life-long partners. The exchange is periodic but not regular. The *soulava* and *mwali* acquire histories, which are related to the villagers by the temporary possessors. The more famous articles lend prestige to the village in which they rest at the moment. ". . . rooted in myth, backed by traditional law, and surrounded with magical rites," the *Kula* has acquired ". . . a halo of romance and value in the minds of the natives [which] have indeed created a passion in their hearts for this simple exchange."[34] In the sea-bound home of the Trobriand Islanders, where tradition and weather impose a homogeneity of experiences, the *Kula* seems to play a role of great significance by providing welcome breaks in routine life patterns. New experiences and recognition are consequences of the Kula's activities. The trips themselves (which also serve an economic trade function) are anticipated with pleasurable excitement and are the subjects of conversation long afterward. It is unlikely that this honored custom could survive an encroaching culture based upon literacy, modern technology, and urbanization. In the absence of these complex cultural factors, however, it is counted among the most valuable of life's experiences.

Similar to, yet distinguishable from, customs such as the *Kula* are the holidays, the special-event days, which characterize almost all cultures. Sociologically speaking, holidays are "cultural punctuation marks." G. K. Chesterton once remarked that it is always three o'clock in Hell. The implications of this for the need for variety should be clear. Likewise, an eternity of Wednesday afternoons would be intolerable. The week end, the holidays, the break in routine (even the "coffee break") are valued experiences which are functions of man's capacity for boredom, his need for a variety of experiences.

This desire for new experience or for variety is manifested even in the field of sensory experiences, and is illustrated by our persistent interest in fire. The fireplace would not hold such fascination were the flame pattern rigid; it is the ever changing pattern of the flames that explains

---

[33] Bronislaw Malinowski, *Argonauts of the Western Pacific* (London: Routledge and Kegan Paul, Ltd., 1953), p. 18. See this source for an elaborate and very readable description of this non-economic commerce.

[34] *Ibid.*, pp. 85–86.

its captivating charm. The same is true of moving water, whether it be a waterfall, the ocean surf, or the ripples of a stream or lake. Few persons find pleasure in sitting for any length of time (even when comfortably warm) merely to watch the shiny surface of a frozen lake, but the patterns created on water by wind or surface craft will hold the attention of spectators for hours. The kaleidoscopic changes of East River traffic are apparently the reasons which explain the building of apartments adjacent to slum areas on the river bank for some of New York City's wealthier residents. For them, at least, the stimulation of the commercial hustle and bustle is preferable to the relatively stable view of, say, the trees, green grass, and shrubs of parkland. Too, the kaleidoscope itself has its value in the infinite variety of patterns of the colored glass bits. This suggests the fascinating topic of the relationship between the desire for variety and aesthetic values. It may, if taken into full consideration, give pause to some of the hitherto unqualified generalizations of certain enthusiastic supporters of the plain, unadorned surfaces of some modern architectural styles. Suffice it to point out that it is not possible to explain or control much of man's social behavior without taking into account this generalized, universally observed, desire for new experience, or, if one prefers, for variety that disperses boredom.

An interesting instance of the exaggerated need for variety is given us by a person who experienced a lack of variety of stimuli for a relatively long period. While isolated for the purpose of doing research near the South Pole, Admiral Richard E. Byrd wrote in his diary:

May 12. . . . The silence of this place is as real and solid as sound. More real, in fact, than the occasional creaks of the Barrier and the heavier concussions of snow quakes. . . . It seems to merge in and become part of the indescribable *evenness*, as do the cold and the dark and the relentless ticking of the clocks. This evenness fills the air with its mood of unchangeableness; it sits across from me at the table, and gets into the bunk with me at night. And no thought will wander so far as not eventually to be brought up hard by it. This is timelessness in its ultimate meaning. Very often my mood soars above it; but, when this mood goes, I find myself craving change—a look at trees, a rock, a handful of earth, and sound of foghorns, anything belonging to the world of movement and living things.[35]

Abnormal situations such as this emphasize for us the fact that man is a curious animal, capable of boredom, and has a need for varying amounts of change and variety of experiences.[36]

[35] Richard E. Byrd, *Alone* (New York: G. P. Putnam's Sons, 1938), 141–142.

[36] Of interest in connection with the discussion of sociogenic motives is a study of grammar school children, the purpose of which was to discover the relevance of feelings of security, insecurity, achievement, and boredom. No difficulty was experienced in classifying items according to these categories and tests of internal con-

The Desire for Response

The desire for response needs little elaboration. That it is akin to the desire for recognition is not to be denied, but it is sufficiently different to warrant separate treatment.[37] It is the need for affection, ranging from that of the parent's love for his children to the informal affectional bonds that unite play groups and congeniality groups. It may have a sexual component, but it is *not* inevitably tied up with sex, a point often misunderstood in our culture, an error which can be the source of social problems. Sex interests and love interests can, obviously, exist independently of each other.

It is particularly important with regard to this desire to realize that the attempt to substitute satisfactions of other needs for the need for affection will fail more times than it will succeed. The child or adult who is in need of affection will not be satisfied in the long run by increases in goods which spell more security, recognition, or new experience. A room full of new toys cannot serve as a substitute for playmates or parents who can provide the needed affection and companionship, nor will a new mink coat or a "nice long trip" always induce the lovesick adult to "forget the whole thing."[38]

In a study of letters intercepted in a reformatory for female delinquents, a marked need for affection was revealed. The home atmosphere had been deficient in this respect.[39] Similar interpretations resulted from a study of female prisoners with problems of alcoholism. "Evidence supported the observations that these alcoholics had been deprived of affection in their home experiences. The inadequate and sporadic affection led to a feeling of isolation, which in turn played a part in the promiscuous behavior and in the excessive use of alcohol."[40]

---

sistency were positive. A positive correlation was discovered between achievement and security feelings, and between boredom and insecurity. The finding that tardiness was positively correlated with feelings of boredom does not come as a surprise. *Journal of Experimental Education*, 27 (1959), 333–340.

[37] Without suggesting that the results can be uncritically transferred to humans, we would recommend that the reader acquaint himself with the excellent studies of nonhuman primate's love needs in Harry Harlow, "Love in Infant Monkeys," *Scientific American*, 200 (1959), 68–74.

[38] Drawing upon his personal professional experiences, psychologist A. H. Maslow writes that psychopathic personalities ". . . are people who, according to the best data available, have been starved for love in the earliest months of their lives and have simply lost forever the desire and the ability to give and to receive affection. . . ." *Motivation and Personality*, pp. 98–99.

[39] Sidney Kosofsky and Albert Ellis, "Illegal Communication Among Institutionalized Female Delinquents," *Journal of Social Psychology*, 48 (1958), 155–160.

[40] D. J. Myerson, "Clinical Observations on a Group of Alcoholic Prisoners with Special Reference to Women," *Quarterly Journal of Studies on Alcohol*, 20 (1959), 555–572.

Still another therapist concludes that the response or love relationship must be reinstated if therapy with alcoholics is to succeed.[41]

The primary groups such as the family, neighborhood, play or congeniality groups provide for this need for response, and it is for this reason that some form of primary group relationship is essential in any society if maladjustment is not to be common. This is just as true of the urban culture as it is of the rural, and it is a common misconception that the city does not provide primary group contacts. Even though a person may not know anything about his apartment house neighbors, he can, and usually does, have a primary group that may spread over the city with regard to residence, but that nevertheless provides the response essential to a well-adjusted personality. This is not to deny, of course, that there are many lonely persons living in cities, for certainly there are.

Just as boredom is the negative side of the desire for new experience, so loneliness is the other side of the desire for response. In sparsely populated parts of the country, the exaggerated importance of such gatherings as church services, socials, weddings, funerals, election gatherings, and other comparable events reflects the need for persons to meet and talk with others. How much such events depended upon the persistent loneliness of isolated families and individuals is revealed in the high mortality of the rural organizations that supported these events once the automobile made daily contact easier than weekly contacts had been when travel was restricted to horse and buggy.[42] The desire for response is present in all normal persons as a motive to social behavior.

The Desire for Recognition

The desire for recognition, or the desire to be noticed, is acquired by every normal individual.

Henry H. Murray has suggested an interesting motivational concept that he labels "ascensionism," which he defines as ". . . an integrate of the need for achievement and a relatively much stronger need for awed attention, for spectacular glory, for sensational prestige, which may or may not be linked with a component of sexuality, the special aim of this compound being to ascend vertically, in a physical, social, or intellectual sense."[43] This is somewhat akin to the need for achievement motive presented by D. C. McClelland, J. W. Atkinson, R. A. Clark, and E. L. Lowell.[44] In both of the motives, however, it is to be noted that the behav-

[41] Giorgio Lolli, "Alcoholism As a Disorder of the Love Disposition," *Quarterly Journal of Studies on Alcohol*, 17 (1956), 96–107.

[42] *Cf.* N. L. Sims, *Elements of Rural Sociology* (New York: Thomas Y. Crowell Co., 1940), pp. 592–619.

[43] "Drive, Time, Strategy, Measurement, and Our Way of Life," in G. Lindzey (ed.) *Assessment of Human Motivation* (New York: Rinehart & Co., 1958), p. 193.

[44] *The Achievement Motive* (New York: Appleton-Century-Crofts, 1953).

ior is never random, but is always in terms of the values subscribed to by the subjects and their significant other. The goal achieved, or sought, gains recognition, security, and so on, for the persons so motivated. As a matter of fact, few, if any, persons exist who do not possess this desire in high degree. Again, the manner in which one can get recognition is determined by his interactive living within a certain cultural milieu. He will select the role which gives him maximum recognition, without losing for him the satisfaction of the other basic needs. The desire for social approval is one aspect of the desire for recognition, but not all of it. We seek social approval for ourselves, but if this is not forthcoming we will seek recognition, even if it does not carry social approval. Witness the so-called "hell raiser" in the schoolroom, the bully in the playground or on the street corner, and the outlaw. We are told that "Exaggerated attention-seeking behavior is an emotional disturbance constituting a misdirection of effort; a defense against the blocking of normal expression of desire for recognition."[45] It is often the case that this socially disapproved form of behavior is the only way the person knows how to get any recognition, and this he will do rather than suffer being ignored.

Another way in which the desire for recognition reveals itself is seen in the multiple "confessions" of guilt which a bizarre and unsolved crime occasionally evokes. Although there are sometimes other explanations for such confessions, the publicity that such persons receive for their "confessions" fulfills a need for the confessors.

The alert parent, schoolteacher, or playground supervisor is aware of this basic need, and provides everyone with an opportunity for recognition in the given primary group. The alternatives are overt, unapproved behavior, or recession into a world of fantasy where the individual conjures up imaginary situations and relationships in which he gains his recognition despite his failure to do so in the world of reality. Analysis of daydreams reveals the basic importance of this desire for recognition. Most of us are reluctant to acknowledge these daydreams, but he who does not experience them is a rare person, if indeed he exists at all. Identification with the heroes of novels, radio, television, movies, and theater provides other ways of vicariously securing recognition.

We have innumerable evidences of the motivating force of the desire for recognition as it operates in the world about us. The whole area of the performing arts is more or less a function of this motivational category. Were man devoid of this impulse, concert halls, and opera houses would be few indeed, and the term *Broadway* would call to mind only a wide traffic thoroughfare. Someone is reputed to have said to Napoleon that

---

[45] *Psychological Abstracts*, 34 (1960, 167; taken from Ruth Wintergerst, *"Erziehung geltungssüchtiger Kinder"* [Guidance of Children with Abnormal Drive for Attention], *Heilpadagogische Werkblatter*, 27 (1958), 249–254.

the medals he awarded to his soldiers were mere toys, to which the little corporal replied, "You call these toys? Well, you manage men with toys!"[46] Certainly badges of recognition are as eagerly sought today as they were in the early nineteenth century, as the status of the Phi Beta Kappa key, the military awards, and the numerous athletic letters and awards will testify. It is unlikely that thousands of men and boys would engage in the hard physical labor of practicing football under weather conditions ranging from blistering heat to subzero temperatures, on frozen ground and in seas of mud, if it were not for the cheers of the packed stands at the Saturday or Sunday game. A football captain of one of the better known university teams in the Midwest once told one of the present authors that he hated football as much as anything he knew, but loved the plaudits of the Saturday game crowd enough to suffer the five (six?) days of hard work which were necessary each week.

Even on the more serious side of life we see the importance of social recognition in motivating persons in the selection of their life jobs. Surely there would be fewer physicians and surgeons if it were not for the high status accorded them. There is nothing uniquely enticing about much of the actual work of these hard working and highly skilled professionals: surgery on the human body has something in common with dissection of other animals (from butchery to taxidermy), not the most eagerly sought of all trades, and the interruption of sleep by emergency night calls is not the most pleasant of experiences. The contacts with the dying and the grief-stricken relatives are not enjoyable; and the facts that these physicians and surgeons have limited time for vacations and possess a shorter life expectancy than some other professional men are real drawbacks. Why, then, do so many desire to enter the field? Surely the desire for social approval or recognition provides a large part of the answer. High esteem is accorded not only to the functions of the physician or surgeon, namely, those of saving and prolonging human life, reducing pain, and repairing broken bodies, but also the mystery which surrounds the work of these men adds to their status. Small wonder that physicians and surgeons enjoy the highest prestige of all professionally trained persons, and small wonder that so many desire to join the ranks of these overworked specialists.[47] They, no less than others, will work hard if the esteem of their fellow men is among their rewards.

It is of interest to note that one of America's better known psychologists believes that "In motivation, the craving for recognition, status, and personal appreciation turns out to be supreme, so much so that our con-

---

[46] E. A. Ross, *Social Control* (New York: The Macmillan Co., 1916), p. 89.

[47] It is true, of course, that many more persons *desire* to become physicians than *will* to do so. Will is constituted of desire, *plus* action that evidences not only the desire but also the intelligence and energy requisite to the attempt at goal attainment.

ceptions of procedure and policy in industrial relations, in education, and in psychotherapy are profoundly affected."[48]

The Desire for Security

The desire for security is reflected in the extreme conformity of a member of the primitive society wherein ostracism is tantamount to death, but it is also manifested in the urbanite's joining a labor union, in his paying taxes for police protection, in his paying relatively large sums for fire and accident insurance, in his spending long years preparing for a profession or other occupation, and in his general conservatism.[49] The term *Social Security* spells predictability for millions of Americans over the age of sixty-five. In our quest for security we perform many unpleasant tasks, but prefer to do this rather than run the risk of loss of security, as we define it in terms of houses, food, comfort, clothes, good health, and social position. The major part of the tax dollar is spent by the government in its efforts to provide security for its citizens; military expenditures, pensions for the old, the ill, the crippled, the blind, the deaf, and the unemployed are all expenditures for security. A study of the four basic wishes made among college students, who were asked to keep a record of their wishes for a week's period, revealed that the majority of the wishes recorded could be classified as wishes for security.[50]

The predictability of social roles on the part of one's associates spells security.[51] To the extent that this is true, the desire for knowledge is a function of the desire for security. Here the "Knowledge as pleasurable means" of Plato is recognized. Another version of security-through-knowledge is the time-honored axiom that "Ye shall know the truth, and the truth shall make you free." Freedom from fear, from uncertainty, from the unknown is bound to have as a consequence an enhancement of the feeling of security.

The reader will note that the desire for security does not have reference to categories of behavior as specific as those of the desires for inti-

---

[48] G. W. Allport, "The Ego in Contemporary Psychology," *Psychological Review*, L (1943), 472–473. Note the comments later in this chapter on the question of whether or not any one motive is strongest.

[49] The negative aspect of this acquired motive is the feeling of insecurity. As one psychologist has noted: "That human fears, anxieties, and feelings of insecurity have wide spread effects upon behavior is almost universally acknowledged." J. S. Brown, *The Motivation of Behavior* (New York: McGraw-Hill, 1961), p. 169.

[50] Maurice H. Krout, "Wishes and Behavior," *Journal of Abnormal and Social Psychology*, XXIX (1934), 253–268.

[51] *See* further discussion of this point in J. E. Hulett, Jr., "The Person's Time Perspective and the Social Role," *Social Forces*, XXIII, No. 2 (Dec. 1944); *also*, "Personality Under Catastrophe," by G. W. Allport, J. S. Bruner, and E. M. Jandorf, where the large part that uncertainty played in the feelings of insecurity among those persecuted by the Nazis is clearly indicated. This article is Ch. XXV of C. Kluckhohn and H. A. Murray, *Personality in Nature, Society, and Culture* (New York: Alfred A. Knopf, 1949).

mate response, recognition, and new experience. In fact, the threat to any of man's biogenic or sociogenic needs is a threat to his security. The deprivation of food, affection, social approval, variety of experiences, material possessions, class standing, or other status items results in feelings of insecurity. If man cannot predict the fulfillment of his needs, both biogenic and sociogenic, with a reasonable degree of certainty—the degree often determined by cultural values—he loses his sense of security. One social psychologist puts it this way:

> . . . security itself is obtained only when all seems to be going, and promises to go, pretty well. Serious frustration of any of man's desires can result in his feeling insecure. Thus, the wish for security has no dependable referent, being a highly generalized and diffuse classification based on a criterion which is essentially negative. It does not make too much sense to say that all people seek security, when the values they seek have only one thing in common; namely, that they seek them and feel disturbed if they fail in obtaining them. However, it is observable that all people seek to predict the future, and this is a positive wish, rather than merely a wish to avoid insecurity.

What other writers might classify as an expression of the wish for security seems in most instances to boil down to the search for prediction. We save money to insure that in the future we will have the necessities which it buys. We strive for education in order to understand our world and to predict what will occur in it. We accept religion, because it assures us that certain truths operate forever and that there is a predictable reward in the world beyond the grave. We accept a philosophy, even a dreary one like Schopenhauer's because in explaining the order of the universe and our relation to it, it renders the future predictable, and thus less terrifying. We lobby for tenure and retirement provisions to enable us to predict our vocational and economic future in the face of growing uncertainty of prediction in our social world. We take out life insurance in order to predict the future of our loved ones, even if we should die. We pass laws and hire men to enforce them in order to predict the behavior of others. We hold on to a mediocre job and refuse to take a chance on a possibly better one merely because the one is predictable and the other is not. Indeed, the lowering of one's level of aspirations or values, or the retreat from the fields of contest found so often among people who feel insecure over a prolonged period of time also seems relatable to this wish for predictability, since reducing one's aims to a level which one can easily reach, or not attempting that which is uncertain of outcome, negative though these actions may be, serves by elimination to increase the percentage of predictability in one's world.[52]

[52] William Bruce Cameron, University of South Florida, from an unpublished manuscript. Quoted with author's permission. (Harry Stack Sullivan, who did much to stress the interactionist approach to psychiatry, preferred to distinguish the motive to security as a function of man's cultural equipment from the motives to "satisfactions" as functions of man's bodily organization. The latter motives lead to

Just what the degrees of certainty are that a person considers to be adequate depends upon both the nature of the culture within which he lives, and the personal social values which have developed from his unique experiences within that culture. Some cultures, particularly the older, stable, and often rural societies, appear to demand a higher degree of security, whereas the newer, pioneering, frontier cultures, or distinctly urbanized societies, seemingly place a premium upon newness and variety at the expense of security and predictability. Although it is true that an act that would be deemed brash in one culture might be considered very conservative in the other, the difference in esteem for security is more apparent than real. The more advanced, complex culture seeks and needs predictability as much as the primitive and rural one, but it can provide it without sacrificing novelty and variety of experiences. Every culture has its own means of providing for security, and every culture that is destined to last will esteem some form of social organization within which predictability is possible. Stable and lasting societies, no less than integrated personalities, require predictability.

The importance of prediction of roles and of knowing one's status as a basis for security is further evidenced by the following passage written about the Ojibwa Indian of Ontario who spends the long winter months in complete isolation from others except for his wife and immature children. Having become adjusted to the lonely life of the winter hunt, he finds that he is not equipped for the communal life of the summer village wherein the families live in close proximity.

> Village life further intensifies his life, but it makes him uneasy. Something akin to claustrophobia sets in. He is irritated by the numbers of people close around him, they hem him in, they invade his privacy, they are *unknown forces he has no means to control*. He feels impelled, therefore, to reduce them to some kind of order; he must achieve the kind of lone ascendency to which he was accustomed in the winter.
>
> But this is difficult. Ojibwa culture does not provide a traditional hierarchy in which a man can find his place and in so doing a measure of stability. He can only continue wary and irritable, wondering about his status in the people's eyes. "What do they think of me? Do they know how many deer I killed? I wonder if they are jealous of me and want to kill me. What did so-and-so mean when he said this, and did not do that? I must watch him. Does he plan to get the jump on me? Does he want to make a fool of me? What is he doing now?"
>
> These are the thoughts of the usual Ojibwa, given expression during drunkenness and in the security of his home.[53]

---

performances in quest of food, drink, and sleep. *Conceptions of Modern Psychiatry* (Washington, D.C., William Alanson White Psychiatric Foundation, 1947), p. 6.

[53] Ruth Landes, "The Abnormal Among the Ojibwa," *Journal of Abnormal and Social Psychology*, XXXIII (Jan. 1938), pp. 20–21. Italics added. *See* p. 431 (fn.) in the present text for additional interpretation of the Ojibwa feelings of insecurity.

The ultimate, it would seem, in this lack of predictability of response is the attitude taken by the paranoid person. In his delusions of persecution, he looks with suspicion upon all persons, not knowing whether they are friends or enemies.

In a discussion of the desire for new experience, it was argued that simple things that are easily learned become ineffective as stimuli, that boredom is associated with repeated presentation of such stimuli, be it a simple song or puzzle. One might ask, then, how it is that in rituals relatively simple events are repeated over and over again, and quite voluntarily. Illustrations are readily available in the bedtime prayers which are so common, in the Lord's Prayer or *Pater Noster*, in the repetitions of "Hail Mary" of the Roman Catholic ritual, in the daily routine of five prayers of the devout Muslim in response to the muezzin's call. The answer seems to be, according to the "four wishes" framework, that these items continue to appeal *despite* their repetition and simplicity, and *because* of their security-giving capacity. The belief that such ritual will guarantee, or raise the probability, that certain desired goals will be reached (predictability), and the feeling of security that is a function or consequence of the ritual, more than offsets the reduced appeal to other acquired desires.

The problem of reconciling such acts as self-destruction (voluntary and accidental) with the desire for security is occasionally raised. Security is not always spelled in terms of physical safety, freedom from pain, or preservation of life. Prediction—sometimes in terms of degrees of probability, to be sure—*may* be best secured by one's committing suicide. The suicides of the Buddhist monks in South Viet Nam—in the very dramatic, highly conspicuous manner of death by fire in public places— were performed in the belief that a treasured value, freedom of Buddhist worship, could best be attained by self-sacrifice. Despite the extreme pain and the ensuing death, the act spelled security for the monks. Those who lose health and lives, gradually or suddenly, for the sake of loved ones or for an ideal, are none the less motivated by the desire that their values shall prevail, and they act thus to enhance the predictability that their goals will be realized, if not by them then by their survivors. Such motives, in the words of Walter Lippman, lead young men to die in battle and old men to plant trees whose shade they will never know.

SECURITY AND SOCIETY

Security involves predictability, and the latter demands a constancy of social structure, which in turn is a function of norms that are sanctioned. One is secure only if his positions within a social system are known and can be counted upon. The individual must know what his rights and obligations are, and others must also agree on the definitions of these rights and duties. When the definitions of the individual and the others coincide, the person is said to have *identity*.[54] He knows what he is supposed to do, others know, and he knows that they perceive his role as proper behavior. When there is disagreement between the perceptions of the person and his significant other, identity is lost, and with it the predictability upon which security depends. Social psychologist Nelson Foote puts it this way:

> Human beings are continually engaged in defining, reiterating, and re-defining their "nature" or character [acquired variable] as a means of regulating their behavior. The hazards of being unable to act in satisfying concert make it vital that these definitions persist, or else change in orderly schedule while keeping a semblance of continuity. Since every episode of social action requires identification of self and other as a premise of action by each, mutual characterization is an outcome of critical moment to all concerned.[55]

A closely related, if not identical, way of conceiving the relationship between the social structure and subjective security is provided by Emile Durkheim's concept of *anomie*.[56] The term has been variously translated as "disorganization," "normlessness," "deregulation." It denotes the social condition in which restraints (norms plus sanctions) upon one's behavior are inadequate, when one's position is poorly defined, or when there is a loss of identity. The latter occurs when circumstances rather suddenly place a person in a position, the norms of which are inadequately understood, that is, wherein a person has not learned and become accustomed to the expected behavior as defined by the norms. Durkheim comments that anomic behavior (suicide in this instance) ". . . results from man's activity's lacking regulation and his consequent suffering."[57] He illustrates this condition by citing the suicides committed by persons who suddenly find their economic position or status changed by economic crashes or panics, or those who have not adjusted to the position of a divorced person. It is not the poverty nor the celibate status that lead to *anomie*, but the novelty of it. Those used to or accustomed to such statuses do not become anomic. Thus, according to Durkheim, ". . . as the conditions

[54] The word *identity* is derived from the Latin *idem*, the same. Thus one attains his *identity* when there is a "sameness" in his and his affective others' perceptions. "*Identity*—the character of a particular self—*accrues from attributions and confirmations provided by significant others who constitute the audience around each other.* While with adulthood he can increasingly effect their responses, they nonetheless constitute him." Nelson Foote, "Anachronism and Synchronism in Sociology," *Sociometry*, 21 (March 1958), 23. Italics added.

[55] *Ibid.*, p. 22. In Ch. 8 this loss of identity in the form of embarrassment will be discussed.

[56] *Cf.* Durkheim's *Suicide* (translated by John A. Spaulding and George Simpson) (Glencoe, Ill.: The Free Press, 1951), pp. 241–276. The translators prefer the less common spelling of *anomy*.

[57] *Ibid.*, p. 258.

of life are [abruptly] changed, the standard according to which needs were regulated can no longer remain the same; . . . The scale is upset; but a new scale cannot be immediately improvised. . . . The limits are unknown between the possible and the impossible, what is just and what is unjust, legitimate claims and hopes and those which are immoderate."[58] Durkheim sums up the relationship of social structure to personal security in this way: "To free [the individual] from all social pressure is to abandon him to himself and demoralize him."[59] Thus security is seen as a constant relationship to norms and to the sanctions that support them, insuring continuity and stability of behavior patterns.

Such, then, are the four wishes. They, like the other secondary or acquired drives, are unconsciously learned.[60] Although it is possible for persons to become aware of their desires in terms of these classifications, it is rare to find persons who consciously label their actions. They remain as unconscious motivations for the most part, and the fact that a single act may fulfill more than one of the basic desires is often overlooked. Instance the remark that "For example, a puzzle once solved, even if accompanied by a burst of elation, no longer attracts the mature individual."[61] By showing others how he has solved the puzzle, one may secure recognition even though he may not derive much satisfaction from it in terms of variety of experience. As a matter of fact, we often attempt to learn complex acts, to solve puzzles of many sorts, primarily to display this technique to our fellow men, and thus to secure the satisfaction of other needs or desires.

COGNITIVE FACTORS AS SUBJECTIVE ASPECTS OF PERSONALITY

We have stressed the functional differences of the central nervous system and the autonomic nervous system. One way to illustrate the differences as they manifest themselves in human thought and action is to take note of the different experiences referred to when we say, on the one hand, "I know," "I think," or "I believe," and, on the other, "I feel." We have dealt with the latter phase of man's subjective equipment, and now turn attention to the former, or cognitive aspects. Just as it is important for clear thinking to distinguish the referents of "feel" and "believe," so is it important to note the tripartite nature of cognition and to define carefully the referents of such words as know, think, and believe. We now turn our

[58] *Ibid.*, pp. 252–253.

[59] *Ibid.*, p. 389.

[60] The question of just how they are learned puzzles all learning theorists. Association learning is apparently the mechanism involved, and is similar to that process as described in Ch. 5, dealing with ANS-CNS learning processes.

[61] Gordon Allport, "The Ego in Contemporary Psychology," *Psychological Review*, L (1943), 468.

attention to this task, noting particularly the relationship of concepts or ideas to motives.

Belief

Whatever definition of knowledge one accepts, there is need for a word that would refer to those cognitive experiences which fall outside of the realm of one's knowledge. This word in English is *belief*, which is a perception that begins where knowledge ends. This does not imply that the distinction between knowledge and belief is always clear. Rather, there is often a hazy and diffuse twilight zone wherein knowledge shades into belief. Nevertheless, beliefs are important in shaping one's behavior.

There are two categories of beliefs. One category is, as it were, "cut out of whole cloth," and numerous examples of this kind of belief are readily available in the child's belief in Santa Claus, the belief in ghosts, fairies, the magical potency of amulets and luck charms, or other objects of fantasy or superstition. The other category of beliefs, very different in character, is made up of the extrapolations of knowledge and is illustrated by the hunches, hypotheses, and theories of the scientifically disciplined person. These are the beliefs that one is logically obliged to develop on the bases of evidence at hand. The former category has no bases (at least no discernible bases) in fact, whereas the latter group is the logical projection of the known into the unexplored phases of experience. Both kinds affect one's behavior, and as far as the subject himself is concerned, both are equally real under certain specified circumstances. As noted, if a situation is *defined* as real, it might as well be real insofar as its consequences are concerned. This is often true, and to ignore these purely subjective beliefs in the study of any sociocultural episode is to omit items which are essential to a full sociopsychological understanding of the situation in question. The following section will provide evidence of this statement.

Concepts, Perceptions, and Motives

Attitudes represent the subjective emotional aspects of personality and, as indicated, are the essence of motivation. However, the action taken in response to these various biogenic and sociogenic motives cannot be explained solely in terms of these impulses to action. If we are to fully understand the "how" and the "what" of persons' actions, we must have recourse to the operation of the central nervous system.[62]

[62] See George A. Kelly, "Man's Construction of His Alternatives," in G. Lindzey (ed.) *Assessment of Human Motives* (New York: Rinehart and Company, 1958), pp. 33–64, for an exposition of the importance of cognition in human behavior. He conceives of *motivation* as an expendable concept. *See also* W. Moore and M. Tumin, "Some Social Functions of Ignorance," *American Sociological Review*, 14 (Dec. 1949).

To each of the countless episodes of his life, the individual brings two kinds of subjective predispositions—his feelings on the one hand and his knowledge (symbols, concepts, percepts, and skills) and his beliefs on the other. The complex of cognitive factors determines in significant degree the nature of the dynamic relationship between the person and the other objects in any particular episode of his life. Whether or not an episode becomes a crisis is as much a function of the knowledge (including skills) and beliefs of the individual as it is of the other inter-acting elements. A moment's reflection reveals to us how knowledge affects what will happen in any given episode; for example, as in a sudden spill into a river or lake, during an examination, in an encounter with an old friend or foe, in a riot, in a highly emotionally charged social situa-tion, or in any of a variety of difficult problems. What a person knows, how he thinks and what his verbal and other skills are—all become criti-cal, even in simple episodes. Although concepts as such will not motivate any action, they are always involved in action or behavior in directing the responses to the motives involved in the episode. The term *mind set* (as opposed to emotional predisposition or *feeling set* or attitude), has been used by some students of the problem to denote the predispositional character of ideas as they operate in any sociocultural episode involving the individual.

An example of the relation of cognitive factors to attitudes is found in a study of eighty-seven high school students who favored greater free-dom for young people with regard to driving automobiles. The subjects were lectured to by a person who advocated stricter control of young drivers. One group was informed of the lecture's content before hearing it, whereas the other group was instructed to evaluate the speaker but was not informed of his topic. It was discovered that those who knew of the topic beforehand found the speaker less convincing than did the other group. Had the topic been one toward which both groups held neutral attitudes, the results probably would have been significantly different.[63]

Nor need one look only to the layman for the distortive influence upon perception and overt behavior of his ideas, or mental sets. Studies have

[63] J. Allyn and L. Festinger, "The Effectiveness of Unanticipated Persuasive Communication," *Journal of Abnormal and Social Psychology*, 62 (1961), 40. Dem-onstration of the relationship between concepts and evaluation is provided by the *semantic differential* approach to the study of personality. This involves the placing in *semantic space* (on a continuum between extremes represented by such terms as "good—bad," "hard—soft," "fair—unfair," "strong—weak," "active—passive," and "positive—negative"), a mark indicating one's judgment of the appropriateness of terms such as these. "Profiles" drawn by connecting these points reveal attitudinal configurations of persons. Denotatively and/or connotatively, these terms involve attitudes. *Cf.* C. E. Osgood, G. Suci, and P. Tannenbaum, *The Measurement of Mean-ing* (Urbana: University of Illinois Press, 1957).

shown that experimenters with different hypotheses come to different conclusions even though the data are the same. In one instance a group of experimenters (Es) was informed that they would probably discover mean ratings of +5 (on a scale of −10 to +10) for all subjects to be rated by them as to their success or failure, and whose pictures were presented to them. A group of equal size was told that they would probably find ratings of −5. Even though the Es read identical instructions to their subjects, "The lowest mean rating [in all studies] obtained by *any* E expecting high ratings was higher than the highest mean rating obtained by *any* E expecting low ratings from his Ss"[64] Here we see carefully drawn evidence of the influence of *mind set* upon perception.

To illustrate further the way in which concepts help us explain social behavior, let us take some situation that is common to several different cultures and observe how the people behave toward this common phenomenon. Mental illness occurs in all cultures and, with few exceptions, attempts are made to return the mentally ill persons to normality in terms of what is normal for that particular culture. However, the means by which this return to normality is attempted vary considerably, and the concepts of mental illness held by the different cultures play a dominant part in the selection of the means. The following examples illustrate the point.

One example of prescientific concepts, which explains the behavior of the people of the community toward psychotics, is found among the Ojibwa Indians of Ontario, who live in an impoverished land where the winter hunt's meager return sometimes leads to psychosis with cannibalistic involvements. For the various forms that this mental illness takes, the Ojibwa have a single term, "windigo."

> Windigo is a mythological and supernatural figure, a giant skeleton made of ice, that flourishes in the wintertime only and is an insatiable cannibal. It epitomizes all those unhappy souls who die of starvation in the winter. It is a frenzied character who howls and crashes through the land, threatening swift and horrible doom. The insane person is said to be possessed by the windigo spirit, compelled to obey its demands.
>
> The mythic windigo, since he is a creature of ice, is said to die in the summer and to be revived in all his malignancy in the winter, and the Ojibwa see in this a rationalization of the fact that windigo pathologies appear in the wintertime and are alleviated in the summer. They will sometimes even suffer a windigo to live through the summer in the hope that this period of relief will effect a cure. It is more common, however, to take advantage of the supposed summer enfeeblement of

[64] Studies by K. L. Fode and R. Rosenthal, reported by R. Rosenthal in "On the Social Psychology of the Psychological Experiment," *Science*, 51 (Summer 1963), 289–270.

the evil spirit to dispatch the violent windigo, killing him and allowing the corpse to smolder for four days.[65]

Clearly, the Ojibwa concepts of the nature of the mental illness direct the response which they make to the fear that the windigo will harm more of them. Without knowledge of their concepts, their behavior would not be fully understood.

In another Indian setting the concepts about mental illness are remarkably different from those of the Ojibwa. In his study of the Mohave Indians in southwestern United States, George Devereux found that the Mohaves perceive mental illness in a modern way, see psychotics as victims of an illness, "charactereologically determined," and treat—them as any sick person would be treated. He reports that the Mohaves are ". . . not only lenient toward the insane but are mildly amused by their odd behavior."[66] The author observed that there was no handicap placed upon the Mohave who had been mentally ill and had recovered. Having perceived the person as being ill, there was no effort at concealment during the illness and therefore no felt need to treat him differently from other well people when he had recovered. It is of interest to note that this "primitive" tribe of American Indians had developed toward their mentally disturbed members an objective attitude which came to western European civilization only in the nineteenth century. The contrast with the Ojibwa conception of mental illness is, of course, most striking.

More familiar to the reader, perhaps, are the prescientific concepts that flourished in the medieval period in Europe. At that time much of the unusual behavior of men, women, and children was explained in terms of the possession of the body by supernatural beings, sometimes the devil and sometimes lesser supernatural functionaries. These beliefs were not restricted to the lower classes, a fact attested to by the following excerpts from a speech by a Burgundian judge in the time of Henry IV of France at the dedication of an abbey:

[65] Landes, op. cit., p. 25. For a different interpretation of this psychosis, see Seymour Parker, "The Wiitiko Psychosis in the Context of Ojibwa Personality and Culture," American Anthropologist, 62 (1960). Parker sees more than the threat of starvation involved in this psychosis. He notes that a "premature and severe training for independence and self-reliance lays the ground work for the very characteristic that it attempts to discourage—dependency cravings." (p. 606). Further, to have failed in hunting also signifies to the hunter that he is "empty and worthless" and that he is ". . . being rejected by significant others in the social environment." (p. 168). Thus the Wiitiko (or windigo) is ". . . a phantasy figure symboling the wider circle of significant others who continue to frustrate the dependency cravings of the adult and constitute threats to his vulnerable self-esteem." (p. 619).

[66] Mohave Ethnopsychiatry and Suicide: The Psychiatric Knowledge and the Psychic Disturbances of an Indian Tribe (Smithsonian Institution, Bureau of American Ethnology, Bulletin 175, U.S. Government Printing Office, 1961), p. 35.

I believe that the sorcerers could form an army equal to that of Xerxes who had one million, eight hundred thousand men. Trois-Echelles, one of those best acquainted with the craft of sorcerers, states that under King Charles IV, France alone had three hundred thousand sorcerers (some read it as thirty thousand). . . . Are we not justified in believing that since those days the number has increased at least by half? As to myself, I have no doubts, since a mere glance at our neighbors will convince us that the land is infested with this unfortunate and damnable vermin. . . . Now to return to our neighbors, Savoie is not yet emptied, since she sends us daily an infinite number of people possessed by devils who, when conjured up, tell us that they were put into the bodies of those poor people by sorcerers . . . the sorcerers reach everywhere by the thousands; they multiply on this earth like the caterpillars in our gardens.[67]

The author tells us that "This inflammatory but very sincere speech voiced a belief and a desire common to millions." With this conception of the nature of man's personality ills, it is not to be wondered at that men behaved toward the psychotic, neurotic, and deviant personality as they did. The expression, "beating the devil" out of someone has come to us from that period, surely. An instance of this behavior is found in the treatment accorded a sixteenth-century girl who was given to abnormal behavior.

Because it is heard that in order to prevent a sorcerer from doing evil, it was necessary to obtain a new broom made of birch wood and to beat with it the said sorcerer, and fearing lest the above-said Francoise be a sorceress, since we saw that what she was doing was something supernatural and beyond human ken, we demanded that a new broom be produced. This was brought to us from the jail; we beat the said Francoise with this broom and hit her on the body several times, doing which however, we used up the broom before the said Francoise came to.[68]

This treatment, however, failed and it was not until the court ordered the head and armpit hair removed that the girl was deemed cured and permitted to leave the court's immediate custody, being placed under the "parole" of a reliable person. There is, of course, an extensive literature that concerns the attempts of the medievalists to treat mental deviants. In general the supernatural conceptions were invoked when natural concepts failed to afford an explanation.[69]

[67] Quoted by Gregory Zilboorg, *The Medical Man and the Witch* (Baltimore: Johns Hopkins Press, 1935), pp. 74–75.

[68] *Ibid.*, pp. 78–79.

[69] One of the most explicit and most interesting documents on this subject is the seventeenth century work entitled *Demoniality*, written by a friar named Ludovico Maria Sinistrari, and translated from the Latin into English by Montague Summers (London: Fortune Press, 1927). *See also* Ari Kiev, *Magic, Faith, and Healing* (New York: Free Press of Glencoe, 1964).

At different times in the history of mental disease, the mentally ill have been looked upon as religiously inspired (Joan of Arc), or as inhabited by devils (*The Bible*, Matt. 8:28), or as possessed by powers of witchcraft and magic (Colonial days). Throughout the seventeenth century (beginning in England and spreading to Colonial America), people were tried, convicted, and punished as collaborators with the devil and his witches. Two hundred and fifty persons were arrested and tried in Salem, Massachusetts, in the year 1691–1692, and of these, fifty were condemned, nineteen were executed, two died in prisons, and one died of torture. Of this Colonial period Deutsch writes,

> The type of testimony that was accepted as truth by the unbelievably credulous judges, and that was instrumental in sending a score of innocents to their death, is exemplified in the interrogation of Sarah Carrier, eight, whose mother Martha was hanged as a witch. Awed by the solemnity of the inquisitors, her mind excited by fears and fancies intensified by leading questions, the child testified in this vein:
> "How long has thou been a witch?"
> "Ever since I was six years old."
> "How old are you now?"
> "Near eight years old."
> "Who made you a witch?"
> "My mother. She made me set my hand to the book."
> "You said you saw a cat once. What did the cat say to you?"
> "It said it would tear me to pieces if I would not set my hand to the book." (that is, the Devil's Book.)
> "How did you know that it was your mother?"
> "The cat told me so, that she was my mother."[70]

This situation continued on into the eighteenth century but the more enlightened population increasingly spoke out against the practice.

> Nevertheless as late as 1716 a woman and her nine-year old daughter were hanged at Huntington, England, after being convicted of selling their souls to the devil. It was not until 1736 that the laws against witchcraft were repealed in the United Kingdom, and local persecutions against the insane suspected of practicing witchcraft and sorcery continued intermittently for a long time thereafter.[71]

These examples of the manner in which concepts shape men's perceptions, which in turn influence their efforts to treat mental illness, it is hoped will suffice to emphasize the importance of concepts in any study of social behavior. The way in which people proceed to solve problems

[70] Albert Deutsch, *The Mentally Ill in America* (New York: Columbia University Press, 1946), p. 35.
[71] *Ibid.*, p. 23.

is dependent upon the way in which they perceive the factors interacting in the problem situation.[72]

Another way of stating the relationship between concepts and motives is to point out that the autonomic nervous system forms the problems (be they fears, desires, loves, or hates) whereas the central nervous system in its higher phases attempts to solve these problems. We desire something because of our emotional learning, (the *why* of human behavior), but we select certain paths toward the fulfillment of our needs (the *how* and *what* of human behavior) through the operation of the cognitive phases of our neurological system. Falling in love, wanting to be a successful person in the eyes of our fellows, or hating an object are all the results of emotional learning. The solutions are intellectual in nature, affected by and closely related to the emotional, but clearly distinguishable from it. Concepts are thus not motivational in scope, but concern themselves primarily with giving direction to (canalizing) our attempts to meet the demands of our motives.

It is important to note, however, that it is not simply the felt need that shapes one's perceptions and his consequential acts. After careful consideration of research in the field of perception, one social psychologist concludes that ". . . there is now enough evidence before us to suggest that not the *amount* of need but the *way* in which a person learns to *handle* his needs determines the manner in which motivation and cognition selectively will interact. . . . On the whole, then, [perceptual] selectivity reflects the nature of the person's mode of striving for goals rather than the amount of need which he seems to be undergoing."[73]

In other words, the parts played by values and habits other than the particular need, such as hunger, must be considered if one is to understand the relationships between the cognitive factors of conception and perception on the one hand and motivation and overt behavior on the other.

HABIT AND WILL

Closely related to motivation, but not identical with it, are the referents of *habit* and *will*. These are commonly used words, by both layman and

---

[72] "The Evasion of Propaganda: How Prejudiced People Respond to Anti-Prejudice Propaganda," by Eunice Cooper and Marie Johada, illustrates the way in which different concepts prevent a meeting of minds in interpreting perceptual experience. *Journal of Psychology*, XXIII (1947), 15–25.

[73] J. S. Bruner, "Social Psychology and Perception," in E. E. Maccoby, T. M. Newcomb, and E. L. Hartley, *Readings in Social Psychology* (New York: Henry Holt & Co., 1958), p. 89. *See* this source for discussion of a more strictly psychological (as opposed to social psychological) *mind set* as a predisposing factor in selective perception, *e.g.*, the part played by surprise in delayed perception of objects. This need not involve *social* factors per se.

social scientist, yet their definition often is something less than precise. The following paragraphs are given to a discussion of these symbols.

Habit

Whimsy, caprice, and irregularity can never be the basis of life. There must be a persistence and regularity in behavioral relationships if the predictability that is the very foundation of security and order can be assured. There is need for a word which denotes the persistent and persevering aspects of human behavior, and *habit* is the word best fitted for that purpose. Repetition is not sufficient to define habit, and such repetitive and complex phases of human action as promptness or brutality are not, per se, habits. Such actions are deliberately effected and guided. Losing one's temper, insofar as this is meant the overt action of throwing a tantrum or striking someone, is not habit. Such action is in part a function of habit, but is not habit as such. The referents of habit are those behavioral aspects which reveal themselves on impulse, in response to sudden demands, which are automatic and therefore nondeliberate, and for which specific conscious attention is not a prerequisite. These predispositions to action are acquired on the cognitive, emotional, and motor levels of learning. "As in common usage, this term refers to a connection between stimuli and/or responses that has become virtually automatic through experience, usually through repeated trials. So, for example, '1492' automatically elicits 'Columbus' from most Americans; a printed word elicits certain manual responses in the skilled typist; a red traffic signal elicits braking in the motorist."[74] Having developed certain concepts and percepts, one does not have to deliberate upon the way in which he perceives an object or event; one does not have to figure out the meaning of such symbols as "Help!", "Fire!", "Your grade is an A." Our attitudes reveal to us, without further experience, how we feel about objects, and when confronted with them we react with characteristic attraction or revulsion. When we speak, write, walk, dance, jump, or play a musical instrument, we do not, unless we are novices, deliberate about our actions. It is, then, this perseveration of attitudes, the consistency of the overlearned perceptions, and the automatic motor behavior that are denoted by the term *habit*.

Will

The concept *will* is of little concern to psychologists and sociologists. One looks in vain for it in the indexes of the social psychological texts, and it is rarely discussed in the literature of psychology or social psy-

---

[74] Bernard Berelson and Gary Steiner, *Human Behavior—An Inventory of Scientific Findings* (New York: Harcourt, Brace & World, 1964).

chology.[75] Does this mean that the concept is unimportant, or that other concepts in social psychology perform its function? Both layman and social psychologist use such phrases as *will power, weak-willed, strong-willed,* and *free will.* What is the referent, (or referents) of the word *will?*

That it denotes something more than the acquired or innate motives seems clear. The old axiom "If wishes were horses, beggars would ride" suggests (among other things) that will is more than desire, more than motivation. A strong-willed person is recognized only by his actions. The referent of will *is* action. Will is a function of: (1) motive in the form of a desire for some goal which is strong enough to induce one to sacrifice other values that are incompatible with goal attainment; (2) a knowledge of the means necessary to goal attainment as well as the nature of the goal; (3) the intelligence and energy requisite to goal seeking; plus (4) *the actual expenditure of energy in a manner appropriate to attainment of the goal.* Another has defined will as "action executed in the pursuance of human desires."[76] Thus, will is a complex of cognitive, emotional, and overt behavioristic components. Motives, knowledge, and beliefs are necessary, but not sufficient, to define will. Will is manifested in action in striving toward a goal, which may or may not be attained. A man of will is a man who tries.

Is Will Free?

Few topics are as capable of evoking overt controversy among today's college and university students as that of "free will." A current religious encyclopedia asserts that the problem of "free will is one of the three or four most important philosophical problems of all time." The assertion that man's will is not free is *willfully* challenged or supported. In part, this is a function of semantics, but in part a matter of well-learned and emotionally bolstered philosophical positions.

Semantically, the problem involves the identification of human freedom with the belief in free will. Had men chosen to use the term *inde-*

---

[75] During the last twenty years, only forty-four entries under *will* are listed in *Psychological Abstracts,* and of these thirty-four are in foreign journals. This contrasts sharply with the thousands of entries under *motive, drive, habit, trait,* and so on.

[76] K. I. Lebedev, "The Question of Presentation of the Theory of Will in Psychological Textbook," *Sovietskaya Pedagogica,* No. 1 (1950), 64–67, as translated for *Psychological Abstracts* by R. A. Bauer of Harvard University. Another writer, M. Dybowski, sees the strength of will correlated with physical racial types, being deficient in "subnordic" and "lapanoid" types. This is curious in view of "iron-curtain" attempts to support the position of the biologist, Lysenko, who saw any biological determinism as incompatible with communism. *Kwartalnik Psychologiczny,* 12 (1947), 53–58. Reported in *Psychological Abstracts.* Since that time Lysenko has fallen into disfavor with the Soviet authorities.

pendent will, or *autonomous will,* in lieu of free will, perhaps the concept would not have become so controversial. Too, the equating of *will* with *wish* adds to the confusion. As we shall see below, there is no incompatibility between the perception of man's will as a learned aspect of human nature and man's freedom.[77]

In the present tri-dimensional interactionist frame of reference, the components of will—cognitive, emotional, and behavioral—are all natural functions of human experience. One's will, as any other aspect of his personality, is not independent of other components. All modern social science supports this view of man's behavior in general and of his will in particular.

But how, one may ask, can man be free if his will is determined, that is, is a function of natural interactive experiences?

Human freedom, both objectively and subjectively, exists when man's biological heritage, environment, and learned or acquired attributes are so constituted and related that his basic needs and desires, innate and acquired, are fulfilled. A free man is the one who understands himself as a human being, whose body is whole and healthy in its cognitive, emotional, and motor potentialities, and whose environment permits the operation of his will in the successful pursuit of life's satisfactions.

The following passage expresses the organism-environment-subject interactionist perception of the nature of human freedom.[78]

> One is born with certain potentialities like thinking, imagining, loving, hating. These potentialities are in some degree realized, actualized in experience—and of course not otherwise. That there are causal conditions involved or required for their realization and conservation is a fact. But that those necessary conditions deprive one of freedom is a curious *non sequitur.* Such a notion probably arises from the deeply ingrained, and at least partly unconscious, belief that to be free is somehow to be able to act without motivation or determination. Such a

---

[77] On this issue see Lawson G. Lowry, "Psychic Determinism and Responsibility," *Psychiatric Quarterly,* 27 (1953), 543–562. Lowry holds that "Determinism and free [as opposed to *independent*] will are not incompatible." One may also wish to look at W. Braunshausen, "Free will in the Light of Experimental Psychology and Modern Science," *Revue des Sciences Pedagogiques,* 9 (1947), 38–46.

[78] We might quibble with an occasional use of words, but in general the passage is acceptable. Others have defined freedom in the absence of a belief in free (independent) will. One holds, in keeping with the Freudian orientation, that "a man is free only to the extent that his behavior is not unconsciously motivated at all." John Haspers, "Meaning and Free Will," *Philosophy and Phenomenological Research,* 10 (1950), p. 329. Another writes: "Although the human will is determined in its functioning, a person experiences freedom to the extent of his capacity for change in the direction of self-realization." Erich Rotthaus, "Concerning the Freedom and Lack of Freedom of the Human Will," *Jahrbuch für Psychologie und Psychotherapie,* 2 (1954), 169–174; as translated by E. W. Eng (Antioch College) for *Psychological Abstracts,* 29 (1955), p. 196.

belief in effect implies that man is in some sense supernatural. To be able to think clearly, to feel intensely, to be able to enjoy the works of nature and art, to be able to love and to hate when objective situations warrant is to be free. . . . The notion that to be genuinely free is to be able to ignore or defy objective conditions is another curious idea.

Because these human abilities do not develop out of thin air but from specifiable conditions of human life and require comparable conditions for their maintenance in no way reduces one to the status of a being or an entity which is the plaything of operant forces. Indeed, the opposite is the case. The important point to notice is that when human potentialities are *not* realized because of conditions which are opposed to human development, then one is *not* free. Then one is the helpless and will-less instrument of other human beings or nonhuman events.

Because man is a natural being in the world, he can exist only by taking advantage of those aspects of nature which are in his favor or can be turned to his account. To be able to use them, to manipulate them, to develop them, or simply to enjoy them is to live in accordance with natural conditions of human life. And to the extent that man can do so he is free, or in other words, man is free when he is determined by the requirements and conditions of his own nature; and only when he expresses his nature can values and ideals have genuine authority or appeal. . .

No kind of freedom is possible for long unless the economic and political conditions of freedom exist. Because man is an inter-personal, or bio-cultural being, his fate is inextricably bound up with that of his society.[79]

So it is that man is free *because* of his ordered relationship between his own dynamic, thinking, feeling, and willing nature and other aspects of nature, and not because he can escape, defy, or deny the natural order. Our hopes for an improved world rest upon our discovering and applying learning principles that will develop the kinds of wills compatible with such a world.

Which Motive Is Strongest?

The anecdote is told of a gentleman visiting his neighbor, an older friend who was baby sitting for his grandson. Upon entering the house, the visitor was met with a most unpleasant verbal squall from the three-year old child who was sitting on the floor. Conversation under these circumstances was difficult, and the visitor finally inquired about the reason for the persistent crying. When told that it was caused by laziness, he expressed doubt that this could be so, but agreed with the judgment when told that the child was sitting on a tack. The implausibility, and

[79] Patrick Mullahy, "Will, Choice, and Ends," *Psychiatry*, 12 (1949), 384–385.

therefore the humor, of this anecdote, arises from the fact that we normally assume that the desire to avoid or escape pain would take precedence over a desire to avoid moving oneself. In general, such an assumption is tenable, but not always. As in the case of any motive, it must be placed in the context of the total situation if its strength or significance is to be understood. The controversy over which motive is the strongest is as time honored as it is needless. As a general statement, it can be said that the deprivation of the means of satisfying any one of these several motives in the adult human being is likely to focus the attention of the person upon that need or motive. It does not seem necessary to belabor the obvious fact that if one is in danger of burning, of freezing, of suffocating, or of being crushed, the needs for optimum temperatures, access to oxygen, or greater freedom of movement, respectively, become paramount at the time of such crises. This is freely granted, even insisted upon.

However, to go beyond this agreement and to designate one of the biogenic or sociogenic motives as *the* primary mover of all men at all times is not warranted. To many a martyr loyalty to a belief or cause took precedence over the motive to avoid pain or to preserve life. In today's culture, the desire for recognition that a slender figure will bring is given primacy over the hunger impulse. Social approval desires inhibit many a sexual impulse, and security needs yield to desires for thrills and novel experiences. The closest to assigning priority to motives in general that one can logically come is to label those goals which are paramount for any given individual or group, *whatever they may be*, as religious. The fact that they have been given priority determines the category, rather than the nature of the motivating goals. We now turn attention to this category of religion as it is manifested in attitudes.

SOCIAL PSYCHOLOGY AND THE RELIGIOUS ATTITUDE

That there is something real to which the phrase *religious attitude* refers is probably not open to serious question. However, just what the referent is cannot be stated at this time in a way that will secure the consensus of either laymen or social scientists. This is not because the concept of religious attitude, or simply religion, has been ignored by the social scientists, for indeed this has not been the case. Religious behavior has long been a favorite topic for research and writing among anthropologists,[80]

[80] Representative sources are: Franz Boas, *General Anthropology* (Boston: D. C. Heath and Co., 1938); J. G. Fraser, *The Golden Bough* (New York: The Macmillan Co., 1922); R. H. Lowie, *Primitive Religion* (New York: Boni Liveright, 1924); B. Malinowski, *Coral Gardens and Their Magic* (London: George Allen and Unwin, Ltd., 1935); E. Sapir and others, *Religious Life* (New York: D. Van Nostrand, 1929); W. D. Wallis, *Religion in Primitive Society* (New York: F. S. Crofts and Co., 1939); W. W. Howells, *The Heathens* (Garden City, N.Y.: Doubleday, 1962).

and to a somewhat lesser extent among sociologists.[81] The subject of religion or religious attitudes is conspicuous by its absence from social psychology text books, though individual psychologists and social psychologists have written about the topic.[82]

However, most of the writings are concerned with the sociological and institutional functions of religions, and have not given much space or attention to the problem of definition of religion or the religious attitude. Nor do the works of those writing from a church-oriented or sectarian view aid the reader much in his quest for a consensual definition.[83] Laymen in general do not use the concept in similar ways.

A study, in which social scientists were asked to give their definitions of religion, resulted in sixty-eight responses, no two of which were exactly alike.[84]

To serve as a significant symbol, the word *religious* must have a more homogeneous referent than is currently assigned by its many users. To some persons religion means adherence to rituals, to others it denotes the seeking or the acceptance of explanations of life's basic problems, and to still others it is constituted mainly of awe-inspiring experiences or security-giving beliefs and practices. However, rather than discuss at length what religion is *not*, we will present a concept of religion that can be understood and tested in every way possible by the reader.

Whereas the anthropologist and sociologist seek to isolate the institutional, organizational, and ritualistic aspects of religion, as social psychologists we will restrict our quest to the identification of the religious attitude, and the part this attitude plays in personality.

The attitude that appears to be common in all religious relationships

[81] E. Durkheim, *The Elementary Forms of Religious Life* (Glencoe, Ill.: The Free Press, 1947); C. Kirkpatrick, *Religion in Human Affairs* (New York: John Wiley and Sons, 1929); W. Goode (*Religion Among the Primitives* (New York: The Free Press of Glencoe, 1951);) J. Wach, *Sociology of Religion* (Chicago: University of Chicago Press, 1944); Max Weber, *Sociology of Religion* (Boston: Beacon Press, 1963); *The Religion of India*, tr. by H. H. Gerth and D. Martindale (Glencoe, Ill.: The Free Press, 1958); *Ancient Judaism*, tr. by Gerth and Martindale (Glencoe, Ill.: The Free Press, 1952); *The Religion of China*, tr. by Gerth (Glencoe, Ill.: The Free Press, 1951); J. M. Yinger, *Religion and the Struggle for Power* (Durham, N. Carolina: Duke University Press, 1946); J. M. Yinger, *Religion, Society and the Individual* (New York: The Macmillan Co., 1957); Gerhard Lenski, *The Religious Factor* (Garden City, N.Y.: Doubleday, 1961).

[82] G. W. Allport, *The Individual and His Religion* (New York: The Macmillan Co., 1960); J. Dewey, *A Common Faith* (New Haven, Conn.: Yale University Press, 1940); K. Dunlap, *Religion: Its Function in Human Life* (New York: McGraw-Hill, 1946); W. James, *The Varieties of Religious Experiences* (New York: Longman's, Green and Co., 1904); Walter H. Clark, *The Psychology of Religion* (New York: The Macmillan Co., 1958).

[83] F. E. D. Schleiermacher, *On Religion* (New York: Harper and Brothers, 1958), pp. 26–27. W. E. Zuurdeeg, *An Analytical Philosophy of Religion* (New York: Abingdon Press, 1958), p. 14.

[84] W. Clark, "How do Social Scientists Define Religion?" *Journal of Social Psychology*, 47 (1958), pp. 143–148.

is a positive emotional relationship, an identification, with some object or objects. However, it would be pointless to label as religious *all* positive emotional relationships between man and his object world. Logic, and the facts presented to us, seem to warrant the retention of the concept religious to denote those relationships wherein people have learned to feel that certain things, material and nonmaterial, are sacred, inviolable, worthy of veneration and protection. *The religious attitude defines man's ultimate values.* These values may have supernatural aspects, but they need not; from the viewpoint of social psychology there may be secular as well as supernatural religious attitudes.[85] This definition is not, the reader may readily recognize, a novel one. It is identical with some and similar to numerous others that have been suggested over the years.

Sociologist Talcott Parson stresses the part played by attitudes in religion. He writes that:

Thus though religious ideas on the sophisticated levels are "philosophical" in content, we will not speak of them being religious so long as the basis of interest is merely intellectual, the solution of baffling cognitive problems. They become religious only so far as a commitment in emotion and action to their implications becomes involved, as, in that sense, to quote Durkheim, they are "taken seriously."[86]

Will Herberg approaches the definition of religious attitudes this way: "If you wish to discover what a person's religion is, find out what it is that he will not tolerate."[87] Theologian Paul Tillich has stated that ". . . religion is what concerns us ultimately."[88] A sociologist and student of religion, agreeing essentially with this starting point, notes that man may develop ". . . a system of beliefs and practices by means of which a group of people struggles with these ultimate problems of human life . . . but they [the problems] express first of all an underlying emotional need, not a group of rationally conceived problems."[89] This statement is quite in keeping with the tri-dimensional frame of reference developed in this text. *As an attitude, religion sets or defines problems, and does not solve them.* Once a value acquires the status of being ultimate, the problem becomes one of how to preserve the value involved, of how to meet the attending problems that this value sets. Death is no problem unless we value life; misery for our children is no problem unless we value their happiness and welfare; interference with the questing of the inquiring

[85] *Cf.* Gerhard Lenski, *The Religious Factor* (Garden City, N.Y.: Doubleday, 1963), for a comparable definition.

[86] "Motivation of Religious Belief and Behavior," in Louis Schneider, (ed.) *Religion, Culture and Society* (New York: John Wiley and Sons, 1964), p. 167.

[87] From a colloqium held at the University of Illinois.

[88] Quoted in J. Milton Yinger, *Religion, Society, and the Individual* (New York: The Macmillan Co., 1957), p. 9.

[89] *Ibid.*, p. 9.

mind is no problem unless one holds academic and scholarly freedom as
a value, and so on. Thus, one is not religious per se, but only with reference to some value which he holds. To say that one is religious reveals
as little as to inform someone that a person loves, hates, or fears. Until we
are informed *what* he loves, hates, fears, or is religious about, we know
little about him.

Herberg's formula for discovering one's religious attitudes is of use
in the study of religious attitudes. When a truly religious person perceives
that his religious objects, those which he judges to be worthy of defend-
ing, are being challenged, he will attempt to thwart or stop any attack
upon the object. The following passage illustrates the point:

> Strong men will be moved to tears by the thought that a cow will be
> or is being sacrificed by Muslims, even though this is done in strict
> seclusion so as not to offend Hindu susceptibilities. The sight of a cow
> being openly led away for sacrifice often arouses Hindus to fanatical
> frenzy, resulting in blood riots; in one of the districts of the United
> Provinces in 1931 eleven Muslims were brutally killed by a crowd of
> Hindus, simply because a Muslim landholder sent a haunch of venison
> to one of his tenants and the villagers, quick to imagine evil, thought
> that it was beef.[90]

Reaction to attack upon a religious object need not be, in fact most
frequently is not, this violent. Yet the pages of history are filled with
episodes in which fortunes, health, family, and life itself have been sacri-
ficed in the defense of religious values. No understanding of a personality
can be called complete that does not comprehend which of one's many
values are to be given priority when, or if, a person is called upon to
choose among them. Everyone has a hierarchy of values, and those values
which he will yield last are, by definition, his religious values.

Can a Person Be Irreligious?

Unless one chooses to define religion in terms of one of the many
varieties of religion, and to judge others ethnocentrically, the reply to the
above query must be in the negative. The only persons who are irreligious are those for whom nothing is sacred, nothing is worth working,
sacrificing, spending, fighting for. It is difficult to conceive of such a
person. It has been suggested that the psychopath is irreligious in that
he cares only about himself, that he has no sense of shame, feels no
obligation to contribute anything to others. However, so long as he has
values that sustain activity in the pursuit of those values, then, however
self-oriented they may be, they are religious. A more likely candidate is
the depressed mentally ill person who has given up trying to remain

90 L. S. S. O'Malley, *Popular Hinduism* (London: Cambridge University Press,
1935), p. 17.

active, trying to remain alive. We also see approximations of this irreligious state in persons who are easily bored, who have no long-run goals toward which they are striving.

SUMMARY

The acquired personal characteristics are those modifications of mental, emotional, and motor potentials which are brought by the individual to each episode or situation in which he participates. These constitute but one category of variables and attributes which, in interaction with other categories, constitute the personality. There is a tendency on the part of people to perceive these subjective features to be the total personality.

The emotional components of personality are comprised of attitudes in the form of biases and prejudices, of guilt and shame, and these make up one's conscience, which is largely but not solely a social product. All motives are attitudes but not all attitudes are motives. The learned, or sociogenic, motives fall into four major categories—the four wishes of Thomas and Znaniecki: for new experience, for recognition, for response or affection, and for security. Categories of sociogenic motives which are comparable to these have been given different labels by other social psychologists.

Cognitive factors of belief and knowledge determine the direction in which one will move in response to his motives, but the former do not themselves constitute motives. Belief denotes two cognitive relationships, the one being an extrapolation of knowledge, such as scientific theories, and the other being "cut out of whole cloth," subjective inventions such as a belief in Santa Claus.

Closely related to motivation are the referents of *habit* and *will*. Habit is the word which best denotes the repetitive and automatic responses to stimuli. Will is a function of motive, knowledge or opinion, energy, and the actual action which is appropriate to the end desired.

Although none of the biogenic or sociogenic motives is, per se, strongest (any given motive may at a particular time, and under special stage settings, assume priority) in every culture and in nearly every individual certain objects are given sacred status and are defended or supported even at great cost to the individual. When this occurs, the supporting attitudes are called religious. The only irreligious person is the one for whom nothing is sacred.

SUGGESTED READINGS

BINDRA, DALBIR. *Motivation* (New York: The Ronald Press, 1959).
BROWN, J. S. *The Motivation of Behavior* (New York: McGraw-Hill, 1961).
DURKHEIM, E. *Suicide*. Translated by J. A. Spaulding and G. Simpson (Glencoe, Ill.: The Free Press, 1951).

GOODE, WILLIAM. *Primitive Religion* (New York: The Free Press of Glencoe, 1951).

HOWELLS, W. W. *The Heathens* (Garden City, N.Y.: Doubleday, 1962).

LENSKI, GERHARD. *The Religious Factor* (Garden City, N.Y.: Doubleday, 1963).

LINDZEY, G. (ed.). *Assessment of Human Motivation* (New York: Rinehart and Co., 1958).

LYND, HELEN MERRILL. *On Shame and the Search for Identity* (New York: Harcourt, Brace and Co., 1958).

MACCOBY, E. E., T. M. NEWCOMB, and E. E. HARTLEY. *Readings in Social Psychology* (New York: Henry Holt and Co., 1958).

MASLOW, A. H. *Motivation and Personality* (New York: Harper and Brothers, 1954).

McCLELLAND, D. C., J. W. ATKINSON, R. A. CLARK, and E. L. LOWELL. *The Achievement Motive* (New York: Appleton-Century-Crofts, 1953).

MOSCOVICI, S., "Attitudes and Opinions," *Annual Review of Psychology 1963* (Palo Alto, Calif.: Annual Review, Inc., 1963).

OSGOOD, C. E., G. SUCI, P. TANNEBAUM. *The Measurement of Meaning* (Urbana: University of Illinois Press, 1957).

Nebraska Symposium on Motivation. (Lincoln, Neb.: University of Nebraska Press, 1953–1964).

SCHOPENHAUER, ARTHUR. *The Essays of Arthur Schopenhauer*, T. B. Saunders (translator) (New York: Willey Book Co., 1937).

SKINNER, B. F. *Verbal Behavior* (New York: Appleton-Century-Crofts, 1951).

SZASZ, T. S. *Pain and Pleasure; A Study of Bodily Feelings* (New York: Basic Books, Inc., 1957).

THOMAS, W. I. *The Unadjusted Girl* (Boston: Little, Brown, and Co., 1923).

WHITE, R. W. "Motivation Reconsidered," *Psychological Review*, 66 (1959).

YOUNG, P. T. *Motivation and Emotions* (New York: John Wiley and Sons, 1961).

Personality,
Personality Types, and
Atypical Interaction

The components of human social behavior, which were analyzed in Chapters 2 through 7, are abstractions that can only be inferred from the study of human behavior. This is true whether the component is a biogenic impulse, a group, an idea, a motive, or a process such as rationalization. In Part II, Chapters 8 through 11, our concern is focused upon actual behavior, the observable actions of man that are both products of, and participants in, the interactive processes described in Chapters 5 and 6. Our conclusions about the observed behavior are syntheses of phenomenal experiences and the concepts which are brought to each episode in question.

Whenever we look at the way in which components of the three basic categories of the triangular model are brought together through one or more of the interactive processes, we are perceiving social psychological reality in its clearest manifestation. It is this behavioral complex that we recognize as personality. In the case of the normal, nonpathological person, understanding of the behavior is possible only if the observer takes into his purview items from the biological heritage, the environment, and the learned or acquired attributes that are pertinent to any given episode. Omission of any one category leaves voids in the understanding of the behavior and thwarts attempts to predict subsequent behavior. This normal, non-pathological personality is described in Chapter 7.

Occasionally, however, for a variety of reasons, one or another of the three basic categories of personality components may embody a factor so extreme in its divergence from the normal (frequently in the direction of what is considered to be pathological or immoral in its nature) that it plays a disproportionately important role in the determination of the person's behavior with reference to others and to nonhuman objects. The factor itself dominates the interrelationships and, by itself, characterizes the personality. When such departures from the normal, or the rational, occur, there arises a rigidity of relationships based almost solely upon the divergent factor, be it biological, environmental, or subjective. In short, the structure of the relationship, of the personality, is known in advance if one is aware of the divergent item. Such conditions are described in Chapters 9 and 10 under the headings of "personality types." Distinction will be made between those personality types which are functions of components drawn from category IV of the triangular model of personality, and those which are functions of category II in its cultural aspects. Although the emphasis is upon the divergent factors in these separate categories, they are still to be interpreted within the interactionist framework.

Very different from these expressions of human behavior is that which occurs in such mob actions as riots, lynchings, stampedes, and panics. Here temporary disorder replaces the usually predictable, legal, and ordered interactions of people. Under the conditions discussed in Chapters 8, 9, and 10, one's daily behavior provides adequate bases for predicting what will come next. The assigned and assumed positions and statuses of an individual permit one to extrapolate into the future the probable behavior of the person or persons in question. In mob actions, the relationship between the positions one normally occupies in a social structure and the dynamic, often violent, social, group behavior is much more tenuous and at times defies one's attempts to predict behavior. Much more than the observed behavior is required if one is to predict accurately future actions. Personality as related to such unusual actions is the topic of Chapter 11.

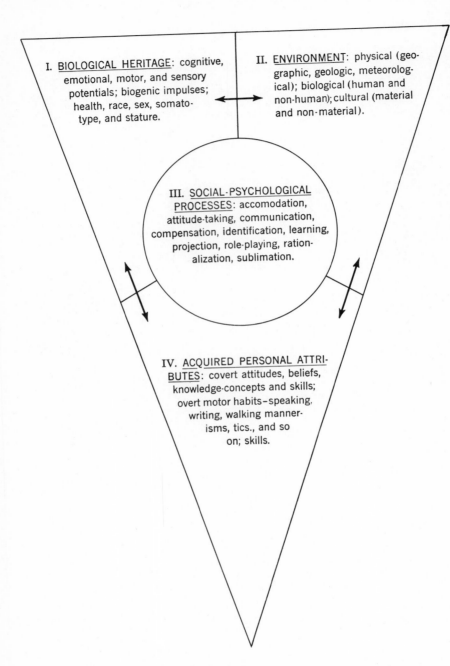

FIGURE 22. Interactionist frame of reference.

CHAPTER 8

PERSONALITY

And all the men and women
merely players.

The interactionist frame of reference comes into clearest focus in its application to *personality*. Except as we recognize personality as a *relationship*, it remains too abstract to be a valuable concept for social psychology. An understanding of personality involves a knowledge of all four phases of personality as shown in Figure 22. One of the temptations that is most difficult to resist, on the parts of both layman and specialist (as noted in Chapter 2), is that of perceiving personality as a subjective, subcutaneous thing; that is, confined to the person himself. This seems so logical. Are we interested in the problem of crime? Then, it appears, we should focus our attention upon the individual criminal (after all, he *did* commit the crime). Is a person distraught or mentally ill or alcoholic? Then, the argument runs, attend to the individual person—*he* is the real thing—so visible, so tangible. Why confuse the issue with extraneous abstractions? —logic seems to ask. That such a view of personality is widely held there can be no doubt—our prison and penal system is grounded largely in this view. Parents and teachers direct attention in large measure to the individual, and are frequently unmindful of other factors. Divorces and other disruptions of marriage and family bear witness to the operation of this view of human behavior, and to its inadequacies.

Earlier in this book, the term *constructionist fallacy* was used. The perception of personality as something restricted to the person, something to be understood apart from other objects, something to be studied in a laboratory, is a clear example of this fallacy. An object by itself is meaningless. Every student of social psychology should commit to memory, and ponder the implications of, Elijah Jordan's statement that "The metaphysically distinct individual is the nearest possible logical definition of nothing." When parents, teachers, spouses, legislators, judges, lawyers, and the like, can fully appreciate the wisdom of these few words, the savings in tears, time, money, and effort will be enormous.

Equally guilty of harboring the constructionist fallacy are the environmentalists who select as *the* factor in behavior one or more aspects of the world of objects external to the person. To find the "causes" of human behavior in slums, in this or that geographic setting, or in the conformist regimen of the American middle class is no less a meaningless abstraction

271

than to explain it in terms of the person himself. Operating under the same kind of fallacy are the biological determinists who see stature or some other feature of body type as holding the key to the mysteries of behavior. Explanations in terms of biological "causes" are still popular with many people, and the genes of the ancestors are selected as the villains on one hand, and the heros on the other. Correlations with size, color, sex, cosmetic presentations, and so on, are pointed out as evidence of the force of heredity in its physical aspects. The use made of such expressions as "blood will tell" and "you can't make a silk purse out of a sow's ear" attests to the conviction with which biological explanations of personality are popularly held.[1]

One may argue that such clearly observable features as a ready smile and a glib tongue are personality features per se; yet they may be perceived as aspects of a "charming personality" by some but as contemptuous and arrogant gestures by others. Even such items as self-assurance, knowledge, and tact can be revealed only through social interaction. Thus *personality is not constituted of subjective attitudes or personal skills, but is the way in which the individual is interrelated, through ideas, action, and attitudes, to the many human and nonhuman aspects of his environment and biological heritage.*[2] The subjective factors are partial determiners of the interaction involving the person, but only in the same manner in which other persons, the geographic environment, and the bio-

---

[1] *Cf.* W. H. Sheldon, Emil M. Hartl, and Eugene McDermott, *Varieties of Delinquent Youth* (New York: Harper and Brothers, 1949), for an analysis of delinquents in terms of body types which is interesting, at times amusing, and not too infrequently frustrating and confusing. Sheldon has modified the older and rather widely known concepts of endomorphy, mesomorphy, and ectomorphy by such terms as "scrub oak mesomorph" and "gnarled mesomorph" and has added a "t" component—the "component of thorough-bredness" as an aesthetic factor (p. 21). On a 7 point scale, 7 being the maximum of this aesthetic factor, Sheldon assigns a ranking of 1.8 to the American people generally.

[2] Comparable, even if not identical, definitions are the following, the first by a psychologist and the second by a psychiatrist: "Personality is that which permits a prediction of what a person will do in a situation . . . . Personality is . . . concerned with *all* of the behavior of the individual, both overt and under the skin." R. B. Cattell, *Personality* (New York: McGraw-Hill, 1950), p. 23; Personality is ". . . *the relatively enduring pattern of recurrent interpersonal situations* [events] *which characterize a human life.*" H. S. Sullivan, *The Interpersonal Theory of Psychiatry* (New York: W. W. Norton, 1953), p. 111. Italics in original.

A study which sought to analyze the nature of the trait of anxiousness into components gives support to the interactionist frame of reference. The three variables of the person's *responses* to the stimulus, the *situation* constituted in part by the person, the stimulus, and other environmental factors, and the *individual differences* of the participating subjects. The variations in the trait of anxiousness were accounted for mostly by the modes of response, next by the nature of the situation, and least by the subjects' individual differences. N. S. Endler, J. McV Hunt, and A. J. Rosenstein, "An S-R Inventory of Anxiousness," *Psychological Monographs*, 76, *No. 17*, Whole *No. 536*, (1962), 1–33.

logical heritage help to determine a given individual's personality. Nothing written here warrants the inference that there is no place for *analysis* of a problem object into its component parts. Indeed, Chapters 3, 4, and 7 have done precisely this. The problem arises when the investigation of human behavior becomes fixed at the level of analysis. Unless we recognize these parts as abstractions and attend to the problem of reassembling them, our efforts come to naught. The synthesizing process is prerequisite to the comprehension of what the components mean. In order to facilitate this process of synthesis, the perception of what constitutes the object, or unit of study, for social psychology must be changed from that of the individual person to the way in which the individual is related to other persons and to nonhuman objects.[3] In Chapter 1 the unit was stated to be the episode, event, or situation.

In the present chapter, the implications of the social cultural conception of personality will be drawn in considerable detail, indicating the relevance of the several component parts as they are connected by the social processes discussed in Chapter 6.

While reading this section it is very important that the reader keep in mind the nature of environment in general and social space in particular as discussed in Chapter 4. It is also important to keep in mind the emphasis given to the differences between subjective and objective perceptions of the world; that attempts at communication are often thwarted by the lack of significant symbols and faulty conception; the fact that men's values, while comparable, are often not identical; that personal social learning introduces novelty and deviation into ideas, beliefs, knowledge, feelings, and behavior; and that every social system, therefore, as an operating structure is different from that defined by explicitly voiced norms, and, furthermore, that most social systems, especially the larger communal and societal ones, have contradictory expectations built into them. If these aspects of the current interactionist framework are brought to bear on the discussion which follows, the chances of false inference will be significantly lessened.

PERSONALITY AND SOCIAL STRUCTURE

The moral concepts that bear such labels as norms, rules, laws, principles, codes, and ordinances are not only real but essential to life—social or biological—for the human beings. These take the place, in part, of

[3] For a recent statement emphasizing the need to attend to the critical aspects of social psychology, a restatement of the interactionist position in the framework of field theory, see J. Milton Yinger, "Research Implications of a Field Theory of Personality," *American Journal of Sociology*, LXVIII, 5 (March 1963), 580–592. Yinger points out the continued restrictions that allegiances to "psychological" and "sociological" frames of references (and "departments") place upon the student of social psychology.

instincts in nonhuman animals. Furthermore, they must approach consensus if such terms as social organization, social order, social structure,
and social system are to have any meaning, regardless of the size of the
groups involved—from a dyad to a nation or group of nations. The moral
terms noted above, the most general of which is *norms*, define what the
relationships *should* be in a social system. They define or delineate what
behavior is *expected* of persons in the system. Although the sociologist,
with his emphasis upon collective action,[4] group behavior in the form
of customs and institutions, can do much with the concepts of social
systems or social structure, the social psychologist, who focuses his attention upon the behaving or acting individual, must of necessity invent a
word or term to denote the individual counterpart of social systems or
social structure, (*i.e.*, the points of interaction, or behavioral junctions,
within the social system), *and* terms to denote the actual behavior of
persons in the social system.

Social psychology's interstitial locus between psychology and sociology is nowhere more clearly defined than in the description and analysis
of the relationship between these normatively defined loci of interaction
within a social system and the actual actions of persons so situated.
Norms define the former whereas *sanctions* plus subjective variables
define the latter. We can define social systems as idealized patterns of
expected ways of relating people to people and people to nonhuman
objects. What people actually do is a function not only of their beliefs,
knowledge, skills, and feelings about the behavior of people and other
objects, but also of the penalties and rewards meted out to them by their
total environment and by their own attitudes. It is very essential that the
social psychologist distinguishes clearly between these two aspects of
his data—the social structure as defined by norms or rules, and the actual
behavior of people in that structure.

Social Location, Position, or Status: Problems of Concepts and Labels

Order and system are essential to all life, to social life no less than to
biological. *The conception of personality as a relationship implies a social
system or organization within which this relationship occurs.* Each individual, by his actions, becomes a junction point within the sociocultural
system—large or small—in which he plays a part. If ordered social interaction is to occur, all persons must be placed—and must know where
they stand—with reference to others in social space. Each actor must be
aware of what is expected of him, must know the parts he is to play in

---

[4] We do not use the term *collective action* as being equivalent to *collective behavior*, the latter being often used to denote unstructured action such as riots and
panics.

—The National Observer

Well son, now that you've found yourself, who are you?

FIGURE 23.   Question of Identity.

the human drama, and must know—more or less accurately—what to expect from others. As noted in Chapter 7, under these conditions the person possesses *identity*. It is, of course, not enough to know what he and his fellows may do; he must also be aware of what he and they must and must not do. These mutual expectations are usually spoken of as rights or privileges on the one hand and duties or obligations on the other. The stability of society is contingent upon individuals correctly perceiving their and others' places in the system of social relationships. Obviously, this involves the process of taking toward oneself the attitudes of others and the development of a self. One must perceive himself as object—must gain personal identity as well as being able to identify other persons in terms of their rights and duties.

In the words of one sociologist: "Society is organized on the principle that any individual who possesses certain social characteristics has a moral right to expect that others will value and treat him in an appropriate way. Connected with this principle is a second, namely that an individual who implicitly or explicitly signifies that he has certain social characteristics ought in fact to be what he claims he is."[5]

This mutual definition of the situation by the occupants of various positions (in terms of rights and privileges) is the *sine qua non* of social order. *Identity* is the individual counterpart to *integration* in the social system. The specificity of definitions ranges from those highly structured systems found in the armed forces and in certain hierarchically organized systems, at one end of the pole, to, at the other end, the almost amorphous situations with which the new boy in the neighborhood is confronted, and in which he must "feel his way" and "play it by ear" before he is "placed" in the neighborhood scheme of things. Without such reciprocal and normative expectations, the predictability upon which personal security is based is unattainable.

What, then, are we to call those social junction points, these places of behavioral interchanges that, taken collectively, constitute customs and institutions and groupings? Consensus on these terms has eluded the social scientist, the one who must cope with these points or places of interaction; the symbols are not yet significant symbols.

Following the lead of anthropologist Ralph Linton (1893–1953), some social scientists, especially sociologically oriented ones, prefer the term *status* to denote the social expectations in terms of rights and privileges which define these points of interaction within a social system.[6] However, a countertrend, sponsored by the popularity of the works of German sociologist Max Weber (1864–1920), has rather effectively changed the meaning of status from that intended by Linton and his

---

[5] E. Goffman, *The Presentation of Self in Everyday Life* (Garden City, N.Y.: Doubleday and Co., 1959), p. 13. See his *Stigma* (Englewood Cliffs, N.J.: Prentice-Hall, 1963), for an extensive analysis of the ways in which biological and personal handicaps are incorporated into personality.

[6] *See* R. Linton, *The Study of Man* (New York: Appleton-Century, 1936), and his *The Cultural Background of Personality* (New York: Appleton-Century, 1945); Kingsley Davis, *Human Society* (New York: The Macmillan Co., 1949); E. T. Hiller, *Social Relations and Structures* (New York: Harper and Brothers, 1947). One sociologist has observed that: "For sometime now, at least since the influential writings of Ralph Linton on the subject, it has been recognized that two concepts—social status and social role—are fundamental to the description, and to the analysis, of a social structure." R. K. Merton, *Social Theory and Social Structure* (New York: The Free Press of Glencoe, 1957), p. 368.

followers by making it roughly synonymous with rank or honor.[7] Followers of Weber tell us that: "Status involves the successful realization of claims to prestige; it refers to the distribution of deference in society."[8]

Both in sociological texts and in social psychological writings this use of the term has gained acceptance. Of the articles indexed under the heading of "status" in the first twenty-six volumes of the *American Sociological Review*, approximately 90 per cent used "status" in the Weberian, not the Lintonian, meaning. Because of this fact, we have chosen to use the more general term *social position*, or simply *position* to denote the points of interaction within a social system.

In one way or another many social scientists use this term and perceive ". . . a position in a social structure as a set of expectations or acquired anticipatory reactions. The job or position is described in terms of the actions expected of the occupant of the position (his obligations) and the actions which he may expect from others such as foremen, subordinates, paymaster, etc. (his rights)."[9]

The following statement expresses well our perception and judgment concerning the term best fitted for the purpose at hand:

> The term position will be used to refer to *the location of an actor or class of actors in a system of social relationships*. The general idea of social location has been represented by some authors with the term status, and by others with position. The two terms have about the same precedent. We have chosen position for this purpose because status connotes the idea of differential ranking among a set of persons or social locations, whereas the more neutral term, position, does not.[10]

As noted above, the social system or social structure is a normative concept, denoting the established and sanctioned ways of behaving.

[7] *See* H. H. Gerth and C. W. Mills (eds. and translators), *From Max Weber: Essays in Sociology* (New York: Oxford University Press, 1946); T. Parsons and A. M. Henderson (translators), *The Theory of Social and Economic Organization* (New York: Oxford University Press, 1947). One sociologist expresses the attitude of some of his colleagues in stating that "Status refers to positions in *all* the systems of society, not just to the prestige systems." F. E. Merrill, *Society and Culture* (Englewood Cliffs, N.J.: Prentice-Hall, 1961), p. 179. It is of some interest to note that, whereas the second edition of *Webster's Unabridged Dictionary* defines *status* with no reference to rank, the third edition gives rank a prominent place in the definition.

[8] Hans Gerth and C. Wright Mills, *Character and Structure* (New York: Harcourt, Brace and Co., 1953), p. 307.

[9] Theodore R. Sarbin, "Role Theory," in G. Lindzey, *Handbook of Social Psychology* (Cambridge, Mass.: Addison-Wesley Publishing Co., 1945), p. 225.

[10] N. Gross, W. S. Mason, and A. W. McEachern, *Explorations in Role Analysis* (New York: John Wiley and Sons, 1958), p. 48. Even though this definition and reasoning coincides with ours, the authors do not spell out the definition of "position" as we believe they must to avoid redundancy with "role."

Thus, position as the individual counterpart of social system is also normatively defined as the way in which the occupant of the position is
supposed to interact, how he is expected to behave with others in the
system. Linton's use of the term persists, even when used by those who
specify its honorific meanings, in such phrases as "marital status," "age
and sex status," "occupational status," and "draft status" wherein there
is no imputation of hierarchical ranking. It appears likely that both meanings will continue in the literature of social science, the meaning being
inferred by the reader from the context within which the term is used.
Furthermore, even when the meaning of deference or rank is incorporated, the term can still be used as a synonym for position with relatively
little chance of its intended meaning being misinterpreted. One such
definition is as follows:

> Although the concept *social status* has been utilized in a variety of
> ways, it may be used here to refer to a person's standing in the com-
> munity, identifiable in terms of the rights, duties, privileges, and im-
> munities that he enjoys by virtue of his position.[11]

However, despite the conviction that the incorporation of hierarchical
meaning into the term status has certain unfortunate consequences for
communication efforts, in the face of current trends it would be unwise
to insist that this is the preferable term. Although both terms will continue
to be used in classroom and in the literature, we believe that the purposes of communication will be better served by adopting the term
position.

*Each position implies a social system or organization, of which it is a
part.* "Teacher" implies a system of education; "widow" and "orphan"
imply a marriage and/or family system; and "priest," "cantor," "verger,"
and "parishioner" imply religious systems or organizations. All institutions, indeed all customs (folkways and mores) are approximations of
ideal group ways that are defined, formally or informally, by societal
norms—norms that, in turn, are enforced by sanctions. Every social system has its normative or moral aspects, and, as the individual counterparts of the social system, *social positions* are thus normatively defined
with appropriate sanctions provided to help insure that the occupants
of these positions behave as expected. In short, the position *is* its relation
to other positions. There are no static concepts in social psychology.

---

[11] T. Shibutani, *Society and Personality* (Englewood Cliffs, N.J.: Prentice-Hall,
1961), p. 218. This social psychologist has written that "Each person is inextricably
involved in a complex web of social relationships and his position within a social
system constitutes his status." *Ibid.,* p. 270. Unless one infers that all positions can
be ranked on a hierarchical scale, this latter definition is clearly synonymous with
our use of *position.*

VOLUNTARY AND INVOLUNTARY POSITIONS

Persons find themselves in various points, or positions, of the numerous social systems for several reasons. A person's social positions are functions of:

1. His having been born into them—for example, race, caste, sex, class, family member.

2. Force—for example, private in armed forces, pupil in school, prisoner.

3. Cultural influences—such as unemployment, residence of village-become-city; attaining leadership; retirement at 65 years of age.

4. His voluntary action—becoming a lawyer, suburban resident, major in history, member of athletic team.

The terms *ascribed* and *achieved* have been used to differentiate the positions which are involuntary from those which the person chose to occupy.[12] Some students of the subject have taken the lead of sociologist E. T. Hiller and added a third category of *assumed* position (status).[13] Even though we find the simple distinction between voluntary and involuntary positions is sufficient, the reader may prefer to use the other terms.

Social Organization, Personal Social Learning, and Role Behavior

Were all customs and institutions functioning perfectly, that is, if everybody involved were behaving exactly as he or she is expected to behave in terms of the societal definitions, and were the larger social system without contradictory or dysfunctional positions or statuses, then to know a person's social positions would permit one to anticipate most of that person's actual behavior. To know that a man occupied the position of judge would be to know that he was wise in the ways of law, intelligent, incorruptible, assiduous in the performance of his duties and meticulous in keeping within the bounds of his prerogatives. However, even under such conditions the inevitable personal social learning experiences would lead to variations in behavior among occupants of identical positions. The jovial and dour judges or physicians may be equally competent; quick and lethargic painters may produce works of equal quality; and calm or excitable auto mechanics may possess comparable skills.

[12] *Cf.* R. Linton, *The Study of Man* (New York: Appleton-Century, 1936).

[13] "In the ascription [ascribed status] of a place, a person is classified in advance of preparation for playing his part; in the assumption [assumed status] of a place, he voluntarily enters it; in an achieved status, he must prove his superiority over other contestants and receive acknowledgment of his attainment." E. T. Hiller, *Social Relations and Structures* (New York: Harper and Brothers, 1947), p. 337.

Furthermore, because of inadequacies in the social system, deficiencies in biological heritage, or failures in the process of communication, socialization, and enculturation, many occupants of social positions fall far short of the behavior expected of them. The inadequate teacher, the corrupt judge or policeman, the stupid father, the deranged physician, the bigoted cleric, and deviants of many kinds do in fact exist. One student of the problem lists the following ". . . awkward empirical facts" that help to account for the something less than perfectly ordered social relationships:

1. Some individuals do not accept even supposedly central values of the society.

2. Individuals vary in their emotional commitment to both important and less important values.

3. This value commitment varies by class strata, and by other characteristics of social position, for example, age, sex, occupation, geographic region, and religion.

4. Even when individuals accept a given value, some of them also have a strong or weak "latent commitment" to very different or contradictory values.

5. Conformity with normative prescription is not a simple function of value commitment; there may be value commitment without conformity or conformity without commitment.

6. When individuals' social positions change, they may change both behavior and their value orientations.

7. The values, ideals, and role obligations of every individual are at times in conflict.[14]

The concept of social position, then, although valuable in permitting the discussion of idealized interpersonal relationships, falls far short of being sufficient in the treatment of actual behavior of persons who occupy these positions. We need a term to denote how people who occupy certain positions behave with reference to the expectations of these positions. *We need a term to denote the parts actually played in life's drama, to focus upon the occupant and not upon the position or social system.* For some, the word *role* seems to suffice. Borrowed from the theater (it originally referred to the scroll or "roll" on which the actor's part was written), role denotes more than what is expected of a given person because of his social position. Thus King Lear had several social positions or statuses which were pertinent to his behavior in the famous drama—he occupied *positions* of king, father, and father-in-law—but his actual behavior was not deducible from these normatively defined posi-

---

[14] William J. Goode, "A Theory of Role Strain," *American Sociological Review*, 25 (1960), 484.

tions. The *part* or *role* played was spelled out by Shakespeare, and no matter who plays the part the lines are the same, and his fate is sealed from the opening words. However, the actor's position, or status, provides some basis for predicting how well or how poorly the various Lears will play their parts.

The problem inherent in using spatial or geometric concepts (position) together with a theatrical concept (role) has been pointed out, and is indeed real. Nevertheless, at this stage in the development of labels for social psychological concepts, there appears to be no reasonable alternative to acknowledging these semantic inconsistencies, but stressing the point that *all* social psychological concepts are dynamic, interrelational, and never static.

No more than in the case of position has consensus been reached for the meanings to be attached to "role." In 1951, a review of some eighty sources led to the conclusion that "The concept role is at present still rather vague, nebulous, and nondefinitive."[15] Later another writer commented that "Although the term role has recently come to have the beginnings of a stable core of meanings, we are a long way from univocality."[16]

One can agree with the view that "The concept role is related to, and must be distinguished from, the concept of social position,"[17] and yet find little agreement as to how this is to be done. A sociologist writes that ". . . the participants in a social system can be thought of as occupants

---

[15] L. J. Nieman and J. W. Hughes, "The Problem of the Concept of Role— a Re-survey of the Literature," *Social Forces*, XXX (1951), 149. At that time they wrote that "There is an increasing trend toward associating the concept role with that of status." This trend, as we have seen, did not continue on all fronts.

[16] Sarbin, *op. cit.*, p. 225. Ten years after the Nieman and Hughes' study another writer commented that: "It is abundantly clear from these findings that there is a great deal of conceptual and terminological confusion in contemporary role theory." B. J. Biddle, *The Present Status of Role Theory* (Columbia, Mo.: University of Missouri, 1961) p. 45. Biddle's is the most exhaustive coverage to date of the literature dealing with role. From this viewpoint it is a valuable contribution, but the definitions of role and status presented, although as valid as most others, do not appear to have solved either the terminological or the conceptual problems. He acknowledges the importance of separating affective and cognitive aspects of role behavior but comments that to "include such a definition within the corpus of role theory at the present time is to open a Pandora's box of additional problems" (*Ibid.*, p. 54). Also, Biddle's subjective approach is bound to contrast with an interactionist approach. He tells the reader that ". . . in the long run, definitions must return to the basic data of persons and their characteristics (*Ibid.*, p. 4). This abstraction of the person is precisely what the interactionist approach argues must not be done. Finally, in view of an earlier discussion of "status," his use of the term in the title of his book is interesting.

[17] D. J. Levinson, "Role, Personality, and Social Structure in the Organizational Setting," *Journal of Abnormal and Social Psychology*, 58 (1959), 172. We agree with those who hold that there is "little to distinguish the two concepts" of role and status or position in Linton's well known and often copied formulation of the concept. *See* N. Gross, W. S. Mason, and A. W. McEachern, *Explorations in Role Analysis* (New York: John Wiley and Sons, 1958), p. 12.

of roles,"[18] whereas a social psychologist counters with the statement that "It is meaningful to say that a person 'occupies' a social position; but it is inopportune to say, as many do, that one occupies a role."[19] Other social psychologists say that "What a typical occupant of a given position is expected to do constitutes the role. . ."[20] but a sociologist tells the reader that "The social role, on the other hand, tells us *what the person does.*"[21] But, writes another, "*Role behavior,* on the other hand, does refer to the actual behavior of specific individuals as they take their roles."[22] *Role enactment* and *role playing* are synonymous for some social psychologists,[23] but others distinguish them, denoting "as if" behavior or play acting by the latter phrase.[24] Another finds it essential to make a distinction between "conventional role," which is the equivalent of our "social position"—wherein "the rights and duties remain the same regardless of who plays the part," and "interpersonal roles"—wherein the claims and obligations depend entirely upon who is involved.[25] That is, the latter are primary group relationships, whereas the former are impersonal and secondary. Still another includes *both* "duties, privileges and obligations which are attached to the positions" and "behavior, beliefs, and attitudes" under role.[26]

These examples of the meanings assigned in current literature to "role," and to phrases involving "role," illustrate how far short of univocality the social psychologists fall in their quest for words differen-

---

[18] Harry Johnson, *Sociology* (New York: Harcourt, Brace, and Co., 1960), p. 48.

[19] Levinson, *op. cit.*, p. 172.

[20] D. Krech, R. S. Crutchfield, and E. L. Ballachy, *Individual and Society* (New York: McGraw-Hill, 1963), p. 310.

[21] J. Fichter, *Sociology* (Chicago: University of Chicago Press, 1957), p. 203. Italics in original.

[22] T. M. Newcomb, *Social Psychology* (New York: The Dryden Press, 1950), p. 330. In this instance Newcomb appears to mean "assume" by the word "take," in the more common meaning of Mead and Coutu, namely, that of taking the attitudes of others toward the subject.

In the book which replaced Newcomb's *Social Psychology*, the authors state that "*Role*, in all these senses—ideal or actual, general or specific, prescribed or emergent —refers to the behavioral consistencies on the part of the person as he contributes to a more or less stable relationship with one or more others." T. M. Newcomb, R. H. Turner, and P. E. Converse, *Social Psychology* (New York: Holt, Rinehart and Winston, Inc., 1965), p. 323.

[23] E. L. Hartley and R. C. Hartley, *Fundamentals of Social Psychology* (New York: Alfred A. Knopf, 1952), p. 488; *also* Shibutani; *op. cit.*, pp. 47–48.

[24] T. R. Sarbin and D. S. Jones, "An Experimental Analysis of Role Behavior," *Journal of Abnormal and Social Psychology*, 51 (1956), 236. The first of these authors, in a previous article, observed that "The positions are collections of rights and duties designated by a single term, e.g., mother, village chief, teacher, etc. The actions of persons, then, are organized around these positions and comprise *roles.*" Sarbin, *op. cit.*, p. 232.

[25] T. Shibutani, *op. cit.*, p. 326. The "interpersonal roles" are constituted of *behavior*, and not of expectations as are "conventional roles" (*Ibid.*, p. 308).

[26] E. H. Bell, *Social Foundations of Human Behavior* (New York: Harper and Brothers, 1961), p. 178.

tiating the expectations that define a social system from the behavior of persons in that system. The proportion of all social psychologists subscribing to one or another of the various combination of terms is not exactly known, but, among those who have published their views, no one use predominates.

Although lack of communication among social psychologists may contribute to the semantic confusion noted here, the problem goes beyond semantics to the conceptions themselves. As was noted above, "The concept role is related to, and must be distinguished from, the concept of social position."[27] This is not an easy thing to accomplish. Although some writers in the field inform us that "We feel that theoretical formulations of role analysis must include these three elements—social locations, behavior, and expectations,"[28] we believe that there are only *two* categories—expected behavior and actual behavior. Social locations, or positions, or statuses can be defined only in terms of the behavior which is *expected* of the incumbents. The models of social positions described by Gross *et al.*[29] are understandable only because the reader perceives these positions as being defined in terms of *expected* behavior. The same authors inform the reader that they use position as an heuristic device, noting that ". . . we never have a position without expectations and behaviors."[30] This statement acknowledges the fact that there can be no static concept in social psychology; every concept must be interactional in nature in terms of either expected or actual behavior. However, we must disagree that a position cannot exist without behavior, if by this is meant without an occupant. Any position may be vacated—a professorship or judgeship may be created and then filled. Resignations, deaths, and dismissals vacate positions. However, roles, or role behaviors, cannot exist apart from a behaving person. This is why it was argued above that one can occupy a position, but not a role; one plays or performs a role.

This point, that one does not occupy, or vacate, a role, has been challenged by the argument that, in strictly dramaturgical analogy, such vacant roles do indeed exist, and Broadway is full of persons competing for vacant roles. This challenge is answerable if one remembers that the language of the theater as applied to social psychology is meant to be only analogous. The position that is empty is normatively defined *not* upon the criterion of the role per se; this is almost invariably set by the script. The position open is defined in terms of current standards of thespian art as these are related to the status of the applicant, to the timbre and tone of his voice, to his gender (although female parts were played more often than not by males in the fifteenth century, it is not

[27] Levinson, *op. cit.*, p. 172.
[28] N. Gross, W. S. Mason, and A. W. McEachern, *op. cit.*, p. 18.
[29] *Ibid.*, pp. 51–55.
[30] *Ibid.*, p. 58.

likely that females will soon be sought for male parts in current drama),
to his race, to his stature, to his intelligence, and so on. Whether or not
Lear, say, will be father or brother to Goneril, Regan, and Cordelia, a
strong or weak character, a success or a failure—these are not open to
question. The position that is open, or vacant, is not defined by Shakespeare (almost any person could play the part of Lear) but is defined by
the director, the sponsor, the anticipated response of critics, fellow actors,
and others. The position open is that of *actor*. Thus, even in the theater,
the position, of which Lear is the role, is defined in terms not deducible
from the role itself. The advertisement might read as follows:

> *Wanted*: Experienced male actor for Shakespearean part; must be of
> at least normal stature and body type, Caucasian, with reputation that
> will attract theater-goers; must agree to stipulations of contract as de-
> fined by director, Theatrical Guild, and sponsor; must cooperate with
> fellow actors regarding times and frequency of rehearsals.

No mention need be made of the role to be played. The position is that
of actor at a given time and place.

We are still faced with the problem of what to call the actual behavior
of the occupant of a position in a social system. *Social role*, or simply *role*,
would suffice, were it not for the fact that a considerable number of persons have chosen to equate it with "position" or, in Linton's sense,
"status." Believing that it is preferable to compromise semantic logic
rather than communicability, we will use the phrase *role behavior* as
an equivalent to *role*. It is hoped that this use of the term will make it a
significant symbol for students of social psychology.

A sociologist has introduced the concept of "role sets," meaning the
several roles played simultaneously by, say, a teacher in his or her relationships to students, school board, superintendent, patriotic organizations, professional organizations, and community at large.[31] This suggests
that each position may have several roles associated with it. The extent
to which this is so is reduced if one gives attention to all the *positions* one
occupies in a social system or in *several* social systems. In the above
example, a person who occupies the position of teacher is not simply a
pedagogue. Equally defined in terms of expected behavior are the positions of faculty member (colleague), employee, member of professional
organization, citizen of country, member of local community, and neighbor, all of which are held simultaneously. The behavior, as incumbent
upon these positions, reflects the corresponding social systems as much
as does the role associated with the position or status of teacher. Roles
are in conflict here because of positional or expectation conflict. There

---

[31] R. K. Merton, *op. cit.*, pp. 369–370. He means sets or groupings of roles, and
not the attitudes or perceptions which are the referents of "response sets" as used in
psychology. The latter is the more established meaning of "set" or "sets."

are role conflicts that are not functions of position or social system conflicts.

This is not, however, to argue that there is a one-to-one relationship between the various points of interaction, (positions or statuses) of a social system and the behavior of occupants of those positions. Lack of integration is especially evident when the subsystems are not integrated into the larger, societal system.

There are the unintended forms of role behavior that are functions of a faulty social system, as, for instance, when the expected behavior is not logical, when the actor is called upon to act in ways that are incompatible with his biological heritage or his subjective variables (attitudes, knowledge, beliefs). In such cases, one finds roles without status, or role performance or behavior without social position. Thus the housewife, subjugated by a dominating and physically stronger male, defined by the culture as less capable, and denied fulfillment of sociogenic needs and desires, becomes a shrew and a nag. Wanting in biceps, she tries her tongue; bored and thwarted, she compensates in the only way open to her—by venting her aggression upon the other family members.[32] Criminals of certain kinds are playing roles that reflect the socioeconomic positions which they occupy. One can make a good case for delineating dysfunctional statuses or positions which yield unwanted role behavior.

Another category of role behavior which is not deducible from the nature of the social system is that which encompasses the boor, the bore, the cheat, certain criminals, and certain mentally ill persons. Such behavior is a function of misperception, failure of self-perceiving and role taking processes, conceptual distortion, ignorance, and other factors. Such role behavior, involving loss of identity, is a product of subjective factors and not of inadequacies of the formal social structure per se.

Culture and Personality

The phrase "culture and personality" denotes a whole separate area of research, and courses by this title appear in many college and university catalogues. The relationship is implicitly noted throughout this book, and the reader is well aware of the differences in people raised in different nations, geographical regions, classes, and in rural and in urban environments. It serves our purposes here to note one or two studies that will illustrate the kinds of research being carried on by social psychologists.

Special funds were made available for research into the influence of college life upon attitudes and values of Vassar College students. An analysis of representatives of the classes of 1904, 1914, 1921–1924, 1929–1935, 1940–1943, and 1956 was made, using portions of the California

[32] *See*, in this respect, Betty Friedan, *The Feminine Mystique* (New York: W. W. Norton and Co., 1963), and Helen M. Hacker, "Women as a Minority Group," *Social Forces*, 30 (Oct. 1951).

Public Opinion Survey.[33] The "F" Scale (32 items) is designed to measure authoritarianism, using such traits and attitudes as compulsiveness, rigidity, intolerance of ambiguity, punitive morality, submission to power, conventionality, and cynicism. The "E" Scale attempts to measure ethnocentrism, and attends to items such as disposition to glorify ingroups, family, country and social class.[34]

The Vassar sample is, of course, not representative of the country as a whole—economically, regionally, ethnically, sexually, or with regard to intelligence. Nevertheless, the temporal changes are of interest and have value, providing the limited scope of the study is kept in mind. It appears clear that the values possessed or acquired during college years tend to persist. Table VIII shows some of the reported differences.

Table VIII
Percentages of Rejection of Selected Items of the Public Opinion Survey*

	1904	1914	1921– 1924	1929– 1935	1940– 1943	1956
	N=85	N=43	N=73	N=50	N=77	N=200
Obedience and respect for authority are the most important virtues that children should learn.	35	49	62	70	77	51
Science has its place but there are many important things that can never possibly be understood by the human mind.	29	58	37	53	42	39

* M. B. Freedman, "Changes in Six Decades of Some Attitudes and Values Held by Educated Women," *Journal of Social Issues*, 17, No. 1 (1961), 26.

One statement, "It is up to the government to make sure that everyone has a secure job and a good standard of living," was rejected by 92 per cent of the 1940–43 alumnae; however, only 72 per cent of the 1929–1935 alumnae rejected it.[35]

The author notes that the alumnae of the 1940's were liberal with reference to certain social and broadly political matters but not in economic values. This is as one would expect. The education at Vassar leads to a better understanding of society in general, but, having succeeded

[33] M. B. Freedman, "Changes in Six Decades of Some Attitudes and Values Held by Educated Women," *Journal of Social Issues*, 17, No. 1 (1961), 19–28.
[34] *Ibid.*, p. 20.
[35] *Ibid.*, p. 27.

under a given economic system, the alumnae are hardly likely to be enthusiastic about changes in the system which, for them, has proved rewarding. However, the differential responses of the 1930's and 1940's alumnae to the question of governmental responsibility for guaranteeing economic security seem to be functions of the former having experienced the economic depression and the latter knowing the boom period of the Second World War. The author concluded that the results of the study suggest that "it seems obvious that social and individual psychological processes parallel one another rather closely."[36] The influence of role taking in the formative years is seen here.

Another study of changing personality in response to changing cultural environment revealed bi-directional changes.[37] From a group of 300 engaged couples tested twenty years previously, Kelly selected 116 couples who were still married and for whom data were available for both time periods. Thirty-three questions were presented regarding respective ages of spouses; who "wore the pants"; homogamy concerning education, religious attitudes, and intelligence; intellectual, aesthetic, ethical, and political attitudes; religious training and disciplining of the children; and attitudes toward premarital and extramarital sexual intercourse. The general trend was toward neutrality of attitudes. Those attitudes which moved from a less to a more important emphasis were:

1. husband and wife should be of same religious faith
2. husband and wife, if congenial, should take their vacations together
3. children should be given religious training
4. children should be held to a strict discipline[38]

There were small but important changes in different directions according to sex on such items as women's economic independence, the female believing this to be more important. Also, whereas twenty years previously the female was significantly more inclined than the male to value highly female virginity at marriage, the attitudes were very similar in the later study.[39] As the author points out, these changes emphasize the fact that persons occupying different social positions can be differently affected by the same cultural changes.

Personality and Religious Attitudes

As noted in Chapter 7, religion denotes the existence of a relationship in which some object is defined as sacred—worthy of being revered and

[36] *Ibid.*, p. 27.

[37] E. Lowell Kelly, "The Re-assessment of Specific Attitudes After Twenty Years," *Journal of Social Issues*, XVII, No. 1 (1961), 33.

[38] *Ibid.*, p. 33.

[39] *Ibid.*, p. 34.

protected. In its more intense form, religion defines objects as ultimate values. Without exception, man is religious in this meaning of the term. The religious attitude is manifested in personality by protective, venerative personal behavior on behalf of some material or nonmaterial object. Clearly, religious attitudes vary in intensity and the greater the intensity, the greater the desire and will on behalf of the religious object. The extremely religious person will not compromise in his quest for his goal or in his defense of the sacred object.

Heroes as well as martyrs are religious products. From a social psychological perspective, the religious component of personality may be supernatural or secular. The personalities of St. Paul, Luther, John Knox, Savonarola, Maimonides, and Servetus reveal unquestioningly the religious attitude, but so do those of Dorothea Dix in her long struggle to improve mental hospitals, Lovejoy's martyrdom on behalf of slavery's abolition, the thousands of Irish and Polish patriots who sought independence for their nations, the many women who dedicated their lives to the attainment of female suffrage, and the signers of the Declaration of Independence; and the pilgrims to Benares, Mecca, Jerusalem, Mt. Fujiyama, Rome, and Moscow are all social psychologically akin. If a person's religious values are known, much of his personality is revealed, particularly in cases of fanaticism.

Religious dedication is a component of high morale and of strong will in the individual and in the strength of in-group solidarity among co-religionists. The ephemeral groupways—crazes, fads, and fashions—are not religion's offspring, but mores are. The religiously oriented personality is characterized by the constancy of the direction of his efforts.

It has not been popular in recent decades to study the social psychological components of religion, but this omission makes for a void in the understanding of behavior. The neglect of religion as a component of personality may be explained by the tendency to identify religion with supernaturalism, sectarianism, superstition, or magic, which are indeed something less than universal and essential human characteristics. Whatever the explanation, it is essential that the referent or referents of the adjective *religious* be sought, identified, and studied by the student of human behavior. These referents appear to be too real, too pervasive, and too persistent to be relegated to an optional category in social psychology. We believe that an understanding of religious attitudes, as defined in Chapter 7, is requisite to an understanding of personality.

THE SELF

In Chapter 6 it was called to the reader's attention that self-perception was in large part, but not exclusively, a function of role taking. Brief mention was made of the self, and we now return to its consideration as an aspect of personality. One of the persistent major problems of social psychological theory concerns the identification of the referent of such terms as *me*, *myself*, *yourself*, *self-consciousness*, *self-condemnation*, and *selfish*. The intellectual giants of the past have wrestled with the problem, and the following paragraph seems almost as appropriate today as when it was written in 1893:

> A man commonly thinks that he knows what he means by his self. He may be in doubt about other things, but here he seems to be at home. He fancies that with the self he at once comprehends both that it is and what it is. And of course the fact of one's own existence, *in some sense*, is quite beyond doubt. But as to the sense in which this existence is so certain, there the case is far otherwise. And I should have thought that no one who gives his attention to this question could fail to come to one preliminary result. We are all sure that we exist, but in what sense and what character—as to that we are most of us in helpless uncertainty and in blind confusion. And so far is the self from being clearer than things outside us that, to speak generally, we never know what we mean when we talk of it. But the meaning and the sense is surely for metaphysics the vital point. For, if none defensible can be found, such a failure, I must insist, ought to end the question. Anything the meaning of which is inconsistent and unintelligible is appearance, and not reality.[40]

Believing that *self* is more than mere appearance, we will attempt to answer the question as to its nature. This is a question that cannot be dealt with by abandoning this and similar terms, because they are too deeply imbedded in the language habits of men. Furthermore, their persistence and prevalence suggest strongly the probability of there being some referent (or referents) that can be objectively known. We have such time honored statements as Descartes' highly provable, "I think, therefore I am," and many such lesser known but equally pointed observations, for instance, that of the nineteenth century philosopher, F. H. Bradley, to wit, "Besides that which at any time is experienced, you have also the thing to which the experience belongs."[41] We would prefer, "the thing which the experience involves," but the essential ideas are the same. However, such statements do little more than emphasize that there is a distinction between self and not-self, while leaving unanswered the question as to just what is the nature of the self. If we are to secure for ourselves a vocabulary that will facilitate objective thinking about, and discussion of, social behavior of the individual person, the object described by the term *self* must be specified. In the next few paragraphs we present as definitive a statement of the problem as research to date permits.

Out of the welter of writings on the subject, two points of general

---

[40] F. H. Bradley, *Appearance and Reality* (Oxford: The Clarendon Press, 1930), p. 55. (This material first published in 1893.)
[41] F. H. Bradley, *Collected Essays* (Oxford: Clarendon Press, 1935) p. 220.

agreement have arisen. The first is that the referents of "self" are not innate or inborn, but are developed as a result of the interaction experiences of the person.[42] The second is that the "self" referent is not identical with the physical organism. Whether it is more than, or less than, the organism, is still a moot point for some persons, but at least *it is not the same as the body*.[43] However, consensus does not go beyond these two points, and we can quote a passage written by William James (who did so much to establish the concept of self in psychology) which is essentially as true today as it was when he wrote it three-quarters of a century ago.

> Ever since Hume's time, it [the problem of the referent of "I" and "me"] has been justly regarded as the most puzzling puzzle with which this psychology has to deal; and whatever view one may espouse, one has to hold his position against heavy odds; if, with the spiritualists, one contends for a substantial soul, or transcendental principle of unity, one can give no positive account of what they may be. And if, with the Humians [The followers of the viewpoint set forward by David Hume in his *A Treatise on Human Nature*, Book I, Part IV, Section VI (London: John Noon, 1739).] who deny such a principle and say that the stream of passing thoughts is all, one runs against the entire common-sense of mankind, of which the belief in a distinct principle of selfhood seems an integral part. Whatever solution be adopted in the pages to come, we may as well make up our minds in advance that it will fail to satisfy the majority of those to whom it is addressed.[44]

Having thus acknowledged the difficulty involved in the problem, we present the following discussion of the self idea as it is to be employed in this book. The reader who would disagree with this conception, or who believes it to be arbitrary beyond warrant, is urged to delve into the writings on this subject of such men as William James, F. H. Bradley,

---

[42] This is made explicit in writings which differ widely in time and emphasis. *See*, for example, F. H. Bradley, *Collected Essays*, p. 218; J. M. Baldwin, *Mental Development in Child and Race* (New York: The Macmillan Co., 1906), pp. 316ff; G. H. Mead, *Mind, Self, and Society* (Chicago: University of Chicago Press, 1934), pp. 135ff; Gardner Murphy, *Personality* (New York: Harper and Brothers, 1947), pp. 480ff; Gordon W. Allport, "The Ego in Contemporary Psychology," *Psychological Review*, I (1943), and M. Sherif and H. Cantril, *The Psychology of Ego Envolvements* (New York: John Wiley and Sons, 1947).

[43] Evidence of this agreement is found in the statement of F. H. Bradley, *Collected Essays*, p. 224, who concerned himself extensively with the problem and who wrote that ". . . we must remember that the body, neither at last *nor at first*, includes all the self; and that at its limits, and again later through nearly all its extent, the body becomes dissociable from self." G. H. Mead, *Mind, Self, and Society*, p. 135, writes that "The self has a character which is different from that of the physiological organism proper," and a current-day psychologist says that the destruction of the body is perfectly compatible with the preservation of the self. I. Chein, "The Awareness of Self and the Structure of the Ego," *Psychological Review*, LI (1944), 311.

[44] William James, *The Principles of Psychology* (New York: Henry Holt and Co., 1890), I, p. 330.

C. H. Cooley, Thomas Henry Huxley, George Herbert Mead, Sigmund Freud, David Hume, Gordon Allport, Isadore Chein, P. Bertocci, E. Goffman, Gardner Murphy, Muzafer Sherif, Harry Stack Sullivan, and Hadley Cantril, who present varied viewpoints, many in direct conflict, of the nature of the referent of self and ego. There seems to have developed in the social sciences, including psychology, a tendency to regard as passé anything that is more than a decade or so old. Many of the insights of the older writers, taken in proper context, are extremely timely even today. The student of social behavior of the person can save himself much time by using the efforts and eyes of others who have wrestled with comparable problems. Certainly a most comprehensive source on the thinking on the self or ego is found in Christopher John Bittner's *The Development of the Concept of the Social Nature of the Self*.[45]

Bittner treats briefly of the ancients' concepts of self or soul, then elaborates the thinking of the modern philosophers, beginning with Descartes, and goes on to show how the treatment of self in modern sociology, psychology, and social psychology has very much in common with the earlier viewpoints of the philosophers. This work is the logical starting point for anyone seeking to know more about the nature of the thinking which has resulted from man's quest for a better understanding of the nature of the referent, or referents, of the *I*, *me*, and *my* words. The reader may also find interest in the early concern of philosopher-psychologist M. W. Calkins with the problem of self.[46]

In the several writings alluded to above, there is much disagreement as to the nature of *self*. Among other things, some equate the terms and some see them as referring to different phenomena. Further, when we study the various viewpoints there appears a common element, namely, *self-awareness*, the ability of man to distinguish between *his* body, *his* person, and *his* personality on the one hand and that which is *not* his on the other. In short, it is the distinction between *self* and *not-self* that is crucial. The process of becoming aware of one's own toes in contrast to the toes of other persons or objects of the world which are not of the body, of one's own social attitudes in contrast to the attitudes of others, of one's own social values in contrast to those of other persons, is the process which gives rise to the self. The reader is reminded of the discussion of the "looking-glass self" concept as presented in Chapter 6. The development of the self goes on along with other social processes, with the development of social preferences, awareness of role playing and of status. The self is not some mysterious thing which is external or internal to the person that pushes the person around or is pushed around by it.

---

[45] (Iowa City: University of Iowa, 1932.)
[46] *See* her *The Persistent Problem of Philosophy* (New York: The Macmillan Co., 1910).

*The self consists of those aspects of the person which the individual per-
ceives and toward which he develops opinions and attitudes, consciously
or unconsciously.* Mead has said that the person acquires a self when he
becomes an object to himself.[47] It is the total person *insofar as he is an
object to that person.* This makes it clear that self is synonymous with
neither the person nor with personality, because it is unlikely that anyone becomes fully aware of the totality of his person or of his relationships with the object world.

It may appear from the above paragraphs that the *unconscious* aspects
of personality are being ignored. This is not intentional. For anyone who
has studied human behavior in more than a superficial fashion, it is clear
that unconscious factors are very important in the explanation of much
of our social behavior. Self-deception is one of man's most highly developed arts, and many of his impulses and motives are unconscious ones.
Instances wherein a person's behavior is motivated by self-interest, often
called ego-involvement, of which he is not conscious are relatively
common. This is particularly true of the person who is not given to
introspection of his attitudes and motives. It is especially noticeable
in children and becomes less common as one matures and becomes more
sophisticated with regard to motivations. As Mead points out, self interest need not involve self-consciousness.[48]

When we state that self involves those aspects of the personality of
which the individual has become aware, we must add the qualification
that this includes the unconscious awareness of personal factors. Unconscious identification with a cause, a person, or an institution illustrates
the point. To ignore this unconscious awareness of items that are self-
oriented would be to omit a significant phase of individual motivation.

The way in which one becomes aware of the nature of his own features, it will be remembered from Chapter 6, is not identical with the
way in which he becomes aware of other objects in his experience. Mead
is clearest on this point, and he writes that:

> The individual experiences himself as such, not directly, but only in-
> directly, from the particular standpoints of other individual members of
> the same social group, or from the generalized standpoint of the social
> group as a whole to which he belongs. For he enters his own ex-
> perience as a self or individual, not directly or immediately, not by
> becoming a subject to himself, but only insofar as he first becomes an
> object to himself just as other individuals are objects to him or in his
> experience; and *he becomes an object to himself only by taking the
> attitudes of other individuals toward himself within a social environ-*

[47] G. H. Mead, *Mind, Self, and Society* (Chicago: The University of Chicago
Press, 1934), pp. 136–140.
[48] *Ibid.*, pp. 150–152.

*ment or context of experience and behavior in which both he and they
are involved.*[49]

It is relatively easy to overemphasize the point made by Mead that
self-consciousness arises as a result of one's taking the attitudes of others,
or what he believes to be the attitudes of others, toward one's own body
and personality. We know what we are like, what statuses are ours, what
roles we will be permitted to play, what success we have met in our
attempts to fulfill our basic needs and desires largely by giving attention
to the attitudes of others as these attitudes are revealed to us by the
behavior of our associates. However, one can know of himself objectively
by means other than attending to the attitudes and actions of others. No
improvement in perceptive accuracy can be explained on a purely social
basis.

It is relevant at this point to note that some students of the problem
have seen fit to divide the self. Thus one distinguishes the "ideal self" as
the self the subject would like to be, the "self" as the subject actually
thinks it is, and the "social self" as the subject believes others perceive
him.[50] We believe this to be a useful distinction, especially in the difference noted between the *total self* which is a function of both social and
nonsocial perceptual influences, and the *social self* which is a product of
the role taking process. All of one's self-perception is not social in origin—
there are, as noted earlier, nonsocial means of learning about one's self.[51]
All of man's relationships are not social, and interaction exceeds the
bounds of social and symbolic processes.

The self, as we have emphasized, is not the equivalent of the person.
The shock which usually accompanies the hearing of one's recorded voice,
or the viewing of one's self on the movie screen for the first time, is suggestive of the many personal aspects of which one may have long been
unaware. Such experiences, incidentally, are valuable in enabling the
person to become aware of his subjective nature, and may enhance his
chances of playing the social role intended for him by his associates, or
at least may enable him to understand better why such roles are intended.
*No aspect of the person, then, becomes part of the self unless he has
experienced it as object.* Part of what is called social intelligence is the
ability to become aware of the way in which others view us; the social

[49] *Ibid.*, p. 138. Italics added.
[50] Gene M. Smith, "Interrelations Among Six Measures of Self Concept Discrepancy and Instability," *American Psychologist*, 11 (1956), 357.
[51] *Cf.* Paul Pfuetze, *Self, Society, Existence* (New York: Harper and Brothers,
1954), which the author describes as ". . . an attempt to state and explore the concept of what I have called 'the social self' from a philosophical, psychological, and
religious point of view, . . ." (p. 1). This stimulating essay seeks to point out the
similarities in the works of George Herbert Mead and Martin Buber.

bore is the person who is oblivious to the evaluations which others make of his physical being and his social behavior. He fails to play the expected role which accompanies an assigned status or position.

Once some aspect of the person is perceived as object it need not always be judged in the same way. The same aspect can have different meanings and be differently valued as other aspects of the personality change. Another social psychologist has stated it this way:

> A person who is judging anyone's act is doing so as a "subject." The act or person being judged is an "object." Any man can be both, simultaneously; having acted, he may make his act an object of scrutiny. He may take as many different stands toward it as his vocabulary permits, just as he may toward another's. His own act may be his object of scorn, denial, dissent, blame, attack, shame, disapproval, a yardstick for further endeavor, a cross to bear, a sign of personal brilliance, or anything else that he has the capacity to view it as. And if he should acquire new terminology through new group participation, he will inevitably reassess certain of his past acts—and himself—in the new terms. The self is no more immune to re-examination from new perspectives than any other object.[52]

This phenomenon may be illustrated from an incident which occurred in a large urban high school. A member of the faculty had a reputation as a boor but did not seem to appreciate the magnitude of his social ineptness. Upon entering the faculty lounge one morning, he noticed that another faculty member was reading a magazine of which he did not approve. He said to his peer, "I thought that would be about the level of reading you would enjoy." The next morning when he entered the faculty lounge, he found all the chairs occupied by other faculty members, each one of whom was busily reading the same magazine. Whether he gained any insight from this social interaction or "group therapy" is not known.

We now turn attention to that which examines the self.

The Ego or "I" Versus the Self or "Me"

In our emphasis upon the importance of the self in human behavior, especially social behavior, we must not overly stress man's nature as a social object, as a mere reflection of the attitudes and actions of others, the significant other. There is also that aspect of the person which is the *subject* or actor, not merely the object or thing acted upon by others and by the person. In Mead's words, "The 'I' is the response of the individual

---

[52] Anselm Strauss, *Mirrors and Masks* (Glencoe, Ill.: The Free Press of Glencoe, 1959), p. 33.

to the attitude of the community as this appears in his own experience."[53] The *I* or *ego* acts in terms of, and toward, more than the self, to be sure, but much of one's social actions involve, one way or another, consciousness of the self as this is socially defined by the attitudes of others which he has learned to take toward his own body, skills, knowledge, beliefs, or feelings. The self represents what is, or is believed to be, whereas the *I* or *ego* is responsible for changes in the person, in the community, and in the relationships between them. The action taken by the person as *I* shapes and reshapes the self of the future, which in turn modifies the behavior of the *I* in subsequent actions.

When the *I* examines aspects of the self, when it looks at the person's characteristics reflexively—generally through the eyes of others, it is pleased with certain aspects, finds others to have relatively neutral stimulus value, and is dissatisfied with still other features. It is the *I* that looks into the social looking-glass described by Cooley.

In a study of attitudes of 196 female and 110 male university students toward their own bodies,[54] certain information was revealed:

Table IX*

Male and Female Dissatisfaction with Physique

Males	*Females*
1. On average wished to be 3 lbs. heavier	1. On average wished to be 7 lbs. lighter
2. One-half of males dissatisfied with weight wished to be lighter	2. All females dissatisfied with weight wished to be lighter
3. All but two males dissatisfied with stature wished to be taller	3. One-half of dissatisfied females wished to be shorter
4. Dissatisfied males wanted wider shoulders, thicker arms and legs; one half wanted larger chests	4. Dissatisfied females wanted smaller hips and waists, thinner arms and legs; nearly half wanted larger breasts
5. Wanted more prominent chins and less prominent ears	5. Wanted bigger eyes, better vision, and more oval shaped faces

* G. Calden, R. M. Lundy, and R. J. Schlafer, "Sex Differences in Body Concepts," *Journal of Consulting Psychology*, 23 (1959), 378. All differences reported were significant at the .01 level.

[53] G. H. Mead, *op. cit.*, p. 196. The treatment of the *I*, the *me*, and the *self* in *Mind, Self, and Society* is something less than consistent. The *me* as synonym for *self* occurs, but also *me* as actor, rather than as object, is made explicit, *cf.* p. 196. Elsewhere *I* and *ego* are equated, *cf.* p. 196. We will use *me* as equivalent to *self* as the object, and *I* and *ego* as actor or subject.

[54] G. Calden, R. M. Lundy, and R. J. Schlafer, "Sex Differences in Body Concepts," *Journal of Consulting Psychology*, 23 (1959), p. 378.

In general, the females were less satisfied with their physiques. When asked to judge samples of Sheldon's somatotypes, both sexes preferred the balanced type, but the females were significantly less inclined than the males to perceive the extreme mesomorph as attractive.

The self-images of these university students seem clearly to reflect the values of time and place as reflected in the attitudes of their significant others. One wonders whether or not a similar study of women under pioneering, frontier conditions of, say, the 1870's, would have revealed the same self evaluations. Here, also, is an illustration of reference groups (those persons who do have the kind of face and figure desired) which are comparison groups and not members of one's significant or affective other. (*See* Figure 9, Chapter 4.) These groups become criteria for measuring oneself but their attitudes are not necessarily significant in influencing the individual's attitudes or actions. We may like the biological heritage which is ours as reflected in intelligence, height, health, curly hair, and clear complexion; we may neither esteem highly nor despise such aspects of our personality as attitudes toward swimming, ability to play cards, color of eyes, study habits, habits of orderliness, or speech habits; and we may heartily dislike our inability to speak effectively before large groups, the ease with which we become bored, our lack of training in music, and the inability to make our own decisions. However, these evaluations of ourselves may well be altered by changing circumstances. *It is in terms of the situation or episode, usually social in nature, in which we find ourselves, a situation which involves our perception of the attitudes of those about us, that the various aspects of the body and personality move into and out of the range of self-consciousness.* The nature of our affective other determines in large part the evaluation we place on various aspects of our personality. The neutral aspects of the moment may become the esteemed or despised ones of tomorrow or next week.[55] A person's inability to swim or ski may be of no consequence, and therefore not consciously considered, if he lives in a part of the country where little or no swimming or skiing is done. But if he moves into an area where water or snowy mountains abound, and everyone swims or skis, he may become acutely aware of the inabilities, and self-consciousness with regard to them may become a signal factor of personal relationships.

An illustration of the process by which latent aspects of the self can become active is provided by a study made of the influence of consciousness of religious affiliation upon opinions concerning such problems as

[55] T. M. Newcomb, *Social Psychology* (New York: The Dryden Press, 1950), p. 248. His view entails the designation of a certain attitude as part of the *self* on one day, but part of the *ego* on the next. *Ego* is, according to Newcomb, "*the self as a value to be protected and enhanced.*" p. 328. This making *ego* an object, rather than subject, conflicts with the established Freudian use.

public versus private school attendance, Europe's problems, birth control, evangelism, and ethics in general.[56] Members of three religious groups were separated into groups which were given the same questionnaire, but under different conditions. The experimental group met in small rooms and were informed that they were all of the same religion; whereas the control group met with members of other religious preference in the regular auditorium-lecture hall. Members of one religious group were used as a control by placing them in a small room similar to the experimental groups, but no consciousness of religious group membership was created.

The individuals of one religious category, who were made aware (self-conscious or ego-involved) of their religious attitudes, marked those items that were pertinent to their beliefs and attitudes significantly different from the way their coreligionists in the control group did. Deviation from the expected answers (in terms of the explicit values of the group) were much higher in the control group (24 per cent) than in the self-involved experimental group (8 per cent).[57] This is seen as evidence of the view that aspects of the self may enter or leave the area of ego-involvement or self consciousness. What the self is at any time depends upon all three variables of the interactionist personality model.

Thus, again we emphasize the importance of understanding the personality as a part of a larger whole, as a relationship to the other factors in social behavior. The things in the personality of which one becomes aware, and the importance assigned to them, are not functions of the subjective aspects of personality per se, but find meaning only when we view the social behavior in all of its aspects—psychological, social psychological, and sociological. We cannot agree that certain attitudes of the individual are ego- or self-involved whereas others are not. All attitudes have as referent the person, and along this line we agree wholeheartedly with the social psychologists who wrote that:

Self-interest is the final generalization which sums up man's audiences, avoidances, appetites, emotions, and cross-conditioned drives. Man's actions, therefore, are always an expression of his self-interest.[58]

[56] W. W. Charters, Jr., and T. M. Newcomb, "Some Attitudinal Effects of Experimentally Increased Salience of a Membership Group," in E. E. Jacoby, T. M. Newcomb, and E. L. Hartley, *op. cit.*, pp. 276–281. Seventy-two questions were asked of all participants.

[57] *Ibid.*, p. 281. The relationship was in the same direction for the other two groups but not significant at the .01 level.

[58] D. Katz and R. L. Schanck, *Social Psychology* (New York: John Wiley and Sons, 1938), p. 288. A similar statement is found in E. B. Holt, *Animal Drive and the Learning Process* (New York: Henry Holt and Co., 1931), p. 237. *Cf. also* Chapter 5 in the present book.

This is not to say that we do not become more acutely aware of the difference between *self* and *not-self* on occasions, for surely we do, as was pointed out above. However, the state of affairs usually indicated by such statements as self-consciousness and ego-involvement are social situations wherein there exists, in the view of the individual concerned, a situation which threatens his well-being, or a situation that serves as an opportunity of fulfilling certain of his felt needs or desires. The matter becomes less mystical and elusive if we keep our attention focused upon the social behavior of man, including, of course, the attitudes of the individual in question. Thus we see as useful such concepts as self-centeredness and egocentricity.

Self-perception, Social Position, Role Behavior

A person's self-image, although partly a result of nonsocial learning, is largely a function of his taking toward himself the attitudes and perceptions, actual or imputed, of other persons, that is, of role taking. There is a close relationship between his self-image, which is a function of his position in a social system, and his role behavior. This relationship is frequently observable in political life wherein the occupant of an elected or appointed office alters his behavior in keeping with the expectations that define the position. In such instances the role behavior tends to coincide more and more with obligations, as well as with the prerogatives, of the position occupied. The political hack who gains an important elected or appointed office is not unmindful of the perception of the office on the parts of a wide variety of persons in his affective other or reference group. The prestige of the office becomes a measure of the occupant, and some interesting alterations in role playing have been observed. An instance that illustrates our point, noted in many American history books, is the case of Chester A. Arthur, who succeeded to the Presidency of the United States upon the death of President Garfield. Arthur had been the pet of the New York political machine, and many, if not most, men "in the know" expected one of the worst, most corrupt administrations in American history. This expectation is summed up by the remark of one contemporary who exclaimed, " 'Chet' Arthur President of the United States! Good God!" However, Arthur's administration turned out to be a pleasant surprise to the supporters of good government. The roles he played were quite in keeping with the rights and duties assigned to the office of the President. He responded to the attitudes he knew the populace had toward the occupant of the presidency. Even those who do not fill the offices they hold as well as did Arthur tend to give at least lip service to the role behavior expected of them. This is true whether the position is that of President of the United States, a father, schoolteacher, businessman, or any other.

FRUSTRATION-AGGRESSION

The authors who formulated the frustration-aggression hypothesis originally wrote that ". . . the proposition is that the occurrence of aggressive behavior always presupposes the existence of frustration, and, contrariwise, that the existence of frustration always leads to some form of aggression."[59] When viewed from the interactionist conception of human behavior, this proposition must be modified. If the latter frame of reference is valid, then no item, per se, is frustrating, that is, serves to block a goal or thwarts the fulfillment of some desire or need. Furthermore, how a frustrating experience is to operate in a person's subsequent behavior is a function of more than the experience itself. What the resolution of the problem of goal frustration (a function of the autonomic nervous system and emotional in nature) is to be, will be determined by the personal variables (the person's knowledge, beliefs, attitudes, and habits) and by the environmental factors, both social and non-social, which are pertinent to the episode in question. The processes that will come into play will relate the several personality items in the ensuing behavior. In Figure 24 items that might frustrate one's plans to play tennis are noted in each of the three personality categories.

Whether or not any of these frustrating variables or attributes will be instrumental in the emergence of aggressive behavior will be determined by the nature of other variables. If one's physique plus acquired skill plus the availability of water permits the substitution of alternate means, such as aquatic sports, the frustration will be attenuated or eliminated by compensatory activity. If the individual's imagination and store of knowledge are adequate, he will have no difficulty rationalizing away the frustrated feeling. His capacity for self deception will permit or deny him the displacement of his aggression from his personal inadequacies to a more vulnerable object. In an impoverished environment one is more apt to accord exaggerated value to the goal sought, and therefore to respond with aggressive action. The presence of several acceptable alternatives (golf, swimming, squash, horseback riding, polishing a car, mountain climbing, and the like) reduces the significance of any single goal. The nature of the significant other helps to define the situation as frustrating or not, and therefore shapes subsequent action.

Thus the frustration-aggression hypothesis becomes meaningful only when applied in an interactionist framework. No experience is frustrating

[59] John Dollard, L. W. Doob, N. E. Miller, O. H. Mowrer, and R. R. Sears, *Frustration and Aggression* (New Haven, Conn.: Yale University Press, 1939), 1. See also Ross Stagner and Clyde S. Congdon, "Another Failure to Demonstrate Displacement of Aggression," *Journal of Abnormal and Social Psychology*, 51 (1955), 695–696. *Cf.* Stuart Palmer, *A Study of Murder* (New York: Thos. Y. Crowell, Co., 1962) for a cogent argument for frustration as a signal factor in homicidal aggression.

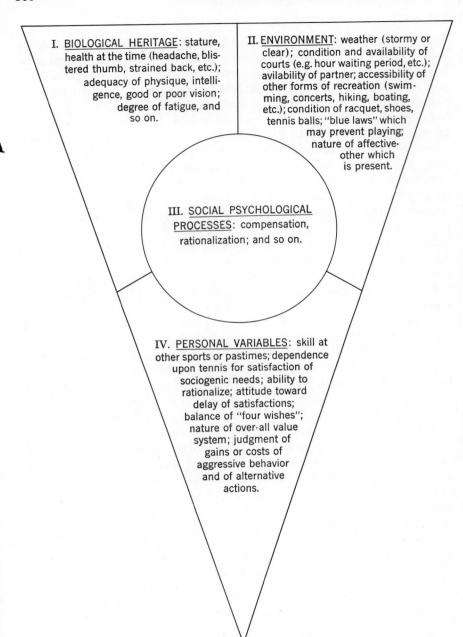

FIGURE 24. Interactionist model of variables potentially interactive in frustration episodes, suggesting sequels other than aggression.

for everyone, and frustration is motivationally significant only under certain circumstances. In short, aggression follows frustration if the person sees it, partly as a product of role taking, as functional. This conclusion has been reached by other students of the problem. One says: "The hypothesis being offered is that the instrumental value of aggression determines the frustration aggression relationship."[60]

SOMATOTYPES AND PERSONALITY

Another form of the particularistic explanation of personality is seen in the readiness with which aggressive, ambitious behavior in short persons, particularly males, is interpreted as compensation for their short stature. In a culture in which the size of many things is deemed better if it is above average, there is a logical basis for assuming that, in certain instances, such contemporary behavior does indeed occur. However, to make this assumption in all instances of aggressive behavior in short persons is to go well beyond the evidence at hand. This uncritical judgment raises certain problems when we find little or no aggressive action in small persons, and much of it in tall ones. As in all stereotypes, there is some truth to this one, but most stereotypes are more often than not incorrect. In Chapter 3 the various somatotypes were briefly described. That there are comparable experiences growing out of the interaction of comparable body structure and comparable cultural factors can hardly be denied. Without a doubt the personalities of these individuals with markedly ectomorphic, endomorphic, and mesomorphic body form do manifest comparable behavior patterns which reflect the comparable somatotype.

Some of the grosser aspects of the influence of body build on behavior can be perceived quite readily by any of us. The thinly muscled, delicately boned ectomorph does not win plaudits as an all-American football player or wrestling star; nor does he earn his daily bread as a puddler in a steel mill. If he turns to crime, it will not be to become a "strong-arm" mugger or robber. Likewise, the overlarge endomorphic mesomorph will hardly make a successful pickpocket, tumbler, or test pilot. A friend of the authors, a physician, wanted very much to be a surgeon, but his gargantuan hands denied him this opportunity. None of the conventional instruments was of sufficient size to fit his hands and fingers, and incisions made by these hands and fingers would have been cavernous indeed. The fact that he turned to making violins, good violins, may well be correctly viewed as compensatory behavior.

However, beyond these grosser limitations that somatotypes place upon man's relationships with the environmental world, just what the

[60] Arnold H. Buss, "Physical Aggression in Relation to Different Frustrations," *Journal of Abnormal and Social Psychology*, 67 (July 1963), 7.

subjective aspects of personality will be cannot with confidence be predicted upon the basis of somatotypes. When it is said of a person that "he is the kindest person I have ever known," it would be foolhardy to attempt to predict the body build of that person. Such crimes as embezzlement are not the monopoly of any one sort of physique, and the gun has long since equalized the prowess of fighters bent upon homicide. There was a time when soldiers were selected because of their large size and mesomorphic qualities; today, however, machines are designed for the average, and the giant is excluded from the cockpits of fighter planes and from many other branches of the armed forces.

One need not look long for instances wherein changes in cultural values have enhanced the chances for good adjustment of persons of abnormal body build. Prior to the advent of basketball's widespread popularity in the United States, the male who grew to heights above six feet and four inches was more than likely to be considered a "glandular goon" and was critically evaluated when scholarships and jobs were awarded. Today such persons are encouraged to play basketball from junior high school on, and, with the advent of semiprofessional athletics in many colleges and universities, are soon feted and pursued by representatives of such colleges and universities. Without such shifts in cultural values, giants would not have the opportunities to gain fame and fortune, nor would it be true that the most expensive buildings on the campuses are not the "halls of learning," but business-oriented basketball spectatoria. In some schools, the physically normal, or physically handicapped, scholar has less chance of gaining entrance than the mesomorph who has developed his athletic potential but neglected his intellectual growth. Such factors cannot help influencing the development of personality.

No better evidence of the varying relationship between physical characteristics of mankind and personality development could be asked for than that which involves the relationship of the nonwhite American to the high esteem most Americans have for athletics of one kind or another. The degree to which the Negro's chances for fulfillment of the desires for recognition, new experiences, and security are evidenced by the many openings in the sport world is great indeed. One has but to think of the paucity of economic and educational opportunities that are available to the lower class Negro to realize the role played by college and professional football, baseball, and basketball. The great contrast between the poorly paid, overworked, barnstorming Negro baseball player prior to the acceptance of Negro players in the big leagues, and today's outstanding Negro baseball players is reflected in the living conditions of their families. Poverty and relative anonymity, on the one hand, and wealth and fame, on the other, reflect the role played by altered cultural values (and the appropriate norms) while personal variables remain the same.[61]

DEPRIVATION AND PERSONALITY

One means of demonstrating the interactionist nature of personality is to observe behavior among several persons when one of the items in the interaction is held constant. One such instance was provided during the Second World War, when a group of volunteers participated in an experiment designed to reveal effects of semistarvation.[62] Thirty-two men began the experiment, two failed to complete the six months of diet, restricted to 1,570 calories per day, and another two were dropped after completing the six-month experiment. Averaging approximately twenty-five years of age, all of the men were healthy, intelligent, and young, but varied widely as to body types, degree of physical fitness, personal and social characteristics, and background. There developed in all of them various degrees of semistarvation neurosis, involving diminution of ambition, ability to concentrate, sex drive, self-discipline, mental alertness, and drive to activity; the "neurosis" also involved an increase in tiredness, appetite, muscular soreness, sensitivity to noise, irritability, apathy, hunger pains, moodiness, and depression.[63] However, everyone did not develop the same patterns of behavior, and the researchers raised the question as to why some men developed abnormal behavior patterns that went beyond the range of the common semistarvation neurosis. The following two cases drawn from the report illustrate the personality differences:

Case No. 2. A 24-year old law student, characterized as having come from an adequate home, had a happy childhood, and was a social and professional leader in college and law school. His physical symptoms

[61] For an interesting observation about the possible relationship between the personality types postulated by Sheldon and Stevens in their *Varieties of Temperament* (New York: Harper and Brothers, 1942) and the cultural types defined by Ruth Benedict in her famous *Patterns of Culture* (New York: Penguin Books, 1945), see Robert W. Janes, "A Note on an Apparent Relationship Between Temperamental Traits and Personality Traits," *Social Forces*, 28 (Dec. 1949), 199–204. Janes finds a significant number of characteristics which are shared by the Zuni Indians and the viscerotonic personality, the Dobuans and cerebretonic types, and the Kwakiutl Indians of the Northwest coastal regions and the somatotonic personality type. He does not press the issue of correlation between somatotypes and personality types.

[62] Ancel Keys, Josef Brozek, Austin Henschel, Olaf Mickelsen, and Henry Longstreet Taylor, *The Biology of Human Starvation*, Vols. I and II (Minneapolis: University of Minnesota Press, 1950). *See also* H. S. Guetskow, and P. H. Bowman, *Men and Hunger, a Psychological Manual for Relief Workers* (Elgin, Ill.: Brethren Publishing House, 1946). Further discussion pertinent to this question of relativity of motives is found in Dorothy Lee, "Are Basic Needs Ultimate?" *Journal of Abnormal and Social Psychology*, 43 (July 1948), 391–395.

[63] *Ibid.*, p. 912.

were average for the semistarvation diet, with the exception of excessive edema (swelling) in the last weeks of the six-month experiment. He was reported as being ". . . lethargic, mildly depressed, and somewhat irritable."[64] In common with the others in the experiment, No. 2 suffered from hunger pains and was preoccupied with thoughts of food, but he seldom talked much about food. His sexual interests dropped off severely rather early in the experiment, and he lost interest in a young lady with whom he seemed to have much in common intellectually. He himself expressed surprise at this lost interest in her friendship. However, he experienced little or no temptation to stop the limited diet, and finished his last semester of law school as well as worked toward a master's degree in political science.[65]

Case No. 234. In contrast to the above pattern of behavior is the case of a young man described as being ". . . Charming, handsome, artistic, and has a 'gift of gab'."[66] Moreover, his standing with the group was high. During the first four weeks, he had unusual dreams of "eating senile and insane people," and was frequently tempted during his stay in the experiment to break the diet, which he did "flagrantly" during the eighth week, eating several malted milks and sundaes. Later he resorted to stealing a variety of objects, and after some resolutions to do better, was dismissed from the experiment. He was judged to be "clearly pathological" on the basis of a well-known personality inventory, the results of which suggested that he was "bisexual with poor integration."[67] Despite his failure to complete the experiment, the experimenters stated that ". . . he appears to have sufficient assets to adjust to the ordinary circumstances of life without much difficulty."[68]

These two cases reveal the multifactor nature of personality. Even though the subjects were matched on many counts, and the only significant variable introduced was the environmental one of a near-starvation diet, the resulting behavior patterns of the subjects were quite different. The interactionist approach to the study of human behavior finds this not at all surprising—in fact it would find any other result quite startling. Each of the thirty-two subjects brought to the experiment a store of attitudes, habits, facts, and beliefs that, in total configuration, was unique in each case. Starvation diets do not mean the same things to all men.

These two contrasting cases demonstrate how comparable environments can yield quite different personality results. It brings to the fore the fact that personality is a relationship of factors both within and without the skin of the individual. The ways in which cases No. 2 and

64 *Ibid.*, p. 881.
65 *Ibid.*, pp. 881–882.
66 *Ibid.*, p. 885.
67 *Ibid.*, p. 885.
68 *Ibid.*

234 were related to the common experience of food deprivation, an environmental factor, were in some instances much the same—both manifested certain common features of the semistarvation neurosis, but each manifested unique relationships to the dietary factor. Under normal conditions of American life both these young men were well adjusted and lived more or less integrated lives. Under conditions of war they shared the minority status of conscientious objectors to military experience, but the day-by-day experiences of case No. 2 had prepared him to meet the rigors of the 1,570 caloric daily intake more successfully than the experiences from which emerged the subjective factors of case No. 234's personal makeup. When the latter was described as being "charming," the description involved a given environmental setting, and again indicates the fact that only part of personality is within the individual. He was something less than charming under the stress of the experiment. The role he played in each episode of his life was a function of external conditions as much as it was of the internal, private aspects.[69]

Inasmuch as few of us are ever really hungry, let alone in danger of starvation, it is more profitable to consider the hunger drive in less critical situations if we are to see its relationship to other needs in our culture. It must be obvious to all that civilized man does not eat every time he becomes aware of the contraction of the stomach muscles and certain hypothalamic states that we have learned to call the hunger impulse; nor does he await that sensation before eating. We eat, for the most part, three meals a day, often when we would not do so were it not for prevailing customs. Furthermore, we eat at the homes of friends during nonmeal hours whether we are hungry or not. After eating a heavy meal, surely surfeited with regard to food, we stuff down the dessert placed before us. It was not without some logic that a physician, some years ago, recommended the eating of the dessert first, for then, he reasoned, only enough of the regular main courses would be consumed to meet the hunger needs. Further evidence of the relative nature of the hunger drive is seen in the common practice of low-salaried young women skimping on lunch money to save enough for the clothes that will assure them the recognition they seek. The quest for affection, social approval, or the security of better health leads many a person to deny himself or herself full satisfaction at the dinner table. Even at starvation levels, as noted above, other motives may become paramount. There were members of the well-known Donner Party in the Sierra Nevada mountains who chose to die of starvation rather than to eat human flesh and live. Thus we see the

---

[69] *See* Viktor Frankel, *From Death Camp to Existentialism* (Boston: Beacon Press, 1959), for further discussion of heterogeneous responses to extreme deprivation in Nazi concentration camps. *Also, The American Soldier* (Princeton: Princeton University Press, 1949), employed enormous amounts of data in the study of wartime deprivation.

influence of cultural values in determining the strength of the hunger impulse as a motive in social behavior. One need not agree with those who postulate a fixed hierarchy of motives in order to see that there is truth in the statement that the motivation of a person at any given time is in large part a function of the degree of satisfaction of all of the person's motives, both innate and acquired. There is no single value that some persons have not considered of paramount importance and therefore worthy of being sought or maintained even at the cost of sacrificing all other values, including life itself. The number of persons—not all of them with martyr complexes—who have deemed life to be a subordinate value is impressively large. In nearly every country in the world the number of suicides exceeds the number of homicides. The ascendancy of any particular value is a function of the particular value system of the person, the presence or absence of persons who constitute one's affective other, and of the many personal variables which the individual brings to the situation in question.

PERSONALITY INTEGRATION AND PERSONALITY CONFLICT

By integration is meant a oneness, a wholeness, an absence of conflicting elements or components. By personality integration we mean a relationship among; (1) the organism; (2) acquired or personal variables; and (3) its environment from which contradictory or conflicting components are excluded. Integration in this sense, as someone has pointed out, is not a datum but is, rather, something one aspires to achieve and probably never completely attains. Such integration can come only after all contradictions among attitudes and traits of the individual and expectations of the significant other have become, by whatever means, resolved. It implies the presence and availability of appropriate physical attributes such as strength, agility, intelligence, and correctly functioning physiological organs; it implies that there is sufficient wealth to meet the reasonable needs and desires of the persons involved, and that the social systems to which one belongs are constituted of complementary and supplementary positions; and it also implies that knowledge, beliefs, and attitudes that have been developed are complementary and not contradictory.

Integration may be judged objectively, regardless of the value system of the judge. For good or ill, integration can occur with a wide variety of value systems, providing all of the supporting and coordinating components are present and protected. The tyrant and the saint, the feudalist and the democrat, the theist and the atheist, the bigot and the unprejudiced—these and many other contrasting personal value configurations can be incorporated into either an integrated or an nonintegrated personality. That certain prerequisite impositions of force or freedom, of censorship and free expression, on the societal level are essential to the existence of some of these integrative personality systems is, for the moment at least, irrelevant to the attainment of personality integration.

The integration cannot be judged on the basis of any single factor, but only in terms of the relationship of the factors. No one of these items by itself demands either a good adjustment or maladjustment. Mental retardation or superior mental endowment may be a component of an integrated or a nonintegrated personality. Although it is true, as Plato pointed out, that poverty can degrade a person, there is a wide range of wealth permitted in personality integration. In order to develop an integrated personality, one must not attempt to satisfy attitudes that cannot be reconciled, nor may he attempt to play contradictory roles. He who would be both saint and sinner, both anti-Semite and friend of the Jewish people, both agnostic and ardent believer, both supporter of Judeao-Christian ethics and participant in shady business deals, is not a candidate for personality integration. Consistency in attitudes, both of individual and significant other, is a prerequisite for this oneness of personality. The person who attempts to play the "all things to all men" role is doomed to disappointment and falls heir to the personality conflicts and attending feelings of insecurity that accompany the attempt to play irreconcilable roles or to occupy conflicting positions. Ironically enough, it is the need for social psychological security which often induce one to attempt the playing of these conflicting roles, roles which can lead only to the intensification of the feeling of insecurity as the person learns that such an attempt results, not in satisfying all, but in satisfying none.

Types of Personality Conflicts

Personality conflicts always involve interaction of personality components, no one component by itself being sufficient to cause conflict. There are three categories of conflict: *First, social-structural conflicts; Second, the less formally structured value conflicts involving the significant other*; and, *Third, subjective value conflicts*.

SOCIAL-STRUCTURAL CONFLICTS

The social-structural conflict is a function of the nature of the social system wherein positions or statuses present contradictory demands or expectations. The conflict may be a result of one person occupying two or more conflicting positions, or it may involve one person whose position is defined in a contradictory manner by different persons or groups.

We have stressed the fact that, other things being equal, human beings tend to be what others expect them to be. Assuredly, variation in personal perceptions, knowledge, and attitudes introduces exceptions to this rule, yet every social system demands this fulfillment of others' expectations. To the extent that the social system is itself integrated, wherein the occupants of its many positions are not required to play conflicting roles, the individuals may develop integrated personalities.[70] Such circumstances prevail only in those small, isolated rural communities from which deviant persons can emigrate. Under such conditions, there is the possibility that a marked homogeneity of values will be developed. In this sacred, rural community where tradition is esteemed and where most attitudes are held in common, it is not difficult to respond positively to all, or nearly all, the attitudes of one's affective other. In other words, it is relatively easy to behave and to feel in accordance with the expectations of the whole community.[71] The Amish communities, so well known in the literature of social science, are illustrative of such environmental conditions. The economy is agricultural, consonant with the Amish feeling, religiously, that this is the only proper means of earning a livelihood. The proper positions of males and females, adults and children are defined unambiguously. The educational values are held in common, and aspirations for college, or even high school, degrees are foreign to the group. The bases for feelings of shame and guilt are explicit and are the same, and the Amish conscience reflects this fact. The affective or significant other of each and every Amishman is restricted to his fellow Amishmen in their rural setting.[72] Rarely does conflict occur because of different definitions of the positions he occupies in the Amish social structure. The Amishman's identity is rarely threatened in his community.

However, such homogeneous social systems are rarely found today, and there are many subsystems wherein the positions are differentially defined. The position of "teacher" is defined quite differently in a Lutheran parochial school, in a Roman Catholic parochial school, in a highly selective private preparatory school, in an isolated, rural, one-room school, and in a large public high school. The world famous "monkey trial," or Scopes trial, in Dayton, Tennessee, illustrates the conflict induced by differential definition of the teacher's position by law and by science.

[70] N. Gross, A. W. McEachern, and W. S. Mason, in their article "Role Conflict and its Resolution," have indicated the many meanings of "role conflict." It has been used to mean the conflicts that involve social positions which are differently defined; some restrict it to only *perceived* incompatible expectations whereas others do not require awareness of conflicts; some see it as function of multiple position occupancy which is simultaneous but others apply it to conflicts in a single occupancy, and still others make legitimacy of the expectations the basis for role conflict. E. Maccoby, T. M. Newcomb, and E. L. Hartley, *Readings in Social Psychology*, 3rd ed. (New York: Henry Holt and Co., 1958), pp. 447–448. It seems best to avoid the concept *role conflict* wherever possible.

[71] It is not necessary to argue that *complete* homogeneity of values exists—this is probably impossible even between two persons. Inasmuch as human adjustment is always a compromise among several competing motives, it is not possible for a resolution of all conflicting and competing values even within a single individual, let alone a plurality of individuals. Compromise of human values is man's destiny.

[72] Recent changes in "the world" have affected the life patterns of Amishmen considerably, with attendant acculturation taking place. Some groups have attempted to move to newer farming areas, farther removed from urbanized, industrialized influences.

Other personality conflicts which result from social positions occupied are:

1. Employee trying to please his shop foreman and union steward on controversial issue.

2. Being highly ethical and also a high-pressure salesman.

3. University student and member of fundamentalist church group.

4. Father-husband in an occupation that takes him away from the family for long periods.

5. Governmental purchasing agent (obliged to buy from lowest bidder) and part-owner of supplying firm (obliged to sell at highest price).

6. Any "marginal man" expected to behave according to contradictory values by peer group and by kinship group. ·

7. The American woman who is expected to play a subordinate role to that of the male, yet expected to do her best in academic and professional areas, which means that she often exceeds her male associates.[73]

That these and many other personality conflicts occur in a society as dynamic and pluralistic as ours is not surprising.

LESS FORMALLY STRUCTURED VALUE CONFLICTS
RELATED TO SIGNIFICANT OTHER

In this category of personality conflict the expectations of others are not functions of established positions in a social system. The values involved may often be functions of personal social learning.

Looking for a moment at our own dominant culture patterns, which are largely urban in setting, we see the extreme heterogeneity of social values, which cannot possibly be incorporated within a single normal personality.[74] In the behavior of those about us, we see evidence of conflicting attitudes toward socialism and capitalism, alcoholic beverages, premarital sex relations, capital punishment, organized religion, divorce, eating of meats, thermonuclear warfare, dancing, public education, sales tax, gambling, Bikini bathing suits, career women, budgets for probes of outer space, labor unions, and so forth, that range all the way from complete approval to violent and uncompromising disapproval. Aesthetic judgments are equally divergent, as reflected in the ardent champions of jazz music contesting with the votaries of classicism, the traditionalists

[73] See Mirra Komarovsky, "Cultural Contradictions and Sex Roles," *American Journal of Sociology*, 52 (1946), 184–189. This well-known article describes a conflict situation that faces educated women today as much as in 1946.

[74] It is recognized that, in a time of rapid communication and transportation, heterogeneity of values—and therefore of expectations—can occur in rural areas.

in architecture protesting against the heresy of a Frank Lloyd Wright, and the gentlemen who prefer blondes failing to see eye-to-eye with those who prefer more pigmentation in their comely companions. In the realm of etiquette there are those who do not question the dictates of, say, an Amy Vanderbilt, and there are probably more who are either indifferent or defiant with regard to the complexities and the niceties of social behavior as dictated by the elite of our culture. The reader can readily add to this list of conflicting social values and the attitudes which define them.

Among the hundreds of persons one encounters during the day or week in towns, cities, or villages, these various and often strongly opposed values are represented. In order to play roles that are at all consistent, one must exclude or ignore certain of these attitudes from one's significant other, while responding, at least overtly, to others. One cannot, for instance, respond positively to opposite ends of the political spectrum, to both religious fundamentalists and avowed agnostics or atheists, and to the dictates of the statutes and the attitudes of associates whose livelihood depends upon breaking these laws. Even on less serious issues, in the realm of the folkways rather than the mores, an individual finds it necessary to select from among incompatible attitudes. For example, a newcomer in some community or neighborhoods will discover that the inhabitants are sharply divided into bridge players and non-bridge players, the one group somewhat intolerant of the other. The newcomer will, perforce, choose between the groups, because he may find it awkward to attempt to move in both. It becomes a problem to arrange one's affairs and to maintain close contacts with both groups in the community. Undoubtedly the reader has had to make such decisions, involving for example, parents and would-be suitors or relatives and friends.

The point should be clear, then, that unless one is to attempt to play the "all things to all men" role, a person must select from among his associates those whose attitudes he will try to respond to in shaping his behavior. As noted in Chapter 6, G. H. Mead has stressed the importance of the process of selecting our friends and associates in terms of their attitudes toward social values. He points out that each individual tends to select, as effective influences, persons whose attitudes are compatible, thus avoiding the necessity of consciously playing a role in the theatrical sense while in the presence of certain associates. Except for the very insecure person, everyone's significant other is more or less selectively developed. Not everyone is involved in the growth of the conscience nor with the self-image that each person acquires.

If one can succeed in avoiding occupying, in the social system, positions demanding contradictory behavior, if he can take toward himself from his significant other only those attitudes that can be reconciled in his behavior and with his value system, then it can be said that he has acquired what G. H. Mead has called a *generalized other*. In the words of Mead: "The organized community or social group which gives to the individual his unity of self many be called 'the generalized other'."[75] More precisely, it is the community, organization, or integration of *attitudes* held by these persons that gives unity or integrity to the self.

Furthermore it is not simply the cognitive process of perceiving correctly how others perceive and feel about us that gives this self-unity. It is the attitude of the individual toward the others that permits him to avoid any feeling that he must, or ought, to modify his feelings, beliefs, or behavior, in ways that will introduce conflict of his feelings, beliefs, or behavior. He must not only recognize that conflicting expectations exist; his attitudes must be such that he feels no compulsion to play contradictory roles. He must be able to play consistent roles without feeling uncomfortable about it, without feelings of guilt or shame. One has a generalized other if he can, in a crowded room, answer any question put to him about any value without first checking to see who is within hearing distance. This does not mean that he must agree on all counts with his associates and friends. It *does* mean that he cannot pretend to share all of their values; he cannot be hypocritical and possess a generalized other.[76]

Nor does it mean that the individual is a commendable human being. In fact, it may be his callous attitude toward the feelings of others that permits his acquiring a generalized other. Conversely, it may be the em-

---

[75] G. H. Mead, *Mind, Self, and Society* (Chicago: University of Chicago Press, 1934), p. 154. There are other definitions in Mead's work, but this is the clearest and least ambiguous. As R. K. Merton and A. S. Kitt point out, Mead seems to gloss over the heterogeneous nature of the significant other. "Contributions to the Theory of Reference Group Behavior," G. E. Swanson, T. M. Newcomb, and E. L. Hartley, *Readings in Social Psychology* (New York: Henry Holt and Co., 1952), pp. 430. Gerth and Mills also restrict "generalized other" to a smaller proportion of society than Mead appeared to do, *op. cit.*, pp. 95–96. See also their use of *significant other* and *authoritative other*.

Unfortunately, the word *generalized* as presented in *Mind, Self and Society* has two meanings. One is given in the above definition, wherein the significant other presents an integrated set of expectations, which Mead illustrates by the baseball team. Thus, the taking of the attitudes (*role-taking* in Mead's terms) of this kind of affective other gives unity to the self. The other use of the term denotes a resolution or generalizing of multiple, often contradictory, forces (social expectations), wherein the person is influenced more by the stronger forces, but is not unaffected by the lesser ones. The situation is comparable to a planet's location being a function of vector resolution. Such a use of the term would be useful for Lewinian Gestaltists. Mead never worked out the implications of the two meanings, nor called attention to their incompatibility.

[76] It is important to keep in mind that the *generalized other* is also a *significant* or *affective other*, but of a special kind. Everyone's affective other must, if he is to maintain mental health, approximate a generalized other. Research suggests that a signal factor in male alcoholism is the inconsistency of values and attitudes in one's affective other. *Cf.* Richard Ingersoll, *Socialization, Inconsistencies, and Alcoholism*, unpublished thesis, University of Iowa, 1965.

pathetic and sympathetic concern of other persons which denies them the opportunity to expunge their affective other of its conflicting demands. Nevertheless each individual is well advised to inspect his significant other to learn whether or not he is needlessly concerned about attitudes that he, in all logic, should ignore without remorse or fear.

Embarrassment. Embarrassment is a social phenomenon, that is, it always involves taking the attitude or attitudes of one's significant other toward himself. It involves a conflict or discrepancy between the position or status occupied and the role or role behavior, but not all such discrepancies lead to embarrassment.

> Embarrassment occurs whenever some central assumption in a transaction has been unexpectedly and unqualifiedly discredited for at least one participant.[77]

These authors list as categories of embarrassment such episodes as:

> forced choices between friends, public mistakes, exposure of false front, being caught in cover story, misnaming, forgetting names, slips of the tongue, body exposure, invasions of others' back regions, uncontrollable laughter . . . .[78]

The reader can supply additional instances of embarrassing episodes which incapacitate the person, temporarily at least, from successful completion of the episode in question.

No longer does identity for the person exist. That is, no longer does his role appear to be appropriate to him and to his significant or affective other. He has violated norms set by himself and/or others; his position and role do not coincide—his self-perception and the perception he imputes to others of the behavior he *should* be presenting are discrepant. This awareness (sometimes a misperception) leads to his loss of poise, loss of confidence in his ability to control the episode to his satisfaction.[79]

It is readily recognized that embarrassment is much more likely for the person whose affective other is constituted of conflicting assumptions as to proper behavior.

The individual who has developed a generalized other, and therefore an integrated personality, is basically unembarrassable. The elite personality evidences this kind of personality.

---

[77] Edward Gross and Gregory P. Stone, "Embarrassment and the Analysis of Role Requirements," *American Journal of Sociology,* LXX (July 1964), 2. See this source for an excellent treatment of the social psychological aspects of embarrassment. *Cf. also* E. Goffman, "Embarrassment and Social Organization," *American Journal of Sociology,* LXII (Nov. 1956), 264–271.

[78] *Ibid.,* p. 3.

[79] *Ibid.,* pp. 3–12.

SUBJECTIVE VALUE CONFLICTS

The conflict here lies with the subject's own attitudes and not among those of his significant other or among his reference groups. Illustrations are found in the person who seeks a reputation as a wise investor *but* who desires items of conspicuous consumption; who wishes to eat heartily *and* also to remain slim; who wishes a perpetual sun tan *but also* an unwrinkled skin; who wishes to play a bassoon proficiently *but* not to practice; who wants the life of a rakish playboy *and* his wife's love and children's respect; who seeks to be wedded *but* not to leave mamma; who enjoys dominating and hurting others *but* wants to be well liked. For the most part these conflicts are functions of the failure to learn to balance his desires, of learning the necessity of compromise among one's desires, in brief, the failure to become socialized. The reorientation is subjective—not necessarily interpersonal per se.

Nothing in the preceding paragraphs should lead the reader to infer that here, at last, are factors which can be understood outside of the interactionist framework. *Why* a person wishes to have a sun tan, a proficiency on the bassoon, a slender figure, or a bank reserve are functions of learning, mostly on the social level. Role taking still plays an important part in the conflict of attitudes, but the situation is one in which, *under the existing* circumstances, the probability is very slight that the resolution can be effected by other than some modification of action or attitude on the part of the subject. In folk axiom, it is illustrative of the fact that "you cannot have your cake and eat it too." In terms of the interactionist frame of reference, it represents an attempt to play simultaneously two or more irreconcilable roles. Frequently these roles are incompatible with the positions occupied by the subject.

The motivational aspects of these multivalent or contravalent attitudes have long been recognized. Writing in the seventeenth century, philosopher Baruch Spinoza presented this axiom:

> If two contrary actions be excited in the same subject, a change must necessarily take place in both, or in one alone, until they cease to be contrary.[80]

In 1957 there appeared in the literature of social psychology a new name for the conflict involving these contravalent attitudes or, at times, irreconcilable opinions or beliefs. The literature sponsored by the presentation of this new label for old concepts is relevant for students of social psychology, especially those interested in personality integration. *Cognitive dissonance* denotes the subscription, by the individual, to ideas,

[80] Joseph Ratner, *The Philosophy of Spinoza* (New York: The Modern Library, 1927), p. 349.

beliefs, or attitudes that are incompatible, inconsistent, or irreconcilable. The referents of cognitive are beliefs, opinions, or "knowledges," as the author of the phrase called them. He illustrates his term by the apparent discrepancy between one's knowing that smoking is inimical to health and the continued practice of smoking. That such behavior is irrational and irreconcilable with his values (providing he also wishes to have good health and long life) is clear. When such discrepancies between what a person believes and how he acts exist, Festinger argues, the individual is motivated to reduce this discrepancy. In his words:

> Cognitive dissonance can be seen as an antecedent condition which leads to activity oriented toward dissonance reduction just as hunger leads to activity oriented toward hunger reduction. It is a very different motivation from what psychologists are used to dealing with, but, as we shall see, nonetheless, powerful . . . .[81]

> The important point to remember is that there is pressure to produce consonant relations among cognitions and to avoid and reduce dissonance.[82]

That man universally wishes to appear reasonable, logical, and consistent in his beliefs and actions is acknowledged by social psychologists generally, and although this tendency is not usually listed with such motives as hunger, sex, and the sociogenic impulses, it is implicitly assumed by social psychologists. It has been discussed, with varying degrees of centrality, by writers from Plato to those of the present day. Festinger's description of how the Ifaluk's belief that man is all good demands the invention of malevolent ghosts to explain man's evil actions is very apt.[83] In our own culture it has been suggested that a similar problem, that of explaining evil in a universe governed by an omniscient, omnipotent, and beneficent God, is handled by the subscription to the concept of free will. Evidence is seen in the felt need of social psychologists, of whatever school, to explain illogical thinking and behavior. This fact, however, does not detract from the importance of one's being aware of the influence of inconsistencies in personality, of cognitive dissonances.[84]

It is not, however, *cognitive* elements which primarily concern the proponents of cognitive dissonance. Rather it is a combination of beliefs, attitudes, and overt behavior, among which inconsistencies are noted,

---

[81] Leon Festinger, *Cognitive Dissonance* (Evanston, Ill.: Row Peterson, 1957), p. 10.

[82] *Ibid.*, pp. 22–23.

[83] *Op. cit.*, pp. 22–23.

[84] For application of the concept of *cognitive dissonance* to situations involving knowledge, values, and overt action, *see* J. W. Brehm, "Increasing Cognitive Dissonance by a *Fait Accompli*," *Journal of Abnormal and Social Psychology*, 58 (1959), 379–382; and J. W. Brehm and A. R. Cohen, "Choice and Chance Relative Deprivation as Determinants of Cognitive Dissonance," *Ibid.*, 383–387.

that are dissonant and nonintegrated. Others working with the concept note that "Thus there is always the implication that the individual does something incompatible with some need or desire."[85] Incompatible ideas, feelings, and actions do not, per se, constitute motives because of their incompatibility. Most Americans are overweight and will live shorter lives because of this fact. Despite the knowledge of this threat to one of man's basic values, it is the rare American who controls his eating habits properly. The total sale of cigarettes has increased since the publication of articles concluding that smoking cigarettes poses a direct and real threat to health. Dissonance of personal variables of personality are motivational only if (1) they are perceived as incompatible, *and* (2) this incompatibility of attitudes or cognitions is perceived as a threat to the person's values. Seen objectively, the dissonance involved in the overeating and in smoking cigarettes is no greater than the conflict of values with which all mankind must cope.

As indicated earlier in the book, life is of necessity a compromise among competing values, and man must learn to live with this condition. The man who weds must support spouse and children, thus spending on them money he would otherwise spend for such items of wealth as travel, cars, and art objects. It should thus be clear that dissonance of values can exist without its being motivationally significant. Many persons hold to belief in both instincts and self determination, undisturbed by their incompatibility. Logic-tight compartments are not only possible, but highly probable among human beings. Furthermore, such inconsistencies or dissonances can be established in customs and institutions. The fact that Judaeo-Christian ethics cannot be reconciled with racial discrimination, imperialism, totalitarian government and certain business, union and city hall practices motivates some to change their behavior, and some to rationalize it, but it leaves others quite satisfied with the status quo. Mankind has frequently gone to war on behalf of, rather than against, cognitive and attitudinal dissonances.

The history of science is a history of the conflict between traditional dissonant thinking and feeling on the one hand and evidence of such dissonance on the other. An individual is as apt to attempt the conservation of dissonances as he is to seek the retention of consonant ideas and attitudes. As Festinger has pointed out ". . . two cognitive elements may be dissonant for a person living in one culture and not for a person living in another, or for a person with one set of experiences and not for a person with another."[86] In brief, objective discrepancies between cogni-

---

[85] J. W. Brehm and A. R. Cohen, *Explorations in Cognitive Dissonance* (New York: John Wiley and Sons, 1962), p. 8.

[86] Leon Festinger, *Cognitive Dissonance*, p. 15. *See also* Maurice N. Richter, Jr., "The Concept of Cognitive Dissonance," *The Journal of Psychology*, 60 (1965), 291–294.

tive or affective elements are not sufficient to motivate persons to lessen or eliminate the objective dissonance. On the subjective side, the role played by the process of rationalization bulks large in cognitive-dissonance explanations.

Before one can properly evaluate the concept of cognitive dissonance, its nature must be more fully studied. In several of the studies to date, the parts played by cognitive and affective factors are not clearly delineated, and the precise nature of the motivation involved is not identified. The parts played by cultural and universal values need to be clarified. Whether the motivational aspects of the observed dissonance reflects intolerance of logical conflicts or the felt need to fulfill the imputed expectations of one's affective other is a question yet to be resolved. The continued research may reveal that the referents are of a single category of behavior or are heterogeneous in nature. Is it merely a recent instance of the "fallacy of the simple" or has it opened up a hitherto unrecognized motivational category? Does it bring new and fuller understanding of behavior? The results to date are not unequivocal and the components of the theory not clearly identified.[87]

Concerning dissonance theory and other concepts of balance and congruity, one writer has concluded:

> Only a theory which accounts for all the data that the consistency principles now account for, for all the exceptions to these principles, and for all the phenomena which these principles should now but do not consider, is capable of replacing them. It is only a matter of time until such a development takes place.[88]

Our only demurrer is that the referents of such concepts may well prove to be too heterogeneous to be subsumed under a single theory.

[87] Cf. E. Aronson and J. M. Carlsmith, "Performance Expectancy As a Determinant of Actual Performance," and T. C. Brock and A. H. Buss, "Dissonance, Aggression, and Evaluation of Pain," *Journal of Abnormal and Social Psychology*, 65 (1962), 178–182, and 197–202; respectively. D. Bramel, "Selection of a Target for Defensive Projection," T. C. Brock, "Effects of Prior Dishonesty on Postdecision Dissonance," and I. D. Steiner and E. D. Rogers," Alternative Responses to Dissonance," *Journal of Abnormal and Social Psychology*, 66 (1963), 318–324; 325–331; and 128–136, respectively. The fact that several of these experiments were "fraudulent" in that the subjects were tricked or lied to, seems to raise questions concerning the conclusions one can draw. Does the fact that some of the dissonances were false have a bearing on the validity of the findings? *See also* the cautious assessment by Brehm and Cohen, *op. cit.*, 309–313. See O. H. Mowrer, "Cognitive Dissonance or Counter Conditioning? A Reappraisal of Certain Behavioral Paradoxes," *Psychological Record*, 13 (1963), 197–211, for arguments, stemming from interpretations of experiments, contradicting the exposition of D. H. Lawrence and L. Festinger, *Deterents and Reinforcements—The Psychology of Insufficient Reward* (Stanford, Calif.: Stanford University Press, 1962). Cf. J. McV. Hunt, "Motivation Inherent in Information Processing and Action," in O. J. Harvey (ed.) *op. cit.*, for further study of cognitive incongruities.

[88] R. B. Lajone, *Public Opinion Quarterly*, 24 (1960), 296.

There is some support for this view. Critics of cognitive dissonance theory have called attention to the fact that it "often concealed a large number of confounded variables."[89]

The reader will recognize that it is in such contradictory relationships among one's attitudes, beliefs, or "knowledges" that the adjustment processes discussed in Chapter 6 are brought into play, consciously or unconsciously, as the person attempts to live with himself and with other aspects of his perceived environment. The person compensates, rationalizes, and accommodates to the multiple demands of his affective other, his own motivations, and the imperatives of the episodic or situational relationships that confront him. He will misperceive, and even invent perceptions, in order to gain a more satisfactory, if only plausible, relationship of the personality's interactive variables.

Personality conflict is, then, many things. At times it is beyond the individual's ability to alter—being intrinsic to the social system, or systems, in which the person finds himself. At other times it is resolvable by a more careful selection of the attitudes to which the individual responds, or attempts to respond; in brief, by modifying the composition of one's affective other. The conflict can also be reduced, when the stage is properly set, by changes in the subject's own attitudes or perceptions. Thus personality conflict can be reduced or modified by changes in one's biological heritage, in one's environment, or by modification of one's subjective feelings, beliefs, and knowledge. In the following pages are presented one model of personality integration and two examples of personalities that fall short of integration of the several components involved.

Figures 25 and 26 show hypothetical patterns of interpersonal relationships, and will serve our purpose of clarifying the nature of personality integration as it involves self-image, role playing and position conflict, and the significant or affective other. In Figure 25 the other persons upon whom Mr. A depends for the fulfillment of his personal needs are described. Taken together these constitute his most significant other, or, more accurately in his case, his affective others. Because of his relationships with these individuals and groups, he takes their attitudes toward himself, and attempts to respond positively to their attitudes. It will be noted, however, that Mr. A does not find it easy to think and act in accordance with these various attitudes. The role behavior demanded by these attitudes are not compatible ones. His emotional identification with all of these persons, however, forces him to attempt to play roles

[89] N. P. Chapanis and A. Chapanis, "Cognitive Dissonance: Five Years Later," *Psychological Bulletin*, 61 (Jan. 1964), 20–21. These critics comment that: "Having now reviewed much of the experimental works supporting cognitive dissonance theory, we conclude that, as a body of literature, it is downright disappointing. Too many studies have failed to stand up to close scrutiny." *Ibid.*, p. 20.

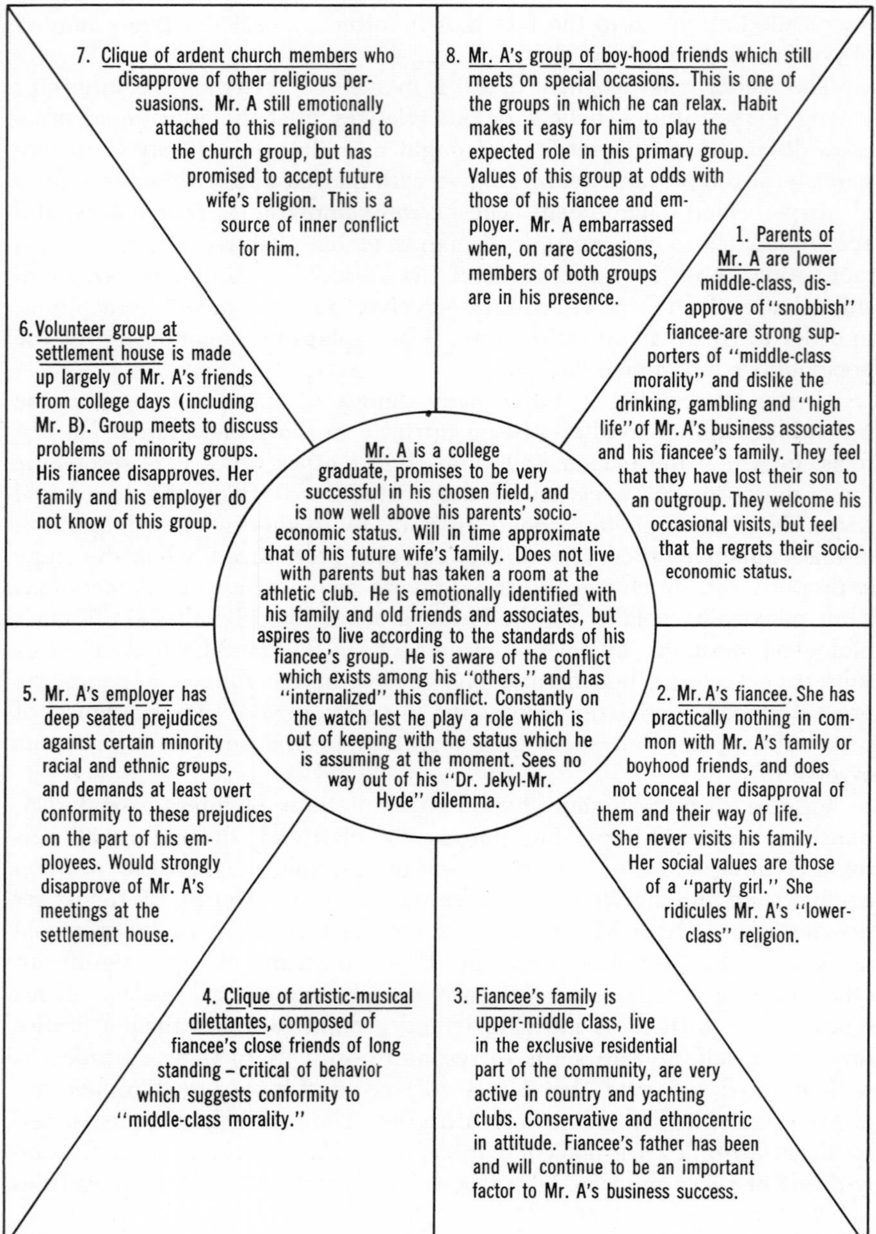

7. Clique of ardent church members who disapprove of other religious persuasions. Mr. A still emotionally attached to this religion and to the church group, but has promised to accept future wife's religion. This is a source of inner conflict for him.

8. Mr. A's group of boy-hood friends which still meets on special occasions. This is one of the groups in which he can relax. Habit makes it easy for him to play the expected role in this primary group. Values of this group at odds with those of his fiancee and employer. Mr. A embarrassed when, on rare occasions, members of both groups are in his presence.

1. Parents of Mr. A are lower middle-class, disapprove of "snobbish" fiancee-are strong supporters of "middle-class morality" and dislike the drinking, gambling and "high life" of Mr. A's business associates and his fiancee's family. They feel that they have lost their son to an outgroup. They welcome his occasional visits, but feel that he regrets their socioeconomic status.

6. Volunteer group at settlement house is made up largely of Mr. A's friends from college days (including Mr. B). Group meets to discuss problems of minority groups. His fiancee disapproves. Her family and his employer do not know of this group.

Mr. A is a college graduate, promises to be very successful in his chosen field, and is now well above his parents' socioeconomic status. Will in time approximate that of his future wife's family. Does not live with parents but has taken a room at the athletic club. He is emotionally identified with his family and old friends and associates, but aspires to live according to the standards of his fiancee's group. He is aware of the conflict which exists among his "others," and has "internalized" this conflict. Constantly on the watch lest he play a role which is out of keeping with the status which he is assuming at the moment. Sees no way out of his "Dr. Jekyl-Mr. Hyde" dilemma.

5. Mr. A's employer has deep seated prejudices against certain minority racial and ethnic groups, and demands at least overt conformity to these prejudices on the part of his employees. Would strongly disapprove of Mr. A's meetings at the settlement house.

2. Mr. A's fiancee. She has practically nothing in common with Mr. A's family or boyhood friends, and does not conceal her disapproval of them and their way of life. She never visits his family. Her social values are those of a "party girl." She ridicules Mr. A's "lower-class" religion.

4. Clique of artistic-musical dilettantes, composed of fiancee's close friends of long standing – critical of behavior which suggests conformity to "middle-class morality."

3. Fiancee's family is upper-middle class, live in the exclusive residential part of the community, are very active in country and yachting clubs. Conservative and ethnocentric in attitude. Fiancee's father has been and will continue to be an important factor to Mr. A's business success.

FIGURE 25. Nonintegrated personality's affective-other; conflicting roles demanded by irreconcilable others.

which are to the liking of the different groups and individuals. The attitudes of groups 1 and 8 are at odds with groups 2, 3, and 4. The "others" numbers 2 and 7 cannot be reconciled, nor can "others" numbers 5 and 6. Mr. A must be constantly aware of the particular "other" with which he finds himself associating at the moment, and be certain that the role behavior is appropriate to the reference group. The nature of Mr. A's affective other precludes the development of what Mead calls the "unity of self." It demands that he play the multiple roles of a "Dr. Jekyll-and-Mr. Hyde" personality, and that each role be played with complete and discomforting awareness of the other roles. Mr. A's unconvincing denial of his parents' accusation that he is ashamed of their socioeconomic status evidences self-conflict. The need to keep reference group number 8 apart from reference groups 2, 3, and 4 further complicates the process of adjustment. In short, Mr. A cannot generalize or harmonize these incompatible others, so neither integrated personality nor generalized other is possible. Persistent maladjustment is his lot under these circumstances.

In contrast is the integrated personality diagrammed in Figure 26, Mr. B's "others" are compatible, and he is possessed of a generalized other. There are no conflicting roles demanded of him as was the case with Mr. A. The overlapping of the reference groups causes no alarm because of the social values held in common. Even when the values are not all shared, the disapproval is so mild that there is no need to keep them hidden from others in the groups of persons whose attitudes Mr. B. responds to positively. In taking toward himself the attitudes of the persons noted in Figure 26, Mr. B is not called upon to play conflicting roles, and he does not have to stop and ask himself, "What do I say now, and how do I act in order to please these people?" He can relax, "be himself," and have no fear of offending the social values of those about him. His personality has a unity or integrity that is supported by the collective attitudes of those about him. His behavior gives evidence of his having developed a truly generalized other.

In a complex, pluralistic urbanized culture such as ours, it is not the common thing to find personalities with as completely a generalized other as we see in the case of Mr. B. The wide variety of social values, the divergent experiences of the many persons with whom we come in contact, and the other exigencies of the environmental situations preclude the development of primary—and secondary—reference group relationships which are free from conflicting demands. Certain situations, as noted above, make rational behavior impossible.

The Multiple Personality

When great discrepancies exist among the components of personality, the person must perform unusual feats in order to compensate for these deficiencies. By dint of hard work, careful planning, and vigilant applica-

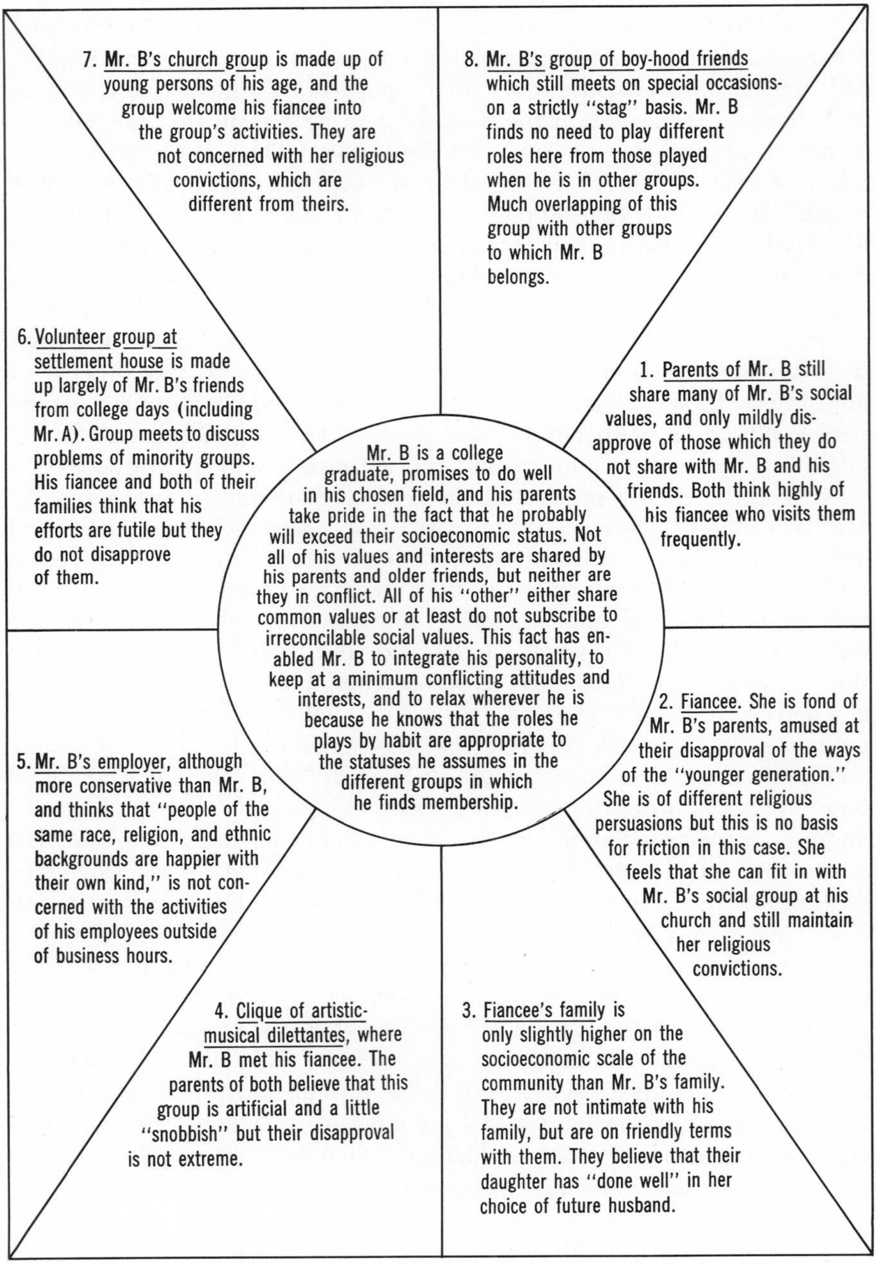

7. Mr. B's church group is made up of young persons of his age, and the group welcome his fiancee into the group's activities. They are not concerned with her religious convictions, which are different from theirs.

8. Mr. B's group of boy-hood friends which still meets on special occasions- on a strictly "stag" basis. Mr. B finds no need to play different roles here from those played when he is in other groups. Much overlapping of this group with other groups to which Mr. B belongs.

6. Volunteer group at settlement house is made up largely of Mr. B's friends from college days (including Mr. A). Group meets to discuss problems of minority groups. His fiancee and both of their families think that his efforts are futile but they do not disapprove of them.

Mr. B is a college graduate, promises to do well in his chosen field, and his parents take pride in the fact that he probably will exceed their socioeconomic status. Not all of his values and interests are shared by his parents and older friends, but neither are they in conflict. All of his "other" either share common values or at least do not subscribe to irreconcilable social values. This fact has enabled Mr. B to integrate his personality, to keep at a minimum conflicting attitudes and interests, and to relax wherever he is because he knows that the roles he plays by habit are appropriate to the statuses he assumes in the different groups in which he finds membership.

1. Parents of Mr. B still share many of Mr. B's social values, and only mildly disapprove of those which they do not share with Mr. B and his friends. Both think highly of his fiancee who visits them frequently.

5. Mr. B's employer, although more conservative than Mr. B, and thinks that "people of the same race, religion, and ethnic backgrounds are happier with their own kind," is not concerned with the activities of his employees outside of business hours.

2. Fiancee. She is fond of Mr. B's parents, amused at their disapproval of the ways of the "younger generation." She is of different religious persuasions but this is no basis for friction in this case. She feels that she can fit in with Mr. B's social group at his church and still maintain her religious convictions.

4. Clique of artistic-musical dilettantes, where Mr. B met his fiancee. The parents of both believe that this group is artificial and a little "snobbish" but their disapproval is not extreme.

3. Fiancee's family is only slightly higher on the socioeconomic scale of the community than Mr. B's family. They are not intimate with his family, but are on friendly terms with them. They believe that their daughter has "done well" in her choice of future husband.

Figure 26. Integrated personality's affective-other; no conflicting roles played; has generalized-other.

tion of knowledge, major discrepancies can be compensated for, but this is not always possible. A bizarre "solution" to inadequate components (they may be in the biological heritage, the environment, or in the personal variables) is the *multiple personality*, sometimes called a split personality.[90] Cameron defines multiple personality as an ". . . hysterical autonomy in which, as a reaction to need or anxiety, two or more organized systems of biosocial behavior develop, with complete amnesia in one system for activities of the other, and in the absence of organ or tissue pathology adequate to account for the development."[91] These multiple systems of social behavior are not reconcilable, and the person, unable to drop either of them and thereby resolve the conflict, develops amnesia; this is carrying the logic-tight compartmentalization of the personality to the ultimate.

This form of adjustment is very rare, but it demonstrates clearly the end process of failure to integrate personality components. Psychiatrist Morton Prince provided the classical description of the multiple personality early in this century.[92] In his famous case, there were several combinations of attitudes and traits occupying the same body, amnesia permitting some of these "persons" to exist without the knowledge of the others. A staid and puritanical person was plagued by a whimsical and capricious person, who (among other things) left the former, who detested smoking, with a tobacco taste in her mouth. In another, and more recent, case, the strain that gave rise to the multiple personality emerged from a situation in which a child was caught between estranged parents, with each seeking the affection and recognition of the child, and each vilifying the other before the child. Being positively identified with each parent, the child was caught in a relationship which she found impossible to resolve by rational methods. Her dilemma led her to develop two personalities, one attuned to the expectations of the mother, and the other reflecting the father's attitudes.

The following description of a multiple personality, although incomplete, will provide the reader with a clearer picture of the kind of nonintegration involved among the personality components.

THE CASE OF MISS EVE BLACK AND MRS. EVE WHITE

This case involves a twenty-five-year-old married woman, mother of one child, who admitted difficulty in her relationships with her mother and anxiety about her own positions as wife and mother. Apparently it was only with strong conscious effort that she was able to carry through

---

[90] See W. Taylor and M. Martin, "Multiple Personality," *Journal of Abnormal and Social Psychology*, XXXIX (1944).

[91] Norman Cameron, *The Psychology of Behavior Disorders* (Boston: Houghton Mifflin, 1947), p. 365.

[92] Morton Prince, *The Dissociation of a Personality* (New York: Longmans, Green and Co., 1905).

with the responsibilities associated with her wife-mother positions. Earlier in her life there had been strong feelings of being rejected by her parents after the birth of her twin younger sisters. During an interview with Mrs. White, the following episode was reported:

> While the therapist, hesitating a moment in wonder, [at Mrs. White's embarrassed reporting of hearing imaginary voices] sought for an adequate reply, an abstruse and inexplicable expression came, apparently unprompted by volition, over Eve White's familiar countenance. As if seized by a sudden pain she put both hands to her head. After a tense moment of silence, her hands dropped. There was a quick, reckless smile and, in a bright voice that sparkled, she said, "Hi there, Doc!"
>
> The demure and constrained posture of Eve White had melted into buoyant repose. With a soft and surprisingly intimate syllable of laughter, she crossed her legs. Disconcerted as he was by unassimilated surprise, the therapist noted from the corner of his awareness something distinctively attractive about them, and also that this was the first time he had received such an impression. There was little point in attempting here to give in detail the differences between this novel feminine apparition and the vanished Eve White. Instead of that retiring and gently conventional figure, there was in the newcomer a childishly daredevil air, an erotically mischievous glance, a face marvelously free from the habitual signs of care, seriousness, and underlying stress, so long familiar in her predecessor. This new and apparently carefree girl spoke casually of Eve White and her problems, always respecting the strict bounds of a separate identity. When asked her own name she immediately replied, "Oh, I'm Eve Black." [Black was her maiden name].
>
> It is easy to say that this new voice was different, that the basic idiom of her language was plainly not that of Eve White. A thousand minute alterations of manner, gesture, expression, posture, of nuances in reflex or instinctive reaction, of glance, of eyebrow tilting and eye movement, all argued that this could only be another woman. It is not possible to say just what all their differences were.[93]

The following is a summary of the differences between the two personalities that inhabited the same body.

Eve White	Eve Black
Demure, retiring, in some respects almost saintly.	Obviously a party girl. Shrewd, childishly vain and egocentric.
Face suggests a quiet sweetness; the expression in repose is predominantly one of contained sadness.	Face is pixie-like; eyes dance with mischief as if Puck peered through the pupils.
Clothes simple and conservative, neat and inconspicuously attractive.	Expression rapidly shifts in a light cascade of fun-loving willfulness. The

93 Corbett H. Thigpen and Hervey Cleckley, "A Case of Multiple Personality," *The Journal of Abnormal and Social Psychology*, 49 (1954), 137.

Eve White

Posture: Tendency to a barely discernible stoop or slump. Movements careful and dignified. Reads poetry and likes to compose verse herself.

Voice always softly modulated, always influenced by a specifically feminine restraint.

Almost all who know her express admiration and affection for her. She does not provoke envy. Her strength of character is more passive than active. Steadfast on defense but lacking initiative and boldness to formulate strategy of attack.

An industrious and able worker; also a competent housekeeper and a skillful cook. Not colorful or glamorous. Limited in spontaneity.

Consistently uncritical of others. Tries not to blame husband for marital troubles. Nothing suggests pretense or hypocrisy in this charitable attitude.

Though not stiffly prudish and never self-righteous, she is seldom lively or playful or inclined to tease or tell a joke. Seldom animated.

Her presence resonates unexpressed devotion to her child. Every act, every gesture, the demonstrated sacrifice of personal aims to work hard for her little girl, is consistent with this love.

Cornered by bitter circumstances, threatened with tragedy, her endeavors to sustain herself, to defend her child, are impressive.

Eve Black

eyes are as inconstant as the wind. This face has not and never will know sadness. Often it reflects a misleading and only half-true naïvete.

Voice a little coarsened, "discultured," with echoes or implications of mirth and teasing. Speech richly vernacular and liberally seasoned with spontaneous gusts of rowdy wit.

A devotee of pranks. Her repeated irresponsibilities have cruel results on others. More headless and unthinking, however, than deeply malicious. Enjoys taunting and mocking the Siamese.

All attitudes and passions whimlike and momentary. Quick and vivid flares of many light feelings, all ephemeral.

Immediately likeable and attractive. A touch of sexiness seasons every word and gesture. Ready for any little, irresponsible adventure.

Dress is becoming and a little provocative. Posture and gait suggest light-heartedness, play, a challenge to some sort of frolic.

Never contemplative; to be serious is for her to be tedious or absurd.

Is immediately amusing and likeable. Meets the little details of experience with a relish that is catching. Strangely "secure from the contagion of the world's slow strain," and from inner aspect of grief and tragedy.

Eve White	*Eve Black*
This role in one essentially so meek and fragile embodies an unspoken pathos. One feels somehow she is doomed to be overcome in her present situation.	Reports that her skin often reacts to nylon with urticaria. Usually does not wear stockings when she is "out" for long periods.
No allergy to nylon has been reported.[94]	

As indicated in the above report, Eve Black was aware of Eve White, but the latter was quite unaware of the immature and irresponsible Eve Black. On one occasion, the therapist reported as follows: "When I go out and get drunk," Eve Black with an easy wink once said to both of us, "*she* wakes up with the hangover. She wonders what in the hell's made her so sick." A third "person," Jane, appeared later in the case's development. The bizarre nature of the case is further illustrated by a note Jane wrote to Eve Black and placed in her jewel case. "I saw what you did this afternoon and I think you are completely selfish. You should be as grateful as Eve W. for what Dr. Luther is doing for us all. I hope you catch cold in that dress—and I don't see how you can very well avoid it. And I wish you'd stop drinking that whiskey. I detest the taste it leaves in my mouth." Two days later Jane found the following note from Eve Black in the jewel box. "Mind your own damn business, snoopy."[95]

This case is different in kind only insofar as amnesia is involved. Each of us plays roles which are very unlike, each normally appropriate to the position occupied at the time. The positions of judge, of clergyman on the one hand, and husband-as-lover on the other, require very different roles. The following verses excerpted from "Plaint of Complexity" describe an unusual person only insofar as the poet was more traveled and perhaps more articulate than most of us.

> I have too many selves to know the one.
> In too complex a schooling was I bred,
> Child of too many cities, who have gone
> Down the bright cross-roads of the world's desires,
> And at too many altars bowed my head
> To light too many fires.
>
> One polished self I have, she who can sit
> Familiarly at teas with the marquise
> And play the exquisite
> In silken rustle, lined with etiquette,

[94] *Ibid.*, pp. 141–142.

[95] Evelyn Lancaster, with James Poling, *The Final Face of Eve* (New York: McGraw-Hill Book Co., 1958), p. 9. This is "Eve's" autobiographical account of her multiple personalities.

Chatting in French, Italian, and what you please,
Of this and that— . . .

And I've a modern, rather mannish self,
Lives gladly in Chicago.
She believes
That woman should come down off her shelf
Of calm dependence on the male
And labor for her living.
She likes men,
And equal comradeship, and giving
As much as she receives.
She likes discussions lasting half the night,
Lit up with wit and cigarettes,
Of art, religion, politics and sex,
Science and superstition. She thinks art
Deals first of all with life, and likes to write
Poems of drug clerks and machines.
She's very independent—and at heart
A little lonely . . .

I've a self might almost be a nun,
So she loves peace, prim gardens in the sun
Where shadows sift at evening,
Hands at rest,
And the clear lack of questions in her breast.

But I've another self she does not touch,
A self I live very much, and overmuch
These latter years.
A self who stands apart from outward things,
From pleasure and tears,
And all the little things I say and do.
She feels that action traps her, and she swings
Sheer out of life sometimes, and loses sense
Of boundaries and of impotence.[96]

SUMMARY

In the description of personality, the interactionist frame of reference is most clearly applicable. Its use enables one to avoid the temptation of seeking simple explanations or of subscribing to the constructionist fallacy, for example, perceiving the acquired subjective components as personality itself. *Personality is the way in which the individual is related, through*

---

[96] Eunice Tietjens, *Body and Raiment* (New York: Alfred A. Knopf, 1919), pp. 13–15. Suggested by its use in P. M. Symonds, *The Ego and the Self* (New York: Appleton-Century-Crofts, 1951).

ideas, attitudes, and action, to the many human and nonhuman aspects of his environment. Personality is a function of one's position in a social system (or systems), and of his actual behavior.

The expectations which people have toward a person in a social system define his *social position.* If it is defined in terms of honor or power, it is called *status.* The actual behavior of the occupant of a *position* and *status* is called *role behavior, role-performance,* or simply *role.*

The *self* is constituted of those features of a person—biological, psychological, or cultural—that are viewed reflexively. A person acquires a self when aspects of the person become objects to him. Self consciousness and ego-involvement are functions of the various social episodes in which one finds himself, and are not constants.

In the interactive processes that give rise to personality, such attitudes as frustration gain meaning only when viewed in terms of other components of personality and need not always result in aggressive behavior. Similarly, type of physique becomes a factor in personality development in terms of such factors as the values of the culture in question and the nature of one's affective or significant other.

Three types of personality conflicts interfere with the development of personality integration: (1) Social-cultural conflicts in which incompatible positions or statuses are occupied; (2) Incompatible expectations from one's significant other which preclude the acquisition of a *generalized other.* Embarrassment is a function of such a situation. (3) *Subjective conflicts* when one's attitudes, beliefs, or behavior are incompatible. Currently the term *cognitive dissonance* denotes various kinds of subjective conflicts, probably quite heterogeneous in character. The precise referents of the concept are yet to be identified.

Two partly hypothetical personality descriptions and an actual bizarre multiple personality illustrate the nature of personality integration and nonintegration.

SUGGESTED READINGS

BIDDLE, B. J. *The Present Status of Role Theory* (Columbia, Mo.: University of Missouri, 1961).

GOFFMAN, E. *Presentation of Self in Everyday Life* (Garden City, N.Y.: Doubleday and Co., 1959).

GROSS, N., W. S. MASON, and A. W. McEACHERN. *Explorations in Role Analysis* (New York: John Wiley and Sons, 1958).

GERTH, HANS, and C. WRIGHT MILLS. *Character and Structure* (New York, Harcourt, Brace and Co., 1953).

HARVEY, O. J. (ed.). *Motivation and Social Interaction* (New York: Ronald Press Co., 1963).

MACCOBY, E. E., T. M. NEWCOMB, and E. L. HARTLEY. *Readings in Social Psychology.* 3rd ed. (New York: Henry Holt and Co., 1958).

MEAD, G. H. *Mind, Self and Society* (Chicago: University of Chicago Press, 1934).

MERTON, R. K. *Social Theory and Social Structure* (New York: The Free Press of Glencoe, 1957).

SARBIN, T. R. "Role Theory," in G. Lindzey, *Handbook of Social Psychology* (Cambridge: Addison-Wesley Publishing Co., 1954).

STOODLEY, G. H. (ed.). *Society and Self* (New York: The Free Press of Glencoe, 1962).

STRAUSS, ANSELM. *Mirror and Masks* (New York: The Free Press of Glencoe, 1959).

CHAPTER 9

PERSONALITY TYPES:

I. Role Behavior Types

> Let me have men about me that
> are fat; Sleek-headed men and such as
> sleep o'nights. Yond' Cassius has a lean
> and hungry look; He thinks too much:
> such men are dangerous.

The reader has heard, and very probably has used many times, the term *personality type*. Is this merely a handy synonym used to spice our writings and conversations, or does it have a referent of its own? If it is simply a synonym for role or position, or if it is used to refer to any and all kinds of collective or shared relationships of individuals, then it warrants no special treatment here, and can be dismissed with a small footnote. However, the literature of social psychology will not relegate the term to this minor and dispensable semantic status. In the literature dealing with man's individual relationships, usually but not always social in nature, there is no dearth of personality type labels.

Personality is, as stressed in Chapter 8, the many ways in which the individual is related through attitude and action to a world of objects. These objects may be animate or inanimate, material or nonmaterial, and include the person's own self. His personality is a function of the ways in which his biological heritage, his acquired attitudes, skills, ideas, and the object world interact. Thus personality types must also be explained in terms of this interactive framework, but the precise referent of the concept *personality type* as it appears in the literature of social science is not always clear. It denotes, to be sure, personality categories, but it is not synonymous with that very general phrase. Occupational categories are also personality categories, as are kinship categories, yet neither the layman nor the social psychologist has these categories in mind when he uses the term *personality type*. The expression, "Oh, you know the type!", denotes a special subclass of personality categories. *It suggests a certain rigidity or fixity in the relationship between the person in question and his environment.* In a rational or reasonable sociocultural setting, prediction and understanding of an individual's behavior require that one possess the knowledge about all three component categories of personality, the biological heritage, the environment, *and* the subjective or acquired variables or attributes. The concept *personality type* implies that understanding, and therefore prediction, of an individual's behavior is possible even if knowledge is restricted to some facet of *only one or two* of the three major component categories of personality. The concept implies a certain inappropriateness of the behavior in terms of the nature of the other components involved in the episode or situation in question. It suggests that the behavior is in some degree illogically or irrationally related to these other components.

The accompanying Figure 27 indicates the conditions under which departure from the normal in any one of the three basic personality component categories serves to define personality types. *Any extreme deviation from the personal, environmental, or biological characteristics which preclude rational behavioral relationships (often, but by no means always, deviations from the normal) sets the stage for the emergence of personality types.* The more extreme the departure, the sharper is the delineation of the personality type, and the more predictable is its behavior, regardless of the nature of the related factors in the situation or episode. These remarks are not to be construed as suggesting that personality types exist, or are to be understood, apart from the interactive frame of reference used in this text. *All* personalities are explained in terms of the interactive processes, but the reader is again reminded of the fact that these processes are functions of the nature of the interactive components, and are not to be understood apart from a knowledge of such components. Too, the degree of adjustment of persons falling into one or another of the personality types is still a function of the nature of the other components in the situation.

Acknowledging the existence of personality types based upon departures from the normal biological structure (such as imbeciles, dwarfs, persons with gross sensory deficiencies), we have chosen to restrict our discussion of personality types to those which are functions of categories II and IV of the triangular model used in this text. We will first discuss *role types*, or *role behavior types* that are functions of the actual behavior, which in turn is a function of divergent, unusual subjective or personal attitudes, beliefs, knowledge, or of biological traits. These subjective variables and attributes cannot be deduced by a study of the formal, explicit, societal structure. A knowledge of the laws, the established mores and folkways, or formalized groups (associations) may well permit the awareness of these personality types to escape the observer. The phenomenologist could be unaware of them, if we take the concept of phenomenology literally. These types are functions of *personal social* learning, rather than functions of institutional processes per se. These types can, and do, occur in every society, regardless of the nature of the formal institutional systems of the societies.

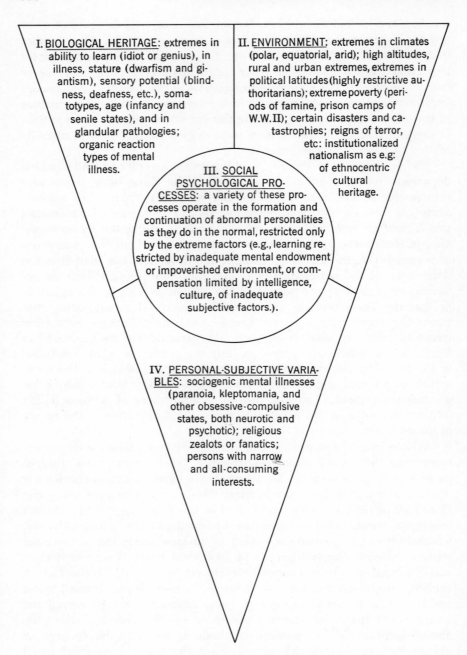

I. BIOLOGICAL HERITAGE: extremes in ability to learn (idiot or genius), in illness, stature (dwarfism and giantism), sensory potential (blindness, deafness, etc.), somatotypes, age (infancy and senile states), and in glandular pathologies; organic reaction types of mental illness.

II. ENVIRONMENT: extremes in climates (polar, equatorial, arid); high altitudes, rural and urban extremes, extremes in political latitudes (highly restrictive authoritarians); extreme poverty (periods of famine, prison camps of W.W.II); certain disasters and catastrophies; reigns of terror, etc: institutionalized nationalism as e.g: of ethnocentric cultural heritage.

III. SOCIAL PSYCHOLOGICAL PROCESSES: a variety of these processes operate in the formation and continuation of abnormal personalities as they do in the normal, restricted only by the extreme factors (e.g., learning restricted by inadequate mental endowment or impoverished environment, or compensation limited by intelligence, culture, of inadequate subjective factors.).

IV. PERSONAL-SUBJECTIVE VARIABLES: sociogenic mental illnesses (paranoia, kleptomania, and other obsessive-compulsive states, both neurotic and psychotic); religious zealots or fanatics; persons with narrow and all-consuming interests.

FIGURE 27. Extreme divergencies in the three basic categories of personality which account for development of personality types and stereotypes.

In contrast are the *position or status types*, which are functions of particular kinds of cultural heritages, with their peculiar cultural content manifested in the attitudes and actions of one's affective other. An examination of the customs, of the formally instituted group relationships, of the explicit and implicit norms (both written and unwritten) enables the investigator to predict some of the personality characteristics of the persons in question. *The attitudes, beliefs, knowledge, and habits of the persons so typed are insufficient to type them. The typing is possible only when one knows the positions or statuses which the person occupies, and it matters not what the person's subjective characteristics are; he is unable to escape the stereotype.* Only by altering the subjective characteristics of *others* in his environment can the type be modified or eliminated from the social stage. Here it is the audience that determines the type, not the actor. A discrepancy exists between the script that the audience ascribes to the actor and the script that the actor wishes to follow. It is a divergence of role and position or status.

ROLE OR ROLE BEHAVIOR TYPES

Most of the personality-type names are of the role type, the following list being representative even if not exhaustive: adrenal, aesthenic, aesthetic, anal, antisocial, athletic, bohemian, born criminal, cerebrotonic, choleric, compulsive, creative, criminaloid, cyclothymic, depressed, economic, erotic, extravertive, gonadocentric, homosexual, idealistic, idiotropic, inner-directed, introspective, introvertive, manic, melancholic, narcissistic, objective, oral, other-directed, perverse, phlegmatic, philistinic, pituitaric, political psychopathic, pyknic, religious, schizoid, schizothymic, sanguine, social somatotonic, syntonic, syntropic, theoretic, tradition-directed, thymocentric, and viscerotonic.[1]

The reader can, of course, supply his own type names which would augment the above list. We have chosen seven role or role behavior types for discussion here: introverted-extraverted; inner-directed and other-directed; Philistine and Bohemian; and the homosexual.

---

[1] *See* Kimball Young, *Personality and Problems of Adjustment* (New York: F. S. Crofts and Co., 1940), Ch. XIII for one of the best treatments of the various schemes of personality typing available. There are, of course, other approaches to the study of the relationships designated here under *personality types*. Erving Goffman accomplishes much the same thing under the concept of *stigma*, which he defines as ". . . an attribute that is deeply discrediting . . . ," *Stigma* (Englewood Cliffs, N.J.: Prentice-Hall, 1963), p. 3. He notes three categories of stigma: (1) "abominations of the body"; (2) "blemishes of individual character" [our acquired attributes]; and (3) "tribal stigma of race, nation, and religion" [our status or position types]. *Ibid.*, p. 4. He emphasizes the first category, which we have elected to omit from our treatment of types. He acknowledges that, in dealing with these stigma, ". . . it should be seen that a language of relationships, not attributes, is really needed." (*Ibid.*, p. 3).

Jung's Personality Types

Carl Gustav Jung, an early associate of Sigmund Freud but later a dissenter in significant degree, has provided a typing of personalities based upon sociopsychological characteristics. He differentiates two general types, *viz.*, the *general attitude types* (the introvert and the extravert), and the function types (in terms of thinking, feeling, sensation, and intuition).[2] Each of the latter types can be introverted or extraverted.

THE INTROVERTED TYPE

An introverted personality is characterized by such terms as shy, reclusive, self-conscious, subjective, asocial, impenetrable, taciturn, and reflective. Other persons are objects to be feared or avoided, and the individual is acutely aware of others taking toward him certain attitudes, sees himself as the focus of their penetrating gaze, and responds with a feeling of discomfort. Psychasthenia is the typical form of neurosis of the introvert.[3]

THE EXTRAVERTED TYPE

In sharp contrast to the introvert, the extravert is characterized by such adjectives as open, sociable, outgoing, objective, doer rather than thinker, friendly, and accessible. Other persons are objects eagerly sought as essential to the fulfillment of self-needs. The extravert appears insensitive, at times even callous, to the attitudes that others take toward him, not expecting complete approbation from others about him. Close association with the external is a must in the life of the extravert. Hysteria is the typical form of neurosis with such personalities.

Jung elaborates on the combinations of the general attitude and the function types of personalities. The distinction is made between the thinking and feeling types as rational types, and the sensation and intuitive types as irrational types. We see no need here to discuss in detail the introverted thinking, introverted feeling, introverted sensation, and the introverted intuitive types, nor the extraverted counterparts. The student can deduce from the nature of the general attitude types the nature of these functional types. One main objection to such typing is the inference often drawn that the types arise from different sociopsychological processes.

[2] C. G. Jung, *Psychological Types, or the Psychology of Individuation* (New York: Harcourt, Brace and Co., 1923), p. 14.

[3] *Ibid.*, pp. 475–478. Pertinent to our discussions of the nature of the self and the ego are Jung's remarks concerning the tendency of the introvert to confuse the nature of these two factors. Although not in keeping with our analysis of personality, Jung's position may be of interest to the reader.

The Inner Directed and Other-Directed Personality Types

The inventors of the labels *inner directed* and *other directed*, wrote an influential book in which they sought to tell

> . . . about social character and about the differences in social character between men of different regions, eras, and groups. It considers the ways in which different social character types, once they are formed at the knee of society, are then deployed in the work, play, politics, and child-rearing activities of society. More particularly, it is about the way in which one kind of social character, which dominated America in the nineteenth century, is gradually being replaced by a social character of quite a different sort.[4]

Our purpose here is not to explore the sociological implications of these character types but merely to delineate them as role behavior personality types. These are, of course, *ideal types* in that they are not intended as description of any actual human being, but rather as a conception of types whose characteristics are shared, in varying degrees, by large numbers of people and enable the group to be recognized and distinguished from other groups.

The type that its creators believe to have been dominant between the Renaissance and Reformation and the twentieth century is called inner directed. These times were given to rapid cultural changes wherein old norms, customs, and sanctions were challenged, bent, and broken. Tradition offered no guide lines for either conformity or success. The cultural changes were neither ordered nor intended, yet this did not alter the fact that the times would be quite selective of those who could, and would, secure for themselves the goals and services, the statuses and positions, that they desired. On stormy and unchartered cultural seas, only those with consistent ideas and motivations are likely to reach their goals. These are the *inner directed* persons, who are capable of handling the novel situations which can be opportunities to them but pitfalls for others who seek nonexisting guideposts from their affective others.

As the authors point out, when the social controls are weakened, "a new psychological mechanism appropriate to the more open society is 'invented'; it is what I like to describe as a psychological gyroscope."[5] This gyroscope is often set going by one's parents. This personality type is very stable, and when he does wander from his inner directed path, the penalty is a feeling of remorse for having violated his own principles. He can usually maintain his behavioral course, even in the absence of

---

[4] David Riesman, Nathan Glazer, and Reuel Denny, *The Lonely Crowd* (Garden City, N.Y.: Doubleday & Co., 1953), p. 17. A third type called the *tradition directed* is not dealt with here, primarily because it is not easily differentiable from the two other types.

[5] *Ibid.*, p. 31. The authors acknowledge that psychologist Gardner Murphy had previously used this same figure of speech in the latter's book *Personality*.

WALL STREET JOURNAL

"We should let Karpf go. He's too inner-directed
to adapt to his peer group."

FIGURE 28.   Too inner directed.

social approval. The authors suggest as an illustration of the inner directed type the stereotyped Englishman who lives the proper life—
dressing for dinner, and so on—even in the tropics.

In sharp contrast is the other ideal type of Riesman, Glazer, and
Denney, the *other-directed* person. Instead of a built-in *alter ego*, the
other-directed type has as his characteristic adaptive mechanism a psychological radar screen with which he learns what is expected of him
by his affective other (which is much larger than the affective other of
the inner directed individual.) "The other-directed person is cosmopolitan. For him the border between the familiar and the strange . . . has
broken down."[6]

> *What is common to all the other-directed people is that their con-*
> *temporaries are the source of direction for the individual. . . . The*
> *goals toward which the other-directed person strives shift with that*
> *guidance: it is only the process of striving itself and the process of*
> *paying close attention to the signals from others that remain unaltered*
> *throughout life.*[7]

The peer group and the mass media are all important in establishing
his values. In contrast to the other types, wherein guilt and shame are

[6] *Ibid.*, p. 41.
[7] *Ibid.*, p. 37. Italics in original.

appropriate sanctions for failure to live up to principles, *anxiety* accompanies the other-directed person's failure, or anticipated failure, to properly interpret the signals from his ever widening significant other. The personality of the other-directed person is far from being integrated and his *other* far from being generalized.

Thomas' and Znaniecki's Social Types

There are attitudinal types based upon Thomas' four basic wishes. The individual whose basic attitude is a desire for security, the marked conformist, the conventional person who seldom if ever attempts anything that he believes might be frowned upon by his neighbors or associates is called a *Philistine*. In contrast, the person who cares little for the security that comes from a predictable future, who is enamored of things that are new and different, who constantly seeks new experiences and thrills is the *Bohemian*. The person who has a balance of these desires for new experience and security, who does not go off on tangents in quest for the new, per se, but who does accept new ideas and ways of doing things if they conduce to his life satisfactions is the *creative man*, according to Thomas and Znaniecki. In the meaning employed in this text, the creative man is not a type, but one whose behavior reflects a logical interplay of personality components. He cannot be typed on the basis of one or two subjective attitudes. It will be noted that these types are based upon only two of the four wishes of Thomas.

A type of personality that reflects the excessive desire for response is found described in Karen Horney's *Neurotic Personality in Our Time*. The author points out that there are many persons who have developed a pathological need for affection, a need to be loved that permeates their whole life pattern to an irrational degree.

Although no one has developed any type centered around the desire for recognition, it would probably not be difficult to verify statistically the presence of such a personality type called, perhaps, an *exhibitionist*. The persons who are constantly in the public eye, or ear, such as the stars of stage, screen, television, and radio, surely have a need for recognition in a degree and kind unlike that of the average person. Although we all require some sort of recognition, most of us get by with much less than the actors mentioned above.

How valid are these types? If we recognize that the inventors of the inner- and other-directed terms are aware that ". . . there can be no such thing as a society or a person wholly dependent on tradition-direction, inner-direction, or other-direction"; we can perceive that such ideal types are discoverable in varying degrees among people in nearly every society. Everyone is, perforce, inner-directed in that he develops habits in the form of attitudes; and everyone is other-directed insofar as he acquires a significant other. As noted above, a *type* emerges only when an extreme departure from the middle ground in the flexibility-rigidity continuum occurs. How easily one is typed, surely, is *in part* a function of where on the continuum current custom rests, yet no culture can survive if its norms dictate behavior at either extreme. Thus one can conclude that the referents of *introverted* and *extraverted*; of *inner-directed* and *other-directed*; and of the type based upon the four wishes are real, and that, within the limitations of any personality type, they can serve as useful concepts.

The Homosexual

The term *homosexuality* denotes the situation wherein the sexual attitudes that are normally directed toward members of the opposite sex (heterosexuality) are turned toward persons of the same sex. For the homosexual male, another male rather than a female becomes his sex object; and the converse is true for the female. Although the concept *homosexual* may be applied to a wide range of relationships within the sexes, all the way from the mild preference for the company of a member of the same sex to overt and specific sexual activity at the genital level, it is toward the latter end of the continuum that the term is most frequently applied. It does not, ordinarily, find use in referring to the preadolescent and early adolescent years when each sex seems to abhor members of the opposite sex, at least in our culture. The epithets of "sissies" and "roughnecks" exchanged between boys and girls at this stage of development definitely are not at the genital level of interaction and no useful purpose is served by using the term in this connection unless it occurs in the context of a general discussion of homosexual behavior. Our present concern is with the persons, of whatever age, whose attitude and overt behavior toward specific sexual activity involve the substitution of one's own sex for the role usually played by the opposite sex. The number of persons whose personalities have so developed is not known exactly, but it is certain that it is not insignificant, probably in excess of 1 per cent of the population. Also, that there are millions of adults in our society to whom the phenomenon of homosexuality is unknown is equally certain. Because it is not a cultural minority but a socially disapproved personal-social one, it provides an elusive subject for research. Because of the social taboos, it is beyond a doubt true that the number of persons with homosexual attitudes is far greater than the number of those who manifest it as a behavior trait. If we add to this the problem of distinguishing the homosexual from the bisexual personality (the person who finds both sexes to be satisfactory sex objects) the identification of this personality type is further complicated. Anyone who has frequented the bright-light districts of our larger cities is conscious of the significant numbers of homosexuals of both sexes. Certain cafes and restaurants are notorious for the large, and sometimes exclusive, patronage by homosexuals. The "arty" districts of these same cities, the studios, the theaters, and the bars always seem to have their quotas of homosexuals.[8] What sort of person is the homosexual? The following paragraphs will enable the reader to know some of the attitudes and traits that do, and some that do not, characterize the homosexual.

THE BIOLOGICAL HERITAGE OF THE HOMOSEXUAL

It is popularly believed that the homosexually inclined individual is identifiable from his or her physical appearance. In general, this is not true; but the whole picture of the relationship between biological factors and atypical sexual behavior is not clear. Studies of the nature of such relationships have provided us with the knowledge that there are certain observable correlations between body type and personality characteristics. An example of these findings is presented in Table X.

Table X
Masculine Component and Personality Trait Grouping*

Personality Trait Groupings	Individuals with Strong Masculine Component (226)		Individuals with Weakness in Masculine Component (27)	
	number	per cent	number	per cent
Sensitive Affect	35	15.5	10	37.0
Unstable Autonomic Functions	29	12.8	7	25.9
Less Well Integrated	31	13.7	7	25.9
Ideational	45	19.9	9	33.3
Creative and Intuitive	11	4.9	5	18.5
Shy	57	25.2	9	33.3
Asocial	18	8.0	6	22.2
Self-driving	31	13.7	5	18.5
Self-conscious	53	23.5	10	37.0
Inhibited	39	17.3	10	37.0
Cultural	42	18.6	12	44.4

* Adapted from Carl C. Seltzer, "The Relationship Between the Masculine Component and Personality," from *Personality in Nature, Society, and Culture,* by Clyde Kluckhohn and Henry A. Murray (eds.), (New York: Alfred A. Knopf, 1948), 91.

[8] See William J. Helmer, "New York's 'Middle-Class' Homosexuals," *Harper's,* 226 (March 1963), 85–92, for a good picture of the life of the homosexuals in a large city.

The *masculine component* referred to in Table X is the mesomorphy of Sheldon, which is described in Chapter 3 of this book, and which is generally recognized as the athletic, broad-shouldered, muscular body type. The Seltzer study, as others like it, shows rather clearly a positive correlation between certain personality traits and attitudes on the one hand and varying degrees of mesomorphy on the other. In this study there is a definite relationship between a lack of the masculine component and a retiring, shy, insecure, self-conscious personality with an unusual interest in ideas and cultural pursuits. Also, the persons with strong masculinity characteristics in body form were revealed to select the natural sciences (traditionally a near monopoly of the male) to a greater degree than those who were weak in this mesomorphic component; but that the latter were shown to prefer the social studies (traditionally a more feminine interest) and the area of arts, letters, and philosophy (in our culture even more a feminine province). In the area of sports, the mesomorphs selected the contact sports of football, baseball, hockey, boxing, and wrestling, where the persons with a minimum of mesomorphy shunned these but were participants in the noncontact sports of crew, tennis, swimming, gym.[9] That there is such a relationship between body form and personality components of attitudes and traits is not to be denied. Complete consensus does not exist, however, in the interpretation of these data. We see no warrant, as shall be detailed later, of interpreting such correlations as evidencing innate preferences or tendencies. This is as true in the above study, which has no reference to homosexuality, as it is in the one to be reported immediately following, which does concern homosexuality specifically.

Terman, Miles, and others, in a study that has become well known in the field of psychology and social psychology, discovered through a series of tests for masculine and feminine social values and attitudes that the passive homosexual male sometimes, though by no means in a majority of the cases, exhibits certain feminine features with regard to body form or amount and distribution of body hair.[10] There is some ground for believing that with more precise techniques used by Sheldon and his associates a higher percentage of endomorphy-ectomorphy might be revealed among the passive homosexuals. Be that as it may, there is still the problem of interpreting the relationship between body types generally recognized as being feminine in character and personality features that are also recognized as feminine. The active or aggressive male homo-

[9] Carl C. Seltzer, "The Relationship between Masculine Component and Personality," from *Personality in Nature, Society, and Culture.* Clyde Kluckhohn and Henry A. Murray, (eds.), (New York: Alfred A. Knopf, 1948), p. 91.

[10] L. M. Terman and C. C. Miles, *Sex and Personality* (New York: McGraw-Hill, 1936), pp. 257–258. See this book for one of the most careful studies of homosexuality, including excellent case studies.

sexual does not exhibit these feminine features in either body form or in attitudes or behavior patterns. The authors conclude, however, that their data failed to reveal any constitutional basis for homosexual behavior, and this seems to be the prevailing view despite some strong convictions to the contrary that are held by certain few persons.[11] Another study reported that sixty of sixty-four male homosexuals were normal physically.[12] An American psychiatrist asserts that "Female homosexuality has no physical, organic, hormonal, or neurological basis."[13] Upon being taken as a guest to a "gay" bar in New York City, a normal male commented as follows: "My reaction to the unusual sight of men embracing each other on the dance floor was one more of curiosity than aversion, probably because the dancers appeared so casual and others in the room so indifferent. I was far more surprised to see no one who 'looked' homosexual. A few were a little too well groomed or elegant in their behavior, and a few were dressed younger than their age (though all looked to be under thirty), but otherwise the only noticeable difference was that everyone resembled the dashing young men in college sportswear advertisements."[14]

HOMOSEXUALITY AND THE CULTURAL HERITAGE

As emphasized earlier, our culture is pervaded with an evaluation of sex as being something less than good, a necessary "evil," a thorn in the side of mankind that is difficult to control or repress and a topic not for general discussion. This conspiracy of silence has given sex a heightened value (so much so that psychiatrist Harry Stack Sullivan calls ours the most sex-ridden of cultures), but also has given rise to pervasive mis-

[11] *Ibid.*, p. 256. For an opposite view see H. Greenspan and J. D. Campbell, "The Homosexual as a Personality Type," *American Journal of Psychiatry*, CI (1944), 682–689. Their position is that homosexuality is always of biological or constitutional origin, and never is learned or acquired. In the light of what is known of the distribution of homosexuality in space and time, this position does not appear to be a tenable one. Sheldon and his associates provide us with some confusing views on the relationship between body build and homosexuality among males. In *Varieties of Temperament*, several of the homosexuals described are extreme ectomorphs, but in the later publication, *Varieties of Delinquent Youth* (New York: Harper & Brothers, 1949), the statement is made that "This group which includes the homosexuals, near homosexuals, and psychiatrically gynandrophrenic men, shows one striking morphological characteristic—absence of pronounced strength or weakness in any of the primary components. There is quite a remarkable avoidance of the whole periphery of the somatotype distribution." (p. 741). This is in contrast to the body types of the homosexuals described in *Varieties of Temperament* (New York: Harper & Brothers, 1942), which shows these ranges: 1—1—7, 2—1—7, and 2—2—5. The reader is probably aware of the "body beautiful" male groups made up of extreme mesomorphs who contribute more than their share to the homosexual population.

[12] *Time*, 71 (June 16, 1958), 44.

[13] Dr. Robert C. Robertiello (Chief Psychiatrist, Long Island Consulting Center, New York), "Female Homosexuals," from *Science News Letter*, 79 (Jan. 14, 1961), 30.

[14] Helmer, *op. cit.*, p. 86.

conceptions about it. Out of this cultural heritage has come a widespread and deep-rooted antipathy for all forms of sexual behavior that are not sanctioned by marriage between adult males and females, and any overt expression of homosexuality is thus taboo. The mores of sexual behavior are reinforced by statutes that make overt homosexuality criminal behavior.[15] There is, of course, no institutionalized form of homosexuality in our culture as there is in some societies. Moreover, ours is a culture dominated by masculine values, a culture in which women can copy the behavior patterns of men, whether such patterns be in athletics, in clothes, in vocations, or other fields, and still maintain accepted social status. The reverse is not true, and the male who enters professions that are generally viewed as effeminate (hairdressing, dress designing, nursing, stenography, and even the fields of drama, the arts, music), runs the risk of losing rank in the eyes of the general public, even of the women themselves who are by no means immune to the dominant male-centered values of the culture. Designers of women's clothes can aid their sales by pointing to the masculine lines of the garments, the manly features of the new styles for women, but not even the most naïve designer or salesman of men's clothing would dare hint that there was a feminine touch in, say, the new fall suits for gentlemen. We compliment a woman golfer by saying, "Say, she swings just like a man!" but who would be so foolhardy as to try the reverse on a male golfer? Even in fields less dominated by males, such as dancing, one rarely hears of a male's dancing ability being attributable to any feminine quality of the dancer. Further, to call a girl a "tomboy" is often meant and interpreted as a compliment, but the term "sissie" has quite a different meaning. The male values by and large dominate our culture, and we must not lose sight of this fact in any interpretation of the attitudes and traits that have a bearing on masculinity or femininity. For the purposes of understanding the homosexual, or anyone who for a variety of reasons cannot live up to the accepted conception of the status of the male, this cultural characteristic of American society must be constantly noted.

Another fact of culture that has a significant bearing on intersex and intrasex social relations in our country is the greater freedom accorded the female insofar as physical intimacy is concerned.[16] Girls and women embrace, kiss, and walk with arms about each other and find cultural sanction for such intimacies, but males just do not do these things without receiving definite and immediate censure from society. Too, as Thompson points out, it is a common cultural practice for unmarried women to

---

[15] As of 1961, private homosexual relations between consenting adults is no longer a criminal act in the state of Illinois.

[16] Clara Thompson, "Changing Concepts of Homosexuality," in Patrick Mullahy (ed.), A Study of Interpersonal Relations (New York: Hermitage Press, 1949), p. 215.

room together in pairs and their action is not a subject of either comment or disapproval, but when two bachelors do the same thing, they become suspect in the eyes of some people.[17] This cultural taboo against males being physically intimate and the approval of such relations (though not, to be sure, sex relations as such) for women sets a cultural stage that is probably significant with reference to homosexuality within the two sexes. The general impression among those who studied the problem is that there is more homosexuality among women than among men. However, those studies which have involved questionnaires and/or interviews report on opposite findings. The following quotation from one of the best known of these studies is revealing:

> There is a widespread opinion which is held both by clinicians and the public at large, that homosexual responses and completed contacts occur among more females than males. This opinion is not borne out by our data, and it is not supported by previous studies which have been based upon specific data. This opinion may have originated in the fact that females are more openly affectionate than males in our culture. Women may hold hands in public, put arms about each other, publicly fondle and kiss each other, and openly express their admiration and affection for other females without being accused of homosexual interests, as men would be if they made such open display of their interests in other men. Males, interpreting what they observe in terms of male psychology, are inclined to believe that the female behavior reflects emotional interests that must develop sooner or later into overt sexual relationships. Nevertheless, our data indicate that a high proportion of this show of affection on the part of the female does not reflect any psychosexual interest, and rarely leads to overt homosexual activity.[18]

However, one can hardly argue the question of which sex in our society is the more homosexual. Males have more sexual experiences generally than do females, and the fact that the intimacies between females are not perceived by them as manifestations of "psychosexual interest" does not settle the issue. There are many degrees of homosexuality—both in attitude and in overt behavior—short of behavior at the genital level. Studies in greater depth than those of Kinsey and his associates are requisite to a full understanding of this problem. For the moment, however, the studies that have gone beyond informal impressionistic reports give pause to anyone who believes females to be more homosexually inclined than males.

Thus, understanding of the nature of the homosexual personality is deficient to the extent that the cultural stage of the action is ignored. The

---

[17] An exception is the lesbian bar which, with its all-female clientele, is highly conspicuous even in large cities.

[18] A. C. Kinsey, W. B. Pomeroy, C. E. Martin, P. H. Gebhard, *Sexual Behavior in the Human Female* (Philadelphia: W. B. Saunders, 1953), p. 475.

social values of the culture, incorporated as they are in the significant others of most individuals, determine to a very marked degree the social adjustment permitted any given type of personality. The homosexually inclined individual is not destined for either adjustment or maladjustment as such, but will find his adjustment tempered by the attitudes and actions of those with whom he or she must come in contact in daily living. This simple fact often is overlooked in the discussion of behavior deviants, be they homosexual or otherwise.

THE HOMOSEXUAL PERSONALITY

The homosexual is a person, not just a term; and as a person he or she is a complex phenomenon. To say that a person is homosexual tells us only that, in varying degree, he or she is attracted sexually to persons of the same sex rather than to persons of the opposite sex. Beyond this one item in the whole personality, the person may be well adjusted or poorly adjusted, may be a dominant personality or a very recessive one, may be a success vocationally or a complete failure, may possess marked physical disabilities or none, and may possess any of the many variations in body style afforded the human being. There is no more reason for expecting greater homogeneity of personality among homosexuals than that which exists among persons who are heterosexual in attitude. Each group has its characteristics, to be sure, but the two groups have more things in common than they have things that distinguish them one from the other. This is demonstrated by the very fact that most social groups in the country include homosexual members, but the only persons who know this are the homosexuals themselves.[19] In fact, many of the readers of these lines who are not themselves homosexually inclined have friends who are, but who have been constrained by society's taboos to keep their sex attitudes secret. As we shall point out, there are some types of homosexuals who are usually recognizable by their overt behavior, but this is not the rule. It is only when the homosexual is forced to live according to the rules of the majority that his minority status comes to light in large numbers. Such a situation exists in the wartime army, and it is difficult for most homosexuals to conceal their nature under conditions that demand close, constant, and intimate contact with large numbers of their own sex. Civilian life permits the homosexual to select his environment

[19] See the interesting comments of Jane MacKinnon in "The Homosexual Woman," *American Journal of Psychiatry*, CIII (1947), 661–664. This is an autobiographical account of homosexual attitudes. In George W. Henry, *Sex Variants* (New York: Paul B. Hoeber, 1948), the reader will find many detailed cases of homosexuals of several types. The interpretations are notable in their noncultural character. However, in his "Impressions," (pp. 1023–1028), Dr. Henry reveals not only his biological bias but also the inadequacy of this approach. Even though the cases were written from this viewpoint, the cultural and personal-social influences are apparent to one with an interactionist frame of reference.

in large measure, to avoid situations that involve primary-group contacts with heterosexual men. This is not possible with men assigned to barracks in random fashion, where decisions as to residence, associates, occupations, sleeping and bathing arrangements are not of the man's own making. To understand the situation into which a definitely homosexual person is thrust by such circumstances, one must realize that it is comparable to having a normal, heterosexually developed person, male or female, assigned to live in a barracks populated by members of the opposite sex, with the added injunction against any sexual activity. It is no wonder that many homosexuals were released from the armed forces after they had been drafted. The screening at induction centers failed to spot all homosexuals, and thus only after induction did the process of more adequate identification take place.

What, then, are the features of the homosexuals that, in our culture at least, distinguish them from the average person? In order to answer this question it is necessary to point to the different categories of homosexuals, namely: (1) the dominant homosexual, the one who plays the masculine role of assuming the initiative and being the aggressive partner in the sex activity;[20] (2) the recessive partner, the one who plays the feminine role; (3) the person who is *bivalent* and shifts from the masculine to the feminine roles; and (4) the bisexual person who is attracted by both male and female sex partners. It is well to keep in mind that among homosexuals, as well as among heterosexuals, there are persons whose sex life is restricted to the attitude or covert level and never manifests itself, perhaps for want of opportunity, courage, or strong motivation, in overt behavior traits.

The Dominant, or Active Homosexual. The dominant or active homosexual type[21] is more easily recognizable among females than males for the reason that the male is "being himself" whereas the female is assuming an inverted role, that of the masculine personality. Mannish clothes, short-cropped hair, masculine mannerisms, and revealed male values of the culture characterize a number of female homosexuals of this "butch" type, but one should assume neither that all active female homosexuals are so identified, nor that all females who dress and act

[20] In all cultures the male does not always play the aggressive role in sex relations, so "playing the masculine role," under such circumstances has a different meaning.

[21] Alfred R. Lindesmith and Anselm L. Strauss, *Social Psychology* (New York: The Dryden Press, 1949), distinguish between inversion as referring to the reversal of roles, as in the passive male and the active female, and homosexuality as referring to sexual or love relationships between members of the same sex. They hold, and in a sense logically, that both partners in a homosexual relationship can not be inverted (p. 422). The reason for not insisting on this distinction by the present authors is their opinion that it does not have sufficient currency to facilitate communication of ideas at this time. The sharpening of denotative meanings is, nevertheless, commendable.

this way are homosexuals in attitude. In the Terman-Miles study, forty-six cases of active male homosexuals showed them to be very masculine in nature, gaining scores on a masculinity-femininity test equal to the average college student. In contrast to the passive male homosexuals, these men liked the rough, contact sports of baseball and football, and were inferior to the passives in terms of education, intelligence, and "culture."[22] Thus the dominant male homosexual cannot, in most instances, be recognized by anything that he does outside of the actual sexual attitudes and behavior.

The Recessive, or Passive Homosexual. Insofar as recognition is concerned, the situation of the passive homosexual is the reverse of that of the active groups. The female with the passive role is typically feminine in her manner and attitude except that she is attracted sexually to the members of her own sex. Her dress, attitudes, and behavior traits are in keeping with those deemed suitable for females in our culture. In every way she appears normal to the nondiscerning outsider, a fact that makes her role a most difficult one to play. One such person writes of her feelings thus:

> What is it like to be this way? You are always lonely. It makes no difference how many friends you have or how nice they are. Between you and other women friends is a wall which they cannot see, but which is terribly apparent to you.[23]

Here we see the maladjustment that comes when one is not prepared to play the role that fits the status to which one is assigned. The comment on loneliness reminds one that a rather average novel called *The Well of Loneliness*, which appeared on the market about a third of a century ago, did as much as any one thing to bring the question of homosexuality before the American public. The passive female homosexual must continue to hide behind this mask of conformity, keeping her attitudes much to herself or to the small circle of her kind that she has contacted. But, as pointed out previously, it is easier in our culture for the female to play this dual role than it is for the male.

The passive male homosexual is less difficult to recognize. A characteristically feminine intonation and inflection in the voice may reveal his predilections. A preference for the upper reaches of his voice range, a flair for color which usually is not permitted the drab male of our culture, a tendency to let the hair grow to "musician's" length, and the mincing gait of the female are all additional features that enable one to recognize this minority group. Among the homosexuals themselves, there is a remarkably high degree of correct guesses as to who is and who is not "one of the boys in lavender." Among the nonhomosexuals, the per-

[22] Terman and Miles, *op. cit.*, pp. 254–255.
[23] MacKinnon, *op. cit.*, p. 661.

centage of correct guesses varies widely, as is the case in almost all of the minority groups. Some persons can distinguish with accuracy between northern and southern Europeans, between Jew and non-Jew whereas others never can tell the difference.

Even though the Seltzer study was not concerned with homosexuals, the data given in Table X show the subjects preferences for things that are usually assigned to the category of "feminine." In almost all of the studies of male passive homosexuals the values of such persons are of this sort. Whereas the typical American boy does everything within his ability to avoid being feminine, the male passive homosexual does just the opposite. As Terman and Miles put it:

> The feminine personality of the inverts appears in their fastidiousness with respect to dress, cleanliness, and care of person; in their preoccupation with domestic affairs; in their preference for feminine types of occupations and for working with women rather than with men: in their fondness for sentimental movies and romantic literatures; in their feminine timidity when faced by physical danger; in their religious interests; and in their liking for literature, art, music, and dramatics. The feminine personality of the inverts is evidenced negatively by their repudiation of everything that is characteristically masculine: aggressive leadership, energetic activity, physical courage, masculine pursuits, and interest in warfare, adventure, outdoor sports, science, and things of a mechanical nature.[24]

When transvestism (wearing clothes of the opposite sex) occurs among the male homosexuals, it is, of course, usually the passives who are involved.[25] They refer to each other as "the girls" and adopt or have assigned to them feminine names. The most permanent of the "marriages" between homosexuals (and the partnerships are referred to as marriages by the homosexuals themselves) are between partners one of whom is active and the other passive. These enduring relationships usually involve complementary personalities and are not founded upon sheer sexual compatibility. This is as true here as with heterosexual marriages, and is a fact often not given its due attention in understanding homosexual partnerships. However, prostitution does occur among homosexuals, as is well known.

The bivalent and bisexual types listed earlier in this chapter are not consistently inverse in the sense that they play the role of the opposite sex, but may play a dominant or masculine role with a younger member of the same sex, or a passive feminine one with an older person, and switch from a male to female partner.

A word of caution is in order lest the reader assume that all emo-

[24] Terman and Miles, *op. cit.*, p. 282.
[25] Transvestism is not to be confused with the masquerading at "drag parties."

tional attachments between members of the same sex are properly called homosexual. Many such partnerships develop between parent and child, between siblings, between close friends or business and professional associates; yet there may be no hint of sexual love involved. If the term is to remain useful, homosexuality must be restricted to mean sexual attraction per se between members of the same sex, with or without love.

These four types help to distinguish the homosexual from the heterosexual person, but among these there are also wide variations of personality patterns. A recent study of homosexuality in England provides the following classification of personalities within the homosexual category.[26]

1. *"The adolescent and mentally immature adults,* many of whom are still in the transitory stage of psychosexual development. Quite often they mistake the part for the whole and erroneously suppose that the recognition of a homosexual component indicates that they are irretrievably homosexual. Latent heterosexuality can exist just as much as latent monosexuality. Such persons can and do react with shame and misery, or overcompensate by bravado. And they can meet an attractive girl, fall in love, and all's well.

2. *"Severely damaged personalities.* Examples are obviously effeminate and flauntingly exhibitionistic individuals (those, contrary to popular belief, are quite rare); grossly inadequate, passive, weak-willed persons; or deeply resentful antisocial types.

3. *"Homosexuality in relatively intact personalities,* otherwise well socialized. Many of them are valuable and efficient members of the community, quite unlike the common conception of the homosexual as being necessarily, or probably, vicious, criminal, effete or depraved.

4. *"Latent and relatively well compensated homosexuals,* who are either not aware of their real difficulty, or else have struggled successfully against it for long periods.

5. "A *homosexual disposition with serious mental disability or disease,* for example, intellectual defect, brain damage or decay, serious mental illness or gross personality disorder (psychopathy)."

As the reader recognizes, these same types exist among the heterosexuals, and the sexual disposition in the sense of its direction is not the critical problem. The personalities noted in category (3) above are as much opposed to the exhibitionistic "flaming faggots" found in category (2) as the normal person is, and certainly do not wish to be identified with the criminals or with the seducers of young children. Even among

[26] *The Wolfenden Report* (New York: Stein and Day, 1963) pp. 119–120. These types noted in special sub-report by Drs. Curran and Whitby.

the "intact personalities" within the homosexual group, there is probably a price paid for having attitudes that they know are not accepted by the larger society. The role taking process affects them no less than it does the kleptomaniac or any other compulsive who, if he yields to his desires, risks censure by both friend and foe. This situation induces them to seek the company of other homosexuals, but this is not always satisfactory. There is no guarantee that a common attitude toward sex will be accompanied by other values that are compatible. The situation in which they find themselves is revealed by the fact that, although a large percentage of homosexuals in one research sample (a reported 96 per cent) answered "no" to the question of whether or not they would like to become heterosexual ". . . if a safe, easy means were available," only 3 per cent said that they would want a child of theirs to become a homosexual.[27] The life of the homosexual is a restricted one, whatever else it may be.

GENESIS OF HOMOSEXUALITY

The sexual impulse, as we have already stressed, is undefined, unchannelized at birth. It is defined in terms of the unique experiences of the individual as he grows up within a cultural setting or settings. Two factors appear to be significant in determining that the majority of persons are heterosexually disposed by the time adulthood is reached. The first is the fact that physiologically the most satisfactory results are obtained from relations with the opposite sex, and second, the culturally transmitted mores and folkways reflect heterosexuality as the norm. In the face of these two factors, it is not difficult to see why some persons are prone to explain homosexuality as the result of biological predisposition. However, the evidence to support this position is slight if, indeed, it exists at all. The observable facts fit better into the theory presented here, that the ultimate disposition of the sex impulse is learned. Early experiences may set the stage for what takes place later, and the time-honored adage about bending the twig to determine the way the tree shall grow is applicable to the sex impulse as it is to other phases of man's drives. Emotional habits built around pleasant physiological experiences are not easily altered, and as one writer in the field says:

> In childhood before the taboos of adults are imposed, a state of uncritical enjoyment of body stimulation exists. When the pleasure is shared, it may be shared with either sex depending to a great extent on propinquity or availability.[28]

This does not mean that a single, or even several, experiences are going to predispose a person to homosexuality, but initiation into sexual

[27] Helmer, *op. cit.*, p. 90.
[28] Clara Thompson, *op. cit.*, p. 214.

activity in this manner, with appropriate subsequent experiences *may* result in the development of a confirmed homosexual. But more than the mere physiological enjoyment of sex is involved in the development of the homosexual person. The inversion of attitudes, the taking of the attitudes of the members of the opposite sex requires specific experience over a period of time. For instance, not even a girl learns to be a girl overnight, but is given appropriate toys, told that girls behave in a certain way, is carefully taught what to do and what not to do, is accorded certain privileges and assigned special obligations that fit the status of the female in our culture. As someone has said, the differentiation begins the moment the boy baby is bundled in blue and the girl baby finds herself surrounded in pink. Even so, there is much overlapping in the personalities of the two sexes, just as there is in physical characteristics. If the members of one sex are treated in ways that are designed in our culture for the other, there is some likelihood that inversion may occur. This is more clearly operative in the case of the male, but perhaps only because we know more about the male homosexuals. It is interesting to note the report of psychiatrists on the nature of the homosexuals dismissed from the armed forces:

> Although the majority had no family history of nervous or mental disease, many were from homes broken by divorce or separation. In many instances the man had been brought up by his mother as a girl, or had been an only son in a large family of girls. About half assumed a "feminine" role, the other half "masculine." Most were either unmarried or had made a failure of marriage.[29]

The items included here find support in the psychosocial formula drawn from the research of Terman, Miles, and associates:

> . . . the psycho-social formula for developing homosexuality in boys would seem to run somewhat as follows: too demonstrative affection from an excessively emotional mother, especially in the case of a first, last, or only child; a father who is unsympathetic, autocratic, brutal, much away from home, or deceased; treatment of the child as a girl, coupled with lack of encouragement or opportunity to associate with boys and to take part in the rougher masculine activities; overemphasis on neatness, niceness, and spirituality; lack of vigilance against the danger of seduction by older homosexual males.[30]

Surely this would turn the child into the channels of interest that, as pointed out, are characteristic of the male passive homosexual. But these influences are not the only ones that may induce a person to abandon the quest for full status of a male in our culture. The positive relationship

---

[29] *Newsweek*, XXIX (June 1947), 54.
[30] Terman and Miles, *op. cit.*, p. 320.

between certain nonmasculine body types (those farthest from the meso-morphic ideal) and feminine social values is often pointed out without any explanation being given. In terms of the frame of reference used in this book, it is logical to suppose that such relationships would be the case. Look at it this way: in order to play the games that are popular with American boys, and particularly in order to play them well, a certain basic physique is a prerequisite. Football, baseball, basketball, hockey, and the rest are not games for "sissies," for those who are not rugged enough to withstand the shocks that are sure to come or who are so poorly coordinated that they cannot fulfill the expectations of their teammates. Anyone who has watched or participated in the "choosing up sides" on an unsupervised sandlot knows the distinct order in which the respective team members are selected. The most agile, largest, and strongest are chosen first, and the less well endowed (from the athletic viewpoint) always show up at the end. If there are too many to play at once, the ones who are left over are candidates for a way of life that is distinctly not typically masculine according to our cultural standards.

A more recent study reports findings of a similar nature.[31] In more than half of the cases studied (106 males) there existed an unusually close mother-son relationship.[32] In nearly one-half of the cases, a dominant wife-mother "minimized" her husband, thus damaging him as a masculine model for the son, and the majority of the parents of the homo-sexual males in this study had poor marital relationships.[33]

In a culture that places extreme emphasis upon physical strength and prowess, where the heroes of boyhood are athletic stars, rugged cowboys, and swashbuckling adventurers, the boy or man who is ill equipped physically to play such roles must ever be a failure or turn elsewhere to gain his needed recognition and companionship. The would-be fullback becomes manager, the ne'er-do-well on the athletic field turns to nonathletic interests such as art, music, and other intellectual pursuits that do not require an agile and rugged physique. Compensation and rationalization enable many such persons to gain satisfaction in what are truly substitute statuses and roles. Were the athletic ideals the *only* values of note in our culture, the person not equipped physically to compete would indeed be in an unenviable status, but although artists, musicians, and scholars do not attract cheering crowds of thirty, fifty, or one hundred thousand, they do know that their efforts are appreciated by significant numbers of persons. In time, the very exclusiveness of the audience, the persons who *really* appreciate the intellectual efforts, becomes a thing valued for its own sake. The recognition by "people who really count for something" is sufficient for personal satisfaction and adjustment; in brief, the significant

[31] Irving Bieber *et al., Homosexuality* (New York: Basic Books, 1962).
[32] Bieber *et al., Homosexuality,* p. 313.
[33] Bieber *et al., Homosexuality,* p. 313.

other is made up of like-minded persons. Much the same observation is provided by a group of psychoanalysts:

> Failure in the peer group, and anxieties about a masculine, heterosexual presentation of self, pave the way for the homosexuals' initiation into the less threatening atmosphere of homosexual society, its values, and way of life. As a group, homosexuals constitute a kind of subculture with unique institutions, value systems, and communication techniques in idiom, dress, and gestures. The tendency to gravitate to large cities may also be extended to residence in particular locales and to "hangouts." Often there is a sense of identification with a minority group which has been discriminated against.[34]

Minority status of this sort can be satisfying. The process of adjustment often follows this pattern: The atypical physique or inadequate perception of self prevents the person from participating fully in the social and play life of the majority and therefore prevents him from gaining satisfactory social approval and response; then through direction of elders, or through chance association with others similarly equipped with nonathletic interests, the person gains new and different interests, finds companionship and affection, and is given the opportunity of securing social approval from a new and different affective other. The taking toward himself of the attitudes of the new group induces him to play the roles esteemed by them. If he is to attain any degree of social adjustment he cannot do otherwise. How successful his new status is varies. Some persons find it completely satisfactory, whereas in another there is a residual desire to "show" the former associates that he can meet them on their own ground, but this he can do only in his daydreaming. Overtly he may scorn the "strong back and weak mind" crew, but secretly he may wish to join their group. To attempt to play overtly such a role would, of course, result in catastrophe unless one is equipped to do so. One must have the status or position of a good athlete before he can play such a role, and this is contingent upon the attitudes of those about the individual. There must be a coinciding of the desire and ability to play the role and the willingness of those who constitute the affective-other to accord that status or position to the person before the needs of the personality can be secured. Intent and ability are essential but not sufficient bases for success in attaining identity.

In understanding homosexual behavior, it is important to keep in mind the fact that behavior and attitudes toward that behavior are not always congruent. Many a woman with little sexual motivation, but with strong desires for affection, recognition, and security has married and tolerated heterosexual relations. The latter behavior is the price she is

---

[34] Bieber *et al.*, *Homosexuality*, p. 317.

willing to pay for the rewards she is seeking. In our culture, at least, there is some truth to the quip that "the female gives sex to gain affection, whereas the male offers affection and security to gain sex." It is plausible, perhaps reasonable, to expect, on the basis of available evidence, that certain homosexuals of both sexes engage in homosexual behavior in return for affection, recognition, and security. The person who is not strongly motivated in either a heterosexual or homosexual direction, but who has been disappointed or rejected in his or her quest for satisfactory personal relationship is a very likely candidate for *either* a homosexual or a heterosexual relationship that promises satisfying social relationships.

Still other persons fail to find in the company of acknowledged homosexuals full satisfaction of their social psychological needs. Students of the problem have observed that:

> . . . Although the emotional need of humans to socialize with other humans keeps many homosexuals within groups, some find the life style incompatible with other held values so that in some cases they come to prefer relative isolation.[35]

Much that has been said here is pertinent to the explanation of the social behavior of males with atypical physiques, and even though it applies to many nonhomosexuals, it is important in explaining some of the homosexuality. If an individual is denied the fulfillment of his basic needs of social approval, new experience, and response or companionship by playing the game according to the majority's rules, then he must turn elsewhere. Furthermore, if the channels left open to him are those which happen in a given culture to be characteristic of the opposite sex, the probability of his altering his significant other in favor of the feminine values is high. Participating in the activities of the opposite sex, he is apt to begin to see things as they do, to adopt their conceptions and evaluations. That his eye-to-eye viewpoint may carry over to the sphere of sex is not unlikely. He becomes identified with a female world of values in all of its many phases, and sex is not excluded. Now, this is certainly not to say that all musicians, artists, and others who are operating in fields that in our culture are open to or identified with women are so oriented. In fact, many males in such occupations are marked mesomorphs in physique and are well equipped for masculine athletic contests. Their interests in such fields are primary, and in no sense substitute or compensatory interests. No more is it true that all passive male homosexuals are possessed of nonathletic builds; their attitudes come from sources other than deficiencies of physique, such for instance, as the factors included in the Terman-Miles "formula" cited earlier in this chapter.

[35] Bieber *et al., Homosexuality*, p. 317.

Initiating factors in female homosexuality are, as would be expected, different from those in the male. One psychiatrist reports that the following factors are found in case histories of female homosexuals: sexually competitive, overly restrictive mothers; brutal, seductive, or overly restrictive fathers; seductive older brother; sexually competitive older sister; and a sibling favored by parents.[36] The lesbian seems to perceive the male-female sexual relationship as being exploitative of the female, and in defense restricts her associations to females.

In concluding our remarks on the homosexuals, it is important to emphasize again the fact that the majority of them are not vicious, degenerative, dangerous persons, and are not necessarily maladjusted. Psychiatrists who dealt with them in the army assert that "at least one half of the confirmed homosexuals . . . were well adjusted to their condition, and neither needed nor would respond to treatment."[37] The majority are useful citizens whose main difficulty lies in the lack of understanding of their nature by the majority of persons with whom they must associate. This statement is found in the English report of 1963: "The object of the treatment is to relieve mental stress by producing a better adjustment. It is perhaps worth adding that for this reason there may be good grounds, from the medical [psychiatric] point of view, for not attempting any fundamental reorientation of the sexual propensity of a homosexual who is already well adjusted and is a useful member of society."[38]

Full understanding by laymen of the homosexual would accomplish two things. First, the lot of the confirmed homosexual would be less difficult, and, second, it is likely that such knowledge would result in a diminution of the supply of homosexuals in our society. The improvement that has taken place in the acceptance of the homosexual is evidenced by the greater freedom they are given to form organizations and to publish magazines for homosexuals' consumption.[39]

CAN HOMOSEXUALS BE CHANGED INTO HETEROSEXUALS?

In order to determine whether a homosexual can be changed to a heterosexual, one must take into consideration the other facets of the personality in question. If the situation is complicated by pathologies of one sort or another, if the person is quite satisfied with his or her status and role, or if he is denied the experience requisite to the relearning of attitudes, the chances are reduced. One psychiatrist bluntly says that "They can be cured if they want to be. The only treatment is psycho-

---

[36] Robertiello, *Female Homosexuality*, p. 20.
[37] *Newsweek*, XXIX (June 1947), 54.
[38] *Wolfenden Report*, p. 111.
[39] W. J. Helmer, "New York's 'Middle-Class' Homosexuals," *Harper's*, 226 (March 1963), 91.

therapy, possibly over a period of several years."[40] Another says of female homosexuals that the patient ". . . at least must have a basic dissatisfaction with herself."[41]

Another group of therapists confidently report that "The therapeutic results of our study [of 100 male homosexuals] provide reason for an optimistic outlook. Many homosexuals became exclusively heterosexual in psychoanalytic treatment. Although the change may be more easily accomplished by some than by others, in our judgment a heterosexual shift is a possibility for all who are strongly motivated to change."[42]

If a homosexual, male or female, is not satisfied with his or her attitudes toward sex and wishes to become heterosexual (granting the difficulty of knowing just when the homosexual genuinely desires to do this), if he can alter the social situation so that all factors in his significant other are favorable to the heterosexual attitude, and can be given the proper emotional experiences over a long period of time, experiences with members of the opposite sex that are pleasurable from both social and physiological viewpoints, it is likely that gains can be made in the direction of heterosexuality. Knowledge that the learning process involves both intellectual and emotional learning is essential to the task, and the emotional process cannot be rushed. A rational program for the reeducation of the homosexual is illegal at the time of the present writing, nor would such a program be approved by the majority of the populace. Nevertheless, any attempts short of this are extremely likely to result in failure. Preaching, scolding, punishing, and any form of mental therapy based upon intellectual approaches or attitudes alone will gain little or nothing with the homosexual. Learning or relearning of anything must involve processes appropriate to the nature of the thing to be learned, be it swimming, liking spinach or snails, or being heterosexual. Desire alone is of no avail. The *will* to change involves appropriate action.

As noted in the Wolfenden Report, however, treatment does not always necessitate change in emotional disposition in order for it to be successful, at least in degree. In the words of the report:

Short of any alteration in the direction of the sexual urge, however, treatment may successfully lead to a better adaptation to life in general. The homosexual, like any other person who suffers from maladjustment to society, may be regarded as successfully treated if he is brought to a more complete adjustment to the society in which he lives. This can happen without any radical change in his propensity itself. It can happen by his being made more fully aware of his condition, and by processes which are directed not to changing it, but towards his fuller

---

[40] Dr. Ben Karpman, *Newsweek*, 57 (May 15, 1961), 94. Dr. Karpman is chief psychotherapist at St. Elizabeths Hospital, Washington, D.C.

[41] Robertiello, *Female Homosexuality*, p. 31.

[42] Bieber, *Homosexuality*, pp. 318–319.

understanding of it and the problems which it raises for him in relation
to society. . . . Treatment may have yet another purpose. It may be
directed simply towards making the man more discreet or continent in
his behavior, without attempting any other change in his nature. This
is not to be despised as an objective, for if it is successful such treatment
will reduce the number of homosexual offenses and offenders.[43]

SUMMARY

The term *personality type* is used often by both layman and social psychologist, and there is no dearth of names of types in our vocabularies.
However, there is no consensus regarding the referent categories of the
names of these many types. The concept *personality type* seems to be
most applicable when some phase of one of the three major categories
of personality—biological heritage, environment, or acquired subjective
variables or attributes—diverges from the normal, which may or may not
be normatively defined. Figure 27 suggests the extreme divergencies
which give rise to clearly discernible personality types. In all personality
types there is implied some degree of rigidity or inflexibility of relationships between the individual and his environment, thus making for behavior that is in some way inappropriate to the situation or episode at
hand.

Those personality types in which the inflexibility rests upon some biological attribute or upon some learned subjective attribute or variable are
called *role behavior types* or simply *role types*. As such the attributes are
functions of the actual attitudes or actions of the persons in question.

The personality types which are functions of the positions or statuses,
especially ascribed positions or statuses, are called *position* or *status
types*. In such types, the rigidity is largely, though not necessarily exclusively, imposed by the social and cultural environment of the individual. The change or removal of the typed relationship awaits changes
in one's affective other. This chapter discusses the following role types:
introverted-extraverted, inner-directed and other-directed, those based
upon the four wishes stated by Thomas and Znaniecki, and the homosexual. In those persons with exaggerated degrees of these characteristics,
one can understand much about individual behavior and can predict with
a relatively high degree of accuracy how the person will behave or act.

SUGGESTED READINGS

GOFFMAN, ERVING. *Stigma* (Englewood Cliffs, N.J.: Prentice-Hall, 1963).
HENRY, GEORGE W. *Sex Variants* (New York: Paul B. Hoeber, Inc., 1948).
JUNG, C. G. *Psychological Types*, or the *Psychology of Individuation* (New
York: Harcourt, Brace and Co., 1923).

[43] *Wolfenden Report*, pp. 110–111.

KINSEY, A. C., W. B. POMEROY, C. E. MARTIN, and P. H. GEBHARD. *Sexual Behavior in the Human Male* (Philadelphia: W. B. Saunders, 1953).

MULLAHY, PATRICK (ed.). *A Study of Interpersonal Relations* (New York: Hermitage Press, 1949).

RIESMAN, DAVID, NATHAN GLAZER, and REUEL DENNY. *The Lonely Crowd* (Garden City, N.Y.: Doubleday & Co., 1953).

Wolfenden Report (New York: Stein and Day, 1963).

YOUNG, KIMBALL. *Personality and Problems of Adjustment* (New York: F. S. Crofts and Co., 1940).

CHAPTER 10

PERSONALITY TYPES:
II. Position or Status Types, Stereotypes, and Resultant Role Types

> In the great blooming, buzzing confusion of the outer world we pick out what our culture has already defined for us, and we tend to perceive that which we have picked out in the form stereotyped for us by our culture.
>
> —*Walter Lippman*

We have discussed in Chapter 9 situations or conditions wherein deviation in biological heritage or the acquired subjective characteristics of the actor himself give rise to rigidity of relationships with the object world. In the category of personality types to be discussed in this chapter, the *audience* is the type maker. The rigidity, and often the cacophony, that exists is a function of actor and audience reading different scripts, with consequential divergent expectations of performance. Only by retreating to certain backstage areas can the actor so typed escape the forces of the coercive expectations of the larger, societal audience. These types have much in common with the typed performer of the theater, for example the comedian who discovers that people tend to laugh at his very serious remarks. Another example is the report that the actor who plays Judas in the well-known passion play at Oberammergau in Bavaria is apt to be stoned on the streets of the town even when off stage. In life's real drama two groups that the audience has typed, regardless of the subjective characteristics of the actors, are the Jews and the Negroes. In the United States especially, these two groups are position or status types. One needs to know nothing more than the mere fact that a person is of Jewish or Negro ancestry, *or believed to be,* in order to understand what certain relationships of the subjects in question will be. The attribution of *role behavior types* to each of these groups is involved in some relationships, but regardless of the actual role behavior, certain fixed relationships can be predicted on the bases of the statuses of Negro and Jew alone. The life chances of a person so identified, regardless of his actual behavior, are limited in a variety of situations.

THE VICIOUS CIRCLE AND PERSONALITY TYPES

A concept that is of value in enabling one to perceive the processes through which *position or status personality types* are related to *role* or *role behavior types* is the concept of the *vicious circle*, the components of which are shown in Figure 29.

The operation of the vicious circle reveals itself in the life experiences of disadvantaged individuals or groups, very few of whom are able to avoid the consequences to their personalities of this circular process. We have employed excerpts from actual case histories to illustrate the vicious circle.[1]

PHASE I. PREJUDICES AND DISCRIMINATION OF DOMINANT GROUPS

Newspapers, magazines, professional journals, court records, and books are filled with evidence of prejudice and discrimination in the dominant group. The laws which prevent the Negro from fulfilling his basic human requirements—biogenic or sociogenic—still exist in the pages of state and local statute books. Most Negro Americans expect their mobility to be restricted in ways that are quite unrelated to the roles they actually play; their racial status by itself is enough to deny them the job for which they are prepared, the meal for which they are willing to pay, the house they would rent or buy, the marriage their love warrants, and the education from which they are prepared to benefit. It would be pointless to detail here the mountains of evidence of the dominant group's prejudiced attitudes and consequent actions of discrimination as these influence the life chances of the disadvantaged status groups.

Although the content of the phases of the vicious circle varies from one disadvantaged status group to another, the general sociocultural processes are much the same as indicated by Figure 29. Some of the differences between Jewish and Negro Americans will be revealed in the following pages. The cultural heritage of the Jewish people is well known. Theirs is the parent religion of Christianity; their language, officially, is Hebrew, although more of them speak a combination of Hebrew and a local native language, the most common being Yiddish, a blend of middle-high German and Hebrew. The nonreligious characteristics of the Jewish

---

[1] This is not to deny that the position and status of the Jewish person has not changed in the past two decades. Will Herberg has reminded us that to be Jewish is no longer to invite immediately the inference that one is a foreigner in a dominantly Protestant country. This is true, but the ascribed position and status of the Jew, for many non-Jews and for a significant number of Jews, still warrant his being characterized as a personality type on the basis of position or status. *See* Herberg's *Protestant-Catholic-Jew* (Garden City, N.Y.: Doubleday and Co., 1956).

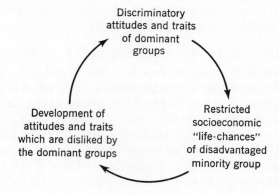

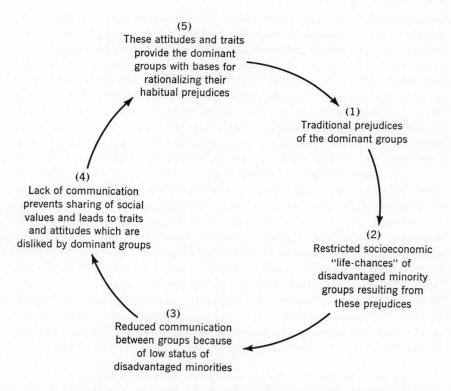

Figure 29. Vicious circle of prejudice and discrimination.

cultural heritage have vestiges of a rural, patriarchal culture. Significant modifications in the Jewish heritage are these:

1. A history of persecution for more than two thousand years that knows no equal in the records of world history. This persecution ranges all the way from mild social ostracism to the violent blood purges that accompanied the Crusades of the Middle Ages, the pogroms of Czarist Russia and Poland, and the merciless, mass murders of the Nazis. This fact is so well stated by one writer that we include it here:

> No *explanations*, however, can change the unalterable fact that Antisemitism has stalked through almost the entire known history of the world irrespective of logic, or morals, or time and space. Antisemitism crossed all frontiers, oceans, and continents, infecting all peoples, penetrating all faiths, languages, cultures, poisoning every environment. Antisemitism existed and exists to this day in Asia and in Africa, in Europe and in America; in the ancient world, in the Middle Ages, and in modern times; under the Pharaohs and under Popes; in the age of handicraft and in the age of highly specialized technology, in the age of radio and radium. Antisemitism appealed to pagans and to Christians and to Mohammedans; to the white and to the colored races; to the yellow and the black, to Semites (Arabs) and to non-Semites; to people speaking Aryan and non-Aryan languages.[2]

2. Until the last quarter of the nineteenth century the Jews were "guests" of other nations, always a people apart, and not candidates for assimilation in any real sense, because prior to the rise of modern seculalaristic urbanism they could not drop their Judaism without adopting another religious creed.

Stereotyped Attitudes of the Dominant Group as Environment

When one attributes role behavior types to the position types the term *stereotype* becomes useful. For the most part these personality types are stereotypes. This term is borrowed from the printing room, and refers to a page or paragraph of type set in type metal, made by pouring the metal into a mold. Once set, it is fixed and cannot be corrected or changed without recasting the whole piece. Walter Lippman, in *Public Opinion*, elected to use this as a basis for an analogy in the description of certain social relationships.[3] He spoke of "pictures in our heads" about other persons; these pictures are rigid, sometimes correct, but often incorrect in whole or in part. All persons sharing positions or statuses are per-

[2] Mark Vishniak, *An International Convention Against Antisemitism* (New York: Research Institute of the Jewish Labor Committee, 1946), pp. 14–15.

[3] Walter Lippman, *Public Opinion* (New York: The Macmillan Co., 1947). *See also* Maurice N. Richter, Jr., "The Conceptual Mechanism of Stereotyping," *American Sociological Review*, 21 (Oct. 1956), 568–571, for an analysis of stereotyping in terms of *empirical generalizations* and *stipulative definitions*. Richter points out how failure to distinguish between these operations yields stereotypes.

ceived as possessing certain traits and attitudes which, in fact, only a relatively small number of such persons possesses. For example, some American tourists are loud, vulgar, and given to ostentatious display of wealth, thus providing a basis for personality typing. Although not all persons with the position of American tourist possess these characteristics, the hotel clerks and others in foreign countries tend to perceive Americans abroad as such, thus forming in their mind's eye a rigid perception of this complex of traits and attitudes, that is, they form a *stereotype*.

The stereotype terms *denote* actual social positions and then *imply* certain roles associated with the positions. The reader is familiar with the picture of the Scotsman as a tight-fisted miser, the humorless and haughty Englishman, the Frenchman as a great lover, and the whole welter of roles attributed to Jews, Negroes, and orientals. The persistent United States stereotype of the Italian as a gangster is illustrated by the fact that a television serial (understandably resented by Americans of Italian ancestry) of fairly recent date became known as "cops and wops." Such terms as "red neck," "down East Yankee," "Texan," and "old maid" are examples of still different kinds of stereotypes. Despite the fact that there is truth in the assertion that almost no stereotype—perhaps *no* stereotype at all—is cut from whole cloth but is a function of actual role behavior on the part of a few, many of the persons caught up in a rigid picture and typed do not in fact behave in the alleged fashion. Thus the concept *personality type* must, as it indeed does in actual practice, include both actual role behavior and *imputed* or *alleged* behavior. This fact provides another illustration of the sometime truth that "if a person defines a situation as real, it is real in its consequences," as W. I. Thomas and Florian Znaniecki reminded us. If one *believes* that persons in certain positions or statuses play, or given a chance will play, given roles, he will consequently behave toward them as if they did indeed act in the alleged manner. Insofar as the particular relationship is concerned, the inaccuracy of the perception is of no consequence.[4] This sensitivity, so difficult to avoid on the part of any problem minority, gives rise to, and is reinforced by, a stereotyped view of the non-Jew on the part of the Jew. For example, there is the belief of a Jewish adolescent that "All Christians have a little anti-Semitism in them. It doesn't come out unless they are disturbed."[5] Such a notion is not quite so unreal as is its counterpart,

---

[4] *Cf.* Robert K. Merton, "The Self-fulfilling Prophecy," in his *Social Theory and Social Structure* (New York: The Free Press of Glencoe, 1963), for an elaboration of this concept which, as Merton correctly notes, is much older than the Thomas quotation.

[5] M. R. Yarrow, "Personality Development and Minority Group Membership" in M. Sklare (ed.), *The Jews: Social Patterns of an American Group* (Glencoe, Ill.: The Free Press, 1958), p. 464. *See also* in this source I. D. Rinder, "Polarities in Jewish Identification: The Personality of Ideological Extremity," pp. 439–502.

belief in the stereotyped Jew, but the result is as much a construct of a rigid mind as is the Jewish stereotype, and reaction to the Gentile in terms of this picture in the mind distorts reality and abets the separation of two groups. Very little attention has been given to this stereotype, but at least two articles, one by a Jewish writer and one by a non-Jew, deal with it specifically. The latter writes:

> During the past five years we have seen the most rapid construction of a literary myth since the carpentry of the Byronic hero. I refer to the conventional Gentile, who was exposed in the novel *Earth and High Heaven*, and subsequently performed on the screen in *Crossfire* and *Gentlemen's Agreement*. By the time he reached the novels *Focus* and *Eagle at My Eyes*, he had already been pared down to a flat uni-dimensional figure with no qualities outside of his attitude toward Jews . . . . How could such a solidly built cliché spring into print in fifteen hundred days?
>
> The answer, of course, is that the Gentile myth is not so new as all that. For this figure can be traced unmistakably to the *goy* of Jewish folklore, shaped out of a thousand years of unhappy history. No Gentile whose life is linked to Jewish communities needs novels to tell him about the goyim.[6]

The stereotype is full of contradictions and, although not subscribed to by many Jews in its entirety, it serves to orientate the reactions of some Jews. There is assumed a homogeneity of attitudes and traits among non-Jews that simply does not exist. The inability or the unwillingness to discern differences among the non-Jewish out-group is a factor in estranging the two groups, as is illustrated by the attitude of one Jewish person, who reports:

> I remember one of my Jewish girl friends telling me that it was absolutely impossible to talk to Gentiles in the same way that one could speak to members of our own group. According to her, there was absolutely no common interest that two people of different groups could discuss.

Experience led another to say ". . . I have come in contact with so much anti-Semitic feeling that I look on most Gentiles as being intolerant until they prove themselves otherwise."

Nor is the Negro without his stereotyped image of the Caucasian. Sitting on a bar stool in East Harlem, a young Negro, unemployed for long months at a time generally considered to be one of national prosperity, was voicing his bitter complaints, not unexpected under the circumstances, to a young white lawyer who had elected to locate his practice in that Negro ghetto. Said the young Negro over his beer, "All

[6] Wayne Clark, "Portrait of the Mythical Gentile," *Commentary*, VII (June 1949), 546.

whites are sons-a-bitches." A wry smile spread over his face as he remembered that his lawyer friend to whom he addressed the remark was white.[7]

Evidence of the existence of the stereotyped Negro is not wanting, as the accompany figures in Table XI reveal.

Table XI
White Stereotypes of the Negro*

Percentage of Whites Who Believe that:	Nationwide	South	Whites Who Had Social Contact with Negroes
	%	%	%
Negroes laugh a lot	85	94	77
Negroes tend to have less ambition	75	88	55
Negroes smell different	71	88	56
Negroes have looser morals	69	89	49
Negroes keep untidy homes	61	72	38
Negroes have less native intelligence	50	73	27
Negroes want to live off the handout	49	71	29
Negroes breed crime	44	58	24
Negroes care less for the family	39	60	24
Negroes are inferior to whites	36	61	17

* Newsweek (Oct. 21, 1963), 50.

SELECTIVE PERCEPTION AND THE JEWISH STEREOTYPE

In a study at Princeton University one hundred students were asked to select from some eighty-four adjectives those which applied to various social groups. The following list shows those most frequently selected as being applicable to the Jewish group: shrewd, mercenary, industrious, grasping, intelligent, ambitious, sly, loyal to family ties, persistent, talkative, aggressive, and very religious.[8]

Illustrative of the fact that the attitudes toward the Jewish group are pervasive in our culture and are not possessed by the dominant white majority alone are the results obtained by another application of the same

[7] For other examples of Negro Americans' stereotyped views of Caucasian Americans, see Thomas F. Pettigrew, A Profile of the Negro American (Princeton, N.J.: D. Van Nostrand Co., 1964), pp. 42–43.

[8] D. Katz and K. Braly, "Racial Stereotypes of One Hundred College Students," Journal of Abnormal and Social Psychology, XXVIII (1933), 280–290.

techniques used in the Princeton study. The picture of the Jewish personality as seen through the eyes of one hundred Negro American college students is comparable to the personality ascribed to the Jew by the white students at Princeton. There is reason to believe that this second study also included persons of different class status than did the first, indicating that prejudicial attitudes are not the monopoly of any one economic class. On the whole, the results were very much like those of the Princeton white group, but there were some differences. The Negro students substituted "deceitful" where the white students had listed "talkative," and the order of the ranking was not the same in both cases.[9] Nonetheless, these two studies indicate how pervasive the Jewish stereotype is, in both its complimentary and its derogatory aspects. It also illustrates the fact that experiencing discrimination is, in and of itself, no guarantee that those discriminated against will not have prejudicial attitudes against other minorities.

Table XII lists the characteristics attributed to the Jewish people in a third study, made by the present authors in a large university and a small liberal arts college in midwestern United States.[10]

The prevalence of the stereotype is further evidenced by a study made in a Chicago High School that is 85 per cent Jewish in its student population. From a check list of characteristics the Jewish students selected these: loud, showy, rich, clannish, well-educated, clever, friendly, and good businessmen.[11] Are these accurate perceptions or merely stereotypes which the Jewish students, as a result of role taking, have assumed as their own? We will take cognizance of this problem later under the heading of *self-hatred.*

Such, then, are the many characteristics which at one time or another find their way into the stereotype of the Jewish personality in our culture. Although the several lists do not coincide exactly, considerable over-

---

[9] J. A. Bayton, "The Racial Stereotypes of Negro College Students," *Journal of Abnormal and Social Psychology,* XXXVI (1941), 100.

[10] No check list was provided, and the otherwise blank sheet of paper had this heading: "We are asking you to participate in a study of minority groups. In the space provided below you are asked to list the characteristics which you feel are typically Jewish. Please include a brief description of any particular experience . . . you may have had which illustrates one or more of these characteristics. Do not sign your name but please fill in carefully the information asked for at the bottom of the sheet." The last sentence refers to questions concerning the number of Jews known personally by the person filling out the questionnaire, circumstances of contacts with Jews, nationality background, religion, and father's occupation. No breakdown of the answers in terms of these background data has been made.

One unexpected reply was: "None of your G——— D——— business. There are enough prejudices and misunderstandings going on in this country and the world as a whole, without a bunch of nosey and trouble-making agitators such as you studying minority groups. Why don't you go out and find a deep hole to fall in?"

[11] A senior honors thesis by Saul Borash (University of Illinois, Department of Sociology and Anthropology, 1950).

Table XII
Stereotypes of Jewish People

Intelligent, very intelligent, intellectual	22
Proud, egocentric, ethnocentric, conceited	19
Crafty, sly, unscrupulous in business	19
Good businessmen	18
Aggressive, forceful	18
Loyal to in-group and especially to family	17
Clannish	17
Mercenary, greedy	16
Nothing characteristic about Jews as such	15
Ambitious, industrious	14
Loud, bold, forward	14
Shrewd in business	14
Ostentatious, showy	12
Good natured, kind	10
Do not care what out-group thinks of them	9
Domineering, must run the show, overbearing	9

lapping does exist. Reported findings of specific research projects on the nature of the Jewish personality usually relate to one or more of these features of the stereotype. The social and psychological situations which initiate and perpetuate the unreasoned, emotional social relationships that we call prejudices are many, and we list a few of the more important ones here:

MISCONCEPTIONS ABOUT THE NATURE OF OUT-GROUPS

There are numerous misconceptions regarding out-groups of all kinds that are not based upon facts. Sometimes they are personal-social items in the personality, but often they are widespread and cultural in nature. The latter type of misconceptions is illustrated by the stereotypes of Negroes as being biologically inferior, less intelligent, innately slovenly, oversexed, and naturally given to criminal acts and by the stereotype of the Jew as being racially different, always wealthy, untrustworthy, conspiring to take control of the world from the non-Jew, archcapitalists and archcommunists at the same time, averse to soap and water, and of lower moral standards than the Gentiles. It is at this level of prejudice that the schools, forums, radio programs, and written articles generally are most effective. An effort on behalf of the refutation of the Jewish stereotype is that of the survey conducted by *Fortune Magazine* as published in Volume XIII of that journal in 1936. This is essentially a survey of the economics of the situation and it pointed out that the Jews are much less in control of the country's economy than is popularly supposed. The situation does not appear to have changed significantly since the survey was made. Sometimes such an erroneous conception of an out-group is actually the foundation upon which the emotional attitudes of prejudice are built, but sometimes it is merely employed as a rationalization of deeply ingrained emotional attitudes that are independent of intellectual concepts. It is clear, too, that misconceptions of human nature in general, and not merely misconceptions of out-groups, are conducive to prejudice. The unawareness of the fact that, "There, except for my unique experiences, go I," is a major factor in biased and prejudiced attitudes.

There is some support for the belief that prejudice may be a function of a particular kind of misconception of an outgroup, namely, perceived (or misperceived) dissimilarity of belief systems.[12]

Stein, Hardyck, and Smith, in a study of forty-four white, ninth grade teenagers, used questionnaires designed to elicit information concerning the subjects' values, perceptions of value differences between them and white and Negro teenagers, and social distance attitudes. This research gave strong support to the Rokeach view, but still found race a significant influence upon social distance in such activities as dining with, dating, or living with the nonwhite persons.[13]

Here the operation of stereotypes in attributing role type behavior to position or status occupants is clearly seen. The subjects are apt to perceive the nonwhite person as subscribing to different value systems. Rokeach and others have shown that it is especially in the absence of adequate knowledge about the out-group member that stereotypes come into play and support prejudice. However, it is a mistake to assume that emotional predispositions, that is, attitudes, can be erased merely by the advent of accurate perceptions of shared values. Although misconceptions of the nature of the object of prejudice can lay the basis for discriminatory practices and the development or perpetuation of prejudices, to suggest a one-to-one relationship between perceptions and prejudices is to oversimplify the situation. The studies by Rokeach and others must be examined with a full awareness of the differences between prejudice and discrimination, between emotional and cognitive learning, and of the parts played by one's significant other group and reference group.[14]

Two episodes help to put the perception of likenesses in appropriate perspective.

1. A female student at a university became aware of the racial misconceptions that she had acquired prior to her graduation from high

[12] Cp. Milton Rokeach, The Open and Closed Mind (New York: Basic Books, 1960). See also Harry C. Triandis, "A Note on Rokeach's Theory of Prejudice," Journal of Abnormal and Social Psychology, 62 (1961), 184–186. Triandis argues that the race factor is more important in prejudice and discrimination than is perception of unlike values.

[13] D. D. Stein, J. A. Hardyck, and M. B. Smith, "Race and Belief; and Open and Shut Case," Journal of Personality and Social Psychology, 1, No. 4 (1965), 281–288.

[14] The material on attitude change in Chapter 5 is applicable here.

school. She learned that her stereotyped attitudes toward nonwhites were founded largely on misinformation, and she chose social work as a career. Her undergraduate training in social work involved working in a neighborhood recreation center, which was located in a racially mixed area of the city. When she first reported for her inservice training, she had to close her eyes and grit her teeth when she first took hold of a Negro girl's hand. The student's relearning at the intellectual level was not sufficient to change deepseated attitudes of prejudice. Only after weeks of close and continued contact with the Negro children did she lose this emotional discomfiture when in contact with them.

2. The second incident involved the reaction to the purchase by a Negro couple of a house in a hitherto all-white neighborhood. The wife, whose slight Negro characteristics were not perceived by the well-tanned housewives of the area, purchased the house while her husband, an Air Force officer, was on a flying mission. Although she was observed several times inspecting the property, no voice of protest was raised. Her clothes and her car were congruent with those of others in the area, and it was not until her husband, manifestly a Negro, arrived that the petition asking them to move was circulated and signed by approximately one hundred neighbors. Only four of the neighbors refused to sign. Here the racial factor was the significant one—not to be counterbalanced by the strong evidence that the couple's values were not dissimilar to those of the others in the neighborhood.

Nevertheless, despite the existence of some unanswered questions concerning the relationship between misperception and prejudice, the interactionist frame of reference and the dual nature of learning support the conclusion that:

> If people of different races encounter one another under conditions favoring the perception of belief congruence (as, for example, in equal status contacts), then racial prejudice should be substantially reduced.[15]

UNFORTUNATE EXPERIENCES WITH NONREPRESENTATIVE
MEMBERS OF OUT-GROUP

The common tendency for persons to generalize their attitudes as a result of contacts with inadequate samples of the environment often sponsors prejudiced attitudes toward out-group members. The following excerpts from actual cases illustrate the operation of this process.

> 1. I recall that one evening my mother had given me fifteen cents to fetch her something from the grocery store at about seven o'clock in the evening. The streets were completely deserted, and as I reached the corner a group of colored boys and girls appeared and beat me up and took my fifteen cents. I remember getting up, after they had pulled at

[15] Stein, Hardyck, and Smith, "Race and Belief: an Open and Shut Case," p. 289.

my hair and slapped and pushed me about, filled with a menacing rage not only because of the beating but because they had called me a dirty janitor's Jew daughter. This was the perfect type of experience to add to my already well-established prejudice . . . . After this experience I never referred to them as anything but "those dirty niggers."

For sake of contrast, we include an excerpt from another case in which fortunate contacts with Negroes fostered a definitely positive attitude toward this minority group.

2. The first contact that I can remember having with a Negro was when I was very young. My family was vacationing on a farm in the poorer section of Alabama. The tenant farmer at one of the neighboring farms was colored and had a son about five years old. I had great respect for him. Not only did his "know-how" command my respect but his daring did also . . . . That summer was a lot of fun for both of us, but, as neither of us then realized, it was also an education in human relations . . . . We did have a colored maid . . . [who] took a personal interest (not superficial) in every member of the family. We all liked her very much . . . . She was the type of person with whom you liked to share your successes and defeats . . . . In the Army I had many contacts with the Negro . . . . A lot of men felt degraded to have to associate with them. I don't know why because they were the best marching platoon on the base. They were good soldiers in every respect. After moving to another base I was assigned to work with several Negroes. My respect for them was increased when two of them taught me how to play golf . . . . Another taught me the fundamentals of boxing . . . . With the acquaintances I have had with the Negroes I could not be anything but tolerant. I have, by mere coincidence, met a better-than-average group of Negroes. (Written by a white, fifth-generation, gentile American.)

The following case is another illustration of strong emotional attitudes built upon early unpleasant experiences.

3. When I was about five years old the little Polocks called me a Christ-killer, and beat the hell out of me, [and] I went home crying. My mother told me they meant no harm, but I told her that I would never like Polocks, and until this day my attitude hasn't changed. My attitude hasn't changed because the Poles have never given me the opportunity to change. I still think they are a bunch of cabbage-eating skunks.

Now, undoubtedly the cited instances in the above excerpts from cases do not tell the whole story. There is the larger picture which supports the traditional antagonisms between Negro and white, and between those of Polish and Jewish background. Both of the individuals in the cases 1 and 3 must have had fights with other persons during their childhood period and perhaps with others in their own in-group, and yet they did not generalize that all such persons are undesirable. Also, the permissive attitude of the parents in case 2 set the stage for pleasant memories of an early childhood contact with the Negro. Nevertheless, such sharply dramatic incidents are significant in providing a basis, if no more than a rationale in some instances, for emotional prejudices for or against outgroups.

PERSONAL DEFICIENCIES

Although there is ample evidence that subjective personal deficiencies often sponsor unreasoned prejudices toward other individuals and toward social groups of which the person is not a member, there still remains much need for research in this field. Just what these deficiencies are, and just how they operate to influence interpersonal relations is not clearly known. Even the carefully conducted studies which have been reported are so restricted in the size and nature of the sample studied, and have been carefully interpreted by too few persons to permit of complete acceptance of their conclusions. Three of the most frequently reported studies are those of Allport and Kramer, Frenkel-Brunswik and Sanford, and Hartley.[16] Although all three of these studies provide definite suggestions as to the probable nature of some of the personal items associated with prejudice, the fact that the samples were all college students enrolled in introductory courses in psychology limits the applicability of the findings.

The Allport-Kramer study revealed that the persons who were more prejudiced were more apt to conform to their parents' ideas and to be less critical of such ideas, to have poorer insight than the nonprejudiced persons, and to be more suspicious in nature. The study by Frenkel-Brunswik and Sanford found that the more prejudiced individual presented a picture of a well-groomed, slightly more superstitious conformist who spoke of great respect for both parents and for authority in general, and who adhered in overt behavior to the tenets of what has come to be known as "middle-class morality," but who were revealed (under indirect research techniques) to have ambivalent attitudes toward parents, to be aggressive and to project upon minority groups some of their own repressed hostility. The Hartley study, in which the subjects were college students from seven different schools, reported characteristics of the intolerant person that agree with some of the findings of Frenkel-Brunswik and Sanford. From the relatively long list of such characteristics, we note

---

[16] Gordon W. Allport and Bernard M. Kramer, "Some Roots of Prejudice," *Journal of Psychology*, XXII (1946), 9–39; Else Frenkel-Brunswik and R. Nevitt Sanford, "Some Personality Factors in Anti-Semitism," *Journal of Psychology*, XX (1945), 271–291; and Eugene Hartley, *Problems of Prejudice* (New York: King's Crown Press, 1946).

these: emotionality rather than rationality, acceptance of conventional mores, and extreme egocentrism.[17]

In a study of Jewish students and their parents in New York City, the conclusion was reached that the more intolerant person was "self-rejecting," that is, unable to admit or accept his hostile and dependency needs, unwilling to bring to consciousness his shortcomings, and manifesting behavior traits of strict conformism, rigid emotional control and lack of insight.[18] That such persons would find need for looking askance at out-groups is certainly plausible, even probable. There are surely other types of personal deficiencies that give rise to the need for projecting personal inadequacies and repressed desires, or cause some people to look for scapegoats and whipping boys. The attitude, typical of the white person of old American stock whose social status is very low, that "at least I am not a nigger, kike, or wop," further illustrates the felt need for someone to look down upon if one is to maintain a semblance of morale. That this is a universal need we would deny, but that it exists in many instances can hardly be questioned.

A much more common type of person is the one which embodies just enough of a feeling of insecurity that the "when in Rome, do as the Romans do" theme dominates much of the individual's social behavior. This is the Philistine type, according to Thomas and Znaniecki.[19] In such persons there may be discrepancies between the covert attitude and the overt social behavior, but the net result is to perpetuate certain prejudices. The following is a case in point:

A young woman moved to a town in which the group she became friendly with was characterized by a slight degree of anti-Semitism. No Jewish people lived in the rural area from which she came and there had been no need to consider the question. However, her desire to enter fully into the social life of her new acquaintances led her to adopt many of the patterns of thought and action which seemed necessary for social success. She learned bridge and poker, acquired a taste for martinis, became more chic in her dress, and joined the Book-of-the-

[17] Eugene L. Hartley, *Problems of Prejudice* (New York: King's Crown Press, 1946), pp. 62, 120. This work contains some interesting cases of different personality types on the basis of tolerance and intolerance. The finding that the tendency to emphasize ethnic group affiliation was not clearly correlated with prejudice (p. 121) seems to be at variance with the Allport-Kramer finding that the anti-Semites were better able to identify Jews from facial features. However, this may not signify a real difference.

[18] Jerome Himelhoch, "Tolerance and Personality Needs," *American Sociological Review*, XV (1950), 81. On this point, *see also* T. M. Newcomb, *Personality and Social Change* (New York: The Dryden Press, 1943).

[19] W. I. Thomas and Florian Znaniecki, *The Polish Peasant in Europe and America* (New York: Alfred A. Knopf, 1947). *See also* Herbert Blumer, *An Appraisal of Thomas and Znaniecki's The Polish Peasant in Europe and America* (New York: The Social Science Research Council, 1939).

Month Club. Among other things, when the occasion arose, she was "properly" anti-Semitic.[20]

Here we see the operation of the affective other in the development of attitudes, or at least of overt behavior patterns. Were it the case that agricultural values dominated our culture, the young lady from the country might not, probably would not, have felt the need to play the role of the anti-Semite for her urban acquaintances. A greater surety of social status would have enabled her to resist some of the demands, or assumed demands, for conformity to the new in-group folkways.

Important as these factors of personality deficiencies or abnormalities may be in our quest for greater understanding of prejudice, realism demands that the quest not be stopped there. *There is good reason to believe that there are persons who are normal, extremely well adjusted, and healthy from both physical and mental viewpoints who do harbor prejudices. It is as much an error to find the explanation of prejudice exclusively in personal deficiencies as it is to ignore them as a source of prejudice.*[21]

Keeping in mind the admonitions which accompany most of these studies, namely, that the samples are small and perhaps not representative of either the populace at large or the college groups themselves, we can tentatively hold that the intolerant, prejudiced person is characterized by:

1. Lack of insight and self-acceptance.

2. Ambivalent attitudes toward authority.

3. Strictly conventional behavior traits, even though there is evidence to suggest incompatibility of these overt traits and covert attitudes.

4. Dominance of emotional over rational behavior.

5. Basic lack of satisfaction with the assigned social position or status.

[20] James A. Bayton, "Personality and Prejudice," *Journal of Psychology*, XXII (1946), 62. It is interesting to note that among the Jewish people there is some evidence of a correlation between feelings of insecurity and patterns of exclusiveness. I. D. Rinder, "Polarities in Jewish Identification: The Personality of Ideological Extremity," in M. Sklare (ed.), *The Jews: Social Patterns of a Minority Group* (New York: The Free Press, 1958), p. 502.

[21] An example of the restricted viewpoint is illustrated by the statement that ". . . the fundamental psychological sources of prejudice . . . are to be found in the quality of parent control used during the formative period of personality organization." Bayton, "Personality and Prejudice," pp. 64–65. It does not seem possible that the differences between the northern and southern regions of this country can be attributed to the "coercive, authoritarian, and capricious parent control . . ." of the southern regions, nor that the anti-Semitism of the Arabs, the Poles, or of the Bostonians of Irish descent is explainable solely in terms of parent-child relationships.

ETHNOCENTRISM

Ethnocentrism is a term described by the sociologists as: ". . . the technical name for this view of things in which one's own group is the center of everything, and all others are scaled with reference to it . . . . Each group nourishes its own pride and vanity, boasts itself superior, exalts its own divinities, and looks with contempt on outsiders."[22] Ethnocentrism is a form of group identification. Figure 30 represents the ethnocentrism of the nations of Europe who, although of the same racial stock, are separated from each other by cultural values that are passed from one generation to the next in the form of language, food habits, dress, and many other items. The cartoon dramatizes the separateness that comes from ethnocentric attitudes. Many of the frictions that develop in and between urban neighborhood areas are traceable to these European-born attitudes.

In Chapter 6 we noted that, of all sociopsychological concepts, the process of identification was one of the most important for the understanding of individual and group behavior. This process takes one beyond sympathy, and he *empathizes* with the individual or group with whom he is positively identified. He actually feels personal satisfaction or pain with the gains and losses of the person or persons involved. All normal persons attain group identifications. The identification process takes place gradually, unconsciously, and it is largely a learning process at the emotional level. Because of this, reward and punishment are not involved, and mere association is sufficient for the learning process to operate. One does not purposely develop ethnocentric attitudes, even though he may purposely feign to have done so if the occasion arises wherein the attitudes of his associates demand such behavioral evidence of such attitudes.

This emotional process respects no status group. Only certain of the mentally ill are exempt. Out of this ethnocentrism come various prejudices, revealed both in attitude and overt behavior traits. It sponsors the traditional fear and distrust of the stranger, as well as aversion to any differences in physical form or social behavior that may vary from racial features to structural pathologies. Just as instances are known where Negroes, seen for the first time, have scared the wits out of white persons, there are also instances where the white missionaries have sent Negroes, the children particularly, into paroxysms of fear by their pallid appearance. The more culturally isolated a person's life has been, the more difficulty he experiences in adjusting to other ways of doing things. The basis for ethnocentrism is, of course, habit, and, as we have stressed earlier in the book, habits, once formed, are not easily broken. Much ethnocentrism is based upon habits of long standing, involving groups as varied as a nation, an athletic team (*e.g.*, the New York Mets, Green Bay

[22] William Graham Sumner, *Folkways* (Boston: Ginn and Company, 1906), p. 13.

FIGURE 30. Ethnocentrism—an international commodity. (Cartoon by Willard Mullin, reproduced by courtesy of *Look Magazine*.)

Packers), a church, or a region or state such as New England, the South, Indiana, California, or Texas. The ethnocentrism that evolves from the process of identification must be counted among the most important factors in the perpetuation of cultural groups, and as a basis for other supporting processes. Whenever group identification occurs, the continued existence and high status of the group in question become values themselves for which the group members will pay high costs. Often this is not a rational process.

Group identification is not necessarily inimical to anyone's welfare; as a matter of fact, group identification is an important ingredient of high morale, as well as an essential aspect of social organization. We recognize it under such names as group loyalty and family devotion.

Illustrative is the experience of a young college professor who was seriously injured in an automobile accident which occurred a long distance from his home. Upon regaining consciousness in the hospital, he discovered two Jewish women who had read of his accident in the paper, had recognized the Jewish name, and had come to proffer whatever help was needed—to contact relatives, to sit with him, or to help financially.

Even when carried to extremes, it need not do harm. The ethnocentric attitude of the Texan is, for the most part, all to the good. On that score, one is reminded of the enthusiastic early settler in Texas who wrote to a friend in the East that all Texas needed was a little better quality of people and more water, to which the friend replied, "Why man, that's all Hell needs."[23] Such anecdotes or replies will not daunt the Texan's morale or loyalty, nor is his identification with his state likely to harm anyone. Ethnocentrism becomes a problem only when it interferes with the freedom and social mobility of others, or with one's own learning and happiness. This happens when a person seeks to make his way of life the only one, or seeks to eliminate or handicap the out-groups, whom he does not invite to join his in-group. It is this ethnocentrism that leads to much of the discrimination against out-groups, and, because it is largely emotional and not rational, its elimination is not solely a matter of preaching or teaching. As a matter of fact, many persons are intellectually aware of the nature of their ethnocentric attitudes, are ashamed of some of them, and yet cannot rid themselves of them.

CULTURAL PREJUDICES

It was stated earlier that there are persons who, although perfectly well physically and mentally, do show prejudices in their social behavior. When social values are shared by a large proportion of the population of a given society, that is, when they are cultural values, there is no guar-

[23] Stanley Walker, "Everything's True about Texas," *Harper's Magazine* (March 1950), 30.

anteeing that they will be rational, unprejudiced values. Growing up in a culture, the young develop the intellectual and emotional pictures of the world from the viewpoint of that culture. They learn what is "proper" behavior, what is "proper" diet, and what is "proper" by way of attitudes. The better their adjustment to the culture, the more fully they will adopt its prejudices. There is no need to postulate personality maladjustment as an explanation for prejudiced attitudes. Prejudice may be no more than effective *enculturation* of the person in question.

By what other means could one explain the historical racial attitudes of some southern sections of this country? Or the attitudes between the Jews and the Arabs in the Near East? Or the antipathies between the English and the Irish, the Turks and the Greeks? There is no more need to suggest that the reason lies in a nationwide neurosis than there is to look in the same direction for the preference of the Japanese for cooler houses or for their diet. Many prejudices are merely the ways in which the persons of a given culture have been taught to conceive of the world and its inhabitants. Habit accounts for the continuation of these prejudices.

Evidence of the cultural bases of prejudices is presented in a study of racial attitudes on the part of university students in 1955 and 1958. No significant changes were recorded because no significant cultural alterations occurred in the three-year interim. The prejudice scores (the higher the score, the greater the prejudice) were as follows: Baptist, 49.8; Roman Catholic, 44.3; Jewish, 39.0; no affiliation with organized religious group, 32.4; residents of communities of fifty thousand or more, 43.3; small town and rural residents, 48.1; majors in pharmacy, 57.3; majors in business administration, 49.9; social science majors, 35.3; residents of east Texas, 55.2; residents of west Texas, 45.5.[24] Here we see evidence of the various cultural positions' influence upon the occupants' attitudes.

Certainly, there are factors leading to prejudice that we have not mentioned here, but it is our position that they can be placed under one or more of the six categories given here. It is important to keep in mind that prejudices are attitudes which may be for or against the social value in question. The term prejudice itself tells us little except that someone has a fairly definite attitude toward some object, group, or way of behaving and is in some degree ignorant of its real nature. Prejudice is not a monopoly of the majority or of the powerful but is found in all persons in varying degrees, and its existence is not to be explained by any single item of personality or of experience. Prejudice may be found in neurotics or in well-adjusted personalities. Prejudice, in short, is not a simple phenomenon, yielding to a particularistic explanation.

[24] R. K. Young, W. M. Benson, and W. H. Holtzman, "Change in Attitudes Toward the Negro in a Southern University," *Journal of Abnormal and Social Psychology*, 60 (1960), 132.

That prejudices are often functions of the enculturation process is further evidenced by the stereotyped views of people who have had little or no contact with the group stereotyped. In Table XIII are recorded the stereotyped characteristics attributed to nine cultural or racial groups by members of a new England high school history class in 1964. The pupils, mostly 17-year-olds, had relatively little contact with most of the groups listed.

Table XIII
High School Students' Stereotypes*

German	Italian	Irish
Industrious	Passionate	Quick tempered
Intelligent	Quick tempered	Very religious
Scientifically minded	Talkative	Witty
Nationalistic	Jovial	Quarrelsome
Aggressive	Quarrelsome	Aggressive
	Very religious	

English	Jews	Americans (U.S.)
Conservative	Shrewd	Materialistic
Reserved	Intelligent	Ambitious
Intelligent	Industrious	Pleasure loving
Sophisticated	Mercenary	Industrious
Practical	Materialistic	Practical
		Progressive

Negro	Chinese	Japanese
Lazy	Loyal to family ties	Loyal to family ties
Superstitious	Tradition loving	Courteous
Musical	Reserved	Industrious
Unreliable	Nationalistic	Intelligent
Sensual	Quiet	Tradition loving

* Source: unpublished research by Richard Dewey.

Discrimination As Environmental Influence

Were the environmental antipathy to remain at the covert, attitudinal, and belief level, the vicious circle would be interrupted in its operation. However, the prejudices are readily translated into overt acts of discrimination. The violence met by both Caucasians and Negroes in their attempts to integrate public services in the United States is well known. Arson, mayhem, and murder provide ample evidence of the prejudiced attitude's viability.

Two reports of trips through southern states reveal clearly the strength of anti-Negro discrimination in its many dimensions. One author is Negro, now a newspaper columnist but then a reporter for a northern news-

paper.[25] The other is a white man who elected to darken his skin arti-
ficially, and to pass as a Negro. The latter is a highly dramatic illustration
of the intrusive nature of the attitudes of one's affective other, as the
following passage reveals:

> I walked to the ticket counter. When the lady ticket-seller saw me, her
> otherwise attractive face turned sour, violently so. This look was so un-
> expected and so unprovoked I was taken aback.
>
> "What do you want?" she snapped. Taking care to pitch my voice
> to politeness, I asked about the next bus to Hattiesburg.
>
> She answered rudely and glared at me with such loathing I knew
> I was receiving what the Negroes call "the hate stare." It was my first
> experience with it. It is far more than the look of disapproval one occa-
> sionally gets. This was so exaggeratedly hateful I would have been
> amused if I had not been so surprised. . . . Once again (in the bus
> station waiting room) a "hate stare" drew my attention like a magnet.
> It came from a middle-aged, heavy-set, well-dressed white man. He sat
> a few yards away, fixing his eyes on me. Nothing can describe the
> withering horror of this . . . .
>
> A Negro reporter sidled over to me. I glimpsed his white coat and
> turned to him. His glance met mine and communicated the sorrow, the
> understanding.
>
> "Where am I supposed to go?" I asked him. He touched my arm in
> that mute and reassuring way of men who share a moment of crisis.
> "Go outside and around the corner of the building. You'll find the
> room." The white man continued to stare, his mouth twisted with loath-
> ing as he turned his head to watch me move away.[26]

The discrimination against an ethnic group is less obvious than that
against members of non-Caucasoid groups, but none the less real, as
these case excerpts show.

1. The first time that I actually felt the blow of anti-Semitism was in
Miami about two years ago. I was spending the summer with my aunt
and I was looking for a job. I applied for a job. I applied for a position
at a neighborhood bank and the personnel manager felt that I could
ably handle the position. As a matter of fact, he told me that I would
be hired after my application was reviewed by the larger down-town
bank. I was called for an interview by the head personnel manager.
He seemed very pleased with my qualifications and went so far as to tell
me what my salary would be. Accidentally I had overlooked the space
provided on the application blank for religion. He asked me what my
religion was and the smile disappeared from his face as I told him that
I was Jewish. He fumbled through his drawer and brought out a piece
of paper which he appeared to be studying intently. He then told me

---

[25] Carl T. Rowan, *South of Freedom* (New York: Alfred A. Knopf, 1952); *See
also* his *Go South to Sorrow* (New York: Random House, 1957).
[26] J. H. Griffin, *Black Like Me* (Boston: Houghton Mifflin Co., 1961), pp. 53–54.

that he was very sorry but he had forgot that the position had been filled by the central office two days previously. He assured me that my name would be kept on file if another position should become available.

2. One day a drunken G.I. came into camp at the end of his pass to Honolulu. He and I had worked, fought, slept, and eaten together, and I naturally thought of him as my buddy. When he caught sight of me he began to call me names and to tell me I was just like the rest of the "dirty Jews," although he had thought I was different. Somehow, the first time I have ever gotten angry, I picked up my loaded rifle, unlocked it and had very carefully started to aim for this fat slob's guts—it hurts most there—when my rifle was hit upwards from behind me and was taken away from me by my C.O. [commanding officer]. After I had cooled down enough to talk I told my C.O. that I would kill this "doggie" at the first good opportunity that presented itself. To prevent further trouble one of us had to be transferred; the army knew it and I believe acted wisely indeed in sending me on.

3. He hated everyone because he was in the Army—and he especially hated the "Kikes," because more than anyone else they were responsible for him being in the Army. For three months it was "Kike this," and "goddam Jew that." Finally it got to the point where it was most [unbearable]. I knew that something was going to happen because after awhile, I just couldn't take it. One day, after a thirty-mile hike Bill started his same line again. I was in no mood to receive it, so without saying anything I picked up a shower clog and broke it in two over his head. Bill was taken to the dispensary, and I was taken to the orderly room.

Captain ——— wanted to know if I made a practice of hitting people on the head. I told him no, and then explained the situation to him. He was rather shocked, and told me if the same situation should ever present itself again to make good use of my other clog.

PHASE II. RESTRICTED SOCIAL AND ECONOMIC LIFE CHANCES

In Figure 31 one sees at a glance something of the Negroes' economic status. This plays an important role in the vicious circle operation. Poverty and segregation set the stage for the learning of roles which are incompatible with the value system of the larger society. The reader is aware of the marked degree to which the Negro American is segregated from his Caucasian countryman, in part because of poverty, but in part because of norms, enforced by sanctions ranging from house burnings and threats of personal violence to discriminatory contracts, usually called restrictive covenants. No region of the country is free of this forced or coerced segregation.

During long centuries of the Diaspora the Jews were not permitted by their host nations in Christendom to own land, nor could they enter

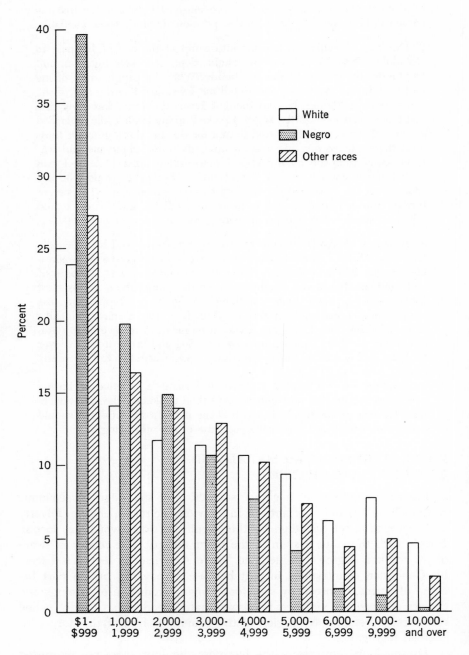

FIGURE 31. U.S. Income According to Racial Groups, 1960. (*Source*: U.S. Bureau of the Census, **I**, *Characteristics of Population*.)

the favored occupations. In Germany, for example, their economic pursuits contrasted sharply with the most prestigious group, the Junkers, who combined land ownership with high military position. These ingredients of high status were closed to Jews, and they were forced into occupations not sought by the more privileged non-Jews, for example, handling money for interest. In America they were often restricted to such pursuits as dealing in scrap iron and rags, or entrepreneurial enterprises which did not involve their being hired by non-Jews.

They were forced for many generations to live within narrowly confined and often walled portions of medieval cities, which have come to be called ghettos. Even in countries that have long since abandoned the walled or legally defined ghetto, there is an informal restriction which accomplishes much the same thing, and the ghetto still exists in the western world, though it may as often be a suburb as a part of the central city.[27]

PHASE III. REDUCED COMMUNICATION BETWEEN MAJORITY AND DISADVANTAGED MINORITY

In one meaning of the term, it is very difficult for any person or group to become isolated from the dominant culture. In the relationships that depend upon *secondary* contacts, for example, upon the advertising media, the readily observable prestige symbols, and many other phases of the larger society's actions that are intrusive in the lives of all of the populace, isolation and segregation are unlikely. However, at the *primary* level, wherein many of the more subtle norms and sanctions operate to develop personal attitudes, knowledge, and skills, isolation is prevalent and pervasive. It is one thing to share esteem for fur coats, white skins, or Chrysler Imperials, but another to share knowledge of table etiquette, desires for college educations, or middle class morality. The effective advertising techniques encounter no immunities in the Americans who happen to have been born into a Jewish or Negro family. Quality of product and popularity of consumer items appeal to all rational human beings. There is no lack of evidence that the majority of Americans, regardless of their statuses, find appealing the items of conspicuous consumption which are so much in evidence in the press and on television. The communication here is between purveyor and consumer and remains on a secondary level. Often, the only primary contacts between the disadvantaged minority group member and the advantaged group members are those in which the prejudices of the latter are made manifest, and in which the role-taking of the former may result in nothing more than the disadvantaged actor taking toward himself only the negative attitude of the other. These contacts are not conducive to learning how the ma-

[27] J. R. Kramer and S. Leventman, *Children of the Gilded Ghetto* (New Haven: Yale University Press, 1961).

jority member acts at the table, toward his relatives and friends, and toward books, art, and other material possessions. Certainly these contacts are insufficient for him to learn about, and to feel positively toward, the values of the majority toward any object except the minority group itself. We now turn to a study of the consequences of this limited primary group contact on, first, the Negro American and, then, the Jewish American.

Reduced Communication Between the Lower Class Negro and the Dominant Majority, Especially the Middle and Upper Classes

The residential segregation of the Negro American, the sharp lines of delineation between the Negro ghetto and the white world, are characteristic of almost every city and many towns and villages in the United States. This is characteristic not only of the South; some northern cities are residentially more sharply segregated than some southern cities. Contacts between lower class Negroes and middle class whites are almost always of a secondary nature. The intimate give-and-take that is essential to the enculturation process is missing. Ignorance of each other's folkways and mores is more extreme than is ordinarily suspected. To each, the other's world is *terra incognita*. The following three items illustrate the segregation and isolation of the groups.

1. In the Randolph Street entrance to the city of Chicago library there was set up a room taken from a Negro slum on the South Side. It was reconstructed as nearly as possible in its original condition, including the dead rat in the corner. The city fathers were accused of exaggerating the conditions, because "no one lives in such conditions today." Evidence that such beliefs were genuine is provided by the next item.

2. An urban sociology field trip to a large American city involved a visit to the slum areas of the city. The students were led on foot through some of the alleys and streets in order to get a first-hand picture of what a slum was like. A few of the girls, suburban residents, became emotionally upset at the conditions of dirt, disorder, and population density in and about the dwellings. Two became nauseated at the sights.

3. During a city election campaign in an American metropolis, a candidate for alderman (later a United States Senator) was invited to a dinner and dance given by Negroes. Not able to attend because of conflicting engagements, he dispatched two of his male assistants to represent him. They were puzzled as to the proper dress, even though the invitation indicated that it was to be a formal affair. Not wanting to embarrass the Negroes, they decided not to wear dinner jackets, but wore dark business suits instead. Upon their arrival at the dinner, they realized that they were the ones who were embarrassed, because all the Negroes were indeed formally dressed, including white ties and tails. This event illus-

trates once more the isolation of white and colored at the primary group level.

Reduced Communication Between Jew and Non-Jew

The century-old schism between Jew and Christian could hardly be expected not to have left its mark upon relationships between the two. Communication has been tenuous, being restricted in many instances to secondary social relations, which may be friendly and courteous but which are hardly primary and intimate. The two basic relations that are characteristic of close primary contacts—intermarriage and dining at each other's table—have been relatively rare in the past and, even today, are not very common. The following excerpts from case histories illustrate the time-honored estrangement of the two groups:

1. I had never dated a boy other than Jewish until I came downstate to school. One night I had a blind date with a fellow whom I later learned was not Jewish. When I returned to the house that night, I remade the vow that I would never again date a non-Jewish boy. I have kept my promise because, for one thing, I would never marry a non-Jewish fellow, and I am not happy when I am on a date with one.

2. My parents are still quite strong in their disapproval of dating between the Jewish and other groups. When I was dating a Jewish boy they often tried to show me that many difficulties could arise from this.

3. In school the Jewish students [who made up one third of the student body] and the Gentiles associated very little and ate at separate tables in the lunchroom. They did not attend the same social functions, and there was no mixed dating.

4. After a class lecture, a student approached the professor and a point in the lecture was discussed for about ten minutes. The young man expressed his appreciation for the time given and started toward the classroom door, only to return suddenly to the instructor's desk. "As a social psychologist you might be interested," he said, "in the fact that you are the first non-Jew that I have had anything like a conversation with for three or four years." The two then talked about the social isolation of Jew and non-Jew, and the student told how his life in a large city was restricted to his own ethnic group, how the same was true of his employment, and how only the most cursory of secondary relationships occurred with non-Jews. Although he regretted the fact of such segregated social contacts, he remarked "It's easier this way."

Under such circumstances, wherein commensualism, intermarriage, and other primary group contacts are minimized, it is reasonable to expect the emergence of different values and of the omission of the out-group from one's affective other. There has been little reward for the assimilation-minded Jewish person over the past centuries. Until very recently his attempts to include the non-Jew in his affective other were futile insofar as his being accepted by the dominant group. Thus it has been that the Jew's affective other is dominated by the Jewish in-group.

PHASE IV.

Development of Divergent Role Behavior and Role Types by Negroes

The current interactionist frame of reference leads one to deduce from phases I through III that the Negro personality will be significantly different from that of the majority of the white group. This is inevitable under the circumstances. Manners, morals, and aesthetic judgments are learned over a long period of time. Enculturation, as the prologue from the *Tea House of the August Moon* reminds us, is "not easy to learn, sometimes painful." The day-by-day, hour-by-hour experiences which give rise to, first, *the knowledge* of what is considered correct, and second, *the feeling* that it is correct, cannot be effected easily at long range, in absence of close and continuous contacts. The roles one learns to play are very largely functions of the attitude-taking process in relationship to the social position one occupies. The conscience is in large part a function of intimate, prolonged learning experiences at the autonomic nervous system level. To expect segregated groups to develop the same or similar value systems, and, therefore, similar personalities, although they are denied primary group relationships, is to expect a violation of the laws of human relationships. From among the almost countless illustrations that could be brought to bear on this subject, we have chosen the following two items:

On a field trip to Chicago, a number of university students were walking toward the Loop through South State Street, a transition area in which are found pawn shops, burlesque houses, bars, and amusement arcades. On the opposite side of the street from the groups were two Negro couples whose raucous laughter, exaggerated gestures, back-slapping, and dress (which most Americans would have considered to be bizarre) attracted the attention of all persons within shouting distance, among them the university group. One of the latter was a Negro student, who cringed and said to the faculty member accompanying the group, "Why oh why do they act like that? Don't they know what fools they make of themselves and what misery they cause other Negroes who do not act like damned fools?" The faculty member suggested that in all probability they were quite oblivious of the attitudes of middle and upper class Americans, that they were quite unaware of the fact that their behavior was disapproved of by anyone.

A well known student of delinquent and criminal behavior makes this same point. In his words:

His [the lower income Negro's] culture provides no incentives for acquiring bathtubs, college degrees, recognition in *Who's Who*, a home of his own on a respectable street, a sedate family. Without incentives and without the example of others, people do not strive, may not even use to advantage (according to middle-class standards) what they do have. This reaction is not a matter of race but of cultural sanctions and of human nature.

In the customs governing sex behavior, the isolation of Negroes from the general culture is easily observable. It is one thing to know what the accepted standards are and then to violate them; such infringements are not uncommon in any class—but it is quite another thing to have no conception of such standards. In a group of ten boys in Chicago, all separated from their own parents and living a footloose existence, an investigator found a near absence of inhibition in their reporting of sex-relations. These boys were not "naturally" immoral because they were Negroes, as white judgments so often indicate; they merely had never known other standards. They reported their sex behavior, which a middle-class schoolteacher would condemn as immoral, as freely and unemotionally as they did their employment records or their love of swimming. With them some forms of sex behavior were taboo, and they had received some warning and instruction from friends, but their sex behavior would indicate that they were thoroughly isolated from accepted middle-class standards.[28]

Isolation of the Negro population is reflected not only in sex standards, but also in modes of dress, standards of cleanliness, types of recreation, attitudes toward parents—particularly toward the father who is so often missing from the scene, and even in modes of speech. On the last item, the segregation is so marked that it takes the whites, the "ofays," some time to catch up with the special idiom that, in its initial stages, is known only to the Negro.

Most Americans know the verb *to dig* means to understand. A great many of us use *like* as verbal punctuation. We know, too, that *cool* means good, that a *cat* is a man and a *chick* a woman. Some of us add the suffix—*ville* to another word and, if we have a headache, describe ourselves as being in *illsville*.

But the above samples, now part of the common vocabulary of Americans, are not original with the beatniks . . . . If it belongs to anyone, it is the language of the people who live in that area of New

---

[28] R. L. Sutherland, *Color, Class, and Personality* (Washington, D.C.: American Council on Education, 1942), pp. 36–37. *See*, for sake of comparison, William F. Whyte's *Street Corner Society* (Chicago: University of Chicago Press, 1943), in which he studies and analyzes the behavior patterns of a lower class white group. There are things that Negro and white groups at this economic level have in common.

York referred to in [the musical comedy] "No Strings" as "uptown, way uptown," or on Chicago's South Side or any place where two Negroes pass the time of day.

To many of these people, the words and phrases borrowed from them are hopelessly out of date. By the time these terms get into the mainstream, new ones have already appeared, though some (such as to *dig* or *cool*) remain staples of the idiom despite wide non-Negro use. A few Negroes guard the idiom so fervently they will consciously invent a new term as soon as they hear the existing one coming from a white's lips.[29]

Whatever the explanation for the Negro idiom—and these are several that have been offered—the fact remains that it could exist only in relative isolation. As Kelley points out, "For many Negroes, this is the only way of speaking they have heard. It is the same with the Chinese child born and raised in America who cannot pronounce "r," or the Italian-American child who speaks English with an Italian accent because it is the only English he has heard in his Bronx neighborhood."[30]

Isolation makes possible the fact that few whites know that Negroes refer to them by such words as *ofay, fay, paddy, gravy,* and *gray.* A few other words, which few *grays* would *dig,* are:

bag (n.): point of view or patterns of behavior
burn (v.): do something well, quickly, or efficiently
cop (v.): take part in, or partake of
fox (n.): a beautiful girl
grit (v.): to eat; (n.): food
happy shop (n.): liquor store
program (v. and n.): proposition
ralph bunche (v.): to talk one's way out of a difficult situation
slam (n.): jail, prison
the man (n.): the police or a policeman
tore down (adj.): very drunk
vines (n.): clothes
woke (adj.): well informed, up-to-date
woof (v.): to brag, boast, talk loudly[31]

But, because of isolation of the races and the motives to keep an idiom, this list may not be *woke*, having been replaced by a new *bag*, idiomatically speaking.

Negro Personality Types

The remarkable changes in the American stage in the parts played by the Negro Americans have done much to alter the stereotyped picture of

[29] William Melvin Kelley, "If You're Woke, You Dig It," *New York Times Magazine* (May 20, 1962), 45.
[30] Kelley, "If You're Woke, You Dig It," p. 50.
[31] Kelley, "If You're Woke, You Dig It," p. 45.

the Negro in the eyes of hundreds of thousands, even millions, of Americans, both Negro and Caucasian. In these changes we see clearly the interaction of cultural environments, unique experiences of individuals, and the general over-all alterations in the personal characteristics of Americans who are significantly involved in the civil rights movements. Although there have come upon the scene new leaders who have been very effective in acting as catalysts in the social ferment, they would have been much less potent were it not for the changed economic conditions, the influences of the wartime period, and the important decisions of the several courts, the United States Supreme Court in particular. However, in the meaning in which we are using the phrase *personality type*, the civil rights movements have not spawned types per se. In the initial discussion of personality types, it was pointed out that, in ordinary, rationally organized behavior, one needed to know all three of the personality component categories in order to understand and to predict behavior. This is the case with such persons as Martin Luther King, James Farmer, and similar leaders. In contrast to the types to be discussed briefly below, these men act in ways that are in keeping with the demands of the situations, the goals they have in view, and the means appropriate to these goals. In brief, they are not rigid or inflexible in their relationship to the world; thus, one cannot predict their behavior without knowing the nature of the situation or episode in question. The same can be said of the persons, Negro or Caucasian, who participated in the sit-in demonstrations in restaurants, bus stations, and other public places. Speaking with such organizations in mind as National Association for the Advancement of Colored People, National Urban League, Congress of Racial Equality, Southern Christian Leaders Conference, and Student Non-violent Coordinating Committee, one observer has said that these organizations ". . . represent the sentiments of a substantial majority of Negro Americans . . . who wish to overcome the barriers of race and enter the main stream of American life."[32] However, such persons are not personality types. That there were, are, and will be, persons involved in the civil rights movement who *can* be typed is readily perceived, but they are in all likelihood a small minority. Moreover, of the three types of Negroes described in the following paragraphs, only one is likely to be represented in most civil rights activities.

There are at least three role behavior type reactions to the Negroes' status in the United States, and in other societies wherein he is assigned a pariah status. The types are

1. The aggressive personality type.
2. The striving-conforming personality type.

[32] Pettigrew, *A Profile of the Negro American*, p. 28.

3. The withdrawing, status accepting, obsequious personality
type.

The person familiar with the Negro American will recognize that these
types are neither mutually exclusive in all instances nor always consistent
within the same individual.

THE AGGRESSIVE PERSONALITY TYPE

One need not subscribe to the proposition that aggression *always* follows frustration to agree that it often does. The lifelong humiliations that
confront most Negroes frequently sponsor a great variety of aggressive
attitudes and traits. Direct, overt aggression is the exception rather than
the rule, because at a very early age the Negro learns of the high cost of
such expression of feelings. The beatings, the loss of jobs and other economic sanctions, the house burnings, and the lynchings are customary
means of forcing the Negro to keep his aggressions to himself in the form
of attitudes. Nevertheless, sporadic overt aggressive behavior has been
an historical accompaniment of Negro-white relationships in this country,
and current events strongly suggest that the end of such violence is not
in sight. In larger northern cities, where both legal forces and folkways
do not always support the case of the white, and where there is less likelihood of immediate extralegal reprisal for such action, aggressive behavior
toward whites is more common. The race riots offer opportunities for a
release of this pent up aggression and for the verification, through action,
of the self-fulfilling prophecy that the world is a hostile camp.

Aggression may be expressed in ways other than direct verbal or
physical conflict. The professional Negro leader, combining aggression
toward the whites with compassion for Negro groups with whom he is
identified, uses such organizations as National Association for the Advancement of Colored People and National Urban League to direct his
feelings into constructive channels. Much as he might like to express his
feelings of frustration and humiliation directly by punching someone in
the nose, he employs a more rational approach to gaining more power for
the Negro.[33] This is not to say that *all* such persons would, upon careful
personality analysis, reveal extreme aggressive attitudes. That all aggressive feelings are not expressed directly is evidenced by the behavior of
the Negro population immediately before, during, and after Negro-
Caucasian prize fights, from Jack Johnson's time to the present. The
vicarious enjoyment of the Negro with every blow landed on a white
man, and with every victory over a white opponent, is a deep-felt enjoyment. The gloom that hangs over Harlem and other areas of Negro
concentration after a defeat, such as that of Louis by Schmeling or of

[33] *Cf.*, James Baldwin, *The Fire Next Time* (New York: The Dial Press, 1963),
for an articulate expression of ambivalent attitudes toward the white world.

Floyd Patterson by Ingemar Johansson, indicates the strength of identification of the Negroes with such a race hero. This feeling is different from
that of the Negroes' pride in Marion Anderson, Roland Hayes, George
Washington Carver, Ralph Bunche, Robert Weaver, or Willie Mays.

THE STRIVING, CONFORMING PERSONALITY

The striving, conforming personality is found in the middle and
upper classes of Negroes. These are the persons who subscribe to the
values of the middle and upper classes of Americans generally and to
the accepted means of attaining these values. They include within their
significant other the respectable persons in the large society, with regard
to moral behavior, social etiquette, aesthetic values, and occupational
statuses.[34] They live a way of life that is not distinguishable from that
of upper middle class whites. Drake and Cayton report that:

> Interview-observation studies of these persons' families revealed extreme
> emphasis on maintaining "a good home" with fine furniture, linen, glass-
> ware, china, and silver much in evidence. Before the Second World War
> the majority kept at least a part-time maid, and a few had more than
> one servant, even during the Depression. The men dressed expensively,
> but conservatively, the women smartly, but to good taste. All of the
> families carried accounts with exclusive downtown shops. The majority
> owned automobiles, and one family had three cars and a chauffeur. All
> were interested in real estate. All thought that Negroes should develop
> more business enterprises. . . They were concerned with "refinement,"
> "culture," and graceful living as a class ideal.[35]

This describes the social status of the upper-class Negro in a northern
metropolis, but the story is repeated, if in fewer cases, in the southern
states. Although Drake and Cayton report that such people in Chicago
". . . talked like ardent Race Men and Race Women,"[36] Sutherland speaks
of "upper class complacency" in referring to the attitudes of the Negroes
who are in the upper income groups. Some of them seem to be relatively
unaffected by the race question. The attitude is much the same as that
of the white American who escapes the slum or blighted area and does
not identify positively with the slum dweller. He seeks to escape the
lowly status and is not bent upon raising the level of all those he left
behind. There is evidence that a significant proportion of Negroes in the
middle and upper classes ". . . are often more preoccupied with their
own social climbing than with forming social contacts across racial
lines."[37] They seek to maintain their social status within their own group,

---

[34] *See* St. Clair Drake and Horace R. Cayton, *Black Metropolis* (New York:
Harcourt, Brace and Co., 1945), Ch. XIX, "Style of Living—Upper Class," and Ch.
XXII, "The Middle Class Way of Life."

[35] Drake and Cayton, *Black Metropolis*, pp. 530–531.

[36] Drake and Cayton, *Black Metropolis*, p. 531.

[37] Sutherland, *Color, Class, and Personality*, p. 44.

and there is little evidence, if any, of a driving desire to associate socially with the white groups. The only thing that distinguishes these particular Negro groups from the white groups of comparable income is the difference in racial features, and often these are slight because of the unusually large number of light colored Negroes in the upper classes. To be sure, the knowledge that the discriminatory attitudes of the whites are still operative is a source of discomfort to the upper class Negro, but his greater education and wealth enable him to avoid their confrontation to a considerable extent. His own clique, his automobile, his own business and residential area are all factors that help to minimize his contacts with either whites or lower class Negroes.

In discussing recent research findings on this type of adjustment, a student of the racial problems has this to say:

> Beyond passive withdrawal is the attempt to insulate oneself as completely as possible from the broader society. Such social insulation is usually only possible for upper-status Negroes. They have attained an economic and professional position which releases them from dependence upon whites, and have many of the material comforts which consumption-oriented America identifies with "success." Why, some of these people ask, should they risk their privileged situation by challenging whites or championing Negroes?[38]

THE WITHDRAWING, STATUS-ACCEPTING PERSONALITY TYPE

This category includes the "peace at any price" type of personality, found in considerable numbers among disadvantaged persons. It is definitely a nonaggressive personality, at least in view of his outward behavior. This is the so-called good nigger, white man's nigger, or Uncle Toms (known to Negro college students as members of the Upsilon Tau Fraternity). The following incident illustrates the type:

> In a university area of one of America's largest cities, I noticed the fellow coming toward me, with a shuffling gait that seemed affected, stooped in a manner as if to deliberately shrink his unusual stature, and effectively giving the impression of obsequiousness. His first words coincided with the picture he presented. "Boss, I's jest a no-good southern nigger and cain't git a job nohow. These Northern niggers are too uppity but they gits the jobs. Could you hep a poor southern nigger to a bite to eat? Please? I's hungry. I ain't et all day long."

Whether or not this man was really an Uncle Tom or, in fact, was a Uriah Heep ("the 'umblest person going"), who exploited the humble exterior in order to further his ambitious and aggressive ends, is a moot question. What does appear to be certain, however, is that not all the "peace at any price" Negroes are either Uncle Toms or Uriah Heeps.

---

[38] Pettigrew, *A Profile of the Negro American*, p. 51.

Some definitely do not have such attitudes, will not flatter the white man's vanity in order to gain their ends, and do not agree with the white's evaluation of the Negro; they will simply avoid any primary contact with white groups. They are tired of fighting, of being insulted and humiliated; they have grown sensitive and tender rather than tough and calloused, have modified and curtailed their aspirations, and have stopped striving and straining. Illustrative of this kind of person is the following reported experience:

> The group of young people from one of the colleges in the hinterland was visiting the large city, "a northern city with a broad southern exposure." Having in the group some Negro students, they sought a place which would serve both groups, and were told that the local YMCA cafeteria was the only place. As we entered the cafeteria, a large one which was nearly filled to capacity, a sudden silencing of the usual "silverware-and-dishes" noises of cafeterias occurred. The stares at the group told us that, even though Negroes would not be denied service there, it most certainly was not a common practice for Negroes to eat there. In response to this sudden silence, a Negro student gave every appearance of being frightened and humiliated. Without being prompted to do so, four of his male companions, all well over six feet in height, began conversing with him, as if to say, "He is our friend, and if anyone doesn't like it, let him start something!"
>
> Later, I asked about his feelings as he entered the cafeteria. He admitted readily that he was hurt and frightened. He added, that he had grown so sensitive that he has often walked miles in cities in order to avoid hearing just once more a pretty white waitress politely and kindly saying, "I'm sorry, but we serve only whites here."

In this type of person, one sees the operation of role taking and the internalization of the stereotype whereby the Negro sees himself in terms of the dominant group's perceptions and attitudes. The previously discussed types refused to accept this stereotyped view.

The withdrawal from contacts with whites may be nearly complete, or it may include only a few limited areas of life. It may be observed among the lower class Negroes and among students in "integrated" colleges and universities, where the physical proximity is present but the social distances are great. In contrast to the striving-conforming personality, who may be awaiting reduction of pressure from the dominant group in order to gain greater social mobility, the withdrawing personality type has curtailed his aspirations and has settled for less in order to avoid further conflict and consequential pain, embarrassment, and humiliation. It is this very reasonable human reaction to discrimination that gives rise to unreasonable accusations by white persons of lack of ambition and initiative on the parts of some Negroes. Until the Negro is in close enough contact to know what is expected of him by the dominant group, and until he can see something to be gained by fulfilling these expectations, it is not likely that he will "act right." Studies show ". . . that lower-class Negro children of school age typically 'give up the fight' and reveal unusually low need for achievement," whereas middle and upper class Negro children possess high achievement goals.[39]

Emergence of Jewish Role Behavior Types

The Jewish people have been a favorite subject for discussion and research among sociologists for decades, and recently the social psychologists and psychologists have become interested. An understanding of the Jewish personality necessitates study of the biological and cultural heritages of the Jews, and much has been done in these fields. Biologically, the Jew is a member of the eastern Mediterranean subgroup of the Caucasian racial group. As such they share the general racial features of all Mediterranean peoples (Spanish, Italians, Greeks, and Arabs) and have certain specific features in common with the eastern Mediterranean peoples, such as the Armenians, the Lebanese, the Arabs, and Iranians. Such peoples have been variously termed *Semitic* (which actually refers to a language base and not to a physical type) and *Armenoid*, but the Levant is not entirely racially homogeneous. The wanderings among the many host nations of Europe, Asia, and Africa have had marked influences upon the Jewish group, and, although it never was a homogeneous group even in the beginning, it is less so now.[40] Many are light in coloring, and it has been estimated that not more than one-quarter of the Jews have the Armenoid or "Jewish" nose. Nevertheless, if we are to be honest and realistic, we must not, because of the fact that the Jews are neither a race nor a homogeneous racial subgroup, jump to the conclusion that, in the United States, it is not possible to recognize the Jew on the basis of physical features. Employers and hotel clerks, among others, are adept at this, as many Jewish persons have learned well. One study of the ability of high school and college instructors and college students to identify Jewish persons among 1,075 elementary school, 1,150 high school, and 650 college students showed the percentage of correct judgments to be 87.[41] The reason for this visibility lies in the fact that the Jews are, for

---

[39] Thomas F. Pettigrew, *A Profile of the Negro American*, pp. 30–31. *Cf. also* Irving Kristol, "A Few Kind Words for Uncle Tom," *Harper's Magazine*, 230 (Feb. 1965), 95–99. The latter article presents an argument for the idea that racial differences will be a barrier to integration even after all cultural differences are removed.

[40] *See* Carleton S. Coon, *The Races of Europe* (New York: The Macmillan Co., 1939), pp. 638–646. For a controversial discussion of the degree of intermixture of Jews, *see* Carleton S. Coon, "Have the Jews a Racial Identity?" and Melville Jacobs, "Jewish Blood and Culture" in Isaque Graeber and Stuart H. Britt (eds.), *Jews in a Gentile World* (New York: The Macmillan Co., 1942), pp. 20–37; 38–55.

[41] Frederick H. Lund and W. C. Berg, "Identifiability of Nationality Characteristics," *Journal of Social Psychology*, XXIV (1946), 77–83. It is of pertinent interest to note that in Germany and Poland Jews were forced to wear distinctive insignia, thus evidencing the fallibility of physical features as criteria of Jewishness.

the most part, the only representatives in the United States of the eastern Mediterranean racial groups, and therefore stand out among a population of which most is from northern Europe. That mistakes are made both ways is common knowledge. A gentile school teacher recently was refused hotel accommodations in a northern Michigan resort because she fitted the physical stereotype of the Jew and could not prove that she was not Jewish. On the other hand, it is probably possible for the majority of Jews to "pass" insofar as their looks are concerned, and thousands do, some sporadically and some permanently. Were the Armenians, Lebanese, Arabs, or Turks equal in number to the Jews in this country, it would then be impossible to identify the persons of Jewish heritage on the basis of physical features. Even in the near absence of these other eastern Mediterranean peoples in America, the segregation of the Jews is not a function of racial prejudice. We cannot hope to discuss or even list all the possible reactions to the awareness of discrimination because of group membership. Those we do select, however, describe the majority of Jewish people.

THE ORTHODOX JEW

Probably not more than 10 per cent of the Americans of Jewish ancestry can be placed in this category. Their attitudes and traits clearly set them apart, and it is not easy to observe all of the traditional features of Judaism in such a secular, urbanized, Christian-dominated culture as that of the United States. The taboo on any work from sundown Friday to sundown Saturday is in marked contrast to the activities of the society in general. Many of these persons are strong supporters of the new state of Israel. Most are older persons whose memories of European persecutions make reconciliation or assimilation with the Gentile world impossible. Continuation of this group is no longer dependent upon pressure from the outside. The reader should not confuse the orthodox with the modified or American orthodox. Few but the Jews themselves constitute the orthodox Jews' significant others. An excellent picture of an ultra-conservative orthodox group is provided by Solomon Poll's *The Hasidic Community of Williamsburg* (Free Press of Glencoe, 1962). This group has maintained its way of life amidst the heterogeneity of urban Brooklyn.

THE DEFENSIVE PLURALIST

The self-perpetuating nature of the interaction involving (1) the larger Gentile group, (2) the Jewish in-group, and (3) the individual's attitudes and traits, is evident in the development of this personality type. We denote this type by the term *defensive pluralist*, rather than simply pluralist, because the desire to keep the group intact is not a self-initiated desire; it is to be explained in part by the defensive attitudes arising from the discriminatory pressure of the out-groups. The social process involved in the creation of the defensive-pluralist is a variation of the marginal-man life cycle:

Step 1. Maintaining original groupways that differ in varying degrees from those of the majority, with no awareness of their evaluation by the larger Gentile out-group.

Step 2. Crisis situation, or series of less dramatic experiences, that brings to acute awareness the significance of being Jewish in a not-too-friendly Gentile world.

Step 3. Withdrawing defensive reaction to this awareness, accompanied by greater identification with the Jewish in-group.

Step 4. Gradual elimination of former Gentile friends and associates from one's significant other (not completely, however, as in case of the orthodox), leading to:

Step 5. Further social isolation of the Jewish group from the Gentile out-group and adherence to the oft repeated admonition, "let the goyim stay with the goyim, and the Jew with the Jew."

This five-step process dates, roughly, back to the French Revolution, when the Jews were relieved of some of the centuries-old disabilities. The earlier ghetto-dominated period did not witness it because of the sharp demarcation between Jew and Christian. It is even more in evidence today, in certain European countries and in the United States.[42]

Original Group ways Which Differ from Those of the Majority. These customs include such items as the Kosher diet and the pleasant memories of the Friday-night lighting of the candles in the home. Illustrative of these influences are the following excerpts:

1. I remember how, when I was a child, my mother worked hard all week, and when the Sabbath came she would have the house cleaned, and she would put a shawl over her head and bless the candles. The softness of the candle-light would change our whole kitchen; the atmosphere was altered to make it a holy place and I could feel the peace of the Sabbath coming into the room.

2. I shall never forget the time I went to one of my Gentile girl-friends' home for dinner. We were all seated at the table and Marilyn's mother served us steak with butter melted all over it. Every morsel of the steak practically stuck in my throat, and I had to absolutely force myself to eat it at all. This is simply due to the fact that we never served milk and

---

[42] The similarity between the defensive-pluralists' development, on the one hand, and the operation of (1) the vicious circle and (2) the development of the "marginal man," on the other hand, is apparent to the student of majority-minority types. *See* E. V. Stonequist's *The Marginal Man* (New York: Charles Scribner's Sons, 1937). *See also* Erich Rosenthal, "Acculturation without Assimilation?" *American Journal of Sociology,* 66 (Nov. 1960), 275–288.

meat foods together at the table in my home. This small, insignificant incident has never left my memory. I have always had the concept that Gentile people prepare their food very much differently than do Jewish people.

3. It was at their [grandparents'] home that I saw the beauties of the Jewish ritual; lighting of the Sabbath candles, the prayers and incantations, exquisitely sorrowful; the joys of the holidays—the meaning of Judaism as a religion.

In such instances we can see the emotional attitudes, developed at early ages, that set the stage for differentiation between Jew and non-Jew and impede movement in the direction of assimilation. Although they may become insignificant in terms of later experiences, they often are used to rationalize an intensification of an in-group attitude, and they are played upon by parents and other elders to keep the in-group intact.

Crisis Situation Which Reveals Antipathies of Non-Jewish People. These two cases illustrate this phase of the process whence emerges the defensive-pluralist.

Finally, I went to high school. I went there because Mom had hinted that perhaps it would be a good idea to become better acquainted with the Jewish girls, since that was where they all went to school. I started out by dating a group of Gentile BMOC's [big men on campus, i.e., popular leaders], and being pledged to the best sorority in school. However, before two weeks were up, one of my "sisters" asked if I were Jewish. Of course I said "yes." The crux of the matter was that Jews weren't allowed here. This was my first taste of discrimination.[43]

On that particular day I was walking to the temple to attend my cousin's bar mitzvah. I paid no attention to the group of boys standing in the alley until one called to me saying he had something to show me back in the alley. Without hesitating (how dumb can you get?) I followed them. Well, they began calling me "kike" and "Jew boy" and did a good job of beating me up. From that day on the *goyim* meant something very different to me.

This step takes different forms sometimes as a long series of minor rebuffs and exclusions from parties and cliques. The end result is, however, much the same awareness of somehow being different and a stranger in any group which is not Jewish, or predominately so.

Withdrawing-Defensive Action, Gradual Elimination of Non-Jews from Primary Groups, and at Times from Significant Other. The withdrawing reaction phase of the "defensive-pluralist" is the most complex

---

[43] The case excerpts included as explanations for prejudices under "Unfortunate experiences with nonrepresentation members of out-groups" also apply here. See pp. 632–633.

and the one most in need of study from the viewpoint of social psychology. The personality components present in this phase are reinforced both from the habituation to and identification with the in-group and by the out-group discrimination. Which is the stronger cannot be said with any degree of certainty, because the in-group pressure is itself in part a function of the discrimination known by the elders. Certainly the desire to maintain the in-group reflects feelings of rejection, frustration, and some aggression; it is rationalization in significant degree. This is illustrated by the social organizations which have grown up within our culture which are exclusively for persons of Jewish ancestry. Illustrative of these are the Jewish (Catholic and Italian as well) fraternities and sororities on college campuses, the Jewish-dominated summer and winter resort areas, and the all-Jewish country clubs. Surely the principal reason for the existence of these associations is the exclusion of the Jews from the older Gentile resorts, clubs, and societies. The provision that one must be Jewish to qualify for membership in many such groups is meaningless except for its symbolic protest value to the in-group. The attitude approaches that of a play on an older saying, "If you can't join 'em, beat 'em."

Added to the mere expediency of saving face are the time-honored ethnocentric attitudes of the in-group. The motivations behind such sayings as the "dumb-goy," "There's no mother love like that of a Yiddische mama," are complex and not to be explained in a cavalier manner. Confronted with a hostile world, the Jew often was given no alternative but to return to his own in-group and in its glorification and perpetuation find a basis for self-approval. This statement illustrates the feeling that supports the in-group solidarity:

> At the end of my second year, I transferred [from a school where the Jews were a small minority] to a school in which the majority of students were Jewish. I immediately relaxed and felt comfortable. I had to make certain adjustments to my new acquaintances but my new feeling of ease was worth these adjustments. I felt, now, that I would be evaluated as an individual instead of a "Jew." These were people with problems like mine and who felt as I did. I was freer in conversation and less on my guard in actions. Since that time the majority of my associates and all of my intimate friends have been Jewish. I am much happier.

Here we see the conscious selection of primary group relations and the narrowing of the affective other to the in-group. Sometimes this restriction is placed upon the individual by the parents, as in the following instance:

> But there is a great deal of chauvinism in my parents' attitudes. "Jews make better husbands." "Jews make fine business and professional men, etc." My parents never cared about the religions of my girl friends, but

> when I began dating, a strict rule was enforced. No dating of Gentile fellows. As my father expressed it: "There are enough Jewish boys in this world to keep you busy."

Again, the motives behind this desire to shut out any but in-group contacts are mixed, involving not only chauvinism, but also a genuine desire on the parents' part to shield their child from injury.

This defensive reaction to the discrimination against Jews reinforces the emotional identification that is already present. As has already been pointed out, when a person becomes identified with a group, it is most often true that the continued existence and prosperity of the group become means to personal security. Note the following:

> 1. Whether or not I am prejudiced is a moot question. Although I do not feel any antipathy for Gentile people and, conversely, "some of my best friends are Gentiles," I have been grouped and categorized, and so I am a Jew. I want to go my way religiously—there I am neither a Jew nor a Gentile; but traditionally, and culturally, I want the Jewish heritage to be kept alive.

> 2. Even though I sometimes heard the comment, "but you're different," I felt the sting of prejudice in its various forms as though it involved me personally as well as the Jewish people as a whole. When I came to college and served in the Army, the bitter prejudices I found strengthened my desire to defend my group more and more, so that I formed a strong identification with the Jewish minority.

Sometimes the identification comes, not as a result of any keenly felt persecution, but as a gradually evolved product of years of subtle experiences with the folkways and customs of the culture, as in the following instance:

> I love Judaism, not as a religion, but as a culture. It would be possible for me to say that I am a Jew only because I was born a Jew if it were not for the fact that a Jew must often be defensive about his religion. I have never encountered any personal anti-Semitism, yet I am always looking for the good things in Judaism . . . . As for culture, I think that the Judaic culture is a wonderful contribution to the world, from the ancient writings up to what the modern Jews are contributing . . . . The Hebrew melodies I know are very dear to me, but again, the holidays and the songs and the writings are not close to me because they are a part of Judaism, but because they are a part of a beautiful culture. You could completely disassociate them from Judaism, and I would still love them as I do. I honestly believe that I do not have one grain of ethnocentrism within me.

It will be noted that under Step 4 of the development of the defensive pluralist type of personality, the point was made that the Gentile group was not eliminated entirely from the person's affective or significant

other. This is particularly true of the second, third, and fourth generation
Jews in this country, and of those who have been middle and upper class
members of a longer time. Such persons, even though they desire to
maintain the Jews as a pluralistic minority, take the attitude of the majority toward themselves in many ways. They are aware of the stereotype
of the Jew and respond by trying to avoid any manifestation of this stereotype in themselves or in their children. One Jewish adult remembers:

> Stern reminders such as "don't be loud" (a trait attributed to the Jews,
> exclusively), "don't be cheap" (another pet characteristic), and a host
> of others. All indicative of the fact that my family had taken on the
> prejudices (attitudes) of the majority group against themselves.

Another defensive pluralist states:

> We have always been careful to steer clear of any sort of "conspicuous
> consumption."

These are representative of attitudes which are common among the
Jewish people, attitudes which indicate that they share the general folkways of the larger culture, and are aware of the unfortunate stereotype
of the Jew. Moreover, the sharing of the larger society's attitudes does
not stop there, but goes on to what has been called Jewish anti-Semitism,
and self-hatred. Indicative of these attitudes are the following excerpts:

1. I began to despise the Jewish women with the characteristic loud
voices, jewelry, and mink coats. I felt that things were being ruined for
people like us and my hostility knew no end.

   There are certain members of the Jewish faith whom I go out of my
way to avoid. The typical stereotype of the Jewish people as being loud,
shrewd businessmen, bargaining, and constantly arguing, though false
as applying to the group as a whole, does apply to a certain percentage
of any type of people. It is against these types that I have a particular
distaste.

2. I then came down here to go to school. Here my environmental and
personal ideas were shocked more severely than ever before. The last
place I expected to find discrimination turned out to be one of the worst.
Housing was short and a friend offered me a place in a fraternity. I
accepted and spent a year observing the social structure of these enlightened organizations.

   It was here I first found Jews drawing lines among themselves. West
side Jews were to be carefully scrutinized before they were allowed
sanction. "Westies" were considered "loud," noisy and much "too
Jewish." This frankly bowled me over. I thought that maybe they were
jesting but they meant every word they said. They frowned on talking
Yiddish in the house or on the street, this latter I never practice, but
the idea was so revolting that a group of us deliberately broke the rules.

On a slightly different note, that of *oppression neurosis*, is this attitude:

3. Another criticism I have is that many Jews have an aggressive attitude toward the majority; they seem to feel that relations with the Gentiles cannot remain pleasant in sustained, close relations, that sooner or later conflict will cause trouble. They seem to look for trouble, and thus relations become more susceptible to conflict. They should realize that if they quit looking for trouble, they would be less likely to find it.

From my family I gained the idea that there were times when I might face discrimination. In fact, the idea that I might not have received certain rewards because of discrimination was encouraged. I almost went around looking for discrimination. I remember feeling that I did not receive certain things because I was Jewish.

Self-hatred and Role Taking. In Chapter 6, in the discussion of communication and learning, we described the process of seeing oneself as others do, of accepting their evaluations of objects, including onself, as one's own. This role taking process operates on all levels of human activity, and any given person's values are largely social in origin. The tendency to share in common with one's affective other a variety of values is pervasive. The concept *self-hatred* denotes one aspect of this process of evaluating oneself as others do, namely, that of derogating oneself in accordance with the standards set by others. That such self-attitudes exist is hardly open to question. There are manifestations of this phenomenon in persons who hate themselves for not measuring up to the standards they have accepted as their own, many of which are first held by others. The causes of this negative attitude may range from failure to be able to speak well before large groups, to being afraid of a variety of objects or being alcoholic, being too thin, too fat, too short, or too tall; individuals often devaluate themselves for being members of a pariah racial or cultural group. The way in which this devaluation of oneself or one's group can operate in the vicious circle process is not difficult to discern.

There is some reason to believe that the concept was chosen with something other than the quest for a denotatively accurate term in mind. A less invective term, such as *self-devaluation*, would have served as well for this purpose. However, as it is frequently used at the present time, self-hatred serves as a bludgeon in a way that other comparable terms could not.

The phenomenon of self-hatred was tragically illustrated on Oct. 30, 1965 when the alleged head of the anti-Semitic Ku Klux Klan of New York City killed himself after a report was published that his parents were Jewish and that he himself was raised as a Jew.

Without denying that there *are* anti-Semitic Jews who are quite willing to participate in discrimination against Jews on almost any score, it seems to be stretching a point to call all of the in-group criticisms noted above "anti-Semitic," or examples of self-hatred. Robert Park, pioneer American sociologist, was among the first to point to this phenomenon of self-hatred. These terms are valuable weapons for the antiassimilationist in general and for those whose life chances are dependent upon the continued existence of the Jewish group as an identifiable and separate social group. For such persons, almost *any* criticism of *any* Jew by another Jew is immediately labeled self-hatred, as is any evidence of an assimilationist attitude. To clarify this point, let us take what seems to be a comparable case, namely, that of the stereotyped American as developed in the minds of many Europeans from their contacts with newly rich American tourists. For them, an American is a person of flamboyant satorial tastes, loud manner, ignorant of the history and culture of Europe, arrogant in manner because of his greater material wealth, extremely chauvinistic in attitude—in brief, a cultural barbarian. If the term self-hatred is applicable to the Jew or Negro who seeks to conform to the prevailing folkways of the United States, and who leans over backward to avoid playing even in limited degree the role of the stereotyped Jew or Negro, then it is equally applicable to the Americans who seek to disabuse the Europeans of their stereotyped view of Americans. In each instance generalizations have been drawn from inadequate samples, and in each instance the desire to fulfill the attitudes of the majority group leads to criticism of the in-group members who abet the stereotype. The prevalence of the concept self hatred is in part the work of those individuals who have become defensively identified with the in-group, and for whom any criticism of that group is a criticism of them. Many such persons might be called aggressive pluralists or even aggressive secessionists. An instance comes to mind of a young graduate couple for whom the term self-hatred was a much-used barb in their attack upon the assimilationist-minded Jew. They were fond of walking through the college halls or the lobby of the student union singing Hebrew folk songs at the top of their voices. Their reply to the criticisms they received from other Jewish students was, of course, self-hatred. The concept was similarly misused by a rabbi on a large university campus who accused all Jewish students who failed to appear at the Sabbath services of self-hatred.

However, the distortion of the concept in such instances should not blind one to the very real social psychological phenomenon that is characterized by the uncritical, and often unconscious, acceptance or adoption of the out-group's values and an accompanying devaluation of the ways of life of the in-group. One young woman reported that:

> I also absorbed the stereotype of Jews and actually believed it. I found Jewish people who fit parts of it, and those who didn't just happened

to be exceptional. In fact, I grew ashamed of being Jewish. I went to college with this attitude and the belief that I would find discrimination.

There is no doubt that self-hatred is a real phenomenon. It may arise from personal-social experiences apart from any group identification, but much of it is a function of role taking by members of disadvantaged groups, be they minority or majority groups. In Chapter 13 the learned preference of Negro children for non-Negro dolls will be discussed. Such behavior is, obviously, closely associated with the concept of self-hatred. Subjected to blatant as well as subtle emphasis upon the superiority of light skin and Caucasoid features, both Negro and Caucasian children are more than likely to respond in similar manner. This is no more surprising than the general preference for prestige motor cars over the less expensive ones, for mink over rabbit in fur coats, or for gold and diamonds rather than aluminum and agates.

But, as we have pointed out, the term's meaning has been expanded to encompass any behavior involving criticism of an in-group by one of its members. Kurt Lewin has noted that this sort of self-criticism by the in-group wanes as the enmity from the out-groups decrease.[44] However, whether criticism is actually self-hatred or sound self-criticism is in large part to be determined by the degree of emotional identification the judge has with the group in question. There is a tendency for those who see the perpetuation of the group as a religious value to view all criticism of the group by current or erstwhile members as being self-hatred.

Another, and very important, fact which operates in the development of the defensive-pluralist personality among Jewish people is the influence of parents. Among such persons the parents play a very important role in their affective other. Just as in the studies which have shown that conservatism and identity with parental attitudes are accompaniments of strong out-group prejudices among the Gentile majority, the facts seem to indicate that such attributes are also characteristic of conservative, ethnocentric minority-group members.[45] In a large number, probably a majority, of the many case studies gathered by the authors, inability or unwillingness to sever family bonds or go against parents' desires is accompanied by defensive-pluralist personalities. As one reported:

> Now I will indulge in the prejudices which I have come more in contact with. I repeat that I was born a Jew and raised in a fairly religious family. It was not Orthodox, but we keep all the holidays and also keep a Kosher home. I have tried to keep most of our religious holidays, and

[44] See Kurt Lewin, "Self Hatred Among the Jews," in his *Resolving Social Conflicts* (New York: Harper and Brothers, 1948), pp. 186–200. Although not in full agreement with the statement, the present authors consider this one of the best treatments of the concept self-hatred.

[45] See the reports of the studies of Allport and Kramer, Frenkel-Brunswik and Sanford, and Hartley, all cited in footnote 17.

when I get married I expect to keep a Kosher home, not because of
myself, but out of respect to one of my favorite "generalized others,"
my father. I think that it would make him happy.

In similar vein another wrote that:

I've always tried to avoid even accepting a date with someone that
wasn't Jewish. Yet about five weeks ago a fellow I had known for about
five months asked me out. I suppose I couldn't have said anything but
"yes" due to my past experiences. I now realize that I like him and that
this 'like' could easily develop into 'love' if I were to break down the
brick wall that I have built up. I also realize that I could never change
my "affective-other" enough to marry him or anyone else outside of
my religion . . . . It is actually my family that I could never fight
against . . . . As it now stands, it's all over.

In summary, the personality called defensive-pluralistic is characterized, insofar as its attitudes toward the Jewish and non-Jewish groups
are concerned, by an emotional attachment or identification with the
Jewish group largely born of oppression from without and because of
this a strong desire to provide for the survival of that group, partly as a
means of protest against the discriminating majority, and partly as a
haven within which they can be certain that they will not be discriminated
against as Jews. Such personalities are usually not without a certain
amount of ambivalence in emotional attitudes toward both in-group and
out-groups, and also a certain amount of confusion with regard to the
nature of the social role which they would like to see the Jew play in
the larger culture. A conflict of generations may play an important part
in the ambivalence and the younger persons do not feel able or free to go
against parents' desires and attitudes. There seems to be less intellectuali-
zation of the role behavior of the Jewish defensive pluralist than in the
case of the assimilationist, which will be discussed in the next section of
this chapter. The attitudes of the defensive pluralist are the products
of the unfortunate experiences of the Jewish people both in their long
history and within our own times and country. If they are irrational, they
also are understandable.

THE ASSIMILATIONIST

Most of the assimilationists share certain attitudes with the defensive
pluralists. They resent the unreasoned discrimination against minority
groups, the Jews among others; and they share common memories of
such discrimination. Also, many of them include the majority in their
significant other and seek to avoid behavior which would assist the anti-
Semites in rationalizing their stereotype of the Jew. Beyond this point,

however, the assimilationist turns into a different social path. He seems to perceive the majority-minority relationships more objectively. Part of this is a reduced emotional identification with the Jewish group and its religion, and this fact removes the feeling that the distinctive aspects of Judaism must, even at high personal cost, be preserved and that the Jewish group must be continued as an identifiable minority within the larger culture. He is more apt to avoid the development of an oppression psychosis than is the defensive-pluralist. If he does not come from parents who themselves are assimilationists, he has strayed further from parental control than the nonassimilationist. He constitutes, to be sure, a minority within a minority, but, although there is no guarantee that his numbers will increase, it seems probable that they will. He is a product of our industrial-urban-secular culture and is illustrative of the fact that, for the first time in the history of the Jewish people, they are now serious candidates for assimilation. They were not candidates before this time because, in the nonsecular world, which relinquished its dominance surely not earlier than the eighteenth century and probably much later, one could not stop being Jewish without becoming a member of some other religious group. Social mobility of the person with neither temple nor church affiliation was so limited that disaffiliation amounted to ostracism, and only such rare persons as philosopher Baruch Spinoza could live in this kind of isolation.

In the present world, the erstwhile Jew can join the growing numbers of erstwhile Catholics and Protestants in the urban and/or secular world without sacrificing a great deal of social mobility. True, such persons constitute a new minority, but frequently they are less of a problem minority inasmuch as they are often satisfied with their associates and friends of the same persuasion. The assimilationist Jews are more apt to be agnostic, and less apt to have any affiliation with a temple, unless it is the secular aspects of the Reform Temple. Are such persons any longer Jews? The answer seems to be that, in terms of social psychology, they are not. Their attitudes and traits are no basis for placing them in the category of Jews. Neither religious nor secular beliefs set them apart from non-Jews who have dropped formal affiliation with church organizations. They do not adhere to dietary laws of Judaism, nor to any of the other identifying traits of Jews. However, they may be Jews from the sociological viewpoint. By that is meant that they have the position or status of Jews ascribed to them by other persons, and because of this share with all Jews certain life chances. If an ex-Jew applies for a position, and is refused because the prospective employer looks upon him (perhaps because of his name or appearance or because he knows the applicant's ancestry) as a Jew, it is hardly realistic to deny that he still has the social status of a Jew. Such an imputed status is probably an inevitable transi-

tional phase of the last stages of assimilation. Three cases will illustrate
the attitude of the assimilationist:

1. Sociologically, I am a Jew. At present, I am in no other sense a Jew.
I do not consider myself a Jew, and the majority of my friends don't
consider me as such, since neither they nor I categorize people in terms
of Jew or Gentile. Therefore, in the restricted social circle of my friends,
even the sociological definition of Jew applies to me only slightly. If,
however, at some future date, I meet a great deal of discrimination
directed against me as a Jew, I am fairly certain that I will have a
violent reaction. I am a marginal man who has been almost completely
assimilated into the culture of the majority. If I am rebuffed by that
majority, there will be a strong emotional reaction on my part. During
the past six years that have gone by since I left home for service with
the armed forces, assimilation has taken place at an extremely rapid
pace. In the process of assimilation, my threshold of sensitivity has been
lowered. I have become so integral a part of the majority group that
I can no longer fall back on the mechanisms of ethnic and religious
pride.

2. At the present time, I am going with a Gentile girl. Her family is
Catholic, but she isn't religious [in the sense of adherence to dogma] at
all. We get along very well together, but our families are the chief
obstacles to our happiness. If I decide to marry this girl, both of our
families would be against it strongly. It is a shame that the attitudes of
both of our families towards one another should thwart our happiness.
My family has always wanted me to marry a Jewish girl. It is their
opinion that anything is better than marrying a Gentile girl. I could
never see the validity of this point of view. I will associate with anyone
I like, regardless of the person's race, religion, or creed . . . . I see
organized, traditional religion as a block to the advancement of our
present civilization, and as a block to the closer harmony between
groups. The Jewish people will be doing a great service to humanity
by associating more freely with outside groups . . . . I identify myself
as a Jew, because society identifies me as a Jew, and I am forced to
accept the responsibilities that are attached to the group. I suffer as
much prejudice as any other member of the group regardless of whether
I practice the religion or not. My attitude is not one that doesn't look
for any hope in the future. Slowly the Jewish people are working towards complete assimilation, and society may change their present
attitude completely.

The assimilationist's role is not an easy one, and the temptations to
withdraw are never completely out of the picture for some. The following
case is illustrative of the problems which face and frustrate the assimilationist.

3. "You are a Jew." My parents told me that at an early age in reply
to the question often asked of them, "What nationality am I?" It was

not these words from their lips which were to deeply influence me and give meaning to that sentence. It was the voice of others, school mates, neighborhood kids, strangers, who were to sing it out, and maybe replace the word Jew by "kike" or "hebe." "What is a Jew?" I asked myself and introspected in a childish way and realized that I had a dark complexion and went to a Sunday School at a synagogue. But this explanation was not enough, not even for my innocent mind because my mother and brother were fair haired and my father was a disbeliever, never setting foot in any religious building.

I felt there was some injustice. Where it was, who it came from, I was not sure of. I was shy and not a fighter. I had no argument to give in return for this discrimination. I knew that I did not like the stigma which seemed to be attached to the name Jew, so I decided, at this tender age, that I would rather not have a finger pointed at me and I would rather not be a Jew. I gave up Sunday School.

My father, artist and actor, was a broad-minded atheist, who preached the hypocrisy of organized religion. My mother had given up hope of converting my father, who had, at one time, studied to become a rabbi until the realization of the disparity of the church and religion came upon him. My mother gave up all customs, dietary laws, and religious membership, but she kept her friends among the Jewish people. Thus, with no compelling force, I had joined a Jewish sunday school just to be with my friends. When I realized that there lay one reason for the discrimination, I decided I would rather not go. I also hated to be seen in front of the synagogue on the High Holidays and I realized that my vacant seat in school on these days would give away my secret to my non-Jewish classmates. I decided to go to school on those days and I would soon be safe from the despised jibes. But I found out that was not enough. They knew. The realization of the somewhat inevitability of being a Jew came upon me. I thus restricted my friends or I should say, my friends were restricted for me. They were all Jewish.

A few years later, my parents moved from this mixed neighborhood into a strictly Gentile one. I thought that with this move, I could find my freedom from the word which I was slowly beginning to despise. I told my new classmates that I was a Lutheran, the name sounding very safe and very Gentile. But after several months they found out my fib. The name calling and finger pointing began and I was alone and without defense. My parents and my brother tried to make my life outside of school bright, to make up for this unhappiness, but for a child, school is the mainstead of life. After two such years, my mother asked for a permit to transfer me to another school. There in the midst of a 10 per cent Jewish enrollment, I was again pushed into a group of Jewish friends by the outside prejudices . . . . But this time the discrimination had decreased and I realized that with numbers, one could stand up so much better. All my school days continued along this trend with a supporting Jewish enrollment for my weakness at the sound of the word Jew.

The above incidents took place in Chicago, the great metropolis, where one would think that he could live in sheltered peace among the masses. Within this great city are a great many factions and each neighborhood is ruled over by one or another. The minorities living in one of these vicinities live a persecuted and unhappy life if they try to become one of the majority. Thus, a small group, as the Jews, found themselves grouping closely together in Gentile neighborhoods, and living small private lives, with little attention being paid to the others in the neighborhood. I learned this after my many unsuccessful attempts at trying to become one of the majority, which in my young eyes had become great and something to strive for.

In later years I joined an action group, whose goal was set at getting Palestine as a Hebrew State. They instilled in all their members the doctrine that the word "Jew" merely designated a religion, the word "Hebrew," a people and an old and great culture from which we were sprung. Again I was misled, for I began to think that the denial of the religion would free me from the stigma. It was not enough. There were always those outside forces, which would not let me shed it.

I began to look at the Jewish people for those distinguishing factors which would make others point that dreaded finger at them. I was looking for them and I found them. I saw that in crowds they were loud, they talked, many of them, with an accent, they disliked Gentiles, and that they were Jewish. Only the last of these seemed to carry any weight with me but I realized with the hatred of the Jews as a minority, these other characteristics had won similar hatred. I still was not a fighter and I am not now. I avoided those among my group who would have those distinguishing characteristics which might stigmatize me.

My mother was from England and my Russian father lost his accent, having been educated in a university. No member of my family has Jewish characteristics and my father is not in any occupation labeled as Jewish. He was an artist and ex-actor and owned a sign shop. All these things made me think that someday, in the same way, I could rid myself of the discrimination that comes with being a Jew. All of these things except my last name.

In college I led a life somewhat sheltered in the midst of a large Jewish group, which I had been forced to be a part of. With my marriage came new realizations and new attitudes. My husband has a good German name and is third generation American. His parents belong to no Church but at one time were Christian Scientists. They know nothing of the Jewish culture. But they are Jewish. Here I thought would be the ideal situation to see if with the name, characteristics, and religion, the stigma could be removed. Our close friends are . . . Jews, non-Jews, and all nationalities, including a Japanese-American, who is one of my husband's closest friends, and a few Negroes. They all know we are Jewish but in a closed mixed group there is nothing ever said of such differences. Here I found that the so-called differences were only in the mind. We all acted the same, speak the same language, and have the same likes and dislikes. Here I also found the basis of establishing a goal for all people in the world.

With all discrimination removed within our closed group, I found out the pressure was still upon us all. My husband applied for medical school with an exemplary record, and a M.S. Degree. Being agnostic there was no need to designate religion on the application forms. He was American. But with the rejection slips, again I sought for a reason and found it. His mother's maiden name had been the give-away clue. With every rejection, the antagonism grew within me. Soon the former attitude I had had of wanting to excommunicate myself from my group turned into an opposite one. I felt that here lay the injustice. I could not be free of this prejudice against me until all those among my group could be likewise freed. I felt objectively sorry for this discriminated group of which I was a part. I had a little antagonism for those few orthodox within my group who I felt to be the origin of the problem and discrimination. But this was overcome by an attitude of defense. I, and people like myself, could save them. I decided to let other people know that I am a Jew, observe my actions, search me for the differences. When they could not find them I would again tell them that I am a Jew. That is one way I believe, that can be the salvation of this small tortured and discriminated group.

With this sentiment towards my own group, I did not feel a corresponding antagonism against the outside group. I saw their guilt lying in their ignorance, the ignorant blinded attitudes and beliefs which needed enlightening in the brotherhood of Man. To be prejudiced against them would be my undoing. They, too, were human beings like myself, who could be easily blinded by the discriminations made by their forefathers which they had blindly accepted. My discrimination towards them would only help fuel the fire of discrimination. Prejudice must be fought where it is found.

My agnosticism is founded not so much on my disbelief or uncertainty, but in my intolerance of the egocentric attitudes put forth in the doctrine of the church.

Here we have examples of the person who does not play the *role* of a Jew, yet has the *status* or *social position* of a Jew. In terms of social psychology, such persons are not Jews, though they are Jews sociologically. There are, to be sure, various degrees of assimilation, and these three cases do not represent all of them. However, it does not appear logical to call a person an assimilationist until he reaches the point that he no longer holds it necessary or desirable to maintain the in-group's identity on any score. Those who have become acculturated to the extent that they draw no lines except those of the primary-group membership and will marry only within their group are *not* assimilationists. They still maintain the two most important barriers to assimilation of the group, namely, dining and marrying only with the in-group members. The assimilationist is kept from being absorbed by the majority only by his inability to drop identifying cultural characteristics, to avoid inaccurate interpretation of the attitudes of the majority, and/or by the unwillingness of the majority to cease imputing minority group membership to him, that is, assigning him minority group position against his wishes. The most important variable here is the pressure from the outside, the continued unreasoned prejudice. Once this is eliminated or greatly reduced, the last basis on which such persons can be called Jews, the sociological, will have disappeared.

The Significant Other and Group Identification

The ways in which the circulatory, accumulative, self-perpetuating processes of alienation (the vicious circle) operate to estrange social groups is infrequently recognized, and even less frequently understood. To understand fully the operation of such processes as they break down the intergroup controls and communication we must turn attention to one of the basic social psychological facts, namely, that the social behavior of any given person or group of persons is determined more by the attitudes of the persons within their affective other than by anything else. Self-control is largely social control; we take the attitudes toward ourselves that our affective other takes, and attempt to fulfill the expectations of that group. The degree to which these controlling attitudes, that is, those of the affective or significant other, are restricted to the in-group, the greater the social isolation of the in-group. The converse, of course, is also true. What is good and bad taste, what is right and wrong is determined by the affective other, and in the extreme cases of social isolation, the in-group and the affective other are synonymous. The conscience is to a marked degree the product of these in-group attitudes, and the out-group attitudes are largely ineffective as social controls.

In the case of a Jewish group, the scope of the affective other ranges all the way from complete inclusion of the larger society to almost complete exclusion of the larger out-group. The affective or significant other of the assimilationist is indistinguishable from that of many non-Jewish groups, but the affective other of the orthodox group includes the larger out-groups only in such matters as essential legal and economic rules. The attitudes which constitute conscience of the orthodox individual are restricted to the primary in-group made up of orthodox Jews. Here the significant other is a generalized other. The defensive pluralist's ambivalent attitudes toward the out-groups are reflected in the composition of his affective other, which is somewhere between those of the assimilationist and the orthodox groups. In some instances such a person is acutely aware of, and responsive to, the attitudes of the non-Jewish out-groups, and this fact is evidenced by such admonitions as "Don't be loud or conspicuous." The taking of such attitudes results in behavior traits that are quite in keeping with the folkways of the larger society, in fact, even *more* in keeping with them than are some of the traits of non-Jews. However, as the social relationships between Jew and non-Jew become *more* estranged, the exclusion of the out-groups from the affective other is apt to go on apace.

Close communication between groups is essential to the development of similar personalities and the process outlined on page 358 is accompanied by a reduction of communication between Jew and non-Jew except on essential economic and political matters. It is this lack of close and constant communication that leads to the development of separate in-groups with attending differences in social values and different affective others. Proper ways of behaving are decided upon by the respective groups with little reference to the attitudes and values of the out-groups, and awareness of what the other groups expect is accompanied by an indifference toward such attitudes and values. When and if members of one or more of the subtypes of groups within the Jewish group (or *any* minority group, for that matter) exhibit behavior traits which are different from those of the dominant majority, the explanation is apt to lie in the absence of communication between that group and the majority. In some instances they do not know, and in other instances they neither know nor care, what the out-group thinks of such divergent behavior. This point is made with the full realization that much of the behavior of the minority group member is only allegedly, and not really, divergent behavior. But at times the behavior is genuinely different, and understandably so. To illustrate, one study, which concluded that the Jewish sample studied was less stable emotionally than the non-Jew, suggests that the Jewish ratings reflect intra-Jewish standards. The authors state that: ". . . the Jew sees himself more or less against the mirror of Jewish circles in which he moves."[46] The external pressures may account for the fact of differential familiarity with one's own in-group's characteristics. One study revealed that, in response to questioning, Jews, Roman Catholics, and Protestants revealed this in-group knowledge in percentages of 71, 57, and 25 per cent, respectively.[47]

Oppression Neurosis As a Function of Discrimination

Regardless of the type of personality developed by members of disadvantaged groups, whether objects of cultural prejudices or of biological deficiencies, there tends to develop in them an *oppression neurosis*, a term we use to designate the extreme sensitivity which characterizes many members of disadvantaged minority groups.[48] It is intended as a descriptive term only, and in no sense a derogatory one. Its origin lies in the reality of the social situation in which there are numerous discriminations

[46] K. Sward and M. B. Friedman, "Jewish Temperament," *Journal of Applied Psychology*, XIX (1935), 75.

[47] Yarrow, "Personality Development and Minority Group Membership," p. 455.

[48] *See* Herbert A. Miller, *Races, Nations, and Classes* (Philadelphia: J. B. Lippincott Co., 1924), p. 32. Miller coined the term *oppression psychosis*, which we have modified.

practiced against such minorities. As a result of such experiences, the individual becomes highly aware of his disadvantaged minority position and is apt to interpret every injury, every social rebuff, every failure as being somehow related to his minority status. Perfectly innocent remarks are interpreted as intentional insults directed toward the minority. Out of reality there has evolved a defensive attitude which distorts the person's perspective, prevents him from correctly interpreting the attitudes of other persons, and creates a genuine neurosis, if by that term we mean a relatively stable pattern of ". . . maladaptive attitudes and responses."[49] We prefer the term neurosis to Miller's term psychosis because the latter has come to mean the more severe forms of mental disorders. Any deviation from the normal in a socially or culturally undesirable direction can give rise to this oppression neurosis; it matters not whether it is biological, cultural, or personal-social deviation. Although it is most likely to occur in the second phase of the marginal man's adjustment cycle, it may be a persistent part of the third phase. The following instances will help to illustrate the operation of this "maladaptive response."

The first involves a Jewish girl student in a small midwestern college. The young lady had been raised in Brooklyn, but upon the advice of a relative enrolled in the inland school where there were no more than a dozen students of Jewish background. One day after tests had been returned to a class in which she was enrolled, she came to the instructor's office, and expressed her desire to discuss the grade which she had received on the test. After a few preliminary questions about the content of the test she inquired, "Didn't I get this because I am Jewish?" The instructor did not know that she was of Jewish background, and was able to convince her of this by pointing to the fact that the highest grade in the test was earned by a Jewish student. For some time the two discussed the problem confronting her, and she reported that all of her life she had associated with Jewish people exclusively. After she had decided to enroll in the small college, several of her friends told her of the rampant discrimination she should expect in a school dominated by non-Jews. Thus prepared, she had misinterpreted many of the actions of those about her as discrimination, especially the supposed cold hostility of her roommate who, it turned out, had a very retiring sort of personality. It was later learned that her roommate did not know that she was Jewish either, because neither name nor her physical and personal characteristics evidenced the fact. Direct consideration of the oppression neurosis enabled her to make a more satisfactory adjustment.

The second case envolves a young man who reported that:

---

[49] Norman Cameron, *The Psychology of Behavior Disorders* (Boston: Houghton Mifflin Co., 1947), p. 9.

I became so hypersensitive to the word "Jew" that I took any reference to the word as being derogatory . . . . Too, I feel the need for social recognition, prestige, and security far more than I do the need for money. For this and other reasons I identify myself with the Yishuv—the Jewish group in Palestine—rather than with the Jewish group in America . . . . I recognize that I am, socially, a pathological case; I'm not at all organized or integrated, socially or psychologically, and I find my outlet in Palestine. It's a good case of projection and of compensation.

This feature of personality, which characterizes a significant number of minority-group members, is no cause for wonder. Suspicious personalities are not the monopoly of any group, and if such personal attitudes occur among the disadvantaged minority groups, the real discriminations that are known to exist afford such persons a firm base upon which to erect fanciful persecutions. However, the failure to get a desired grade, a job, a date, or a membership in a social organization; the failure to gain acceptance into college or graduate school; or the failure to be accorded courteous or friendly treatment raises certain questions even in the cases of persons not abnormally suspicious as to the motives of the persons withholding the desired permission or actions. How can the member of a disadvantaged minority be certain that discourteous behavior or the denial of a request is not motivated by prejudice against all members of such a minority? The existence of prejudices against certain groups places the members of such groups in the unenviable position of having to develop an unusual ability to interpret the attitudes of those about them. They must be able to distinguish accurately between the real and the fancied discriminatory practices of their associates. When in fact persons who are members of the advantaged minorities or of the majority develop feelings of persecution it is logical to expect an even greater number of members of problem minorities to do likewise. Thus the "chip on the shoulder" attitude has two bases; first, the minority member's resentment of very real prejudiced treatment, and second, the misconstruing of all limitations upon social mobility as being motivated by anti-minority group prejudices. The latter leads to belligerent defensiveness on the one hand, and to rationalization of all failures on the other. Reduction of this oppression neurosis requires a greater understanding of human nature by both the members of the underprivileged minorities and those who are not members of such groups. This hypersensitivity decreases even further the already circumscribed social mobility of such minorities by increasing the prejudices of the out-groups and by inducing the minority members to withdraw from contacts with the larger society.[50]

[50] Erving Goffman observes that the persons ". . . may perceive, usually quite correctly, that whatever others profess, they do not really 'accept' him and are not ready to make contact with him on 'equal grounds'." *Stigma* (Englewood Cliffs, N.J.: Prentice-Hall, 1963), p. 7. This is another way of describing the oppression neurosis.

SOCIAL STRATIFICATION AND PERSONALITY TYPES

Social class has come to mean more than simply differences based upon income or possession of wealth. Instead of differentiating between classes which are defined on the basis of comparable chances for goods and services on the open market, and status groups which are differentiated on the basis of honor or prestige in the manner of Max Weber,[51] today's social scientists have incorporated the prestige items as well as the economic power in the concept social class. This has led, in the writers' opinions, to a marked degree of both heterogeneity and ambiguity in the concept "class," in contrast to the clear-cut distinction made by Weber.[52] Moreover, the social scientists have yet to reach consensus concerning the exact nature of the "ways of life" that cons' te the various class strata and concerning the influence upon the personalities of the persons involved. That marked differences in either material wealth or marked deferential treatment are important shapers of personality cannot be doubted, even though the precise nature of the relationships cannot be fully comprehended at this time. Our concern here is with the extreme differences as these affect the development of personality types as we have defined types. If we are to restrict the concept *personality type* to those sociocultural relationships in which there exists a rigidity of attitude and action on the part of the subject or others in his social environment, a rigidity which carries with it a certain inappropriateness of behavior, then it must be concluded that class in the economic sense probably will not give rise to personality types. Except in the extreme cases, wherein poverty leads to malnutrition and starvation with its characteristic starvation syndrome as described in Chapter 8, there is much heterogeneity among people of the same economic classes. The homeless bums on Skid Row, the agricultural serfs of the Medieval centuries, the sharecroppers of the American South, the religious orders that impose poverty vows, the impecunious conscientious objector to the income tax-supported war effort who lives on less than six hundred dollars per year—these do not reveal any significant common personality characteristic.[53] There seems

---

[51] See his "Class, Status, and Party," in Hans H. Gerth and C. Wright Mills (eds. and trs. from Max Weber), *Essays in Sociology* (New York: Oxford University Press, 1946), pp. 180–195.

[52] *Cf.*, William H. Sewell, "Social Class and Childhood Personality," *Sociometry*, 24 (Dec. 1961), 340–356. *See also* W. Lloyd Warner, *Social Class in America* (Chicago: Science Research Associates, 1949); August B. Hollingshead, *Elmtown's Youth* (New York: John Wiley and Sons, 1949); J. A. Kahl, *The American Class Structure* (New York: Rinehart and Company, 1953); Kurt B. Mayer, *Class and Society* (Garden City, N.Y.: Doubleday and Co., 1955); Egon Bergel, *Social Stratification* (New York: McGraw-Hill Book Co., 1962).

[53] *See* Oscar Lewis, *Five Families* (New York: John Wiley and Sons, 1962), for an attempt to discover some of the ways of life which are common to a "culture of poverty." Again, the intrusion of the values extant in Mexico into the lives of these

to be, however, among certain impoverished societies or portions thereof a common attitude toward material wealth insofar as its immediate use is concerned. The writers have acquired the opinion, after reading from anthropological literature and from reports of domestic impoverished groups, that poverty, when carrying with it a genuine shortage of food, leads to the operation of the pleasure principle rather than the reality principle. There is so little hope that any significant accumulation of wealth is possible that the emphasis is upon the here-and-now aspects of consumption of whatever wealth is available. Although there is some evidence to support such a perception, we readily grant that it is impressionistically rather than scientifically grounded. Anthropologists and other travelers into areas of primitive and poverty-stricken cultures often comment upon the "childish" and impulsive attitudes toward material wealth. Even in this country those who hire impoverished individuals on a temporary basis have learned not to pay these workers too often, lest they simply disappear on payday, not to return until their money is gone. Beyond such characteristics there appears to be little that one can point to by way of personality types which are functions of economic class position.

The other aspects of social class or stratification, however, do provide some basis for personality typing. "Of all the dimensions of stratification, status seems the most directly relevant to the psychology of the person."[54] Status or stratification, as has often been noted, requires someone to *claim* the prestige, and others to *honor* the claim, and is thus clearly a social phenomenon. Role taking plays a large part in the establishment and continuity of any stratification system.

In any discussion of stratification, the distinction must be made between the honor that attaches to the person, usually denoted by the term *esteem*, and the honor that attaches to the *position* independently of the person who occupies it, indicated by the term *prestige*. Stratification is based upon prestige, not upon esteem. Furthermore, it is essential that honor can be claimed and accorded, both in esteem and prestige, without leading to social stratification. One can honor a person for some objective accomplishment, for some *achieved* status, without being involved in deferential behavior which is not logically related to the basis for honor. One can honor the skilled surgeon or the great artist, even though he

---

impoverished people appear to the reader to modify significantly the effects of poverty, thus to obscure whatever generalities there may be among impoverished people regardless of cultural environments.

[54] Hans Gerth and C. Wright Mills, *Character and Social Structure* (New York: Harcourt, Brace and Co., 1953), p. 325. See this source for a more extended discussion of stratification and personality, especially Ch. XI. The analysis rests basically upon Max Weber's concepts of class and status.

may be without such trappings of stratification as differential modes of dress, privileges of exclusive residence, special insignia, or special entrances to buildings. Social stratification is not the same as social differentiation on the basis of skills, knowledge, service. Social stratification and division of labor are not synonyms. *The essence of social stratification is some combination of hierarchical relationships, invidious comparisons, extraneous privileges, and subjective judgments.*[55] Stratification requires both actors and audience for its existence.

There are many facets of the stratification-personality relationship, but our concern here is the relatively narrow one of the relationship as it serves to develop personality types, and with only three of the several possible types. We will briefly comment upon the *elite*, who both claim and are accorded high prestige, the personality of the *extremely low status* person, and the snob who seeks high prestige as an end in itself, by whatever means available to him or her.

The Elite As Personality Type

The elite are not, to be sure, a distinct species of man, but the particular cultural setting within which their personalities develop and operate leaves its distinctive marks. They are a minority group with many of the characteristics of minority groups, such as limited mobility spatially and socially. There are a limited number of residential areas open to them, a restricted list of proper hotels, schools, summer and winter resorts, and occupations. A glance at a recent *Social Register* confirms this compressed socialcultural world of the elite. There is an amazing concentration of the elite in terms of residential areas, both the permanent homes and the "dilatory domiciles," that is, the summer or winter places of residence. Only a very restricted number of colleges and universities appear often enough to warrant abbreviations.

Although mobility into and out of the elite has increased in recent decades, entrance, particularly, is still difficult. Money alone is never sufficient to gain entrance for those on the outside, but it is a mistake to assume that high prestige can be maintained for long without money. As Gerth and Mills have pointed out:

> The facts of the *nouveau riche* (high class without high prestige) and of the broken-down aristocrat (high prestige without high class) refute the complete identification of upper-prestige and upper-class position,

---

[55] Although the reader may infer from this statement certain of the writers' views on stratification, we will not become involved in the time-honored argument about the functional nature of stratification. This is a more strictly sociological problem, although it has important social psychological aspects. *See* Kingsley Davis and Wilbert Moore, "Some Principles of Stratification," *American Sociological Review*, 10 (April 1945), 242–249, and the response which this article elicited from Melvin M. Tumin, plus the "Reply" and "Comment" by Davis and Moore respectively in *American Sociological Review*, 18 (Aug. 1953), 387–397.

even though, in the course of time, the broken-down aristocrat becomes simply broken-down, and the son of the *nouveau riche* becomes a man of "clean, old wealth."[56]

Two personal attitude categories which characterize the elite as personality type are: (1) ethnocentric exclusiveness; and, (2) social aplomb or self-assurance.

ETHNOCENTRIC EXCLUSIVENESS

It is difficult to exaggerate the "we-group" feeling of the elite. The exclusiveness provided by their status does much to satisfy the desire for recognition and social approval. Although, as we shall emphasize later, the out-groups are not a very significant part of the elite group's generalized other, the latter are vaguely aware of the mass of people outside of the pale and know of their own superior status with reference to *hoi polloi*. A certain hauteur seems to be a product of this knowledge, and the following incident serves well to illustrate this "we" feeling: A reporter, who was not too well acquainted with the difficulties associated with gaining even the most cursory of personal contacts with members of the elite, decided to telephone and make an appointment with a feminine member of an exclusive eastern seaboard group. The description of his experience is as follows:

> He called, got the butler, and explained his mission. Then, because of an upstairs telephone complication, he got the lady's son (just seventeen years old). Again he explained his position and desire. "Who are you?" he was asked. Believing the man hard of hearing, he repeated his name and his magazine affiliation for the third time. "I know," snapped the man, "but *who* are you?" The reporter put down the telephone.[57]

This emphasis upon *who* a person is, not *what* he is, is still the all important question with regard to elite status. This is the most difficult of minority groups to join; the "we" and "they" distinction is one of the sharpest. By violating the unwritten rule of endogamy, members of the elite have been expelled from the *Social Register*, and there seems to be some evidence to support the assertion that the females of the species have preferred spinsterhood to marrying out of the group. There came to the present authors' attention an instance wherein a person from a very wealthy family came under the care of a psychiatrist because of his inability to enter the closed circle of the elite in his city.

Those who do enter the group by ways other than being born into it must adhere to the strictest of rules of behavior. After the most careful

---

[56] Gerth and Mills, pp. 316–317.
[57] Cleveland Amory, "Newport: There She Sits," *Harper's Magazine*, CXCVI (Feb. 1948), 119.

negotiations, often under the tutelage of a member of the elite, a person with proper means and attitude may gain social access to the elite members and become a candidate for membership. When this stage is reached, meticulous attention must be given to the learning of the folkways and mores of the in-group; any breach immediately removes the candidate from consideration for acceptance. Such candidates must learn purposely and consciously the ways of behavior that persons born into the elite cannot help following out of habit. It is for the use of the newcomers, or would-be newcomers, that the rules of social ritual are made explicit in such books as those written by Amy Vanderbilt.

SOCIAL APLOMB OR SELF-ASSURANCE

Perhaps the most striking personality characteristic of the truly elite is their taking for granted that their actions are socially right. This social aplomb results from their minority group's social status—a high prestige status, which is based upon a relatively guaranteed continuity, stability, and exclusiveness.

The significant other of a member of such a group is very largely restricted to the in-group, and if he adheres to the folkways and mores of his own group, he cares not what the judgment of any out-groups may be. Such adherence is easy because it is habitual with him; the social ritual of the group has taken care of that. Here we see clearly Mead's point that self-control is essentially social control.[58]

The enrollment of the children in the proper private schools is but a continuation of the training begun at home, and there is no need to learn new ways of doing things at school, because there are no ways that do not coincide with those taught at home. The rules are well-established through several generations, and one has no more need to ask himself what is proper behavior than he has to inquire as to his own name. The following paragraph describing the attitude of a member of Boston's elite illustrates the aplomb that is characteristic of the elite generally:

> Basically unembarrassable, the First Family lady is *so secure in her position* [status] in Boston that she has no fear of looking ridiculous. With rarefied aplomb she does not hesitate to carry in public an assortment of bundles which would bring a blush to the cheek of her upstairs maid, and she faces with complete indifference such feminine tragedies as being caught with a run in her stocking or wearing her galoshes on a sunny day. *Rules are made for others, not her.* She jay walks freely on Boston streets and in a crowded store, while never pushy in the vulgar sense, she does not hesitate to go direct to the department head for service, rather than wait her turn in line. Carefully brought up never to raise her voice, she rarely lowers it either. In a public place where

[58] G. H. Mead, *Mind, Self and Society* (Chicago: University of Chicago Press, 1934), p. 255.

others are talking in low tones she feels free to carry on a conversation with a friend in the same well-bred but clearly audible pitch she would use in her own drawing room.[59]

It should be noted, however, that such self-assurance as this, and of the Chicago social leader who admonished her daughter that "Whatever I do is *right* because I do it," is the possession of those who are long-time members of the in-group. This certainty of social role is a product of stability and continuity, of ways of behaving which have become institutionalized through being used by several generations, and of guaranteed economic status. The aplomb of the elite comes from the fact that members of that group are the taste makers. They do not have to learn what is the correct thing to do; they do it automatically because it is habitual with them. It comes from the fact that the ones who would disapprove of their actions are not within the generalized other of this exclusive group and therefore such disapproval is of no avail in controlling behavior or of influencing attitudes of "the 400" members. It would be a mistaken salesperson who would attempt to make a sale to a member of the elite by telling him or her that "everybody is wearing this." What everybody is doing is of not of the slightest interest to the taste makers who, as a matter of fact, are apt to drop any fashion just as soon as "everybody is doing it." It is much more likely that they will pursue ways of behavior simply because everybody is *not*, and cannot, do likewise. Thorstein Veblen's *Theory of the Leisure Class*, even though written in another generation, still has much of value for those who would seek to understand the ways of the elite. His terms *conspicuous leisure, conspicuous waste*, and *conspicuous consumption* are nearly as applicable today as they were when coined. The in-group of the elite engages in these practices, which are designed to demonstrate to others of the group and to the world that *they* are a group set apart, as a matter of custom and habit. The newly rich, the persons who seek membership in the elite, are very apt to overdo these things and to open themselves to charges of vulgarity by the Old Guard elite. However, the uninitiated might find it difficult to differentiate between the "ins" and the "would-be-ins" in terms of overt behavior.

Perhaps one of the best present-day illustrations of the status symbol in Veblen's meaning of the term involves the British motor cars, the Rolls-Royce and the Bentley. The only difference between these automobiles is the radiator design, the Rolls costing three hundred dollars more than the Bentley. The established elite are more apt to purchase the Bentley, whereas the newly rich prefer, even insist upon, the Rolls. The elite symbolization of the cars becomes clearest when they are sold a second

---

[59] Cleveland Amory, *The Proper Bostonians* (New York: E. P. Dutton & Company, 1947), p. 110. Italics added.

or third time. The least expensive of them sells for approximately sixteen thousand dollars when new, with the three-hundred dollar differential noted, but on the used car market there will be a difference, in a five year-old car, of two thousand dollars in favor of the Rolls. The fact that everything is identical except the radiator's appearance matters not to the seeker after the prestige symbol. The self-assured member of the elite does not feel the need for the Rolls, preferring the Bentley.

In summary, the elite as personality type reflects a strong in-group orientation and a self-assurance which leads to his behaving in ways which are inappropriate to the totality of the social situation or episode in question. One can predict that he will expect deferential treatment, that he will expect others to accord him privileges not warranted by the nature of the stage setting as this is viewed objectively. That there are many rationally oriented behaviors characterized by some elites is not denied, but is readily recognized and acknowledged. This does not alter the existence of a certain rigidity of relationships, which exceeds the bounds of rational personal interrelationships.

The Snob As Personality Type

Snobs occur among the elite, especially among the newly arrived members of this exclusive group, but they are not found only among the top prestige groups. Snobbism or snobbery has as its essence the quest for reputation, especially without the bother of attaining skills or other bases upon which prestige is built. The snob seeks to gain the reputation merely by association with others who, by whatever means, have acquired prestigious reputations. The following passage states it well:

> Prestige, the esteem of others, can be gained and lost in countless ways. To acquire "the bubble reputation," people may go quite literally to the length, the height, and the depth Shakespeare suggests. Reputation is found not only "in the cannon's mouth" but in many equally deadly places.
>
> The savage by wearing a lion's mane hopes to impress on others that he slew a lion; in a sense he hopes to increase his status by incorporating that of the lion. That is also the aim of the cannibal who eats the slain enemy: he hopes to acquire his qualities by incorporation; mainly, he hopes to appropriate the enemy's fame; sometimes literally to appropriate his name, too.
>
> Likewise, a hostess may bag a famous "lionized" man to get some of his reputation and enhance her status, in short, to partake of the deference paid him. She reverses the cannibal's procedure—she usually feeds her man—but she hopes for the same result. Hostess and cannibal have discovered that by association, such as eating or feeding each other, one can take over some of the fame and of the *mana* of one's victims or guests. This is also the belief of many of the faithful who incorporate the religious hero through ritual eating—direct or symbolic

—of his body. Totemic feats and communal meals are part of many religious observances.

Hostesses discovered something primitives did not know: a reputation can be built without achievements or deeds of valor simply by being associated in the public eye with those who have high status. One can manipulate status without changes in the status base. A cannibal after all has to beat his man before he eats him. The hostess only needs to entice her lion to feed him. With this discovery *snobbery* was born.

. . . To raise his status, a man may seek to associate with famous people or status groups above his own. He can claim to have succeeded by "dropping names" or by indicating participation (even mere presence) at status-conferring events such as exclusive parties or premieres. Other "firsts," attendances and achievements, or "mosts" serve too. He may try to be the first man through the newly dug tunnel or to set foot on the Jungfrau, or eat the most pancakes, or sit longest on a flagpole. The quality of the achievement is less important than the renown it brings. The bizarre competes with the great and defeats the unspectacularly good without trying. "Firsts" enhance status perhaps because to be first (princeps, primus: whence prince, principal, primary, primate, and so forth) originally meant to lead. And to be presented with something first meant a recognition of leadership status. However, to go to premieres or to race through the new tunnel first is neither assumption nor recognition of leadership nor even any longer actual presumption. It expresses at most a yearning, possibly unconscious, to be thought to belong to a high status group. One does if enough others think so.

. . . The snob does not try to achieve a high status by doing what is required—by leading in slaying enemies, making money, or writing poems. He tries to sneak into the high status by associating with those who have it. But even the association is not genuine. The snob does not hope, as the cannibal does, to acquire the famed person's qualities, nor is he moved by admiration for the achievement of the high status group. He does not wish to emulate it for any intrinsic merit he finds in it. The snob craves fame, deference, or reputation, not the qualities that won it. He is not interested in anything he does but for the effect it may have on his status.[60]

The difference between the snob and the person with the high prestige is that the snob is willing, even impatient, to secure undeserved honor. This type of personality occurs in various sectors of a society. The person who seeks the reputation of the scholar without having learned, the one who is basically interested in a college degree rather than a college education, is a snob. As Van den Haag has pointed out, there are many kinds of snobbery; it may be based upon intellectual, literary, sexual, aesthetic, or political grounds. He also notes that it becomes involved in

[60] Ernest Van den Haag in Ralph Ross and Ernest Van den Haag, *The Fabric of Society* (New York: Harcourt, Brace and Co., 1957), pp. 158–159.

prejudiced actions. Certainly it is an operative factor in the vicious circle as this accrues to the disadvantage of the powerless groups. The snob does not necessarily have any basic antipathies for the out-group, but he would not want to have one as house guest or neighbor because of the effect upon his or her reputation. The snob's affective other, or reference group, is made up, more or less exclusively, of the persons whom he considers to be *the* prestigious sector of his society. It is in this manner that the rigidity enters to define the snob as a social type. Much of his action will be inappropriate in terms of objective factors.

The Low Status Personality Type

When the social distance between the person low on the stratified scale is exaggerated, a demoralization appears to set in which helps to type the persons involved. Observation appears to yield the perception that it is the lowest status Negro in the United States who "gives up the fight," who does not take advantage of the opportunities available to him. He views the distance to be traversed as too great to warrant his making any attempt to gain ground in the status competition. This is especially characteristic of the person in any culture who has little or no status. If what he possesses by way of esteem or prestige is not worth protecting, what motivation is there for him to take the attitudes of others toward him in shaping his actions or attitudes? The classic illustration is the slave, who, no matter what he does, cannot hope to better his position beyond a very limited extent, and often not at all. The vestige of the slave heritage is still strongly reflected among many Negro Americans, a fact to which many hypercritical Americans of white ancestry are oblivious. The rigidity of response which types this low status person is, basically, this demoralization which is reflected in his overdependence upon rationalizations, projection of hostilities, and general ineptitude. Hopelessness is most characteristic of the person at the bottom of a hierarchically organized social system. Certain forms of *anomie*, that is, deregulation or normlessness, also are observable among the low men on the stratified social totem pole. The "Uncle Toms" are functions of low status, and "Tomism" tends to disappear quickly with a rise in status and the attendant acquisition of hope.

In a study involving interviews of 701 persons, there seemed to be evidence to support the argument that anomia (essentially despair as used here) is a function of failure to gain access to the means of achievement of life's goals.[61] The persons so handicapped were disproportionately persons of low socioeconomic status. The authors raise the question as to whether the despair might have given rise to the variables rather than vice versa.

[61] Dorothy L. Meier and Wendell Bell, "Anomia and Differential Access to the Achievement of Life Goals," *American Sociological Review*, 24 (April 1959).

SUMMARY

In the case of the position or status personality type, the audience is the type maker. Two such types of "made" personalities are the Jews and the Negroes, as they are related to other groups in the theater of western European culture. A concept which is valuable in the attempt to understand these position or status personality types is the vicious circle. The first phase of the vicious circle is the *prejudice* and *discrimination of the dominant group*. This involves the attributing or role type behavior to persons on the basis of perceived positions or statuses in the social system, and thus stereotypes develop. Prejudice stems from a variety of sources, some of which are

1. misconceptions about the nature of the out-group.
2. unfortunate experiences with nonrepresentative members of the out-group.
3. personal deficiencies which give rise to projection and displacement of these deficiencies.
4. ethnocentrism, which is a universal and normal characteristic of groups.
5. cultural prejudices which are both consciously and unconsciously acquired.

There is no lack of evidence of the prejudice and discrimination which operate in the vicious circle. Furthermore, it is apparent that these attitudes and actions are not restricted to the dominant groups.

Phase II of the vicious circle is seen in the *restricted life chances* politically, socially, and economically which result from Phase I of the process. Segregation is a function of these reduced chances, which in turn brings into being Phase III: the *reduced communication* between the dominant and disadvantaged groups. Secondary contacts are retained, but the intimate, face-to-face relationships essential to a shared system of values are not possible. Phase IV is characterized by the development of *divergent role behavior* and *role personality types*, which in turn are perceived by the out-group as justifying the prejudices and discrimination constituting Phase I of the vicious circle.

Phase IV gives rise to three personality types among the Negro Americans: aggressive types, striving-conforming types, and withdrawing status-accepting types. Among the Jewish groups there arise the orthodox, the defensive-pluralists, and the assimilationists. Adjustment mechanisms —such as self-hatred and oppression neurosis—are observed among certain of these role types as functions of the positions and statuses to which the persons are assigned or ascribed.

Minor position or status personality types are observed among groups which are differentiated and given prestige on the basis of material wealth and/or social honor. Snobbism is often an accompaniment of these class or status types, but not always.

SUGGESTED READINGS

ALLPORT, G. W. *The Nature of Prejudice* (Cambridge, Mass.: Addison-Wesley Publishing Co., 1954).

BALDWIN, JAMES. *The Fire Next Time* (New York: The Dial Press, 1963).

BRINK, WILLIAM, and LOUIS HARRIS. *The Negro Revolution in America* (New York: Simon and Schuster, 1964).

GOFFMAN, ERVING. *Stigma* (Englewood Cliffs, N.J.: Prentice-Hall, 1963).

HERBERG, WILL. *Protestant, Catholic and Jew* (Garden City, N.Y.: Doubleday and Co., 1956).

LIPPMAN, WALTER. *Public Opinion* (New York: The Macmillan Co., 1960).

LOMAX, LOUIS. *The Negro Revolt* (New York: Harper and Brothers, 1962).

POLL, SOLOMON. *Hasidic Community of Williamsburg* (New York: Free Press of Glencoe, 1962).

SIMPSON, G. E., and J. M. YINGER. *Racial and Cultural Minorities* (New York: Harper and Brothers, 1964).

SKLARE, M. *The Jews: Social Patterns of an American Group* (Glencoe, Ill.: The Free Press, 1958).

STONEQUIST, E. V. *The Marginal Man* (New York: Charles Scribner's Sons, 1937).

YOUNG, KIMBALL. *Personality and Problems of Adjustment* (New York: F. S. Crofts and Co., 1940).

CHAPTER 11

PERSONALITY IN
RIOTS, MOBS, AND PANICS

An unremitting control is needed, for the moral habit of one generation does not become the instinct of the next.

—*E. A. Ross*

In preceding chapters attention has been paid to the ordered, customary, and institutionalized behavior of man. However, as the reader well knows, not all of man's actions are patterned in this way. The processes of socialization and enculturation always, in one way or another, fall short of the goals their bearers have set for themselves and their fellow man. Uncontrollable variables of many kinds, inadequate knowledge of means-ends relationships and of learning principles, plus the intricacies of personal social learning, render sanctions ineffective, permit the violation of norms, and the departure from established groupways. There arise, from time to time, group as well as individual actions in which subjective, often latent, personal variables and attributes play more important roles in defining action than they do in the routine episodes of daily living. Episodes of group action such as riots, mob behavior, panics, collective manias, and stampedes are examples of this nonpatterned, partly unpredictable actions of groups of people.[1]

---

[1] Many sociologists include such actions of groups under the heading of *collective behavior*, along with ". . . mass behavior, public opinion, propaganda, fashions, fads, social movements, revolutions, and reforms." Herbert Blumer, "The Field of Collective Behavior," in Alfred McClung Lee (ed.), *Principles of Sociology* (New York: Barnes and Noble, 1955), p. 167. Our preference is to avoid this term, for several reasons. First, the items thus gathered together constitute a category of behavior which is too gross, too heterogeneous to permit the development of significant generalizations about them. To illustrate, what is there in common in a seemingly spontaneous riot in the wake of a school boy football game, a panic in a burning building, and a carefully planned, meticulously propagandized revolution or reform movement? Second, as Blumer points out, "From one point of view practically all group activity can be thought of as collective behavior." Third, our concern is not with those collective, group actions which are preludes to the development of social order, (*ibid.*, p. 169), nor are we ". . . concerned with the rise of new societies and new social units, insofar as they are formed in the efforts of societies and social groups to act collectively." (*Ibid.*, p. ix.) For an interesting and more recent attempt to systematize the study of collective behavior, see Neil Smelser, *Collective Behavior* (New York: John Wiley and Sons, 1963).

Our concern here is with those ephemeral, dynamic, sometimes violent group actions as they are related to personality.[2] The data with which we are concerned do not involve collective action of the type upon which social order, and therefore individual and group freedom, are based. The following collection of accounts of these unpatterned, noninstitutionalized, informal, collective actions is not meant to be comprehensive, merely illustrative.

ITEM 1: RACE RIOT

The *Chicago Tribune* for Wednesday, June 23, 1943, carried this news item on its front page:

> Detroit, Mich., June 22 (AP). Under orders to "load your guns and don't take anything from anybody" United States army troops patrolled Detroit streets today, restoring calm to this great armament center after 24 hours of racial conflict that brought death to 28 persons and injuries of varying degrees to at least 750 others.

The rioting had been precipitated Sunday night, June 20, at Belle Isle, a playground and beach for Detroit. Just what event acted as the precipitant will probably never be known accurately, because several "true versions" exist. Whatever the event, the fight that started on Belle Isle Bridge that Sunday night in June, 1943, soon spread rapidly from the recreation area to the Negro ghetto near downtown Detroit. Rumors that spread among the whites were matched by those spread among the Negroes, and an event which might, under slightly different circumstances, have been confined to a few persons on the bridge, soon involved thousands of both Negroes and whites and lasted for several days. By the end of the week, some of the restrictions that had been placed upon the city's normal social life were still not withdrawn.[3] During the days of the riot's most intense phase, gangs of both races roamed the streets beating up members of the out-groups, and looting by Negroes of the white-owned stores in the Negro ghetto was extensive. Covert attitudes of prejudice and hate and overt behavior began to coincide as the rioting spread, and the increased numbers of participants seemed to sanction or

---

[2] The term *collective dynamics* has been applied in a way which more closely approximates the category we are discussing here. Kurt and Gladys Engel Lang use the phrase to denote social actions which are "spontaneous and unstructured and therefore not reducible to a social structure." (*Collective Dynamics* (New York: Thomas Y. Crowell Co., 1961), p. 11. However, insofar as their data include such patterned behavior as fashions, public opinion, mass communication, and social movements, the rubric possesses some of the limitations previously observed in *collective behavior*.

[3] Most of the information about the riot used here is taken either from the Chicago and Detroit newspapers or from Alfred McClung Lee and Norman D. Humphrey, *Race Riot* (New York: The Dryden Press, 1943).

to cover up the rioters' extralegal behavior. As noted in the extract above, armed forces were finally needed to stop the rioting. The Detroit riot of 1943 was not the only one of the period. That same year, there occurred both the short but severe riot in Harlem in New York City and the "zoot-suiter" riots of Los Angeles.

An observation made in another book appears to be as appropriate today as it was in 1951:

> Nor is it likely that we have seen the last of such events, because many of the ingredients of the riots still exist in large cities of the United States, and a slight shift in the social setting, plus a seemingly insignificant hostile social act involving members of out-groups, may again precipitate the rioting.[4]

The next item is illustrative of the fact that the stage for riots is still set.

ITEM 2: RACE RIOT

In the City of Angels last week, a 50 square-mile piece of the American dream had turned, after four nights of apocalyptic fury, into a nightmare. The fighting in the streets had subsided at last. But the scars remained. In the war zone called Watts, whole blocks lay in rubble and ashes. Black men and women—the human debris of war—queued up in bread lines at makeshift relief stations. Jeep loads of heavily armed soldiers warily prowled the streets, an American army occupying part of America's third largest city. And outside a pillaged store, a Negro teen-ager—himself a ruin before he ever reached manhood—surveyed the wreckage without a whisp of remorse. "You jus' take an' run," he said, "an' you burn when they ain't nothin' to take. You burn whitey, man. You burn his tail up so he know what it's all about."[5]

A Negro business man who lived outside of the Watts area reported the following:

> "The crowd called the ministers [Negro ministers who were assisting two white adults who had been beaten by the mob] hypocrites. They cussed them and spit on them. Some Negro officers tried to disperse the crowd, but they were jeered at, sworn at, called traitors and stoned.
>
> The Negro officers were given a worse time than white officers.
>
> Light-skinned Negroes such as myself were targets of rocks and bottles until someone standing nearby would shout, "He's blood. He's a brother—lay off."
>
> As some areas were blockaded during the night, the mobs would move outside, looking for more cars with whites. When there were no

[4] Richard Dewey and W. J. Humber, *The Development of Human Behavior* (New York: The Macmillan Co., 1951), p. 694.
[5] *Newsweek*, LXVI (Aug. 30, 1965), 13.

whites, they started throwing rocks and bottles at Negro cars. Then near midnight they began looting stores owned by whites.

Everybody got into the act—children, grownups, old men and women, breaking windows and going into stores.

Then everybody started drinking—even little kids eight and nine years old.[6]

ITEM 3: LYNCHINGS

"Experts working from dental charts and other evidence identified today the three bodies found buried deep inside a cattle-pond dam as those of three missing civil rights workers."[7]

The victims, two whites and one Negro, had been arrested for a minor traffic violation, then released from the Philadelphia, Mississippi jail late at night. They were never seen alive again by anyone except the lynchers. The FBI arrested twenty-one men in December, 1964, in connection with the lynch slaying of the civil rights workers. Included in the group of suspects were law enforcement officers.

Queretaro, Mexico, March 29 (AP). A second lynching in two weeks was reported today by the authorities of the town of Juarez. They said two men accused of witchcraft had been hanged by a mob.[8]

The following item bore the headline, "Whole Family Lynched."

Atlanta, Ga., Jan. 15, [1915]. Dan Barber, his son Jesse, and two married daughters, Bula and Ella Charles, negroes, were taken from the Jasper County Jail at Monticello, Ga., last night by a mob and lynched.

The lynchings resulted indirectly from a fight that recently occurred at Dan Barber's home, when J. P. Williams, Chief of Police, attempted to arrest him on a charge of selling whiskey without a license. Barber appeared to have peaceably surrendered when he suddenly seized a revolver, and opened fire on the officer. Barber's son, Jesse, and the two Charles women then joined in beating him severely. Negroes living nearby notified the county authorities, and the four were placed in jail.

Late last night, according to Sheriff Ezell, a mob of 100 white men entered the jail, overpowered him, took his keys, unlocked the cells, and took the Negroes from the building.

The Negroes were lynched one at a time, first being hanged, then shot. Their bodies, riddled with bullets, were found on the outskirts of town today.[9]

[6] Robert Richardson, *New York Times* (Aug. 8, 1965), 8.
[7] *New York Times* (Aug. 6, 1964), 1.
[8] *New York Times* (Mar. 30, 1955), 26.
[9] *New York Times* (Jan. 16, 1915), 1.

In the next case the heading stated, "Negro Burned by Mob."

New Albany, Miss., Sept. 20 [1925] (AP). L. I. Ivy, negro timber cutter, was burned at the stake by a mob which had taken him from officers near here this afternoon. Ivy, according to Sheriff John W. Roberts, confessed that he had attacked the daughter of a farmer in Etah Community, eighteen miles from here, Friday. He was returned to the scene of the attack and burned to death . . . . While about 400 were lynching him many of the others were searching for three negroes alleged to have been implicated by Ivy in the crime.[10]

ITEM 4: MOB ACTION AND RIOTS

The stage setting for this social action was a middle- and lower-middle class residential area on Chicago's South Side. It was a neighborhood made up of white, native-born Americans whose ancestors came from the British Isles, a considerable number of whom were city employees. Because of the proximity of the area to Negro residential districts, the local population had become apprehensive about the possibility of the invasion of the area by Negro residents. Local "improvement" and "protective" societies were formed, and signs reading "This House Is Not for Sale" were displayed on many houses. The person against whom the disorders were directed described the situation in a radio broadcast, excerpts of which are given below:

I recently bought a home on Peoria and 56th Streets. I moved in on October 17. Shortly after, on November 8th, I invited friends over to my house, both Negro and white . . . . We have both Negro and white members of our organization, and I invited them over to my house for a social evening. About ten o'clock that night, a mob of people gathered in front of my house. I walked outside and asked what the trouble was and one of the hoodlums by the name of ———— said to me . . . , "If you put your hard earned money down on this building, you'd better get the niggers out of the house and keep 'em out if you and your family want to be OK and if you want the building to stand where it is." I immediately told him that I, as an American citizen, have the right to invite whomever I want over to my house and that I intend to maintain that right. . . . (complaints were registered with police and with the Mayor's Commission on Human Rights.) I came home that night (Wednesday, November 9th) around six o'clock. Around seven o'clock a crowd began to gather in front of my house. We made repeated calls to the police department, to the local police station . . . . I went outside and I asked the policemen that were there to please disperse the crowd but they refused to do it. Around ten o'clock that night, the crowd grew to about 300 people. . . . When I got home that night (Thursday) I

[10] *New York Times* (Sept. 21, 1925), 8.

found there were a number of people standing in front of the house. As I got out of the car, a bunch of kids ran toward the car and started calling me all sorts of anti-Semitic and anti-Negro names. Thursday night, around eight o'clock, large crowds began to gather. Again I went outside and demanded that the police move the crowds from in front of my house, and the policeman outside told me that he received orders just to clear the front of my house. The crowd had formed a horseshoe in front of my building. There were about a hundred policemen out there at that time and while they were standing out there the hoodlums began to throw rocks at the building. After they broke one window I went outside and I asked the sergeant in charge, I said, "How many windows do they have to break before you move the crowd away from the house?" Shortly thereafter, a mob of about a hundred or two hundred people tried to push through the police and to get into the house. They shouted, "Get the damn Jew nigger-lover and lynch him." And standing in the background were kids of ten and twelve yelling, "let's start a race riot, let's start a race riot!"[11]

On Friday evening, the 11th, the owner of the house was visited by a representative of the protective association who offered to arrange a peace meeting with the neighbors if no more "undesirables" were invited to the house. Refusal of the offer brought forth the reply that the house owner would not be able to live comfortably in that community.

The action was not restricted to this one home owner, but spread out in the general neighborhood, first in the form of anti-Negro acts, but later including acts of violence against Jews or persons taken for Jews, and still later to University of Chicago students. Teenage groups beat up persons who could not prove that they lived in the neighborhood.

ITEM 5: RELIGION AND RIOT

During the months of March, April, May, and June, there occurred in Ceylon a riot described at its height as an ". . . explosion of religious hatred and nationalist ambition."[12]

Late in May ". . . tensions reached fever pitch when hooligans and fanatics attacked shops, vehicles and individuals."[13] Sinhalese mobs (some of them illiterate) tarred Tamil signs in Colombo.[14] Among them were Buddhists who had forsaken Buddha's doctrine of nonviolence.[15] One hundred and fifty nine deaths resulted and over six thousand were arrested.

[11] Material taken from an unpublished research paper.
[12] *New York Times* (June 25, 1958), 5.
[13] *New York Times* (May 26, 1958), 9.
[14] Farzie Vittachi, *Emergency 1958: The Story of Ceylon Race Riots* (London: Deutsch, 1959).
[15] *New York Times* (May 26, 1958), 5.

ITEM 6: RELIGIOUS RIOT

New Delhi, March 26, (AP). His voice heavy with emotion, Prime Minister Nehru appealed today to the people he had led for 17 years to halt the bloody religious rioting that is sweeping India . . . .

He made a special appeal to Christian Adivasi tribesmen, a bow-and-arrow people in eastern India whose entry into the rioting in the past 24 hours helped push the death toll to nearly 300 . . .

Adivasis, many of whom are Christians, joined the Hindu-Moslem fighting when they heard tales of anti-Christian atrocities allegedly committed by Moslems in nearby East Pakistan.

Adivasis poured down from the hills, in groups reported to be as large as 1,000, burned two villages in their search for Moslem victims and said the torch would be put to two more.

Thousands of army troops, some airlifted across the subcontinent from a central reserve in New Delhi, have been able to keep the lid on the major cities and towns but have been unable to stop mobs roaming the countryside.[16]

ITEM 7: GENTLEMAN IN A STADIUM

Mr. G. has driven some three hundred miles to see his university team play an old rival, and he is but one of approximately eighty thousand like-minded persons who fill the stadium on this perfect autumn afternoon. The game has entered the final quarter and the star halfback of Mr. G's team has just run a kickoff back ninety-five yards to score and to put his team back in the lead. In response to this feat Mr. G., no longer a young man, is yelling at lung-bursting level, dancing and gesturing in a manner wild enough to satisfy even the most ardent adolescent, and jeering at a few glum supporters of the opposite team who happen to have seats near him. The behavior of Mr. G., in the packed stadium, three hundred miles from home, is in sharp contrast to his normal behavior. Usually he is a quiet man, conservative in both dress and manner, and, like so many fathers, given to cautioning his children against boisterous displays and noise making. "Nice people don't behave that way," he tells them.

ITEM 8: LADY AT A CONCERT

In conjunction with a festival of modern art which was sponsored by a large American university, a concert was presented by Duke Ellington and his orchestra. Even though this group of jazz musicians is usually considered to be a dance band, the auditorium was filled with persons who came to listen, not to dance. The lady in question appeared to have come under some form of coercion or assignment, or perhaps out of sheer curiosity. Whatever the motivation that induced her to come,

[16] *Washington Post* (March 27, 1964), A–14.

she seemed to be singularly immune to the emotional influence of the music which was evoking enthusiastic participation of those about her. Throughout most of the first half of the two-hour concert she sat almost motionless, making only feeble gestures of applause at the end of each number. Gradually, however, her attitude seemed to change, and her overt reaction more closely approximated that of the rest of the audience as the evening wore on. Finally the apparent disdain which she had shown earlier in the evening gave way to an unrestrained enthusiasm, until, after the last encore, she was jumping up and down in a most undignified manner, shouting with the rest of the audience, "More! More!"

ITEM 9: YOUTH RIOT WITH JAZZ OBLIGATO

Newport, R.I., July 2. The Newport Jazz Festival erupted into a riot tonight as hundreds of youthful toughs unable to get seats, turned on music enthusiasts.

The rioters tore open the gates at Freebody Park, the scene of the holiday week-end concerts, knocking down spectators and taking over seats from some of the capacity audience of 16,000 persons inside.

Yelling and shouting youths, said to number 3,000, had been bunched on the streets around the park.

They spilled into the downtown area, attacking policemen, kicking in store windows and manhandling residents of the community . . . .

Several stabbings were reported. When the police tried to clear the streets around the park the crowd, mostly youngsters who had been driving through the clogged streets of Newport and drinking beer since early in the morning, fought back with bottles and beer cans, empty and full.

The police lobbed tear gas bombs into the crowd in an attempt to break it up. High pressure fire hoses were also turned on. After each assault by the police the crowd retreated a little but the barrage of cans and bottles continued.

Several police and civilians were hit in the head with filled beer cans and bottles and knocked unconscious. A call went out from the state police to police departments throughout the state to send all available supplies of tear gas and extra night sticks. The air police, the shore patrol, and the Marines were called in . . . .

The rioters were mostly college youths aged 17 to 20, according to Police, Joseph A. Radice.[17]

ITEM 10: PANIC—MARTIANS VS. YANKEES

Long ago it was said that if a person defines a situation as real, it is real in its consequences. The truth of this statement was clearly demonstrated by the consequences of a broadcast on October 30, 1938, of a special radio adaptation of H. G. Wells' *War of the Worlds.* An object

[17] *New York Times* (July 2 and 4, 1960).

which at first was believed to be a meteor was reported to have landed in New Jersey, but much to the consternation of the observers, a hatch began to open and weird beings began to tumble out of the huge contraption. In brief, they were Martians attacking the earthmen, and they had poisonous gases and other weapons at their disposal. The script lent realism to the supposed invasion from Mars by using as commentators on the radio fictitious scientists (from real and fancied universities), a Secretary of State, and other governmental and military officials. The use of the names of well-known places in and around New York, mostly in New Jersey, added to the feeling of authenticity, and this technique, plus the high caliber of the actors, proved to be effective because, as one who studied the panic reaction reported, "Long before the broadcast had ended, people all over the United States were praying, crying, fleeing frantically to escape death from the Martians."[18]

The reader will probably recognize this as the now famous Orson Welles Mercury Theatre broadcast that precipitated panic among large numbers of Americans.

A woman in Pittsburgh tried suicide, preferring that to death at the hands of the Martians; others drove frantically on the highways leading from the New Jersey area; still others were arrested for speeding in their attempts to reach and rescue loved ones from the danger zone. Those readers who are too young to remember the broadcast will find interesting the newspaper and magazine reports for that time. More than a quarter of a century later, it seems quite fantastic. How many thousands reacted, for longer or shorter periods, to the broadcast as being real will never be known, but the number must have been large. Reactions were far from uniform.

ITEM 11: PANIC—MARTIANS VS. ECUADORIANS

Quito, Ecuador, Feb. 13. An enraged mob that hurled gasoline and flaming balls of paper took fatal vengeance here last night for a panic caused by an Orson Welles-type radio dramatization of an "Invasion of Mars." The mob attacked and burned the building of the newspaper, *Comerico*, which housed the radio station, and killed fifteen persons and injured fifteen others . . . .

Hysteria drove most of the population of Quito into the streets before the program director learned how much consternation they had caused. Frantically they appealed to the people to be calm, and assured them it was all fictional.

When the people finally were convinced, they swept upon the

[18] Hadley Cantril, "The Invasion from Mars," in T. M. Newcomb and E. L. Hartley (eds.), *Readings in Social Psychology* (New York: Henry Holt and Co., 1947), p. 619. *See also* the more extended account of the panic in Hadley Cantril, Hazel Gaudet, and Herta Hertzog, *The Invasion from Mars* (Princeton, N.J.: Princeton University Press, 1940).

Comerico Building, which housed Ecuador's principal newspaper, showering it with stones and driving occupants to the upper floors.

Groups set fire to the building at various points, and some of the occupants leaped from the third-story windows as the flames trapped them.

Police aid was slow to rally because mobile police units had been sent to nearby Cotocallao, scene of the radio-reported "invasion," to investigate. Police officials said they thought Cotocallao was the scene of the broadcast, which gave realistic witness accounts.

The broadcast mentioned well-known Government officials and newsmen as being at the scene of the Martian landings, and an actor impersonating the Minister of Interior in an appeal to the people.

The people, many of them only half clad, fled into the streets in wild display of terror—when they learned it was a hoax, they were just as wild in their wrath.[19]

ITEM 12: MORBID CROWD

Albany, N.Y. A 19 year old youth who threatened to leap from a 12th story hotel ledge was coaxed to safety by his 7 year old nephew while onlookers below jeered and chanted "Jump! Jump! Jump!"

The youth, ———, who has been under psychiatric care in the Albany medical center, perched on the 37 inch wide ledge for two hours, staring down at the crowd—on the lawn of the state capitol across the street—numbered up to 4,000 persons.

While spotlights played on the distraught youth and members of his family, several policemen and a Roman Catholic Bishop spoke to him from the roof of the hotel. As the crowd gathered across the street on the lawn of the state capitol, shouts of "Jump! Jump! Jump!" echoed.

"Aw, c'mon, you're chicken!" one teen ager shouted. "Jump! What's the matter, ya yellow?" another shouted. One word became a chant from a cluster in the crowd: "Jump-jump-jump." At times it seemed the youth would obey the taunts.

"I wish he'd do it, and get it over with," a young woman told her companion. "If he doesn't hurry up we are going to miss our last bus."

Down on the lawn betting began. One elderly man said aloud, to nobody in particular: "Five bucks says he don't jump." A quick answer came back: "What odds you giving?"

A fire truck crew started to raise a ladder, but the youth threatened to leap and the truck withdrew.

"I hope he jumps on this side," a well-dressed man remarked. "We couldn't see him if he jumped over there."

Once ——— moved to the edge of the ledge and spread his arms as though he were perching for a swan dive from a springboard.

Several onlookers again called to him to jump. He lowered his arms, and shouted "Shut up!"

[19] *New York Times* (Feb. 14, 1949), 1, 7, 14.

————'s nephew, ————, persuaded him to leave the ledge. ———— leaned over the roof wall, put out his right hand, and said: "Come on, Uncle Dick. Take my hand."

The youth took ————'s hand, and was quickly caught by the policeman. A spokesman said ————'s family had consented to have him committed next Friday to the Rome state school for the mentally retarded.[20]

SOCIAL PSYCHOLOGY OF CROWD AND MOB BEHAVIOR

As in the many instances of highly organized, formalized, and instituted action, the unpatterned behavior is a function of the interactive processes as these involve items from all three categories of personality variables.

The above items are heterogeneous in many respects but do have in common: (1) collective, socially stimulated behavior; and (2) unstructured characteristics involving expediency and to some extent unpredictable and/or unlawful action. There are no special principles of human behavior which explain such action. The behavior involved cannot be predicted on the basis of knowledge about the positions the participants in such behavior occupy in a regularized and formalized social system. Occupational categories or marital status are not bases for predicting such action. Except when the divergence is marked, knowledge of the individual's biological heritage is not adequate for predicting that the individual will engage in such collective action. Neither will one gain an understanding of such behavior by concentrating his attention upon either the acquired personal attributes or the environment per se.[21]

Biological Heritage and Crowd Behavior

Little needs to be said regarding the influence of biological heritage upon mob behavior. The individual must have the physical energy, intelligence, sensory equipment, and knowledge required to participate in collective, unstructured action. The bedridden and the idiots can neither riot nor lynch, neither do blind-mute people yield to crowd enthusiasm at football games or jazz concerts. Beyond recognizing these palpable facts, it is not essential to devote attention to the relationship of biological endowment and such collective behavior. Certainly violence in riots is not restricted to mesomorphs.

Environment and Crowd Behavior

There are minimal environmental requirements for every social action regardless of the number of participants involved. In brief, the stage must be set, the props must be in place, the audience, if any, must be

---

[20] *The Milwaukee Journal* (Apr. 15, 1964).
[21] It has been pointed out that occupancy of certain official positions is related to one's initiating action in problem situations. However, the action is appropriate for the position occupied and quite unlike the unstructured crowd or mob action.

properly constituted, and the prompters and "shills" must be in their places. Personal social variables no less than customary and cultural ones, must have the proper setting. Riots, mob actions, and panics are not characteristic of tightly organized social systems, or those communities within which customs and supporting norms are homogeneous and where primary groups dominate. When individual and community values coincide, when each person has acquired a generalized other, the shared values are not violated by mob action.

The cultural script for any mob action must be of a special nature— the norms against it cannot be too strictly drawn, and the sanctions designed to control it cannot be applied too quickly or surely. For those who do not participate directly, often the audience, there must be a basis for rationalizing their failure to stop the illegal and riotous action. Table XIV shows the states within which mob lynchings have been most numerous between the years 1882 and 1946.

Table XIV
Lynchings by State and Race, 1882–1946*

Negro		White	
1. Mississippi	533	1. Georgia	381
2. Georgia	487	2. Texas	143
3. Texas	346	3. Montana	82
4. Louisiana	335	4. Oklahoma	82
5. Alabama	299	5. Colorado	66
6. Florida	256	6. Kentucky	64
7. Arkansas	226	7. Arkansas	59
8. Tennessee	203	8. Louisiana	56
9. South Carolina	155	9. Missouri	51
10. Kentucky	141	10. Tennessee	47
11. Virginia	83	11. Alabama	47
12. Missouri	71	12. Kansas	35

* J. P. Guzman (ed.), *Negro Year Book* (Tuskegee, Ala.: Tuskegee Institute, 1947), p. 306.

The social setting for the majority of lynchings in the United States is a dull one. The most characteristic setting is one which is rural, isolated, and economically poor. In the "lynch level" community, the level of education is low; rarely does anyone having more than the average number of years of formal education participate in the disorderly lynch mob. Provincialism, a life devoid of satisfactory departures from a dull, day-by-day routine, and a low educational level are important ingredients in the lynch mob behavior. The lynching noted in Item 3-(a) had such a setting, and had general community sanction. The lynching procedure is to be explained as much by its function as a divertive, self-aggrandizing recreational event as it is by any *personal* feelings which the mob may have toward the intended or actual victim. Many lynch victims are not known to the lynchers, and even when they are known, personal animosity is not part of the motivation. It is not yet known how many were actors and how many audience in the lynching of the three civil rights workers. In any event, the stage was such that few of the audience would dare protest the lynching.[22] Many of the onlookers do not participate in the actual lynching, but give tacit approval of the act and support the acting mob by their very presence. It is often for them that the mob puts on its act of violence. It is obvious that lynchings rarely occur in communities which strongly oppose them, and in which one would lose status and his freedom were he apprehended in such action. William Faulkner's novel, *Intruder in the Dust*, describes well this kind of setting.

When formal channels of justice are inaccessible, violators of local mores, regardless of race, are likely to be subjected to arbitrary and impulse directed retribution. The mob lynching of white men ceased almost completely with the frontier's disappearance, as governmental agencies became established and the rationale for vigilantism disappeared. Negro lynchings continued in those areas where formal judicial procedures were not accessible to nonwhites and where local authorities failed to play the roles appropriate to the positions held. The entrance of the policing agencies of the United States Government upon the local stage, a function of judicial, executive, and legislative action, plus the increased willingness of local police to resist the mobs, have accounted in part for the dramatic reduction of mob lynchings openly carried out in public view.[23] Other alterations in stage settings include a less avid audience, changed in part by the unfavorable image which the area has gained through modern communication techniques, and by the economic costs of mob action. Table XV shows this decrease. However, only the most uninformed believe that the practice of illegal killings, either by mobs or by individuals, has ceased. The church burnings and bombings, and the killings, known to police and sometimes recorded, evidence this fact. Furthermore, our knowledge of the nature of emotional habit and of attitudes does not permit us to believe that the negative attitudes that were instrumental in the explicit, exhibitionistic lynchings of previous decades have disappeared from among the people. The major explanation for the altered behavior, for the substitution of clandestine lynching for the

[22] William Bradford Huie, *Three Lives for Mississippi* (New York: Trident Press, 1965).

[23] Joe Jordan, "Lynchers Don't Like Lead," *Atlantic Monthly*, 177 (Feb. 1946), reprinted in E. A. Schuler, T. F. Hoult, D. L. Gibson, M. L. Fiero, W. B. Brookover (eds.), *Readings in Sociology* (New York: Thomas Y. Crowell Co., 1960).

Table XV
Lynchings in the United States, 1882–1962*

	White	Negro
1882–1889	669	534
1890–1899	429	1111
1900–1909	94	790
1910–1919	53	563
1920–1929	34	281
1930–1939	11	119
1940–1949	2	31
1950–1959	0	6

* J. P. Guzman (ed.), *Negro Year Book* (Tuskegee, Ala.: Tuskegee Institute, 1947), p. 307; *World Almanac* (New York: World Telegram and the Sun, 1963), p. 310.

carnival type, lies in environmental change and not in subjective modifications. As noted above, the increased willingness of law enforcement officers to obstruct, or attempt to obstruct, the torture and illegal executions primarily accounts for the modification in the lynching techniques and the actual reduction of illegal homicides.

Acquired Personal Attributes and Crowd Behavior

What about the person involved in the lynch mob? The personal characteristics of the lyncher in communities where lynching is still accepted as an institutional pattern of social control—communities in the "lynch level" area—probably are not significantly different from the rest of the people in the community.[24] However, there is good reason to believe that in the disorderly lynch mob are inadequate personalities of many sorts who find lynchings to their liking. Those of low status seem particularly adept at entertaining the crowd by acts of violence and sadism. Even under the stimulation of the lynch mob, it takes an abnormal person to apply a blowtorch to the face and chest of a person, to dismember a living body, or to drag a dead and disfigured body through the streets. No well-adjusted person, for whom the assigned social position and the preferred social roles coincide, is a candidate for such culturally abnormal action. The person who has little or no status to lose, who is starved for recognition and social approval, is a ready candidate for mob action, as are the sadist and the individual whose aggressive tendencies have been frustrated.

It is the person for whom the social structure as it now exists has

[24] See *The Mob Still Rides* (Atlanta: Commission on Interracial Cooperation, 1936), pp. 16–17, for further discussion of the nature of lynch mobs and "lynch level" communities.

failed to provide the satisfactions of basic needs who seeks them in atypical and socially disapproved fashion. As Raper says:

> Moreover, manhunts and lynchings make it possible for obscure and irresponsible people to play the roles of arresting officers, grand jurors, trial jurors, judges, and executioners. An added attraction is that they often afford an avenue of emotional escape from a life so drab and unilluminated that any alternative is welcomed.[25]

The active participant in the *disorderly* mob (as contrasted with the orderly lynching group in the "lynch level" communities), be it a lynch mob or any other, is the personal-social deviant who sees in the lynching or rioting an opportunity to satisfy some basic social need, or to give expression to pathological impulses.

Much that has been said of the lynch mob applies equally well to the Detroit and Los Angeles race riots and the threatening mob on Peoria Street described briefly in this chapter. These race riots were not institutionalized, nor were they sanctioned by the majority of the population of the communities. To be sure, it was not an accident that the riots occurred in Detroit and Los Angeles; the stages there were fully set for such events. The general tension of the wartime period in Detroit, a large number of Negro and white migrants from southern states, plus the inept handling of the riots by the police and other officials were important components of that riot situation. The latent anti-Negro attitudes of many laymen, and of some police as well, added to the difficulties. In Los Angeles the riot-ridden Watts area has, except for the skid-row area of downtown Los Angeles, the lowest per capita income of the entire city. Because of absentee ownership the Negroes' identification with the residential and commercial buildings was largely negative. The burned and looted stores were not theirs.

Riots are not cut from whole cloth, but are put together with parts that already have been cut to fit such social actions. The attitudes that support the overt behavior of the riots are not created overnight but are revealed by the nonstructured social situation in which the conventional controls fail. One of the principal reasons why such controls fail is inactivity on the part of those formal organizations whose function it is to see that the institutionalized norms are enforced. In this sense the riots are sociologically explained. However, the reason why the social roles of policemen often fail to coincide with the assigned position of law-enforcers is also a question for social psychology. At this point, the personal social experiences and attitudes of the policemen reveal themselves despite the fact that they do not fit the ascribed social positions

---

[25] A. F. Raper, *Tragedy of Lynching* (Chapel Hill, N.C.: University of North Carolina Press, 1933), p. 9. Even though written more than a third of a century ago, this observation is still applicable today.

of policemen. The same is true of the laymen in their participation in the riots. Under cover of the crisis situation, latent hatreds and fears spill out into the open. Anything that symbolizes the subordination of the Negro to the white, such as the police, the pawn shops, and the white-owned stores where the Negro can buy but cannot work, become the objects of attack by certain groups of Negroes.

The types of personalities involved in riots are much like those in the lynch mobs. More apt to be young than old, lower class than any other, and not overly burdened with education or approved social status, the active participants were subrepresentative of the culture at large. Culturally ingrained myths and prejudices, added to personal social short-comings, prepared the actors for active roles in the riots, roles about which rioters bragged afterwards. Their affective other, or audience, was composed of persons who would in most instances condone their actions. The chances of the Caucasian or Negro rioters coming into primary group relationships with other Caucasian or Negro persons who would con-demn their actions were and still are slight. Once the formal, third-party, impersonal urban controls broke down, there was little to hold such persons in line. All they required for action was some assurance of im-punity in the situation. Their consciences, built upon a significant other that did not share the larger society's values, were not designed to control their actions once the law-enforcing agencies proved ineffective.

The Peoria street riots are of the same pattern. The subcultural group of the area supported the anti-Semitism and the anti-Negro behavior pat-terns. Police action gave at least tacit approval to the mob's attitudes, and even most religious organizations in the neighborhood failed to raise voices in protest. The same types of inadequate personalities as those found in lynchings, and Detroit, Jacksonville, and Los Angeles mobs appear here, seeking an improvement of the social status or the release of frustrations, and taking advantage of the situation to gain recognition and other personal satisfactions through acts of violence.

The behavior revealed in Items 5 and 6 is religiously oriented, and ostensibly the mobs were acting with unified purpose, yet it is unlikely that all participating persons defined the situation in an identical manner. Here, as in other mob actions, uniform behavior obscures a variety of motives. Such remarks are also applicable to the "Youth riot with jazz obligato." One young couple at the scene observed that, just prior to the onset of the disorder, the youths who were thwarted in their desire to attend the jazz concert appeared to be "accidents looking for some place to happen." This couple, along with some others, correctly assessed the situation and departed from Newport. In this Newport episode, the frus-tration-aggression interpretation appears to be a valid one, at least for some of the participants who seemingly displaced their aggression to the likeliest and most available object. It is to be noted that, aside from their function as supportive audience, the majority of the youths played no signal roles in the disorder. Items 10 and 11 enable us to see the parts played by the actors' definition of similar objects in terms of different cultural values. Although the persons who believed the North American version of the story to be true, for whatever length of time, were drawn from all walks of life, it seems clear that those with greater knowledge were able to check the validity of the report sooner than were others. Also, those of more critical habits of thinking were prone to doubt the broadcast from the beginning and to seek objective checks to remove the slight doubts that might have been engendered by the clever realism of the broadcast as it was presented by Orson Welles and his company. The broadcast was not something different in kind from other experiences in which individuals are called upon to differentiate the real from the unreal. The medium of the radio and the caliber of the personnel in charge of script and dramatic presentation added to the difficulty of checking the true nature of the report, but at best the difference is one of degree. Anyone at all familiar with advertising or sales techniques is aware of the varying gullibility among potential customers. Moreover, many who mistook the true nature of the Martian "invasion" were to be found among the believers of the many racial and ethnic myths upon which are based current prejudices. Radio itself has been used to dupe large numbers of persons by certain medical charlatans, for instance, who added much to their financial profit by their airborne "cures." The strength of the reaction to the "War of the Worlds" broadcast lies in the fact that, as Cantril points out, the Martian invasion seemingly threatened the very lives of the listeners.[26] Furthermore, the panic aspect of the fear was augmented by the absence of any institutionalized or habitual way of meeting the threat. It is this lack of adequate preparation for any event that defines the event as a crisis for the person involved. Whatever resentment was felt by the North Americans toward the broadcasters of the Martian invasion was repressed, but in many instances the reaction was embarrassment, not anger; rationalization and not aggression. The South Americans, in contrast, were quick to project upon the perpetrators of the hoax their feelings of wrath, and to express that wrath in vengeful form. Although it is not warranted to say that such a reaction should have been anticipated (their fellow countrymen in charge of the broadcast apparently failed to do so), the violent reaction is at least in keeping with the stereotype attributed to the South Americans, and, in retrospect, is not perceived as being out of character. In both "Martian invasions," moreover, differential social positions were operative in selection of those credulous people who reacted in fear. Differences in knowledge, belief,

[26] Hadley Cantril, "The Invasion from Mars," in T. M. Newcomb and E. L. Hartley, *Readings in Social Psychology* (New York: Henry Holt, and Co., 1947), p. 627.

and feelings helped to set the stage for credulity in some and skepticism in others, whether they were *Americanos del norte or del sur*.

Abstract and Concrete Crowds

In any unstructured crowd action, the explanations require knowledge of the personality categories of the triangular model. Failure to perceive this interactionist nature of such collective action has given rise to the belief that something called the mob spirit, or crowd contagion is the independent variable in mob actions. It is not to be denied that the socially stimulating behavior of the crowd (either the actor or the audience) is an essential ingredient explaining any given individual's participation; however, such stimulation is not sufficient to account for that participation. The active, concrete, compact, or acting crowd, however, does not come into being out of the blue, but is drawn from a pre-existing passive, abstract, diffuse, or latent crowd made up of persons with comparable attitudes.[27] The nature of the attitudes, and the attending values, determine that active or concrete action in which one is likely to participate.

Each person in his day-by-day living selectively acquires attitudes, perceptions, and misperceptions which make him susceptible to some crowd influences but which render him immune to stimulation by other crowds. No one is swept off his feet or carried away in violation of basic values. Negroes do not lose their critical faculties in riot or lynching situations and attack other Negroes. Jews do not yield to the crowd pressures and desecrate temples and synagogues. The Tamils did not join Sinhalese mobs and destroy Tamil property or attack fellow Tamils. There is no "mob spirit," a "group mind" apart from the subjective values of the actors and the supporting affective other. Even the lady at the jazz concert was prepared, albeit unconsciously, to respond belatedly but positively to the crowd's and orchestra's stimulation. The morbid interest of the audience for the would-be suicide cannot be explained by the argument "everybody was doing it," but was acquired over a long period of time.

If actions can be induced against an individual or a group, it is only because of the prior existence of an appropriate abstract or passive crowd or group. The Hindu-Muslim riots that followed partition of India were predicated upon centuries of irreconcilable religious attitudes and values. The stage is set in some parts of the world for discrimination and antagonisms between Christian and non-Christian. In America we have not seen

[27] *See* Leopold von Wiese and Howard Becker, *Systematic Sociology* (New York: John Wiley and Sons, 1932), pp. 455 ff., for an early discussion of abstract and concrete crowds. G. H. Mead *also* made use of these concepts. *Cf., Mind, Self and Society* (Chicago: University of Chicago Press, 1934), p. 157.

the last of racial and ethnic strife, but a person would be foolhardy indeed were he to attempt to initiate an anti-Scandinavian campaign. The abstract crowd upon which to base the action is simply nonexistent.

Finally, even if there exists an abstract group that might serve as a basis for an active or concrete crowd, the environment may be so well ordered governmentally that the attitudes remain covert, never being transformed into overt behavior.

SUMMARY

The processes of socialization and enculturation do not operate equally among all members of complex societies. Personal-social backgrounds prepare certain actors in the various theaters of culture to participate in forms of collective behavior that are departures from custom and violations of cultural norms. Riots, mob actions, panics, morbid interests, and stampedes occur when the normal sanctions fail. Despite the heterogeneity of these types of collective behavior, they do have in common (1) collective, socially stimulated behavior, and (2) unstructured relationships involving expediency and, to some extent, unpredictable and/or illegal actions.

There are no special principles of social psychology that explain such actions. The behavior cannot be predicted on the basis of knowledge about the participants' positions in the social system, but the collective behavior is explainable in terms of the tri-partite interactionist frame of reference. Unless the stage is set with the appropriate props, the audience favorably disposed to the action taking place, and the individual prepared by habit, attitude, and belief to perceive the situation as an opportunity to fulfill certain needs or to express pathological impulses, no riot or other mob action occurs. There is no "mob spirit" that operates apart from the three basic categories of personality.

SUGGESTED READINGS

BLUMER, HERBERT. "Collective Behavior," in A. McClung Lee, New Outline of the Principles of Sociology (New York: Barnes and Noble, 1946).

CANETTI, ELIAS. Crowds and Power. Translated by Carol Stewart (London: Gollancz, 1961).

CANTRIL, HADLEY, HAZEL GAUDET, and HERTA HERTZOG. The Invasion from Mars (Princeton, N.J.: Princeton University Press, 1940).

CAUGHEY, J. W. Their Majesties the Mob (Chicago: The University of Chicago Press, 1960).

LAPIERE, RICHARD T. Collective Behavior (New York: McGraw-Hill, 1958).

LEE, ALFRED MCCLUNG, and NORMAN D. HUMPHREY. Race Riot (New York: The Dryden Press, 1943).

RUDE, GEORGE F. The Crowd and the French Revolution (London: Clarendon Press, 1959).

Smelser, Neil. *The Theory of Collective Behavior* (New York: The Free Press of Glencoe, 1963).

Turner, R. H., and L. M. Killian. *Collective Behavior* (Englewood Cliffs, N.J.: Prentice-Hall, 1957).

Vittachi, Farzie. *Emergency 1958: The Story of Ceylon Race Riots* (London: Deutsch, 1959).

Westley, William A. *Formation, Nature, and Control of Crowds* (Montreal: McGill University, 1956).

PART III

Social Psychology
of Age Groups

They have their exits and their entrances,
And one man in his time plays many parts. . . .

Thus far we have concerned ourselves with the definition and interpretation of the basic concepts of social psychology that are essential
to an understanding of the development of human nature in its social
aspects. In the remainder of the book we want to see how these concepts enable us to understand the individual's social behavior at
different stages of his life and in the many and varied positions and
statuses in which he finds himself, and the ways he plays or fails to
play the social roles appropriate to these positions and statuses. The
student who has mastered the ideas advanced so far will be interested in learning how these ideas become keys to understanding why
human beings behave as they do when they interact with others.

One element that distinguishes the age roles in the American
and Canadian cultures is the associational structures of communities. These associational affiliations tend to be age graded and initiation into them marks movement from one age role position to
another. Schools are, of course, formally age graded. But so also
are more adult associations such as clubs, churches, and unions. We
shall learn in the ensuing chapters who are the significant people
in this associational network that inform each person as to what it
means to be age five, twenty-one, or sixty. In Chapters 12 to 16 the
personality characteristics of each age group, infancy and the preschool years, childhood, adolescence, adulthood, and old age, will
be discussed with reference to the physiological and cultural environmental factors involved in the social situations.

Social scientists view human life as a totality and endeavor to
study the specific functions and roles of the different ages of life

within the framework of the whole. If life is viewed as a meaningful *gestalt* and not merely as a process of growth and decline, the role behavior appropriate to each age of life becomes quite meaningful.[1]

Age groups as the basis of sociological and sociopsychological positions and roles are noted in all cultures, but they vary in accordance with the particular cultural values. Berelson and Steiner refer to these age groups as the "age grades of society" and it is claimed that these age grades are roughly correlated with the stages of biological growth.[2] Fortes describes the relationship of age grading and physiological growth as follows:

> Though these phases do not invariably conform to stages of physiological growth, in relatively homogeneous social systems there is a close parallelism between them. For in such societies the basic educational tasks required to produce an adult person capable of playing a full part in maintaining and transmitting the social capital seem to be complete at about the same time as the attainment of physical and sexual maturity and therewith the capacity for replacing the parental generation in productive and reproductive activities. But what I want particularly to emphasize is that the maturation of the individual and his proper passage through the life cycle is of paramount concern to society at large. This is shown in the widespread occurrence of institutionalized procedures for legitimizing each step in it, and especially for terminating the period of jural infancy, whether it ends with adolescence or extends into the stage of physical adulthood.[3]

Chronological age provides a rough approximation of the age positions, statuses, and roles, but both between cultures and within a given culture there are marked variations in the obligations, rights, and roles or role behavior which are associated with a particular age. The Andaman Islanders are reported to have had twenty-three terms which they used to describe the various age groups, whereas the Masai tribe of East Africa used but three—boy, warrior, and elder. The following classification was used by the ancient Incas of Peru, and it can be seen that the categories are based partly upon

---

[1] *See* Charlotte Bühler, "Theoretical Observations About Life's Basic Tendencies," *American Journal of Psychotherapy* (1959), No. 13, 561–581.

[2] Bernard Berelson and Gary A. Steiner, *Human Behavior* (New York: Harcourt, Brace & World, 1964), p. 82.

[3] Meyer Fortes, "Introduction" in Jack Goody (ed.), *The Development Cycle in Domestic Groups.* Cambridge Papers in Social Anthropology, No. 1 (Cambridge University Press for the Department of Archaeology and Anthropology, 1958), pp. 1–14.

physiological maturation and partly upon social statuses assigned to the persons in certain of the categories.[4]

1. Punuc rucu (old man sleeping), 60 years and upward.
2. Chaupi rucu (half old), 50–60 years. Doing light work.
3. Puric (able-bodied), 25–50 years. Tribute payer and head of family.
4. Yma Huayna (almost a youth), 20–25 years. Worker.
5. Coca palla (coca picker), 16–20 years. Worker.
6. Pucllac Huamra (8–16 years). Light work.
7. Ttanta raquizic (bread receiver), 6–8 years.
8. Macta puric, under 6.
9. Saya huamrac. Able to stand.
10. Mosoc caparic. Baby in arms.

One American social scientist designates the years from birth to twenty as the preparation phase of life, the years from twenty to sixty as the performance phase, and the years from sixty to death as the phase of relinquishment.[5] These terms do suggest the nature of the roles played by the several age groups, particularly in our culture. Chronological age is not the sole determinant of the positions that are assigned to the various age levels, and the variation in age positions and statuses from society to society is explainable largely in terms of cultural values. To be sure, the age factor is indirectly responsible for such differences in assigned statuses in such instances as, for example, when cultural factors have made it possible to raise the average life expectancy from thirty years to more than seventy years as has been done within the last century or two in some countries. The greater proportion of older persons is itself a determining factor in what people are expected to do, can do, and actually do.

The variation in the cultural evaluation of age levels is evidenced by the fact that the Inca category of "old man sleeping" begins at an age when many persons in our culture reach the peak of their performance. The Presidency of the United States, sometimes called the toughest job in the world, has usually been occupied by men in their fifties and sixties. Dwight Eisenhower was seventy years of age upon retirement from the Presidency and the Late John F.

[4] C. R. Markham, *The Incas of Peru* (London: Elder, Smith, 1910), pp. 161–162.
[5] Robert J. Havighurst, "A New American Dilemma: Life After Sixty," *The University of Chicago Magazine*, XLII (Feb. 1950), 2.

Kennedy was unique in that he was the youngest President (age 43) ever elected to this office.

Because chronological age by itself is more often than not inadequate as a basis for establishing age categories that are significant from the viewpoint of social psychology, we must give our attention to culture patterns. In order to avoid the imposition of subjective judgments of what constitutes behavior appropriate to the several age groupings, the criteria for distinguishing these groups must come from careful observation of the positions actually assigned to such groups, and the roles actually played by members of these groups. To be sure, overlapping of positions and roles is inevitable because of the absence (in our culture) of sharp disjunctures between the age groups. Nevertheless, there are certain positions and behavior patterns that are characteristic of any given age category, and that are denied to, or voluntarily shunned by, other categories. For instance, our society permits children to cry when they pinch their fingers or have their "feelings" hurt, but withholds approval from adults who do likewise; it denies the right of contract to the young, but expects this right to be exercised by adults; and it expects, and gives approval to, dependence of adolescent children upon parents for decisions, but frowns upon adults who look to their parents for such decisions. Thus the criteria for judging age categories in terms of social behavior must be derived by study of the culture pattern of the group in question. It logically follows, then, that these criteria are applicable only within the culture from which they were derived. We will make references to other cultures, but only for purposes of contrast and comparison. The cultural limitations of any age-group criteria must be recognized if such criteria are to gain objective meaning. In short, the influence of age upon behavior must be studied within the interactionist framework and related to biological heritage, environment, and personal variables.

CHAPTER 12

INFANCY AND THE
PRESCHOOL YEARS

> At first, the infant,
> Mewling and puking in the nurse's arms.

In this chapter we will focus our attention on the interpersonal behavior of the infant during the preschool years of life. At first observation it might seem that there is little interactive behavior of real significance in the early months of life. Yet, as we shall see, it is in these earliest experiences with other people that the child first learns who he is and what the world is like. A child becomes aware of himself and his characteristics through his perception of how other people feel toward him, and these feelings are established very early in life in relationship to those who are closest to him. Family members, playmates, teachers and other members of the infant's primary group are the important members of the child's affective other, and it is in terms of their expectations, and in terms of their views of the world that the child develops his own concepts, attitudes, and beliefs.

There is almost complete consensus today among social scientists that the quality and character of child rearing practices provide an important key to an understanding of infant personality development.[1] Behavior scientists are interested in the relationship between personality and culture and in the way in which society's customs, beliefs and value systems become incorporated into the self concepts of each individual. While there is consensus that the infant's personality development is intimately associated with his early experiences with the persons responsible for his care, there is as yet little research that has confirmed any specific relationships between particular infant training practices and personality traits. In the absence of consensus among the "experts," there has been, and still is, a broad spectrum of recommended child training practices prevalent in our own culture.

---

[1] L. J. Newson, "Contemporary English Infant Rearing Practices," in *Proceedings of the Sixteenth International Congress of Psychology* (Amsterdam: North Holland Publishing Co., 1960), p. 418.

FASHIONS AND FADS IN INFANT TRAINING PRACTICES

Stendler has studied what she calls the "fads" in child training as they have been presented by magazine writers in women's periodicals over a period of sixty years.[2] Table XVI summarizes some of her data, which indicate that, in terms of the popular reading material of the day, there have been wide swings in attitudes toward child discipline and training. The trend from the early loose, sentimental, and indulgent parent-child relationship through the Watsonian "let them cry-it-out" period to the more recent self-regulating procedures is apparent.

Table XVI
Percentage of Methods of Child Training Practices Recommended by Writers for Women's Magazines Since 1890 by Decades*

	1890	1900	1910	1920	1930	1940	1948	1960
Tightly scheduled	0	22	77	100	75	33	0	0
Loosely scheduled	100	78	23	0	0	0	0	0
Self-regulated	0	0	0	0	25	66	100	100

* Celia B. Stendler, "Sixty Years of Child Training Practices," *The Journal of Pediatrics*, XXXVI, No. 1 (Jan. 1950), p. 126. Research for 1960 is by authors.

Three different schools of thought have prevailed during this period with regard to how children should be raised. The 1890's and 1900's saw a highly sentimental approach to child rearing; 1910 through the 1930's witnessed a rigid and disciplinary approach; beginning with the 1940's the emphasis had shifted to self-regulation and understanding of the child. Bronfenbrenner lists the following major changes in parental behavior in relationship to child training in the last twenty-five years, as follows:

1. Greater permissiveness toward the child's spontaneous drives.
2. Freer expression of affection.
3. Increased reliance on direct "psychological" techniques of discipline (such as reasoning or appeals to guilt) versus direct methods (like physical punishment, scolding or threats.)
4. In consequence of the above shifts in the direction of what are predominantly middle class values and techniques, a narrowing of the gap between social classes in their patterns of child rearing.
5. In succeeding generations the relative position of the father vis-a-vis the mother is shifting with the former becoming increasingly more affectionate and less authoritarian and the latter becoming relatively more important as the agent of discipline, especially for boys.[3]

[2] Celia B. Stendler, "Sixty Years of Child Training Practices," *The Journal of Pediatrics*, XXXVI, No. 1 (Jan. 1950), 122–124.

[3] Urie Bronfenbrenner, "The Changing American Child—A Speculative Analysis," *Journal of Social Issues*, 17, No. 1 (1961), pp. 6–18.

DRAWINGS BY
Whitney Darrow, Jr

1890: "Love is the mighty solvent." 1920: "Let 'em cry it out."
1950: Babies need love and affection.

FIGURE 32. Fads in child care.

Thus each period has had its share of fads and theories concerning the best manner of influencing the behavior of children. Today's grandparents and great-grandparents must be amazed at the apparent inability of pediatricians, psychologists, and social psychologists to make up their minds about what kind of child training is best. Orlansky's review of studies of the effects of various child training practices on child development makes it clear that many of the recommendations that have been made on the subject of child training practices are not based on any substantial body of experimental evidence.[4] Watsonian behaviorism was probably in part a reaction to the heavy sentimentalism and moralism of the turn of the century. Freud's emphasis upon the child's needs for security and affection in a permissive environment is certainly in part a reaction to the emphasis on objectivity and sophistication of the 1920's. Stendler's research referred to earlier showed that one of the major shifts in parental attitudes toward child training over a sixty-year period was the change in emphasis from character development to personality development. However, the firing of the first Sputnik set off still another abrupt trend in child training, namely, the current near obsession in child development on *achievement* instead of *adjustment*. Bronfenbrenner detects in this development a return to the more explicit disciplinary techniques of an earlier era.[5]

[4] Harold Orlansky, "Infant Care and Personality," *Psychological Bulletin*, XLVI (1949), 1–48.
[5] Bronfenbrenner, "The Changing American Child—A Speculative Analysis," p. 16.

CROSS-CULTURAL COMPARISONS OF CHILD TRAINING PRACTICES

Child training practices differ in many ways from one society to another. How these varying practices influence the behavior of the infants of these societies has been the object of studies by anthropologists and sociologists. Whiting and Child have demonstrated how certain culturally patterned methods of child rearing become internalized as attitudes common to the members of that society. The main causal sequence is as follows:[6]

maintenance systems[7] → child training practices →
→ personality variables → projective systems[8]

Thus the authors propose that the primary institutions of society, together with the child training practices associated with them, are responsible for the underlying personality characteristics of each society. This reasoning comes full circle when it is realized that the resulting personal attributes of the members of the society largely determine the kinds of secondary institutions and associations (schools, churches, economic systems) that shall prevail.

The relationship between child training practices and personality development can be seen in various anthropological studies. Thus Dubois has described the adult population of Alor, an island in the Dutch East Indies, as suspicious, distrustful, anxious, and hostile. Dubois attributed these characteristics to the infant child rearing practices of the Alor culture. These practices appeared to Dubois to be extremely frustrating for the infants of the island because the mothers soon leave the infants to the care of older children or anyone else who may be available. The discipline of the island children is inconclusive and unpredicable. Deliberate training is unknown. Instead the children, when they misbehave, may be

---

[6] John W. M. Whiting and Irvin L. Child, *Child Training and Personality* (New Haven: Yale University Press, 1953), p. 310.

[7] By maintenance systems the authors mean "economic, political, and social organizations of a society—the basic customs surrounding the nourishment, sheltering, and protection of its members, which seem a likely source of influence on child training practices." An example would be the marriage structure prevailing in a culture. "The form of marriage is one aspect of social structure which appears to be clearly related to child training practices. Most of our societies may be classified into three groups, according to the form of marriage: monogamy, sororal polygyny (in which co-wives customarily are sisters), and non-sororal polygyny (in which co-wives are not sisters). The implications of marriage form for child training practices have to do primarily with a contrast between sororal polygyny and the two other forms of marriage. Societies with sororal polygyny are found in general to be more indulgent in the initial care of the young child, and less severe in subsequent socialization than either of the other groups of societies." (Whiting and Child, *Child Training and Personality*, pp. 310–311.)

[8] Projection is used in this study to refer to the fact that adults relate to other people in terms of their own anxieties, frustrations, and personal needs.

shamed, intimidated, or ridiculed. Dubois reports that the children do not respond to such treatment with open hostility but express covert aggression toward one another in sly teasing and pinching. A pattern of parental rejection and denial is established early and continues as the children grow older.[9]

By contrast, Gorer, in describing the Japanese attitude toward infant training and nurture emphasizes the indulgence with which the Japanese culture regards infant feeding. Japanese babies are offered the breast even before there is evidence of hunger, and Gorer believes this is related to the lack of hunger anxiety in the Japanese culture, the latter being somewhat indifferent to meal schedules. However, toilet training in the Japanese culture is more rigidly required and the inference is therefore made that the Japanese preoccupation with rituals and neatness in adult life stems from this early anal training.[10]

However, not all cross-cultural material shows this same close correspondence of infant feeding and training habits and later personality traits. Thus, Underwood and Honigmann report that ". . . the Kaska personality norm is introvert and the Haitian extrovert, although in both societies babies are fed when they so desire, receive no pressure to control elimination, are comforted and handled when irritable or playful, and suffer no discipline for emotional willfulness."[11]

It is against this background that we compare American child rearing practices with those of other societies. The American standard for many of these comparisons is the findings of Davis and Havighurst who in the early 1940's interviewed and observed 200 families, representing an equal number of white middle and lower class and Negro middle and lower class families.[12]

The results of that study indicated that lower class homes in this sample, more than middle class homes, assumed a more permissive attitude toward the child's direct satisfaction of organic as well as social needs. Davis and Havighurst reported the following differences which, according to their sample, characterized lower and middle class training practices:[13]

[9] Cora Dubois, *The People of Alor* (Minneapolis: University of Minnesota Press, 1944), pp. 39–49.

[10] G. Gorer, *Themes in Japanese Culture.* Transactions of New York Academy of Science, 5 (1943), pp. 106–124.

[11] Frances W. Underwood and Irma Honigmann, "A Comparison of Socialization and Personality in Two Simple Societies," *American Anthropologist*, 49 (1947), 557–568.

[12] Allison Davis and Robert J. Havighurst, "Social Class and Color Differences in Child Rearing," *American Sociological Review*, 11, (Dec. 1946), 698–710.

[13] Davis and Havighurst, "Social Class and Color Differences in Child Rearing," p. 703.

1. More lower class than middle class babies are breast fed only.

2. More lower class babies are fed at will.

3. More lower class (white) babies have the breast or bottle longer than twelve months.

4. Lower class children are weaned later.

5. Bowel training is begun earlier (on the average) with middle class children.

6. Bladder training is begun earlier (on the average) with middle class children.

7. Middle class children are expected to be home earlier.

8. Middle class children are expected to assume responsibility earlier.

9. Lower class children stay up later, stay in the streets later, and go to the movies more often.

Whiting and Child made a cross-cultural comparison of middle class child training practices (using the Davis and Havighurst study as the American norm).[14] When compared with the child training practices of forty-seven primitive societies it was found that while the American training procedures are rather extreme in the severity of their socialization practices they do not fall outside the range of the primitive societies in this regard. However, American habits in this comparison, are tied with the two most extremely nonindulgent societies out of the forty-seven societies in the sample. "The average degree of initial indulgence is found to vary from an average rating of 10 for the Tanala and Dobuans to an average rating of 17 for the Siriono. The median is at 13. Our American middle-class group has an average rating of 10, and they are thus extremely low in average indulgence. . ."[15]

These cross-cultural comparisons of child training practices are based, as we have indicated, on the findings of one urban midwestern study made by Davis and Havighurst a generation ago. The groups studied by Davis and Havighurst were very likely less permissive in their child training practices and attitudes than a similar group would be today. Furthermore, the study has been criticized because it was restricted to the Chicago area, which is probably not representative of the entire United States. As we suggested earlier in this chapter, American practices in child training procedures do not stay put, at either the professional or the lay level of experience. It is not surprising, therefore, that more recent studies in Boston and in California do not confirm all of the class differences in child rearing practices identified in the earlier Davis

[14] Whiting and Child, *Child Training and Personality*, pp. 305–324.
[15] *Ibid.*

and Havighurst Chicago sample.[16] White found none of the class differences in weaning and toilet training practices reported by Davis and Havighurst. In fact, White's data suggest that contemporary middle class mothers (as compared with working class mothers) appear to be *more* permissive in their child training practices, more open and responsive to new ideas in child training and more willing to rely on outside experts in these matters. In view of the change over the years of expert ideas on child training practices, and because middle class parents are highly responsive to such professional opinion, it is likely that contemporary middle class practices reflect this change. Bronfenbrenner's findings also indicate a definite narrowing of class differences in child training practices. All classes, according to Bronfenbrenner, are presently oriented toward permissive child training practices.[17]

Having called to the reader's attention some of the concepts and practices of child nurture, we shall now turn to a consideration of the contemporary findings regarding personality development in the preschool years. Following the frame of reference developed in the first part of the text, we shall pay attention to the maturation, socialization, and development of personality in the infant.

BIOLOGICAL MATURATION

One-celled animals like the amoeba or paramecium possess no infancy—they are literally born grown up. Three days after birth the guinea pig can take care of itself. Anyone who has observed the behavior of a newborn colt knows how quickly it gains the use of its legs and is ready for life. At the other extreme is the human infant, completely dependent upon adults both physically and culturally for many years.

Apparently those creatures least dependent upon ready-made mechanisms of adjustment are most dependent upon growth and education to develop a repertoire of skills and habits that will enable them to survive by their own efforts. For these higher and more complex organisms a long infancy is necessary to allow time for the maturation of structure and education in its use. The human child, with the longest infancy, is the most educable of all creatures. The absence of stereotyped and ready-

[16] Martha C. Ericson, "Social Status and Child Rearing Practices," in T. M. Newcomb and Eugene L. Hartley (eds.), *Readings in Social Psychology* (New York: Henry Holt and Co., 1947), pp. 494–501. Martha Sturm White, "Social Class, Child Rearing Practices, and Child Behavior," in Neil J. Smelser and William T. Smelser (eds.) *Personality and Social Systems* (New York: John Wiley and Sons, 1963), pp. 286–296. Ethelyn Henry Klatskin, "Shifts in Child Care Practices in Three Social Classes Under an Infant Care Program of Flexible Methodology," *The American Journal of Orthopsychiatry*, 22 (Jan. 1952), 52–61.

[17] Urie Bronfenbrenner, "The Changing American Child—A Speculative Analysis." *Journal of Social Issues*, 17, No. 1 (1961), p. 348.

made patterns of responses makes him more adaptable and flexible. His responses are not limited to those with which he was born. He is, because of the absence of established instincts, capable of achieving a maximum of freedom in developing a wide repertoire of adaptations to his world. This fact is one of the advantages man has over all other less educable creatures.

Of course, the child is not born devoid of all automatic and pre-established mechanisms. Fortunately, his basic physiological functions are automatic and need not be learned. Reflexes and the nervous system, which gives rise to them, appear as needed. But over-all, one of the chief distinctions among the structures in the evolutionary scale is the ratio of infancy to length of life. The more complex the growing organism, the longer the period of infancy. Figure 33 illustrates this phenomenon.

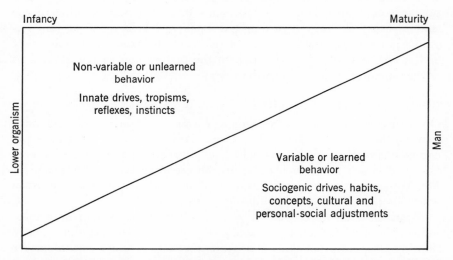

FIGURE 33. Diagrammatic representation of the relative dependency of lower and higher organisms upon learned and unlearned types of behavior. (Adapted from Peter Sandiford, *Foundations of Educational Psychology*, New York: Longmans, Green & Co., Copyright 1934, p. 260).

Civilization generally has encouraged the prolongation of infancy and adolescence to a point where even within the human race there are wide differences in the length of childhood dependency. Among human cultures the more stress that is placed on formal education, the longer becomes the dependency of the child.

Maturation, an important term in the discussion of physical development, refers to the process in which the organic potentials of the organism ripen and unfold. Jersild distinguishes between growth and maturation as follows: "Growth and maturation have a meaning in common. However, maturation denotes not solely a change in the physical equipment of the organism but also a change in function, in *capacity to perform* through the use of this equipment."[18] The maturation of structure is not an automatic unfolding of capacities, but is dependent upon the appropriate stimulation of environment, including diet, affection, education, exercise, and so on, all of which facilitate, modify, retard, or destroy the ultimate development of innate structure potential.

The kind of behavior that the organism ultimately exhibits is dependent upon the nature of its physical structure. Different organisms react differently to similar stimuli, depending upon the nature of their structure and constitution and their experiences up to the time the stimuli are encountered. Education, training, and exercise are effective depending upon the capacity of each organism to respond to these stimuli.

The complementary relationship between hereditary structure and environmental stimulation can be seen in situations where a developing organism is placed in an environment that is substantially different from the animal's native habitat. Thus psychologists have sometimes been interested in the capacity of an infant chimpanzee to adapt to and respond to the stimulation of a human home environment. Hayes and Hayes adopted a chimpanzee named Viki a few days after her birth. Viki was brought up in the experimenter's home and, with very few exceptions, was accorded the treatment usually provided a human child. Viki, as a result of this exposure, was able to acquire many behavior patterns much more complex than would be true of chimpanzees raised in their native milieu. In spite of these achievements, the chimpanzee's physiological structure placed limits on her learning ability. These limitations were centered about her relative failure to acquire human language symbols. The investigators felt, on the basis of their experience with this one animal experiment, that man's superior ability to use language skills may be his only really important genetic advantage over the chimpanzees. The importance of language skills is, of course, a major advantage since it makes possible still other advantages, including the sharing of knowledge.[19]

An older classic study by Kellogg and Kellogg is even more pertinent to our study because it involves both an infant chimpanzee and a human

[18] Arthur T. Jersild, *Child Psychology*, 4th ed. (Englewood Cliffs, N.J.: Prentice-Hall, 1954, p. 19. It is important also to distinguish between learning and maturation. Valentine makes the following comment in this regard, "This term (maturation) refers to that aspect of growth and development which is due to the inherent ripening of the elements and organization of the nervous mechanisms (including the brain cells) concerned with any form of activity, as distinct from the organization or coordination which is due to learning through practice or training." C. W. Valentine, *The Normal Child* (Baltimore: Penguin Books, 1956), p. 50.

[19] Keith J. Hayes and Catherine Hayes, "The Intellectual Development of a Home-raised Chimpanzee," *Proceedings of the American Philosophical Society*, 95 (1951), 105–109.

FIGURE 34. Gua and Donald. (From *The Ape and the Child*, by Kellogg and Kellogg. Copyright, 1933. Courtesy of McGraw-Hill Book Co.)

sibling raised in a human home simultaneously.[20] The aim of the study was to investigate the possibility that the ape with its particular constitution could profit from a human environment in the same manner as a child with a structure different from the ape's.

The story of this investigation is as follows: A chimpanzee, a female named Gua, was introduced into the investigator's home at the age of seven and one-half months and was treated as a sibling to their son, Donald, two and one-half months older than Gua. Every effort was made to control the similarity of physical and affectional stimulation for both Donald and Gua. The chimpanzee was treated in every way, including punishment and endearment, the same as was the human child. Playthings, cribs, food, and clothing were the same. The experiment lasted nine months, during which time accurate measurements were obtained

[20] W. N. Kellogg and L. A. Kellogg, *The Ape and the Child* (New York: Whittlesey House, McGraw Hill, 1933).

of the learning ability of both infants. Gua surpassed the human infant on many of the experimental tasks even though she was chronologically younger. At the age of twelve months Gua could respond accurately to twenty commands, while Donald at the same age could accomplish only three. However, by the end of the experimental period the child's development was advancing more rapidly than was Gua's and if the experiment had continued, it is likely that the human child would have excelled the chimpanzee in all activities except those involving strength and physical agility.

Thus we see that the influence of exercise and culture will vary with the nature and maturity of the structure of each organism. The chimpanzee, or any of the animals lower on the evolutionary scale than man, would sooner or later reach a point where further education would be of no use because of the limitations of structure and constitution. As we shall indicate later, this is true among members of the human race as well as among various organisms of different genus. That is, as native endowment differs among human beings, so will the effectiveness of education and culture vary.

Biological Maturation Follows an Orderly Sequence

The development through maturation of physical structure proceeds in the infant in an orderly progression. The growth of the organism follows a maturation sequence that is roughly comparable from infant to infant. So regular is this sequence for most children that norms or standards have been set up to guide the pediatrican and parent in the progress of the child's growth. Gesell, who has devoted much of his life to developing these norms, writes that:

> The child's personality is a product of slow and gradual growth. His nervous system matures by stages and natural sequences. He sits before he stands; he babbles before he talks; he fabricates before he tells the truth; he draws a circle before he draws a square; he is selfish before he is altruistic; he is dependent on others before he achieves dependence on self. All of his abilities, including his morals, are subject to laws of growth. The task of child care is not to force him into a predetermined pattern but to guide his growth.[21]

Because there is a sequential growth pattern for the development of all structures, it is apparent that the infant will be able to make certain responses when a particular structure has matured and not before. For example, the child does not ordinarily walk before he can stand, does not reach for a dangling object before he has first learned to fixate his eyes.

[21] Arnold Gesell and Frances L. Ilg, *Infant and Child in the Culture of Today* (New York: Harper & Brothers, 1943), p. 403. *See also* Helen Thompson "Physical Growth," in Leonard Carmichael, (ed.), *Manual of Child Psychology* (New York: John Wiley & Sons, 1954).

Exercise and training of the infant must recognize the necessity of physical readiness of the child to learn a particular task. To return to our earlier illustration of the champanzee and the human infant, it would be foolhardy to try to teach the latter tasks with his slower maturation sequence that would be quite appropriate for the chimpanzee with his earlier maturation patterning. This is as true of symbolic learning as it is of motor learning. Piaget's research leads him to conclude that, "It is a great mistake to suppose that a child acquires the notion of number and other mathematical concepts just from teaching. On the contrary, to a remarkable degree he develops them himself, independently and spontaneously. When adults try to impose mathematical concepts on a child prematurely, his learning is merely verbal; true understanding of them comes only with his mental growth."[22]

Some social psychologists have held that the use of specific exercise and education may be ineffective and unnecessary since maturation appears to move forward without much help in the way of educational aids.[23] Early studies of twins by Gesell and Thompson[24] and McGraw[25] indicate that phylogenetic functions (behavior characteristic of the race based on organic structure) are not materially affected by exercise or special training. Control children isolated from special opportunities to develop such activities as walking, climbing, and toilet training developed these skills at about the same age as the trained, experimental child.

Unstructured experiments, as among the children of the Hopi, illustrate similar findings. There is no statistically significant difference in the average age of first walking between those Hopi children raised for months on a cradle board and those Hopi infants not so restrained.[26]

However, other studies suggest a degree of caution in assuming that an infant will develop normal motor skills if his freedom of exercise is seriously curtailed in certain ways. Dennis found that institutionalized babies in crowded places who did not have an opportunity to get off their backs in their cribs, were distinctly retarded in their ability to sit, creep, stand and walk. A baby, according to Dennis, cannot learn to creep simply by lying on his back in a crib.[27] In short, interaction is a prerequisite to learning.

Other authorities also have called attention to the necessary reciprocal

[22] Jean Piaget, "How Children Form Mathematical Concepts," *Scientific American* (Nov. 1953), 74–79.

[23] Reported in Jersild, *Child Psychology*, p. 20.

[24] Arnold Gesell and H. Thompson, "Learning and Growth in Identical Infant Twins: An Experimental Study by the Method of Co-Twin Control," *Genetic Psychological Monographs*, VI (1929), 1–24.

[25] M. B. McGraw, *Growth: A Study of Johnny and Jimmy* (New York: Appleton-Century-Crofts, 1935).

[26] W. Dennis, *The Hopi Child* (New York: Appleton-Century-Crofts, 1940).

[27] W. Dennis "Causes of Retardation Among Institutional Children," Hectographed (Brooklyn, N.Y.: Brooklyn College, 1949), 20, p. 137.

relationship between physiological maturation and a favorable, active, and stimulating environmental support. Thompson and Melzack experimented primarily with dogs. Consequently, their work has little specific bearing on human development. However, their experiments bear out a point of view that behavioral interactionists have claimed about humans, namely:

> any animal needs varied sensory stimulation in order to develop normally, just as it needs food and drink. This is a fact that has frequently been neglected by psychologists. It has long been assumed, either explicitly or implicitly, that all behavior is governed by a basic need to minimize tensions and disturbances in order to preserve the stability of the organism. This is evidently not so. Organisms like to be disturbed (as by an exciting novel, climbing a mountain and so on). And indeed they cannot live normally and fully if they are not. Especially during the early, plastic period of life, they must have a good deal of stimulation in their environment. If they do not, they may remain forever immature.[28]

Similarly, the Harlows have demonstrated, using monkeys as well as children as subjects, that learning ability is not purely innate. The "learning how to learn" phenomenon, which the Harlows have demonstrated strongly suggests that the acquisition of problem solving ability is directly related to the development of *learning sets* that are acquired as a result of learning experiences. "All these data," say the Harlows, "indicate that animals, human and subhuman, must learn to think. Thinking does not develop spontaneously as an expression of innate abilities; it is the end result of a long learning process.[29]

Provence and Lipton reported on the similarities and differences in the behavior of infants nurtured in institutions and those nurtured in family situations. The institutionalized babies were able to match the family babies in the maturation of their neurological structures but were not able to fully utilize these maturing systems in their adaptation to life.

> One of the central hypotheses of the study is that adequate development and learning in the first year comes about through an interaction of the infant's inborn maturing systems and the forces of the environment. One of the needs of the baby is that the maturing systems be organized into "action units" in order that they can emerge as functions and be used in his adaptation. Our data reveal that in many aspects of development this organization does not occur in the absence of the variety of stimuli and communications that are a part of mothering. The most important

[28] William R. Thompson and Ronald Melzack, "Early Environment," *Scientific American* (Jan. 1956), 42.
[29] Harry F. Harlow and Margaret K. Harlow, "Learning to Think," *Scientific American* (Aug. 1949), 36–39.

aspect of the infant's environment in his first year is adequate maternal care with all that this implies.[30]

The obvious conclusion for our understanding of child development is that activities dependent upon maturation of structure for their appearance will not appear earlier nor improve significantly as a result of special training alone. However, unless the organism is nurtured and stimulated by appropriate environmental activity, including appropriate maternal care, organic maturation may fail to achieve its full potential. Martin and Stendler arrive at a similar conclusion, ". . . maturation is essential to learning, but proper environmental conditions will insure the development of those kinds of behavior for which the organism is ripe."[31]

Differentiation and Integration in Maturation

The process of maturation progresses from the general to the specific, from the random movements to the well ordered, from the axis outward, from the head downward. These are well established and observable phenomena that each child reveals in his own maturing behavior.

Behavior in the beginning is mass movement. The fetus' movements are organismic from the start; they are, however, random, unrefined, and undifferentiated. Studies of human infants removed by Caesarean section show that the random mass movements of these early months of life precede the more specific reflex units of the latter months.[32] By birth the child is still refining his motor activities as growth of specific muscles and reflexes makes that possible. We have already described the maturation sequence that has been carefully observed and recorded for children in general. This process is from the whole to the part, from the random to the orderly, and from the general to the specific. Maturation and differentiation develop from central to peripheral movements, as for example, the child can use his shoulder muscles before he can use his wrist. The use of fingers in holding a spoon comes still later. Maturation behavior proceeds along the physiological gradient, beginning in the head and progressing throughout the organism in the direction of the feet. Not only is this true of motor development; it is equally true for the learning process involving mental and emotional maturity. William James's description of the baby's world as a "great big blooming buzzing confusion," becomes in time, in a normal and healthy environment, orderly and reliable phenomena.

---

[30] Sally Provence and Rose C. Lipton, *Infants in Institutions* (New York: International Universities Press, 1962), p. 161.

[31] William E. Martin and Celia B. Stendler, *Child Development* (New York: Harcourt, Brace & Co., 1953), p. 40.

[32] Gardner Murphy, *Personality, A Biosocial Approach to Origins and Structure* (New York: Harper & Brothers, 1947), p. 63.

Maturation Is Not Uniform for All Children

While the authorities have observed and plotted the sequence of maturational development in children, there are wide individual differences of growth within those norms.[33] The individuality of child development has been observed by Gesell, Ilg,[34] and Thompson,[35] among others, who have recorded the significant variation of rates of maturation for individual children. Meredith observed eighteen anthropometric measures on boys ranging in age from birth to eighteen years of age.[36] He found wide physical differences in physical measurements of children of the same age. The heaviest two-year old in his study weighed more than the lightest eight-year old; and the heaviest eight-year old youngster was about the same weight as the lightest boy of eighteen years.

These differences in rate of physical development become a significant cultural variable for the infant whose physique at a particular time may differ from the norm of his family or play group. Kagan and Moss, in a fourteen year longitudinal study, investigated the life histories of 71 infants and reported a relationship between infant physique and certain later adult personality characteristics. They hypothesized that a child with a low muscle mass might be predisposed to adopt a passive posture toward his social world (might withdraw from attack or avoid strange new social situations), and that in future encounters with the environment might exaggerate these initial responses. Their investigation presented evidence that suggests that there is an association between such passivity in adulthood and slight body form and low muscle mass during the first three years of life.

> Boys with small muscle mass are likely to have more difficulty perfecting the gross motor and self-defense skills encouraged and rewarded by young boys and, therefore, less likely to gain acceptance by the same sex peers. Moreover, a boy with little muscle and small frame perceives that he deviates markedly from the culture's definition of a masculine physique, and he is apt to anticipate difficulty in obtaining acceptance from men and love from women.[37]

The child who develops rapidly for his age, who is stronger, more agile, taller, heavier than his associates of the same age, is treated differently from the child of normal or subnormal development. Those people

[33] Harold W. Bernard, *Human Development in Western Culture* (Boston: Allyn & Bacon, 1962), p. 71.

[34] Gesell and Ilg, *Infant and Child in the Culture of To-day.*

[35] George G. Thompson, *Child Psychology* (London: George Harrap & Co., 1952), Ch. II.

[36] H. V. Meredith, "The Rhythm of Physical Growth," *University of Iowa Studies in Child Welfare*, XI, No. 3 (1935).

[37] Jerome Kagan and Howard A. Moss, *Birth to Maturity* (New York: John Wiley & Sons, 1962), p. 276.

who are a part of his affective other may, because of his physical maturity, extend or endow him with qualities of leadership which he accepts as his own. The writer is acquainted with a young man whose early years were characterized by physical development that outdistanced that of his companions of similar age. Because he was larger, he was a better athlete and was more often than not chosen as the captain of the sandlot and school teams. Looking at himself through his interpretations of his friends' ideas of him, he began to accept for himself the status of the robust leader and played the appropriate roles. By adolescence, youngsters of his same age had caught up with him in physical development and he no longer had the edge over most of them in physical stature and agility. Nevertheless, he had so long played the role of the athletic leader, the aggressive leader, that it was difficult for him to think of himself in any other light. A shift in social status was not accompanied by an appropriate shift in social role. Although this youngster was endowed with more than average mental and scholastic ability, he tended to select friends and business acquaintances as an adult that supported his concept of himself as a robust personality rather than as a professional man. Under other circumstances of maturational development or in a cultural setting where athletic prowess is less highly esteemed, he might have conceived of himself as a scientist, clergyman, lawyer, and so forth.

The Integrating and Patterning Functions of Maturation

Whereas physical maturation proceeds by differentation and progressive economy of movement, a patterning and integration of physical behavior is being accomplished at the same time. At the same time that mass activity is becoming specific and random movements are becoming particular, organization of elements of behavior is taking place. Both differentiation and integration are concomitant functions. Murphy divides the maturation process into three levels:

1. A level of global, undifferentiated mass activity.
2. A level of differentiated parts, each acting more or less autonomously.
3. A level of integrated action based upon interdependence of the parts.[38]

The third and highest level of integration can take place only when the first and second levels have been accomplished. Murphy points out that the process is sometimes reversed as in disease or in frustration so that there may be regression to earlier, unorganized behavior.

The patterning of behavior through organization of cells, tissues, and muscles makes possible the particular movements of behavior that enable

[38] Murphy, *Personality: A Biosocial Approach to Origins and Structure*, p. 66.

the organism to adapt itself to its environment. A behavior pattern is defined as "a movement or action which has a more or less definite form."[39] Thus the organization of the visual functions makes it possible for the infant to "take hold of the physical world with his eyes."[40] The development of the eye-hand coordination enables the child to select and manipulate particular objects in the environment. Thus the infant develops patterns of behavior through maturation that enable him to take greater advantage of environmental opportunities and to improve his adjustment to the many stimuli that fall upon his sense organs. The fact that the child's maturation of behavior patterns involves higher nervous centers means that he is not imprisoned in unlearned, stereotyped behavior characteristic of the instincts of lower organisms. The human infant develops behavior patterns that are consistent with his structure and function but which do not so restrict him that he cannot adapt, modify, and improve by exercise, education, and insight the use he makes of his unlearned basic behavior.

Sex-Role Identification As a Determinant of Behavior

An obvious role differentiating category in human relationship is sex typing. Culture assigns particular values to male and female statuses and the occupants of these positions are expected to satisfy the role expectations associated with these categories. Traditional sex-role standards are early communicated to the infant by the members of the child's affective other. Children who are denied the opportunity to clearly identify with these ideal female and masculine standards are likely to suffer confusion of sex role all their lives. In a study of hermaphroditic children it was observed that the critical stage for sex identification occurred prior to the age of two and one-half years. Infants raised as members of one sex and subsequently changed to the other sex were able to achieve this shift in status if it was accomplished prior to this age. If the shift in sex status was attempted after this time it was usually associated with traumatic experiences on the part of the infant.[41]

Many behavior characteristics are clearly associated with and governed by the infant's desire to conform to society's definition of the male or the female model. Sex-role identification is central in directing the selective adoption and maintenance of the appropriate behavior systems. Thus aggression, competitiveness, passivity, dependency or sexuality is governed, in part, by the infant's evaluation of the conformity of behavior with the prevailing sex-role standards.

Kagan and Moss, in their longitudinal study of infants to adults,

---

[39] Gesell and Ilg, *Infant and Child in the Culture of To-day*, p. 16.

[40] Gesell and Ilg, *Infant and Child in the Culture of To-day*, p. 17.

[41] J. Money, J. B. Hampson, and J. L. Hampson, *Archives of Neurology and Psychiatry*, 77 (1957), p. 333.

report that, "Even the children who were reared by families that did not consciously attempt to mold the child in strict concordance with traditional sex-role standards responded to the pressures of the extra-familial environment. The aggressive girls learned to inhibit direct expression of overt aggressive and sexual behavior; the dependent boys gradually placed inhibition on urge toward dependent overtures to others. . . . The individual's desire to mold his overt behavior in concordance with the culture's definition of sex-appropriate responses is a major determinant of the patterns of continuity and discontinuity in his development."[42]

Other investigators have confirmed the relevance of sex-role typing in behavioral choices.[43] These studies indicate that the infant early learns to differentiate and accommodate to the culture's definition of masculine and feminine characteristics. Those who do not so conform are likely to find themselves isolated from conventional peer group relationships.

SOCIALIZATION AND ENCULTURATION

Social growth is achieved by a reciprocal give and take with cultural models that influence the infant's pattern of behavior development.[44] The baby, "bristling with sense organs," only recently emerging from the womb where all his needs were cared for automatically, is very much aware of, and in need of, attention, stimulation, and affection.

The infant first meets the socialization process at those points of

---

[42] Kagan and Moss, *Birth to Maturity*, p. 268.

[43] W. W. Hartup and E. A. Zook, "Sex Role Preferences in Three and Four Year Old Children," *Journal Consulting Psychology*, 24 (1960), 285–302.

[44] There is mounting evidence that learning begins even before birth. Thompson reports that when pregnant mothers were exposed to four types of extreme emotional stress (conditioned anxiety, electric shock during pregnancy, electric shock before pregnancy, adrenalin injection), statistically significant behavioral changes occurred in the offspring. W. R. Thompson, "The Effects of Prenatal Experience on Behavior," in *Proceedings of the Sixteenth International Congress of Psychology* (Amsterdam: North Holland Pub. Co., 1962), pp. 409–410. Montagu reports that "there is good evidence that the mothers' emotional states are, at least in the chemical form, transmitted to the foetus." M. F. Ashley Montagu, "Constitutional & Prenatal Factors in Infant and Child Health," from M. J. E. Senn (ed.) *Symposium on the Healthy Personality* (New York: Josiah Macy, Jr., Foundation, 1950), pp. 148–175. Spelt demonstrated that the foetus in the last two months of pregnancy can be taught to respond to the secondary association of a primary original stimulus. D. K. Spelt, "The Conditioning of the Human Fetus *in Utero*," *Journal of Experimental Psychology*, (1948) 38:338–346. In earlier studies Sontag found that fatigue in the pregnant mother will produce hyperactivity in the foetus. Mothers who suffer severe emotional stress in later pregnancy, according to Sontag, generally have babies who are hyperactive, irritable and have feeding problems. Such a baby, says Sontag, "is to all intents and purposes a neurotic infant when he is born—the result of an unsatisfactory foetal environment. In this instance he has not had to wait until childhood for a bad home situation or other causes to make him neurotic. It has been done for him before he has even seen the light of day." L. W. Sontag, "Differences in Modifiability of Fetal Behavior and Physiology, *Psychosomatic Medicine* (1944) 6:151–154.

biological need that are not automatically cared for by the reflex actions of the organism. No creature in all evolution is so dependent upon any other organism as is the infant upon the members of the family who care for him. The parents induct him into the rhythm of the demands of the adult world, and more particularly into the world of the immediate family, with its particular attitudes, habits, and needs. In this connection, Gorer, in his essay on our national character, makes the point that, "Societies continue, though their personnel changes." This, according to Gorer, is so only because of "the present generation of children who, as adults will have habits similar to their parents."[45]

Parent–Child Relationship

Since the gestation period of humans is about nine months, the infant is not exactly a surprise to the new parents. His coming is usually anticipated with great expectations and preparation for his arrival. Although all cultures do not look upon birth with equal enthusiasm, it frequently is accepted as a happy and memorable event. This attitude of acceptance and readiness of the parents for the new baby is, of course, important for the basic security of the infant.

The infant is met by the personalities of its parents with their expressed and unexpressed personal needs, wishes, and fears. The strengths and weaknesses of the parents as individuals, plus their attitudes towards each other, are part and parcel of the primary culture that molds the child's early behavior patterns. Probably the single most powerful factor in the personality development of the child is the happiness and stability of the primary group environment in which he spends his early years.[46]

"The Children's Charter" adopted by the 1930 White House Conference on Children and Youth, states that every child is entitled to "a home and that love and security which a home provides." But there is a growing class of unwanted American children who are dependent for their existence on institutional care or foster home living. The Child Welfare League estimates conservatively that there are more than 100,000 such children in the country today. Many of these children receive the affectional benefits of well-planned adoptive homes but too often, in spite of the best intentions, some of these children become the victims of dis-

---

[45] G. Gorer, "The Concept of National Character," in J. L. Crammer (ed.), *Science News* (Harmondsworth, Middlesex: Penguin Books, 1950), No. 18, 105–122.

[46] Although in the United States and Canada the home is the agency most frequently employed to socialize and enculturate the child in the early years, it is not the only one. Orphanages, nurseries, foster homes, creches and baby sitters are also utilized, and in the kibbutzim of Israel, the family and home, as we know it, is hardly a fact. *See* Stuart A. Queen *et al. The Family in Various Cultures* (Chicago: J. B. Lippincott Co., 1961).

organized adult behavior. For some children the concept of home is an anachronism as is illustrated in the following case:

> He was barely a year old when his mother tried first to choke him and then kill herself. She was hospitalized and placed under mental observation, and Ralph's father disappeared from home. Ralph was sent to an institution for "temporary" foster care.
>
> As the years went by, his life took on a strange pattern. From the institution, he was moved first to one set of foster parents and then another. Sometimes he was returned to his own home for another chance at living with his mother since adjudged sane. But such stays were brief. Always, for one reason or another, she found an excuse to return him to foster care. Ralph developed an amazing string of symptoms. He set fire in the homes of foster parents, he stole, he soiled his clothing and wet the bed—though he was old enough to go to school— and he began to engage in unnatural sexual experiences with other boys.
>
> He ended up finally in Spurwink School, a center in Portland, Maine, for emotionally disturbed boys. By then he had lived with twelve foster parents and he had been in eleven hospitals and one custodial shelter in seven years. Today at nine, after two years of understanding care by a staff of professionals at the school, Ralph is beginning to trust adults again. But it is unlikely that he will ever return home.[47]

The primary group environment (home, orphanage, kibbutzim) need not be characterized by a high level of education, a high standard of living, or even a large degree of success in meeting its problems, important and desirable as they may be. We mean by a happy and stable primary group one in which there is affection and consideration among the members for each other; one in which the individual members are emotionally secure and mentally healthy. Attitudes are contagious, and a child born into a home where there are anxieties and distrust (or security and fulfillment) is likely to identify with these models in a manner that will make them part of his own repertoire of adaptive techniques. The development of primary affectional and social bonds is less cognitive than emotional. *It is likely that given any kind of strong emotional arousal a young child or animal will become identified with any individual or object with which it is in close contact for any length of time.* Both positive and negative emotions can contribute to a social relationship. In infancy, emotions that might ordinarily be considered punitive may produce an effect similar to more rewarding emotional experiences.

> An animal (and perhaps a person) of any age, exposed to certain individuals or physical surroundings for any length of time, will inevitably become attached to them, the rapidity of the process being governed by the degree of emotional arousal associated with them. I need not dwell on the consequences for human behavior, if this conclusion should

[47] Richard Haitch, "Children in Limbo," *The Nation* (April 6, 1963).

apply to our species as well as to other animals, except to point out that it provides an explanation of certain well-known clinical observations such as the development by neglected children of strong affection for cruel and abusive parents, and the various peculiar affectional relationships that develop between prisoners and jailers, slaves and masters, and so on. Perhaps the general adaptive nature of this mechanism is that since the survival of any member of a highly social species depends upon the rapid development of social relationships, a mechanism has evolved which makes it almost impossible to inhibit the formation of social bonds.[48]

The coming of the first child may be interpreted by one or both parents as the final confirmation of the marriage relationship. Biologically, the sex cycle is complete only when the male sperm successfully fertilizes the female ovum. The parents may feel that with pregnancy any thought of escaping the marriage relationship is now voided by the responsibilities about to ensue and by the demands society will make upon the parents to care for a new citizen. Fortunately, most children are welcomed and wanted, but too frequently the infant is, originally at least, rejected unconsciously or consciously by one or both parents. The male, more frequently than the female, may unintentionally resent the third member of the union who detracts from his single supremacy in his wife's affections. The writers knew of one father who, on the occasion of the birth of his first child, began using intoxicating liquors to excess and continued to do so all the while his many children were growing up. This practice of intermittent inebriation continued until the last child had grown up and left the home, at which time he reverted to his earlier practice of sobriety. At no time, apparently, was he consciously aware of the relationship between his drinking problem and the presence of children in the home.

Role Learning in Infancy

George Herbert Mead described at length the ease with which normal healthy infants learned their particular place in the family constellation. Mead proposed that this role learning is accomplished in association with the parents or surrogates in which both infant and parent simultaneously learn his or her role in relationship to the other.[49] Cumming and Cumming have described this process in the following perceptive statement:

When a boy and his father are together, the father is constantly revealing through various cues the kinds of behavior he thinks appropriate for a son. The son, in order to be able to respond appropriately to his

[48] J. P. Scott, "Critical Periods in Behavioral Development," *Science*, 38 (Nov. 30, 1962), No. 3544, p. 954.

[49] G. H. Mead, *Mind, Self, and Society* (Chicago: University of Chicago Press, 1934), p. 150.

father, must learn a good deal about his father's motives and feelings. His ability to perceive what his father expects of him in any situation means that he has also learned something of the father role. By the same token, the father relives his earlier role of son to his own father in the course of interacting with his child. In this way, the two come to understand each other and to act firmly in their own roles while "taking the role of the other" in order to understand the interaction.[50]

This dual process, in which both members of an interacting pair learn each other's role, is ultimately extended to include the *significant other*. Thus, a child must learn not only his own role in relationship to his parents, but he must learn also the respective roles of his siblings and their role relationships to each other as well as to him. The child thereby is able, by symbolically *playing the role of the others* to predict what the other members of the family are likely to do in particular situations. Thus, by anticipatory role behavior, his actions become appropriate and meaningful both to himself and to the other members of his primary group. By this means he is able to locate himself in the family of which he is a part and thereby achieve a working conception of what he is to do and what the other members of the group can expect of him and he of them. This process is of course soon projected beyond the primary family group to the neighborhood play group, the schoolroom and ultimately into secondary group relationships in the broader community. But it is in the initial relationships with his own parents that he begins to learn who he is and what his role is to be in relationship to other people. Thus, he learns to develop a role repertoire by internalizing the attitudes, feelings, and actions of the various adult models he experiences, first at home and later in the community.

Sigmund Freud in the posthumously published *Outline of Psychoanalysis* (1940) referred to "the common assertion that the child is psychologically the father of the man and that the events of the first years are of paramount importance for his whole subsequent life." He further concluded that the central experience of this period of childhood is the infant's relation to his mother. Freud's teachings have influenced the thinking of behavioral scientists for two generations and have caused researchers to stress inappropriate mothering (and more recently, maternal deprivation) as a major cause of later personality aberrations. Whereas mother identification is a necessary primary relationship in infancy, each child, as he matures, normally achieves an identification with the parent of the same sex. This identification is exhibited in the child's emulation of the parent's behavior, feelings, and attitudes. Many studies have tended to emphasize the importance of personality for-

[50] John Cumming and Elaine Cumming, *Ego and Milieu* (New York: Atherton Press, 1962), p. 20.

mation in relationship to one parent only—minimizing the importance of the social matrix of the family. Freud saw the family social system as consisting not exclusively as the mother-child dyad, but as a father–mother–child relationship. Winch has pointed out that, "The structure of the nuclear family is of crucial relevance to the identification of children."[51] As an example, Winch cites the experience of Negro families that, since the days of slavery, have been characterized by a relatively high incidence of absence of fathers and the presence of the maternal grandmother. The relevance of this familial structure for the identification of Negro children was noted in an earlier study by Frazier as follows:

> The dependence of the child upon the mother, who is the supreme authority in the household, often creates a solidarity of feeling and sentiment that makes daughters reluctant to leave home with their husbands and brings sons back from their wanderings. . . the mothers on their part show equally strong attachment for their grown sons and daughters.[52]

Thus, in many Negro families, the grandmothers were highly esteemed as repositories of wisdom and as the most responsible members of families—the ones who kept "the generations together when father and even mothers abandoned their offspring."[53]

Clinical evidence indicates that the child's perceptions of the father as well as the mother are an important variable in personality development,[54] and that the fantasy lives of infants separated from their fathers were less masculine oriented and less aggressive than were the fantasies of children whose fathers were not absent.[55]

Earlier in the chapter we pointed out the changing patterns of parental role responsibility in the American culture with reference to child rearing habits and attitudes. Urie Bronfenbrenner raises a question concerning the kinds of children that develop in families where the father plays an affectionate rather than a disciplinarian role and where both parents share equally the disciplinary function. He offers one answer to this question from his own research as follows:

> A tentative answer to this question is supplied by a preliminary analysis of our data in which the relation between parental role structure and adolescent behavior was examined with controls for the family's social

[51] Robert F. Winch, *The Modern Family* (New York: Holt, Rinehart and Winston, 1952), p. 11.

[52] E. F. Frazier, *The Negro Family in the United States* (Chicago: University of Chicago Press, 1939), p. 144.

[53] Frazier, *The Negro Family in the United States*, p. 150.

[54] Eve Jones, *Raising Your Child in a Fatherless Home* (New York: The Free Press of Glencoe, 1963).

[55] George R. Bach, "Father Fantasies and Father Typing in Father–Separated Children," *Child Development*, 17 (1946), 63–80.

class position. The results of this analysis were summarized as follows:
. . . Both responsibility and leadership are fostered by the relatively
greater salience of the parent of the same sex. . . Boys tend to be more
responsible when the father rather than the mother is the principal
disciplinarian; girls are more dependable when the mother is the major
authority figure. . . In short, boys thrive in a patriarchal context, girls
in a matriarchal. . . The most dependent and least dependable adolescents describe family arrangements that are neither patriarchal nor
matriarchal but equalitarian. To state the issue in more provocative
form, our data suggest that the democratic family, which for so many
years has been held up and aspired to as a model by professionals and
enlightened laymen, tends to produce people who "do not take initiative," "look to others for direction and decision," and "cannot be
counted on to fulfill obligations."[56]

Other writers, for somewhat different reasons, are also concerned
about the changing role relationships between adults and their children
and the impact of this change upon the self-esteem of the latter, although
such contentions are not yet supported by published research.[57]

How mothers and fathers feel about their children is of special interest
to the social psychologist and, as Thoma has pointed out, "comparative
studies help us distinguish between universal and culturally patterned
responses." As an example of such cross-cultural studies, Thoma compared the degree to which Norwegian, Indonesian, and United States
mothers tended to accept their children's emotional deviation (as defined
in terms of their respective societies).[58] Each mother had a child between
eight and ten years of age and the child was defined by the school authorities in each society as having an emotional problem. The results are
reported as follows: "The Indonesian mothers in the sample are more
accepting of their children recognized as having emotional problems than
the United States mothers . . . the Indonesian mother represented by the
sample is less threatened by the perceived criticism of others and her
feelings around the problem are invested in the child rather than in
herself."[59] The Norwegian mothers, in contrast with the United States
group, were significantly more accepting of their deviant children and
less threatened by the criticism of others. These findings are consistent
with other investigations which reveal a similar parental anxiety and ego

---

[56] Bronfenbrenner, "The Changing American Child—A Speculative Analysis,"
pp. 6–18.

[57] Edgar Z. Friedenberg, The Vanishing Adolescent (New York: Dell Publishing
Co., 1959).

[58] Elizabeth Thoma, "A Comparative Culture Study of Mothers' Attitudes," in
Proceedings of the Sixteenth International Congress of Psychology (Amsterdam: North
Holland Pub. Co., 1962), pp. 291–295.

[59] Thoma, "A Comparative Culture Study of Mothers' Attitudes," p. 293.

involvement by the parents of middle class American children in the success and happiness of their children's lives.[60]

The socialization and enculturation process transmitted by parents meets the maturational development in such fundamental physiological training as feeding, toilet training, and cleanliness. Such training usually falls to the mother who controls absolutely the education of the child in these phenomena which Cameron calls "visceral ethics." The mother can reward or punish in terms of affection, kissing, disapproval—all of which become significant gestures for the infant. The infant learns early to recognize these gestures even though he may not be ready or agreeable to obeying them. It is important to recognize how the mother's own personality becomes involved in this training. Says Cameron:

> The effects of these early lessons in visceral ethics. . . are never quite lost. They become especially obvious in the behavior disorders. In both neurosis and psychosis one finds endless confusion of cleanliness with godliness, of genital function and problems of evacuation with social wickedness, of eating with pregnancy and social sin. One encounters disguised visceral ethics in the worried or self-righteous preoccupation over diet, digestion, elimination and reproductive rhythms that so many hypochondriacs show. They are more afraid of malfunction and more proud of good function, than the circumstances of their adult life can possibly justify. The same criticism can be made of many ritualistic performances seen in the compulsive disorders. In terms of adult verbal logic they seem aimless and bizarre. The neurotic or psychotic person who is caught in this type of ethical confusion does not suspect and cannot recognize its infantile and early childhood origins. But to the student of behavior pathology its genesis is early in the child's misunderstanding of cultural demands made upon him very early, and quite emotionally in the name of right and wrong.[61]

Training in these particular phenomena, related as they are to biological needs, is more likely to persist than are lessons learned in terms of acquired habits that are not so closely related to physiological development. Hence, there are relatively fewer personality confusions over training (enculturation) in music lessons, social dancing, or learning the multiplication table. These latter are not so closely related to emotional or physical phenomena, nor are they learned so early, nor in such an intimate way with the parent.

We can see in these early training habits not only the development of physical habits that will be beneficial to the child and acceptable to the

---

[60] Davis and Havighurst, "Social Class and Color Difference in Child Rearing," *American Sociological Review* (Dec. 1946); Arnold W. Green, "The Middle Class Male Child and Neurosis," *American Sociological Review*, XI (1946), 31–41.

[61] Norman A. Cameron, *The Psychology of Behavior Disorders* (New York: Houghton Mifflin, 1947), p. 623.

demands of the larger society; but we also recognize that the child's moral development, no less than other aspects of his social development, emerges out of just such an intimate and spontaneous teaching relationship between parent and child. Infant feeding is only one of the ways in which a mother makes herself know to her baby. Infant feeding involves more than the incorporation of food, as can be seen in the works of Erikson, an eminent child psychologist. The infant's first encounter with society, according to Erikson, occurs

> when the newborn, now deprived of his symbiosis with the mother's body, is put to the breast. His inborn and more or less coordinated ability to take in by mouth meets the breast's and the mother's and the society's more or less coordinated ability and intention to feed him and to welcome him. At this point he lives through and loves with his mouth; and the mother lives through and loves with her breasts. For her this is a late and complicated accomplishment, highly dependent on the love she can be sure of from others, on the self-esteem that accompanies the act of nursing and on the response of the newborn. To him the oral zone, however, is only the focus of a first and general mode of approach, namely, *incorporation.* He is now dependent on the delivery of 'material' of all kinds directly to the receptive doors of his organism. For a few weeks at least, he can only react if and when material is brought into his field. As he is willing and able to suck on appropriate objects and to swallow whatever appropriate fluids they emit, he is soon also willing and able to 'take in' with his eyes what enters his visual field. (As if nearly ready also to hold on to things, he opens and closes his fist when properly stimulated.) His tactile senses too seem to take in what feels good.[62]

Critical Stages of Learning

Critical *periods* of learning are more appropriately called critical *stages* of learning when used with reference to humans. This phenomenon is best illustrated in the primitive imprinting common in the socialization of many animals. Imprinting refers to the process of primary socialization in which a young animal achieves certain emotional identifications that establish basic and lasting behavior patterns and relationships. These primary social bonds are effective and durable when they occur at certain optimal and critical periods in behavioral development. This phenomenon may be illustrated as follows:

> A number of years ago I was given a female lamb taken from its mother at birth. My wife and I raised it on the bottle for the first ten days of life and then placed it out in the pasture with a small flock of domestic sheep. As might have been expected from folklore, the lamb became attached to people and followed the persons who fed it. More surpris-

[62] Erik H. Erikson, *Childhood and Society* (New York: W. W. Norton, 1963), rev. ed., p. 71.

ingly, the lamb remained independent of the rest of the flock when we restored it to the pasture. Three years later it was still following an independent grazing pattern. In addition, when it was mated and had lambs of its own it became a very indifferent mother, allowing its off-spring to nurse but showing no concern when the lamb moved away with the other members of the flock. Since following the flock is such a universal characteristic of normal sheep, I was impressed by the extensive and permanent modification of this behavior that resulted from a brief early experience.[63]

The phenomenon of imprinting has been experimentally demonstrated by many researchers. Berelson and Steiner describe imprinting as an adaptive process that combines an innate behavioral pattern with the influence of experience: the response is wired in and constant, but the specific object that will elicit it is established during one short but critical experience shortly after birth.[64] It is also assumed to be self-reinforcing. Imprinting is also effective only at certain optimal and critical periods.

It has not yet been demonstrated that imprinting is a phenomenon that characterizes the primary social learning of human behavior. However, there is evidence that in human beings there are stages of development at which time certain identifications and relationships can be achieved and which, if denied at that particular time, may be permanently lost or at least modified. Some students consider the effects of early social deprivation to be comparable to the process of imprinting in animals. According to Gray, imprinting occurs in humans by means of an immutable bond formed between the infant and other humans between the ages of six weeks and six months—consequently serious social deprivation (or conversely, social enrichment) at this particular time may have lasting effects.[65] Harlow's monkeys that were isolated socially from birth for six months or longer, never were able to achieve normal play or heterosexual relationships with their peers. Harlow comments:

Our first few experiments in the total isolation of these animals would thus appear to have bracketed what may be the critical period of development during which social experience is necessary for normal behavior in later life. . . The indications are that six months of isolation will render the animals permanently inadequate. Since the rhesus monkey is more mature than the human infant at birth and grows four times more rapidly, this is equivalent to two or three years for the human child. On the other hand, there is reason to believe that the effects of shorter periods of early isolation, perhaps 60 to 90 days or even more, are clearly reversible. This would be equivalent to about six months in the

[63] Scott, "Critical Periods in Behavioral Development," p. 949.

[64] Bernard Berelson and Gary A. Steiner, *Human Behavior* (New York: Harcourt, Brace & World, 1964), p. 41.

[65] Philip H. Gray, "Theory and Evidence of Imprinting in Human Infants," *Journal of Psychology*, 46 (1958), 155–166.

development of the human infant. The time probably varies with the individual and with the experiences to which it is exposed once it is removed from isolation. Beyond a brief period of neonatal grace, however, the evidence suggests that every additional week or month of social deprivation increasingly imperils social development in the rhesus monkey. Case studies of children reared in impersonal institutions or in homes with indifferent mothers or nurses show a frightening comparability. The child may remain relatively unharmed through the first six months of life. But from this time on the damage is progressive and cumulative. By one year of age he may sustain enduring emotional scars and by two years many children have reached the point of no return.[66]

One of the earliest experiments in human social deprivation occurred in the thirteenth century when Frederick II became curious about the language development of infants.

> . . . he wanted to find out what kind of speech and what manner of speech children would have when they grew up if they spoke to no one beforehand. So he bade foster mothers and nurses to suckle the children, to bathe and wash them, but in no way to prattle with them or to speak to them, for he wanted to learn whether they would speak the Hebrew language, which was the oldest, or Greek, or Latin, or Arabic, or perhaps the language of their parents, of whom they had been born. But he laboured in vain, because the children all died. For they could not live without the petting and joyful faces and loving words of their foster mothers. And so the songs are called "swaddling songs," which a woman sings while she is rocking the cradle, to put the child to sleep, and without them a child sleeps badly and has no rest.[67]

Infants deprived of normal adult affectional relationships in the first months of life appear to be permanently handicapped emotionally.[68] This finding was confirmed in a study of children separated from their mothers at birth or almost immediately thereafter and institutionalized for the first two to four years of life. The author makes this comment regarding these children: ". . . the chances of re-educating (these) severely hospitalized children are at present viewed with great pessimism. It appears that the condition cannot be cured either by psychotherapy or by educational measures. A considerable number of inmates of detention homes for juvenile delinquents and many adult criminals are people who were deprived of maternal care in early childhood. Others, who were neglected and unable to establish a reliable emotional relationship during the first year of life tend to fail, especially as marriage partners and in the roles

[66] Harry F. Harlow and Margaret Kuenne Harlow, "Social Deprivation in Monkeys," *Scientific American* (Nov. 1962), 8.

[67] J. R. Stone and J. Church, *Childhood and Adolescence* (New York: Random House, 1957), p. 3.

[68] Provence and Lipton, *Infants in Institutions*, p. 160.

of mothers and fathers. The responsibility to avoid hospitalization of children under public care lies with the community."[69]

A review of the literature leads to the conclusion that certain roles are learned by the infant at determinable ages and, once these relationships have been established, it becomes increasingly difficult to modify this learning. Similarly, what has been learned up to a particular point becomes critical for whatever learning is to follow. Jersild refers to the "snowballing effect" of significant early experiences in early life.

A child who is slow in learning to read, and who is pressured or ridiculed, may become discouraged about school and about himself, and what began as a moderately slight handicap may become a very serious one. A youngster who early in life becomes suspicious and distrustful of others because of neglect or abuse may develop attitudes which make it hard for him, as time goes on, to develop friendly relations with friendly people. An adolescent boy who is an "early maturer" at a time when size and athletic ability have a strong influence on a boy's popularity may continue, even after others have caught up with him in their physical development, to harvest the benefits of greater self-confidence and poise.[70]

In the very early stages of the developing embryo, a cell can be transplanted to a new location and it will develop appropriately and conformingly in terms of the character of its new milieu. However, if this same cell is transplanted at a later stage, it will not take on the character of its new environment, but will maintain its original integrity and thus create a structural abnormality. Both the location and the time sequence are important in developing a proper relationship among the various organs. As Stockard has pointed out, there is a particular time sequence for the development of each organ, and any organ which misses its time of ascendency is not only doomed as an entity; it endangers at the same time the whole hierarchy of organs.[71] The failure of a particular aspect of a growing system to appear at the critical time not only results in the temporary decrease in the potency of that organ but makes it impossible for that part to again become ascendent in the structural relationship. Thus, its effectiveness is permanently changed.

A similar organizing process may characterize primary social learning. There are some interesting parallels in the growth system of embryonic

[69] Lotte Schenk—Danzinger, "Problems of Social Adaptation of Children Deprived of Maternal Care in Earliest Childhood," in *Proceedings of the Sixteenth International Congress of Psychology.* (Amsterdam: North Holland Publishing Co., 1962), pp. 394–397.

[70] Jersild, *Child Psychology,* p. 24.

[71] C. H. Stockard, *The Physical Basis of Personality,* (New York: W. W. Norton, 1931), p. 138; T. Dobzhansky, *The Biological Basis of Human Freedom* (New York: Columbia University Press, 1956).

cells and the achievement of behavioral differentiation in organisms. It can be hypothesized that there is a general organizing principle here which requires that once a system becomes organized, whether in cell structure or in behavioral differentiation, it becomes increasingly difficult to modify or reorganize the system. Once a system is set, or established, it resists further reorganization. Moreover, modification of existing organization systems can be accomplished only during the active growing processes leading up to closure of the system. It is this freezing of the organizational structure that makes crucial the critical stages of development and learning in infancy and childhood.

The significance of critical stages for learning primary social behavior has also been observed by psychoanalytic researchers. The early psychoanalysts identified certain regions of the body's orifices as zones of psychological significance for emotional health and illness. These zones involve oral, anal, and genital development and certain modes of behavior are associated with each stage of their growth. The normal, healthy child evolves through these successive stages in a manner that is both satisfying and reinforcing. Each stage represents particular achievements that make possible the emergence of the next level of self-realization. Each stage is critical for the developing child. Children who have not mastered a particular level of achievement may become fixated and dependent at that stage in their development. Such children continue to grow physically but remain trapped at a limited level of emotional development. Emotional afflictions may be associated with fixations or regressions to particular infantile zones and stages. Whiting and Child's cross-cultural study of the relationship of childhood experiences to adult behavior in various cultures is organized about the assumption that personality development is to be examined in terms of these fixations: "Psychoanalytic theory has suggested that extreme frustration or extreme indulgence of a particular form of behavior in childhood may produce a continuing fixation of interest on that particular form of behavior.[72] Examples would be oral aggression, dependency, or any of the ego defenses. A fixation can, of course, take any form and be associated with any mechanism.

> Addicts, for example, depend as the baby once did, on the incorporation by mouth or skin of substances which makes them feel both physically satiated and emotionally restored. But they are not aware that they yearn to be babies again. Only as they whine and boast and challenge are their disappointed and babyish souls revealed. Manic-depressive patients, on the other hand, feel hopelessly empty, without substance, or full of something bad and hostile that needs to be destroyed, or again so permeated with sudden goodness that their sense of power and exuberance knows no bounds and accepts no limitations. Yet they do not

[72] Whiting and Child, *Child Training and Personality*, p. 315.

know either the source or the nature of all these inner goodnesses and badnesses. Hysterics, if they are women, act as if strangely victimized, attacked, and revolted by things and yet fascinated by them, while genitally frigid, they are preoccupied with events which, on analysis, dramatize the women's inceptive role. They are unconsciously obsessed with their sexual role, although (or because) it became unacceptable far back in childhood. All these tormented people, then, whether addicted, depressed, or inhibited, have somehow failed to integrate one or another of the infantile stages, and they defend themselves against these infantile patterns—stubbornly, wastefully, unsuccessfully.[73]

Whether these critical stages of socialization are defined formally as in psychoanalysis, or are described operationally as in the work of behaviorists, it is important to recognize and more clearly identify these sensitive areas in infant and child development. With increasing knowledge it may be possible to speed up or delay the socialization process depending upon the particular needs and growth rate of each child. The postponement of closure in the learning process may avoid premature crystallization of the organizational system at an immature level of achievement.

Scott believes there are some benefits to be gained by modifying the onset and termination of these critical stages in infant and child development:

> . . . since the development of fear responses limits the period of primary socialization, we can deliberately extend the period by reducing fear reactions, either by psychological methods or by the use of tranquilizing drugs. Or, if it seems desirable, we can increase the degree of dependency of a child or pet animal by purposely increasing his emotional reactions during the critical period. Again, if infantile stimulation is desirable, parents can be taught to provide it in appropriate amounts at the proper time.[74]

Allport, Orlansky, and Knapp, as well as others are not inclined to accept completely these hypotheses concerning the finality and irreversibility of particular traumatic experiences in infancy.[75] Orlansky, in a comprehensive review of the experimental studies of infant nurture, arrived at two conclusions: (1) that it has not been demonstrated that the personality configuration of the child is necessarily established in the first few months of life; and (2) that the particular manner in which

---

[73] Erikson, *Childhood and Society*, p. 61.

[74] Scott, "Critical Periods in Behavioral Development," p. 957.

[75] Gordon Allport, *Pattern and Growth in Personality* (New York: Holt, Rinehart & Winston, 1961); Harold Orlansky, "Infant Care and Personality," *Psychological Bulletin*, XLVI (Jan. 1949), No. 1, 38; Robert H. Knapp, "The Psychology of Personality," in *The Behavioral Science Today*, Bernard Berelson (ed.) (New York: Berec Book, 1963); Bernard Berelson and Gary A. Steiner, *Human Development* (New York: Harcourt Brace & World, 1964).

parents handle the conditioning of primary physiological activities is not nearly so important as is the total situation in which the discipline takes place.

> We conclude that the rigidity of character structuring during the first year or two of life has been exaggerated by some authorities and that the events of childhood and later years are of great importance in reinforcing or changing the character structure tentatively formed during infancy.
>   . . . we are led to reject the thesis that specific nursing disciplines have a specific, invariant psychological impact upon the child. Instead, it appears that the effect of a particular discipline can be determined only from knowledge of the parental attitudes associated with it, the value which the culture places upon that discipline, the organic constitution of the infant, and the entire socio-cultural situation in which the individual is located. In short, it is contended that personality is not the resultant of instinctual infantile libidinal drives mechanically channeled by parental disciplines, but rather that it is a dynamic product of the interaction of a unique organism undergoing maturation and a unique physical and social environment.[76]

Pursuing the same argument, Pearson, in an early study at the Philadelphia Child Guidance Clinic investigated seventy-two problem children with reference (1) to their visceral training, and (2) to the relationships existing between the child and parents.[77] The object of the study was to determine whether physiological events such as length of nursing period, duration and method of weaning, nature of toilet training, health of mother during pregnancy, nature of delivery, and so forth, were more or less significant in the personality development of these children than the social-psychological influence as indicated by the child's birth order, attitudes of each parent toward the pregnancy and the birth of the child, and the attitudes of parents toward the child and toward each other. Pearson's conclusions were:

> . . . the parental attitudes exert a more important influence on the formation of the child's personality than actual events. . . There is no question that the physical situations of the child's life bear a definite relation to the formation of his personality, but the number of associated etiological factors renders it impossible to consider any single situation as causative. This study does indicate, however, the marked importance of parental attitudes. . . The child forms most of his ideas about the world of humanity from his impressions of his parents and their attitude to him. . . (The child's relationships with his parents) affect the formation of his personality to a far greater degree than the

[76] Orlansky, *Infant Care and Personality*, p. 39.
[77] G. Pearson, "Some Personality Factors in the Formation of Personality," *American Journal of Orthopsychiatry*, I (1931), 284–291.

length of his birth or the duration of his breast feeding. The events of a child's life enhance and crystallize the parental attitude toward him. . . and the child reacts to the parental attitudes through its association with the events of his life rather than to the events themselves.[78]

Knapp, in a historical review of child development theories, reports that the finality and irrevocability of childhood experiences is much less certain today because of the failure of researchers to confirm the central importance of these early experiences. "There is a growing amount of evidence to indicate that significant personality changes may occur in adolescence and even in maturity, and that, in part, the capacity for such changes may depend upon maturation."[79]

None of these investigators questions the major significance of the primary years in developing human nature, but several students of the subject do believe that research studies indicate that the infant's later experiences have the power to interact with his personal variables in such a manner as will confirm or vitiate many aspects of the earlier learning.

The Sibling Relationship

The decisive influence in personality development ascribed to the parent–child relationship should not blind us to the importance of other primary social bonds in infancy. Infant to infant contacts can also play a significant part in determining the peer relationships and the sexual role of the adult personality. Although we do not wish to dwell on animal research in this writing, it should be noted that Harlow was able to demonstrate that infant rhesus monkeys, motherless, or raised by inadequate mothers were able to achieve normal social bonds when exposed during early infancy to sufficient infant to infant interaction.

Our observations sustain the significance of the maternal relation, particularly in facilitating the interaction of the infant with other infants. But at the same time we have found compelling evidence that opportunity for infant–infant interaction under optimal conditions may fully compensate for lack of mothers, at least in so far as infant–infant social and heterosexual relations are concerned. It seems possible, even likely —that the infant–mother affectional system is dispensable, whereas the infant–infant system is the sine qua non for later adjustment in all spheres of monkey life.[80]

The brothers and sisters of the infant play a very important part in bringing patterns of culture to him. These siblings are, of course, also acquiring behavior patterns of their own at the same time that they are

---

[78] Pearson, *Some Personality Factors in the Formation of Personality*, pp. 284–291.

[79] Knapp, "The Psychology of Personality," p. 163.

[80] Harlow and Harlow, *Learning to Think*, p. 38.

influencing the behavior of their contemporaries. This interaction of culture among children extends to other youngsters not members of the immediate family, and their influence, too, is significant, but usually not until after the first eighteen months or so of infancy. Shirley has observed that infants up to forty-three weeks of age do not pay very much attention to each other at baby parties. Their attention is attracted primarily to seeking and acquiring toys and manipulating them, crying, and smiling. Infants in nursery school concentrate more on the equipment and playthings than they do on other children.[81] "Two year olds in nursery school bump into one another and sometimes congregate in one spot, but they are usually bent on their own private play enterprises."[82]

The attitudes a child develops toward himself are determined in part by the position accorded him by the other members of the family. For example, a dull child born into a family of brilliant siblings is likely to develop different attitudes toward himself than the dull child brought up among brothers and sisters whose mental capacity is similar to his own.

In a large family the children have many opportunities to play many kinds of different roles in relationship to one another. One of the most conspicuous forms of specialization of roles among the siblings in a family results from the order of their birth. Bossard reasons that the relationships among the members of the family are influenced at every turn by the sequence of sibling birth order.[83]

Only children obviously suffer from a lack of sibling playmates and thus miss the richness of experience that can come only from various social relationships with older and younger brothers and sisters. Except for the youngest child, the *only* child is the only member of the family who never experiences the arrival of a younger sibling and potential rival. His place in the family is never challenged by the admission of a new family member. In this regard, Winnicott makes the following observations:

> One thing the only child especially lacks is the experience of finding hate turn up; the child's own hate, as the new baby threatens what seemed to be a settled and safe relation to the mother and father. It is so usual as to be called normal when a child is upset at the birth of a new one. The child's first comment is not usually polite: "It's got a face like a tomato"; in fact parents should feel relieved when they hear the direct expression of conscious dislike, and even violent hate, at the birth of a new child. This hate will gradually give way to love as the

[81] Mary M. Shirley, *The First Two Years: A Study of 25 Babies* (Minneapolis: University of Minnesota Press, 1933).

[82] Ruth Strang, *An Introduction to Child Study* (New York: The Macmillan Co., 1959), 4th ed., p. 65.

[83] James H. S. Bossard, *Sociology of Child Development* (New York: Harper & Brothers, 1954), p. 108.

new infant develops into a human being, who can be played with, and, of whom one can be proud. The first reaction, however, can be one of fear and hate, and the impulse may be to put the new baby in the dust-bin. I think that it is a very valuable experience for a child to find that the younger brother or sister for whom love is beginning to develop is the same as the new baby who was hated a few weeks ago and actually wished away. For all children a big difficulty is the legitimate expression of hate, and the only child's relative lack of opportunity for expressing the aggressive side of his nature is a serious thing. Children who grow up together play games of all kinds, and so have a chance to come to terms with their own aggressiveness, and they have valuable opportunities for discovering on their own that they do mind when they really hurt someone they love.[84]

The oldest child begins his life with the status of an only child but this position changes with the birth of a sibling. The oldest child is usually reported to be the more conservative, inner directed, and serious.[85] He is more likely to exhibit qualities of leadership and is more often reported in Who's Who than are the other siblings. Bossard and Boll report that the oldest child in large family groups is more likely to be dissatisfied with his family position than are the middle or youngest children.[86] The following report from their files is illustrative:

I do not like being the oldest member of a family of six children. All my life I have been set up as an example for them to follow, and knowing this has made me overly conscious of all I fail to accomplish. . . . As the oldest child I have had to pave the way for my other brothers and sisters, and of course this means my parents were much stricter with me in childhood than they are on the other children now. It seems that automatically a certain responsibility falls upon you and I am ashamed to admit that at times I bitterly resented this responsibility. One thing I am certain I am not, is spoiled. That is why I would not like to be the youngest child in a family, because I have seen how spoiled my sister became before the baby was born, and even now she expects to be pampered as she was then.[87]

The in-between child's position is the preferred position according to siblings who were asked about this.[88] However, the problem of identity is greater for the middle-ranking child since he is likely to be "lost" some-

[84] D. W. Winnicott, The Child and the Family (London: Tavistock Publications, Ltd., 1957), p. 109. The reader will recognize the moot question of this author's assumption that aggression is "natural."

[85] C. McArthur, "Personalities of First and Second Children," Psychiatry, 19 (1956), 47–54. Robert R. Sears, "Ordinal Position in the Family as a Psychological Variable," American Sociological Review (June 1950), 397–401.

[86] James H. S. Bossard and Eleanor Stoker Boll, The Large Family System (Philadelphia: University of Pennsylvania Press, 1956), p. 205.

[87] Bossard and Boll, The Large Family System, p. 208.

[88] Bossard and Boll, The Large Family System, p. 221.

where in the middle, never gaining the position of oldest or youngest. Bossard and Boll summarize the situation for the middle-child, as follows:

> . . . the middle place in the birth order is the most coveted position among the children reared in large families. Older children carry too much responsibility, they are too often the practice child, they tend too often to be exploited. All children, regardless of birth order, recognize these facts. Youngest children most often like their position, but other children know why and do not envy their place nor their treatment and resultant characteristics. It is the middle position that avoids both extremes. Such children profit from having others precede them but avoid their responsibilities; they are followed by younger children and have the advantages of those who are at the lower end of the birth order.[89]

The youngest child, like the only child, is never dethroned by a new sibling. He retains his position as the youngest and as the last. However, Bossard points out that the youngest child grows up in a more complex atmosphere than does any of the other children, for there are now, in addition to the parents, all the siblings and the many interpersonal relationships toward each other as well as toward him.[90]

After about eighteen months the child becomes aware of people outside the immediate family. The infant meets the mailman, the family physician in his office, the bus driver. He no longer plays exclusively with his own parents, his brothers, and sisters but with other children, too.

Thus the processes of socialization and enculturation continue to develop in an ever-broadening way, but the origin and the primary pattern of attitudes upon which new attitudes are built were established in those early years when his emotional pattern was set by the interactions among the members of his immediate family.

THE DEVELOPMENT OF SELFHOOD AND PERSONALITY IN THE INFANT AND PRE-SCHOOL CHILD

The biosocial behavioral development that we have been discussing as maturation and socialization of the infant is not complete without taking into consideration the infant's own reaction to these processes. The child may grow up physically healthy; he may be exposed to the finest social stimulation; but all of this is of value only insofar as he can respond to these forces by the development of feelings of selfhood. An infant is not a static object that can be molded from within by innate biological forces and from without by social forces. The infant reacts to, interprets, and finally modifies these phenomena in terms of his own needs, wishes, and developing self concept.

[89] Bossard and Boll, *The Large Family System*, p. 209.
[90] Bossard, *Sociology of Child Development*, p. 115.

The process of the development of self is one of the most complex and interesting of all the phenomena of social psychology. Dai makes these observations:

An individual is born with only biological needs, but acquires a self in the course of maturation and socialization. But with the growth of the self, the needs for security in self-other or inter-personal relations become as important as, and very often more than, the needs for biologic satisfaction. In fact, the self-system tends to exert an over-all control over all the needs of the individual, biologic or otherwise, any serious disturbance of which control may result in varying degrees of anxiety.

It follows from the foregoing that the nature of the self-system an individual acquires in the course of socialization depends largely on the kind of personalities he is associated with and the culture after which his activities are patterned, what the significant people in the environment think of him and the ways in which the socialization program is carried out.[91]

When we discussed the biological maturation process, we observed that the development began with large undifferentiated movements in the larger muscles; this was followed by a process of differentiation in which specialized functions began to make their appearance; and finally the whole procedure resulted in an integrated muscular coordination that made affective action possible. Murphy has suggested that a similar process characterizes the emergence of the self, unfolding in the three steps of (1) egocentrism, (2) differentiation, and (3) integration.[92] We shall review the development of selfhood in the baby according to these three levels.

In the beginning the infant responds to himself either as a physical object or as a social object without adequately distinguishing between his own organism or his own thoughts and those of his environment including objects and people. The infant does not distinguish between himself and the rest of the world at first. Initially he is all ego, and he assumes that he and the world are one.[93]

At birth the baby does not even identify the various parts of his body with himself. It is a notable day when he first realizes that his toes belong to him instead of to the world in general. He is doubtless perplexed during the first year by the fact that his shoes come off at night when his feet do not.[94]

[91] Bingham Dai, "Some Problems of Personality Development Among Negro Children," in Clyde Kluckhohn (ed.), *Personality in Nature, Culture and Society* (New York: Alfred A. Knopf, 1953), p. 547.

[92] Murphy, *Personality: A Biosocial Approach to Origins and Structure*, p. 344.

[93] Jean Piaget, *The Moral Judgment of the Child* (Glencoe, Ill.: The Free Press, 1932), p. 88.

[94] Ruth Strang, *An Introduction to Child Study* (New York: The Macmillan Co., 1959), 4th ed., p. 77.

The child may strike at the objects in the room with a mallet, first the floor, then a chair, at other people, then at his finger. When he strikes a finger the reaction is different from that than when he strikes at other things. By such incidents does he begin to think of his fingers as different from other things, though not yet does he integrate the fingers into a generalized concept of self.

In the same way, infants do not initially distinguish between their own ego structures and those of others. The infant tends to project his own ego upon all others and to assume that all the world thinks, sees, and feels as he does. For the first four or five years of life the child usually continues to assume that others see the world as he does. The following quotations illustrate how children project upon others what is a part of their own subjective nature:

> Arabella, aged two and a half years, lay in her bed in a room in a "railroad apartment" in New York City. She knew from his vocalizing that Paul was in his bed three rooms away. Arabella had proudly mastered the "tumbleset;" and since achievement calls for a spectator, she shouted the length of the hall, "Paul, see what I can do," and did another tumbleset for him to see. This was no summons for him to come down the hallway; his answering voice showed that he had heard, and nothing more was necessary for Arabella's happy continuance of the performance in the presence of a witness.[95]
>
> Paul himself at five noticed a scarlet tanager. His father remarked that some people couldn't tell a scarlet tanager from a grosbeak. "Oh yes, they could; they'd notice his black wings and he's redder." "But, Paul, some people don't know; they never noticed how red he is, or how black his wings are." Paul was not convinced. He had studied minutely the color plates showing the tanager and grosbeak, and he knew every detail; the details were there to be seen, and no one could miss them; everyone's experience was like his own. The fact that others perceive differently from oneself can come only later, after long experience with the differences in people's testimony as to what they perceive and when the sharpness of self-awareness is brought into relation with these different worlds of experience.[96]

The child who never learns to differentiate between his own ideas and those perceived by others may arrive at adulthood with a rigid and inflexible personality. It is only when the concept of the self is sufficiently sharpened that it is possible for the child to look upon himself as a social object, as different from other people's egos as his finger is from the chair or the finger of his playmate. One of the chief values in the child's learn-

---

[95] Murphy, *Personality: A Biosocial Approach to Origins and Structure*, p. 340.
[96] Murphy, *Personality: A Biosocial Approach to Origins and Structure*, p. 341.

ing by contact with other children is the realization that other children have mothers and fathers, too; that these playmates do not share exactly the same concept of the world as he does, and that they are individuals as he is himself. He learns that his role is not unique and that he shares his social status of childhood with others. These products of learning are aspects of the socialization process.

The infant's primary identification in the early months of life is with the mother. Initially, the infant does not distinguish between himself and his mother, but in healthy children this differentiation is gradually accomplished. The infant learns that he is expected to act differently in the presence of the father than he is in the presence of the mother. The child also learns to discriminate the appropriate role relationships between the sexes, between adults and children, and between his family and other families.

At the same time that he is differentiating among people, he is beginning to identify himself as an individual. He is developing an image of himself in different roles, as he sees it reflected in his interactions with others.

> At first an infant reacts soberly to his mirror image without sustained interest. Next he responds to it as to a playmate. Between six and seven months of age he begins to react toward his image as if he were attempting to relate the mirror image to himself. At about one year, his behavior suggests true self recognition.[97]

He also begins to understand himself in terms of his interpretation of the attitudes and expectations of others toward him (in terms of his role taking). Our earlier discussion of Cooley's "looking-glass self" is useful here for it points up the fact that the child begins to gain self-insight by evaluating the acts and attitudes of others toward him. His evaluation may be incorrect or blurred, but whatever the interpretation may be, it will determine his self-regarding characteristics. The individual becomes aware of himself in the process of interaction with people. Infants do not, as it is sometimes stated, react to their own appearance, intelligence, or dress, in a manner that directly influences their personality development. Rather, the infant or child reacts to his evaluation of other people's attitudes toward his appearance, intelligence, or manner of dress. In this fashion does the child become a social object to himself as well as to others. The child learns early to refer to himself in the third person. "Johnny did it," or "Johnny is hungry." The child also learns to take the attitudes of others toward him and to reflect their attitudes toward him as "Johnny is a good boy," or "Johnny is bad." As we said earlier, self-

---

[97] Strang, *An Introduction to Child Study*, p. 69.

consciousness arises only as a result of one's taking the attitude of others toward one's own body and personality. We know what we are like, what roles we shall be permitted to play, what success we have met in our attempts to fulfill our needs and desires, only in giving attention to the attitudes and expectations of others as these are revealed to us by other people's behavior in relation to us. If the child accurately interprets what these attitudes and expectations are, he develops more objectivity and insight into his own self-understanding than is otherwise possible. The child who first sees himself in a snapshot, in a mirror, or first hears himself on a recording may not recognize himself. The adult seeing himself on a taped television show for the first time may sympathize with the child's initial alarm at recognizing himself as others really see him.

Language and the Development of Self

The development of self-identification is closely associated with the emergence of language. The ability to communicate symbolically is essential to any culture. Lower animals cannot achieve a culture as we know it because they do not possess the cortical structure that makes possible complex symbolic communication. When we discussed Donald and Gua earlier in this chapter, one of the chief advantages that the boy gained over the ape was in the former's language development. The ape did not accomplish language communication, not so much because of an inadequate vocal apparatus but due to inadequate cortical development which makes verbal communication possible.

The infant's language is at first meaningless babble which gradually becomes differentiated as random sounds become identified with meaningful objects and concepts. As the child learns to speak, some of his sounds become effective in communication and others drop out because they do not achieve a desired response. Thus, an infant in an English speaking family may inadvertently employ sounds that would only be effective in another language culture, but these sounds are not retained in his repertoire because they are not part of the repertoire of his immediate in-group and hence are ineffective in achieving responsive behavior. Sounds or gestures that do produce results are reinforced and repeated and thus become an established part of the infant's language.

Piaget points out that the infant's early vocalizations do not represent "socialized speech," (speech articulated for the benefit of others). Initially the infant talks aloud but primarily to himself and usually without any meaningful reference to other people. At this early stage in his development the infant does not distinguish clearly between his own perspectives and those of others. It is only later that he is able to take the role of others and articulate his thoughts in a language that is socially and symbolically meaningful. Piaget indicates that as the child grows older the ratio of egocentric to socialized speech diminishes and an increasing portion of his language is directed to others. As might be expected, the child gradually learns to limit his communications to those verbal symbols and physical gestures to which other people are able to respond.[98] We have noted these gestures earlier in the discussion of Mead's "significant symbols."

The child learns to perceive himself through the use of language. Language is a form of self-communication. When the child talks to others he also talks to himself. He can and does react to his own words. The child talks to himself as he expects others would talk to him. When the infant internalizes these self-communications we call it thinking rather than conversation. Thinking, in such instances, has been described as subvocal speech. A child learns through these self-conversations to become an object to himself. Thus a child achieves self-objectification and can become aware of that part of the environment which is himself. Through language he can achieve a degree of self-objectivity by addressing himself as a distinct somebody. He thus learns who he is as he becomes a self-regarding person. In Pfeutze's words, "The self, through language and role taking can turn back upon itself, can become its own object, talk to itself, see itself as others see it, distinguish itself from other selves, judge itself from the standpoint of others."[99] This capacity for man to "get outside" himself and see himself as part of his own environment can only be accomplished by an organism that can think abstractly and symbolically. It is largely in this process of symbolic interaction (with himself, with others, and with objects) that a person achieves full self-realization.

The child learns through language development to play appropriate roles and to assume the statuses associated with them. The ideas an individual forms of himself usually have a social reference. The conception of self may involve a role one intends, or is expected to play in a social situation. In fact, it is seldom possible to understand fully the meaning of any specific characteristic or attitude of the child except in terms of the role the individual is playing in a particular social situation. The child learns to assume or play those roles which are appropriate to his image of himself—an image of self that he has learned through his role-taking experiences with others. Through these processes, the affective other becomes an important factor in the child's personality.

The concept of self develops out of those interactions the infant

[98] Jean Piaget, *The Language and Thought of the Child*, Marjorie Gabain, translator (New York: Harcourt, Brace & Co., 1926).

[99] Paul E. Pfuetze, *Self, Society and Existence* (New York: Harper & Brothers, 1961), p. 74. This view of the self as object is, of course, a paraphrase of G. H. Mead's *Mind, Self and Society*, a work which strongly influenced Pfuetze.

experiences with other people. These experiences are internalized and he types himself in terms of the language imagery available to him through these interactions. In the emergence of the self the child incorporates some of the responses of his affective others into himself and makes them his own. He learns to act toward himself as he believes others would act.

In this fashion, the child, growing in physical strength and interacting with his primary cultural models, develops feelings of self-hood and personal identity. Thus are represented the three variables always interacting in human development: the physical heritage, the social heritage, and the personal subjective characteristics. Change or modify any of the variables and the whole pattern changes, so interdependent are all three factors in the development of the child's personality structure.

SUMMARY

Parents, siblings, playmates, and teachers are the most important members of the infant's and pre-school child's affective other. It is in terms of their expectations and attitudes toward him (and toward each other), their treatment of him, and their beliefs and feelings about the world that the infant gains many of his early personality features.

The infant achieves personality; he is not born with it. Being human is an acquired status, it is not a position into which we are born. Through the interaction of organic, cultural, and personal influences, the child develops behavior traits at the sociocultural level. None of these three variables becomes of value in developing personality unless the infant himself experiences the interacting variable.

The development of an awareness of self is achieved as the infant learns to differentiate between himself and other persons, when, in Mead's words, he perceives himself as object. The infant learns to respond to himself both as a physical object and as a social being. It is in the process of social interaction with others that the child begins to take toward himself the attitudes that he believes others are taking toward him. Language plays a large part in this process of self-awareness. As a form of self-communication, the child talks to himself as, he believes, other members of his affective other would talk to him. It is through these self-conversations that the child becomes a reality to himself. The child also learns through language development to play appropriate roles and to assume the positions associated with them.

Infancy and the preschool years together constitute an extremely important age period insofar as the development of the subjective aspects of personality is concerned, but opinion is divided regarding the permanency of the personal variables established at this time. Although the primary years are of major significance in subjective personality development, the experiences of later years will determine the extent to which these early dispositions are actualized. In keeping with the interactionist frame of reference, L. Guy Brown[100] has summarized the age relationships in these terms:

> The idea that the first five years of a child's life are the most important is one of these [misconceptions stemming from thinking in terms of cause and effect]. Too much emphasis has been placed on childhood experiences *per se*. In reality, subsequent experiences determine the importance of these early activities. They can have meaning in adulthood in no other way. The individual is not a product of his childhood but is the result of what adolescence, youth, and adulthood do to childhood experiences. Each subsequent period becomes a testing place for the human nature developed in a preceding period. Childhood experiences, like the experiences of any other period, must be viewed as an interactive part of a process. Each new experience makes childhood reactions a part of a new totality. These new experiences may continue the childhood patterns but they may also change them. If childhood patterns reach adulthood it is because the experiences of youth and adulthood were of a nature to foster rather than to change them.

SUGGESTED READINGS

BERNARD, HAROLD W. *Human Development in Western Culture* (Boston: Allyn and Bacon, 1962).

CHURCH, JOSEPH. *Language and the Development of Reality* (New York: Random House, 1961).

CUMMING, JOHN and ELAINE CUMMING. *Ego and Milieu* (New York: Atherton Press, 1962).

ERIKSON, ERIK H. *Childhood and Society*, rev. ed. (New York: W. W. Norton, 1963).

JERSILD, ARTHUR T. *Child Psychology*, 4th ed. (Englewood Cliffs, N.J.: Prentice-Hall, 1954).

KAGAN, JEROME and HOWARD A. Moss. *Birth to Maturity* (New York: John Wiley and Sons, 1962).

PROVENCE, SALLY and ROSE C. LIPTON. *Infants in Institutions* (New York: International Universities Press, 1962).

STRANG, RUTH. *An Introduction to Child Study*, 4th ed. (New York: The Macmillan Co., 1959).

[100] L. Guy Brown, *Social Pathology* (New York: F. S. Crofts & Co., 1942), p. 11.

CHAPTER 13

CHILDHOOD

Then the whining schoolboy, with his satchel
And shining morning face, creeping like snail
Unwillingly to school.

PHYSIOLOGICAL DEVELOPMENT

In contrast to the accelerated growth of infancy and the thrusts of early adolescence, the years of childhood, in between, are not characterized by sudden or dramatic events. By the time the child is ready to enter kindergarten at approximately the age of five he has usually established himself as a healthy physical specimen who is likely to be around for many years. He has weathered the rigors of relatively high infant mortality and has built up sufficient resistance to disease to withstand all but the most severe attacks upon his physical well being.

While growth continues at a rapid rate, the child is settling down to assimilate some of his early progress. During this period the child grows very little in height.[1] Physical growth during these grade school years is negatively accelerated as revealed by growth curves of averages for large numbers of children. However, this is not only based on a general average for many children but is also based on an average for various kinds of physical growth. Figure 35 shows the differential among three kinds of physical growth. The genital development is, of course, more or less dormant during these preadolescent years; the lymphoid development is unique in its early acceleration and later decline in puberty, while the development of the nervous system is negatively accelerated, having achieved its greatest development very early. Further breakdown of these phenomena of growth by sex would show that girls grow a little faster than boys, and arrive earlier at puberty. The average six-year-old girl has developed bone structure as mature as the average seven-year-old boy. Boys, on the average, are heavier than girls at all ages except from the age of eleven to fourteen when girls respond to the puberty thrust earlier than boys.

The slowing down in the over-all rate of growth is most clearly demonstrated when one considers the achievement in physical structure, for

[1] William E. Martin and Celia Burns Stendler, *Child Development* (New York: Harcourt, Brace & Co., 1953), p. 224.

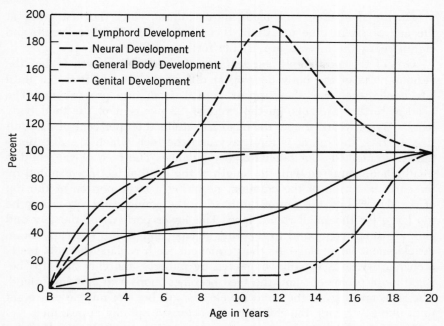

FIGURE 35. This graph shows differential rates of growth for various parts and organs of the body. (From S. Harris, *The Measurement of Man*, Minneapolis: The University of Minnesota Press, 1930. Reprinted by permission.)

instance, during the first year of life compared with any single later year. For example, the differences in growth between the second and third year are very much greater than between the seventh and eighth year.

Gesell and Ilg consider the age of five for most children to be a year of consolidation of earlier gains preparatory to further growth:

The five year old has come a long distance on the upward winding pathway of development. He will have to travel 15 years more before he becomes an adult, but he has scaled the steepest ascent and has reached a sloping plateau . . . Five is a nodal age; and also a kind of golden age for both parent and child. For a brief period the tides of development flow smoothly. The child is content to organize the experiences which he gathered somewhat piecemeal in the less deliberate fourth year. As an expansive four year old, he was constantly going out to meet the environment, making his thrusts in an almost harumscarum manner. In contrast, the five year old is self-contained, on friendly and familiar terms with his environment. He has learned much; he has matured. He takes time to consolidate his gains before he makes deeper excursions into the unknown.[2]

[2] Arnold Gesell and Frances L. Ilg, *The Child From Five to Ten* (New York: Harper & Brothers, 1946), p. 62.

Having shed their milk teeth, most children enter the first grade at the age of six in time to exhibit their first molars. In the seventh and eighth years, the incisors are usually forthcoming.

One of the most significant features of childhood growth is that the various parts of the body develop at differing rates and it is not until late adolescence that they approximate their mature proportions.[3] The head at birth represents, on the average, 22 per cent of the total body length. By six years of age, the head has attained 90 per cent of its adult size. In fact, the infant is top-heavy and the feet, which are disproportionately small, do not facilitate easy balance. The face of the child is small when compared with the length of the head, a fact necessitated by the early maturing of the cranium, requiring a large portion of the top of the skull. Thus, the top of the head in the young child appears to be too large for the small round face. The lower portions of the jaw and chin are small compared to the enlarged portion where the early brain development takes place. As the permanent teeth replace the milk teeth, a change which is usually completed by puberty, the chin and lips become more prominent and the face becomes more oval and less round. The arms and legs of the child develop length but not muscle or weight until puberty, giving the child the characteristic spindly appearance.

Within these patterns of growth, characteristic of child development in general, there are wide individual differences which must be understood in terms of the particular heritage and culture of the child. Not all children grow at the same rate. Some children grow faster, some slower than the average. Anyone who has ever sold children's ready-to-wear clothing in a department store can appreciate the wide range of sizes that fit children of the same chronological age.

THE RELATIONSHIP OF PHYSICAL FEATURES
AND SELF CONCEPT

The child's emerging self image is related to his physical development insofar as the latter becomes a cultural object. It is of course not realistic to assume a direct relationship between self-esteem and any particular physical feature. The child learns who he is, what he is like, and how he compares with others, through his interaction with other people, primarily through rôle-taking. The child's feelings toward his own organism, how it compares with the group norm and what he can do with it become crystallized through his experiences with parents, peers, teachers, and other significant adults. These personages communicate to him their feelings and attitudes toward his physical features and he incorporates into himself these significant evaluations. Such communications may be ap-

---

[3] Helen Thompson, "Physical Growth," *Manual of Child Psychology* (New York: John Wiley & Sons, 1954) Ch. 5.

proving or disapproving, articulated or unspoken, reinforcing or punishing. The important point here is that the emergence of self attitudes as they develop in relationship to physical growth are to be understood within the frame of reference of the child's experiences with other people.

Cultures assign particular status to various physical features. Those who occupy these positions are expected to comply with the behavioral expectations associated with this status. Such physical features could include sexual identification, racial characteristics, or any physical deviation (temporary or permanent) from the group norm.

We discussed sex typing in the previous chapter. Of the many roles an individual may be expected to play, the position of boy or girl is probably the most rigid. Parental expectations are usually very explicit on this point, femininity being highly valued and gravely reinforced in girls, and masculinity similarly being highly valued and reinforced in boys. Sears speculates on the parental role in this communication of cultural patterns:

> The sex of her child provides an important stimulus to a mother. It places the child in a social category that has enormous implications for training. She knows the many differences in the roles that apply to the two sexes; she has expectancies that are congruent with these roles. Even by the age of 5, the child elicits some kinds of behavior from the mother that are direct responses to the fact of the child's being a boy or a girl.[4]

Role behavior is specified not only in terms of sex typing, including attitudes and concepts regarding masculinity and femininity, but is also related to acceptable overt behavior including language, inhibition or expression of sexual curiosity, or passive-aggressive behavior.

Kagan and Moss in their longitudinal study of a group of infants from birth to maturity were impressed with the degree to which cultural rules relating to sex-role behavior in children carried over from childhood to adulthood.[5] Passive and dependent behavior is consistently approved and reinforced in our culture for girls and women while such behavior is disapproved and punished for men. These cultural expectations for each sex are communicated by *role models* to the children who are rewarded or punished to the extent to which they conform to the approved behavior. Kagan and Moss demonstrated in their study group that childhood passivity and dependency are related to adult passivity and dependency behavior in women, but not for men.

The extent to which a child learns sex identification or any role behavior from his parents is also a function of the relationship that exists

---

[4] R. R. Sears *et al.*, Patterns of Child Rearing (New York: Harper & Bros. 1957).
[5] Jerome Kagan and Howard A. Moss, *Birth to Maturity* (New York: John Wiley and Sons, 1962), p. 268.

between children and parents in a more general way. The readiness of a child to accept or reject a particular position is related to other considerations including the mother's own sexual needs and satisfactions, the relationship between the parents and the family authority structure, and so on.

The child's peer group relationships also reinforce or punish role behavior which does not conform to the expectations of the primary group. Later in this chapter we will note how the curriculum content of the school also reinforces the boy-girl expectations of the adult culture.

The same relationship between physical characteristics and personality traits may be noted with reference to racial features. Specific behavior is sometimes expected of people who occupy particular positions because of their race. Racial features may evoke stereotyped role expectations which are difficult to escape. Sometimes the child who occupies the assigned position accepts these cultural definitions for himself, feeling more comfortable and less anxious when he fulfills these expectations than when he rejects them.

Clark and Clark were able to demonstrate some of the effects of cultural expectations on the self-esteem of Negro children (ages three to seven years). Dr. and Mrs. Clark presented to these Negro children four dolls, two of which were colored brown with black hair and two of which were colored white with yellow hair. Each child was asked, "Which doll is most like you?" Approximately two thirds of the children stated that they were most like the brown dolls. When the children were asked which doll they preferred, the majority of children at every age rejected the brown dolls and indicated an unmistakable preference for the white dolls.

> One little girl who had shown a clear preference for the white doll and who had described the brown doll as "ugly" and "dirty" broke into a torrent of tears when she was asked to identify herself with one of the dolls. When confronted with this personal conflict some children looked at the investigator with terror and hostility. Many of the children had to be coaxed to finish the tests.
>
> The only children who reacted with such open demonstrations of intense emotions were northern children. The southern children when confronted with this personal dilemma were much more matter of fact in their ability to identify themselves with the brown doll which they had previously rejected.[6]

Any physical deviation can gain significance if assigned a particular status value by the culture. Thus a child who develops at a rate different from other children, or who may become sensitive about a dispropor-

[6] Kenneth B. Clark, *Prejudice and Your Child* (Boston: The Beacon Press, 1955), p. 45. The United States Supreme Court cited Dr. Clark's research in its decision of May, 1954, which ruled that laws requiring or permitting racial segregation in public education are unconstitutional.

tionate development of a particular physical feature, may develop feelings of anxiety about his situation. Such feelings are accentuated by the tendency of each culture to assign particular status to various physical features, and each individual is expected to play a social role consistent with this position. Such a position, assigned on the basis of physique alone, may be inappropriate for the chronological or emotional age of the child.

Breckenridge and Vincent report the following case:

At eight years and five months, A. S. was as tall as the average twelve-year old girl, as heavy as the average eleven-year old and had a mental age of twelve years, two months. In one year and three months she had gained 3⁴⁄₁₆ inches and 10⅝ pounds. Her feet had grown so rapidly that she wore an adult size six shoe at the end of the year, in contrast to a size thirteen (children's size) at the beginning. During the year she had complained of being tired and it had been necessary for her to miss about two days of school each month in order to relieve this fatigue. In addition, a certain degree of restlessness was indicative of fatigue. This was noticed when she visited the Child Development Laboratory for her yearly measurements of growth. In school she was reported by her teacher as a disciplinary problem and lacking in initiative. The conflict between teacher and child was solved when it was discovered that her seat and desk were not adjusted to her size. It had been necessary for the child to place her feet in the aisle in order to have any degree of comfort. With the adjustment of the chair and desk her behavior improved. Out of school, she generally selected children of her own size as playmates which meant she was playing with ten to twelve year olds. When the pressure of keeping up with children two years or more older became too great, she selected children of her own chronological age. Thus she had two sets of playmates which she alternated according to her immediate needs, playing with the older children when rested, with the younger ones when tired. In this way, she had solved her own problem of play, but of course, could not solve her own problem in school.[7]

A recent Broadway play, *A Thousand Clowns* illustrates considerable insight into this problem as can be seen in the following conversation between a precocious twelve-year old boy and his uncle:[8]

Nick: The past couple months I have been thinking about different names and considering different names because in four weeks I'm gonna be thirteen and I gotta pick my permanent name, like we said.
Murray: Why don't you just go on calling yourself Nick? You've been using it the longest.

[7] Marion E. Breckenridge and E. Lee Vincent, *Child Development* (Philadelphia: W. B. Saunders, 1943), p. 37.
[8] Herb Gardner, *A Thousand Clowns* (New York: Random House, 1961), p. 106.

Nick: Nick is a name for a short person. And since I am a short person
    I do not believe I should put a lot of attention on it.
Murray: Whaddya mean, where'd you get the idea you were short?
Nick: From people who are taller than I am.
Murray: That's ridiculous.
Nick: Sure, standing up there it's ridiculous, but from down here where
    I am it's not so ridiculous. And half the girls in my class are taller
    than me. Especially Susan Bookwalter. (Nick sits dejectedly).
Murray: (Crouching over next to him) Nick, you happen to be a nice
    medium height for your age.
Nick: (Pointing at Murray) Yeah, so how is it everybody crouches over
    a little when I'm around?
Murray: (Straightening up) Because you're a kid. (sits next to him).
    Listen, you come from a fairly tall family. Next couple of years you're
    gonna grow like crazy. Really, Nick, every day you're getting bigger.
Nick: So is Susan Bookwalter.

Instances of children's concern about their own growth pattern, particularly in comparison with other children of similar age, are not always
solved when in late adolescence the various bodily functions usually come
into balance and earlier disproportions within the body or in relation to
other people have been lessened. This is so because the child tends to
perpetuate inaccurate concepts of himself picked up during those periods
when he was particularly self-conscious about his physical deviations.
Thus, unless the child understands and appreciates the temporary nature
of his awkwardness, why he is smaller or taller than others, he may develop false concepts of his own capacities. He may generalize from the
self-depreciating attitudes associated with particular physical characteristics to situations having nothing to do with the physical aberration. He
may develop habits of compensation and adjustment to satisfy a particular
thwarted need which may become a part of his permanent "style of life"
long after the original cause has been forgotten. The persistence of habit
can, in this fashion, perpetuate role behavior that was once effective but
which may be inappropriate in new situations.

As we have seen, physical deviations may become problems to a child
if the culture in which the child lives defines such deviations as defects
and if the child takes the same attitude toward his physical structure as
does his affective other. It is generally true that healthy and intelligent
children, on the average, have a better chance of developing more effective and satisfying behavior than do those who suffer culturally defined
limitations. A wholesome example of a culturally defined physical characteristic and the problem it presented to one family is clearly indicated
in the following quotation:

    . . . we Americans admire size, high coloring, robust bearing in children.
We go to vast trouble—rich milks, gallons of orange juice, liver soup,

sun lamps, summer camps, early bedtime, organized sports—to achieve our tall, big-boned, heavy-muscled, rosy-cheeked darlings. I tried to assume a decent modesty the day I enrolled Patrick in his Paris *lycee*, but my heart swelled with pride when I saw my handsome son next to the poor, pale, spindling, meager lads in his class.

"Imagine," I told my husband afterward, "they wouldn't believe he was only eleven years old. They kept saying, '*Tiens!*' and '*Est-ce possible!*'"

Mother and Daddy, true-blood Americans, chuckled with satisfaction.

One week later, I was grimly cutting the legs off Patrick's long American trousers. Richard, after indignant protests, bought him the fancy tweed jacket with the narrow lapels, the tight back, half-belt and nipped-in waist; also striped shirts with high-starched collars, the black string necktie, the pointed light brown shoes. His crew haircut took six weeks before he could douse it with pomade and make a careful waved lock over his right eye.

But alas, even disguised in short pants and long hair, Patrick was still *Le Monstre* to his best friends. Enemies or bystanders had a whole battery of nicknames for our poor, beleagured Monster. Pat was *Le Chimp* (pronounced Sheeempppp, for chimpanzee); *Monsieur Fee-Fi-Fome* (from Jack and the Beanstalk); *Le Roi Kong* and *Le Turc Terrible.*

Patrick's teacher, a kind, warm-hearted lady, assured me she greatly pitied my poor son. He suffered, she supposed, from some grave malady of the glands?

"He isn't any bigger than lots of American boys his age!" I retorted, stung.

"Ah, yes," Mlle. Reffier sighed. "One has heard. These afflictions are so sad. One feels for the mothers, as well as for the children."[9]

Most children enter school for the first time between the ages of five and seven years. This represents a major transition to a new primary group situation. The child brings to his first school experiences his organic heritage which becomes interactive in the educational situation. In this regard it may be noted that many schools are planned for the child of average scholastic aptitude and of average physical size. The curriculum is suited to the pace of the student of average mental alertness. Desks, blackboards, lunch and playground equipment are designed for the student of average height, visual, and auditory capacities. Neither the brilliant nor the dull student is challenged by the learning process that assumes that all children have an intelligence quotient of 100.

The comparisons of behavior at various levels of intelligence indicate that children with average mentality are better adjusted than are chil-

[9] Ruth McKenney, "Paris, City of Children," *Holiday* (Apr. 1953), 63–68. Reprinted by permission of the author. Copyright © 1953 by the Curtis Publishing Co.

dren either brighter or duller than most youngsters. This is to be expected in a world where the environment is adapted to the average level of mentality. Though Terman reported only 11.9 percent of unselected school children to have intelligence quotients above 115, Anderson found 17.3 percent of the children at the child-guidance clinic at that level. Similarly, Terman found that 11.2 percent of unselected school children have intelligence quotients below 85; in the child guidance clinic 20.3 percent were in that group. An examination of Anderson's data indicates that the greater the deviation from normal intelligence, the more numerous were cases of problem behavior.[10]

The child whose organic heritage deviates from the norm will respond to the school experiences in a manner which emphasizes his own frustrations or boredom. The problem is more complex than might at first be apparent. There is no simple solution to the school adjustment problems presented by the range of individual differences in size, health, aptitudes, intelligence, interests, family background, chronological age, and emotional maturity among the children in almost any classroom. Not only do the children vary among each other in these attributes, but each child varies within himself, (i.e., his chronological age may not correspond to his emotional age). The instructor with a large teaching load will not always be able to "tailor-make" a curriculum to suit each child's changing needs and capacities.

The current practice and the expectation of the community is that children will begin school and progress according to their chronological age. Chronological age, as we have indicated before, is a very rough and inadequate index of general maturity. Figure 36 (p. 530) illustrates this phenomenon.

The biological differences that present themselves in the classroom are not independent variables in the learning process. We cannot neatly isolate the successful or the failing student and lay the cause to physiological deviations alone. These traits of physique and mental capacities profoundly influence the behavior of children in school as elsewhere, but they must always be seen in relationship to the cultural background and the personal resources of each student.

CHILD DEVELOPMENT AND THE CULTURAL PROCESSES

While the child is gaining physical strength he is also interacting with the cultural environment and thereby continuing the socialization and enculturation process begun in infancy. He is learning new social roles as his contacts widen with his ever increasing physical mobility and

---

[10] Harry N. Rivlin, *Educating for Adjustment* (New York: Appleton-Century-Crofts, 1936), p. 29. *See also* J. Wayne Wrightstone, "Individual Differences and School Adjustments," in *Elementary Educational Psychology*, Charles E. Shenner (Ed.) (New York: Prentice-Hall, 1945), pp. 185–211.

powers of communication. Piaget's studies of the relationship of age and social interaction show that pre-school children (ages two to seven years) move through three stages of play: (1) isolated or egocentric play (2) parallel play, and (3) cooperative or competitive play. Piaget also noted that the size of the group in which children play increases with age.[11]

The child's human behavior is accomplished through his associations with other people. A child does not become human simply by growing up inside his own skin. Almost everybody grows up in group situations and thereby learns to communicate by means of symbolic (language) skills. How important these human associations really are in the development of personality can be seen in those isolated situations where a child has been deprived of normal human contacts for prolonged periods of time.

Kingsley Davis describes one such case as follows:

Isabelle was isolated from her family and practically all human association (except her deaf mute mother) until she was 6½ years of age. The child's mother was unmarried and the seclusion was an effort to conceal Isabelle's existence. Because of the mother's muteness, Isabelle had no opportunity to develop speech except by means of gestures. When discovered by the authorities she was in poor health and was so bow-legged that the soles of her shoes came nearly flat together when she stood up. Her behavior toward strangers, especially men was almost that of a wild animal. In lieu of speech she made only a strange croaking sound. She seemed to be entirely unaware of human relationships of any kind. At first it could not be determined if she had a hearing loss because her senses had never been practiced. The specialists at first thought her to be feebleminded. Although the prognosis was not favorable, the professionals in charge initiated a concerted training program. It required one week of intense effort before she made her first attempt at vocalization. Gradually she began to respond, however, and after the first hurdles had at last been overcome, a curious thing happened. She went through the usual stages of learning characteristic of the years from one to six, not only in proper succession, but far more rapidly than normal. In a little over two months after her first vocalization she was putting sentences together. . . . She covered in two years the stages of learning that ordinarily require six. . . . To-day she is over 14 years old and has passed the 6th grade in a public school. Her teachers say that she participates in all school activities as normally as other children.[12]

There can be no doubt that children deprived of human associations such as Isabelle do not become human by themselves or solely in terms

[11] J. Piaget, *The Moral Judgment of the Child* (New York: Harcourt, Brace & World, 1932).

[12] Kingsley Davis, "Extreme Isolation of a Child," *American Journal of Sociology*, 45 (1940), 554–565. Copyright 1940 by the University of Chicago.

of their own organic maturation. Isabelle, as any other child, was able to acquire her distinctly human behavior patterns only when she had an opportunity to interact with people to whom she could relate and who could also communicate with her.

National legislation has taken cognizance of the likelihood that mental handicapping can come from cultural as well as from biological defects. Testifying on mental health and mental retardation legislation before a subcommittee of the United States Senate, Professor Nicholas Hobbs recently (March, 1963), had this to say:

> By far the largest number of the retarded have no identifiable physical, biochemical, or medical deficits or disorder. They are victims of inadequate opportunities to learn from infancy on. They have not had the stimulus to acquire the motivations, the concepts, the skills that are necessary for effective functioning in our society.[13]

The Child's Role Learning Experiences

The process of personality development through socialization and enculturation is a dynamic undertaking that involves learning a series of social roles to conform to the altered positions accompanying physical growth and maturation.

Kagan and Moss recognize three primary group role learning experiences during the age period of six to ten years which they regard as essential to achieving important changes in the child's emerging behavioral organization.

1. Identification with parents and the concomitant attempt to adopt the values and overt responses of the parent.

2. The realization that mastery of intellective skills is both a cultural requirement as well as a source of satisfaction.

3. The encounter with the peer group . . . which experiences force the child to accommodate, to some degree, to the values and evaluations made by peers. For some children, peer experiences strengthen patterns of dominance, social spontaneity, and positive self-evaluation. For others, peer rejection and a perception of marked deviation from peer-valued attributes lead to social anxiety, social submission, and a sense of ineffectiveness.[14]

The child's first role behavior in the family was consistent with his position as the new baby in the family. His responsibilities here soon became well defined, and he could anticipate and thus become familiar with the kinds of responses his parents and siblings expected of him. However, (unless he remains an only child) his position as *the baby* was

---

[13] Nicholas Hobbs, "Statement on Mental Illness and Retardation," *The American Psychologist*, 18, No. 6 (June 1963), 295–299.

[14] Kagan and Moss, *Birth to Maturity*, p. 272.

soon preempted by a younger brother or sister. The child who has learned to live a certain role, with certain affectional relationships well established, may feel seriously threatened by the challenge of a rival near his own age. Until now he has looked in only one direction, toward older people for understanding and affection. Now he has to look in both directions, still toward older people but toward younger children too. The younger sibling not only competes with him for parental affection but also requires something of his affection. Now there is someone in the house more helpless than himself. He may respond enthusiastically to this ego-inflating idea that he is expected to be more self-sufficient than someone else and that he is partly responsible for someone else. Or, if he interacts with this situation with insecure personal resources he may, in order to regain the position he knew earlier, regress to the role playing of the former position characterized by enuresis, crying, or the use of "baby talk." In other instances, he may take refuge in phantasy and withdrawal behavior, a reaction sometimes favored by parents since it creates less trouble for them, but the results for the child's own development may be no less serious.

Sibling rivalry can be a serious business for children, involving as it does competition for the affection of the parents, particularly the mother or the mother surrogate. A new baby in the family is a threat to the child who until this time has occupied the position of the youngest. At such a time the sibling needs the reassurance and security that comes from a close relationship with the parents, particularly the mother. The following quotation indicates one mother's response to this need:

Melanie, the mother, bent her head; her light breath stirred the tuft of pale hair, gently, with love.

"I'm glad it's a boy," she said, "*Un bealu garcon comme son papa, n'est-ce-pas?*" she added, in a proud whisper for the baby alone to hear.

"Do you like boys best?" Cosette, the six year old foster child, said casually, fiddling with the ribbons on the lace pillow, in a way she was told not to do.

Melanie glanced at her. Her eyes danced as she said very gravely:

"But naturally, little silly. I have already a girl, *voyons!* What would I do with another."

"Oh!" said little Cosette, her mouth open. She seemed struck with this idea, then her spirits soared and soared. She greeted Soeur Bernarde with a beaming smile and went, without fuss, into the garden. There was no longer any need to cling to the Flower Room on such a lovely day, now she was sure they needed her. It just made all the difference.[15]

The affection which children feel for the mother may set up in the child feelings of ambivalence toward the father involving competition

[15] Oriel Malet, *My Bird Sings* (Garden City, N.Y.: Doubleday & Co., 1946), p. 154.

for the mother's time and affection. The vast contemporary literature concerning the Oedipus complex is pertinent here.[16]

In these intra-family relations, and particularly in play, are rehearsed in spontaneous situations many of the roles the child will be expected to play in the larger community. The child without siblings or companions is frequently denied this opportunity and may in phantasy satisfy some of his needs for socialization. The imaginary playmate is not uncommon among lonely children. Names and elaborate ego-satisfying situations may be invented by the child to fill the social void.[17]

Bossard and Boll point out that siblings in large families frequently function as parental surrogates. The problem of discipline as well as affectional satisfactions while growing up may become real problems to younger siblings in large families. This can be illustrated from the following case:

> "As time went on," writes one of seven, "my older sister more and more took on a double role; a substitute for the head of the house and a big sister to whom all would look and whose judgments and decisions all came to respect. Thus my mother and sister came really to be copartners in the operation of the house. As it was, mother referred most things to my sister. In consequence of all this, she was robbed of a normal teen-age and early twenty development. And, too, because of her exalted position, she gradually became a little managerial in her attitude toward her brothers and sisters."[18]

Family size is a factor in sibling and parental relationships. Small families appear to provide fewer opportunities for interpersonal relationships and large families seem to offer vastly increased potential connections between family members. As the size of the family increases the number of potential relationships accelerates much more rapidly than does the increase in the number of individuals in the family.[19] The number of these relationships is not infinite and can be quantitatively determined by the following formula:

$$\text{P. R.} = \frac{N^2 - N}{2}$$

where P. R. equals the potential relationships available and N equals the number in the family. Thus a family of four would have 6 possible relationships and no more. However, since the relationships between sub-

---

[16] E.g., William Golding, Lord of The Flies (New York: G. P. Putnam's Sons, 1959).

[17] Norma E. Cutts and Nicholas Moseley, The Only Child (New York: G. P. Putnam's Sons, 1954).

[18] James S. Bossard and Eleanor Stoker Boll, The Large Family System (Philadelphia: University of Pennsylvania Press, 1956), p. 160.

[19] A. Paul Hare, Handbook of Small Group Research (New York: The Free Press of Glencoe, 1962), pp. 228–230.

groups in the family as well as between individuals are important, a more complete parameter of relationships is made available by another formula:

$$P. R. = \frac{3^n - 2^{n+1} + 1}{2}$$

This formula yields the total number of intra-group personal relationships available for a family of a given number including subgroups, *i.e.* grandparents, grandchildren, and so on. Table XVII shows the rapid increase in relationships with the addition of a member of a subgroup, *i.e.*, the addition of a grandfather to a family of five (two parents and three children) will add 211 potential relationships available to the members of that family.[20] Conversely, in the same situation, the loss of a single member of the original primary family means the group will actually lose 70 per cent of their relationships.

Table XVII*
Increase in Potential Relationships (x) with an
Increase in Group Size (N)

Size of Group	Number of Relationships
2	1
3	6
4	25
5	90
6	301
7	966

* Hare, *Handbook of Small Group Research*, p. 229

Thus it would appear that the number of potential relationships in a family can become so large in comparison with the size of the group that most of these relationships become nonoperative. It is quite likely that a child could become "lost" in a large family because of the overwhelming number of relationships which are available but which simply cannot function because of the overwhelming weight of the whole structure. These formula raise interesting questions concerning the optimum size of a family, including subgroups, for the maximal participation and involvement of the members in the life of the family unit. Bossard and Boll are convinced from their studies of happy and unhappy large families that the size of the family group is only one variable in determining the character of the interactive processes that develop among its members.[21]

[20] W. M. Kephart, "A Quantitative Analysis of Intra-Group Relationships," *American Journal of Sociology* (1950), 55, pp. 544–549.
[21] Bossard and Boll, *The Large Family System*, p. 104.

In analyzing the *happy* (large) families, type of community and a friendly attitude by parents toward large families were not found to be significant per se, but the cultivation of family rituals, conscious efforts of parents to promote family group life, and especially administrative and managerial ability on the part of the mother, were revealed rather clearly as important factors in the development of happy large family living.

A study of the unhappy large families emphasizes the importance of the father's misbehavior, such as drinking and vile temper, the mother's ineffectiveness; the disorganization that appears in immigrant families because of intergenerational conflicts; and the death of a parent, followed by the subsequent remarriage of the other parent, with additional "blocks" of children.[22]

Neighborhood Relationships

The emergence of the child into the community is not a sudden event. He first comes to know those people who come to his house to see his parents or brothers and sisters or to deliver the paper or bring the groceries. Some of these people come especially to see him, as the family physician or the grandparents. Gradually he goes out with the family on picnics, to other people's houses, and to church. All this increases the socialization of the child. But thus far all of it is under the supervision and tutelage of the people who created his whole social world in the early months of his life. When he does begin to venture out on his own, to the corner store, to the mail box, or across the street to the playground, he loses some of the primary group status his parents afford him at home. He meets his peers who treat him without all the special considerations he has learned to expect at home. This is something new for him to experience.

In the neighborhood play group the child finds another kind of primary group relationship where he meets people face to face, now of his own age and without the constant restraint, reassurance, and supervision of the original primary influences. The socializing effect of these new experiences is related to the degree of correspondence that exists between the neighborhood peer group and the family position.

The child, whether or not he has siblings, who has learned to play only one kind of role thus far at home may be ill suited to participate in the many-sided activities of children hard at play. The child overtrained in particular kinds of role behavior will not easily modify his behavior to satisfy new expectations defined by new positions. Such a child's affective other may have become so stereotyped in terms of his parents' expectations of him that he cannot readily enlarge his view of himself to include

[22] Bossard and Boll, *The Large Family System,* p. 105.

the attitudes and feelings of others toward himself. Consider the following case:

Jimmy Allen, an only child of eight years, is brought to the psychological clinic by his parents at the insistence of his teachers. The parents are much incensed and regard all this as a direct insult to the family. They raise a thousand complaints against the school and are completely at a loss to understand the situation. Jimmy, they tell us, is a delightful child at home. He has his moments now and then, but on the whole he is his Mother's and Daddy's darling, the center of a comfortable suburban home. Jimmy plays with a group of younger children whom he completely dominates, much to the delight of his father. His slightest wish is his parents' command. His manners are delightful with adults, and he speaks like a polished young gentleman. With the adults at the clinic, he is calm, poised and helpful, too helpful for a child of eight. The parents feel the school must be a very terrible place, for they point out that Jimmy just hates to go there and cries and begs to stay home. He has even made himself sick over it and had to stay home because he got so upset.

The report from the school on Jimmy presents a vastly different picture. His teachers complain that he is "not bright," stubborn, and a "very nasty child." He does not get along well with the other children, beats up the younger ones, and buys off the older ones with lollipops and licorice shoestrings from the store across the street. In class he is constantly talking and showing off. He must always be the center of attention. He likes art work, and this is the only thing he does well. Whenever his work is displayed, he brags insufferably. He has been known to cheat on exams. When he lost the lead in the play recently, he skipped school for three days in a row. With forty children in class, the teacher is at wits' end to know what to do with him.

Jimmy joined the local Y, went four times and never went back again. The boys' work director says Jimmy never got along with any of the boys, stuck to the director "like molasses" and only wanted to swim. He refused to go to gym classes and stayed out of clubs entirely. He was an excellent swimmer, however, and enjoyed this sport immensely until the day he was sent home for holding two younger boys under. He hasn't been back since.

When we see this child as he sees himself, his behavior becomes understandable. While we might analyze his behavior in terms of many specific needs all these become a function of the one dominant aspect— the need to protect and to enhance his own self-concept.

Thus, Jimmy has developed at home a concept of himself as being very important, as indeed he is, to his parents. He feels completely adequate, loved, wanted and safe. His every wish is granted by indulgent parents, who in no sense deny his concept of himself. When he moves from this sheltered atmosphere, however, to the wider world of school and community, his associates do not react to him in any such light. They are unwilling to accept him at his value of himself. On the contrary, they are not even aware of the values he places on himself but react to Jimmy in terms of his behavior. All this must be very puzzling to him. Since his concept of himself is not accepted by his associates, he is forced to defend himself, and this he does by "stubbornness," being nasty, and cheating on exams. In his attempts to gain what he feels is his rightful due, he buys off the older boys and beats up the younger ones; he sticks close to the director of the Y and, of course, brags of his accomplishments and enjoys what he can do well.

A delight at home to his parents, a nuisance away in the community; his need for self-esteem surfeited at home, opposed in the community— seen in this way, Jimmy's behavior becomes consistent.[23]

What the child learns in the neighborhood play group about himself will, in turn, influence his attitudes and behavior at home. This participation in play with his peers supplements the experiences in group interaction and socialization his siblings have already provided him at home. The difference between the attitude of his family at home and the attitude of the play group toward the child is great, however, in that the peer group is usually indifferent to any special rights or privileges of the child, and the youngster has to play and compete without the immediate protection or intervention of those who feel responsible for shaping his destiny. This factor of indifference is significant, for it puts the child on his own mettle and requires that he socialize his needs on the basis of nonsubsidized competitive situations.

It is in this rough and tumble, trial-and-error interaction with the peer group that positions are assigned by the attitudes and expectations of the group. One can sympathize with the child, striving to define his position in the neighborhood play group. Unlike the adult who usually plays well-defined roles in his daily behavior, the child's behavior is usually uncharted. Within the home the child may play a fairly consistent role, but outside the home his place is not so well defined. In the neighborhood play group the child may shift his role frequently. He can be a "policeman" one hour and a "bandit" the next. He can shift his role to suit the changing demands of the social situation. Play activity provides the child an opportunity to develop a repertoire of social skills by playing kaleidoscopic roles. As he moves from the unorganized, individualistic play to the game stage he also learns the functions and responsibilities of role playing.[24] Thus, in team play the child learns that the first baseman's job is to be the first baseman and not the pitcher or the second baseman. He also learns that others also have their responsibilities to perform. Through play he learns to play his part in terms of the responsi-

[23] Donald Snygg and Arthur W. Combs, *Individual Behavior* (New York: Harper & Brothers, 1949), pp. 58–60. Copyright 1949 by Harper & Brothers. Reprinted with the permission of Harper & Row, Publishers, Inc.

[24] *See* G. H. Mead's reference to the part played by games in Chapter 5.

bilities and obligations of reciprocal role relationships. Through these experiences in role differentiation he learns that group action becomes possible. Learning to play a consistent role is one of the important lessons of childhood. A child may grow up and because of his chronological age and his physical dimensions gain the position of an adult citizen; but if he has never learned to live the role consistent with adult position, he will be an ineffective individual. Adjustment occurs if the position assigned by the group and the role played by the individual are compatible. Piaget noted that the ability of a child to find his place in society, including an awareness of the primary rules or laws which characterize the local social sanctions, are learned slowly but progressively. At first a child is content merely to imitate the models of his seniors. Later he learns it is to his advantage to follow rules. Still later, as has been pointed out by still other social psychologists, he learns to give up something of his own "rights" in order to gain concessions from others. This progression from anarchy to government by consensus and codes is learned through reciprocal participation in cooperative primary group activities.[25] These positional adjustment experiences are not always smooth and comfortable for the child. Berelson and Steiner have pointed out that the closer the correspondence of values and mores between socializing agencies such as the home, church, and school, the more rapidly and certainly does the socialization process take place. Conversely, the more the conflicts between them, the slower and more uncertain the process.[26]

> If such conflict reaches a high degree of intensity, as felt by the subject, he will tend to renounce one agency in favor of the other, or renounce both, or become psychologically disturbed. In a study of Oriental Jews in Israel, for example, the gulf between the parents and the schools resulted in early school-leaving on the part of the children, poor grades, poor attendance, etc.[27]

While the position which the child knew at home and the role which he plays in the community are not always consistent, his position and roles outside of the home are influenced by the child's family status. A child's position in the community is influenced by many factors including his color, ethnic group, and the family social class.

As Davis has pointed out:

> Our knowledge of the social-class training is now sufficient to enable us to say that no studies can henceforth generalize about "the child." We shall always have to ask, "A child of what social class, in what

---

[25] Piaget, *The Moral Judgment of the Child*, pp. 1–69.

[26] Bernard Berelson and Gary A. Steiner, *Human Behavior* (New York: Harcourt, Brace and World, 1964), p. 71.

[27] S. N. Eisenstadt, *From Generation to Generation: Age Groups and Social Structure* (Glencoe, Ill.: The Free Press, 1956).

cultural environment?" Very few of the statements which we may make concerning the physical growth, the socialization, or the motivation of slum children, for example, would hold for upper-middle-class children.

The child's social learning takes place chiefly in the environments of his family and its friends, and of his own play-group. All these groups, we now know, are restricted in the range of their social and cultural participation by social-class barriers. Thus the culture of both the child's family and his play-group become class-typed. This social-class patterning of the child's learning, as exerted through the family, extends from control of the types of food he eats and of the way he eats it to the kinds of sexual, aggressive, and educational training he receives.[28]

The behavior of the children in the neighborhood is a reflection of the socioeconomic background of their family. Thus Davis, who studied 200 Chicago families, divided equally among Negroes and whites, with half the families being from lower socioeconomic positions and the other half from middle class socioeconomic situations, reported that physical aggression among the lower class families was not only countenanced but was frequently encouraged by peers and parents.[29] Such aggression was the procedure commonly used to solve problems in the community and within the family. Sexual activity in its several manifestations and at an early age was tolerated among the lower social class children in Davis' study and the young child soon learned that some of the adults in this group were promiscuous in such matters. Abstinence was a mark of disesteem. The affective other of Davis' lower class child was more frequently than not commended for the kinds of behavior which were considered to be either illegal or immoral by the larger society.[30] Because there was little communication between the lower and upper classes, the children of this group had relatively little opportunity to learn during their formative years the mores of the upper classes. If they did interact with the other social class mores, little was learned because they had been taught to ridicule or reject them. Here we see the operation of the vicious circle principle.

The middle class children studied by Davis were more restrained in their overt behavior. These children were taught self-discipline and the substitution of persuasion, logic, or indirection for a frontal, aggressive attack on their adversaries. In the middle class family, aggression took the form of ambition and initiative. Sexual behavior was more restrained, and anxieties about sexual taboos were frequent. For example, masturbation was found to be more frequent among Davis' middle class than

[28] Allison Davis, *Social Class Influences Upon Learning* (Cambridge: Harvard University Press, 1948), pp. 11–72. Reprinted by permission of the publishers. Copyright 1948 by the President and Fellows of Harvard College.

[29] Davis, *Social Class Influences Upon Learning*, p. 35.

[30] Davis, *Social Class Influences Upon Learning*, p. 36.

lower class children. However, the middle class child, because of his social position, had wider opportunities to sublimate his aggressions into socially approved behavior.[31]

When the children of the various social classes reach school for the first time, they, of course, carry with them their class distinctions. It has already marked them in terms of vocabulary, social skills, and behavior patterns, but even more important, the child has marked himself in his own mind. For example, he takes toward himself the same attitudes as does his affective other's social class. Children assemble according to neighborhood cliques and behavior patterns, and the social class differentiation is thus perpetuated. One report, however, indicates that this is somewhat less aggravated than in the out-of-school relationships. Stendler observed the class-conscious attitudes of children in grades 1, 4, 6, and 8 in a New England community. Each child was catalogued according to his economic and social class, tested, and interviewed. A significant difference appeared in the sociometric pattern between the student's "in-school" and "out-school" choices of friends. In the school situation 23 to 42 per cent of the first graders selected friends from their own class; but in the out-of-school situation the same students chose 76 to 89 per cent from their own group. Similar differences characterized the choices of students in the higher grades.[32] This again indicates the importance of recognizing that personality is not a solely subjective, under-the-skin phenomenon.

School Relationships

When a child enters school it is essential that, among many things, two factors be well established. The first is the ability to communicate in and understand the language; secondly, the child should already have acquired his first lessons in group behavior. Like the home, and the neighborhood playground group, the schoolroom is also a primary group relationship. As indicated in Chapter 12, a child becomes aware of himself and what he is like through his perceptions of how others feel about him. Feelings about self are developed early in life in relationship to those primary models or significant figures including mother, father, siblings and later the child's teachers. Davidson examined over four hundred elementary and secondary school children to determine the relationship which might exist between a child's perceptions of his teachers' feelings toward him, and how these perceptions might be related to such variables as self-concept, achievement in school, and social class background. A

---

[31] Davis, *Social Class Influences Upon Learning*, pp. 22–37. It would be a mistake, however, to attribute to middle class Americans a disdain for physical aggression. See Ch. 4.

[32] C. B. Stendler, *Children of Brasstown* (Urbana, Ill.: Bureau of Research and Service, University of Illinois, 1949).

check list of thirty adjectives (shy, helpful, wise) was used by means of which each child (1) rated himself, and (2) how he thought the teacher rated him in terms of these same characteristics. Davidson reported the following:

1. A moderately high correlation between self-perception scores and the child's perception of his teachers' feelings toward him, that is, the child who has a more favorable self-concept is likely to perceive his teachers' feelings as more favorable toward him.

2. The girls perceive their teachers' feelings as more favorable to them than do the boys.

3. The better the child's achievement in school and the higher his social class position, the more favorable is his perception of his teachers' feelings toward him.

4. Even when achievement is held constant, social class operates to determine the degree of favorability of the child's perception.[33]

The teacher, depending upon the sex, frequently becomes a maternal or paternal surrogate for the child. The classmates may become rivals for the affection and attention of the teacher. As the school takes the children at ever younger years—originally at the age of six in the first grade, then at five in kindergarten, and now at four in nursery schools—the school assumes an increasing share in the education and socialization of the child.

Children who have not been able to establish a solid emotional relationship in the early years of life with a parent or adult surrogate may have special difficulty in the classroom. A study of children deprived of such a relationship (institutionalized from birth) indicates the special problems of these children in the classroom.

A careful study of (these) children's behavior and motivations showed, that they were driven towards aggressiveness by jealousy. A child who grows up without roots in the family is unable to adopt toward his teacher that friendly but matter-of-fact and rather aloof attitude which is characteristic of the family-child, whose emotional life is centered in, and supported by the attachment to his parents. Children who had not been attached to a mother in early childhood seek in vain to secure the exclusive attention of every adult they meet. The normal child's claim for exclusive possession of his mother is extended to the teacher by the hospitalized child. He wants the teacher all to himself, hence his jealousy of all the other children, each of whom is an enemy, if only

[33] H. H. Davidson, "Children's Perception of Their Teachers' Feelings Toward Them Related to School Achievement and Social Class," reported in *Proceedings of Sixteenth International Congress of Psychology* (Amsterdam: North Holland Publ. Co., 1960), pp. 423–424.

because he is there and may perhaps get more attention. Thus the formerly hospitalized child lives in a state of constant, hopeless and aimless longing; his striving is bound to be continuously frustrated which causes a permanent tension, a constant feeling of injury, a mood of hostility, which is released in apparently reasonless acts of cruel aggression.[34]

While the school is bringing to the child in a formalized way his knowledge of the world in which he is to live, the child is also learning his personality in a second home, in associations within the classroom and on the playground with other youngsters and under the supervision of an adult who is concerned about him but also about many other youngsters as well.

Students learn from each other as well as from the teacher and from books. Students are formally oriented in the classroom around the teacher, but their spontaneous and informal relationships are directed toward each other. The spontaneity and informality of the inter-pupil relationships provide the children with ample opportunity to try themselves out socially. The playground and classroom situations develop social organization as each child endeavors to establish his own role in the activity. In these experiences the child learns resourcefulness, teamwork, and develops a variety of social roles which will be useful in adult living. The child brings to the school all the biological and acquired needs learned earlier. He works out these needs in the company of new friends and rivals.

Whenever children are together in groups for any considerable time a peer-group society comes into being and the relationship within the group becomes structured in terms of the status won by each child or youth on the basis of roles played effectively. So in every classroom there are high-prestige children in peer-group terms. There are regular belongers who are sure of the roles they will have on the playground and in their neighborhoods; and there are "fringers" who sometimes can win particular roles, and sometimes cannot, depending upon the activity and the make-up of the group at the moment. There also are rejected children who are denied participation by the group either because of lack of knowledge and skill or because their behavior does not conform to the codes and customs of the group. Finally, there are isolated children, persons who do not matter to the other children because they are so lacking in capacity, experience background, or initiative that they cannot make a beginning at playing roles in 'he peer-group.[35]

[34] Lotte Schenk-Danzinger, "Problems of Social Adaptation of Children Deprived of Maternal Care in Earliest Childhood," *Proceedings of the Sixteenth International Congress of Psychology* (Amsterdam: North Holland Publ. Co., 1962), pp. 394–397.

[35] Daniel A. Prescott, *Factors That Influence Learning* (Pittsburgh: University of Pittsburgh Press, 1958), p. 38.

Not only does each child try to define his own position in the school situation, but his peers help establish his role for him. The role played in the classroom may be very different from that played on the athletic field. Recognition and achievement are gained by different means in each situation. The classroom provides the intellectually aggressive child an opportunity to exhibit verbal leadership with subordinate roles assigned to the less agile.

One child may win recognition by his report card, another through his athletic prowess, and still another by antisocial activity, each person adapting according to his human nature and the exigencies of the situation. These children communicate ideas, techniques of adjustment, and culture to each other in a most effective way. It is probably as important for a child to be stimulated by interesting and significant classmates as it is to be taught by effective teachers.

Character Development and Curriculum Content

The schools traditionally have encouraged the development of conforming, dependent behavior. Independent thinking and aggressive adjustment in such situations have been discouraged, while the conforming behavior of the retiring student is rewarded. Rivlin writes that "The traditional school is planned for the introvert."[36] When one realizes that the teacher must be not only instructor but also administrator of the classroom, it is not surprising that she is sometimes concerned more with order than behavior.

The Wickman investigation endeavored to identify those behavior traits which teachers and mental hygienists rate as most serious and as least serious.[37] Teachers emphasized as most serious those traits which are extraverted in their manifestations and disturbed orderly classroom activities. Covert behavior symptoms were rated as least serious. The mental hygienists, rating the same traits, arrived at very different conclusions, rating withdrawing and covert behavior as most serious and aggressive activities as least significant. Perhaps if the hygienists had also the responsibility for managing the children as well as diagnosing and treating their behavior, their observations might have been closer to those of the teachers. Twenty years after the original Wickman investigation, the study was repeated by other researchers. The theoretical expectation was that over a period of a generation the gap between teachers' and mental hygienists' attitudes toward classroom behavior problems would have narrowed and conversely that teachers' ratings in the two generations might have widened in the direction of closer conformity to those evidenced by the mental hygienists. However, the latter study did not

---

[36] Rivlin, *Educating for Adjustment*, p. 79.

[37] E. K. Wickman, *Children's Behavior and Teachers' Attitudes* (New York: Division of Publications, The Commonwealth Fund, 1928).

indicate that this had occurred and in fact the results showed a marked correspondence between the ratings of the teachers of 1944–1945 and those of the mid 1920's.[38]

Another investigation of similar behavior ratings, this time the ratings being made by child psychologists, parents, and teachers, revealed that while ratings made of behavior problems were similar to the results obtained in the Wickman study, it was also observed that the teachers' ratings were much closer to parents' ratings than they were to the ratings of the child psychologists.[39]

A study of the relationship existing between character development and the content of children's textbooks was reported by Child, Potter, and Levine at the Institute of Human Relations at Yale University.[40] The object of the investigation was to determine the probable effect on children's behavior of the reading they are required to do as a part of their education. The authors examined the various characters depicted in the reading material of third graders, defined the problems that confronted these characters, observed how the characters solved their problems, and recorded the success of their endeavors as described in the stories.

The authors did not engage in an experimental examination of the effect of this reading material on personality development but contented themselves with analyzing, classifying, and recording the representation of the characters and incidents in the reading material. The authors felt that "the effect of a sequence of symbolic behavior are in many important ways similar to the effects which the corresponding sequence of real interaction with the environment would have if it occurred."[41] If children enlarge their knowledge of adjustment techniques through reading about how others manage their problems, it is important that they learn from situations which are worthy of their emulation. After examining the literature read by these third-grade children, the authors arrived at various conclusions among which are the following:

1. The stories consistently emphasize the rewards of hard work and solid endeavor as the approved means of succeeding in life.

2. Independence of thought and action is discouraged in children except when such autonomous behavior is sponsored by an adult. "There can be no doubt that if children continue to be trained in this way as they grow older, the effect on their poten-

[38] Sophie Ritholz, *Children's Behavior* (New York: Bookman Associates, 1959).

[39] C. E. Thompson, "The Attitude of Various Groups Toward Behavior Problems of Children," *Journal of Abnormal and Social Psychology*, XXXV (Jan. 1940), 120–125.

[40] Irvin L. Child, Elmer H. Potter, and E. M. Levine, "Children's Textbooks and Personality Development: An Exploration in the Social Psychology of Education," *Psychological Monographs*, LX, No. 3 (1946), 1–54.

[41] Child, Potter, and Levine, "Children's Textbooks and Personality Development," p. 8.

tialities as adults will be a bad one. It may indeed be that a considerable proportion of adult maladjustment in marriage and occupational life is due to the discouragement of autonomy and independence by the educational system up to the point where an adolescent or young adult leaves it.[42]

3. The characters depicted in the reading material encouraged "unrealistic optimism" by suggesting that success and reward are commonplace and that failure is unheard of. Not enough attention is paid to unsuccessful adaptations. The characters depicted do not provide any information about what people do when they fail, and ignore the necessity of developing alternative adjustment techniques when the present adjustment is unsatisfactory.

4. Male characters are depicted two and one-half times as frequently in central roles as are females. Males are portrayed as "the bearers of knowledge and wisdom," and as the persons through whom knowledge can come to the child.[43] Females are portrayed as "sociable, kind and timid, but inactive, unambitious, and uncreative." There can be no excuse for this greater attention to males in the claim that males have achieved more in society and hence that there is more to write about them. These stories, with few exceptions, are not about individuals of outstanding achievement but simply about the life of everyday people. The implication of this difference for a girl is that being female is a pretty bad thing, that the only people even in everyday life who are worth writing about or reading about are boys and men. If the content of these readers is typical of other social influences, small wonder that girls might develop for this reason alone an inferiority complex about their sex."[44]

5. The children in these stories are depicted as conforming and adaptable in their behavior. In contrast with adults, they are depicted as being more socialized and obedient.

The content of the readers, then, is likely to point out to children certain rewards and punishments that, for them, follow upon the display of approved or disapproved behavior, but to suggest that these rewards and punishments may stop when they grow up to be adults. Such a lesson, which to be sure is also often made in a child's everyday life, may be satisfactory for the short-sighted parent or teacher, who knows that his immediate responsibility for the child will cease when the child becomes an adult. But as a background for educational policy it seems

---

[42] Child, Potter, and Levine, "Children's Textbooks and Personality Development," p. 46.

[43] *Ibid.*, p. 48.

[44] *Ibid.*, p. 49.

deficient to anyone who looks at child-rearing or education as a task of preparing children to become adequate adults.[45]

More investigations of this kind which identify the factors involved in conceptual learning will contribute to the improvement of the techniques of formal education. Not enough attention has been given to the understanding of how the school contributes to the development of children's attitudes, character, and human nature. With a few notable exceptions, investigations of school life have been primarily concerned with the factors which contribute to the learning of content material. It has been pointed out that in some respects the classroom peer group society is itself a significant part of the curriculum of any school.[46] This peer group society is experienced by all the school children and thereby much social learning and role playing is accomplished. The prudent teacher will be aware of each pupil's peer group status, of the roles he plays effectively and of the experiences he is obtaining from peer group participation.

The Influence of the Class Structure on Learning Experiences

For social psychologists, the examination of social class differences has many attractions for it contains the requirement of an experimental variable within a natural field setting. Since the schools are a part of society they will reflect the economic and social distinctions among the people of that culture. That these differences in the community are real can be gathered from studies made throughout the United States and Canada regarding the educational opportunities of children in several socioeconomic groups.

Davis points out that social-class membership is only one of the systems of social rank in the United States which restrict and limit the learning opportunities of children and young people.[47] It is unlikely that children and young people (to say nothing of adults) are aware of the extent to which they are ethnocentric in certain group practices and behavior, nor are they always conscious of the degree to which their behavior is influenced by their membership and hence their position in one of these several class groups. The prestige values of the social classes are ranked by the inhabitants of a culture into lower, middle, and upper class groups, with subgroups within each grouping. Prestige value is determined by such things as place and type of residence, financial worth, occupation, education, social skills, club and church membership, and so on.

[45] Child, Potter, and Levine, "Children's Textbooks and Personality Development," p. 51.
[46] Prescott, *Factors That Influence Learning*, p. 40.
[47] Davis, *Social Class Influences Upon Learning*, p. 4.

Toby has shown from a review of the literature that by almost any index of school achievement, it is apparent that "for every age level, the average grade of middle-class urban children is higher than that of lower-class children."[48]

Several hypotheses are offered as to why middle class children should be more successful in their studies than lower class children. The most common hypothesis, advanced by several researchers, is that the schools are predominantly middle class in their instruction and orientation. Most teachers are themselves products of middle or lower middle-class culture and reflect the various judgments of this experience in their teaching, their personal habits, and in their attitudes. However, all children do not bring the same subjective experience to the school inasmuch as they have experienced different parts of a heterogeneous society. The lower class child probably has a more difficult time adjusting to the attitudes and expectations of the middle class teacher than do the children of middle and upper middle class families. The teacher's social status group and class have not been in the affective other of the lower class child. This is particularly so if the lower class child is of an ethnic or racial group with strong minority feelings. The child whose personal social traits find favor with teachers and middle or upper class people, will have a far better chance of succeeding both socially and academically than will the child whose behavior and personality habits are offensive or unpleasant to middle class people. Consider, for example, the limited opportunity to succeed in school of the young man whose attitudes, outlook on life and grammar are as follows:

> Jim lackadaisically walked from class to class, often without his note-books or textbooks. He sat in study hall daily, dreamily looking out the window. When the teacher told him to get to work, he would slowly reach into his desk, take out a Western magazine or a comic book, and read it for the rest of the period. Jim thought the best thing for him to do was to join the Navy. He said he was going to do this just as soon as he was 16. After the outbreak of war, he was more convinced than ever that this was his destiny. The day he was 16, he quit school; the day after, he joined the Navy. Jim believed his mother had to work too hard for him to achieve a high school diploma; besides, "What good is it? I know a lotta guys at the Mill; they ain't finished eight grade." His father didn't care whether he went to school or not, but he thought in a vague way that it would "be a good thing if Jim finished" high school.[49]

The child whose behavior reflects a social background that differs from the teacher's and other students will react toward his school experi-

---

[48] Jackson Toby, "Orientation to Education as a Factor in the School Adjustment of Lower-Class Children," *Social Forces*, 35 (1957), 259–266.

[49] August B. Hollingshead, *Elmtown's Youth* (New York: John Wiley & Sons, 1949), p. 178.

ences in a manner which is characteristic of his own perceptions and needs. The tendency has been to encourage this child to modify his personality patterns to suit the requirements of the school situation. Conflict between school and home may become active at this point.

Another hypothesis proposed to explain why the lower middle class child does poorly in school is that the latter is not so much thwarted by the teacher's middle class morality nor by his own socioeconomic status, but rather by his own lack of interest and motivation. It is not only the teacher according to this view, but also the student who brings certain judgments and attitudes to the school situation which preclude a congenial learning atmosphere.

> Whereas the middle-class child learns a socially adaptive fear of receiving poor grades in school, of being aggressive toward the teacher, of fighting, of cursing, and of having early sex relations, the slum child learns to fear quite different social acts. His gang teaches him to fear being taken in by the teacher, of being a softie with her. To study homework seriously is literally a disgrace. Instead of boasting of good marks in school, he conceals them, if he ever receives any. The lower class individual fears not to be thought a street-fighter; it is a suspicious and dangerous social trait. He fears not to curse. If he cannot claim early sex relations his virility is seriously questioned.[50]

Unfortunately, when the lower class child drops out of school for failure or lack of interest, he cuts himself off from one of the few ladders of mobility open to him. By separating himself from the educational system he is likely to become a permanent prisoner of his own class position.

> The withdrawees' job skills are limited to what they have learned from contact with parents, relatives, friends, and through observations and personal experience, largely within the community; no withdrawee has any technical training for any type of job; furthermore, few have plans to acquire it in the future. . . The boys have some acquaintance with working on farms, washing cars, loading and unloading grain, repairing cars, driving trucks, doing janitor work, clerking in stores, and odd jobs, but their lack of training, job skills, and experience combined with their youth and family backgrounds severely limits their job opportunities.[51]

In contrast to the lower middle class child, the middle class child brings a different set of attitudes to the school situation. Toby says that the middle class child ". . . is caught in a neighborhood pattern of academic achievement in much the same way some lower-class boys are caught in a neighborhood pattern of truancy and delinquency."[52] While

[50] Davis, *Social Class Influences Upon Learning*, p. 30.

[51] Hollingshead, *Elmtown's Youth*, p. 369.

[52] Toby, "Orientation to Education as a Factor in the School Adjustment of Lower-Class Children," p. 260.

the lower class boy or girl has cut himself off from channels of social and economic mobility, the middle class member maintains his social class position because of family reinforcement but also because he more easily identifies with the goals of the teacher and of the prevailing educational atmosphere.

It is interesting to note that in England the state schools are utilized to accomplish "sponsored mobility." At the age of eleven years, on the basis of intelligence and achievement examinations, 20 per cent of the children are selected for grammar school which is preliminary to entry into the universities.

> There is thus built into our educational system a decision point where children are told, through the operation of the selection machinery, whether they are sheep or goat. They are informed of their future destiny; working class children, by virtue of being selected for the grammar school, begin their social climb; likewise, middle class children, not so selected and sent to schools where most of the pupils come from upper and lower working class homes, begin their downward mobility.[53]

Two studies from England indicate that it is intelligence more than social class membership which finally determines how the child looks at the world around him.[54] Intelligence, according to Himmelweit, is seen as a motivating force, "its influence being more important than social class in shaping attitudes in the case of the very intelligent child and that of the child of below average ability."[55] Intelligence in this writer's view provides not only the intellectual power needed to acquire knowledge, but intelligence also provides the aspiration and the impetus needed for mobility.

"Further," says Himmelweit, "because of the very different social learning experiences that face the able and the less able child, we suggest that intelligence exerts indirectly a causal influence upon the child's drive to achieve." Jayasuriya reported similar conclusions in his research. "One of the most revealing findings of the whole inquiry has been the demonstration of the extent to which social class influences are overlaid by differences in intellectual ability."[56] These groups of studies purport to show that children of similar mental capacity but of differing socioeconomic backgrounds and class statuses in England hold remarkably

---

[53] Hilde T. Himmelweit, "The Role of Intelligence in Modifying Social Class Differences in Outlook," in *Proceedings of the Sixteenth International Congress of Psychology* (Amsterdam: North Holland Publ. Co., 1962), pp. 273–281.

[54] Himmelweit, "The Role of Intelligence in Modifying Social Class Differences in Outlook," pp. 273–281; D. L. Jayasuriya, *A Study of Adolescent Ambition Level of Aspiration and Achievement Motivation* (University of London, Ph.D. Thesis, 1960).

[55] Himmelweit, "The Role of Intelligence in Modifying Social Class Differences in Outlook," p. 275.

[56] Jayasuriya, *A Study of Adolescent Ambition Level of Aspiration and Achievement Motivation.*

similar aspirations and expectations in terms of social mobility. Certain of the conclusions of these English scholars are similar to the findings reported by Havighurst (reported more completely in Chapter 14).[57] In the latter study, it was shown that mobility in the United States, while not "sponsored" to the same extent as it is in England, is increasingly made possible by educational ladders. Those children who do drop out of school isolate themselves from these avenues of upward mobility.

One's immediate response to these English studies is likely to be that of perceiving a conflict with American studies and certainly with the nature of motivation as presented in this text. However, one of the English authors presents information which significantly modifies his perception of intelligence as a motivating factor. He writes, "Compared with a more intelligent child, he (the less intelligent one) is less open to stimulation and is also less encouraged to do so by his family, be it middle or working class. It is probably that the drive to achieve relates to social learning experiences first at home and later at school. An intelligent child when he tries new things tends to succeed or show promise of success so that he is further encouraged by adults around or even rewarded."[58] Thus the author acknowledges that the motivation is learned and that intelligence is instrumental to success in the same way that a mesomorphic physique is instrumental for a person motivated by values of physical prowess. The acknowledged value system of the English and the critical part played by schooling in social mobility set the stage for intelligence to play its important instrumental, not motivational, role.

PERSONALITY DEVELOPMENT IN CHILDHOOD

As the child grows and interacts with an increasingly complex environment, he develops a personality unique to his own heredity and experiences.

Sometimes we assume that boys and girls are the same the world over. But children vary in their so-called "human nature" according to the culture in which they live. The subjective personality that emerges from the interaction of organic and cultural experiences is reinforced by all the expectations and responses to which the child is exposed, resulting in an increasing specificity of the organization of predictable personality traits. The effects of this process can be seen in an illustration taken from a charming article written by Ruth McKenney in which she describes Paris not as a city of gaiety and glitter, but as the "City of Children." The reasons for the adoration reigned upon *les petits choux*, "the adored little cabbages," by the Parisians is due to the fact that there are so few chil-

---

[57] Robert J. Havighurst, *et al.*, *Growing up in River City* (New York: John Wiley & Sons, 1962).

[58] Himmelweit, "The Role of Intelligence in Modifying Social Class Differences in Outlook," p. 280.

dren in Paris (a result of two world wars, a declining birth rate for fifty years, and metropolitan sterility.) "Paris in real life is the city of children. They are its true cult. All the rest of the world may love a lover; all Paris loves a child. . . . The children of Paris are surrounded by the most tender and anxious affection from the very day they are born, which accounts, I think for their grave charm, their endearing manners."

One little boy in Paris, named Georges, behaved as follows:

Georges was nearly always polite, gay and charming. He shook hands with other little boys he met in the park, he came when *Maman* called, he brushed the mud off his white shoes and took extreme care not to drip ice cream down the front of his ruffled yellow or pink silk shirt. He sat patiently while Grandma curled his hair and tied it with a blue-satin bow; he begged to see Punch and Judy, but accepted—with a certain almost ironic resignation—the fatal words, "some other time."

Georges had a little sailboat which he loved with a great love; one day the wind blew it out to the deeper reaches of the pond.

"Georges!" Grandma called anxiously.

Poor Georges! His arms were stretched out prayerfully after his darling treasure; he hesitated.

"*Mais*, Georges!" Grandma was surprised.

"*Oui, Grandmère*," Georges said sadly, and abandoned his sailboat as he apparently thought, to the vasty deep and *pour toujours*. At last when I took off my shoes and waded in after the precious *bateau*, Georges was so beside himself with joy he jumped up and down, lost his blue bow, and had to be recoifed before launching his clipper ship again, this time on safer waters.

"How do they manage him?" I asked Richard. "I don't understand it. I've never heard any of them use a really cross, let alone harsh, word to Georges. Spank him, jerk him about—unthinkable! And yet, when Grandma called, sailboat or not, Georges came."

"*Doucement*," Richard said, "*Doucement*. They've been telling him that since the day he was born. Besides, they expect him to behave with a certain *noblesse oblige*. Georges has so much love, he must be responsible to it."[59]

Unless Georges moves to another culture, these personality characteristics will continue to be reinforced by the affections and experiences of an adoring milieu. It is not difficult to see in these culture patterns the reinforcement which gives French gentlemen the distinctive qualities of *noblesse oblige*. Once established, personal factors become interactive in determining the further adaptations of the child to new experiences and situations. Every reaction habit that the organism makes to satisfy a need or wish reinforces a pattern of habitual responses which itself becomes a force in determining the future needs and opportunities to which the

[59] McKenney, "Paris, City of Children," p. 66. Reprinted by permission of the author. Copyright © 1953 by Curtis Publishing Co.

child will be sensitive. The way in which a child satisfies a need today makes it easier to satisfy that same need in a similar way tomorrow, providing the social situation has not changed. The manner in which personal tensions are reduced today establishes a precedent for the same practice tomorrow and makes it less likely that other substitute mechanisms will be utilized. This is simply saying what we already know, that as a person grows older he is likely to become fixed in his traits, concepts, and attitudes, and he finds it increasingly difficult to modify his role behavior to meet new social expectations. Thus the web of personal attributes established as a means of satisfying the basic needs of life, both biogenic and sociogenic, becomes itself a factor in determining the new situations to which the individual will be sensitive and to which he will respond, as well as influencing the kinds of responses the individual will make.

It has been claimed that it is sometimes possible to predict roughly, even before birth, what a child's character will be if one knows the family and the culture in which the child will be brought up. The predictability of certain personality traits from infancy to later years has been demonstrated by the Fels Research Institute which has for the past thirty years conducted multidiscipline longitudinal studies on a group of three hundred children from before birth to adulthood. Among the many findings of this study has been the apparent stability of many behavioral and personality characteristics of these children from birth to adulthood. For example, forty-four boys and forty-five girls of this group were rated as children (ages 0 to 14) in terms of aggressive behavior. As adults (age range twenty to thirty) they were rated again by an examiner who had no knowledge of the longitudinal data. The latter's rating correlated significantly with the earlier ratings made when the subjects were children. The authors report, "Aggressive behavior in school age boys is a fairly accurate predictor of predisposition to aggressive behavior in adulthood. This behavior is less stable for girls because aggression is subject to more severe socialization pressures in girls than in boys."[60]

When the child reaches the age of five, he comes into contact with teachers and playmates in a formalized association in the school where, without the backing or the intervention of his parents or relatives, he has to put into practice the personality he has been learning at home for the

[60] L. W. Sontag, J. Kagan, and H. A. Moss, "Stability of Aggressive Behaviors from Childhood Through Adulthood," reported in *Proceedings of Sixteenth International Congress of Psychology* (Amsterdam: North Holland Pub. Co., 1962), pp. 154–157. See also Stuart Palmer, *A Study of Murder* (New York: Thomas Y. Crowell Co., 1960) for an interesting study of the influence of early frustrations upon aggressive actions later in life. After careful comparison of fifty-one murderers and a control group of the offenders' brothers, Palmer argues cogently that early frustrations bred in each murderer a ". . . tremendous reservoir of aggression [that] had to have some escape." p. 156.

first five years. Until now there has been a "unity" and "oneness" (usually) in the home regarding the way one does things. To a large extent the infant has identified his own security and ego with the stability and singleness of the attitudes and expressions of faith he knows at home. Now in school, he meets under formalized supervision people whose ideas, feelings, and practices may differ from those he has always known. If he has not already done so, he may begin to question the authority and omniscience of the parents. If the role or roles that he has learned to play at home have been stereotyped and inflexible, he may have difficulty adapting himself to the new status which the classroom and the playground require of him. The child carries to school all the concepts and feelings toward himself and others that he has learned up to that time. These are expressed as personal traits and as such sensitize him to certain stimuli in the environment and insulate him from others.

The social influences outside the home which come into contact with the child and, in greater or lesser degree, have some responsibility in developing the child (such as the school, YMCA, church, or scout troop) cannot undo in a matter of a few hours a week the emotionalized habits and self-regarding concepts established during the years of infancy at home. Nevertheless, these forces outside the home which supplement the influence of the home, while not changing fundamentally the core of the child's personality, will modify and redirect some of the child's habits of adjustment. Probably the greatest influence of all beyond the home will be the children with whom this child plays; for with them in unstructured and spontaneous play situations, the child will act out his conflicts and emotional needs. And as the child practices his personality and is reinforced, encouraged, or rebuffed by the responses of others toward his behavior, he develops the personal organization which progressively becomes more stable, predictable, and unchanging.

SUMMARY

The childhood years are characterized by organic growth patterns which are fairly stable and predictable, especially when compared with the rapid initial growth of the infant and the latter thrusts of adolescence. Deviations from the group norm in any particular physical trait may contribute to personality development if the culture as well as the child defines the structure as unusual. The child's reaction to the awareness that his culture defines certain aspects of his organism as unique will depend upon the personality characteristics (already developed in infancy) with which he experiences this situation.

The child, at home, in the playground, and later in school achieves a certain position and learns to play social roles consistent with the place assigned to him by the group. In play activities at home, in the neighborhood and in school, the child develops facility in social relationships. In play the child has an opportunity to test himself and his environment, and in the primary neighborhood group he has a chance to try himself out in situations where he is not immediately under the benevolent protection of his home. The school provides still a further extension of his growing independence. Each child approaches the school situation in terms of the particular socioeconomic status assigned to him by his class membership.

The child's subjective traits will interact with his culture in terms of his needs, resources, and frustrations. The child will profit from some experiences and he will not respond to others. The personality variables already achieved will act as a selector of the stimuli to which he will respond. A child who goes out from his home with feelings of personal adequacy will profit far more from the interactions with environmental opportunities than will the rejected or dependent youngster.

We must not overlook the possibility that the child who feels himself to be inferior and has accepted that definition of himself as true, may when the opportunity presents itself, interact with that opportunity with compensatory motivation in such a manner as to gain for himself unusual recognition for successful achievement.

SUGGESTED READINGS

ALLPORT, GORDON W. *Pattern and Growth in Personality* (New York: Holt, Rinehart and Winston, 1961).

BOSSARD, JAMES S. and ELEANOR STOKER BOLL. *The Large Family System* (Philadelphia: University of Pennsylvania Press, 1956).

BRECKENRIDGE, MARION E. and E. LEE VINCENT. *Child Development* (Philadelphia: W. B. Saunders, 1960), 4th Ed.

DAVIS, KINGSLEY. "Extreme Isolation of a Child," *American Journal of Sociology*, 45 (1940), pp. 554–565.

KAGAN, JEROME and HOWARD A. Moss. *Birth to Maturity* (New York: John Wiley and Sons, 1962).

PRESCOTT, DANIEL A. *Factors That Influence Learning* (Pittsburgh: University of Pittsburgh Press, 1958).

SMELSER, NEIL and WILLIAM SMELSER (eds.). *Personality and Social Systems* (New York: John Wiley and Sons, 1963).

CHAPTER 14

ADOLESCENCE

And then, the lover,
Sighing like furnace, with a
woeful ballad
Made to his mistress' eyebrow.

George Bernard Shaw, in his *Back to Methuselah*, depicts a scene in the year 31,920 AD. In this scene a large egg rests upon an altar located in a wooded glade; the egg begins to rock; the egg hatches and presently reveals "The Newly Born, a pretty girl who would have been guessed as seventeen in our day." She "sits up in the broken shell, exquisitely fresh and rosy, but with filaments of spare albumen clinging to her here and there." She has been growing up in the egg for two years and thereby spared herself "a development that once cost human beings twenty years of awkward stumbling immaturity after they were born."[1]

Unfortunately, we are living in the twentieth century, and Shaw's whimsies are yet far from realization. Consequently, it is still necessary to attend to the "awkward stumbling immaturity" of the years that lead to adolescence and finally adulthood.

PHYSIOLOGICAL DEVELOPMENT

Sexual maturity completes the biological cycle. Physiologically, the organism's health and growth seem to be pointed toward the maturation of the reproductive processes. With their realization, other growth functions are soon matured and the organism relaxes in the fulfillment of its physiological destiny.

The adolescent years are transitional from childhood to adulthood and represent a major shift in role behavior expectations. It is a big step from the position of child to the position of adult, perhaps the greatest of all the age-divides in the human life span. Most societies recognize this shift in age position by ceremonies which have been called "rites of passage." Primitive societies recognize the incidence of puberty as a symbol of adulthood and mark the occasion with celebration and initiation into the responsibilities of adult society. In more industrialized societies,

---

[1] George Bernard Shaw, *Back to Methuselah* (New York: Oxford University Press, 1947).

the role behavior of adolescence, which begins with puberty, is extended by social controls until the individual is self-supporting and has completed his formal education.[2] Hollingshead has pointed out that in western society the position of the adolescent is often ambiguous, and the roles he is expected to play are not well defined. Adolescence as he sees it is:

> . . . an ill-defined no man's land that lies between the protected dependency of child-hood, where the parent is dominant, and the independent world of the adult, where the person is relatively free from parental controls. This no-man's land is a place where the maturing person works out the extremely important developmental tasks of freeing himself from his family, making heterosexual adjustments, selecting a vocation, gaining an education and establishing a home of his own . . . . The adolescent's ambiguous position in the society may be a product of the loss of function for this age group in our culture.[3]

Puberty is a physiological phenomenon, but as an age-grade symbol it is experienced differently by boys and girls. Ruth Benedict, in a comparative anthropological study of several primitive cultures concluded that,

> The clear physiological facts of adolescence . . . are first socially interpreted even when they are stressed . . . a survey of puberty institutions makes clear a further fact: puberty is physiologically a different matter in the life cycle of the male and the female. If cultural emphasis followed the physiological emphasis, girls' ceremonies would be more marked than boys': but it is not so. The ceremonies emphasize a social fact: the adult prerogatives of men are more far-reaching in every culture than women's and consequently as in the above instances, it is more common for societies to take note of this period in boys than in girls.[4]

Adolescence is not only the occasion for physical maturity in reproductive matters. It is also the occasion for the final achievement of physical growth in such areas as height and weight, intelligence, and muscular coordination. G. Stanley Hall, who was among the first to focus scientific attention upon the adolescent period, identified it as a time of storm and stress characterized by sharp physical and psychological up-

[2] Bernard Berelson and Gary A. Steiner, *Human Behavior* (New York: Harcourt, Brace and World, 1964), p. 84.

[3] August B. Hollingshead, *Elmtown's Youth* (New York: John Wiley and Sons, 1949), p. 236.

[4] Ruth Benedict, *Patterns of Culture* (New York: The New American Library, 1946), p. 37. For a well known discussion of the ways in which different cultures treat adolescence *see* Margaret Mead, *Coming of Age in Samoa* (New York: William Morrow and Co., 1928), and *Growing Up In New Guinea* (Garden City, N.Y.: Blue Ribbon Books, 1930). *See also* Stuart A. Queen, *et al.*, *The Family in Various Cultures* (Philadelphia: J. B. Lippincott Co., 1961); Mischa Titiev, *Introduction to Cultural Anthropology* (New York: Henry Holt and Co., 1959).

heavals.[5] Although there is an acceleration of growth in many fundamental bodily functions during this period, we shall show later that these developments are not particularly sudden or sharp.

Margaret Mead in one of her early anthropological studies set out to determine if the stress and strains of adolescence as she saw them in our society are a universal phenomenon resulting from the physical changes associated with puberty. As is well known, she discovered in Samoa that the adolescent is no more anxious or troubled than in earlier or later periods of his life. Her conclusion, which has never been seriously challenged, was that adolescence is not a universal phenomenon which can be characterized by any particular syndrome, but is a personality variable which differs markedly from culture to culture.[6]

Adolescence and preadolescence are characterized by an acceleration of growth in height and weight. Growth curves based on average increments in height and weight for individuals representative of each age group tend to obscure the significance of these phenomena. Longitudinal studies made on the same group of individuals over many years indicate that this period is characterized by a moderate, though not sudden, increase in height and weight. This acceleration in height begins for boys between the ages of eleven and sixteen with the year of maximum growth, on the average, being the fourteenth year. Girls realize their greatest growth in height between the ages of eight and fourteen years, with the maximum growth, usually, at twelve. The maximum acceleration in weight for both sexes follows closely after the year of most rapid height increase. Other physical properties, such as breathing capacity, muscular strength, and heart and liver weight, also show slightly accelerated development at this time.[7]

---

[5] G. Stanley Hall, *Adolescence, Its Psychology and Its Relation to Physiology, Anthropology, Sociology, Sex, Crime and Education* (New York: Appleton-Century-Crofts, 1904), 2 vols.

[6] Mead, *Growing Up in New Guinea*. It need not be inferred from Mead's research that a stressless adolescence necessarily implies an idyllic society. Adolescence is less stressful in certain other societies. However, in such societies, high birth and death rates prevail, early marriages and pregnancies are accepted, even welcomed, and early death is commonplace. Also, very modest expectations accompany the attainment of adult status. But in complex industrialized societies a stressless adolescence may be incompatible with the facts of low death rates, accompanying demands for population control, and for prolonged periods of preparation essential to the fulfillment of the expectations of the adult culture. At the present time, biological maturation in the form of sex impulse, child bearing capacity, and the achievement of physical prowess, on the one hand, and social psychological maturation in the form of knowledge and attitudes appropriate to adult life in a complex industrial civilization on the other, rarely coincide. The situation is one in which cultural evolution has outdistanced biological evolution. Under these conditions, anxiety, stress, and temporary frustration are to be viewed as normal accompaniments of this period of life in a complex industrial society.

[7] John E. Horrocks, "The Adolescent," in *Manual of Child Psychology*: Leonard Carmichael, Ed. (New York: John Wiley and Sons, 1954), p. 707.

The pituitary gland is a primary influence in the rate of body growth. The pituitary gland is also responsible, at the appropriate time, for stimulating the development of the sex glands consisting of the testes in the male and the ovaries in the female. Not only are these sex glands or gonads responsible for producing the cells necessary for reproduction, but they secrete internal hormones, which are responsible for the physical changes characteristic of pubescence. These sex hormones also inhibit the effect of the pituitary in stimulating further general physical growth. This is why a child who is premature in sexual development may fail to achieve further significant growth in a characteristic such as height. Conversely, the youngster whose pituitary gland is slow in stimulating the maturation of the sex glands will probably achieve prolonged physical growth until sexual maturity is attained.

The age at which puberty arrives in a given individual is related to standard of living and good health. The impression that primitive or tropical cultures stimulate earlier sexual maturation is not true, although earlier sexual activity, encouraged by relaxation of sex taboos in these cultures, obscures the age of puberty. When standard of living is taken into account, there are relatively unimportant differences in age of puberty by race in this country. The onset of puberty varies with individuals, culture, climates and socioeconomic position. Mills noted that girls in central North America achieve sexual maturity earlier than anywhere else on earth. By comparison the girls of South America are retarded one year in terms of sexual maturity. Even later menarche has been observed among rural South African girls.[8] These data are probably a reflection of other than climate factors such as nutritional values and standard of living. Greulich believes that food and dietary habits, health, and a favorable environment are conducive to the early onset of puberty.[9] It is also of interest to note that the average menarcheal age has for the last thirty years been falling in the United States as well as in central and northern Europe. Such changes, if they represent a long term trend, would have significant implications for educational planning and heterosexual adjustments.[10] Menarche does not usually coincide with ovulation. Menarche signals the approach rather than the arrival of the capacity to reproduce. American girls reach puberty between the ages of nine and seventeen with the mean age falling between twelve and fourteen years depending

[8] C. A. Mills, "Geographic and Time Variations in Body Growth and Age at Menarche," *Human Biology*, 9 (1937), 43–56; J. M. Tanner and B. O. Keefe, "Age at Menarche in Nigeria School Girls," *Human Biology*, 34 (1962), 187–196.

[9] W. W. Greulich, "Physical Changes in Adolescence," in *Adolescence*, Part I of 43rd Yearbook of National Society for the Study of Education (Chicago: University of Chicago Press, 1944), pp. 8–32.

[10] John E. Horrocks, "The Adolescent," in *Manual of Child Psychology*, Leonard Carmichael, Ed. (New York: John Wiley and Sons, 1954), Chap. 11.

upon the study and the nature of the population in the sample.[11] The mean age of menarche for a population of girls from a high socioeconomic group in Cleveland is 12.5[12] or a mean age of 13.5 for a low socioeconomic group living in an orphanage in New York City.[13] Boys achieve puberty one to two years later than girls, or between the fourteenth and sixteenth years. These data must be recognized as averages, and allowance must be made for unusual cases which may exceed these limits. Murphy is inclined to hold out for the importance of cultural suggestions and habits as a powerful influence in stimulating endocrine secretions affecting sexual maturation. He points out that Danish girls living in the United States menstruate six months earlier than do Danish girls living in their native land.[14] Certainly no one factor alone contributes to the maturation of the reproductive functions.

More important for the individual than tables of anatomical development are the deviations from these norms that are obscured in the general averages. It is the person who varies (or believes he varies) most conspicuously from the norm of his peer group in terms of height, weight, or general appearance who is most likely to experience difficulties of adjustment. Sensitivity to the will of the crowd makes the adolescent particularly self-conscious regarding his own physical maturity and appearance. If he matures early or late, if he suffers from acne or other culturally defined deviations from normal health, if he feels that he is physically out of proportion in one way or another, and if he believes these features are not valued by his peers, he will experience anxiety and perhaps a loss of self-esteem.

In one study of adolescents, Bayley and Jones described a group of late maturing boys who were discontent and ill at ease in their adjustment.[15] They felt different from their peers who were growing away from them in interests and physique. This late maturing group became shy, irritable, and confused in their peculiar immature physical states. They could not live up to the expectations of their affective others. Certainly, this situation is common for young men and women who, during the years in which they are most anxious to conform and most sensitive to any sign of difference between themselves and their peers, find themselves at least temporarily with characteristics not consistent with accepted group stand-

[11] Horrocks, "The Adolescent," p. 703.

[12] F. K. Shuttleworth, "Sexual Maturation and the Physical Growth of Girls Aged 6 to 19." Monograph. *Social Research Child Development*, 2 (1937).

[13] E. Engle and M. Shelesnyak, "First Menstruation and Subsequent Menstrual Cycles of Pubertal Girls," *Human Biology*, 4 (1933), 431–453.

[14] Gardner Murphy, *Personality: A Biosocial Approach to Origins and Structure* (New York: Harper and Brothers, 1947), p. 100.

[15] N. Bayley and N. C. Jones, "Some Personality Characteristics of Boys with Retarded Skeletal Maturity," *Psychological Bulletin*, XXXVIII (1941), 603.

ards. The values of the larger culture play a significant role in the good or poor adjustment of persons with such atypical physiques.

Stone and Church have pointed out that, in the eighth and ninth grades, there is a spectacular developmental mismatching of boys and girls. "The average junior high school is populated by young ladies and male children."[16] This can be seen most conspicuously at any junior high school dance. Cole describes the resulting problems as follows:

Adolescents often make quite extreme reactions to compensate for their size. For instance, a tall girl may never go to dances because she is certain to be taller than most of the boys she dances with. Or a large girl may go in for athletics, politics, masculine clothes, and a career because she cannot be "cute" and feminine. Or a small-sized boy may become a "grind" largely because he cannot compete on equal terms physically with other boys—and may, if he attempts games even be beaten by girls. Very tall boys also have difficulties of adjustment. Chairs, desks, beds, driving seats of cars, and even doorways are too small for them. Whenever they are on their feet, they cannot help feeling conspicuous, and they are constantly being reminded of their height by inquiries about the condition of the atmosphere up where they are, and by similar pleasantries. The writer knows one girl of six feet two who was so miserable in American schools that she went to Sweden for her education, where her excessive height would be less conspicuous and where she would not be forced every week into three hours of gymnasium work and four hours of participation in some game—all of which made her acutely miserable. Fat girls and boys are among the unhappiest of adolescents and are almost always maladjusted.[17]

One girl in late adolescence described her feelings about her physical development in these words:

My basic physical growth and maturation was slower than the average girl's in my class but gradually by the age of sixteen I had reached my maximum height of 5' 9½" and weight of 130. By that time I had filled out in the right proportions and the snide remarks and nicknames had ceased. But my height began to pose another problem. I was taller than most of the boys in my class. Because of the recognition and accentuation of my height by my classmates I "couldn't possibly" go out with anyone shorter than myself. Having a natural inclination and the body type (ectomorph-mesomorph) for athletics, I began to take more interest in them in order to improve myself and excel in some fields to compensate for what I lacked in others. As I grew older and the boys did too, my height ceased to be the great disadvantage it had been

[16] Joseph Stone and Joseph Church, *Childhood and Adolescence* (New York: Random House, 1957), p. 286.

[17] Luella Cole, *Psychology of Adolescence*, 5th ed. (New York: Rinehart and Co., 1959), p. 28.

previously. I now had developed new attitudes and feelings toward my height and became less conscious of the reactions of others. My attitude began to change from resignation and acceptance to that of preference, a rationalization which subdued my previously hostile attitudes toward my height. Although my selection of a mate will still be limited and I think of all the wonderful boys I know who will have to remain a "buddy" I now feel that my height is an advantage. Because of my height and basic body build I will not have to worry about gaining undesired weight in later life. My chubby little friends from early adolescent days now envy my figure.

Figure 36 shows the physical differences between two girls of the same chronological and mental age, in the same grade in school, and from similar socioeconomic backgrounds. One might expect that people would react differently toward these two girls because of their physical variations. Barker, Wright, and Gonick investigated this possibility and asked (without revealing the purpose of the study) various members of each girl's generalized other to check their own reactions toward each girl's maturity.[18] The results are recorded in Table XVIII. It can be seen that girl A, who is the same age as girl B, is considered more mature and is accorded more freedom and responsibility, probably because people assign her a position consistent with the physiological traits of an older person. Girl B, on the other hand, is accorded the position of a younger girl and is expected to play the role of someone younger than her own chronological age. Such differences in attitudes based on acceleration or retardation in physiological developments are the culturally defined variables that contribute to the formation of personality differences. It is by means of these kinds of experiences, in which a child endeavors to fulfill the expectations of the significant members of his culture, that he gains his own self-regarding attitudes and ego identity.

Rapid increase in height precedes menarche in girls and is coincident with the appearance of secondary sexual characteristics in boys. Maximum rate of weight growth seems to coincide with these signs of sexual maturity in girls and follows puberty in boys. Children who are most advanced in physical growth usually are furthest along in terms of achieving sexual maturity. This means that children who are heavier, taller, and more developed physically usually are nearer sexual maturity than children less advanced physically.

The mental growth curve in adolescence does not show the same positive acceleration characteristic of other physical traits in this period. This may be a characteristic of the measures used to test mental development,

[18] R. G. Barker, B. A. Wright; and M. R. Gonick, *Adjustment to Physical Handicap and Illness: A Survey of the Social Psychology of Physique and Disability* (New York: Social Science Research Council, 1946), p. 24. *See also* rev. ed. Bulletin 55, published in 1953 by the Social Science Research Council.

Table XVIII

Adult judgments of Social Maturity of Two Girls of the Same Chronological and Mental Age*

Activities judged	Child A Judges					Child B Judges			
	M	F	T	T+	T	A	F	T+	T
1. Go to movies alone	x	x	x	x	x				
2. Attend dances unchaperoned			x	x	x				
3. Not play "house"	x		x	x	x				
4. Conduct class recitation	x			x	x				
5. Buy school dress	x	x		x	x	x			
6. Stay alone over night				x	x				
7. Play bridge		x	x	x	x				
8. Decide how to wear her hair	x	x		x	x	x	x	x	
9. Teach SS class of younger children		x		x	x	x			
10. Go out with boys		x		x	x				
11. Not receive physical punishment	x	x	x	x	x	x			x
12. Overnight camping trip	x	x		x	x	x	x	x	
13. Buy winter coat	x	x							
14. Not enjoy playing on "slide"		x		x					
15. Participate in adults' conversation		x		x	x	x			
16. Not wear ¾-length sox	x	x	x						
17. Plan and conduct party		x		x	x	x			
18. Run household for a day		x	x	x	x				
19. Decide what movies to go to	x	x		x	x	x	x	x	
20. Choose her own friends	x			x	x	x	x	x	
21. Not play "London Bridge"	x		x	x	x				
22. Wear high heels		x		x	x				
23. Evening party at friend's	x	x	x	x	x	x	x	x	
24. Decide how to spend $5 gift	x	x		x	x				
25. Not wear "little girl" dresses	x	x	x	x					
26. Pluck eyebrows				x	x				
27. Social engagement alone at night				x					
28. Use rouge and lipstick		x		x	x				
29. Decide what to wear to party	x	x	x	x	x	x			
30. Use nail polish		x	x	x	x			x	
Total, mature judgments	16	19	13	28	26	11	5	6	1
Mean			19				6		

x indicates that the judge considers the child sufficiently mature for the behavior indicated.

F   father of the girl   T+   same teacher for each of the pair
M   mother of the girl   A   aunt with whom B lived
T   teacher of the girl

* R. G. Barker, B. A. Wright, and M. R. Gonick, *Adjustment to Physical Handicap and Illness: A Survey of the Social Psychology of Physique and Disability* (New York: Social Science Research Council, 1946), p. 26. *See also* the rev. ed. Bulletin 55, published in 1953 by the Social Science Research Council.

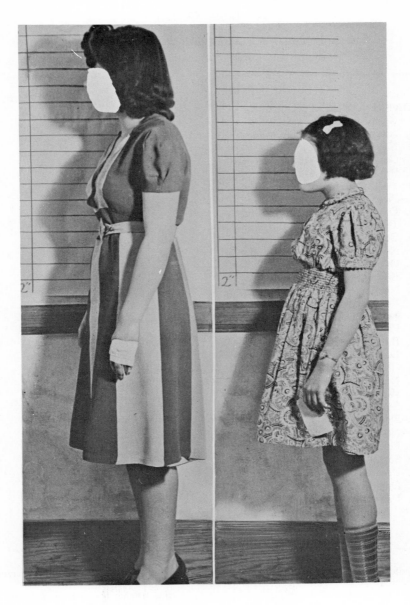

Child A
13 yrs.-2 mos.-27 days

Child B
13 yrs.-1 mo.-8 days

FIGURE 36. Contrast in physical maturation. (Reproduced from R. G. Barker, B. A. Wright, and M. R. Gonick, *Adjustment to Physical Handicap and Illness*, New York: Social Science Research Council, 1946, with permission of Roger G. Barker.)

but the findings we do have agree that mental growth is steady but is not positively accelerated during these years. Like the other forms of growth, however, mental growth achieves final development at the end of adolescence, or about the age of twenty-one.[19] Children of less mental ability achieve their ultimate mental maturation at an earlier age than do those of advanced intellectual capacity. Children of less mental ability mature more slowly intellectually and reach their maximum growth at an earlier age than do the average. Children who are above average in mental ability mature more rapidly in this regard and continue to develop longer than other youngsters. Again as in other forms of growth, there are wide variations from the mean. It is unwise to try to guess mental age from chronological age, or to guess mental capacity from grade attained in school because there are wide individual differences in mental capacity within each age group and schoolroom. There are also differences within an individual regarding his aptitudes for various kinds of mental activities. In Chapter 3 we reported that intelligence is not a single unitary trait. Intelligence is composed of a number of specific abilities positively correlated with one another. The growth curves we have described above are based on measurements of the kind of intelligence important in thinking abstractly and academically. Such IQ scores may not, for example, clearly identify the young person with creative talent. Thus, in assigning a particular role to a person based on his mental capacity, it is essential to specify which measure of intelligence is employed in making this judgment.

Hsu points out that the American adolescent is early taught the importance of self-esteem and the value of self-reliance. Hsu feels that the adult culture does not necessarily do all it might to prepare the adolescent for the achievement of these values and, in effect, sends him out into the world to make it "on his own" without close continuing family support in case of failure or disappointment. The child is taught to achieve his own success, either immediately in school or later in a career, and in this endeavor the family, as they are able, will support him emotionally and financially. However, the family in the American culture does not intend that this support be permanent, nor does it expect that the adolescent will someday come back home to become an adult member of the original household. The young person is instead encouraged to form his own home, to establish his own career, to join his own clubs and in short to develop his own peer group relationships. There are conspicuous exceptions to this system of values and expectations, as in the case of

[19] Florence L. Goodenough, "The Measurement of Mental Growth in Childhood," in *Manual of Child Psychology*, Leonard Carmichael, ed. (New York: John Wiley and Sons, 1954), p. 479. David Wechsler, *The Measurement and Appraisal of Adult Intelligence*, 4th ed. (Baltimore: Williams and Wilkins, 1958).

the unmarried male or female who remains a part of the parental establishment. This, says Hsu, is very much in contrast with the parental experiences of young Asians, who are oriented toward a vertical social relationship rather than a horizontal one and thus become more intimate with and sensitive to their elders than their peers.[20] Conversely, American adolescents are fundamentally oriented toward a horizontal relationship than a vertical one, being more intimate with and sensitive to their peers than to their elders.

Sometimes in an endeavor to keep close to his peers the adolescent may overidentify with the heroes of cliques and crowds. This is sometimes carried to a point where individual identity is obscured in the obsession with collective behavior. Edgar Friedenberg in his interesting book, *The Vanishing Adolescent*, fears that the emphasis on group adjustment and crowd behavior which sometimes characterizes modern life may interfere with the central developmental task of adolescence which is the achievement of individual self-esteem.

> Adolescence is the period during which a young person learns who he is, and what he really feels. It is the time during which he differentiates himself from his culture, though on the culture's terms. It is the age at which, by becoming a person in his own right, he becomes capable of deeply felt relationships to other individuals perceived as such. It is precisely this sense of individuality which fails to develop, or develops only feebly in most primitive cultures or among lower-status social groups. A successful initiation leads to group solidarity and a warm sense of belonging; a successful adolescence adds to these a profound sense of self—of one's own personality.[21]

THE PEER GROUP CULTURE

Within each age-grade there are various subcultures centered about certain ways of thinking and behaving. These shared behavioral characteristics are unique to each group and are acquired only by interaction with those who already share and embody, in their belief and action, the subculture way of life. Adolescence is an age that is particularly fertile for the development of subcultures. The need for peer group approval is probably higher at this age grade than at any other, and hence cohesive collective behavior is highly valued at this time.

The need for peer group approval is seen in the subculture of the adolescent gang or club. As criminologists have pointed out, most crimes are committed in groups, suggesting the delinquent's endeavor to find a

---

[20] F. L. K. Hsu, *Clan, Caste, and Club* (New York: D. Van Nostrand Co., 1963), p. 202.

[21] Edgar Z. Friedenberg, *The Vanishing Adolescent* (New York: Dell Publishing Co., 1959), p. 30. A well-written novel which deals with this theme is J. D. Salinger's *The Catcher in the Rye* (Boston: Little, Brown and Co., 1951).

primary group loyalty that will support his need for recognition and response at a level consistent with his own moral code. Thrasher found in his study of adolescent gangs that the size of the gang was usually a function of the number of boys who could maintain face-to-face relationships at one time.[22] A controlling need, insofar as size is concerned, was that when the gang all met at one time any one boy could easily be heard by all the others. When the gang became larger, common experiences became more difficult to share and the gang tended to fragment.

The gang age (nine to sixteen) is a crucial phase in the process of socialization. It is in this experience that boys usually first learn to practice role behavior in a primary group relationship of their own creation. Helanko divides the gang age into two subgroups: the *first* gang period (nine to twelve) is characterized by *introversion* interaction.[23] That is, the boys find their interests exclusively within the closed circle of their own gang. This in-group force leads to the growth of a firm organization, which is manifested in the formation of gang clubs in a repellent attitude toward other neighborhood gangs. The *second* gang period (twelve to sixteen) is *extraversive*. As the ages of the boys increase, there gradually develop competing outside interests that weaken the intense inner cohesion that characterized the younger childhood gang. The group, however, remains clearly identified as a gang with primary peer group loyalties and symbolic commitments prevailing.

Some gangs persist as subculture groups beyond adolescence. Whyte describes such a gang of "corner boys" (ages twenty to twenty-nine) in which the peer group relationships are clearly defined in terms of primary group identifications and values:

> The corner-gang structure arises out of the habitual association of the members over a long period of time. The nuclei of most gangs can be traced back to early boyhood, when living close together provided the first opportunities for social contacts. School years modified the original pattern somewhat, but I know of no corner gangs which arose through classroom or school-playground association. The gangs grew up on the corner and remained there with remarkable persistence from early boyhood until the members reached their late twenties or early thirties. In the course of years some groups were broken up by the movement of families away from Cornerville, and the remaining members merged with gangs on nearer corners; but frequently movement out of the district does not take the corner boy away from his corner. On any evening on almost any corner one finds corner boys who have come in from other parts of the city or from suburbs to be with their old friends. The resi-

---

[22] F. Thrasher, *The Gang* (Chicago: University of Chicago Press, 1927). *See also* Albert K. Cohen, *Delinquent Boys* (New York: The Free Press, 1955).

[23] R. Helanko, "Peer Groups and Personality," in *Personality and Social Systems*, Neil Smelser and William Smelser, Eds. (New York: John Wiley and Sons, 1963), pp. 238–247.

dence of the corner boy may also change within the district, but nearly always he retains his allegiance to his original corner.

Home plays a very small role in the group activities of the corner boy. Except when he eats, sleeps, or is sick, he is rarely at home, and his friends always go to his corner first when they want to find him. Even the corner boy's name indicates the dominant importance of the gang in his activities. It is possible to associate with a group of men for months and never discover the family names of more than a few of them. Most are known by nicknames attached to them by the group. . . .

The code of the corner boy requires him to help his friends when he can and refrain from doing anything to harm them. When life in the group runs smoothly, the obligations binding members to one another are not explicitly recognized. Once Doc asked me to do something for him, and I said that I welcomed the chance to reciprocate. He objected: "I don't want it that way. I want you to do this for me because you're my friend. That's all."

It is only when the relationship breaks down that the underlying obligations are brought to light. While Alec and Frank were friends, I never heard either one of them discuss the services he was performing for the other, but when they had a falling-out over the group activities with the Aphrodite Club, each man complained to Doc that the other was not acting as he should in view of the services that had been done for him. In other words, actions which were performed explicitly for the sake of friendship were revealed as being part of a system of mutual obligations.

Not all corner boys live up to their obligations equally well, and this factor partly accounts for the differentiation in status among them. The man with a low status may violate his obligations without much change in his position. His fellows know that he has failed to discharge certain obligations in the past, and his position reflects his past performances. On the other hand, the leader is depended upon by all the members to meet his personal obligations. He cannot fail to do so without causing confusion and endangering his position.[24]

The need to conform to and be approved by his peers requires that the adolescent accept the position and play the appropriate role assigned him by his contemporaries. The insightful young person will know what this position is, what role he is expected to play, and why he is assigned this particular position in the group. One of the writers was acquainted with a young man who found he was expected to play a role which was not consistent with his own personal needs and expectations, even though he enjoyed the position's status and prestige assigned him by the group. This young man grew up in a family of strict moral character but of cosmopolitan interests. He enroled at a college with a strong sectarian orientation which was not congenial to his own training or experiences.

[24] W. F. Whyte, *Street Corner Society: The Social Structure of an Italian Village Slum* (Chicago: University of Chicago Press, 1943), pp. 253–263.

He was not an athlete so did not find friends in that group. Neither was he sufficiently a scholar to enjoy the company of the "intellectuals." Because he adhered to dominant, middle class mores and was a pleasant and aggressive young man, he found himself in the foreground of the more conservative religious students. His character was consistent with their moral standards; but as one of their leaders, in the position assigned to him, he was expected to play the role of an evangelist for the group's religious point of view. While he enjoyed the status of leader, it was not possible for him to fulfill the role expectation required of him. At the end of the semester, he transferred to a more cosmopolitan institution where he could develop a significant other more consistent with his own background and interests.

The need to conform and be like his peers may bring the adolescent into conflict with his own family. Nieman and Stouffer have pointed out how the divergence in norms and attitudes between the family group and the peer group may create conflict situations for the individual.[25] It is the unusual parent who can successfully compete with an adolescent's peers for places of prominence in his affective other. The sensitive young person, anxious to please his parents, also feels compelled to maintain prestige in the eyes of his own generation. Physically, he feels equal to many adults, yet he is required in various ways to submit to parental and adult domination. This is also the age when the adolescent is beginning to experiment with and test his own assertion of authority. This may result in open or covert rebellion against parental authority, or it may resolve itself in overt obedience. The adolescent may feel guilty about his ambivalent feelings toward authority figures such as his parents. Conflicting roles and responsibilities within the primary group relationship may characterize the most pleasant home atmosphere. A neighborhood example of normal parent-child conflict came to the writer's attention in a family where the father and his thirteen-year-old son found themselves in disagreement over the proper operation of the boy's morning newspaper route. The problem was finally resolved when the father defined his own position in relationship to this responsibility by writing the following letter to his son:

Dear Bob:

I thought I had better put this down in writing so we would have it as a matter of record. I want to talk to you about your paper route.

Originally your mother and I were not enthusiastic about your having a morning route. As you have demonstrated your capability in

[25] Lionel J. Nieman, "The Influence of Peer Groups Upon Attitudes Toward the Feminine Role," in *Personality and Social Systems*, Neil Smelser and William Smelser, Eds. (New York: John Wiley & Sons, 1963), pp. 248–254; Samuel A. Stouffer, "An Analysis of Conflicting Social Norms," *American Sociological Review*, 14 (1949), 707–717.

handling it, I have become more optimistic about your continuing with this. However, as you know, I have been unhappy that you have not done those things which would have made it easier for me to help you where you needed it. This has resulted in my frequently nagging you, setting deadlines and in general confusion. I am not going to do any of that any more and I want to tell you why.

This is *your* route. It is not *mine*. It is not *our* route. So I should let you run it yourself. Your boss is your *Sentinel* manager, not me. He will hold you responsible. I would like to help you set it up properly, but this is really not my job. All my life I have run things, and I would like to see you run your route properly also. But this I should not do because it is *your* route.

So in the future I will not interfere or volunteer advice or help unless you ask for it. If you get in a jam I will do what I can, although you will have to take what is available under the conditions you present at the time you need me. You will also have to take the consequences and the rewards of doing this thing by yourself. This way you may learn responsibility and I will not be upset.

The only conditions your mother and I set are health and school-work. If you are in bed at 8:30 and keep your work up to standard you may continue. But just as we will not interfere in your route, we do not want you to interfere with our plans either, and I refer to vacations and other things which may require your extra planning, etc.

Dad

The approval of the peer culture is essential to adolescent adjustment. It is a troubled young person who believes his affective other (which in these years includes most importantly his peer culture) disapproves of his physique, dress, speech, or anything else about him, especially if he cannot or is not permitted to change these characteristics. But the adolescent's family also remains a part of his affective other and even though he may consciously reject the idea, he usually is still emotionally dependent upon the approval and support of his original primary group. This brings us to a discussion of the adolescent's behavior traits as they are related to his home experiences.

FAMILY CULTURE PATTERNS AND ADOLESCENT BEHAVIOR

Social scientists are agreed that the values and behavior standards of a family do exercise an influence upon the character and personality traits of its members. Some authorities see these behavioral characteristics being transmitted via family culture patterns[26] and others believe these traits develop as a result of the family authority structure.[27]

[26] Walter L. Slocum, "Family Culture Patterns and Adolescent Behavior," *Bulletin 648, Institute of Agricultural Sciences* (Pullman, Wash.: Washington State University, Oct. 1963).

[27] Urie Bronfenbrenner and Edward C. Devereaux Jr., "Family Authority Structure and Adolescent Behavior," in *Proceedings of the Sixteenth International Congress of Psychology* (Amsterdam: North Holland Pub. Co., 1962), pp. 414–418.

Family culture patterns as defined in sociological terminology by Slocum refer to those values and standards which when internalized by the family members, serve as guides for conduct outside the family as well as within the parental home.[28] "If transmission of family culture patterns were complete and if other influences did not intervene, we might expect brothers and sisters to react identically when confronted by identical social situations. We know, however, that substantial differences sometimes exist in the attitudes and behavior of brothers and sisters when confronted by the same situation; consequently, some may wonder if family values and standards are really so important after all."[29]

In order to determine the impact of family culture patterns on adolescent behavior, Slocum examined by means of anonymous questionnaires students in six different high schools in the state of Washington (1,307 boys and 1,194 girls). These questionnaires gave the young people an opportunity to anonymously rate their own families on four variables: (1) family democracy; (2) affection among family members; (3) cooperation among family members; and (4) fairness of discipline. Each student was himself rated in terms of his scholastic interest and achievement, his participation in school and extracurricular activities, and dating, plus several nonschool recreational activities.

Slocum, after examining the data, came to the conclusion that in this study the hypothesis that families exercise important, though differing, influences on adolescent interests and activities was confirmed. The study indicated that families which were rated high by the students in terms of the four criteria generally produced adolescents who were high on school related activities and low on delinquent behavior. Adolescents in these high rated families tended to perceive their families as concerned about them and their welfare as persons more than did those adolescents who came from families that did not rate high on these four scales. However, it was also observed that the *bulk* of the variations in teenage behavior could *not* be accounted for by the family culture patterns. Slocum concluded that ". . . peer group standards and expectations may in many cases be more important and more powerful influences than family standards and expectations."[30] It is pertinent to recall at this point Nieman's investigation of the impact of family culture patterns which indicated that the efficacy of such variables (family culture patterns) was in part a function of time; peer patterns becoming more influential and family patterns less potent as the adolescent grew older and more independent.[31]

Bronfenbrenner and Devereaux investigated certain adolescent be-

[28] Slocum, "Family Culture Patterns and Adolescent Behavior," p. 6.
[29] *Ibid.*, p. 4.
[30] *Ibid.*, p. 31.
[31] Lionel J. Nieman, "The Influence of Peer Groups upon Attitudes Toward the Feminine Role," *Social Problems*, 2 (1954), 104–145.

havior variables, considering how they might be related to the family authority structure. Four hundred students in the tenth grade of Ithaca High School, Ithaca, New York, ". . . responded to a questionnaire designed to yield information about their families, with respect to such matters as "family composition, types of child rearing techniques employed both by the father and the mother, division of labor between the parents in household tasks, and authority structure in the family."[32] The adolescents were also exposed to measures of their own behavior and personality. Independent validation of these assessments was made by direct interviews with a sample of the experimental population. The families were classified in terms of types of family authority structure such as (1) patriarchal, (2) matriarchal, and (3) equalitarian.[33] There are many ramifications in the study but we are primarily interested in that part of the inquiry which concerned itself with the impact that these various types of home situations may have had on the adolescents who grew up in them. When rated by their teachers the boys from the various types of homes were described as follows:

1. Boys from patriarchal homes are seen as relatively high on responsibility, leadership, daring, persistence, and academic achievement and as somewhat low on sensitivity to the feelings of others. The authors suggest that this type of boy seems to resemble the traditional entrepreneurial person of earlier generations.

2. The teachers viewed boys from equalitarian families as spontaneous, outgoing, and expressive but also as more childish, mischievous, and irresponsible. Their school achievement was lower than that of the other groups, and their profiles resembled the team-playing "Organization Man" of W. H. Whyte.

3. Teachers saw boys from the matriarchal families as responsible, controled, and persistent, as cooperative and well-behaved but also as submissive, shy, and noncompetitive. They held high levels of aspiration and were high achievers in schoolwork. The authors regarded these adolescents as compulsively disciplined, bureaucratic personalities.

4. The findings regarding girls were more ambiguous. Girls from equalitarian homes resembled boys from equalitarian homes, but girls from matriarchal homes had many of the characteristics of boys from patriarchal homes. The authors believe that what is important here is whether the strong parent is of the same or the opposite sex. Thus, girls in matriarchal homes are described as

[32] Bronfenbrenner and Devereaux, "Family Authority Structure and Adolescent Behavior," p. 415.

[33] Patriarchal was defined in the study as a family situation in which the father had the final say, matriarchal, where the mother's word was final, and equalitarian where mother and father made decisions jointly.

relatively high on leadership, daring and dominance, whereas in patriarchal homes they are seen as submissive, noncompetitive, adult-oriented, and apprehensive.

5. Social class differences did not seem to make any great difference in these results although there were some exceptions. Thus, in patriarchal families, if the father has only a secondary education, both boys and girls tend to rate high on masculine attributes, activities, and interests. Among patriarchal families with college-educated fathers, however, although the girls still show a strong masculine profile of attributes, the boys in our sample show rather consistently a more submissive, feminine pattern.

While Bronfenbrenner and Devereaux make it clear that the findings reported above are tentative and have not yet survived the criticism and evaluation of repeated investigations, they do make the following interesting observation:

> The general pattern which seems to be emerging from these findings, if substantiated in further research, raises some rather sobering questions about recent trends in family structure in America and elsewhere: what is the price of the equalitarian family, with its democratic atmosphere of warmth and "togetherness." Will the spontaneous, outgoing and emotionally expressive adolescents from these families develop into forcefully creative adults? Or are these values bought at the expense of responsibility and self-discipline? Is it possible that somewhat firmer parental discipline, or somewhat clearer role differentiation between the parents, are essential for the development of emotionally mature and effective adults? In a world of organization men, who will be the leaders and achievers?[34]

FAMILY CLASS POSITION AND ROLE BEHAVIOR

The adolescent experiences vastly increased mobility and he interacts more frequently with the culture beyond his own family and neighborhood. As a child he has learned that his position in the larger society is not determined solely by his own interests, talents, and human nature, but is already established by his family background, place of residence, religion, race, and nationality. Initially, as a child, and more consciously as an adolescent he learns to regard himself and his family in terms of this position assigned him by the larger culture. How he behaves, where he goes, and who his friends may be are functions of his social status and positions.

Acceptance of his positions and attending status as defined by his affective other and by himself in his home community means that oppor-

[34] Bronfenbrenner and Devereaux, "Family Authority Structure and Adolescent Behavior," p. 417.

tunities for social mobility and personality growth are limited to behavior patterns consistent with his and society's concept of his place in the community. As long as the young person remains in the community in which these positions are derived, and as long as he accepts these definitions as his own, he will function in a well-prescribed and predictable manner consistent with the roles associated with his positions.

Hollingshead has explored the relationship of adolescent behavior to family background and has concluded that, in the community that he studied (a midwestern city of 10,000 population), ". . . the social behavior of adolescents is related functionally to the position their families occupy in the social structure of the community." He points out that,

> . . . the family and neighborhood sub-cultures not only set the stage upon which the child acts but they also provide him with the ways of acting and definitions of action. In addition, they make him realize that he will be rewarded for some kinds of behavior and punished for others. They provide him with roles, teach him how to play them, and accord him different status position as he plays such roles as child in the family, pupil in the school, or little boy in the street. As he participates in successive social situations, he learns to act in certain ways, to regard himself as a valued member of the group or as an unwanted person. Unconsciously, he is being molded into a personality that is simultaneously a creature of his experience and a creator of new situations in which he will act as a molder of conduct.[35]

Hollingshead found that Elmtown families could be grouped into five social classes, from Group I, which represented the highest status in the community, to Group V, which was lowest in such a classification. The following summary description of the influence of membership in one of these classes upon childhood and adolescent behavior is worthy of our thoughtful consideration:

> Children reared in class I, II, and III homes are taught be "polite," to have "good manners," to be "refined," and to use "judicious" speech. They are taught also that personal aggression is extremely dangerous from the viewpoint of social acceptance. By precept and example, they learn that one's aims are to be achieved by stratagem and subterfuge rather than by combativeness. They are taught not to play with hoodlums, to watch their manners, to select carefully their friends, hobbies, and recreational pursuits. There is continual pressure from parents to study, to avoid the lower classes, to go to Sunday School regularly. The parents generally know the parents of the children with whom their children associate. If these friendships do not meet with their approval they ordinarily bring pressure to bear on the child to drop the friends and activities which do not conform with parental expectation. They are not always successful, but the pressure is active. On the whole,

[35] Hollingshead, *Elmtown's Youth*, p. 445.

though, children in these three classes are guided by their parents along lines approved by the class cultures with remarkable success.

By way of contrast, the class V child reared "below" or "near" the canal learns very soon that his family is stigmatized in many ways—area of residence, kind of residence, occupation, reputation, number of children—and that he is held in contempt by boys and girls in the higher classes. He learns to resent his family but he must rely upon it for food, clothes, and shelter. However, he has almost unlimited freedom to do as he desires, for his father is generally away from home, at work, or in search of pleasure, many times in jail, and his mother is busy trying to eke out a bare existence for her many children by means of a job outside the home. Since there is little or no room in the severely over-crowded small house where he may play, he plays along the river and the canal, in and near the coal chutes, and along the railroad tracks. His parents admonish him to be a "good" boy (a "little lady" in the case of a girl), but there is little effective control over his play. From the age of 5 or 6 he is faced with the responsibility of looking out for himself in the neighborhood, in school, and around the community. By the time adolescence is reached he has assumed full control of himself and his activities. He earns his own money, makes his own choices, and believes that he is acting as a "free agent." Actually he does what he and his fellows have learned they must do if they are to play the roles appropriate for their age and class statuses. In his thoughts and actions, he is bolstered by his clique mates (and it is not coincidence that almost all are class V's, and the rest are class IV's) as well as by older youths and adults in the social circles in which he moves. He insists upon absolute freedom in the spending of his money. If one tells him he is foolish to spend his money for old cars, flashy clothes, liquor, gambling, and sex one will be told forcibly—we experimented on this point with a few class V's we knew well—"No one can tell me how I am going to spend my money. Did you earn it?" This insistence upon freedom to do what he desires brings him into conflict with the law with significantly greater frequency than the other classes. This situation, however, is accepted by the class V youngster as something he must expect for he has seen it happen with parents, relatives, and friends.[36]

It should be noted that these are customary rather than legal definitions of behavior. The law does not require that people relate to each other in this manner, nor does the law insist that people behave in a manner consistent with their positions. It is also noteworthy that the individuals, and particularly the adolescents themselves, accept these definitions. The effect of such social controls is nonetheless effective in establishing and maintaining the *status quo*.

If the young person moves to another community, he will carry with him these same self-regarding attitudes. Whether or not they will persist in influencing his behavior will depend upon the affective other he ac-

[36] Hollingshead, *Elmtown's Youth*, p. 444.

quires in the new community and upon the positions the new culture assigns to him. The adolescent away from home, whether on a job, in college, or on a visit will probably feel uncomfortable and strange until once again he tests his new environment and knows what kind of behavior is expected of him.

In the adult world the most urgent adjustments the adolescent will be required to make are represented by the achievement of marital, educational, vocational, political, and religious maturity. The achievement of heterosexual interests to replace interests in self (characteristic of childhood) and to replace interests in members of one's own sex (characteristic of prepubescence) is a very real problem for some people in our culture.

THE ACHIEVEMENT OF SOCIAL MATURITY

The growth of social maturity, progressing from infancy to adulthood, may be outlined as follows: The baby is fully egocentric, and is concerned only with its own feelings. Self-manipulation and self-interest are characteristic of this period. The child soon learns, as his interests broaden, that in order to satisfy all his needs he must sometimes be dependent on others. He feels kindly toward those who do things for him. As he moves out of the home to the level of play with other children, he begins to learn the necessity for cooperative interaction. The gang age places prime values upon close in-group loyalties with members of the same sex. Heterosexual interests emerge with pubescence and there is a still further extension of the adolescent's ego developed in an emotionalized way with another person or persons of the opposite sex. If heterosexual interests culminate in marriage and family, the individual has achieved adult status and responsibilities that may represent a high order of social maturity. Fortunately many people are able to achieve a continuing development of self-realization through shared interpersonal experiences in the larger community. In this regard Pfuetze says:

> One grows by giving and receiving within a community. The human organism is born into, nourished by, participates in, communicates with a world of persons. Thus the individual comes to full stature as a human person in the reality of relationship with other persons and things and events—and, Buber would add, with God. In the mutual recognition of other selves, like myself yet different; in response to their behavior, often unexpected and disturbing, vis-a-vis my own thought and meaning and behavior; in acknowledgment of the mutual claims which persons as persons have upon each other the human self develops and has its being.[37]

[37] Paul E. Pfuetze, *Self, Society, Existence* (New York: Harper Torch Books, 1961), p. 233.

This sketchy outline of the emergence of social maturity has been included here to emphasize how a person's development can become arrested on any level of social growth. Every psychiatrist and clinical psychologist meets many people who have never emerged beyond an immature level of self-realization. These separated and isolated people have developed a social role that, in childhood, was sufficient to meet their needs at a time when such a role was appropriate to the expected behavior of the individual. But they overlearned this role, and, because it satisfied their childhood needs so completely, they were never motivated to move on to new roles of responsibility in keeping with new positions. Habits of self-manipulation in babyhood may signalize self-love and self-curiosity, appropriate attitudes at that age; but as substitutes for normal, outgoing interests in people of one's own generation, they represent an infantile fixation.

Happy adjustment at each age is excellent preparation for the next stage of living, but it sometimes happens that the comforts and pleasures of a younger age are made so complete that there is little motivation to prompt the child to strive for adult maturity. The problem is similar to the treatment a child receives in sickness. If the illness is made a particularly pleasurable experience, in which the child gains recognition and attention he would not receive otherwise, he may appropriate the illness as an adjustment mechanism, setting the basis for a malingering and hypochrondriacal personality. Each succeeding age development should hold forth the promise of new responsibilities and rewards that will challenge the neophyte to outgrow his present position.

Sometimes this process of self-realization can be cut short by economic or health catastrophies as can be witnessed in the following report.

The economic situation in our family was due to the death of my father at the age of forty, when the oldest boy was sixteen and the youngest was one year of age. There was no social security nor insurance for occupationally incurred diseases in those days. After my father's death, my sixteen-year old brother seemed suddenly to mature. On the day of the funeral, he turned to my mother and said: "Don't cry Mom. I'll take care of you." And to this self-imposed task as head and breadwinner of the family, he gave himself with all the eagerness of youth . . . . He never married. He lived with his mother until his death. His life was short, he worked hard, but I am sure he had more satisfaction than others who live only for themselves.[38]

Most social psychologists regard learning as the fundamental process in understanding human behavior. Human learning and the achievement

[38] James H. S. Bossard and Eleanor Stoker Boll, *The Large Family System* (Philadelphia: University of Pennsylvania Press, 1956), p. 121.

of self-realization, as we have been discussing them through these various age stages of growth, is not an automatic or guaranteed process. The phenomenon of "learning how to learn" (Harlow) which we discussed in Chapter 3 is pertinent here. Each person achieves social and emotional growth by actively learning to play the various roles associated with the positions appropriate to each age. An infant must learn the role of the infant before he can achieve the position of a child, and the child must learn the role behavior appropriate to childhood before he can assume the position of an adolescent. Similarly the adolescent must learn his part in the matrix of role relationships before he can assume the position and status of an adult. Cumming and Cumming have pointed out that this process of learning roles and role relationships ". . . does not automatically organize itself but requires an active process of simultaneously internalizing new role relationships and integrating them with those already internalized."[39] Erikson similarly makes the point that a child grows in ego strength as he learns the repertoire of role skills that makes possible the successful achievement of the next stage of human development. Cumming and Cumming have described Erikson's observation succinctly in the following paragraph:

> A child in his [Erikson's] view, increases both his skills and his drives as he matures, but, at the same time, society makes culturally determined demands of him and signifies culturally approved opportunities for action. For example, at a certain point in his life, a child must go to school, and there he may further increase his mastery of the environment. Such changes may coincide with more fundamental epigenetic phases of development and these inner and outer changes together will require major reorientations on the part of the child, both to himself and to the world around him. These needs for reorientation are essentially problems to be solved. If he solves each problem adequately as he meets it, a child will be better able to solve the next—in short, his ego will be stronger and more capable of further problem solution. If the child fails to resolve one crisis his ego remains weak and less able to resolve the next one.[40]

With the beginning of puberty, childhood comes to an end and the adolescent experiences what Erikson calls a "physiological revolution" within himself that threatens his body image and his ego identity. The adolescent becomes preoccupied with what he appears to be in the eyes of others as compared with what he feels himself to be. Adolescence is seen by Erikson as the stage in life when a positive, dominant ego identity

---

[39] John Cumming and Elaine Cumming, *Ego and Milieu* (New York: Atherton Press, 1962), p. 23.

[40] Cumming and Cumming, *Ego and Milieu*, p. 20. The reader may perceive that Erikson's use of *ego* is much the same as the older concept of *will* as discussed in Ch. 7.

must be established in order that he may experience the establishment and re-establishment of continuity with his preadolescent experiences.

> The sense of ego identity then, is the accrued confidence that the inner sameness and continuity . . . are matched by the sameness and continuity of one's meaning for others, as evidenced in the tangible promise of a "career."[41]

The adolescent, according to Erikson, must re-establish his ego identity in the light of his preadolescent experiences and accept his physical changes and libidinal feelings as part of himself. If identity is not satisfactorily achieved at this stage of self-development, there is the danger that role confusion will thwart further subjective development. The adolescent achieves selfhood and maturity in his experiences with the significant interpersonal relationships including religion, education, sexual behavior, and a career.

ADOLESCENCE AND RELIGION

It is not surprising that adolescence is frequently a time of idealism and philosophical self-searching. During childhood, morality and religion, like so many other things, have been the parents' responsibility. As the adolescent puts on his strength, moves out from the influence of the family circle and endeavors to locate himself in the adult world, he assumes greater personal control in matters of philosophical orientation and personal commitment.

Berelson and Steiner note that in many Western countries, adolescence is the most idealistic period in life:

> The young person growing to maturity, begins to see in adolescence the disparity between the moral precepts taught him as a child and the real conditions of life, and he often turns to a high moral and political altruism in reaction to his elders and in anticipation of his own imminent immersion in the actualities of life. This response includes rebellion against the parents, attachment to "causes," strong criticisms of the going order . . . .[42]

Similarly Ackerman has observed that:

> Adolescence is a groping, questioning stage, a phase in which the adolescent condenses the values that will guide his social perspective for the major part of his life. It is exactly here that he confronts the challenge of bringing into harmony his view of self and his view of the world. He must now link his life striving with a personal philosophy.

---

[41] Erikson, *Childhood and Society*, p. 228. In the interactionist frame of reference, the use of *ego* to modify *identity* is superfluous.

[42] Berelson and Steiner, *Human Behavior: An Inventory of Scientific Findings*, p. 84.

The adolescent asks: "What is life? Who am I? What am I good for? Where do I fit? Who are my real friends? Who are my enemies? What must I fight? With whom? Against whom? For what life goals? And finally, Is life really worth the struggle?"

This kind of feverish, anxious searching for identity, values and social orientation is paralleled by an expanding interest in social and economic conflicts, in religion and philosophy. In the service of this search, the adolescent mobilizes his intellect and exploits it as a defense against his anxiety. Such struggles deeply affect the adolescent's choice of group associations. In a time of testing of parental images and temporary dissolution of self, the adolescent seeks to identify with something larger than himself. His urge is to ally with a cause greater than his own. Economic and religious affiliations offer such an opportunity.[43]

At this age the adolescent comes to grips with certain physical and social realities, which, if he has escaped them earlier, can be postponed no longer. Military obligations, college education, courtship and marriage, sickness and death, career planning, political identifications, and religious orientation become subjects requiring personal decision. The young person brings to each of these areas of evaluation the knowledge, the concepts, and personality traits he has acquired in the experiences of infancy and childhood.

Undoubtedly religion represents for some young people an uncritically accepted set of values. Mature religion involves an attempt to come to grips with certain values about which philosophers have argued for centuries. As noted in Chapter 7, the only irreligious man is he for whom nothing is really sacred. Such a person lives only within himself and is not related to other people in terms of shared goals and values. All cultures have been characterized either by monolithic or pluralistic forms of religious life and it is in this manner that people have endeavored to relate themselves to one another in the celebration of common goals and shared values.

The adolescent brings to the classroom the values of his affective other. Some of these values, which he has experienced and with which he has identified, may be challenged by the philosophies and sacred attitudes of a more complex affective other. Old values and commitments may be challenged by new and sometimes unique experiences, which may not coincide with existing value systems. The accommodation of values that accompanies the achievement of new positions or statuses can be threatening and painful. Serious conflicts may arise with parents or friends over changing religious convictions and attitudes. The adolescent may find himself in conflict with his own past beliefs and faith. The relatively small number of persons who shift significantly from the religious view of par-

---

[43] Nathan W. Ackerman, *The Psychodynamics of Family Life* (New York: Bone Books, 1958), p. 215.

ents indicates the strength of habit in the formation of adult attitudes. These religious patterns are crystallized in each person into a system of attitudes and beliefs which are sometimes called conscience. Hopefully, this conscience is sufficient in its scope to embrace the wide areas of adaptations required of a growing and questioning adolescent. There is no escape from a provincial set of religious values except into a more meaningful system of religious expectations.

Adolescence is a time of anticipation of unattained yet obtainable values. This quest for meaning and purpose in living is perhaps more immediately pertinent to the adolescent needs and aspirations than for any other age. Life's unattained possibilities, the awareness of the difference between what is and what might be, sets the stage for expectation and fulfillment. "Salvation," according to Allport, "comes only to him who ceaselessly betters himself in the pursuit of objectives that in the end are not fully attained."[44]

ADOLESCENCE AND EDUCATION

By the time the adolescent reaches high school age his personality structure is well on the way to final crystallization. When a child reaches the adolescent years three interactive variables (Chapter 2)—(1) organic heritage, (2) environmental forces, and (3) the resulting subjective variables—all have had an opportunity to make their mark on the character and personality of the young person. His health and physical characteristics (including intelligence) are visibly taking shape; his home background has exerted its full impact with results that are clearly discernible, and the outlines of his unique personality are readily identifiable by others. Researchers are generally agreed that by the beginning of the adolescent years it is possible to predict with reasonable accuracy the kind of adult adjustment toward which each child is headed.[45] Underlying this prediction, of course, is the assumption that the personality of each adolescent is already locked into a combination of realities that most young people are likely to accept rather than resist. In fact, resistance and motivation are themselves discernible personal traits, which, if present, can be identified and thereby enhance the prediction.

Fortunately there are enough exceptions to these predictions to make the researcher humble in his prognostications. There are avenues and ladders of upward and downward mobility in the social class structure which can enable some of the young people to escape the predictions of the computer. The primary ladder in this regard is formal education. For adolescents this means high school and college.

[44] Gordon W. Allport, *Becoming: Basic Considerations for a Psychology of Personality* (New Haven, Conn.: Yale University Press, 1955), p. 67.

[45] Percival M. Symonds and Arthur R. Jensen, *From Adolescent to Adult* (New York: Columbia University Press, 1961).

In the community which they studied, Havighurst *et al.* call the high school the only reasonable avenue from adolescence to adulthood.

> Schools provide the only pathway to adolescence in River City, and high school is the only easily traveled route through adolescence to adulthood. For the third of the River City youths who do not finish high school the way to adulthood is not an easy one . . . . drop outs have the greatest difficulty in growing up successfully. They are the most vulnerable to delinquency. They get the poorest jobs if they get jobs at all. They have the most trouble with marriage. The churches see very little of them.[46]

A high school education has become the prescribed route for the adolescent on his way to adulthood. The quality of education in high schools has continued to improve in the last generation; but knowledge and technical skills learned in high school are not the only things the adolescent gains in this experience. High schools also provide young people opportunities to practice and develop social and leadership skills, opportunities to experiment with new ideas and attitudes, and a chance to experience and participate in cultural values. High school is a vehicle by means of which young people can practice becoming adults, hopefully even more alert and knowledgeable than their sometimes proud parents.

The fact that most high school graduates do better in life by almost any measure than do the dropouts is not *entirely* due to the impact of high school education. Many of these alert and well motivated young people would succeed even without a high school degree although it would be difficult even for them. A high school degree has in itself become very nearly a minimal requirement for successful adult living—it is part of the folkways of our culture; to ignore it in this education-conscious generation is tantamount to isolating oneself from significant peer group relationships.

Two respected studies have been made of the children and young people of anonymous midwestern communities, namely *Elmtown's Youth* and *Growing Up in River City*.[47] Both studies focus much of their attention on the educational and class structure systems of their respective communities and comparisons of the findings are pertinent to our study of adolescent development. *Elmtown's Youth* was published in 1949, while *Growing Up in River City* was published in 1962. Both studies were made under the auspices of the Committee on Human Development of the

---

[46] Robert J. Havighurst *et al.*, *Growing Up in River City* (New York: John Wiley and Sons, 1962), p. 64. For an excellent treatment of the general social and cultural influences of the school experiences, *see* Wilbut B. Brookover and David Gottlieb, *A Sociology of Education* (2nd Ed.) (Cincinnati: American Book Co., 1964).

[47] Hollingshead, *Elmtown's Youth*; Robert J. Havighurst *et al.*, *Growing Up in River City*.

University of Chicago. The former study covered a more complex range of subjects, while the latter contented itself with a longitudinal observation of a parameter of children, following them from age twelve to young adulthood. Both studies regard social class as a major determining characteristic of the children of their respective communities. *Elmtown's Youth* was written about young people who grew up during Depression days, while the children of River City lived in a time of postwar prosperity. The former investigation found class structure unyielding. Even the school structure in Elmtown tended to reinforce social class status and discouraged social mobility. The River City study found that a similar class structure characterized that particular community but that the social classes appeared to be working together in an atmosphere of reasonable harmony. Furthermore, the children of River City had available to them a school system that provided ladders of upward mobility in the social class structure.

Let us look more closely at the children of River City as investigated by Robert J. Havighurst and his colleagues.[48] The study began in 1951 with four hundred boys and girls all of whom were in the sixth grade of River City (a midwestern community of 45,000 population) public schools in 1951–1952, plus some children from parochial and private schools of the same grade level. Also included were some children from special classes who were physically or mentally handicapped, but at the same grade level. The progress of these twelve-year-old children was observed until they reached the age of twenty. It is in essence a study of what happened to a typical group of children in the decade of the 1950's in a medium sized midwestern city.

As might be expected all of these children were classified in terms of their family background, intelligence, and personal and social adjustment. Several conclusions pertinent to our discussion can be derived from this exhaustive investigation:

1. The children who do well in high school in River City are those who are endowed with the greatest advantages, including mental ability, and families who encourage them in their studies. As might be expected from our interactive frame of reference the advantaged take further advantage of their resources and opportunities, and the disadvantaged tend to dig themselves into even deeper holes.

2. Thirty-five per cent of the River City young people do not finish high school. Those who drop out of high school generally do not find work a satisfactory alternative pathway to adulthood. The same factors which produce a poor school record usually guar-

[48] Havighurst *et al.*, *Growing Up in River City*.

antee a similarly poor work record. The authors regard dropping out of high school as a clear sign of rebellion against society's folkways resulting in an unfavorable prognosis for the future. Dropping out of school in 1930 to take a job was reasonable but in the 1960's it is a sign of general maladjustment to society.[49]

3. The educational systems of River City offer the adolescents an opportunity to rise above the level of their parents on the socioeconomic scale. For many young people it requires great effort in terms of educational achievement to avoid falling behind their parents in this regard. Young people generally must secure more education than their parents in River City in order to maintain the socioeconomic level attained by their parents.

4. Educational achievement in River City is the accepted way and the usual way to climb in the social structure. For girls marriage may present an alternative route, if they marry higher placed and better motivated men.

5. Successful social adjustment in the peer group is just as important if not more important than intelligence as a means of succeeding in school and doing well in adult life. The authors are quick to point out that social adjustment here does not mean peer conformity, but rather such qualities as leadership, acceptance of others, autonomy, and a sense of personal worth.

Education beyond high school is becoming increasingly available to young people. In the River City study, nearly 30 per cent of the population surveyed eventually enrolled in college. These figures can be compared to the national average. In 1900 only 4 per cent of the college age population of the United States enrolled in institutions of higher learning, in 1956 this had become 35 per cent; in 1966 the percentage is expected to be 45 per cent. In 1970 it is anticipated that half the college age population will be enrolled in college or universities. Some affluent and striving communities are already witnessing 80 per cent and even 90 per cent of their high school graduates entering college.[50]

A thoughtful evaluation of the adolescent's perceptions of his peer group relationships includes the observation that academic achievement is not accorded a high status in most schools. It is the concern of some educators that while we are developing programs for gifted children which will isolate them still further from their contemporaries, we are abandoning the majority of high school students to their hedonistic

---

[49] Employment opportunities for high school dropouts continue to dry up in almost all communities. Employment of adolescents, ages sixteen and seventeen, is only half what it was fifty years ago.

[50] Nevitt Sanford (ed.), *The American College* (New York: John Wiley and Sons, 1962).

pleasures.[51] In a two-year study of the "climate of values" in nine mid-western high schools, Coleman came to the conclusion that "despite wide differences in parental background, type of community, and type of school, there was little difference in the standards of prestige, the activities which confer status, and the values which focus attention and interest."[52] When the various measures of position and status were evaluated by the high school students in this study, social success, either through athletic achievement or by gregarious friendliness consistently rated highest. Scholarship and academic achievement had relatively low position in *all* schools studied. This finding by Coleman was found to be true not only in small town schools, working class schools, and upper class suburban schools, it was true even in a private university laboratory school where the students were selected on the basis of their academic orientation. In the latter institution the student leaders reported that the "thing to do" to be part of the crowd was to get reasonably good grades without expending special effort in doing so. In all schools studied the investigator detected "a norm against working too hard on one's studies." Coleman likens the situation to the condition, which prevails in some office or factory situations, where employees jointly bring group sanctions against the "rate busters." In the school situation the name for rate buster would be "curve raiser" or "DAR" (damned average raiser). A more extreme example cited by Coleman is any jail where there is a collective response to the demands and restraints of the jailers. "The fact that prisons do not rehabilitate, but largely confirm offenders in criminal ways, is almost solely attributable to the fact that each prisoner is subject to the society of the inmates, with its deviant norms and values, and cannot be reached by the professed goals of the prison."[53] So is it in the school or in the employment situation, where the peer group holds down effort to a level which can be maintained by all. Coleman does not evaluate this reaction but merely notes that this behavior is a logical response to this particular system of rewards and punishments. The school behavior is no different from the reactions of some workers who, in return for their pay, will do as much work as is necessary but no more, or inmates of jails who respond with no more cooperation than is necessary to gain certain privileges; and in both situations those isolated persons who would like to break out of this static pattern are likely to be sabotaged by their peers. Coleman's suggestion is that educators must either rescue

---

[51] Hilde T. Himmelweit, "The Role of Intelligence in Modifying Social Class Differences in Outlook," in *Proceedings of the Sixteenth International Congress of Psychology* (Amsterdam: North Holland Pub. Co., 1962), pp. 273–281. *Cf. also* James B. Conant, *Slums and Suburbs* (New York: The McGraw-Hill Book Co., 1961).

[52] James S. Coleman, "The School and Personality," in *Personality and Social Systems*, Neil Smelser and William Smelser, eds. (New York: John Wiley and Sons, 1963), pp. 212–229.

[53] Coleman, "The School and Personality," p. 221.

these highly motivated students from the tyranny of their materialistic peer culture or substitute a new climate of rewards and punishments. In this connection he recommends for consideration Deutsch's significant study in which the latter compared the effects of learning in "competitive educational situations" with "cooperative educational situations."[54] In this investigation the "competitive" classes were composed of five members each who were advised that they would be scored on the basis of their comparative ranking within the class during the semester of study. The "cooperating" classes, also composed of five members each, were advised that each class would be ranked as a class from 1 to 5 on the total showing the class made in solving the same problems to which the competitive groups were exposed. At the end of the semester, the ranks of the five classes were averaged, and the members of each class were graded according to their class's average rank. Thus, in the competitive situation, each student was compared with his classmates while in the cooperative situation each class was compared with other classes. Deutsch found that the results favored the cooperative learning situation not only in terms of knowledge gained, but also in terms of improved interpersonal relations which in the cooperative group were more reinforcing and positive. The structure of rewards in this comparative situation leads Coleman to suggest that the majority of high school students would be more highly motivated to achieve academically if scholarship, like sports, were based on total school or total class effort as opposed to a system which rewarded pupil-to-pupil competition. However unrealistic and remote this suggestion may be, it is nevertheless a novel and suggestive approach to modifying the nonchalance of the adolescent culture toward scholastic matters in such a manner that the adolescent's expectations will reinforce rather than conflict with education's goals.

SOCIAL EXPECTATIONS AND THE SEX ROLE

The basis of sexual motivation is of course biological; however, the direction that this sex interest will take and the objects to which it will become attached are culturally determined. This applies to sexual practices as well as to sexual objects. Furthermore, every known society imposes some restrictions upon sexual activity and enforces periods of abstinence which may have very little to do with physiological considerations.[55]

Adolescence as a distinct phenomenon is a problem only in human civilized communities. Subhumans are concerned not at all by the achievement of sexual maturity. Adolescence as a problem is unknown in many

[54] Morton Deutsch, "The Effects of Cooperation and Competition Upon Group Process," in Group Dynamics, D. Cartwright and A. Zander, eds. (Evanston, Ill.: Row, Peterson, 1953), pp. 319–353.

[55] Clellan S. Ford and Frank A. Beach, Patterns of Sexual Behavior (New York: Harper and Brothers, 1951).

primitive cultures, perhaps because of the presence of other and more demanding problems such as high mortality and death rates, precarious food supplies, and so on. In such cultures, the transition from childhood to maturity presents few problems and few social restrictions. Malinowski reports that the only sexual taboo among Trobriand Island children is incest. These children have no problem resulting from a change in attitude toward members of the opposite sex because promiscuous behavior is encouraged in children by their parents from an early age.[56]

A similar indulgent treatment of heterosexual play can be illustrated from the customs of the Baiga:

> Baiga children grow up free and unrestrained . . . . Their sexual consciousness is developed very early. Parents may insist on their children going to work and to work hard, but they rarely interfere with their pleasures . . . . Even when they see their children indulging in erotic play, they simply laugh tolerantly. "Sometimes we say, 'Why do it now? Wait a little,' But the children grow excited, so what should they do?" Lahakat might be expected to adopt this tolerant attitude, but Dhan Singh, a much stricter and chaster man, echoed it. "If a child of seven goes to a girl, what does it matter? It does no harm. But of course when they are grown up and go to the bazaars, then there is something in it." Sujji of Kawardha told me that "If I catch my young daughter with a boy I let her alone. I don't beat her or abuse her; otherwise the neighbors may say, 'Is she your wife or your daughter that you are so jealous? Why are you making trouble, you impotent old man? Let her do what she likes'."[57]

Our culture does not tolerate this kind of behavior. The development of strong family ties, important in a democracy, assumes that procreation will be limited to those who will be legally responsible for rearing and caring for the child. In our culture a high standard of living is associated with long education, late marriage, and consequently a longer period of adolescence. Berelson and Steiner note that in a complex society such as the United States, the factors of chronological age (years since birth), biological age (relative maturation), and social age (assigned roles) are not always identical.[58] For example authorities believe that the sexual drive reaches its peak in boys by the age of sixteen, but somewhat later for girls. This means that by the time of marriage most men have already passed the peak of their sexual capacity which occurs sometime in late adolescence.[59] Washburn comments on this disparity as follows:

[56] B. Malinowski, *Sex and Repression in Savage Society* (New York: Harcourt, Brace and Co., 1927).

[57] Verrier Elwin, *The Baiga* (London: Murray Co., 1939), p. 230.

[58] Berelson and Steiner, *Human Behavior: An Inventory of Scientific Findings*, p. 83.

[59] Berelson and Steiner, *Human Behavior: An Inventory of Scientific Findings*, p. 303.

Modern medicine and diet have accelerated puberty by about three years over what it was in the beginning of the 19th century. On the other hand, social developments have tended to postpone the age at which people take responsible positions. For example, if puberty is at fifteen and a girl is married at seventeen there is a minimum delay between biology and society. However, if puberty is at twelve, and marriage is at twenty, the situation is radically different. In terms of college entrance, people tend to enter older but to have grown up younger than formerly, and nothing in our system takes account of these facts.[60]

It is to be noted, however, that the age of marriage has been decreasing in the United States since 1900 and this trend continues today. The median age of first marriage for women was 22 in 1900, was 20.6 in 1950, and, for the first time, dropped below 20 in 1960.

A period of long adolescence may serve many useful functions in a complex industrialized economy characterized by a high standard of living as well as a highly interdependent matrix of role relationships. This bridge from childhood to adulthood provides the young person an opportunity to differentiate among the many adult models which compete for a place in his affective other. As the adolescent learns these distinctions he internalizes them in an orderly manner. If play is important to the child's development in achieving a repertoire of social skills, so is it important for a young person to explore and develop similar skills in interpersonal relationships at the heterosexual level. Such social experiences in the courtship game during adolescence are regarded by some authorities as a desirable prelude to satisfactory sexual behavior in adult life.[61] If the adolescent period is pointed at the achievement of marriage and the establishment of a home, it becomes important that the adolescent enjoy a sufficient breadth and variety of social contacts with members of the opposite sex to make a discriminating and happy choice of a marriage mate.

Except in some subcultural groups, we do not have in the United States well-defined and widely established customs regarding courtship procedures. Each family and more particularly each individual proceeds in courtship in terms of his personal social needs and cultural background. The sex role behavior of the adolescent is a function of his socioeconomic level, his religious background, his peer group expectations, and his concept of his own sex image. Thus the role the adolescent perceives as appropriate to him and to the members of the opposite sex evolves out of his own past experiences and his relationships with the significant

[60] Sherwood Washburn, *personal communication* (1961) in Berelson and Steiner, *Human Behavior: an Inventory of Scientific Findings*, p. 83.

[61] Berelson and Steiner, *Human Behavior: An Inventory of Scientific Findings*, p. 301; Ford and Beach, *Patterns of Sexual Behavior*, p. 197.

adult models that make up his affective other. However, there is consensus among students of sex role learning that, at least in the United States, the young people learn specific sexual behavior more from their peer culture than they do from adults.[62]

Courtship is the social form which provides the stage upon which the adolescent acts out and practices his multiple sex roles. "Falling in love," is not exclusively, or even primarily, a sexual matter. Erikson contends that adolescent courtship and love is largely ". . . an attempt to arrive at a definition of one's identity by projecting one's diffused ego image on one another and by seeing it reflected and gradually clarified. This is why many a youth would rather converse, and settle matters of mutual identification, than embrace."[63] The courtship game, of course, has definite sexual implications, and success in dating is construed as achievement in fulfilling the expectations of position of sex partner. A person's success in dating influences his impression of his own sexual image, but it should not be assumed that success in dating is necessarily a good predictor of happiness in marriage. Levine points out that, "Within our culture relatively little emphasis is placed upon psychological characteristics and the relationship between them and the ability to love, to be concerned about others, or to fulfill [play] the role of a husband or wife."[64]

The courting game is a highly intricate system of shifting and delicately balanced role relationships which require a repertoire of social skills and a capacity for anticipatory behavior for which many adolescents are not prepared. Consider the following composite picture of the peer group's expectations of one popular high school girl:

A girl's "reputation" is a crucial matter among adolescents. A girl is caught in a dilemma, a dilemma suggested by the importance of good looks on the one hand, and a good reputation on the other. A girl must be successful with the boys, says the culture, but in doing so she must maintain her reputation. In some schools, the limits defining a good reputation are stricter than others—but in all the schools, the limits are there, and they define what is "good" and what is "bad." The definitions are partly based on behavior with boys, but they also include drinking, smoking, and other less tangible matters—something about the way a girl handles herself, quite apart from what she actually does.[65]

---

[62] Berelson and Steiner, *Human Behavior: An Inventory of Scientific Findings*, p. 301.

[63] Erikson, *Childhood and Society*, p. 228.

[64] Louis S. Levine, *Personal and Social Development* (New York: Holt, Rinehart and Winston, 1963), p. 240.

[65] Based on questionnaires administered to the students in nine public high schools in the midwest. Coleman, "The School and Personality," p. 216.

In many cultures, the courtship activity is so completely institutionalized that the adolescent's progress toward marriage is prescribed by the
adult culture. The freedom with which our young people approach courtship assumes, rightly or wrongly, that trial-and-error methods will enable
the adolescent to choose a marriage mate wisely. Romantic love, as the
basis for a marriage relationship, is a relatively new cultural phenomenon
and is dominant only in the western world. In many other cultures the
marriage relationship is arranged by interested older adults. In ancient
Greece, and until recently in China, the bride and groom never saw each
other before the marriage ceremony. The period of courtship is for the
adolescent in the American culture an opportunity to develop sufficient
significant friendships with members of the opposite sex to permit him
to choose, when he so desires, the kind of marriage mate who will enable
him to live most completely and usefully.

During the adolescent years the young man or woman has to make
some decision about his economic future. Since most young women expect
to and eventually do marry and become housewives, this vocational
decision is seldom of the same importance as it is to the young man; but
for both sexes, the time comes sooner or later when they leave the family
nest either for a job and/or for marriage.

PLANNING A CAREER

We have already indicated the extent to which educational attainment
can define one's social class position. Of course, there are involved other
status factors, such as wealth, power, and family background. But, increasingly, our culture is defining class position in terms of education
and knowledge. It is a stalwart person today who will defy the status
symbols attached to a diploma or degree representing the attainment of
particular knowledge or skills. Moreover, trade unions, government
bodies, and business houses frequently require minimal schooling
achievements for consideration in their respective operations.

The industrial revolution, which began more than a century ago, continues unabated today. The introduction of business machines into the
offices of the country has extended the automation process to classes of
jobs not formerly effected by the industrialization of the economy. Automation is making unnecessary many of those jobs that require repetitive
types of work. For example, entire floors of some government and industrial offices, where hundreds of girls used to perform tedious clerical
functions, are now populated by business machines instead of girls. In
spite of this revolution in human relations, however, there are more jobs
available, and more people are working now than ever before. But they
are working fewer hours and in less tedious and repetitive activities than
heretofore. Also more education and skills are required. Jobs are drying

up for people who have nothing to offer but brawn or willingness to endure boredom.

The President's Committee on Youth Employment (April, 1963) made the following comments concerning the changing nature of the labor market:

The world confronting young people today is different from the world of their grandparents or parents. Old answers are outdated.

Before 1910 or even in the 1920's, many jobs were open to young people. Youths were needed on farms, were employed in local distribution and service trades, in factories, shops, and even mines. Nearly everyone could count on finding a job he could do with relatively little schooling.

These conditions no longer prevail. Our living and working standards as well as our job requirements now impose greater demands.

Automation, mechanization, and scientific advances are causing many unskilled jobs to disappear. Today's and tomorrow's jobs require higher skills, more maturity and judgment, and more experience.[66]

The new jobs that are opening up are likely to be in the fields of recreation, service industries, or health and public welfare. Thus, girls who once might have become file clerks or bookkeepers may now become waitresses or housekeepers. Men who once worked as elevator operators or as assemblers may turn up as taxicab drivers or hospital attendants. These significant shifts in the employment picture are requiring the learning of new skills, new manner of dress, and new modes of living.

The young man or woman who has had some work experience before assuming full time employment will have an advantage in adjusting to the demands of the economic world. At home and in school, the young person has seldom fully tested himself in a situation where the responsibility for success was almost entirely on his own shoulders. In spite of enlightened personnel policies, most industrial firms cannot run their businesses to suit the particular needs of each and every individual. The individual is expected to adapt himself to the pattern of life set down not only by his supervisors, but by his fellow workers. His attitudes toward business authority and particularly his boss will not differ greatly from the attitudes he built up over the years toward his own parents. Good vocational guidance will enable each young person to assay his own aptitudes, interests, and temperament, in order to select the vocation that will best meet his own needs and his own capacities to produce. These adjustments place upon the neophyte a responsibility for self-determination that may have been unknown to him at home and in school.

[66] "The Challenge of Jobless Youth," President's Committee on Youth Employment, W. Willard Wirtz, Chairman, Secretary of Labor (Apr. 1963), p. 3.

Among the resources available to the adolescent in selecting a career appropriate to his own aptitudes and temperament are the vocational and counseling services offered by many universities, high schools, community agencies, and private professional services. Such evaluation can be of value in aiding the uninitiated to anticipate his best chances for a satisfying life in a job appropriate to his own needs and capacities. In this connection, Donald MacKinnon attributes the following story to Mark Twain. The story is about a man who sought the greatest general who ever lived.

> Upon inquiry as to where this individual might be found, he was told that the person he sought had died and gone to Heaven. At the Pearly Gates he informed St. Peter of the purpose of his quest, whereupon St. Peter pointed to a soul nearby. "But that," protested the inquirer, "isn't the greatest of all generals. I knew that person when he lived on earth, and he was only a cobbler." "I know that," replied St. Peter, "but if he had been a general he would have been the greatest of them all."[67]

It is unfortunate when talent is recognized only after it is too late to acquire the appropriate education and experiences for its appropriate nurture. It is important that parents and educators worry about cobblers who might have become generals and about all those who fail to become what they are capable of, because neither they nor others recognized their potentialities and nourished their realization.[68]

Several students have pointed out that choosing a vocation is more than a matter of simply identifying aptitudes. The choice of a career is a developmental process which extends over many years.[69] Blau *et al.* point out that "There is no single time at which young people decide upon one out of all possible careers, but there are many crossroads at which their lives take decisive turns which narrow the range of future alternatives and thus influence the ultimate choice of an occupation."[70] It is the social structure, together with its institutionalized patterns of activities, interactions and ideas among various groups—which sets the stage for occupational choice.

> The social structure affects occupational choice in two analytically distinct respects, as the matrix of social experiences which channel the personality development of potential workers, and as the conditions of occupational opportunity which limit the realization of their choice.[71]

[67] Donald W. MacKinnon, "The Nature and Nurture of Creative Talent," *American Psychologist*, 17, No. 7 (July 1962), 484–495.

[68] MacKinnon, "The Nature and Nurture of Creative Talent," p. 484.

[69] Donald E. Super, "A Theory of Vocational Development," *American Psychologist*, 8 (1953), 185–190. Peter M. Blau, John W. Gustad, Richard Jessor, Herbert S. Parnes, and Richard C. Wilcock, "Occupational Choice, Participation, and Social Mobility," *Industrial and Labor Relations Review*, 9 (1956), 531–543.

[70] Blau *et al.*, "Occupational Choice, Participation, and Social Mobility," p. 560.

[71] Blau *et al.*, "Occupational Choice, Participation, and Social Mobility," p. 570.

PERSONALITY DEVELOPMENT IN ADOLESCENT YEARS

Anna Freud described a composite picture of the adolescent personality as follows:

> Adolescents are excessively egoistic, regarding themselves as the centre of the universe and the sole object of interest, and yet at no time in later life are they capable of so much self-sacrifice and devotion. They form the more passionate love-relations, only to break them off as abruptly as they began them. On the one hand they throw themselves enthusiastically into the life of the community and, on the other, they have an overpowering longing for solitude. They oscillate between blind submission to some self-chosen leader and defiant rebellion against any and every authority. They are selfish and materially-minded and at the same time full of lofty idealism. They are ascetic but will suddenly plunge into instinctual indulgence of the most primitive character. At times their behavior to other people is rough and inconsiderate, yet they themselves are extremely touchy. Their moods veer between light-hearted optimism and blackest pessimism. Sometimes they will work with indefatigable enthusiasm, and at other times they are sluggish and apathetic.[72]

This description is of course an ideal construct and probably no single adolescent has ever possessed all these traits in exactly this particular configuration. Nevertheless, it is likely that all of these traits have appeared as characteristics in different adolescents at different times.

How the adolescent reacts to physical changes in himself and how he responds to the social forces of his culture in these years will depend upon his personality needs and the role behavior repertoire which he has developed over the years. The child brings to the adolescent years the attitudes, concepts, and defense mechanisms he learned at home, on the playground, and in grade school. We cannot forget that the product of biosocial forces produces personal characteristics which themselves become forces in determining thenceforth what the individual will be sensitive to in himself and in his culture. Countless people are buffeted by similar biosocial forces but come out quite differently because, since they were not the same persons when they experienced these forces, the experiences did not mean the same thing to each of them.

Whether adolescence is an explosive period of disruptive fear and anxiety is largely dependent upon the personality traits of the individual who approaches this age *and* upon the cultural setting in which the person finds himself at this time. The way in which a child or adolescent perceives himself and others has an important bearing upon his own behavior. The adolescent whose self-concepts are unrealistic or debilitating

[72] Anna Freud, *The Ego and the Mechanisms of Defense* (London: Hogarth Press, "The International Psychoanalytical Library," No. 30, 1937), p. 149.

will relate to people quite differently than will the person who likes himself and who sees himself as a worthwhile person.

The inflexible, insecure, and dependent person will not readily adapt to the new physical and social demands of this adolescent age. Such a young person will be sensitized to certain changes and insulated from others. Adolescence can be for him a period of anxiety and apprehension. Adolescence is less taxing for the self-accepting and insightful adolescent who has already learned to shift comfortably to meet the changing expectations of his culture and of himself. The problems of adolescence are only in part created by civilization and the physical changes associated with puberty. Each adolescent personality brings its own unique resources to the challenge and opportunities of this particular age.

Jersild deplores the fact that many adolescents will grow into the adult years with inadequate or inaccurate concepts of self and others and that these inappropriate concepts can create for the adolescent years of unnecessary unhappiness. The following quotation from Jersild summarizes this observation:

> A large proportion of children will move into adulthood troubled and unhappy about many things. Many will be afflicted by irrational fears which do not represent dangers in the external environment but unresolved problems within themselves. Many, as adults, will suffer from attitudes of hostility, vindictiveness, and defensiveness which are not a response to hostile forces in the outside world but represent attitudes carried over from unresolved childhood struggles. Many persons similarly will acquire persisting feelings of inferiority or other unhealthy attitudes regarding their personal worth which represent either an irrational estimate of themselves or a failure to accept themselves realistically as they are.[73]

Symonds, who observed and studied the life experiences of twenty-eight adolescents as they grew into adulthood, reports that "One of the outstanding findings of this study is the remarkable persistence of personality trends over this thirteen year period. Growing out of adolescence does not mean giving up certain personality trends and taking on others, but rather meeting life's experiences with the same personality equipment one has been provided from earlier years . . . . Becoming an adult does not mean shedding one personality for another, but rather using the personality that one has to meet the exigencies of adult years."[74] These findings concerning the persistence and stability of personality traits throughout life are about what would be expected. One of the basic principles of behavior theory is that behaviors that are rewarded tend to persist. The adolescent years witness the result of behavior, both adaptive

---

[73] Arthur T. Jersild, "Self-Understanding in Childhood and Adolescence," *American Psychologist*, 6 (1951), 123.
[74] Symonds and Jensen, *From Adolescent to Adult*, p. 196.

and maladaptive, that has persisted and become stereotyped, because, in one way or another, it has been rewarded and reinforced by life's experiences.

Although the personality and self-concepts of the child are well crystallized by the time of the adolescent years, they are not static; they continue to be modified within the limits set by the person's maturation and his unique life experiences. Such modification can, of course, be increased by specific psychological and therapeutic techniques calculated to enlarge upon a person's self-concepts and make his insights more realistic and appropriate. Carl Rogers flatly states that, "We know the attitudes which, if provided by a counselor or a therapist, will be predictably followed by certain constructive personality and behavior changes in the client."[75] Vargas is similarly optimistic concerning behavior changes resulting from psychotherapy and relates the change to a person's capacity to achieve self-insight. "According to the counselor-judgment criterion, there is a positive correlation between success of therapy and increasing self-awareness, the change in self-awareness is evinced in an increasing proportion of self-descriptions of self, decreasing repetition of old self-perceptions, and increasing emergence of new (previously unknown or unacceptable) aspects of self."[76]

As we noted earlier, the adolescent works out his adjustments under the scrutiny of his parents as well as his peers. Consequently the adolescent will meet his problems largely in terms of techniques and attitudes practiced at home and in the neighborhood. The kinds of adjustments he makes in this adolescent period will open some doors of opportunity to him and close others. Some friends will be selected and others rejected. Decisions will be made concerning education—where, how much, and for what purpose. Some vocations will be chosen and others rejected, and one will be pursued with obvious influence on his own standard of living and success experiences. The period of courtship will enable him to meet, select, and marry one of the members of the opposite sex. In these deci-

---

[75] Carl R. Rogers, "Implications of Recent Advances in Prediction and Control of Behavior," *Teachers College Record*, 57 (Feb. 1956), 316–322; Carl R. Rogers, *Psychotherapy and Personality Change* (Chicago: University of Chicago Press, 1954).

[76] Manuel J. Vargas, "Changes in Self-Awareness During Client-Centered Therapy," in *Psychotherapy and Personality Change*, Carl R. Rogers and Rosalind F. Symond, eds. (Chicago: University of Chicago Press, 1954), p. 164. It should be noted that there is by no means consensus that psychotherapy is an effective variable in producing behavior changes. Conclusive evidence is yet lacking to support the claims of various schools of psychotherapy. In all fairness it must be observed that adequate research criteria for measuring behavior change is elusive. When specific and measurable behavior changes are the object of psychotherapy (*e.g.*, changes toward a more positive attitude regarding sexual behavior) the results are more conclusive. Joseph Wolpe, *Psychotherapy by Reciprocal Inhibition* (Berkeley: Stanford University Press, 1958). When more general claims are made for behavior change as a result of psychotherapy the results are as yet unimpressive. Berelson and Steiner, *Human Behavior: An Inventory of Scientific Findings*, p. 287.

sions and in the behavior which follows from them the adolescent makes his own unique impact upon his milieu and he is himself modified further through these experiences.

SUMMARY

Adolescence is a bridge between childhood and adulthood. The adolescent years witness the initiation and culmination of the final physiological thrusts of maturational development. The person's physical structure will be modified in the years beyond adolescence but such changes are more a result of environmental factors than of maturation.

The physical changes of these adolescent years are important in themselves and also for what they may mean to the individual young person. The fulfillment of sexual maturity requires the adolescent to assume a new position and to satisfy the attendant new role expectations as assigned by his culture. New dimensions in height, weight, and other physical features, plus improved muscular coordination, give the adolescent a new place in society. Probably more important than the physical changes that accompany the adolescent years is the personal interpretation the young person makes of these changes in himself and in others of similar age. Some young persons gain the impression that their peers disapprove of elements of their physical structure, because they are different from the norm. The fact that not all physical changes occur simultaneously may place special burdens on those whose rate of maturation is accelerated or retarded and is thus inappropriate for the chronological age. The approval of the peer culture is ardently sought after by the adolescent.

The peer group is a large and important part of the adolescent's affective other, and, when he cannot conform to the group's expectations of him, he may become a troubled young person.

An important part of adolescence centers about two decisions which are likely to influence the remainder of life and which are usually decided at about the same time. These include the selection of a vocation (including the extent and nature of his education) and the courtship period leading to the selection of a mate. The young person will interact with these situations with the personality he has already acquired. These new experiences will also influence his future development, for his work and his own home will become increasingly significant as part of his affective other.

SUGGESTED READINGS

BERELSON, BERNARD and GARY A. STEINER. *Human Behavior* (New York: Harcourt, Brace and World, 1964).

COLE, LUELLA. *Psychology of Adolescence* (New York: Holt, Rinehart and Winston, 1964) 6th Ed.

CUMMING, JOHN and ELAINE CUMMING. *Ego and Milieu* (New York: Atherton Press, 1962).

FRIEDENBERG, EDGAR Z. *The Vanishing Adolescent* (New York: Dell Publishing Co., 1959).

HAVIGHURST, ROBERT J. *et al. Growing Up in River City* (New York: J. Wiley and Sons, 1962).

LEVINE, LOUIS S. *Personal and Social Development* (New York: Holt, Rinehart and Winston, 1963).

QUEEN, STUART A. *et al. The Family in Various Cultures* (Chicago: J. B. Lippincott Company, 1961).

SMELSER, NEIL and WILLIAM SMELSER (eds.) *Personality and Social Systems* (New York: John Wiley and Sons, 1963).

STONE, J. R. and J. CHURCH. *Childhood and Adolescence* (New York: Random House, 1957).

SYMONDS, PERCIVAL. *From Adolescent to Adult* (New York: Columbia University Press, 1961).

TITIEV, MISCHA. *Introduction to Cultural Anthropology* (New York: Henry Holt & Co., 1959).

CHAPTER 15

ADULTHOOD

> Then, a soldier,
> Full of strange oaths, and bearded like the pard. . . ,
> Seeking the bubble reputation
> Even in the cannon's mouth. And then, the justice,
> In fair round belly, with good capon lin'd,
> With eyes severe, and beard of formal cut,
> Full of wise saws and modern instances. . .

If we remove a few beards from the above quotation, Shakespeare's observations about the adult positions and roles of the sixteenth century are not amiss today. Then, as now, the years of adulthood were characterized by changes in positions, statuses, and roles, albeit less drastic than the age levels which preceded and followed them. A person's self image develops and changes through the experiences of the passing years as he becomes aware of and responds to the expectations and evaluations of others. The adult's self image is a compilation of the images of him which others have presented to him by their gestures of approval or disapproval. By the time a person has reached the adult years, this image of self, though dependent in varying degress upon the current appraisal of others, is usually sufficiently independent to persist in terms of its own personality organization developed through the years. The adult has incorporated into his own self image the many appraisals, expectations, and models which others have presented to him and which (depending upon his own perception of them) have become a part of his own subjective organization. Thus the stability which characterizes most adult personalities is a function of one's own subjective organization and comparable organizations in the individuals who comprise his affective other. Habits, attitudes, traits, and perceptions (even misperceptions) become mutually reinforcing components of personality.

When perceptions of self are an accurate view of reality they make for good mental health. But when they are based on a misconception of self, the resulting behavior may be maladaptive or abnormal. Shibutani contributes the following example:

> Among the Exemplary Novels of Miquel de Cervantes is a fascinating tale of a man, temporarily deranged, who believed that he was made of glass. Whenever people approached him, he screamed and implored

them to keep their distance lest they shatter him. He always walked in the middle of the street, glancing apprehensively at the rooftops for loose tiles that might fall upon him. On one occasion, when a wasp stung him on the neck, he did not dare strike it nor shake it off for fear of breaking himself. He refused to eat anything as hard as meat or fish and insisted upon sleeping only in beds of straw. Since glass is not only thinner than the skin but also transparent, he claimed that the peculiar construction of his body enabled his soul to see things more clearly, and he offered to assist those facing perplexing problems. Before long he became famous for his astonishing astute observations. People followed him everywhere, seeking his advice. Whenever mischievous boys threw stones at him, he cried so loudly and desperately that adults came running to his assistance, and finally a wealthy patron hired a body-guard to follow him about and to protect him against hoodlums.[1]

As Shibutani points out, not many people outside mental hospitals believe themselves to be made of glass, but there are persons who regard themselves as being rather fragile.

Those who believe that they are unusually susceptible to cold, heat rashes, blisters, or freckles go out of their way to avoid exposure. Those who believe that their angelic children might become contaminated by contact with the filthy urchins who live in poorer neighborhoods take special care to see that their youngsters play exclusively with others of their own kind. All this suggests that much of what men do volun-tarily depends upon what they conceive of themselves to be; Cervantes was merely pointing to an exaggerated instance of a common process.[2]

In our treatment of adulthood, or maturity, we shall note the relation-ship between the biological heritage and the cultural environment. We will first consider the nature of the biological factors in maturity.

ADULTHOOD AND PHYSIOLOGICAL CHANGES

In contrast to the periods of life which precede and the one which follows it, the adult or mature phase of man's life is characterized by relative stability of biological factors. It is, by all odds, the longest of the five major periods of life as we present them. Changes in the body continue to occur, to be sure, but they are usually covert and less drastic, and therefore, less influential in shaping social behavior. The increased pro-portions of the waistline are viewed with alarm by some, eyeglasses are required or need adjustment, and cosmetics become more important to the females in our culture; but such changes do not require the specific demands for adaptation comparable to those found in infancy, childhood,

---

[1] Tamotsu Shibutani, *Society and Personality* (Englewood Cliffs, N.J.: Prentice-Hall, 1961), p. 213.

[2] Shibutani, *Society and Personality*, p. 214.

adolescence, and old age.[3] In maturity, as in the other age groups, the processes of growth and change are not uniform for the whole body. Sensory equipment matures and declines at varying rates, and head hair disappears or turns gray or white at widely varying ages. And, as emphasized in the previous three chapters, there are wide variations among individuals with regard to these changes. Wolff points out that aging can begin early in some people.

> Arteriosclerosis is not solely limited to advancing age, and calcification of the aorta can, indeed, begin at the age of 20. Other investigators believe that age pigments are an important characteristic of the process of aging but already at the age of 7 the first traces of yellow pigment can be observed in several types of nerve cells in men . . . Acid-fast age pigments appear frequently in human cardiac muscle as soon as the age of 20 and increase thereafter.[4]

An exception to the generalization that the bodily changes of maturity are gradual and slow is found in the alterations which take place in the reproductive organs, especially in the female. The "change of life," or climacteric, often is associated with some dramatic event. Webster's defines the climacteric as that period of life ". . . in which some great change in the constitution, health, or fortune takes place, or is supposed to take place or to be especially likely to occur." Modern knowledge concerning this phase of the life cycle tends to support the skepticism noted in Webster's definition. The term "change of life," or climacteric, has come to mean more than just biological changes, and often is believed to be a time when there is some biological predisposition to mental illness or "nervousness." That there are distinct physiological changes is clear, especially in women.

It is at this time that the menopause occurs. This is the cessation of the menstrual flow, and with this change are associated ". . . the periodic occurrence of hot flushes, or flashes, a shrinkage of the uterus and to some extent of the vagina, and changes in the breasts due to the atrophy of the milk glands."[5] Kinsey's inquiries indicated that nearly 20 per cent of women began menopause by the age of forty-six; slightly more than half by age fifty, seven-eighths by age fifty-four, and all but one in thirty by age fifty-six.[6] Menopause in women usually terminates reproduction,

---

[3] However, Lansing points out that after the age of about forty there is an increasing lack of capacity for adaptability to environmental changes. A. I. Lansing, "Some Physiological Aspects of Aging," *Physiological Review*, 31 (1951), 274–284.

[4] Kurt Wolff, *The Biological, Sociological and Psychological Aspects of Aging* (Springfield: Charles C. Thomas, 1959), p. 8.

[5] Amram Scheinfeld, *Women and Men* (New York: Harcourt, Brace and World Co., 1944), p. 236.

[6] A. C. Kinsey *et al.*, *Sexual Behavior in the Human Female* (Philadelphia: W. B. Saunders, 1953), p. 719.

though one student of the problem claims that this is not necessarily so, and holds that reproduction in very healthy women can and occasionally still does occur because the ovulation cycle continues, even though the menstrual flow ceases.[7] It is now generally agreed among medical men that menopause does not signalize the end or even any significant slackening of sexual potency for women.[8] The belief that it does, however, is often subscribed to by many women, and this belief may adversely affect their personality adjustment.[9]

Whether or not there is a climacteric in the male which parallels that in the female is still a moot question. Most books on the subject of marriage either do not mention the possibility of a "change of life" in men, or are very vague about it. Some authorities do not support the possibility of such a period at all.[10] Others vigorously insist that the climacteric in men is represented by a temporary period of impotency, and is accompanied by an anxiety which may last for a year or two.[11] Further research is needed on this point. However, that there are changes in social behavior and in personality adjustment at this period of life is well established. Whatever the physiological changes per se may be, they seem to be less important than the attitudes toward such changes on the part of the individuals involved.

Our culture places such high value upon youth, vigor, and sexual potency that any sign that the individual is growing old or impotent is likely to give rise to feelings of anxiety and distress. During adulthood the battle with the aging and sometimes sagging organism is entered into full tilt by both consumer and entrepreneur. Vitamins, reducing diets, exercise courses, hair restorers, flattering clothing that reveals or conceals, and of course all manner of cosmetics are advertised and slanted toward the adult who wishes to maintain the proper body or physical "front" in keeping with the emphasis upon youth in our society.

The physiological changes that occur in the female at this time are

[7] M. C. Stopes, *Changes of Life in Men and Women* (New York: G. P. Putnam's Sons, 1936), p. 23.

[8] Kinsey, *Sexual Behavior in the Human Female*. In the population Kinsey studied, the maximum sexual responsiveness for the male occurred in the late teens and early twenties and for the female, the late twenties. Furthermore, the females' sexual capacities (in the group Kinsey studied) remained at a fairly stable level throughout most of life, while the males experienced a gradual decline from the peak years into old age.

[9] Kinsey, *Sexual Behavior in the Human Female*, p. 736. Kinsey's study indicated that two-fifths of the 127 cases questioned reported that menopause had no effect on their sexual response and no change in sexual activity, but half of the same group reported decreases in both respects. However, some of the women in the latter group are reported to have never been particularly interested in sexual activity.

[10] *See* Oscar J. Kaplan (ed.), *Mental Disorders in Later Life* (Stanford, Calif.: Stanford University Press, 1945), p. 45.

[11] Stopes, *Changes of Life in Men and Women*, p. 39.

dramatic enough to act as a reminder that many of the so-called best years of life have sped by. More than that, these physical changes may coincide with social changes which threaten her status. In our culture the principal source of recognition for a woman comes from her activities as a housewife and mother. As the children grow older and become less dependent upon her, she feels less important and may be unhappy in the thought of her lowered status. Should this change in social status coincide with menopause, the resulting reaction of the person may be serious. *Involutional melancholia* is the term used to denote the depression which occurs at this time in some individuals.

In the man, the changes in personality that take place may have little or nothing to do with any alteration in the reproductive organs, but may result from a gradual awareness that he is getting old, that he has not made his mark in life as he had aspired to in earlier years, and that he probably will never be able to do so. He becomes depressed at this thought, and may become mentally ill for a shorter or longer period. The fact that fewer men than women are listed as being ill with *involutional melancholia* may be a function of the division of labor in our culture. The peak years in business or professional activity for the male coincide with the period of menopause and depression for certain women. It seems that if the life pattern is a continuing one through these years, there is very little likelihood of personality maladjustment resulting. Some people are simply too busy to become mentally ill in this manner. The woman who is approaching the late years of maturity is well advised to seek activity which will be sufficiently rewarding from the viewpoint of social psychological needs. If this is done, the menopause period is reduced in significance, is less climactic. Such activity, coupled with the knowledge that menopause has little if anything to do with sex expression, and probably nothing to do with mental illness unless misinterpreted to be so related, will serve to remove the crisis from the change-of-life period.

There are other changes which occur in many individuals' physical equipment that call for an altered way of life. Figure 37 suggests some of these changes which are compatible with the maturation of the organism. In some instances, poor physical condition and lack of appropriate exercise, rather than advancing years, may be the basis for the need to take things easy. However, the less vigorous activity that is normally associated with the full and later years of maturity can be quite satisfying if the person has prepared himself for behavior that is appropriate to these years. Oftentimes, it is only those who have perpetuated the social values of youth and young adulthood who are sorely concerned with the need to become less active physically. As we shall indicate below, part of the process of maturing socially is the acceptance of the reality of the situation. In this instance the reality concerns a less flexible, a less adaptable physical mechanism.

FIGURE 37. Must you slow down after 35? (Illustration from *Better Homes & Gardens Magazine.*)

THE BIOLOGICAL HERITAGE AND THE JOB

We have had occasion to point out that society places certain values on particular biological features of people, and it is in terms of the individual's perception of and reaction to such evaluations that he achieves certain of his social arrangements. In the adult work situation the problem is no different. Personal physical features do play a part in determining an individual's place in the professional and business world. This is true not only for the indirect influence that people's attitudes toward an individual's physiology may produce in that individual but for the direct effect that physiological efficiency or clumsiness will have upon his productivity. Among the various physiological factors which influence one's vocational adjustment may be included mental ability and aptitudes, physique, health, and appearance.

Mental Ability and Aptitudes

As indicated in Chapter 3, one's mental potentialities are determined in large measure by the efficacy of the neurological structure which provides the basis and which, together with appropriate environmental stimulation, sets the limits to learning ability. Although there is a positive correlation between measured mental ability and work success (as measured by level of responsibility and authority), the relationship is not so high as might be expected because there are many variables in addition to intelligence which help determine vocational success. Among these are motivation, judgment, experience, and opportunity. The various vocations roughly distribute themselves according to levels of measured mental ability; scores made by inductees in World War II on the Army General Classification Test demonstrate clearly the manner in which vocational groups distribute themselves on such a test.[12] Accountants, mechanical engineers, medical students, writers, chemical engineering students, lawyers, and teachers were among the highest of the vocations on this test in terms of their mean ability scores. On the other hand, lumberjacks, farm workers, teamsters, and miners were among the lowest of the vocational groups. Not only is there a wide range of mean scores among the various occupational groups on this test, but there is a wide range of scores within each occupational group. Some of the occupations at the lower end of the distribution include individuals whose scores were comparable with some of the persons functioning in the occupations at the higher extreme. This overlapping can be seen, for example, when the top group (accountants) is compared with the lowest scoring group (lumberjacks). Ninety per cent of the accountants made scores on this test of 114 or better. Yet 10 per cent of the lumberjacks were also able to

---

[12] Richard Dewey and W. J. Humber, *The Development of Human Behavior* (New York: The Macmillan Co., 1951), p. 645–647.

equal or exceed that same score. This wide range of mental ability scores suggests the danger of offering vocational guidance on the basis of such test scores alone.

A man's measured intelligence will influence his vocational choice most particularly at those points where he is required to learn the fundamentals and techniques of the job. The ability to master the schoolwork is a prerequisite for many vocations. This is particularly true of the professions, but it is also true to a lesser degree in the skilled trades. Once the technicalities of the job have been mastered, the judgment, reasoning ability, and motivation of the employee become prime factors in his effectiveness. While abilities can be improved through experience and training, both the native constitution and the character of the milieu set limits to such development.

An individual's motor and sensory capacities are much more heterogeneous than are his intellectual skills. Whereas there is a positive correlation among both motor skills and mental capacities, there is much less homogeneity among the former than among the latter. Hull has indicated that an individual's best potentialities for vocational achievement are almost three times as great as his poorest.[13] The range will vary with different people. In the case of the individual whose talents are closely clustered about one activity, there is not much of a problem of vocational decision. But the many-talented individual will have the opportunity to choose among his talents in terms of his interests and job opportunities. The measurement and identification of special aptitudes are important considerations in making sure that a person does not overlook some particular facility he might develop into a vocational skill.[14] Psychometrics has helped many individuals identify their particular aptitudes and relate them to specific jobs. The selection and distribution of talent according to appropriate aptitude have reduced the frequency of many of the distressed and misplaced employees of former years. But the emphasis that in recent years has been placed on psychometrics may, by stressing technical competency, overlook the larger needs of the individual as he endeavors to meet the social demands of his job. The following statement of Mayo is appropriate:

> The fact that the United States has developed a successful series of tests for technical skills does not prove any extenuation of psychology. Within its narrow limits, this is useful, and indeed excellent. But the general effect is to concentrate on technical problems and to blind us to the importance of the problems of human cooperation—social skill.[15]

---

[13] C. L. Hull, *Aptitude Testing* (Yonkers: World Book Co., 1928), p. 48.

[14] J. P. Guilford, *Psychometric Methods*, 2nd Ed. (New York: McGraw-Hill, 1954).

[15] Elton Mayo, *The Social Problems of our Industrial Civilization* (Boston: Harvard University, Graduate School of Business Administration, 1945), p. 20.

Physique

In Chapter 3 we classified the various physical types according to three somatotypes: the endomorphs, the mesomorphs, and the ecomorphs. The evidence regarding the bearing that these body types may have on vocational orientation is inconclusive. However the public has developed such stereotyped ideas of what a detective, professor, minister, or sales-man, is supposed to look like that individuals probably tend to oblige this theory of somatic determination by fitting themselves into these vocations according to these culturally determined classifications. The "fat butcher," the "skinny preacher," and the "muscular soldier" fit the usual expectations. The skinny butcher, the muscular preacher, the fat soldier do not fit the public's expectations of these vocations.

It is likely that some practical considerations may be involved in distributing individuals according to somatotypes for particular jobs. Thus it would be impractical for an obese person to engage in an activity requiring agility or making it necessary for him to work in space which for him would be cramped. However, the reader will be able to recall several exceptions to this general statement. Likewise, the ectomorphic individual will not be ideally suited to outdoor activities requiring ex-posure and endurance. Nevertheless, every police force and every fire hall has among its members competent individuals of this type of physique, but these are the exceptions.

A practical application of these body types to work situations is reported in an investigation conducted by C. W. Dupertuis, an anthro-pologist for the United States Navy.[16] In this investigation, Dupertuis somatotyped forty Navy divers plus forty-one other subjects who were members of the Navy such as scientists, cooks, and physicians, but who were not divers. These men were then exposed to rigorous tests to meas-ure their reactions to diving conditions. It was concluded that not only are the mesomorphs best suited to this aspect of naval activity, but that "Navy diving tables on how fast to bring a man to the surface will be revised in terms of body types and body densities. Each diver may have a sort of custom-made formula that is safest for his particular physique. And eventually, all Navy men may get a body-type score to be used in an assignment."[17] Other evidence was also forthcoming from this study which included the observation that the mesomorphs make the best pilots for the high speed planes. "Neither the round-soft nor the very lean men are too good as fighter pilots. As for the extreme round-softs, most of these probably would be eliminated or else given desk or kitchen jobs."[18] This investigator went on to hypothesize that not only do these physical types

---

[16] C. W. Dupertuis, "Shaped to Fit," *Newsweek*, XXXV (June 5, 1950), 57.

[17] Dupertuis, "Shaped to Fit," p. 57.

[18] Dupertuis, "Shaped to Fit," p. 58.

make for various best fits in vocational placement, but that there is associated with each physical type certain temperaments which must also be considered in job classification. However, convincing evidence for the correlation of body types with temperament is still lacking.

Cureton examined the physiques of men studying medicine at the University of Illinois and compared them with the physiques of male students in the department of physical education at Springfield College.[19] The results appear in Table XIX and indicate as might be expected that the mesomorphs predominate in the school of physical education while the endo-mesomorphs are more heavily represented in the medical school. The fact that these percentages do not add up to 100 indicates that not all people lend themselves to clear-cut physical typing. The results do indicate the tendency of people to distribute themselves vocationally according to their physical dimensions.

Table XIX
Comparison of Types of Student Physique in Two
Different University Curricula

	Illinois Medical Group (per cent)	Springfield College Physical Education Majors (per cent)
Mesomorphs	6.36	44.27
Ecto-mesomorphs	16.36	39.58
Endo-mesomorphs	18.18	3.42

The major consideration in judging the effects of body type on vocational placement and success is to be found in the individual's own interpretation of the position society assigns him and the role he is expected to play because of his particular physical features. We believe it is in terms of this phenomenon rather than in terms of any inherent structure-temperament relationship which will help determine an individual's effectiveness in the industrial and professional world.

Health and Physical Handicaps

The handicapped person is disabled not only physically but in terms of his opportunities for normal personality satisfactions in the industrial world. Cultural values define the extent to which a physically handicapped person feels rejected or crushed by his environment. In cultures which assign high position values to physical achievement, appearance and agility, the physically handicapped person is certain to develop

[19] T. K. Cureton, *Physical Fitness, Appraisal and Guidance* (St. Louis: The C. V. Mosby Co., 1947), p. 113.

feelings of dependency, withdrawal, and perhaps, guilt. These feelings may be encouraged by his peers who may reinforce his dependency needs.

One study reports that co-workers are likely to accept the presence of physically handicapped persons when the handicap shows. But when the handicap is concealed as in hernia, respiratory, or cardiac disorder, the co-workers are likely to develop feelings of hostility toward what they consider to be malingering work habits which require the others to carry part of the disabled person's work load.[20] Some individuals with a personality disorder may seize upon a physical accident or handicap as an effective and socially acceptable defense against their own psychological weakness. As Gelb says, "Neurotic dependency may 'look good' when one is (physically) handicapped. . . In many cases the injury or physical illness establishes a situation which is more congenial for the practice of a pre-existing neurosis or psychosis. It is, therefore, understandable that some individuals would welcome a physical illness or disability." Gelb contributes the following case:

> The patient, a thirty-year old welder, sustained a superficial one-inch laceration of the right forearm. Eighteen months later he was referred to the Institute by an insurance company. Before referral he was seen by at least 12 consultants, none for psychiatric evaluation. Yet because of bizarre and inconsistent neurological findings, most of these physicians felt the patient had a conversion reaction. Two of them advised surgery. Despite a variety of treatments, he reported that his arm pain increased. The patient would not use his arm. He had stellate ganglion blocks, steam packs, paraffin baths, ultra sound and other physical therapy.
>
> At the Institute he was not considered physically handicapped. Evaluation in the Social Adjustment Service revealed a man with very little anxiety. He casually spoke of somatic symptoms and related stories of poor treatment following his accident. He had resented his mother's and nine siblings' expectation that he contribute to their support; he had married but left home four times; he had had a succession of many jobs in 10 years. In psychological testing he made a minimum of effort and actually reacted with amusement to repeated failures. The patient's buoyancy and joviality reflected his satisfaction in proving his inability to function and his expectation that others would now have to take care of him. The patient was diagnosed passive-agressive personality with hysterical and paranoid features. He would not accept anything but physical "treatment" and he left the Institute to continue passively to receive this elsewhere.[21]

[20] G. Brighouse, *The Physically Handicapped Worker in Industry*, Bulletin 13 (Pasadena, Calif.: Institute of Technology, Industrial Relations Section, 1946).

[21] Lester A. Gelb, "Personality Disorganization Camouflaged by Physical Handicaps," *Mental Hygiene*, 45 (Apr. 1961), 209–210.

It is commonly assumed that there is a close association between cardiovascular disease and the strains of employment pressures, particularly at the executive level. Studies, however, do not indicate that hypertension and arteriosclerotic disease are more frequent among executives than among non-executives (white collar workers). Lee and Schneider report, "Analysis of group data revealed no relationship between the level of responsibility and the incidence either of hypertensive disease or of myocardinal infarction."[22] These data probably should not be taken to mean literally that the executive is less subject to stress than are other members of the organization. Stress is a relative and subjective matter and it may be that the executive is better able by reason of superior health, insight or personal organization to cope with these pressures. Perhaps, the same factors that cause him to be selected for executive responsibility also operate to protect him from the pressures of the job. People react to pressure in terms of their own personal resources. For example, the Presidency of Harvard University would ordinarily be regarded as an executive pressure situation. However, on the occasion of President Eliot's retirement from Harvard, President Eliot is reported to have replied to a newspaper reporter's question by saying, "I look back upon my administation as President of Harvard as 25 years of sheer boredom."

Appearance

The way in which one's culture evaluates one's appearance will, of course, influence a person's vocational adjustment. Or it may be that the individual will begin to imagine from some small and insignificant cue that his appearance is the object of amusement or ridicule on the part of his affective other. The writers are impressed with the frequency with which young men (successful as well as unsuccessful) mention the sudden loss of their hair as the most unpleasant experience they have ever had. When the inquiry is pushed to ascertain the reason for this severe reaction, the explanation seems to lie in the fact that each person has taken a new attitude toward himself following this physical change. This new attitude which he takes toward himself is based on his evaluation of the shift in attitudes which he believes his friends have taken toward him because of the unfamiliar and sudden physical deviation.

The superintendent of a machine shop who had suffered a sudden hair loss would, subsequent to this event, wear a hat on all occasions and if he was invited to some place where the removal of a hat was mandatory, would not attend. For this reason he brought his lunch and ate it in his office rather than eat in the company dining room as had been

[22] Richard E. Lee and Ralph F. Schneider, *Journal of American Medical Association*, V 167 (1958), 1447–1450.

his earlier custom. This self-inflicted isolation increased to a point where he finally voluntarily removed himself from the company.

Each individual will, of course, react to this or similar physical deviations in terms of his own needs and personal resources. The following case will illustrate how a physical aberration may influence self perception and personality development.

Frances L. was referred to the psychologist by her supervisor who indicated that the girl wanted to leave the company in spite of the fact that she said she liked her work and was doing an excellent job. The young lady explained to the psychologist her displeasure with the job in terms of a working companion whom she had come to dislike so completely that further association with her was impossible.

In the course of the examination Frances was given a piece of white typing paper and was asked to draw on it a picture of a man and a picture of a woman.[23] The result of her drawing appears in Figure 38. Inquiry regarding the faceless girl elicited the response that such details were unimportant. When it was pointed out that most other details, including the man's face, were clearly drawn, the subject became disturbed. She was told that in this kind of a situation, the individual is likely to project his own self regarding attitudes into a drawing. It was also pointed out that the fact that the girl had been an art student did not influence the validity of the instrument. With this explanation the girl began to verbalize some feelings of anxiety which she had not been able to express earlier. As she talked it became apparent that the girl in the drawing was an unconscious representation of her feelings about herself. The lack of a face symbolized her own self-rejection.

When she was a little girl she had been considered very homely. Her father referred to her as the "ugly duckling" and compared her unfavorably with her younger sister. Her difficulty was associated with crooked and protruding teeth which were not corrected. She compensated for her unattractive appearance by obtaining good grades in school and was able to aid her younger sister who was not so successful academically. Because of her disability she had never expected and in fact did not have any dates. At the age of 24 she had saved enough money to obtain the necessary medical and dental attention which was so successful cosmetically that no one would suspect that she had ever suffered a facial malformation. Unfortunately, although the physical aberration had been corrected, Frances had over-learned adaptive habits calculated to avoid any situations which might prove embarrassing, and the change in physical structure was not accompanied by modifications in her behavior. After she returned to her job ·from the hospital she reported that as she would walk down the halls she imagined that the girls would whisper to each other, "There's the girl who had her teeth

[23] The projection test used here is an adaptation of procedures suggested in Karen Machover, *Personality Projection in the Drawing of the Human Figure* (Springfield, Ill.: Charles C. Thomas, Publisher, 1949).

FIGURE 38. An example of personality projection in drawing the human figure.

straightened." The girl with whom she was working and upon whom she had fastened all her hostility may have served as an image of her younger sister with whom she had been compared so unfavorably in her early years. Frances' problem involved the development of new insights into herself, a reevaluation of her life goals in terms of the new opportunities opened to her by this physical correction and the practice of a new set of living habits geared to gregarious living rather than to isolation and self-rejection.

SOCIAL PSYCHOLOGICAL MATURITY

That such a thing as a mature personality exists cannot be doubted, but no consensus as to the precise components of maturity has been reached. In the interactionist frame of reference, maturity involves adult status on the biological level, but also embodies the social cultural environment as well as the subjective attributes which the adult has acquired over the years. In Table XX we have presented the interactive components which appear to us to constitute the mature personality. Alterations in any one or more of the components may reduce the degree of maturity of the personality in question, albeit the objective measures of maturity in any of the components are elusive. Nor would we assert that all of these items are universal for mankind, and are not reflections of cultural biases on the part of the authors.

Table XX

Social Psychological and Sociological Aspects of Maturity

Social System as Environment	Positions (Defined in terms of privileges and duties)	Roles or Role Behavior (Defined in terms of actual behavior)	Attitudes (Emotional relationships)	Cognitions (Intellectual relationships)
Viable and integrated; encourages and permits individuals to act in congruence with nature of man's nature; orders, rather than forces, relationships; facilitates socialization and enculturation; provides for exigencies by appropriate compensation, sublimation, and rationalization. Positions or statuses, norms, and sanctions clearly and consistently defined.	Occupants of various ascribed, assumed, and achieved positions which are functional in maintaining the social system in viable and integrated form; detailed below.	Reflects awareness of privileges and obligations of positions occupied; based upon reality rather than pleasure principle; modified when novel conditions warrant it.	Desire to do that which one ought to do in terms of positions held and in keeping with demands of changing conditions of environment.	Acquired knowledge, beliefs, skills appropriate to positions held and which are functional for viable and integrated social system. Ability to think rationally and to avoid beliefs which give rise to unwarranted attitudes, e.g., fears, prejudices, over-dependency.
Basic Institutions	Positions	Roles	Attitudes	Cognitions
Marriage. Purpose: assumption of responsibility for children in	Spouse and parent; Privileges: sexual intercourse and parenthood	Behavior in keeping with ideals as defined under positions, but	Desire to establish orderly relationship with member of oppo-	Knowledge of the reasons for norms and sanctions of marriage

Basic Institutions	Positions	Roles	Attitudes	Cognitions
terms of initial socialization and enculturation, by providing for needed protection, affection, social stimulation, and so on. Applies secondarily to spouse.	which may result; making own decisions regarding dwelling location, and so on. *Obligations*: care of children as outlined under institution.	modified in terms of exigencies of time and place; personal social factors need not threaten fulfillment of obligations.	site sex and to fulfill obligations to offspring should they come. Desire to make own decisions and to accept full responsibility for one's actions.	institution; knowledge appropriate to fulfilling obligations to children and to spouse.
The Economy. *Purpose*: to create, and allocate wealth. (*wealth* defined as any item or service which contributes to welfare of man.)	Occupation or vocation—ranges from that of the self-sufficient agriculturalist to the narrowly trained specialist. *Privileges*: access to areas, tools, knowledge, and people that is denied to others; use of certain position or status symbols, *e.g.,* titles, insignia, and so on. *Obligations*: maintenance of standards of performance in keeping with purpose of economy as institution.	Same as above.	Desire to work (*i.e.,* to create, preserve, or allocate wealth); Veblen's "instinct of workmanship"; to accept some position as vocation or "calling" after appropriate trial-and-error experience.	Acquisition of requisite facts, ideas, and skills appropriate to fulfillment of obligations and development of congruent attitudes. Awareness of function of roles played in over-all economy, and of the rewards and liabilities of various vocations, both in short run and over a vocational lifetime.

Table XX (Continued)
Social Psychological and Sociological Aspects of Maturity

Basic Institutions	Positions	Roles	Attitudes	Cognitions
Education. Purpose: to discover, preserve, and transmit knowledge, attitudes, and skills which are congruent with the nature of man.	Layman, teacher, researcher, student, librarian, laboratory technician, museum curator, inventor, and so on.	Same as above.	Desire for, and pleasure in, learning; no fears of the consequences of learning; of searching intellectually; emotional acceptance of the implications of new knowledge.	Acquisition of knowledge in addition to that requisite for vocation; awareness of nature of objective and subjective ideas; subscription to scientific conception of the nature of man and universe.
Religion. Purpose: To define those values worthy of supreme devotion and the sacrifice of time, energy, wealth, and even life itself if necessary for their protection and preservation.	Laymen, students of religion, clergy, and other special functionaries. *Privileges:* to take action appropriate to the purposes of the institution of religion; to act as professional conscience of community. *Obligations:* to act in a manner congruent with the preservation of the objects,	Same as above.	Strong feelings that religious objects must not be violated and must be supported, augmented, and preserved; willingness to sacrifice in manner necessary to such ends.	Awareness of what ought to be defined as religious objects and thus justify the strong attitude and attendant action. Knowledge of what is appropriate action for the support of the values deemed religious. Recognition of implications of one's religious attitude and action.

Basic Institutions	Positions	Roles	Attitudes	Cognitions
	material or immaterial, defined objectively as religious. To make certain that action taken on behalf of religion is not merely a projection of one's subjective or ethnocentric values.			
Government. Purpose: To set the cultural stage so that the other basic institutions are able to function effectively; to establish the order which is essential to man's fulfilling his basic needs and desires.	Voter, citizen, legislator, executive, member of judiciary, protective functionaries, *e.g.,* police and firemen; recorders, clerks, and so on.	Same as above.	Desire for order that is requisite for human freedom; motivation to play roles congruent with viable systems of norms and sanctions; willingness to curtail own impulses in keeping with requirements of societal order and freedom. Desire to acquire the knowledge and skills which are essential to successful participation in governmental process in terms of one's social positions.	Awareness that independence and freedom are not synonyms, that norms and sanctions are essential to freedom; recognition that the adjectives "public" and "governmental" are not synonyms; knowledge of the skills required for successful governmental participation and leadership.

The acquired attitudes and cognitions, together with the attendant behavior, of the mature persons described by the chart could not develop in all environments. The prison, certain boarding schools, hospitals for the mentally ill, families, communities, associations, and societies under authoritarian rule or those characterized by illiteracy and extreme poverty are not supportive of mature personality development. These environments deny the person the opportunity to want to be independent and the chance to make one's own decisions or to assume responsibility for such decisions. Unless the basic institutions function effectively in congruence with the nature of man, maturity is not attainable, regardless of the strength of the subjective personal desires.

Having once been a child, and having been exposed to both cultural and personal social experiences which are not designed to prepare the person for mature status, it is not to be wondered at that even after chronological adulthood has been attained, there are different degrees of maturity, with some persons eliminating many more of the attitudes and traits of childhood and adolescence than other persons are able to do.

Lawrence K. Frank summarized the matter very nicely:

> We need only remember that underneath the outer mask of adult size and dignity, behind the official position, rank, or prestige of the grown-up man or woman, there is always a little boy or little girl, still living over the hurts, the injustices, the unhappiness of a forgotten childhood. It is these little boys and little girls who run our social life and create the social problems and difficulties we suffer from—not because they are deliberately wicked, sinful, selfish, or antisocial, but because they are dominated by these childish feelings which govern their lives and direct their conduct. Usually they are unaware of the long forgotten occasions for the resentments and anxieties that so potently influence their present lives; but as we gain insight into personality development and trace back the individual's adult career to these early emotional experiences, we can see how the need to "get even" with parents and teachers, to build up defenses against early anxieties, to atone for guilt over childish misbehavior, are all operating as effectively as if the individual were indeed a little boy or little girl.[24]

In contrast to the sporadic focus of attention which is characteristic of the child, a constancy of both attitude and behavior characterizes the adult. There must be the recognition that human life is a compromise of competing needs and values, and that one must often postpone the fulfillment of immediate satisfactions in order to attain more lasting and significant pleasures at a later date. This is, of course, the mature reality principle as opposed to the pleasure principle of the immature, the

[24] Lawrence K. Frank in *Parent Teacher Magazine* (Dec. 1938), quoted in Robert G. Foster, *Marriage and Family Relationship* (New York: The Macmillan Co., 1950), p. 136.

disorganized, and the neurotic person.[25] The constancy of the mature adult is a function of his having occupied a position within a stable social system, of having established firm emotional relationships with values which are not ephemeral, and of having acquired knowledge which permits him to modify his environment *or* subjective attributes in keeping with the more permanent value system. The knowledge which permits him to perceive more accurately the nature of the world, social and non-social, within which he must live also enables him to escape the bonds of unwarranted fears, prejudices, and other emotional attachments which are functions of ignorance. Furthermore, it enables the actor to sort out the many heterogeneous pressures from *his others* and to move toward the goal of a generalized-other. It enables him to act in a rational manner.

A person is capable of thinking rationally if: (1) he is aware of his needs and wants and of the things which will fulfill these needs and wants; (2) he is aware of the means by which he can attain these ends; and (3) he takes into account the full consequences of this acceptance of goals and the selection of appropriate means.[26]

On the question of increased knowledge as a measure of maturity, it is safe to say that wisdom is a near-monopoly of adulthood, and in saying this we must distinguish between mere accumulation of facts which is a function of rote memory and the meaning of these and other facts which goes well beyond sheer memorization. Child prodigies are not uncommon in the physical sciences, in mathematics, and in some of the arts, but there is no record of one ever having shown up in the fields of the social sciences or in philosophy. The experiences that are required for the development of competence in the latter fields are rarely if ever available to the child, and the necessity of experience leads us to the next point in our discussion of maturity.

Maturity and Change

Maturity, as we perceive it, goes beyond the precise fulfillment of the expectations that define the status or position which the position occupies. Such coincidence of position and role, were it possible, would lead to stagnation of cultures and thwart any change. The mature person perceives when to adhere to the letter and spirit of the norms, and when to depart from them. In a sense, the mature person is both a conservative and a liberal, in that there will always be values to be preserved intact, and others which, in response to the demands of the hour, ought to be

[25] *See* Douglas H. Heath, *Explorations of Maturity* (New York: Appleton-Century-Crofts, 1965), for a summary of research findings concerning maturity. The author deals with the difficult problem of distinguishing between organization and maturity, and between disorganization and immaturity.

[26] This formulation is a slight modification of the German sociologist Max Weber's definition of rational thinking. It is argued by some that unless the ends sought are reasonable, the action cannot be considered to be rational.

modified or destroyed as having served their purpose. The mature person, therefore, never seeks a set of rules by which he can always calculate what is appropriate for the situation or episode in question. Freedom comes from order, but at times order is best served by change rather than by stability of established custom.

It is inconceivable that the perfect social system will arrive wherein there will be no need to meet and cope with failure. Accordingly, there must always be the opportunity, afforded by the social environment and accessible to the individual, to compensate, rationalize, sublimate, and accommodate without loss of freedom or status. It is for this reason that these adjustment processes are not perceived as pathological.

The Cultural Definition of Maturity

Each culture ascribes, permits, and restricts certain obligations and privileges to the adults of the society. The established rights and duties constitute the adult, or mature, positions or statuses of a given society. If we are to understand the personalities which have developed within a culture, we must know what these mature positions are as they have been defined by that culture. Some are peculiar to a given society, whereas others are merely variations upon positions which are common to man wherever he successfully survives in a society. Table XX notes some of the many possible positions, but does not consider the celibate adult. What is his status from the point of view of maturity? Surely, both from the point of view of the larger society and from that of the individual celibate, any given culture may well be improved by its bachelors and spinsters. The greater social mobility which the unmarried adult has in certain of life's phases often accrues to the benefit of the culture at large. The history books attest to the significant contribution to civilization made by the unwed adult. Furthermore, the implications of the population explosion for evaluation of celibate status is not fully comprehended at the present. Moreover, if seeking heterosexual relationships is a function of maturity, then it is clear (as pointed out elsewhere) that the celibate, especially the female, is denied this mature behavior because of the unwed state. Here, it would appear, modification of the cultural environment is a requisite to the celibate's attainment of full maturity.

Myth and Maturity

In a scale which is designed to measure degrees of maturity there is included as one of its items of social maturation the realization on the part of the child that there is no Santa Claus or Easter Bunny in the literal sense.[27] The recognition of such fairy tales as symbolic is generally

---

[27] Edgar A. Doll, *Vineland Social Maturity Scale* (Minneapolis: Educational Publishers, Inc., 1947).

taken as a measure of growing up, and if this principle is extended, we find that as a criterion of maturity it carries us well beyond the distinguishing of obvious items of fantasy. As the maturation process of the individual progresses along this line, there comes a time when myths, particularly culturally established ones of long standing, are distinguished from reality only by those who give special attention to study and research in the field in question. The pointing out of certain of these myths for what they really are is accepted in certain instances, but strongly resisted in others where personal interests (economic, political, or personal social) are involved. This raises the provocative question of whether or not the persons who continue to believe in the myths, even though they be the majority, are mature in this one respect. Few, if any, cultures, are devoid of such myths.

Illustrative of the differences between cultures in the interpretation of maturity is the following incident which is reported to have happened in the Malay Peninsula. The story has it that a group of European and American scientists were en route to some inland jungle area to study certain biological specimens peculiar to that region. On the second or third day on the journey, which was on foot and entailed the assistance of several native porters and guides, the latter happened upon a local feast or celebration and decided to stay over for it. The time-conscious representatives of Western European culture were violently opposed to the delay in their probably very tight schedule, and became quite emotional upon finding that the men were not to be dissuaded, by either pleas or threats, from their planned attendance at the feast. The scientists berated the men as immature and childish for putting such pleasure above the scientific purposes of the trip. On the other hand, the native men, not products of a clock-oriented society, were amused at what they considered to be the immature show of emotion merely because of the delay of the trip for a single day. These same Asians might find it difficult to comprehend why it is that adults of the United States can perform vigorous dances of domestic and foreign origin without being called immature, yet could not play hop-scotch or skip rope with the same impunity from criticism and possible loss of status.

Furthermore, within the history of a given country social changes bring with them altering bases for judging maturity. Football, baseball, and boxing would not be deemed mature activities in Colonial New England where even violin playing was banned as too frivolous.

Chronological Age and Maturity

The reader will recall seeing in the Introduction to Part III the designation of different age groups in an ancient civilization. Just when a person becomes a mature person is not agreed upon among different cultures, nor in the society from one time or place to another. Recently a passenger on the Burlington Zephyr was heard to exclaim in amazement and to gesture excitedly toward a large tractor being driven across the prairie. The cause of his behavior was that the tractor was being driven by a boy who appeared to be no more than nine or ten years old. To this observer, who lived in a state where eighteen is the legal age for securing a driver's license, it seemed outrageously dangerous to permit such a child to handle the tractor, but to the other occupants of the car it seemed rather commonplace. On many farms the rule about using equipment is, "if they are big enough, they are old enough." The passage of child-labor laws, it must be acknowledged, was motivated partly by compassion for overworked children, and in part by the desire to eliminate children from the competition for jobs which adults needed. Whatever the reasons, occupational maturity now occurs at a much later chronological age than was the case several decades ago. The reasons are frequently economic and cultural, rather than physical, immaturity of the persons who would enter the job market.

Even though no laws have been changed for many years with regard to holding political office, the voting age of twenty-one is more remote from the age at which persons enter such offices than it was when the country was first established.

The U. S. Constitution specifies that the lower house of the Congress shall have no members younger than twenty-five years of age, the Senate none under thirty years, and the President must be at least thirty-five. These ages were decided upon at a period in the country's history when men assumed obligations much earlier than they do generally today. One wonders whether or not the ages would be so young were the Constitution to be drawn up today. Support for the belief that they might not be so young is found in the fact that both elected and appointed officials of the U. S. Government have grown progressively older through the years since the ratification of the Constitution. Senators and Representatives were on the average about forty-five and forty-three years old, respectively, in 1799, whereas the comparable ages were sixty-five and fifty-three, respectively, in 1925. In 1963, more than one-fourth of the members of the United States Senate were over sixty-five years of age. The median age of the President's Cabinet increased from age forty-seven in 1789, to age sixty in 1945, and to 60.5 in 1957, but dropped to approximately 54 years in 1964. The median age of the top ranking generals of the Revolutionary War was thirty-nine, the Civil War, forty-nine years, and World War II, fifty-nine years. Present day leaders in legislative, judicial, diplomatic, military, naval, religious, and educational responsibilities are older today than were their predecessors holding the same positions.[28]

[28] *Cf.* Harvey C. Lehman, "The Age of Eminent Leaders, Then and Now," *American Journal of Sociology*, LII (Jan. 1947), 343.

A quick glance at history and the current scene in other cultures will show the variation in chronological age of persons who are by almost any criteria mature in role and position. Children may drive farm tractors in our country, but that a nine-year-old boy in our society could order his family, parents included, out of the house and make them camp for several days in the front yard is a preposterous idea, yet this very situation is reported by anthropologist Ralph Linton to have taken place in a Marquesan tribe (South Pacific island group).[29] Among the Marquesans, the culture ascribes to the eldest son, regardless of age, the hereditary title of chief, and it would be unthinkable that others would oppose his desires or orders. In this instance which Linton chanced upon during one of his visits, there had been a quarrel between the nine-year-old chief and his father, and the enraged son banned the whole group from the house. Alexander the Great began his leadership of armed men at the age of sixteen, and as king he led what were then huge armies into battle in his early twenties. He is but one of many young persons who have been in circumstances favorable to early maturation and have fulfilled the obligations of the ascribed positions which they held. The cultural values, known to the individual largely through the attitudes of those about him, determine within very wide limits the position to be assigned to any age group. The time when a person is deemed capable of making decisions for himself and assuming responsibility for his actions is determined as much by culture as by biological factors.[30]

The Achievement of Adult Status Through Direct Experience

In the acquisition of adult mature position, not only must one have a *breadth* of experience as he acquires knowledge of the world, but he must also have *appropriate* experiences. This is particularly true in the case of the development of emotional attitudes. However assiduously one may study and investigate all aspects of the world, and no matter how adequate his intellectual attitudes and concepts are, unless he has certain direct experience with the world about him and the people in that world, he may well remain in a state of emotional immaturity. Returning to our earlier emphasis (Chapter 5) upon the need to recognize the different processes involved in intellectual and emotional learning, we point to the need for specific experiences as the means of attaining mature status with regard to heterosexual attitudes and traits. Awareness of the cultural sex values and of the ways in which such sex values are developed is of no consequence to the person if he has not been able to develop the culturally approved heterosexual attitudes. Not only is the acquisition

[29] Ralph Linton, *The Study of Man* (New York: Appleton-Century-Crofts, 1936), p. 120.

[30] One anthropologist of note states that culture is more important than biology in assigning social position (Linton, *The Study of Man*, p. 119).

of culturally sanctioned desires dependent upon prior experiences, but the ability to fulfill these desires is equally contingent upon having had certain long-run experiences. Failure of the home situation to develop adequate identification of the male children with the father's role and identification of the female children with the mother and her role will often result in the development of culturally atypical sexual attitudes and deny the individual mature status insofar as sex and family relations are concerned. Bach studied the father fantasies of children (ages six to ten) separated from their soldier fathers for periods ranging from one to three years.[31] The separated children at the time of the study showed a feminine and idealistic fantasy picture of the father. When compared with a similar group of children not separated from their fathers the author concluded that a child's perception of his father is an important ingredient in human development.

Heterosexual attitudes, desires for wife or husband, and acceptance of children are developed unconsciously and gradually. Nothing is quite so futile as the homosexually oriented person wishing that he were of heterosexual inclination, a person wishing he were not afraid of the dark, or the nonswimmer sitting on the bank and wishing that he could swim. In each case actual learning of the proper kind, which can occur only with appropriate experiences, must take place if the desires are to become anything except desires. A homely variation on this theme is found in the old adage, "If wishes were horses, beggars would ride." Granting the improbability of ever separating completely the emotional and intellectual aspects of personality, it is equally unproductive of understanding to view them as identical processes. Our earlier discussions of learning theory are applicable here. The baseless fears and unwarranted prejudices that are more characteristic of children and adolescents are the products of intellectual misconceptions and of selective emotional experiences. Salter perceived that "human emotional problems are the result of personal miseducation . . . only by learning new emotional habits can the neurotic learn to be happy."[32] If the enculturation process is to alter these concepts and attitudes, not only must the appropriate replacement of facts occur, but also there must take place experiences which will permit an emotional reorientation. For example, what appears to be a pervasive immature attitude on the part of Americans toward races other than the Caucasian is a product of both intellectual misconceptions and selective contacts with these other races. Controlled observations, in a sense experimental in nature, have demonstrated the need for day-by-day

---

[31] George R. Bach, "Father Fantasies and Father Typing in Father-Separated Children," *Child Development*, 17 (1946), 63–80.

[32] Joseph Wolpe, Andrew Salter, and L. J. Reyna, *The Conditioning Therapies* (New York: Holt, Rinehart and Winston, 1964), p. 21.

primary-group contacts with members of the out-groups if habitual prejudices are to be altered. It goes without saying that the social setting is important, and that the same contacts in Alabama as those in New York are not likely to produce identical results.[33]

Successful Marital Adjustment As a Product of Appropriate Preparatory Experiences

Tolstoi, in a perceptive sentence from *Anna Karenina* wrote, "Happy families are all alike; every unhappy family is unhappy in its own way."[34] Sociological studies of happy and unhappy families confirm this literary observation. Successful marriages are more homogeneous in terms of the character of their interpersonal relationships than are unsuccessful marriages.[35]

Two studies of the factors involved in marital happiness illustrate clearly the relationship between adult attitudes and appropriate experiences in earlier years. Both studies emphasize, and one explicitly states that experiences that augment the process of enculturation (*i.e.*, acquiring or learning the social values of the culture in question), are highly significant for adjustment in marriage. Adjustment here, as in other social situations, involves the willingness and ability to play social roles in keeping with the assigned or assumed social position or status, in this instance, marriage. Background factors that indicate socialization into the culture are found to be positively correlated with success in marriage. Such factors include level of education, frequency and duration of attendance in church and Sunday school, number and sex of friends prior to marriage (generally numerous friendships with persons of both sexes were common in the early lives of those who adjusted well to marriage), active participation in social groups, and residence in a neighborhood of single-family dwellings.[36] In a later study, Burgess and Locke found that successful marriages are related to the length of the period of acquaintance, courtship, and engagement. This latter study also indicated that, on the average, marriages based on comradely affection turned out happier than those based on romantic attitudes.[37]

These are, to be sure, correlations and not causal relationships. Never-

---

[33] *See* the studies reported in Ch. 9.

[34] Translation by C. Garnett (New York: Modern Library, 1950).

[35] A good reference book on this subject is: Robert Winch, *Marriage and the Family* (New York: Holt, Rinehart and Winston, 1963).

[36] Ernest W. Burgess and Leonard S. Cottrell, *Predicting Success or Failure in Marriage* (New York: Prentice-Hall, 1939), p. 345. For comments on the value systems of the authors, *see* W. L. Kolb, "Sociologically Established Family Norms and Democratic Values," *Social Forces*, XXVI (1948).

[37] Ernest W. Burgess and Harvey J. Locke, *The Family*, 2nd Ed. (New York: American Book Co., 1953), p. 431; Alfred McClung Lee and Elizabeth B. Lee, *Marriage and The Family* (New York: Barnes and Noble, 1961).

theless, these items are suggestive of the type of life which makes for socialization, and which, therefore, prepares one well for married life which is continued in terms of the values of the culture.[38] Burgess and Cottrell further point out that their research into the lives of over five hundred married couples yielded the information that the children of happily married couples have much better than average chances for happiness in their own marriages. Too, close attachment between parents and the children seems to be a condition favorable to success in marriage.[39] Similarly Bossard and Boll, in the family structures they studied, concluded that "children reared in happy homes are more likely to be happy in their own marriages than children reared in medium or unhappy homes."[40]

Unconscious influences in the selection of a marriage partner are revealed in the observation of Burgess and Cottrell that children appear to select mates that resemble the parent of the opposite sex if the affectional relationships between the individual and that parent have been satisfying.[41] If such relationships with the parent of the opposite sex have not been satisfying, particularly if conflict has characterized the relationship, the individual is apt to select a person for marriage who is quite unlike the parent. However, this does not seem to result if frustration rather than conflict characterizes the parent-child relationship.

The same study revealed that birth-order was related to success in marriage. The greatest number of very happy marriages occurred when both of the marriage partners were oldest children, the fewest number of happy marriages occurred when both partners were youngest or only children. The least number of unhappy marriages occurred when middle children married.[42] In Bossard and Boll's studies, the oldest child, especially girls, did not rate high in marital happiness; the middle child did rate highest in this regard.[43] The sharing experiences that are often denied the single child but which are commonplace in the life of the child from the larger family, are favorably related to marital success. Bossard and Boll's study of large families indicated that large family products are usually good matrimonial risks. The following illustration

---

[38] George Simpson has criticized the marital happiness prediction studies by Burgess and his various collaborators as being naïve and superficial. Simpson believes that these studies are inadequate in at least two respects: (1) the criterion of success is based on a limited middle class definition of happiness; (2) the investigation failed to take into account the unconscious needs and motivations of the subjects. George Simpson, *People in Families* (New York: Thomas Y. Crowell Co., 1960), pp. 218–228.

[39] Burgess and Cottrell, *Predicting Success or Failure in Marriage*, p. 244.

[40] James H. S. Bossard and Eleanor Stoker Boll, *The Large Family System* (Philadelphia: University of Pennsylvania Press 1956), p. 304.

[41] *Ibid.*, p. 345.

[42] *Ibid.*, pp. 9–10.

[43] *Ibid.*, p. 304.

from one of their records indicates some of the things an only child may miss:

> Mother and Dad were relatively young when the first five of us came along and they played with us, and we all loved it. Dad used to chase Mother with a mop and she used the broom to get after him. We all squealed with delight for we knew that it was all in fun. People who came to the house to sell things often doubted the presence of Mother because of the great shrieks of laughter and accompanying noises that came from our house. In the summertime, we enjoyed many parties in the playhouse. If a cake "fell" we had a party, and we used to pray that the cake would fall. Every birthday was a grand occasion, presents or not. Everyone always had a cake. They are special ones, too. Mine was always chocolate with white icing, red teaberries, and pink candles.[44]

Berelson and Steiner surveyed the recent literature concerning the factors involved in marital adjustment and report findings consistent with those discussed above. They found that marital adjustment and happiness are more likely:

1. the more alike the marriage partners.
2. the better the adjustment of the partners during the period of courtship.
3. the happier the partners perceive their own parents' marriage to be.
4. the higher the level of education of the partners, or their socio-economic status.
5. the more religious they are.
6. the less psychologically disturbed or anxious they are.[45]

There are many exceptions to these generalizations, but the persons who have these items in their backgrounds are favorably situated with regard to playing the roles demanded of the marital status of marriage in our culture. Both intellectual and emotional factors are involved, and it is difficult to separate them. However, it is easier to change ideas and opinions, and this is often done without altering the emotional attitudes which handicap a person in his social relationships. Courses in marriage and the family result in changes in knowledge and beliefs more often than they accomplish change in attitudes. Unless these attitudes are based upon intellectual misconceptions, the preparation is only partly accomplished. Emotional habits of long standing are not easily changed, and then only when the appropriate experiences have been encountered. For example, the crux of any therapeutic endeavor is related to the achieve-

[44] Bossard and Boll, *The Large Family System*, p. 89. However one should not equate marital stability with marital happiness. A family may be broken social-psychologically while remaining together in the same household.

[45] Bernard Berelson and Gary A. Steiner, *Human Behavior* (New York: Harcourt, Brace and World, 1964), p. 310.

ment of insight on the part of the patient, and as Monroe has pointed out this involves not mere intellectual insight, but, "the actual *experiencing* of aspects of one's personality which have been made defensively unconscious."[46] The inertia of habit makes it very unlikely that any significant changes are going to occur in the personality of an adult whose attitudes are not those which are required for assumption of the adult position of marriage.

Familial Status Relationship

Most human beings in western culture are members of a family organization. The almost universal nature of this familial primary group relationship is an essential unit of social control in the stable organization of most societies. The family, in one form or another, channels sexual activity, provides a quality of economic protection, regularizes child bearing and child training and gains a place for the members of the family in the social system. While premarital arrangements are tolerated in many societies, extramarital behavior is usually discouraged. When illegitimacy occurs both parents as well as offspring are likely to be punished in one manner or another. Just as all societies provide for some kind of family arrangements, so do most societies provide sanctioned methods for dissolving the marriage relationship.[47]

Probably because of the expectations of the marriage arrangements in most cultures, most adults ultimately marry. Of course the form of the family organization will vary from society to society. However, society rather than the individual determines the marriage form which is acceptable in each culture. Kenkel points out that "Nowhere is the individual allowed to decide for himself. In all societies there is a particular marriage form that is well ingrained in the culture; and most frequently there is only one form that meets with high social approval."[48] Davis and Blake note that it is primarily in urban-industrial societies that the proportion of women who never marry by the end of the reproductive years exceeds 10 per cent.[49] By contrast, in many underdeveloped areas, the percentage of women unmarried at the end of the fertile years is much less. Davis and Blake provide the following comparative data:

[46] R. Monroe, *Schools of Psychoanalytic Thought* (New York: Holt, Rinehart and Winston, 1955), p. 520.

[47] Bernard Berelson and Gary Steiner, *Human Behavior* (New York: Harcourt, Brace and World, Inc., 1964), p. 308; *Cf.* George P. Murdock, *Social Structure* (New York: The Macmillan Co., 1949).

[48] William F. Kenkel, *The Family in Perspective* (Appleton-Century-Crofts, 1960), p. 28.

[49] Kingsley Davis and Judith Blake, "Social Structure and Fertility: An Analytic Framework," *Economic Development and Cultural Change* (Vol. 4, No. 3), April 1956, p. 219.

Table XXI
Percentage of Women Unmarried at End of Reproductive Span in Various Cultures*

Belgium (1930)	13.3	Switzerland (1941)	20.1
England & Wales (1931)	16.8	India (1931)	0.8
Ireland (1946)	26.3	Ceylon (1946)	3.4
Sweden (1949)	20.9	Malaya (1947)	3.3

* Kingsley Davis and Judith Blake, "Social Structure and Fertility: an Analytic Framework," *Economic Development and Cultural Change*, 4 (April 1956), 218–219.

Within the typical middle class family in the United States and Canada, the father is the task leader and the mother the social emotional leader.[50] However, this is not always the situation in other cultures nor is it necessarily the norm in all subcultures in the United States. In highly cohesive family groups there is usually agreement among family members concerning the respective tasks and functions which characterize each member's position and role. Role differentiation within the family makes possible the smooth operation of the family organization.

It is obvious that in the family structure, or in any small group situation of a primary group nature, it is important that the place and role assignments of the members of that group be unambiguous and compatible. *Role collision* may occur in a family when the parental positions are not clearly defined, such as responsibility for child discipline or in economic responsibilities. Source of authority and disagreements as to who is responsible for a particular task may create confusion and tension. *Role incompatibility* may occur in those situations where any member of the family is expected to occupy two or more positions which are mutually exclusive. Role incompatibility is more likely to occur in situations where in-laws live within the nuclear or conjugal family domicile. If the wife's father lives in the home, the wife is faced with possible incompatible role expectations from her husband as well as from her father. Her husband's expectations of her in her position to him as his *wife* may be in conflict with her father's desire for her to function in terms of her position as an obedient *daughter*. The situation for this lady may be further complicated by children who expect her to fulfill their expectations of *mother*. Whether these respective statuses and positions of *wife*, *daughter*, and *mother* are compatible will of course depend upon the skill of the central actress but also upon the willingness of the various members of the family to recognize the many positions they are asking their

[50] A. Paul Hare, *Handbook of Small Group Research* (New York: Free Press of Glencoe, 1962), p. 116.

heroine to occupy simultaneously. Role incompatibility may also be a problem for husbands whose job demands conflict directly with their positions as father and husband. Presumably many physicians face this problem in determining whether the expectations of the family will be pre-empted by the emergency expectations of patients.

Still another problem in role differentiation within the family is that of *role confusion.* The effectiveness of any member of the family is diminished to the extent that that member permits or promotes ambiguity in the definition of his status or position. Inconsistency in family rules, indeterminant leadership, and lack of clarity in role assignments can, by creating role confusion, detract from family cohesiveness. Spiegel has pointed out that "In general, contradictions in the role expectations [positions or statuses] for a family member tend to make that individual more self-aware and on guard, forcing him constantly to make decisions about his role behavior. This type of family situation appears to foster more disturbed children."[51]

The Affectional Role in Marriage

Of all the affectional relationships in life none offers more opportunity for fulfillment or frustration than the love relationship. Not all heterosexual love occurs within marriage. Nor are all sexual relationships within marriage love relationships. Sexual behavior and the love relationships are not necessarily to be equated. Loving is an active process in which the lover realizes his own self-fulfillment and deepest sense of realization through his contributions to the self-fulfillment of another person. Cavan has stated the matter precisely as follows:

> The motive of sex is selfish, the release of one's own tensions. The sexual object is merely a means to an end. At this level, sex is often spoken of as carnal, low, animalistic, and its expression usually is kept secretive. Because of the definition of sex as unworthy, some justification must be found for it. A social justification through the birth of children formerly was the highest motivation for sex, strictly limited to marriage. Now, with a more personal definition of marriage, sex has found a new justification—as the expression of love. Although love and sex are now closely related and the deepest experience of love and sex may occur between the same pair, they are not identical simply because they coincide.[52]

Students of sexual behavior agree that sexual competency in the marriage relationship is not necessarily identical with affectional gratification.

---

[51] J. P. Spiegel, "The Resolution of Role Conflict Within the Family," *Psychiatry,* 20 (1957), pp. 1–16. Quoted in A. Paul Hare, *Handbook of Small Group Research* (New York: Free Press of Glencoe, 1962), p. 121.

[52] Ruth Shonle Cavan, *The American Family* (New York: Thomas Y. Crowell Co., 1953), p. 402.

Ellis bluntly states that "the best coital partner may not be one of the best sex partners because intercourse is only one way to satisfy the sex needs of the average female." "A man," says Ellis, "may be an excellent *lover* without necessarily being an excellent *copulator*. . . Indeed as I often tell my marriage counselling and psychotherapy clients, a man who had no penis whatsoever could be an excellent lover, just as a woman who had no vagina could be a perfectly satisfactory sex partner for the average man if he or she did not have overpowering pro-coital prejudices."[53]

The affectional relationship in marriage is dependent for its fulfillment upon the reciprocal needs, capacities, and attitudes of the parties involved. The affectional relationship may take many forms, whether sexual, romantic, or economic. Cavan puts the matter into proper perspective as follows:

> When two people love each other, they tend to identify themselves with each other. Part of this identification is on a psychological level; that is, they probe each other's thoughts and feelings and seek similarities and develop new common attitudes. They like to do things together and especially to build up activities shared by themselves alone. When a man and a woman love each other, shared sex experiences become a symbol of their identification. Our culture requires privacy and secrecy for sex relations. It also approves only of sex relations between one pair over a period of time. Intercourse therefore becomes the ultimate in exclusive shared experiences and an almost ideal symbol of identification sought by those who love each other.[54]

Not all people are equally prepared by their life experiences for the sexual role in marriage. Our culture has placed high value upon certain physical features which are presumably related to potency in sexual behavior. There is no evidence that sexual potency is related to any particular physical features or characteristics. Yet some people have assigned themselves to impotent role relationships because of culturally defined (or imaginary) genital, or vaginal deficiencies. Hussain reports the following case from his own practice:

> A thirty five year old white male and his thirty four year old wife were both referred for psychiatric opinion, since they had been married for ten years and no sexual intercourse had taken place. The wife suffered from dysparenuia, anxiety, and various somatic complaints. The husband was alleged by the wife to be impotent.
>
> Both were treated by hypnosis. During the trance, the wife's anxiety was inhibited by relaxation responses. Later on she was advised to try vaginal dilators for building up confidence. The husband was also

[53] Albert Ellis, *The Art and Science of Love* (New York: Institute for Rational Living, 1960), p. 117.

[54] Cavan, *The American Family*, p. 402. *See also* Clifford Kirkpatrick, *The Family* (New York: Ronald Press Co., 1963).

treated with relaxation responses. The anxiety responses in both were inhibited, and for the first time in ten years, sexual union resulted. Both were overjoyed with the effects of the treatment, which took eight weeks altogether. No symptom substitution took place, and they have continued to enjoy married life as never before.[55]

The Role of the Celibate

Kimball Young arbitrarily selected the age of 30 as the age when a person who is not, and has not been married is defined as a celibate.[56] (Figure 16 in Chapter 4 provides recent census data concerning the marital status of the United States population by age and sex.)

Over the years, the celibates have become fewer in number as the sex ratio dips below 100, the frontiers disappear, and the culture becomes more mature and stable. The minority position of these people is not culturally designed but results from personal social experiences of the persons involved. In fact, the cultural preparation for the adult years, except in rare instances, is not for celibacy but for marriage. The "playing house" which is so common among the children of our culture always is built around father and mother roles, not around single positions. Marriage some time in the future is taken for granted by almost all young people, and their personalities are developed in anticipation of assuming marital roles in adulthood. The unknown variables are the time and the person involved.

An important factor in the adjustment of the adult to celibacy is the acceptance of marriage as the norm, the *good* in our culture. The many ceremonies and institutions which surround marriage and the anticipation of it are not matched by similar ones for celibacy with the sole exception of the religious celibates. The modern variation of a dowry, the hope chest, the engagement and the accompanying parties or showers for the bride-to-be, the giving and wearing of the engagement ring, and the marriage ceremony itself are important experiences in their own right, as well as means to the end of entering the world of married people. Because this is true, the bachelors and the "unclaimed treasures" are deprived of these personally satisfying experiences to which the vast majority of the young people, the young women especially to be sure, aspire. In addition to giving immediate personal satisfaction to the participants, these culturally approved experiences also are evidence to the world at large that the person involved has gained a culturally esteemed position, that he is *wanted* by someone. This fact cannot be overlooked

---

[55] A. Hussain, "Behavior Therapy Using Hynosis," in *The Conditioning Therapies*, Joseph Wolpe, Andrew Salter, and L. J. Reyna, eds. (New York: Holt, Rinehart and Winston, 1964), p. 59.

[56] Kimball Young, *Personality and Problems of Adjustment* (New York: Appleton-Century-Croft, 1940), p. 572. Young used this definition in connection with his discussion of single women only.

in the study of the personality of the unmarried female. Actually, the status of a married person is sought by some women even more than is the *role* of the married woman. This is a result of the personal social variations in the premarital experiences of the young women of our culture. Whereas, the culture ascribes high status to marriage, and in general prepares the young to play marital roles as adults, the many unique experiences of any given person may ill prepare him to play the role of the married person. Much marital friction results from the discrepancy between the person's desire for the status of husband or wife and his or her ability to play the role which normally accompanies that status. Persons who for a variety of reasons have failed to develop maturity in terms of assuming responsibilities for decisions, or sex attitudes and traits, may desire the status of spouse without the obligations of it. This situation is illustrated by an instance brought to the attention of the present authors wherein six college-senior girls, all of whom were engaged to be married, revealed degrees of sexual frigidity which ranged from complete revulsion at the thought of the sex act to complete indifference to kissing and caressing. When questioned as to the seemingly illogical act of becoming engaged under these circumstances, the young ladies replied that they were motivated by the prestige which accompanied being "pinned" or engaged by the time they were seniors. "You just *have* to be engaged by that time or lose face!" seemed to characterize the attitudes of these girls who were poorly prepared to play the role of married women. At least one young lady of this group, once graduation was accomplished and she was no longer in the immediate presence of her affective other, broke her engagement, stating that she knew she could not at that time fulfill her obligations as a wife.

The dilemma faced by such persons is that they feel the social pressure to attain the societal position of a married person, but cannot bring themselves to want to play the accompanying role. Because of the cultural arrangement of insisting that the male, ostensibly at least, must make the advances in the request to marry, society tends to assume that the unmarried women are the unwanted women. This imputation gives rise to many unhappy situations, even though the person in question may prefer to remain single because of her sexual adaptation, her career ambitions, or for other reasons. If she has had proposals for marriage, she feels the need to tell her associates so. Such a situation is not a happy one. The single male, on the other hand, is assumed to have chosen his marital status and therefore, he finds no social pressure comparable to that faced by the female celibate. The bachelor has a much better chance of becoming well adjusted than has the single woman because of this difference in the imputed involuntary position of the latter. However, it is a very real question as to whether such female celibates are less well adjusted than are the women who, despite personal social development which is incompatible with marriage roles, proceed to become married. Except for the discomfort of occupying a socially disesteemed position, the spinster is apt to be less maladapted if she is playing the role for which her past experience has prepared her, than the married woman of comparable experience who is forced to play a role for which she is ill fitted.

An attractive single lady, age forty-one, summarized her feelings about her celibate status as follows:

> I have heard the question, "How did you ever manage to remain single?" so often that I am conditioned to respond automatically, "It wasn't easy." Seriously, I think that, in most cases, it is a matter of circumstances and social contacts. You have to be at the right place at the right time. To catch fish, you must go near the water—when I finally went to the water, the fish were caught. Also, women are at a disadvantage in that they have to wait to be asked; often, those that ask aren't necessarily the desired ones. Some women, perhaps like myself, are much too fussy in view of what they have to offer. I don't think anyone sets out deliberately to remain single—it just happens. No one is as surprised as I am that I am still single, but in my case, I think that it is a good thing as perhaps I am more suited to play this role. I admire married women very much; in fact, I am in awe of them as the older I get, the more complex and difficult the marriage role appears to be. Most women, if unmarried, are miserable, but they are probably the type who would be miserable single or married—"the grass is always greener . . . ." One advantage of getting older is that the things that seemed so important a few years back, no longer matter. A few years ago, "old maid" was a "dirty" word—an appellation that I never wanted applied to myself; yet, here I am enjoying the so-called "fate worse than death." The fear of being an "old maid" has driven more than one woman to marriage for the sake of marriage. Thank goodness that I never became that "scared."

In the instance of the unmarried woman who is involuntarily so, there is no question as to the maladjustment. She has developed a personality which anticipated marriage and the accompanying roles of sex partner, wife, and mother; yet she is forced to play another role. Attuned to a desire for heterosexual experience, because of cultural taboos against such experience outside of wedlock she is denied it in large measure. Certain studies indicate that there is considerable discrepancy between prescribed practice and what is actually done by these single persons.[57] Denied sexual experiences in marriage, the single person is offered four other possible outlets, only one of which is socially sanctioned: (1) complete repression or sublimation of the sex impulse; (2) homosexuality;

---

[57] Alfred C. Kinsey, *et al.*, *Sexual Behavior in the Human Female* (Philadelphia: W. B. Saunders, 1953).

(3) autoeroticism; or (4) extramarital heterosexuality. How successful the first of these is cannot be stated with surety; but there is doubt that it occurs frequently except in the instances of persons whose sex impulse is characteristically weak or not oriented in the heterosexual direction.[58] For the person who desires marriage and normal heterosexual experience, this adjustment probably is but rarely a satisfactory one. Homosexuality was discussed in Chapter 9. Autoeroticism or masturbation does provide a substitute sex outlet for the unmarried adult. Kinsey's studies showed masturbation to be common in single men and women but the frequency of the need was much less in single women than in single men.[59] Earlier studies of this factor in single women show that it is a consideration in their sex adjustment.[60] These studies suggest that probably more than one-third of the single women studied employ this means of satisfying the sex impulse.

Even in the increased urbanization of our culture, with the greater opportunity for anonymity of social behavior, it is not likely that a large proportion of female celibates finds extramarital heterosexual outlets to be satisfying. There are still the hazards of loss of status, of pregnancy, and of guilt and shame feelings. We are not entirely free, by any means, of the double standard for sexual behavior which permits the male experiences that are denied the female. Culturally, what is sauce for the goose is not deemed suitable sauce for the gander. In truth, none of these four possibilities of satisfying the sex needs of the unmarried female is apt to prove successful except in rare cases.[61] In a culture which provides one, and only one, approved means of adult sexual expression, it is likely that those who are sociopsychologically prepared for, but who are denied, this single outlet, will not become well adjusted socially or sexually. Such persons are members of a personal social minority for which our culture provides no satisfactory status. Even in nonsexual affairs, the single person, particularly the single female, presents a problem. Many of the social events, such as dances, card parties, and even social gatherings of less formal nature, often are couple-centered, and the celibate is apt to be left out of it or if invited is likely to feel superfluous. To remain in the world of "the girls" is usually the adaptation of the female celibate. To the single woman upon whose shoulders falls the task of caring for aging

[58] Cf. Alfred Kinsey et al., Sexual Behavior of the Human Male (Philadelphia: W. B. Saunders, 1948), pp. 205–207. Some of the major and often valid criticisms of the Kinsey study do not invalidate his observations on sublimation and the low frequency of sex outlet among females.

[59] Kinsey et al., Sexual Behavior of the Human Male, pp. 71–76.

[60] Cf. R. L. Dickinson and L. Beam, The Single Woman: A Medical Study in Sex Education (Baltimore: Williams and Wilkins Co., 1934); K. B. Davis, Factors in the Sex Life of Twenty-two Hundred Women (New York: Harper & Brothers, 1929).

[61] Cf. Young, Personality and Problems of Adjustment, pp. 584–585, for further comment on these attempted adjustments.

parents society accords a certain approbation and the recognition given for this worthy assignment helps the individual accept her deprivation with some grace. The old saying that, "It is a poor family that cannot provide at least one old maid" has reference to this role of the unmarried daughter.

The sole exception to the rule that our culture fails to institutionalize single status is found in the celibate religious orders. Both the male and female organizations of this kind provide for their members a satisfactory status and the persons assuming these statuses usually find the roles compatible. This is so because the persons who enter these orders and remain in them are carefully selected in terms of habits and attributes which permit them to play the expected roles successfully. They are not random samples of the persons in the societies from which they are drawn. In the rather severe and lengthy preparatory periods involved in becoming a priest or a nun, the persons whose personal attributes are ill fitted for the role of the celibate and other atypical experiences are eliminated from the running. The successful individuals are those whose sex drives, *for a variety of reasons,* are less demanding or are sublimated in a manner which is not typical of the larger society. The unique experiences of the religious celibate and/or a less-than-average innate sexual drive are especially attuned to the celibate existence. Although most of those who are not thus prepared are eliminated early in the career preparation for religious celibacy, occasionally, as is well known, there occurs an abandoning of the acquired position in favor of the conventional sexual adjustment through marriage, but this is the exception. Of comparable nature is the bachelor who marries years after the average age of marriage. The formation of the celibate, religious or otherwise, begins very early in life and is not the result of a few years of intensive training in late adolescence and early adulthood. The average person, male or female, is not likely to be a successful candidate for such a position. Celibacy is usually not a burden for those who voluntarily enter it; the coincidence of position and role in such instances spells good social adjustment.[62]

Celibacy, then, is a minority position for which, except in the cases of religious celibate orders, our culture makes no positive provisions. It is a residual category peopled by those persons who do not fit into the major institutionalized patterns, sometimes because they have not developed social roles in keeping with the normal statuses, and sometimes despite the fact that they have developed such roles. Social mobility is limited, and in most instances this situation presents a problem. The problem's dimensions are measured in terms of the discrepancy between the social

---

[62] *Cf.* L. B. Holman and B. Schaffner, "The Sex Lives of Unmarried Men," *American Journal of Sociology,* LII (1947), 501–507; R. Reed, *The Single Woman* (New York: The Macmillan Co., 1942); R. R. Willoughby, "The Emotionability of Spinsters," *Character and Personality,* XV (1937), 215–223.

position of a person and the willingness and/or the ability of the person to play the accompanying role. It is safe to say that the majority of the celibates, especially the females, find their marital status a socially unsatisfactory one. Their unique experiences have not prepared them for roles demanded by the social position which society accords them.

However, the individual with adequate mental and physical endowment, who lives in a cultural environment which provides a variety of specialized positions, and who is equipped with a truly liberal education, often utilizes the adjustment processes or mechanisms of compensation, rationalization, and sublimation so that he perceives his life as entirely worthwhile.

Adult Positions and Job Satisfaction

Among the many goals to which a mature adult may aspire is career achievement. Much of the adult life is centered about the realization of job satisfaction and the roles associated with the position of a particular career responsibility. Most adult men find their lives polarized about two centers of orientation: the home and the job. There are of course additional or supplemental areas of interest such as club, church, or other extra-curricular activities. Hsu would in fact claim that one of the unique characteristics of the American culture is its obsession with belonging to various kinds of social organizations at every age grade.[63] This affiliation is sought after, says Hsu, to satisfy certain social needs denied by the culture's emphasis upon the importance of the self and the high value placed upon individual freedom. Certainly the club, the labor union, the employer's association, the church, and so on, all afford opportunities beyond the home and the job for the satisfaction of social as well as more utilitarian needs. The importance of the job in satisfying self esteem and social affiliation needs beyond the ordinary monetary considerations is readily apparent.

The adult career position and role for women is less complex and sometimes is more frustrating than it is for men. The male is not so completely dependent upon the success and the happiness of home as is his wife. A man may be unhappy at home but successful at work or vice versa, but for most women this choice of position is not available. In our culture the affective other for most women requires that she shall achieve her major satisfactions within the home or as an extension of her family's place in the community. While there are an increasing number of women whose affective other does not include this definition of female position, the overwhelming majority of women do identify their career with homemaking and its related activities and many seem to enjoy it.

[63] F. L. K. Hsu, *Clan, Caste, and Club* (New York: D. Van Nostrand Co., 1963) p. 227.

In this connection, *The Feminine Mystique*[64] revives a vital theme that has not been heard for a long time. Just as Whyte's *Organization Man* described the modern industrial employee as a prisoner of corporate life, so does Mrs. Friedan describe the modern American housewife as a prisoner of her home. Mrs. Friedan in this volume decries the failure of American women to achieve a satisfactory identity. American women, according to Mrs. Friedan, have accepted a position which is a function of what she is pleased to call the *feminine mystique* and they try desperately to satisfy the role expectations of that assignment. This mystique, according to Friedan, requires that an intelligent American woman will aspire to self-realization solely by means of her femininity in a passive sexual role as mother, wife, and adjunct to her husband's career and home. The feminine mystique is described as follows:

> The feminine mystique says that the highest value and the only commitment for women is the fulfillment of their own femininity. It says that the great mistake of Western culture, through most of its history, has been the undervaluation of this femininity. It says this femininity is so mysterious and intuitive and close to the creation and origin of life than man-made science may never be able to understand it. But however special and different, it is in no way inferior to the nature of man; it may even in certain respects be superior. The mistake, says the mystique, the root of women's troubles in the past is that women envied men, women tried to be like men, instead of accepting their own nature, which can find fulfillment only in sexual passivity, male domination, and nurturing maternal love.[65]

It would be Mrs. Friedan's contention that while American women have achieved legal equality, they have failed to acquire psychological equality. With the help of the slick women's magazines and with the assistance of Freudian psychoanalysis (which is, according to Friedan, masculine oriented, *i.e.*, she regards Freud's concept of "penis envy" as a highly presumptive and provincial thesis), women have been persuaded to satisfy the expectations of the feminine mystique and have doggedly endeavored to play the passive role associated with such a position. Such a role can, for the intelligent and educated women, lead only to a sense of futility and lack of self-realization. Mrs. Friedan quotes with satisfaction the famous speech made by Nora to her husband in Ibsen's *Doll House*, at the time when Nora is about to slam the door on the feminine mystique of her generation:

> You have always been so kind to me. But our home has been nothing but a playroom. I have been your doll wife, just as at home I was Papa's doll child; and here the children have been my dolls. I thought it great

[64] Betty Friedan, *The Feminine Mystique* (New York: W. W. Norton, 1963).
[65] Friedan, *The Feminine Mystique*, p. 37.

fun when you played with me, just as they thought it fun when I played with them. That is just what our marriage has been, Torvald. . . .

How am I fitted to bring up the children? . . . There is another task I must undertake first. I must try and educate myself—you are not the man to help me in that. I must do that for myself. And that is why I am going to leave you now . . . I must stand quite alone if I am to understand myself and everything about me. It is for that reason that I cannot remain with you any longer. . . .

For a man to be successfully engaged in a worthwhile occupation is generally defined in our culture as desirable. Involuntary unemployment is usually regarded as a condition to be avoided, not only because of the resulting lack of income, but because it symbolizes to the unemployed person, and to others, that his skills are not highly valued in the market place. The consequences for self-esteem as a result of denied opportunity to pursue work is readily apparent. This is true not only for the physically handicapped and the older worker but also for those denied the opportunity for work success because of minority status. If work is an important organization of the American male's value system, then one needs to consider not only what success in the system says about a man, but also what curtailed or denied success does to his self-esteem.

As society becomes more complex, the dependency upon a job increases. A man without a job is a man who doesn't belong. Involuntary unemployment in the North American culture frequently means loneliness, separation from active people, rejection, loss of position and identification as a vital and valued person. What a man does vocationally is one of the identifiable labels of achievement and worthfulness.

Nor is permanent leisure usually considered in our culture to be a satisfactory substitute for job responsibilities. Even those who for reasons of financial good fortune do not need to work find it undesirable socially to be without some kind of job identification lest they be left unlabelled. If a person earns or inherits money in sufficient quantities to make him financially independent, retirement is not in most communities accepted among younger men as a reasonable form of occupational adjustment. Such fortunate individuals, if they are to maintain prestige with their peers, are expected to achieve some kind of recognition in the business or professional world which will give them a career. In recent years politics has, for some members of the leisure class, offered opportunities for public service and the role playing satisfactions associated with these assignments. The importance of titles and medals has helped build nations and win wars. Status symbols objectify in a very concrete way the individual's apparent attainment as it has been judged by others. Their importance in business and industry cannot be overemphasized.

J. F. is married to a woman whose wealth and social position make special demands upon him. He is an ordinary sort of fellow of average intelligence and without any education beyond high school. Because of his wife's wealth he does not have to work to support the family, but the men in his social set are all engaged in interesting work and he has no such identification. He is embarrassed when at cocktail parties people ask him where he works and he cannot identify himself with any particular segment of the industrial or professional world. He is not capable on his own merits of holding down a job of significant responsibility and so has bought an interest in a small company where he has an executive title but does not interfere with the operations of the organization. When people ask him what he does he can now tell them he is an officer of a company, thus he gains the status without playing the role of the successful executive.

In ancient Greece only the wealthy people could become citizens because the state required so much of their time that labor was out of the question. This was why Aristotle observed that those who must labor in order to live could not become citizens.

There are cultures today in which earning a living is important only for its money income. In some oriental cultures it is (or at least was) a mark of distinction to be at leisure even at a poverty level. Many a Chinese could retire without social disapproval under such circumstances. Such an individual in the older Chinese culture was respected, for work as such carried no enviable prestige.

But the American ethic assumes that people will work for a living. We are a nation of workers, of producers. To a large degree our lives are vocationally oriented. We gain status through our jobs, our work titles, and our incomes. Success in our culture is commonly measured in terms of vocational achievement. Aaron Levenstein observes that, "A man's closest link to his society is his job or profession. Dislocation in that area means trouble for both the community and himself. The health of the individual and the health of the society depend on how they are linked to each other. And the most significant link is in the work relationship."[66]

This is not exclusively a North American phenomenon. Alexandre Vexliard of France notes that, "Our time has been characterized as a 'civilization of work' . . . At no time in history has the active part of the population been so important in proportion to the total population. The leisure classes, poor as well as rich, were much more numerous formerly . . . It is only nowadays, since the thirties, that a positive attitude toward work has become quasi-universal in the great global industrial societies."[67]

[66] Aaron Levenstein, *Why Men Work* (The Crowell-Collier Press, 1962), p. 20. *Cf.* Robert Dubin, *The World of Work* (Englewood Cliffs, N.J.: Prentice-Hall, 1958); Edward Gross, *Work and Society* (New York: Thomas Y. Crowell Co., 1958).

[67] Alexandre Vexliard, "Variability of Ethical Attitudes Toward Work," *Proceedings of the Sixteenth International Congress of Psychology* (Amsterdam: North Holland Pub. Co., 1962), p. 630.

However, some sociologists see an ethic of leisure replacing the Protestant ethic of work. C. Wright Mills indicates that, "What is psychologically important in this shift to mass leisure is that the old middle-class ethic—the gospel of work—has been replaced in the society of employees by a leisure ethic, and this replacement has involved a sharp, almost absolute split between work and leisure. Now work itself is judged in terms of leisure values. The sphere of leisure provides the standards by which work is judged; it lends to work such meanings as work has."[68]

There is no doubt that a dichotomy is developing in the work force between those who work a given minimum, and those who work according to their own needs. The former are likely to be those whose jobs are assigned through union contracts in which work rules and in some cases laws prescribe the hours a man may work. As a result of this shortening of the work week, in an industrial city like Milwaukee, Wisconsin, it is not uncommon for a man to hold down two full-time jobs simultaneously. Such "moonlighting" is, of course, frowned upon by those who regard such motivation as unsporting. On the other hand, professionals and executives who more or less set their own work load (or have it set for them by the demands of their clients) generally work longer hours than do those at hourly paid levels. Wilensky reports that, "At every level there is a group or category where about a third work at least 55 hours—lawyers, professors, lower middle-class managers, upper working-class youngsters."[69] The writer attended a conference of social scientists recently, in which the opinion was expressed that by the end of the century, work would probably be regarded not as something a person does in order to earn enough money to live well, but rather as a privilege in self-realization. The opinion was expressed that by the year 2000, only those who can make a contribution will be able to enjoy the creative satisfaction of work and many may live out their lives without ever knowing work as we know it today. "The problem," said one astute observer, "will be to teach those who are not chosen for work that a life of leisure is not shameful."

Work and Role Expectations

An important postulate of social psychology is that a person's attitudes and beliefs are a reflection of the position he occupies in a social system. Furthermore, as a person's position changes in society, his attitudes are likely to be influenced by the nature of the expectations of the new status.

---

[68] C. Wright Mills, *White Collar* (New York: Oxford University Press, 1951) p. 116. *Cf.* also in this connection Thorstein Veblen's *Instinct of Workmanship* (New York: The Macmillan Co., 1914).

[69] Harold L. Wilensky, "The Uneven Distribution of Leisure; The Impact of Economic Growth on 'Free Time'," *Social Problems*; a publication of the Society for the Study of Social Problems, 9, No. 1 (Summer 1961), pp. 33–36.

Thus Lieberman has demonstrated that when rank and file workers are promoted into the ranks of foremen, their attitudes become more management oriented, while those rank and file workers who are elected union stewards become more pro-union in their attitudes.[70] Conversely, when members of either group are demoted to their former position, their attitudes also tend to revert to the earlier orientation.

A change in roles almost invariably involves a change in reference groups. Old reference groups may continue to influence the role occupant, but new ones also come into play. The change in reference groups may involve moving into a completely new group (as when a person gives up membership in one organization and joins another one) or it may simply involve taking on new functions in the same group (as when a person is promoted to a higher position in a hierarchical organization). In both situations, new reference groups will tend to bring about new frames of reference, new self precepts, and new vested interests, and these in turn will tend to produce new attitudinal orientations.[71]

When a man moves his family into a new community, the neighbors want to know "where he works," and "what he does." These are not idle questions, because when you know a man's job, you may also know a good deal about the man, how he lives, his attitudes, and what his family may be like. The job usually requires the worker to play a role consistent with the stereotype associated with that kind of work. Men tend to take on the character and qualities of their job. When a young lady announces her engagement, her family and friends want to know about her fiancé and particularly, "What does he do?" The answer to this question will tell a good deal about the standard of living the young couple will probably enjoy but will also indicate something of the kind of young man this is, or is about to become. A young lady who marries a physician is likely to live a different kind of life than the girl who marries a sales engineer. And the man who becomes a foreman is going to live a different kind of life than a man who becomes a school teacher. Men take on the personalities of their jobs. Men assume the role expected of a particular career.[72] An individual derives his perceptions of himself in part from the reactions

[70] Seymour Lieberman, "The Effects of Changes in Roles on the Attitudes of Role Occupants," in *Personality and Social Systems*, Neil J. Smelser and William T. Smelser, eds. (New York: John Wiley & Sons, 1963), pp. 264–279. A question which remains unanswered is the extent to which a person may be promoted because he may already possess some of the attitudes which will make him effective in the new position and vice versa.

[71] Lieberman, "The Effects of Changes in Roles on the Attitudes of Role Occupants," p. 277.

[72] Chris Argyris, *Personality and Organization* (New York: Harper and Bros., 1957), pp. 76–122.

of others toward his job and himself. Investigations of particular kinds of jobs reveal the influence of the work situation upon the attitudes and behavior of the worker in those jobs. Such studies of particular vocational experiences include, "The Personality of Artists,"[73] *The Saleslady*,[74] *The Hobo*,[75] and *White Collar*.[76] Still others are Cottrell's, "Of Time and the Railroader,"[77] and Whyte's *Organization Man*.[78] In each of these occupations it is apparent that the job assigns the man a particular position together with specific roles which he must play in order to satisfy the expectations of his affective other.

PERSONALITY DEVELOPMENT IN THE MIDDLE YEARS

The personal attributes in these middle years are ordinarily fully matured and it is not often that life has many new surprises for the average adult by way of new surges of talent, energy, or personal developments. The adult person has emerged from the interaction of nature and nurture over many years. The adult has had a great deal of practice over the years in over-learning particular role behavior to correspond to the expectations of particular aspects of his culture. This role behavior, once acquired, becomes an attitudinal and perceptual set which resists further modification. Most persons perseverate in these habits, opinions, and attitudes and resist any change that threatens a break with reinforced practices and concepts. However, the wish to believe that people can change their personal orientation at will is a strong one. People harbor a desire, fostered by sentimentalists, that a new life awaits the person who will only change his way of thinking, feeling, or believing. The latter of course can be accomplished, but only by the intervention of particular experiences which happen to be appropriate to the needs and physical capacities of the person involved. People do not change *by themselves*. Interaction with an outside agency or event or series of events, which meets the needs of the individual at an appropriate time, is necessary to accomplish this, and this kind of dramatic turn of events is rare in the adult world.

The life of the French painter Paul Gauguin is sometimes referred to as an example of a man who dramatically changed the direction of his own life. Popular descriptions of the life of Gauguin, in order to heighten the dramatic interest, like to depict his decision to leave his position with the bank, to abandon his family, and to involve himself completely in painting as a sudden and abrupt event. However, even a single reading

[73] Anna Roe, *Journal of Educational & Psychological Measurement*, VI (1946), 401–410.

[74] F. R. Donovan (Chicago: University of Chicago Press, 1929).

[75] Nels Anderson (Chicago: University of Chicago Press, 1923).

[76] C. Wright Mills (New York: Oxford University Press, 1956).

[77] W. F. Cottrell, *American Sociological Review*, IV (Apr. 1939), 191–198.

[78] William H. Whyte (New York: Simon and Schuster, 1956).

of Gauguin's life in a good encyclopedia makes it clear that this development in his life was clearly forecast and that the only surprising thing about it was that the break did not occur earlier than it did.

Adults are not nearly so mobile, modifiable, or flexible as is sometimes presumed. We have indicated elsewhere how people resist change in attitude and belief. But this is also true in terms of more overt behavior. People tend to marry within their own social or economic class, within their own religious group, and even within their own neighborhood. The last point is particularly interesting in view of the fact that mobility has increased the opportunity for marital choice in this country. Freedman reports that:

> Numerous studies of choice of marriage partners which have been made by sociologists over the years . . . indicate that even in our largest cities . . . where modern transportation facilities make possible quick and easy movement, approximately one-quarter of all marriages are contracted by persons living within five blocks of one another and half are contracted by persons living within twenty blocks of one another.[79]

Furthermore:

> The selection of a wife was once for most persons a selection from a small set of eligible girls. One might think that urbanization alone radically increases the number of eligibles. Yet this is not so, as at least one study has shown: in a class bound and residence-bound society (France before World War II) the effective range of selection of marriage partners was as low in Paris as in the most isolated hill communities, and lower than in midlle-sized towns.[80]

That the majority of people in the adult years have settled down and become ethnocentric in their personal adaptations is so obvious that it hardly needs further exploration. That some people are more flexible and open to change than others is also obvious. The ability to adapt to new role expectations is of course in itself an acquired or learned capacity. Education, diversified experiences, and an open society are desirable and necessary exposures that make possible the greatest expectations for personality growth and accomplishment in the adult years.

The adult personality is a product of the interaction of biological forces, life space, and the individual's own developing ego organization. But man, particularly as an adult, is capable of *modifying* the environment (both cultural and physical) that nourished him. To paraphrase Luria we can say that man can alter the relative strength of the stimuli acting

[79] Ronald Freedman, Amos H. Hawley, W. S. Landecher, G. E. Lenski, and Horace Miner, *Principles of Sociology* (New York: Holt, Rinehart, and Winston, 1956) p. 81.

[80] Berelson and Steiner, *Human Behavior*, p. 307. Quoting from an unpublished paper by James S. Coleman, 1958.

upon him and he can adapt his behavior to the influences thus modified.[81] Thus most men do not always respond passively to the forces of nature and nurture. Man, as he achieved maturity of personal organization, can assume some responsibility for his own destiny. He can become modifying variable in the interaction processes of which he is himself a product. Some men can accomplish this more easily than others. Some men are dependent and passive, others are more self-reliant and dominant, depending upon their own talents, self-evaluation and life experiences.

The social phenomenon of leadership is most clearly discernible in the adult years. Leadership appears in all the age grades but it is more *consequential* for social change in the adult years. Political or business leadership is not ordinarily chosen from among children or adolescents. The genuis of leadership can sometimes be seen among younger people and among children in the creative arts or in science, but seldom does such youthful leadership appear in political or business arrangements.

The impact of leadership on culture is related to the "great man" theory of history. To what extent do men, or specifically one man, influence the course of events? Does leadership merely respond to the needs and fulfill the role expectations of the group? The answers to these questions are related not only to the capacity of the leader but also to the power structure and the particular needs of the group.

Borgatta and his associates demonstrated in their research into the interaction of group and leadership behavior that in the populations they studied, "great men" tended to *make* "great groups" in the sense that both major factors of group performance—productivity and satisfaction of the members—were satisfied.[82] However, Berelson and Steiner report that a leader is better liked the closer he conforms to the accepted norms of the group, while the less he appears to conform to the group the less will he be accepted by the group. Furthermore, the personal qualities or style of the leader are influenced more by the expectations of his followers and by the requirements of the situation than by the personal characteristics of the leader himself. Nevertheless, very high ranking leaders who are secure in their position enjoy a certain tolerance of "eccentricity" and do not need to conform as strictly to the group norms as do individuals of middle ranking. Moreover, the most successful leader is able to involve his followers in terms of their own private goals as well as in the group goals.[83]

Leadership then varies with the needs of the group and with the

[81] A. R. Luria, *The Role of Speech in the Regulation of Normal and Abnormal Behavior* (New York: Liveright Pub. Co., 1961).

[82] Egard F. Borgatta, Arthur S. Couch, and Robert F. Bales, "Some Findings Relevant to the Great Man Theory of Leadership," in A. Paul Hare *et al.* (eds.), *Small Groups: Studies in Social Interaction* (New York: Alfred A. Knopf, 1955), pp. 568–574.

[83] Berelson and Steiner, *Human Behavior*, pp. 339–349.

leader's own personal attributes. Thus the leadership may be active in terms of guiding, persuading, coercing; or it may be passive in terms of mediating or negotiating (or serving as a model to the group).[84]

The fact that adult behavior is ordinarily predictable and responsible in its manifestations makes it attractive in terms of the power structure of business and political leadership. The adult group has arrived, it has been over the course, it presumes to know where it is going and offers itself as a model. Younger people sometimes presume to rebel against the authority figures of the adult culture, but the majority finally respond to the adult models and symbols of social control. The father figure of the male adult, or the mother image of the female is common in literature and religious symbolism. The adult is ordinarily cast in the role of authority either in the family situation, in the school room, in the police or military establishments, and in the power structure of the job. Adult personalities range themselves along an axis of dominance-submission in which some adults are more active, aggressive, persuasive, or coercive than others; at the opposite end of the continuum are the permissive or dependent followers. However, very few leaders are dominant in all situations, nor are all followers dependent in all relationships. A man may be dominant in the work situation and passive at home, or vice versa. A man may be dependent in relationship to his wife and authoritative in his relationships with his children. Each adult responds to the expectations of social position in terms of his own personal characteristics as well as in terms of the needs of the group to which he endeavors to be related in each particular social situation or episode.

SUMMARY

The period of adulthood or maturity is the longest of the five age groups. The biological aspects of maturity are more stable than in the other periods of life, and the "change of life" or climacteric is the only dramatic change common to the period. This is clearly known in the female but the male counterpart is only vaguely understood. Reactions to the biological changes seem to be more important than the changes themselves. There is no necessary connection between the physiological changes taking place at this time and personality maladjustment. If the personality and social environment are adequate, no disability results at this period of life. If the person has had experiences which prepare him to play the roles compatible with adult status, the tapering off of strenuous physical activity evokes no serious maladjustments.

Adult status in our culture involves (1) marriage, (2) gainful employment, (3) independence of decision and action, (4) assumption of

[84] Berelson and Steiner, *Human Behavior*, p. 344.

responsibility for these decisions and actions, and (5) conformity to the folkways prescribed for adults. To the extent that an individual does not conform to these obligations and privileges, he has failed to attain full, mature social position in the culture.

The mature person has attained an emotional maturity which prepares the way for his adult roles and positions, and he has attained an intellectual maturity which involves both knowledge and the ability to think rationally. The attainment of full mature social position or status and personality requires appropriate experiences in childhood and adolescence. These experiences make possible the socialization and enculturation of the person that is essential to adjustment in adulthood.

There are adults whose life experiences have not prepared them with the attitudes and behavior traits demanded of those occupying the adult positions and statuses. Maladaptive behavior may develop from the fact that such persons are denied the status of adults, and no alternate provisions for their basic needs are provided by society. Examples are the single women or men who desire marriage and a family but who, for one reason or another, have not achieved this relationship.

The adult personality is usually sufficiently mature to function in a modifying capacity in terms of the culture which nourished it. Society relies for its survival upon those men and women whose personal attributes suit them for positions of responsibility and leadership. Such personalities, who are themselves products of nurture and nature, are thus able to influence the character of their own culture through the leadership they can provide the various groups with which they identify and which in turn identify with them.

SUGGESTED READINGS

ARGYRIS, CHRIS. *Personality and Organization* (New York: Harper and Bros., 1957).

BERELSON, BERNARD and GARY A. STEINER. *Human Behavior* (New York: Harcourt, Brace and World, 1964).

BOSSARD, JAMES H. S. and ELEANOR STOKER BOLL. *The Large Family System* (Philadelphia: University of Pennsylvania Press, 1956).

CAVAN, RUTH S. *The American Family* (New York: Crowell-Collier, 1963).

FRIEDAN, BETTY. *The Feminine Mystique* (New York: W. W. Norton, 1963).

HEATH, D. H. *Explorations of Maturity* (New York: Appleton-Century-Crofts, 1965).

KINSEY, ALFRED (*et al.*). *Sexual Behavior in the Human Male* (Philadelphia: W. B. Saunders, 1948).

KINSEY, ALFRED (*et al.*). *Sexual Behavior in the Human Female* (Philadelphia: W. B. Saunders, 1953).

LEE, ALFRED MCCLUNG and ELIZABETH B. LEE. *Marriage and the Family* (New York: Barnes and Noble, 1961).

LEVENSTEIN, AARON. *Why People Work* (New York: Crowell-Collier, 1962).

WINCH, ROBERT. *Marriage and the Family* (New York: Holt, Rinehart and Winston, 1963).

WOLFF, KURT. *The Biological, Sociological and Psychological Aspects of Aging* (Springfield: Charles C. Thomas, 1959).

CHAPTER 16

OLD AGE

With spectacles on nose and pouch on side,
. . . and his big manly voice,
Turning again toward childish treble, pines
And whistles in his sound. Last scene of all
That ends this strange, eventful history.
Is second childishness and mere oblivion,
Sans teeth, sans eyes, sans taste, sans everything.

There are no unmistakable signposts that will indicate just when man enters this stage of post-maturity which Shakespeare so dolefully describes. If the transition from adolescence to adulthood is a gradual change, so much more so is the one which occurs between adulthood and old age. Chronological age is even of less value at this juncture than it was in the earlier periods. Nevertheless, we will look at the variables involved in one's growing old that we may better understand the social status, positions, and roles of the aged in our culture.[1] Emphasis is placed upon the ways in which physiological and cultural factors become incorporated in personality. But, first let us look at some recent background statistics that show the size and some of the trends in this growing segment of the population. The social psychological implications of these facts will be discussed in the following pages:

1. In 1900, one person out of twenty-five was sixty-five and older; today one out of every eleven is sixty-five years and older.

2. In ten years, 1950–1960, the aged population (age sixty-five and over) increased by nearly 35 per cent. The general population increased only 19 per cent.

3. In contrast to the sixty-five-plus population, the population aged 45–64 has grown only at about the same rate as the total population, 17.4 per cent, between 1950–1960.

4. The aged population is expected to more than double in the forty years between 1960 and 2000.

[1] Despite popular belief, man has the longest life span of all creatures with the exception of the great tortoises. Elephants have been known to live as long as sixty years and parrots fifty-four years. Carl V. Weller, "Biological Aspects of the Aging Process," in Clark Tebbetts and Wilma Donahue (eds.), *Aging in Today's Society* (Englewood Cliffs, N.J.: Prentice-Hall, 1960), p. 123.

5. Women are outliving men. The ratio of women to men in the over-65 age group is 114 women to every 100 men; over-85 age group, 157 women to every 100 men.

6. Nationally, there are 121 aged women for every 100 aged men. On farms, however, there are only 84 aged women for every 100 aged men.

7. Nearly one-half of the aged are widowed, single, or divorced. Seven out of every ten aged men are married, while only one out of every three aged women is married.[2]

PHYSIOLOGICAL OLD AGE

Some of the changes that occur in the body as one moves beyond adulthood are obvious, whereas others are not. Reduced agility and speed of motion, lessened strength, a less steady hand, and increased difficulty of movement generally are known even to the small child who has observed his grandparents or other old people. National Health Survey data (1960) shows that two out of every five persons over age sixty-five have a chronic condition which limits their usual activity. About one out of every five aged is either confined to the house or has trouble getting around by himself. The health picture grows worse with advancing age. Among those seventy-five or older, for example, about every third person is confined to the house or needs help getting around outside.[3]

One of the less obvious changes is the progressive loss of hearing acuity at the extremes of the sound range, with some differences on the basis of sex; males reporting less loss in low frequencies, and females in the high frequencies.[4] Eyesight fails, but in many instances this appears to be a continuation of processes begun early in life. Certain deficiencies occur, however, that are not overcome by corrective devices, among them deficiencies in memory.[5]

In reaction time the decline usually begins in the third decade of life, but there is wide variation from individual to individual in this respect. In any given age group, about one-third of the individuals have reaction times that are equal to or less than the average reaction times of the group that is ten years younger.[6] Thus the old are not necessarily slow

[2] *New Population Facts on Older Americans 1960* (U.S. Government Printing Office, Washington: 1961).

[3] *New Population Facts on Older Americans.*

[4] Wilma Donahue, "The Human Machine at Middle Life," in *Aging in Today's Society,* Clark Tebbetts and Wilma Donahue, eds. (Englewood Cliffs, N.J.: Prentice-Hall, 1960), p. 106.

[5] Nathan W. Shock, "Physiological Aspects of Mental Disorders in Later Life," in *Mental Disorders in Later Life,* Oscar J. Kaplan, ed. (Stanford, Calif.: Stanford University Press, 1945), p. 46. *See also* Jeanne G. Gilbert, "Memory Loss in Senescence," *Journal of Abnormal and Social Psychology,* XXXVI (1941), pp. 73–86.

[6] Shock, "Physiological Aspects of Mental Disorders in Later Life," p. 48.

in reaction time. Homeostatic control does not function as well in the old who cannot tolerate extremes of temperature. Heat control is less efficient, resulting in greater sensitivity to cold and certain weaknesses in hot weather.[7]

Whether or not mental ability decreases with age depends upon which definition of intelligence is employed. William James referred to intelligence as *sagacity* and by this definition it is likely that many older people retain alert mental functioning to the end of life. But, if one defines mental ability in terms of the capacity to meet and solve new and unique problem situations as measured by various psychometric devices, the answer is less optimistic. Mental ability in this latter sense does decrease progressively with age, although this deterioration is a very gradual process that begins imperceptibly in young adults. Nor is the decrease in mental alertness uniform for all people. The differences within any age group are far greater than the mean differences between age groups. Cerebral arteriosclerosis and other types of mental degeneration may hasten the process in some of the less fortunate.

Generally, it may be said that older people retain their ability to make judgments in areas consistent with their own past experiences, but that the average older person is less able to meet and solve problems requiring the utilization of material (particularly conceptual material) foreign to their own life experiences. A rough index of the degree of loss of mental alertness is provided by a psychometric device such as the *Shipley Institute of Living Scale.*[8] This testing procedure is based on the assumption that in mild degrees of mental deterioration, vocabulary (as an index of memory retention) is relatively unaffected, but the capacity for abstract (conceptual) thinking declines. The Scale consists of a vocabulary test and an abstract reasoning test and any loss in mental capacity due to impairment is indicated to the extent that the subject's abstract thinking score falls short of his vocabulary score.

These, then, are some of the changes which occur in the later years of life. They do not take place with any uniformity within or among individuals. One person may have been wearing a hearing aid since his middle years, but still have jet black hair and good vision. Some individuals may have become so incapacitated by age changes that at fifty they are not able to carry on any sustained effort, whereas, others are as active at seventy or eighty as they were twenty or thirty years previously. Sir Winston Churchill was sixty-six when he became Prime Minister of the United Kingdom in 1940. After leading his country to victory through

[7] Edward J. Stieglitz, "The Personal Challenge of Aging," in *Aging in Today's Society*, Clark Tebbetts and Wilma Donahue, eds. (Englewood Cliffs, N.J.: Prentice-Hall, 1960), p. 47.

[8] *Shipley Institute of Living Scale*, The Institute of Living, Hartford, Conn.

the dark war years, he was defeated for reelection at the age of seventy-one, but again became Prime Minister at the age of seventy-six. After his retirement due to ill health, he wrote the four volume, *History of the English Speaking People*, and other works. Just why these extreme variations occur in the aging of people is still one of the prime problems facing the physiologists. The implication for personality development and changes is obvious. Because of the variation in aging from the biological viewpoint it does not make much sense to attempt to state in terms of years just when old age begins. As has been pointed out, the arbitrary selection of a given age, say sixty or seventy, means that for some individuals old age lasts but a few years, whereas, for others it may be thirty or more years in length.[9] Accordingly, physical old age must be considered as only one of several criteria of old age.

In our culture, the age of sixty-five is generally accepted as the proper age for retirement. But many men are physically ready to retire much earlier than sixty-five, whereas others are competent to continue at their jobs for years beyond this age. An industrial psychologist encountered a gentleman recently who applied for a job at the age of sixty-five. He was informed that that was the age of retirement in the firm where he was applying for work. His story was that he had already been placed on retirement at his former place of employment even though his company regretted the necessity of following this tradition since his work was more than satisfactory. His appearance, mental alertness, and physical agility signalized a man of many years younger. He admitted that this apparent youthfulness had troubled him all his vocational life, that people never believed his age so that he had to carry his birth certificate with him.

Such a person because of his chronological age is assigned a position by society, but he is not prepared to play the role associated with that position. Workers in this predicament are likely to find it difficult to reconcile successfully the apparent discrepancy between society's definition of their age status and their own definition of the situation.

It should not be assumed that psychological changes in old age result exclusively from changes in anatomical or physiological structures. One authority reports that,

> In those cases showing the most marked psychological deterioration, the diagnosis of "senile dementia" or of "psychosis with cerebral arteriosclerosis" is usually made. In making one of these diagnoses, most psychiatrists have given as the causal factor the changes in the parenchyma, the cortex, and the vessels of the brain. Recent formulations and recent findings of a number of investigators indicate that the anatomical changes that occur in the central nervous system constitute only one of

[9] Ruth Shonle Cavan, E. W. Burgess, Robert J. Havighurst, and Herbert Goldhamer, *Personal Adjustment in Old Age* (Chicago: Science Research Associates, 1949), p. 8.

many factors that enter into the psychological changes in deteriorated individuals.[10]

The evidence from many studies suggests that changes in behavior of the elderly may be related to organic deterioration, but that factors in the life experiences of the individual may also be involved to the extent that a one-to-one relationship with organic cause is not the rule.[11]

OLD AGE IN CULTURAL PERSPECTIVE

No social psychological definition of old age is possible without a knowledge of the culture of the group involved. In Bali the meaning of old age is altered by the fact that the dominant belief in that culture is in reincarnation, and hence, endless life. Under this belief older people do not order their lives toward a terminal destiny but continue to be interested in improving themselves, even learning complicated new tasks into their late sixties.

In a hunting, nomadic culture the inability to contribute to the food supply and to keep up with the group in its wandering quest for food determines that old age is measured largely in terms of physical fitness. Under such conditions, the persons no longer able to do their share of the work and who become burdens to the others, may be left behind to die, may voluntarily leave the group and go off by themselves, or may request a younger member of the group to kill them. This latter practice is found among the Chukchee Eskimo group.[12] Another cultural item which makes this practice of killing the aged seem less harsh is the belief of the Chukchee that they will appear after death in the same physical state in which they left the world, and none wishes to spend eternity in a state of physical deterioration. One can surmise that this interpretation of the afterlife evolved from the necessity of making the abandoning of old people more palatable. Be that as it may, the socioeconomic setting of the Eskimo leads to a definition of old age that is very different from that known to industrialized, urbanized cultures, or in more affluent rural areas.

The family unity system of the Chinese peasant culture assigns a high status to all members of the family, including the elderly and the dead. On a visit to his father's native village in China, an American boy had the following conversation with one of his older Chinese relatives:

> Heng-Shen: And what of your family—the Wangs in America? Where are they going? You haven't told me much about that.

[10] Lawrence Greenleigh, "Some Psychological Aspects of Aging," *Understanding the Older Client* (New York: Family Service Association of America, 1951–1955), p. 10.

[11] Hollis E. Clow, "A Study of One Hundred Patients Suffering from Psychosis with Cerebral Arteriosclerosis," *American Journal of Psychiatry*, XCVII, No. 1 (1940), 16–26.

[12] *See* Gladys A. Reichard, "Social Life," in *General Anthropology*, Franz Boaz, (ed.) (Boston: D. C. Heath and Co., 1938), p. 481.

George:	We don't think in America of families going anywhere— it's more the individual.
Heng-Shen:	Oh, yes, I have heard that in America (it is the same in Europe, is it not?) the family means only the man and his wife and their children. When the man or woman dies, or they part, that is the end of the family. It seems very strange. Can it possibly be like that?
George:	I am afraid it is. . .
Heng-Shen:	With us it is very different. The Chinese family is buttressed against misfortunes that happen to individuals in the family. There is continuity. The family includes the dead, the living, and those not yet born. The land and other property belong to the family, not to individuals. At the core of the Chinese family is the father and son. . .[13]

We now turn our attention to various features of our sociocultural environment which have important implications for adjustment and achievement in the later years of life.

Urbanization-Industrialization

The sedentary, highly specialized nature of many occupations and professions in North America sets the stage for a very different definition of old age than those just described. The greater productivity of the farms and factories permits the society to support a large number of economically nonproductive people, and the frail physique of the older person does not preclude his or her contributing to the general progress and welfare of the society in general and of the smaller primary groups. This is, of course, especially true of those whose contributions are based upon mental abilities and skills and not upon physical prowess and strength. The Justices of the United States Supreme Court have no counterparts in the widely dispersed, nomadic groups of the world. However, the change from the rural-farm economy of the early nineteenth century to the dominantly urban-industrial economy of the present has not been without loss to the old persons of the country. In the late eighteenth century approximately nine out of ten persons lived on farms, by 1920 this ratio had dropped to less than one in three, by 1940 only 23 per cent of the population was located on farms, and today less than one in fourteen of our people calls a farm their home.

The influence of the urbanization-industrialization process is shown quantitatively in the estimated changes in the proportion of persons sixty-five years and older who are gainfully employed. In 1890, 70 per cent of these males over sixty-five were in the labor force; in 1900 this

---

[13] Len Peterson, "Family Patterns: China and the U.S.A.," in *Growing Old in Today's Society*, Clark Tebbetts and Wilma Donahue, eds., (Englewood Cliffs, N.J.: Prentice-Hall, 1960), p. 187.

had become 65 per cent; in 1950, 43 per cent; and in 1960 the porportion had shrunk to 34 per cent. Interestingly enough the percentage of females over sixty-five gainfully employed has increased since 1890 when only 8 per cent were employed, until today more than 11 per cent of women over sixty-five are in the labor force.

These shifts in residence, occupation, and age of retirement hold important implications for the older citizens of the country. On the farm the physically less capable can find much to do that is of service to the family. The minor chores of gathering eggs, feeding the fowl and other stock, making minor repairs on clothing and machinery, giving advice to younger people and in general making themselves useful convey an accompanying gain of *feeling* that they are still important in the larger scheme of things. The process of growing old is less abrupt and more of a "tapering off" process, a fact that is of importance to personality adjustment. Not so, however, in the industrial-urban scene where work-for-hire is the order of the times. The highly competitive nature of the economy makes it mandatory in many instances to hire and retain only the most efficient workers. Industrial and commercial firms which hire between 30 and 40 per cent of all nonagricultural workers have maximum hiring age limits. Usually these ages are forty-five for unskilled persons and fifty for skilled workers.[14] Government agencies frequently follow a similar hiring pattern. Many firms do not hire people over fifty because of the pension plans which require a person to participate for a minimum of fifteen years (retire at sixty-five) in order to be eligible for the benefits of the plan. For the same reason many people will not shift jobs in middle age because of their investments in these pension plans. Thus pension plans have had the effect of freezing people in their jobs and thus reducing industrial mobility. Alan Harrington puts the problem specifically, as follows:

> I would say that the key principle in corporate life is the one governing the annuity and insurance program. This is the frame and prop of all other corporation values. Without it the moral structure of the company, on which life in the Crystal Palace rests, probably could not sustain our operation in its present form. . .
>
> To be dropped out of the company insurance plan would not be the end of the world. Most of us at the Crystal Palace would look on such a prospect with utter horror. Why? Should a more interesting job come up, a job in which we could express ourselves more freely (a job, who knows, that might encourage us to live longer), must we first inquire: "But . . . but what kind of insurance plan do you have?"[15]

[14] J. E. Nordskog, E. C. McDonagh, and M. J. Vincent, *Analyzing Social Problems* (New York: The Dryden Press, 1950) p. 76.

[15] Alan Harrington, *Life in the Crystal Palace* (New York: Alfred A. Knopf, 1959), pp. 30–32. It should be noted that this observation is equally as true of government and educational institutions as it is in private industry.

Absenteeism attributable to advancing years is not acceptable in most urban occupations. The complexity of a tightly scheduled and efficient economy does not have a place for the man who cannot maintain the pace. The work relationship is an either-or proposition and the possibility of keeping employed by doing less demanding tasks, as is possible on the farm, is rarely possible on the urban scene. There is little noteworthy advice that, say, a drill press or power sewing machine operator can give to the younger replacement. Retirement in the urban world is, for the majority of workers, an abrupt break with the culture's main stream. Retirement often carries with it a feeling of being tossed on the scrap pile, of being discarded.

The following real life scene occurred in the office of the manager of the public relations department of a large and benevolent corporation when one of the retired executives returned to offer a suggestion:

Mac Tyler slapped his hand on the table. "Art," he said, "the problem that you describe so well is one we're up against all the time. But what's the idea you were speaking about?"

Our visitor returned his attention to the paper in his hand. "I thought this," he said. "I've drafted a memo on it, which I will leave with you. The idea is, why don't we get up a program to inform the public about our activities—to do away with the general ignorance on the subject?"

It was one of the few times I have seen the chief of the Crystal Palace's public relations department taken aback. "Well," he said, "I think that's a fine idea, Art. In fact, right now we're trying to mount a major—"

"They told me you'd like it," the old man nodded, and there came into his dim eyes a foxy gleam. "What I want to tell everybody now is that I'm ready to go to *work* on this program in any way I can, the sooner the better. That is, I'm ready and willing—"

"We *know* you are, Art," said Mac Tyler, rising from his chair. "And on behalf of everybody I want to tell you how mightily we appreciate your taking the time to come and visit us, and give us the benefit of your valuable thinking."

"If I could be of some use, is what I mean," said the old man as Mac Tyler pumped his hand, "I'd be willing to come out of. . ."

"You can be certain that we'll remember you, Art, boy; now be sure to come around more often in the future. Do you hear?"

In another minute the mournful annuitant had reached the doorway, and Mac Tyler accompanied him to the corridor. Tyler came back and sat down. "God, isn't that too bad!", he said, and passed his hand quickly in front of his face to wipe away the sad image that had been projected on us. "Those poor guys!" he exclaimed, and we looked at one another.[16]

[16] Harrington, *Life in the Crystal Palace*, pp. 174–175. Copyright © 1958, 1959 by Alan Harrington. Reprinted by permission of Alfred A. Knopf, Inc.

The cessation of work can be a tragedy in our society not only from the viewpoint of loss of income, but also because of the work ethic which characterizes our culture. The status of the adult depends upon his obtaining and holding a position of gainful employment, and except for the very wealthy, lack of this work position is a major handicap. In some cultures this is not so, as for instance in rural China where a man will retire as soon as possible, even on a very poor pittance, but will prefer idleness at the poverty level to a higher level of living which entails work.[17] He would find it hard to understand the self-pity of the old people in our country who have retired, forcibly perhaps, upon a well-earned but small income.[18]

Present and Future Age Structure

As a matter of fact, the person of sixty-five today can look forward to only a few more years than a person of that age could a century ago, or even at the time of the Roman Empire. The reason, of course, lies in the fact that medical science, improved sanitation, and good diets have kept alive many persons who would have died from the rigors of earlier periods. If a man lived to the age of sixty in the time of the Roman Empire he was of sufficiently rugged constitution to survive many more years. The significant changes which do affect the old of the present period are the ones in age distribution. If we arbitrarily take the sixty-fifth year as the threshold of old age, we note from the census report (Figure 39) that 3.1 per cent of the population has attained this age in 1900, 16.6 per cent were over sixty-five in 1960, and that in the year 2000, it is estimated that about one-third of the population will be over sixty-five.

An important aspect of the environment is found in the quantitative features of the population. For our immediate purposes, the fact that we are becoming an older society is pertinent. Although it is frequently assumed that the span of life (*i.e.*, the extreme length of life that is characteristic of the species) has increased greatly, such is not the case. The increased *life expectancy* is attributable to the curtailment of premature deaths, especially in infancy and childhood. Life expectancy (in contrast to life span) is an average, a *mean*, which is readily increased by reduction of mortality in the younger years. The man or woman whose life has lasted a century is a rarity and is likely to remain so in the foreseeable future.

[17] See Hsiao-Tung Fei, "Peasant and Gentry; An Interpretation of Chinese Social Structure and Its Changes," *American Journal of Sociology*, LII (July 1946), 1–17.

[18] Half the older couples in the United States have a cash income of more than $2,530.00, and the other half have less. *The Older American*, The President's Council on Aging (Washington, D.C., U.S. Government Printing Office, 1963), p. 9. *See also* Max Kaplan, *Leisure in America* (New York: John Wiley & Sons, 1960); Robert W. Kleemeier, ed., *Aging and Leisure* (New York: Oxford University Press, 1961).

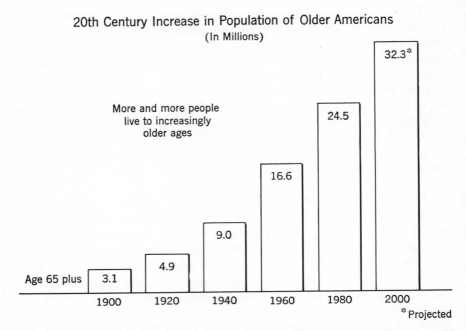

FIGURE 39. 20th Century Increase in Population of Older Americans (*Source*: 1900 through 1960, *Census of Population*; 1980, U.S. Bureau of the Census, "*Current Population Reports; Estimates*," Series P-25, No. 251. For population 2000, *Division of the Actuary, Social Security Administration.*

Age of Retirement

We have already pointed out that the urban world is dominated quantitatively by the people in the ages between twenty and fifty, and that this is sure to result in the values of this age group dominating in large measure. One means of discovering the values of this age group is to look into the ages at which persons are permitted, expected, or forced to retire. This cultural fact gives us a measure of the time of life when those in power, for whatever reasons, believe that a gainfully employed person in our urbanized-industrialized economy should retire from active participation in the economy. A few instances of this view are noted here. In a recent survey of some thirty contracts between labor unions and employers, most of them contained retirement provisions at the age of sixty-five. The Railroad Retirement Act does not provide for compulsory retirement from service, but permits railroad employees to continue in service as long as they are physically fit. However, the railroader can retire at sixty-five if male, at sixty if female, with full benefits. Post office employees may retire at sixty, clerks and carriers must retire at sixty-two, and superintendents at seventy. In the college teaching field, the retire-

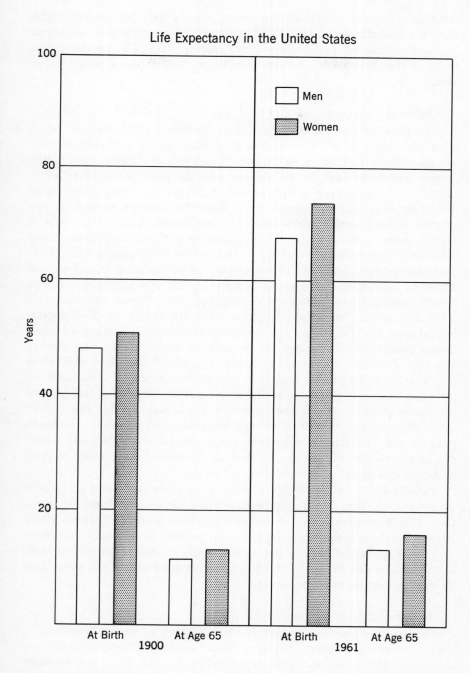

FIGURE 40. Life Expectancy in the U.S. [*Source*: U.S. Department of Health, Education and Welfare, *Trends* (1962).]

ment age is almost always in the sixties, usually sixty-five or sixty-eight. Both the opportunity and the need to retire at these ages have important implications for the personality of the older person. The trend appears to be in the direction of further compulsory retirement at even earlier ages.

Cultural Provisions for the Old

The principles of aid to the indigent, including aged persons, which were laid down in the Elizabethan Poor Law of the sixteenth century served as the basis for care of the poor in this country until very recently. A most important item in the old law was the principle of "least eligibility." This was the rule which provided that no one being cared for at public expense was to receive more than the amount earned by the poorest self-supporting individual. The motivation behind this rule is logical enough, namely, that of discouraging persons from abandoning their gainful pursuits and seeking a place on the public relief rolls. However, the resulting low level of support led to innumerable hardships and added to the fear of growing old. In recent years, the principle has been greatly modified, and the newer principle is that of need, but even this takes into account little more than the basic nutritional needs of physiological man. Too, the stigma attached to receiving charity makes the small money grants even less acceptable to many of the recipients. Our culture has not yet found the happy formula which will stimulate individual initiative in self-support, and still permit the giving of assistance in instances where it is fully warranted without the loss of social respect for the recipient. A step in that direction which may provide the answer is the phenomenal growth in old-age insurance and pensions which are paid for prior to retirement by both employer and employee, and which the latter receives not as charity, but as something that he has earned and contributed to.

In 1935 about 1,100 employers had pension plans and about 2.2 million employees of their families were thus covered. Today, there are more than 25,000 company plans covering 23 million workers.[19] There is no stigma attached to the receiving of such a pension or insurance payment. The coverage of the old-age pensions is being constantly expanded both in public and private fields, and to the higher paid executives as well as to other categories of wage earners.

Low Prestige of the Aged

Our country has been popularly characterized as having a culture in which the youthful, brash, brawling, flashy, and novel aspects of life are dominant. This characterization is not without some basis, and because

---

[19] *The Older American*, President's Council on Aging (1963), p. 5.

of this the lot of the aged has not been too happy. This is not to say that parents and grandparents are not loved and protected by children and grandchildren. But though they may be loved they are not too frequently honored and respected, neither for their age as such nor for their views and accomplishments. This is not the place to argue the merits of age; our only concern is with the cultural setting as it bears upon the personality of the old person. In other cultures the old are respected to a degree not known here, and because of this they remain active in community affairs much longer than they are apt to in our culture. One has but to run through the ads of representative newspapers or magazines to learn of the esteem with which we hold the values of the young. Almost any article announced for sale appears to have its sales appeal heightened by the use of some adjective which will emphasize its close relationship to youth and the earlier adult years. Ours is a culture in which huge stadiums are jammed with tens of thousands of enthusiastic spectators at athletic events, in which the achievements based upon youth, strength, and beauty are followed by publics numbering in the millions, but in which the carefully garnered results of long years of efforts are esteemed by small minorities. The lectures of the philosopher draw numbers which need no huge stadiums, but can be comfortably accommodated in small meeting halls or private houses.

Our culture does not give to the aged the power of control that is found in preliterate or nonliterate cultures. Literacy, formal education, open class systems—all these have operated to give to youth and younger adults the opportunities to seize control of much of society, and these opportunities have not been ignored. Unable to monopolize the sources of information and power, the elders have had to meet younger and more aggressive adversaries on other than their own terms. It is sometimes stated that there is a "cult of youth" extant in the United States and Canada. A society that stresses the values attainable only by a minority of the population—between the ages of eighteen and thirty-five years—sets the stage for a reduction of social honor and prestige for its older citizens. With the spectacular growth in that portion of the population living beyond retirement age such a value system grows less and less realistic.

PERSONALITY AND OLD AGE

The points outlined and discussed below are presented as bases for understanding the nature of the personalities of the older citizens of our society. All of these propositions tend to emphasize the view that personality is not a static entity, but is a relationship that exists between human beings.

There is no personality of old age as such. There are no particular sets of traits, attitudes, and habits that distinguish older persons as a group from all other groups. That there are certain uniformities in physical decline and deterioration is surely true, but the behavior traits and attitudes that result from these physical changes are not the same in all individuals. Even some of the physiological changes which are usually associated with advanced age may result from pathological causes earlier in life, and the reactions to the changes at times approximate reactions of older persons to age-induced changes. There is as much variety among the personalities of the oldsters of our culture as there is among other age groups.

While the old age group as such is as heterogeneous as any other in its characteristics, it is also true, as Neugarten has demonstrated, that the personality of each older person becomes "institutionalized with the passage of time." An older person, according to Neugarten, becomes "increasingly like himself" and the personality structure of an older person is more clearly identifiable and clear cut than is true of a younger person.

> Not only do certain personality processes become stabilized and provide continuity, but the individual builds around him a network of social relationships which he comes to depend on for emotional support and responsiveness and which maintain him in many subtle ways. It is from this point of view that the typical aging person may be said to become, with the passage of years, a socio-emotional institution with an individual structure of supports and interactional channels and with patterns which transcend many of the intrapsychic changes and losses that appear.[20]

Personal characteristics in advanced age are largely determined by whatever characteristics existed in adulthood. A person's attitudes toward his own aging are shaped by the feelings and attitudes which the significant older people in his primary group took toward old age when he was an impressionable youngster. Thus the manner in which the person's parents, grandparents and other important adult figures managed their own aging problems helped determine the individual's self-concept toward his own aging process. Such attitudes are, of course, modified as the person develops through his own unique life experiences. The "As the twig is bent . . ." axiom is as applicable to the old as to the adolescent and adult. The habitual attitudes and traits which the person has established through the years of childhood, adolescence, and adulthood are not easily sloughed off when the status of old age is reached. Persons' likes and dislikes, prejudices and biases, fears and hopes, are very apt to be carried from year to year with no marked break at any given time. Political, religious, class, status values, and attitudes remain much the same as one makes the transition from adulthood to old age. Even in the support of such movements as the Townsend Clubs of the 1930's (bigger and better pensions for the aged), old age was not the only variable. The wealthy

20 Bernice L. Neugarten *et al., Personality in Middle and Late Life* (New York: Atherton Press, 1964), p. 198.

old persons were not interested in any significant degree. As one student of old-age behavior points out, age itself is often assigned as the cause for things which in reality are attributable to lifetime personality factors.[21] The same writer holds that those persons who have not been able to face reality, who have "kidded" themselves as to their roles and status, find adjustment to old age difficult. Acceptance of reality at whatever age is a prerequisite to good adjustment.

Sociogenic needs persist in old age. Even though the sex drive and other innate impulses to action may wane, the needs that arise from the social interaction of persons continues into old age. The needs for social approval or recognition, for companionship and affection, for security, and even in some degree for variety of experiences are as much a part of the older person's needs and wants as they are of the younger person's. A wide variety of defense mechanisms may be employed by the older person to protect himself against the anxiety resulting from the threatened loss of social status. Greenleigh has pointed out that,

> . . . because of the decreasing physical stamina and the decreasing energy for tolerating the stresses of adaptation to older age roles, positions, and functions, certain compensatory mechanisms may be mobilized by the average individual. These are related to his experience, his knowledge, his special skills, his interests, and his positive motivations. Should his defense mechanisms be insufficient, the individual shows signs which are fairly typical and which lead the casual observer to remark, "He's just getting old, that's all."[22]

Aristotle saw the older people of his age, in comparison with the youths and middle aged, as weak and querulous. He wrote of them, as follows:

> Their fits of anger are sudden but feeble. Their sensual passions have either altogether gone or have lost their vigor; consequently they do not feel their passions much, and their actions are inspired less by what they do feel than by the love of gain. Hence men at this time of life are often supposed to have a self-controlled character; the fact is that their passions have slackened, and they are slaves to the love of gain. They guide their lives by reasoning more than by moral feeling; reasoning being directed to utility and moral feeling to moral goodness. If they wrong others, they mean to injure them, not to insult them. Old men may feel pity, as well as young men, but not for the same reason. Young men feel it out of kindness; old men out of weakness, imagining that anything that befalls any one else might easily happen to them.[23]

---

[21] S. W. Hartwell, "Mental Diseases of the Aged," in *New Goals for Old Age,* George Lawton, ed. (New York: Columbia University Press, 1943), p. 140.

[22] Lawrence Greenleigh, "Some Psychological Aspects of Aging," p. 11.

[23] Aristotle, "Youth, Age, and the Prime of Life," (384–322 B.C.).

Aring makes the point that old age and its problems must be evaluated in terms of the basic life needs of the human being.

> If one's environment is unloving and painful and without prestige or status, what would be more natural than escape into the past? Almost universally, the older person had more status and was more successful in some of his endeavors in bygone years. The only retreat possible is that afforded by the human mind, which can escape a situation while remaining in it, by such psychological mechanisms as repression or regression (flight). The pathological signs of the latter are quite common to senility—sexual exhibitionism, disheveled dress, and soiling—all of which are universal manifestations of the early phases of human existence. The aged are sensitive to the rejection with which they are usually met and they react hostilely with the commonly seen anger, irritability and querulousness. Their inability to adapt, their lack of flexibility, are not only due to the physical stiffening that goes with aging, but also to the blow that is inherent in the acceptance of new ideas which implies that those previously held were less good. Since the aged are not accepted as par in the human family, their interests narrow; old ways are looked upon as the best, and there is reciprocally a loss of interest in the present. Their lack of love they attempt to compensate by the techniques of loving themselves—"If no one loves me, I'll love myself." Thence the boastfulness and bragging so common to advanced years.[24]

Authorities have referred to the older persons' progressive disengagement from life, a process which is seen as a gradual withdrawal from social interaction between the aging person and other people in the social systems to which he belongs.[25] Neugarten speaks of this process as the interioration of personality in the aged.

> Along with increased interiority there seems to go a certain reduction in the complexity of the personality. With the shrinkage in psychological life space and with decreased ego energy, an increasing dedication to a central core of values and to a set of habit patterns and a sloughing off of earlier cathexes which lose saliency for the individual seem to occur.[26]

Adjustment of the aged, as it is for any age group, is spelled in terms of the compatibility of the social positions and the social roles of the person. Whether or not a person is going to be well adjusted in his or her old age cannot be known by looking only at either the ascribed posi-

[24] Charles D. Aring, "Psychological Aspects of Neurology," in *Clinical Neurology* (Summer 1952).

[25] *See* Elaine Cumming and W. E. Henry, *Growing Old* (New York: Basic Books, 1961) *and* R. J. Havighurst, Bernice L. Neugarten, and S. S. Tobin, *Disengagement and Patterns of Aging.* Paper read at the International Research Seminar on Social and Psychological Aspects of Aging (Markaryd, Sweden: Aug. 1963).

[26] Neugarten, *Personality in Middle and Late Life*, p. 198.

tions or statuses or the role which the person plays. The way in which they are related is the important factor, and only when the total situation is known is one in a position to judge which of the two is the independent variable. In certain instances the status assigned to the aged person and the positions which they can occupy are such that few persons who have known full adult status are willing to play the accompanying old age roles. After years of assuming responsibilities both in business and family relations, it is not easy, and at times it is not possible, for a person to shift abruptly to the role of an inactive person. Such situations occur when a person loses his job suddenly because he is summarily dismissed, because of economic crisis, because of ill health, or retirement. He is unprepared to live the routine demanded by the new situation, and is faced with a period of maladjustment, or, as some prefer to call it, unadjustment. Charles Lamb worked for 33 years as a clerk in a humdrum London job which finally became so frustrating to him that his employers surprised him one day by offering him immediate retirement at two-thirds his usual pay. He was delighted at this sudden turn in his fortunes. He describes his feelings in the days that followed:

> For the first day or two I felt stunned—overwhelmed. I could only apprehend my felicity; I was too confused to taste it sincerely, I wandered about, thinking I was happy, and knowing that I was not. I was in the condition of a prisoner in the old Bastile, suddenly let loose after a forty years' confinement. I could scarce trust myself with myself. It was like passing out of Time into Eternity—for it is a sort of Eternity for a man to have all his Time to himself. It seemed to me that I had more time on my hands than I could ever manage. From a poor man, poor in Time, I was suddenly lifted up into a vast revenue; I could see no end of my possession; I wanted some steward, or judicious bailiff, to manage my estates in Time for me. And here let me caution persons grown old in active business, not lightly, nor without weighing their own resources, to forego their customary employment all at once, for there may be danger in it.[27]

Any culture which fails to find some means of awarding the old men and women with a satisfying status can be assured of acute problems of maladjustment among this age group. However, even when the culture does provide a social position in keeping with the abilities of old persons, it cannot guarantee good social adjustment for all its aged citizens. There are those individuals whose experiences have been such that they have developed unrealistic attitudes toward themselves and their age groups. Such conditions are found in the persons who, for a variety of reasons, have refused to consider the time when the activities of full and robust maturity must be abandoned in favor of activities more in keeping with

[27] From "The Superannuated Man," Charles Lamb (1775–1834). *The Essays of Elia* (New York: A. L. Burt, Pub., 1885), 233.

altered status based upon altered physiological age, or upon altered social status, which accompanies the later years. The person whose social satisfactions have been secured solely as a result of her physical beauty, her role as mother, or some other function which is incompatible with the later years of maturity or old age is poorly prepared to play the social roles appropriate to these later age levels. The social disapproval of the attempt to deny one's age and to appear years younger than one actually is only tends to intensify the maladjustment resulting from this unwillingness and inability to play roles in keeping with the other aspects of the personality, namely, the physiological aspects and the cultural environment. The following case illustrates this:

> The situation that exists when beauty is all important is illustrated by the case of a 55-year old woman who, as a result of an early disturbance in her relationship with her mother, felt unlovable and undesirable. She attempted to protect herself from any further trauma in this sensitive area by settling for an inferior substitute for love—admiration. Moreover, she needed admiration to combat her own unacceptable picture of herself. Since she was a very pretty woman, it was not difficult for her to produce the effect upon men that she desired. This held her own feelings of worthlessness in abeyance for years. When her beauty began to fade, however, she felt extremely threatened. She spent long hours looking into the mirror to reassure herself. She went on frequent shopping tours looking for clothes that would enhance her beauty. When these efforts failed to hold her doubts in check, she became seriously depressed. It was only when she felt sure of her own lovability, after more than a year of psychotherapy, that she could accept aging with relative tranquility.[28]

Bühler, who has intensively studied the problems of the aging, arrived at the conclusion that,

> . . . the predominantly emphasized factors of functional decline and insecurity are not necessarily the decisive factors for old age maladjustment. More decisive even than illness, I found in a number of cases the individual's self-assessment as to whether he did or did not reach fulfillment; whether he accomplished in and with his life what he feels he ought to or wanted to accomplish.[29]

Bühler would categorize older people into four categories, as follows: (1) Those who feel that they did their lives' work and they are content to relax in this achievement; (2) Those who feel that their active life is never over and that they will continue doing things of interest to the

---

[28] M. H. Hollender, "Individualizing the Aged," in *Understanding the Older Client* (New York: Family Service Association of America, 1951–1955) p. 11.

[29] Charlotte Bühler, "Old Age and Fulfillment of Life with Considerations of the Use of Time in Old Age," in *Proceedings of the Sixteenth International Congress of Psychology* (Amsterdam: North Holland Pub. Co., 1960), p. 127.

end; (3) Those who are not satisfied with the life they led or with what they accomplished, but lack the strength or capacity to go on struggling. Their mood is characterized by a degree of resignation and discontent. (4) Those who feel they have led meaningless lives, or who feel they went out for all the wrong things and now feel guilty and regretful about it. These latter may blame their environment as well as themselves for their frustration and feelings of unfulfillment. Bühler concludes by suggesting that ". . . old age can be lived as the period of that fulfillment to which a person has been looking forward if he conceived of his life as a whole with a sequence of goals and an end-goal to be reached." [30] The following example is illustrative:

> A woman of 69, never married, who worked in her native Vienna as a housekeeper in various families, lives now, and has for several years in retirement under rather distressing circumstances. She suffers from ill health and is also very poor; she is losing her eyesight and is consequently nearly disabled. Her very small income affords her a small room and board in a country home. Her Nazi relatives disowned her in every sense during the Nazi period, when she refused to be drawn into their antisemitic excesses.
>
> While herself without much help or hope, Anna, as we may call her, spent all her energies on helping two of the Jewish families, in whose houses she had found friendship and kindness, to get out of the country. Poor and without resources as she was, she found ways to provide them with some of the most necessary means for their survival and their escape.
>
> When, after it was all over, she found herself exhausted and lonely in her own little abode, the memory of the great thing she had been able to do, to help some valuable human beings to survive and to find a new place in the world, was what sustained her and what gave her strength as well as self-esteem. This, she considered, had been the most meaningful accomplishment of her life, which gave her a sense of fulfillment and of the worthwhileness and dignity of her existence.[31]

The ability to develop in the prime of life interests which can be carried on, even with the coming of physical disabilities resulting from advanced age, is one way of assuring greater adjustment to the later years. Such pursuits as sedentary games (cards, checkers, chess), interest in spectator sports, in listening to music, and membership in clubs where age is not a significant favor, tend to minimize the sharpness of the transition to a less active way of life. There are in the city of Milwaukee large numbers of old persons, mostly of German ancestry, who spend long hours in the parks, in their homes, and in clubs playing a card game called *Schopskopf* (Sheepshead). It affords them much

---

[30] Bühler, "Old Age and Fulfillment of Life," p. 128.
[31] *Ibid.*

pleasure and also provides a bridge with earlier periods because they have been playing it for years. The only difference is that they now have more time for it than they had when they were gainfully employed. If they had not played it when they were younger, it is unlikely that they would have become so attached to it in their later years. The need to learn forms of recreation and leisure-time activity that can be carried on through the years of adolescence, adulthood, and old age is clear. Any such activities provide a continuity of behavior that is conducive to minimizing the anxiety concerning growing old, and to smoothing away the corners which one must turn as his body ages. The role of a liberal education in preparing the way for adjustment in the age levels through which one must pass is illustrated in the following exerpt from a letter written by a retired librarian in her seventies:

> From a really settled abode in the attractive college town of Claremont in the foothills, I send you greetings.
>
> By the end of the school year at Pepperdine, June 2, I was ready to let up on library hours, and eager to have my own things around me in a little apartment in Claremont, where I have long spent holidays and weekends among old friends. I was fortunate to find a cozy three room apartment, in a patio of over forty unusual plants and trees—camellias, Australian orange, banana, acacia, orchid and guava trees, ferns, holly, ivy walls—one block from old friends, two blocks from Community Church, five to ten minutes' walk to shops and Claremont Colleges. The Los Angeles bus stops at my corner—a little over an hour into downtown Los Angeles.
>
> I've stayed in California this year, just enjoying its variety; weekends with old friends in Long Beach, Santa Ana and Arrowhead mountains; a January drive over the desert to Palm Springs; Easter at Desert Hills Guest Ranch on Lucerne Valley Desert; La Jolla, Laguna and Santa Barbara by the sea. A June drive to Camp Sierra in the Pines of northern California gave me a stimulating week at the Friends World Affairs Conference, in discussions with leaders recently from Africa, Asia, Cuba, and Russia.
>
> I've enjoyed activities in Los Angeles and Claremont with A.A.U.W., Delta Kappa Gamma and Pi Lambda Theta teachers. Claremont Chambers of Commerce bus tours took me to the picturesque "Ramona" Pageant in San Jacinto Mountains, to the Living Pictures Festival of Art in Laguna, and Hollywood Bowl Viennese Night. I've been to the China Society dinner in China Town, Intercultural dinner at the Russian Refugee Center, Mexican fiesta at Padua Hills above Claremont, and to AAUW Southern California Council at Balboa. A friend and I have had summer matinee jaunts into Los Angeles for "My Fair Lady," "Sound of Music," "Guys and Dolls." San Francisco Opera in Los Angeles was a treat in "Lucia Di Lammermoor" and "Madame Butterfly." Now for the winter in Claremont are lectures on world problem areas, artist and Los Angeles Symphony concerts and travel films at

Claremont colleges, Pomona Adult Education Forum, and African Seminar, church groups, Democratic Club. I'm enjoying having students from India, Japan, and Korea to my apartment for supper, old and new friends in for teas and suppers. Once a month, I am glad for an opportunity to talk Japanese, when I go with a Church World Service group to meet Japanese immigrant ships bound for Brazil.

I've had a variety of library work, over the year—reference with Pepperdine College students, now part time Reader's Adviser and reference with the variety of people in Pomona Public Library, and some special jobs in the library of Scripps College. It's good to have some leisure, too, to enjoy the many interests and people of Claremont.

The good life which this enthusiastic spinster lives is not a function of her present environment alone. The same advantage was taken of her surroundings in Kansas, Illinois, and Japan. Her love of people and knowledge, in all forms, makes accessible to her the human and cultural resources of whatever environment in which she lives.

There are a few, unique older people who have lived vigorous lives and who with good health look forward to retirement as an opportunity to begin a new career. For these few, retirement is not a problem of adjustment but a challenge and an opportunity. One such man, who had been president of a large corporation, upon retirement, began a new business—his own. It was an entirely new career for him. He worked harder than ever and seemed to enjoy it. His old friends are glad to see him not just because of old times sake but because he is creating something and is not living in the past. He has something which other people *need* and he knows it. Another gentleman who was head of a large engineering department has elected to take early retirement at age sixty. Although he enjoyed a brilliant career in engineering, he had never had a formal education. He has enrolled as a freshman at a state university and is having the time of his life. Of course, these are unique people. They were not dependent people in their own lifetimes and if good health prevails they will continue to live useful and satisfying lives for many years.

Another aspect of the adjustment of role to the situation involves the reaction to a less strong and agile body, and to one with altered glandular activity. All persons do not react in the same manner to these body changes; some are regretful to the point of frustration; others accept the altered biological endowment. Following are some pertinent comments which have come to us across many centuries:

"You don't come to see me, Socrates, as often you ought: If I were still able to go and see you I would not ask you to come to me. But at my age I can hardly get to the city, and therefore you should come oftener to the Piraeus. *For let me tell you, that the more the pleasures of the body fade away, the greater to me is the pleasure and charm of conversation*. Do not deny my request, but make our house your resort and keep company with these young men; we are old friends, and you will be quite at home with us."

I replied: "There is nothing which for my part I like better, Cephalus, than conversing with aged men; for I regard them as travellers who have gone a journey which I too may have to go, and of whom I ought to inquire, whether the way is smooth and easy, or rugged and difficult. And this is a question which I should like to ask of you who have arrived at that time which the poets call the 'threshold of old age'—Is life harder toward the end, or what report do you give of it?"

"I will tell you, Socrates," he said, "what my own feeling is. Men of my age flock together; we are birds of a feather, as the old proverb says; and at our meetings the tale of my acquaintance commonly is—I cannot eat, I cannot drink; the pleasures of youth and love are fled away; there was a good time once, but now that is gone, and life is no longer life. Some complain of the slights which are put upon them by relations, and they will tell you sadly of how many evils their old age is the cause. But to me, Socrates, these complainers seem to blame that which is not really at fault. For if old age were the cause, I too being old, and every other old man, would have felt as they do. But this is not my own experience, nor that of others whom I have known. How well I remember the aged poet Sophocles, when in answer to the question, How does love suit with age, Sophocles—are you still the man you were? Peace he replies; most gladly have I escaped from a mad and furious master. His words have often occurred to my mind since, and they seem as good to me now as at the time when he uttered them. For certainly old age has a great sense of calm and freedom; when the passions relax their hold, then, as Sophocles says, we are freed from the grasp not of one mad master only, but of many. The truth is, Socrates, that these regrets, and also the complaints about relations, are to be attributed to the same cause, which is not old age, but men's characters and tempers; for he who is of a calm and happy nature will hardly feel the pressure of age, but to him who is of an opposite disposition youth and age are equally a burden."[32]

A few substitutions of terms, for example, traits, values, and attitudes for "character and tempers," and the passage has a decidedly modern ring. The essence of the passage, *viz.*, that it is not old age itself that is the cause of maladjustment, but the meaning assigned to old age by the particular cultural context and by the individual's subjective evaluation, is the point we wish to emphasize here.

A case in point is found in the reaction of women to menopause, as was noted in Chapter 15. There is nothing about this biological change which leads directly to neurosis or psychosis, but the fact that a depression termed *involutional melancholia* is sometimes an accompaniment

[32] Plato, *The Republic*, Book I.

of this "change of life" has given rise to such a belief. The neurosis or
psychosis that come at this time is a reaction to the menopause as a
signal to the individual that something very important to the continued
recognition and security of the person is slipping away.[33] Women in our
culture depend upon their physical attractiveness, their care of the
children, their fertility, and their roles as sex partners in marriage, for
satisfaction of their sociopsychological needs. The menopause acts as a
precipitant of neurosis or psychosis because some women incorrectly
interpret it as signaling the end of their sex life, a warning of approaching old age, and because it often occurs at the time when their statuses
as housewives and mothers are being altered by the fact that the children
are growing up, leaving the parental home, and setting up homes of
their own.

Betty Friedan, in *The Feminine Mystique*,[34] argues for the rejection
of an image of American women which image would limit their position
to that of housewife and mother. The role expectations of the feminine
mystique are such that a woman's "fulfillment" is accomplished and over
when her children have grown up and moved away from the home.

After years of having played the role of confidante, mother, and
counselor to her children, she now finds herself no longer needed. What
then? Unless substitute activities are found, maladjustment is apt to
result. This is not because the person is growing old, but because of
the altered social relationships and the need to play different roles.
Some means will be made to secure the recognition and attention lost
by the children's leaving home. Intellectual awareness of the physical
changes accompanying old age, and acceptance of these limiting factors,
can do much to adjust role to status. The following brief case illustrates
this:

> Miss S, over eighty years of age, lived with her spinster sister who was
> some seven years her junior, in the home in which they had grown up.
> For twenty-five years Miss S taught botany in a small mid-west college,
> and had retired at the age of seventy. When she returned to the home
> town to take up residence with her sister, she renewed many old ac-
> quaintances of earlier years, entered into church and other group activi-
> ties, and took an active interest in the young couples who rented the
> upstairs apartment of the old home. She was acutely aware of her
> advanced years, often joking about how "stupid" she was becoming,
> but was careful to restrict her activities in terms of her physical and
> mental abilities. As time went on she noted that she was no longer able

[33] *See* Norman Cameron, *The Psychology of Behavior Disorders* (Boston: Houghton Mifflin, 1947), pp. 521–522; and also by the same author, "The Neurosis of
Later Maturity," in Oscar Kaplan, (ed.) *Mental Disorders in Later Life*, 2nd ed.
(Stanford, Calif.: Stanford University Press, 1956). The latter is much more detailed
in its treatment of neuroses attending old age.

[34] Betty Friedan, *The Feminine Mystique* (New York: W. W. Norton, 1963).

to serve capably as secretary of a small social group because of her failing memory. Rather than becoming resentful at herself or the situation, she accepted this as inevitable, and resigned from the position. She continued to attend the meetings and to participate to the extent of her abilities. Her knowledge of the nature of her limitations and the rational reaction to them permitted her to adjust easily, if not without some regret, to the situations in which she found herself. The social approval she received for this explicit awareness of her limitations probably was satisfying.

The more clearly the status of the aged is defined by the culture, the easier it is for the aged person to play the appropriate roles.[35] People age most successfully when they are able to fit into the social structure of their own culture in ways which will insure prolonged influence and security. One of the difficulties attending the adjustment to old age in our culture is the lack of any clearly defined positions for old age.

Simmons has pointed out that stable societies provide a structured framework of participation for the aged.[36] In such mature societies, positions and roles are clearly defined in terms of age grades. When the age grade pattern stays fixed over many generations, the aging have a lifetime in which to fit in and entrench themselves.

> The general principle seems to be: In the long and steady strides of the social order, the aging get themselves fixed and favored in positions, power and performance. They have what we call seniority rights. But when social conditions become unstable and the rate of change reaches a galloping pace, the aged are riding for an early fall and the more youthful associates take their seats in the saddles.[37]

In our change from an agricultural to an industrial economy, the former status of the aged has been dropped but nothing has taken its place. No institutional (customary) provisions for relationships between children and elderly parents have been established. The trial-and-error efforts of the welfare agencies, both public and private, are attempts to find some solution to the question in terms of subsistence. There remains the question of the noneconomic status of the old persons. The picture is still fuzzy, and as long as it remains so, the old persons of our country will have difficulty in adjusting to their old-age status.

Adjustment in old age is possible to the extent that the younger persons have knowledge of the positions which will be theirs later, and learn to anticipate life in those societal positions. If a person can look forward to the things that the given age levels expect of him, and can visualize

---

[35] *See* Leonard S. Cottrell, Jr., "The Adjustment of the Individual to His Age and Sex Roles," *American Sociological Review*, VII (Oct. 1942), p. 619.

[36] Leo W. Simmons, "Aging in Modern Society," in *Toward Better Understanding of the Aged* (New York: Council on Social Work Education, 1958), p. 7.

[37] Simmons, "Aging in Modern Society," p. 7.

himself in those positions, playing the appropriate roles, he is less apt to become maladjusted to the new positions when he must assume them. He does not then come upon the necessity of playing a given role with no preparation for it because "resignation gently sloped the way."

Adjustment in old age is facilitated by the opportunity of the old people to have their own primary groups made up of their peers. There are numerable instances where elderly persons have resisted entering a home for old people, only to discover afterward that they are happier there than they have been for years. The reason seems to be the opportunity to live with their peers as far as age is concerned. Common problems, common memories, and the assurance that they are not to be rejected merely because they are old are positive virtues of such peer groups.

A full life in earlier years is conducive to satisfaction in old age. An old person full of memories of innumerable and various experiences is more apt to find adjustment in old age, other things being equal, than those of limited experiences. If a person can find something familiar in almost every book he picks up, in many a chance remark of his associates, in the things he hears over the radio, the more meaningful life will be for him and the less is his chance of being bored and unhappy. The rereading of books is often a pleasant reliving of earlier experiences. The story is told that a friend of the late Oliver Wendell Holmes found him, during the Chief Justice's last illness, reading from the writings of the Greek historian, Thucydides. When the visitor expressed some mild surprise at the book selected, Holmes replied that *everyone* ought to reread Thucydides when he reaches ninety! Too, reminiscences of significant, emotionally identified experiences of years gone by with friends or associates can give much pleasure to the old. The more complete the earlier experiences, the more there is to draw upon for such purposes; a poverty of experiences in adolescence and adulthood prepares the way for a hollow old age. In their study, *The Psychology of Radio*, Professors Hadley Cantril and G. W. Allport found that the older adults preferred the old song favorites to the currently popular tunes. The more songs they knew and the more varied the associated experiences, the greater the pleasure upon rehearing them. Frequently one hears old persons express regrets that they had not taken time to attend a certain exhibition or fair, had not seen Babe Ruth play, Sara Bernhardt on stage, nor heard Caruso sing, even though such opportunities had been theirs. A realistic view of retirement as something which emerges as a result of and a continuation of a complete and alert life is contained in the following quotation:

. . . the letters from our annuitants, most of them, reveal that joy long deferred is a diminished joy. Joy must be *practiced*. The capacity for excitement must be exercised, or when the time comes for you to summon it up it won't be there. Yes, our annuitant travelers, like most old people, appear to enjoy scenery very much. They enjoy renewing the acquaintances of old associates who have settled in far-off places. But apart from the scenery and these occasional "cutting up old touches with the Bill Smiths" and "we spent a pleasant day and night reminiscing with the Eliot Wheelocks," our correspondents seem hardly aware that they are away from home. The impact of new people, architecture, and the living history of a strange land that so often rocks and moves and excites a younger visitor simply cannot excite an old traveler in the same way unless he has kept alive and open for adventure during all his young years.[38]

There are wide variations from person to person in the number of names and events which would be familiar in the reading say of a book such as Frederick Lewis Allen's *Only Yesterday*, a rapid-fire description of the colorful highlights of the 1920's. All of us can read it as history, but for those who participated in the news-crammed decade between the end of World War I and the early years of the depression, the book has additional emotional meaning. The prestige accorded the persons who have traveled extensively in other times and other lands is of no small consequence for a person who no longer can create significant experiences, but must draw upon the past for his satisfactions. The consciousness of this need in later life affords the younger persons chances to purposively store up these things of which memories are made.

Religion and Old Age

Argyle's studies have shown that religious concern is most evident in the years of adolescence and again in old age. The years thirty to thirty-five are described as the time of least religious activity.[39] The heightened interest in religion in adolescence differs from the religious interests of people in the latter half of life:

> In adolescence there is a great intellectual perplexity and doubt coupled with emotional turmoil: young people suddenly change their whole orientation one way or the other. In old age, when both intellect and emotions are dimmed, there is no worry about the niceties of theology, nor is there any emotional excitement about religious matters; old people increasingly take part in religious practices which have long been habitual, and in belief are primarily concerned with the central facts of God and the after-life.[40]

[38] *Life in the Crystal Palace*, p. 183.
[39] Michael Argyle, *Religious Behavior* (Glencoe, Ill.: The Free Press of Glencoe, 1959), p. 69.
[40] Argyle, *Religious Behavior*, p. 66.

Adolescence is less a time of heightened religious activity than a time of religious questioning, decision and commitment. Belief in specific religious dogmas declines with age and belief in deity and immortality increases. One study reports that 71 per cent of the males and 83 per cent of the females in the sixty to sixty-four age group were certain of an afterlife, but that this percentage for both groups increased to 100 per cent for the persons over ninety.[41]

As we noted earlier, the adolescent is seeking self-identity in his relationships with the social world. The aging person, on the other hand, is endeavoring to retain and preserve his identity. If a person's self esteem is a function of his social relationships, then old age, (which by its very nature means a loss of friends and members of the significant other through infirmity or death), means increasing social isolation and separateness. It is not surprising that in this sense of increasing isolation, an aging person may endeavor by various means to strengthen his ties to shared values in this world or in one projected into the future.

Aged people face the reality of impending death which in the end will overwhelm them. The subject of death is often avoided, postponed, or suppressed in our culture. We will talk around the subject but seldom do we come to terms with its meaning for us. Within our frame of reference it is likely that it is less the destruction of the life processes which is so threatening as it is the end of the self which is feared. The survival of the self is the real objective in life or death. Each person, whether young or old, will face the reality of death with whatever personal resources he brings to this final act of life. Some will be satisfied with immortality of self in their children and in their deeds; others will find it in the lives of people with whom they have lived significant relationships. Still others will regard death as a part of the life process, but not necessarily as final isolation from their affective other.[42]

SUMMARY

Except in extreme form, when the person reaches the "sans everything" stage, biological age is only one of several factors determining socio-psychological old age. In fact, in many instances there are greater dif-

[41] Cavan, et al., Personal Adjustment in Old Age, p. 67.

[42] In this connection we are using affective other as Pfuetze employs generalized other to describe the psychological equivalent of the historical concept of God. "Since the 'generalized other' is the symbol which stands for Society, for Humanity, for the Whole Community, and since Mead had his roots deep in the soil of humanism and positivism, and since he conceived of religion as the extension of social attitudes and relations to the universe at large, one may fairly raise the question as to why he did not see or why he was unwilling to grant the use of the Generalized Other as a religious equivalent for God." Paul E. Pfuetze, Self, Society, Existence (New York: Harper Torchbooks, 1961), p. 86. As noted in Chapter 8, G. H. Mead failed to use "generalized other" consistently. Pfuetze uses one of the meanings here.

ferences induced by factors other than age. The variations in physical fitness among persons of the same age are remarkable. More important than the physical old age itself is the person's reaction to it. The cultural setting for the aged person must be taken into consideration if any attempt to understand the personality of old people is made. Our culture is one in which there are few institutional provisions for a definite old age status, and one in which the active adult dominates the scene. The dominant values are those of the adult in the prime of life, as revealed by the tendency of our urban-industrial economy to employ younger men, and to hesitate to hire them if they have attained the age of, most usually forty-five. Our fiction and advertisements reveal the youth-and-adult orientation of the culture. There is considerable confusion and ambivalence in the treatment of the old, with attending confusion in the makeup of old persons' personalities. The increasing proportion of the aged in the population structure may alter this picture in time.

There is no such thing as an old-age personality as such. The attitudes and traits of the old person are usually but a continuation and intensification of those attitudes and traits already present in the personality during the years previous to old age. Greater variations occur between sexes, occupational groups, and educational levels. Adjustment in old age is dependent upon the compatibility of social positions occupied by the aged, and the roles played by the aged. This compatibility rests upon: (1) the degree to which the positions are clearly defined; (2) the extent to which the younger persons have knowledge of the forthcoming positions and learn to anticipate playing the appropriate roles; (3) and also upon the extent to which the person is able to live a full life in his earlier years, and in so doing "pile up" experiences which make for full memories; and finally (4) upon his access to a primary group made up of his peers. Given such conditions, old age may attain that degree of adjustment and contentment suggested by Oliver Goldsmith's words in "The Deserted Village":

> O blest retirement! friend of life's decline,
> Retreats from care, that never must be mine,
> How blest is he who crowns in shades like these
> A youth of labor with an age of ease;
> Who quits a world where strong temptations try
> And, since 'tis hard to combat, learns to fly! . . .
> But on he moves to meet his latter end,
> Angels around befriending virtue's friend;
> Sinks to the grave with unperceived decay,
> While resignation gently slopes the way;
> And, all his prospects brightening to the last,
> His heaven commences ere the world be passed.

SUGGESTED READINGS

NEUGARTEN, BERNICE L. *Personality in Middle and Late Life* (New York: Atherton Press, 1964).

The Older American. The President's Council on Aging, 1963, U.S. Government Printing Office, Washington, D.C.

SHOCK, NATHAN W. (Ed.). *Biological Aspects of Aging* (New York: Columbia University Press, 1962).

TEBBETTS, CLARK and WILMA DONAHUE (Eds.). *Aging in Today's Society* (Englewood Cliffs, N.J.: Prentice-Hall, 1960).

Toward Better Understanding of the Aging. Council on Social Work Education, New York, 1958).

Understanding the Older Client. The Family Service Association of America, New York, 1951–55.

PART VI

APPENDIX

And you would say the same of the conception of the good? Until the person is able to abstract and define rationally the idea of the good, and unless he can run the gauntlet of all objections, and is ready to disprove them, not by appeals to opinion, but to absolute truth, never faltering at any step of the argument—unless he can do all this, you would say that he knows neither the idea of good nor any other good; he apprehends only a shadow, if anything at all, which is given by opinion and not by sciences; —dreaming and slumbering in this life, before he is well awake here, he arrives at the world below. and has his final quietus.

—Plato

SOCIAL PSYCHOLOGY
AND AXIOLOGY

The mores can make anything right.

—*William Graham Sumner*

That what is Law, is, in different countries, widely different; while that which *ought to be*, is in all countries to a great degree the same.

—*Jeremy Bentham*

. . . All ethical statements [are] necessarily ethnocentric—relative to some culture.

—*George Lundberg*

But the questions of human values are inescapable, and those who banish them at the front door admit them unavowedly and therefore uncritically at the back door.

—*Morris Raphael Cohen*

The above quotations—some old and some relatively new—are but four of many which could have been selected to indicate the marked divergence of opinions concerning the relationship between science (knowledge) on the one hand and ethical judgments on the other. Quite clearly the problem is a perplexing one, but one that we believe to be worthy of consideration by serious students of social behavior. There is a term—not commonly used today—that denotes this problem area. *Axiology* is defined as "the theory or study of values, primarily of intrinsic values . . . but also of instrumental values . . . particularly with reference to the manner in which they can be known or experienced, their nature and kinds, and their ontological status."[1] It is our purpose in this brief Appendix to pursue the problem of the relationship between axiology and the concepts and facts of social psychology as they have been presented in the preceding chapters. The core of the controversies over the nature of the science-axiology relationship is found in the assertion of the one group that human values are discoveries, and the equally confident assertion of the other group that human values are inventions. The former believe that human values are universal relationships that are sought, consciously or unconsciously, by all human beings; the latter argue with conviction that human values are creations of this or that society, group, or individual. The readers of these lines

[1] *Webster's Third New International Dictionary, 1965.*

will be, of course, divided on this social science-axiology issue. Some will perceive as incredible the view that one cannot know what is right and wrong, moral and immoral, whereas others will find it no less difficult to accept the idea that one's ethical standards are functions of his knowledge. The one insists that monogamy is good, that justice must (or must not) be extended without regard for sex or race, that segregation of races is good (or bad), and so forth. The other judges such views to be merely the products of one's having lived in a given cultural environment and of having become habituated to certain items which he values highly. The latter group would subscribe to Sumner's famous dictum that "The mores can make anything right.", which is the view held by the majority of American social scientists, at least as the latters' views are revealed in print. It is their view that, on matters of value, the social scientist is no better prepared to make ethical or moral judgments than are the laymen; regardless of the quality or quantity of knowledge acquired, it can never become an objective basis from which to derive ethical or moral judgments. Following are two statements that express this position, the first by a political scientist and the second by a sociologist.

> The difficulty lies in the fact that value judgments cannot be derived logically from factual data, but must be justified by some other means; they are not either true or false in the empirical verifiable sense.[2]

In like vein is the second statement:

> As a science, sociology is necessarily silent about questions of value; it cannot decide the direction in which society ought to go and it makes no recommendations on matters of social policy. . . . sociology cannot itself deal with problems of good and evil, right or wrong, better or worse, or any others that concern human values. . . . There is no sociological warrant, nor indeed any other kind of scientific warrant, for preference in values.[3]

Although, as the following paragraphs would seem to evidence, there is a trend away from the value-neutral position, at least one sociologist perceives the persistence of an opposite trend. He writes that:

> The dominant drift in American sociology is toward professionalism, the growth of technical specialists, toward the diffusion of the value-free

---

[2] R. Bierstedt, E. J. Meehan, and P. A. Samuelson (New York: McGraw-Hill, 1964), p. 212.

[3] *Ibid.*, pp. 9–10. See Bierstedt's earlier elaboration of the value-neutral position in "Social Science and Social Policy," *Bulletin of American Association of University Professors*.

outlook to the point where it becomes less of an intellectual doctrine and more of a blanketing mood.[4]

Another group, although of the persuasion that value judgments are not outside of science's province, is represented by the opinion that:

> . . . the important thing to bear in mind is that the social scientist, as far as moral values are concerned, is a layman and an amateur, in no position to tell even the meanest of his brother citizens in a democracy what *ought* to be done—if by "ought" we imply the choice of a goal rather than a means toward it.[5]

Thus the former group argues that the social scientist cannot, *despite his acquisition of knowledge,* make objective value judgments. The latter argue that the social scientist cannot make objective value judgments *because of his lack of knowledge* about human nature. However the science-values issue has not been resolved by the prevalence and persistence of these protests in favor of the value-neutral position or of the "we are not yet ready" view of the social scientists role in judging what is right or wrong. The literature in professional journals reflects a continuing probing into the problem.

The authors of some recently published articles represent another group of social scientists who are persuaded that the arguments, noted above, for the scientists' reluctance or refusal to judge values are both untenable. They argue that social scientists *do* have knowledge which better equips them (vis-a-vis the layman) to make judgments, that they *ought* to make value judgments on the basis of knowledge, and that they *will, inescapably,* make such judgments. One cannot objectively estimate the proportion of social scientists who do not subscribe to the value-free or value-neutral idea, but the number appears to be growing, if at something less than a mad pace. Representative of this group is a sociologist who holds that human values have *ontic,* or objective, status. ". . . that somehow in the structure of the universe values objectively exist independently of their apprehension and espousal by man. Thus if it is objectively wrong to commit murder it is wrong even though no man knows it and no man espouses it." [6] In short, the group of sociologists represented by this statement believe there is a distinction to be made between subjective values and universal, human values, the former

---

[4] A. Gouldner, "Anti-Minotaur: the Myth of a Value-Free Sociology," in *Sociology on Trial,* M. Stein and A. Vidich, eds. (Englewood Cliffs, N.J.: Prentice-Hall, 1963), p. 44. Indicative of an incipient trend away from the value-free position is Gouldner's departure from a previously strongly supported value-free position.

[5] R. B. Cattell, "Ethics and the Social Sciences," *American Psychologist,* 3 (June 1948), pp. 194–195.

[6] W. Kolb, "Values, Positivism, and the Functional Theory of Religion; the Growth of a Dilemma," *Social Forces,* 31 (May 1953), p. 306, footnote 4.

being products of invention whereas the latter exist to be discovered. Sociologist Claude C. Bowman, although affirming the fact that the detachment which resulted from the value-neutral approach served to support scholarly research in "unsympathetic environments," the need for this is now past and sociology lags in that it does not actively engage in shaping culture.[7]

Evidence of the fact that social scientists in general, and sociologists in particular, have not been loath to act upon their values is seen in the layman's oft-spoken opinion, borne out by facts, that social scientists are often sharply critical of the current cultural values.[8] The opposition of both extreme leftists and rightists suggests that the connection between values and social science may not be as tenuous as many social scientists assume or wish it to be. The works of the late C. Wright Mills (1916–1962) reveal a willingness on his part to support values as functions of his sociological knowledge.[9]

THE PSYCHOLOGISTS AND VALUES

On the other side of the mountain, a larger number of psychologists than sociologists appear to have concerned themselves with the problems involving the relationship between values and science or knowledge. They appear to have paralleled the sociologists in the range of their views on values, but seemingly fewer of them have believed or felt it necessary to protest as strongly the mixing of values and science.

In a study of value orientations among psychologists, one writer examined four categories of criteria for values: [10] (1) Naturalism, under which the physiological processes of the body which are functional to biological survival are the sole bases; (2) Culturalism, in which one's own culture is the measure of things. (3) Humanism, wherein certain native characteristics of man are chosen as criteria, and, (4) Theism, in which man's redemption is sought in following a personal God's directives. Each of these categories he finds wanting, and concludes that ". . . differences in value orientation cannot be resolved, each

[7] "Is Sociology Too Detached?" *American Sociological Review*, 21 (Oct. 1956), p. 565. *See also* his article "Must the Social Sciences Foster Moral Skepticism?" *loc. cit.*, 10, pp. 709–715 and J. Schneider's critical comment on same; *loc. cit.*, 11, pp. 637–639.

[8] *Cf.* R. W. Leeper, "An Analysis of Action on Science Legislation in the Last Congress," *American Psychologists*, 2 (1947), pp. 127–136.

[9] *See* his *White Collar* (New York: Oxford University Press, 1951); *Power Elite* (New York: Oxford University Press, 1956); *Sociological Imagination* (New York: Grove Press, 1959).

[10] C. M. Lowe, "Value Orientations," *American Psychologist*, II (June 1956), pp. 688–690. Under this heading of "Naturalism" he places B. F. Skinner as his views were revealed in *Walden Two*. *Cf.* J. W. Krutch's critique of this in *The Measure of Man* (New York: Boobs-Merrill, 1954).

orientation having adherents whose beliefs should be respected. . . . We further suggest that psychologists . . . turn these [their] biases to fullest advantage by being of professional assistance to the special interest groups with which their values coincide." [11] Neither the ontic nor the subjective nature of these biases is apparently of any import, and any interest group—conservative, radical, anti-Semitic, racist, or eleemosynary—may find its professional psychologist to aid its cause. This position parallels that taken by many sociologists who see attention to means as legitimate, but delineation or judgment of goals as out of bounds for the social scientist.

Another psychologist, well known in the field, believes that ethical values lie within the sphere of science, and that ". . . the social sciences have the possibility of ultimately becoming the source of a science of ethics, i.e., of bringing ethical principles on to the same plane of objectivity as predictive principles . . ." [12] However, in his opinion the time when this will come to pass is not near, because of our present ignorance of man's nature.

Another is less modest in his claims for social science, psychology in particular, and holds that:

> Because his education, training, and experience are related to so many of the community's needs, the psychologist is not only more aware of these needs, than the average layman, but also may be familiar with the probable ways of meeting these needs.
>
> Our [psychologists in public service] job is not *only* to give service, but to improve the society we live in. [13]

However, whether or not the psychologist is poorly or well equipped with knowledge about human values, he must act, and his actions will, whether he wishes it or not, reflect some, if not all, of his values.

> But the psychologist cannot help making choices, as scientist, teacher, therapist, or human engineer. The choices may be witting or unwitting, responsible or irresponsible, but they are made, and they entail consequences. Acceptance of one's culture as given and beyond reconsideration implies a conservative choice; it can add the psychologist's voice in fact, to the crescendo urging total conformity, a trend which in the long run maybe not at all conservative of our traditional values. And the claim to a value-free science, when it goes beyond insistence on a disciplined regard for fact whether or not it accords with our wishes, only obscures the value elements in the choice of problem, of research set-

[11] *Ibid.*, p. 692.
[12] Cattell, *op. cit.*, p. 196.
[13] L. S. Rogers, *American Psychologist*, 11 (June 1956), p. 312–313.

ting, of conceptual framework, in the decision as to when to rest with negative findings, when results are reportable, and so on endlessly.[14]

Even more than the psychologist-as-researcher is the psychologist-as-counselor involved, often inadvertently, with values—his own, those of his clients, and those of the latters' affective others. Regarding the problem of the counselor's relation to values and his responsibility to clients, one person's views are these:

> We can approach the problem of social responsibility by asking three basic questions:
>
> 1. Is human behavior controllable? Overwhelming experimental evidence in fields of motivation, conditioning, and personality development indicates that this is true.
>
> 2. If so, is it desirable or wise for psychologists to continue research in these fields? Psychologists have no choice but to continue their research. The findings can be used just as meaningfully to help man as to hinder him. Further, methods of counter control can be developed. The danger is *not* in the research findings but in their potential misuse.
>
> 3. What safeguards can be incorporated into this type of research? The answer to this is the crux of the psychologist's dilemma. First, a code of ethics such as that of the A.P.A. is a good first step, but certainly not enough. An ethical code merely says that the psychologist will not deliberately misuse his findings. It does not go into the more basic question of the psychologist or behavior controller's value system. If we see him as one who is in a position to change or modify other's behavior, this implies a value decision as to what is "good behavior," what is "mental health," and what is desirable adjustment. To deny control is to do a disservice and, in effect, to hide one's head in the sand like the proverbial ostrich. The fact that the behavior controllers are professional individuals is no guarantee that behavior control will not be misused. We have only to turn to the role of German physicians in medical atrocities as evidence of misuse by a supposedly professional group.[15]

Other counselors pursue these questions, asking:

> Whom or what should a profession serve? The nation? Its own economic interests? The public? The will of God? Humanity? Creative evolution? Or what? . . . It is often argued that pure science is ethically neutral, or even that ethical statements simply cannot be meaningfully made in

[14] M. Brewster Smith, *American Psychologist*, 9 (Sept. 1954), p. 575. It may be the problem of values which has led to one psychologist's remark that: "Indeed, it often seems that the correlation between goodness of design and importance of project is remarkably high, and negative." Ann Roe, "Man's Forgotten Weapon," *American Psychologist*, 14 (June 1959), p. 262.

[15] L. Krasner, "Behavior Control and Social Responsibility," *American Psychologist*, 17 (April 1962), p. 202. *Cf.* A. Mitscherlich and F. Mielke, *Doctors of Infancy* (New York: Henry Schuman, 1949).

the language of science. If this is true, must a profession look elsewhere for moral sanctions? If, on the other hand, it is false and all science has ethical presuppositional, how may these be discovered?[16]

Do we counselors believe that in counseling "anything goes" or that any kind of development behavior is as good as any other? Do we believe that the fullest growth of one individual inevitably enhances the fullest growth of all other individuals? Are there no relevant and valid standards of growth in individuality? Must any individual choose between the bipolar opposite of absolute autonomy of an individual and object and supine conformity of the individual to someone's (or society's) imposed standard of development—are there no other options to choose in developing one's life?[17]

In the opinion of this author:

It seems clear to me that we cannot and indeed should not attempt to eliminate some consideration of values from the counseling situation.[18]

Some specific evidence that the counselor's values do matter is reported in a study which concluded that:

Patients who improved tended to revise certain of their moral values in the direction of their therapists; while the moral values of patients who were unimproved tended to become less like their therapists.[19]

To the extent that therapists' and teachers' values do count, it becomes more important to take such values into account explicitly and to attempt some judgment of them.[20]

With regard to this problem of values, it appears reasonable that:

What is needed most crucially now is an attempt to think things through on a level which might be called philosophical, and perhaps

[16] R. F. Creegan, "Concerning Professional Ethics," *American Psychologist*, 13 (June 1958), p. 27.

[17] E. G. Williamson, "Value Orientation in Counseling," *Personnel and Guidance Journal*, 36 (April 1958), p. 523. The "Standards of Ethical Behavior for Psychologists," *American Psychologists*, 13 (June 1958) do not help answer these questions. The admonition to show ". . . sensible regard for the social codes and moral expectations of the community in which he works, . . ." is but another version of "When in Rome, do as the Romans do," and "The mores can make anything right." p. 268.

[18] Williamson, *op. cit.*, p. 525. Charlotte Bühler also makes this point in her book *Values in Psychotherapy* (New York: The Free Press of Glencoe, 1962).

[19] D. Rosenthal, "Changes in Some Moral Values Following Psychotherapy," *Journal of Consulting Psychology*, 19 (Dec. 1955), p. 435.

[20] It is of interest to note that Professor Cattell, despite his pessimism ab[...] social scientists ability to make value judgments, recommended that "It sh[...] first task of responsible social scientists to weigh the characters as well [...] tual capability of those who become professional social scientists." [...]

there might follow from this some attempts to strengthen both the
in-service work and the more strictly academic courses.[21]

A sociologists' observations implicitly support the above psychologists' plea for a direct confrontation of the science-values problem. His
apprehensive evaluation of the current status of the conception of a
value-free social science is stated thusly:

> I fear that there are many sociologists today who in conceiving social
> science to be value-free, mean widely different things, that many hold
> these beliefs dogmatically without having examined seriously the
> grounds upon which they are credible, and that some few affirm a
> value-free sociology ritualistically without having any clear idea what
> it might mean.[22]

A LOOK AT THE VALUE-NEUTRAL IDEA

If it is true that the idea of a value-free social science is poorly
understood, as the sociologist quoted above argues, then, indeed, it is
worth one's while to look at the problem philosophically, as suggested by
the psychologist. We have seen expressions, in the preceding paragraphs,
of some of the problems and implications of the attempts to hold to the
value-neutral position. With full awareness of the incompleteness of the
examination, it is our intention to look at the problem through the
framework of the interactionist concepts developed in the preceding chapters. That it is in large part speculative and deductive is freely
acknowledged, but one is reminded that much of science—biological,
physical, and socio-cultural—is of necessity also speculative and deductive. The problem which we have set for ourselves is distinguishable
from those which appear to be more empirical in nature by its complexity, and not by the applicability of methods or techniques of
research. The adequacy of the concepts or facts which can be mustered

---

[21] Creegan, *op. cit.*, p. 272.

[22] A. Gouldner, *op. cit.*, p. 37. This article attempts to explain the cultural conditions which gave rise to the German sociologist Max Weber's (1864–1920) plea for
separation of science and moral judgments, which Gouldner claims was not as stringent as is uncritically assumed by many American sociologists. This point has, of
course, been made by others. W. L. Kolb credits philosophical positivism, rather than
cultural relativism, with having induced ". . . most theoretically sophisticated sociologists to accept the view that value-judgments have no basis of validity in reality and
are simply expressions of personal and group preference. Positivism transforms
Weber's humility before values into one of arrogance." "Values, Positivism, and the
Functional Theory of Religion; the Growth of a Dilemma." *Social Forces*, 31 (May
1953), p. 306. A more extensive treatment of the nature of Weber's ideas of science
and values, and their misinterpretations, is Howard Becker's, "Supreme Values and
the Sociologist, or, Our Roles and Their Loyalties," being pp. 281–305 in his *Through
Values to Social Interpretation* (Durham, North Carolina: Duke University Press,
1950).

for the assault on the problem are to be judged in terms of the nature of the problem and not against other and simpler tasks.

Can Social Psychology Be Value-Neutral?

In the discussion which extended through the first seven chapters of this text, attention to man's cognitive and affective nature was persistent and necessary. The fact that man's motivational characteristics were emotional in nature was spelled out in detail. It was emphasized that although in human behavior or action the functioning of the cognitive and emotional processes cannot be separated, understanding of behavior demands that they be distinguished conceptually. The objects of attitudes are values, and insofar as one holds attitudes toward objects, he also possesses values. Whether these attitudes are attached to illusory, subjective, and purely phenomenal objects or to real, ontic, or objective values is, for the moment, irrelevant. The pertinent fact at this time is that man's every action, however simple or complex, is manifest evidence of the existence of his value system, variously defined by combinations of biogenic and sociogenic motivations as these operate within his behavioral environment. One of man's values may be that of attempting to perceive the world objectively, undistorted by personal-subjective concepts and attitudes. This is but another way of defining the scientific orientation, but it is a value nevertheless. The problem with which one is presented when he attempts to study and gain an understanding of human behavior involves selecting which of many values will be operative in his research activity. These values will be, of course, functions of what the individual knows, believes, and feels, and of the human and non-human objects around him. The value-neutral person would be an inert one insofar as behavior is concerned. The closest one can approach such a state is in some form of pathology—mental or otherwise—as in the last, vegetative stages of schizophrenia. The only other conceivable instance of a person being value-neutral lies well within the limbo of absurdity, and would be a human counterpart of Balaam's legendary ass, which, caught exactly midway between two cocks of hay, starved because of his indecision as to which he should eat. Thus the problem is not whether the social psychologist should be value-neutral, but is one of which values should motivate him. When it is viewed in this way, consensus is evident among scientists who, by their commitment to science are thereby committed unequivocally to the value of objectivity, to the goal of perceiving the object world as it is, in its own terms and not as reflections of a subjective perspective. This commitment, logically, rules out solipsism, a point argued in Chapter 6.

However, even though consensus might be gained in these terms, and all agree that no one is or can be value-neutral, the implications for ethical judgments of the commitment to the scientific attitude involve unsolved problems. Could one agree to all that has been written thus far in this Appendix and still hold that science must be silent on questions of value? We now turn to one means of attempting to solve this problem.

MAN AS SCIENTIST AND MAN AS CITIZEN

One should not be led to the conclusion that social scientists do not become involved in ethical or value controversy, because indeed they do, even those who explicitly avow an ethically neutralist position. How is this possible? One answer proposed is that the individual acts in two capacities, in the societal position of scientist and the societal position of citizen. In the one he must eschew any judgments of social values, must avoid being drawn into expressing an opinion, must, as one sociologist has said, take ". . . seriously the famous remark of Jeremy Bentham, that the word 'ought' ought never to be used, except in saying it ought never be used."[23] However, as citizen, it is argued, he may make judgments of value about a variety of things without sacrificing his status as scientist. This line of argument holds that as scientist the anthropologist cannot say that segregation is moral or immoral, good or bad, a value to be supported or attacked, but as citizen the anthropologist may take either side without fear of losing favor in the eyes of his fellow scientists.

The question which one who subscribes to the interactionist frame of reference for social psychology is logically obliged to raise is whether or not such a separation of roles or positions is possible, or at least is probable. What is the probability that the acquired knowledge concerning the nature of man, and of race, is likely to be independent of the attitudes which one forms toward factors of race and the attending relationships in which the racial factors have become significant? Is the person who believes that there are significant differences in the presence or absence of instincts among races, differences in moral capacity and intelligence among races, likely to acquire the same ethical attitudes as the one whose research has led him to doubt such differences? Is the criminologist whose life has been devoted to the study of crime and criminals likely to judge the penal systems of any given country in the same way that an individual who had never given attention to such problems does? What is the probability that the willful destruction of a Rembrandt or Cezanne painting, or a Greek temple, will be valued equally by a highly educated person and an illiterate provincial? Is the attitudinal response to the beating of a wife by her six-foot, two-hundred

---

[23] Robert Bierstedt, "Social Science and Social Policy," *American Association of University Professors Bulletin*, 34 (Summer 1948), 312.

pound spouse likely to be the same among all persons, regardless of their understanding of the nature of human nature? Is the sacrifice of human beings to appease the gods, as was done by the ancient Incas, viewed with the same attitudes by the ignorant and superstitous on the one hand and by the educated and informed on the other? These are the questions with which the reader must concern himself if he is to judge the logic of the "as scientist" and "as citizen" bifurcation. In brief, is it probable that one can occupy the position of scientist, play the role of scientist, and still subscribe to values, (that is, hold attitudes) which do not reflect his position and role?

Values as judgments of the individual and as judgments of the species.

Another approach which might appeal to some readers, an approach which may permit them to resolve the problems raised by axiology, is to conceive of values as being characteristic of the species, and not as subjective, personal-social inventions of the individual or group. If one approaches the axiological questions with this conception of values, it may be that an apparent dilemma can be resolved. With this in mind, we use the remaining lines to speculate about the nature of the *good* and the *bad*, the *moral* and the *immoral*, the *ethical* and the *unethical* in human socio-cultural relationships.

Within this axiological framework, the *given* becomes the nature of man's cognitive, motor, and emotional potentials. One must look to the universal, species-wide characteristics for the criteria in axiology. This is no easy assignment, and immediately it becomes clear that the solution of all axiological problems awaits that time when man has attained a much greater understanding of man's nature—biologically, psychologically, social psychologically, and sociologically. As one philosopher has reminded us, the solution of problems of axiology ". . . presupposes the knowledge of the world in all its aspects."[24] The good life, the truly ethical relationships of man to his environment, is a function of a sound biological heritage, a rich environment, and complex, ordered, and functional subjective attributes at the motor, cognitive, and emotional levels. The values to be discovered, the ontic values, are matters determined by the rational human being who has been afforded the opportunities to learn the nature of objects in his environment, the nature of his own biogenic and sociogenic motivations, the nature of relationships which are essential to the fulfillment of the needs of *the species,* and not merely those of the individual, subjectively perceived. When we are in

[24] Elijah Jordan, *The Good Life* (Chicago: The University of Chicago Press, 1949), p. 13.

possession of surer knowledge about the nature of things, then, and only then, will the criteria for solution of axiological questions be available in a form that will lead to consensus by men of knowledge.

In the meantime, what is the most reasonable path to pursue? Is there any alternative except to rely upon those individuals whose knowledge appears, by all tests available to one, to be the most objectively based? Immediately one perceives the seriousness of the problems which this commitment presents. Who is to say what is the best solution to controversial issues? The first lesson to be learned is that the question is an improper one. The logical (scientific if you will) question is *"How do you know?"*, not *"Who* knows?" Truth or objectivity is never a function of who asserts this or that proposition. The proper question is one which leads to the inquiry into the manner in which the person in question came to his conclusions. If all of the severe restrictions imposed by the simple phrase *scientific method* have been brought to bear upon the problem at hand, have we any alternative to choosing the consequent judgment over the conclusion which was reached on the basis of sheer tradition, local custom, or "intuitive" judgments? The axiology of which we speak is man-centered, admittedly, and thus the criteria must center upon an understanding of man's nature. It is in terms of the nature of the species, of the strivings and will of mankind that objective evaluations must be made. There is no logical alternative. To the extent that we can judge objectively, what values should be preserved and which should be abandoned, are discoveries available only to the man of knowledge. That this approach demands that one return to basic problems of epistemology, to the epistemic problem, is readily recognized. That there *is* a major difference in the things which are valued by the man of knowledge, in contrast to the man of gross ignorance, seems to be undebatable. The extent to which this book has contributed to the reader's knowledge about the nature of man's social psychological being, to that extent he is better prepared to answer axiological questions. The degree to which this knowledge is adequate is a question to be answered by the tests of logic and time. These tests will determine whether or not the hoary axiom *De gustibus non disputandum est* will be abandoned in favor of *mores ex scientia*.

SUGGESTED READINGS

Ayres, C. E. *Toward a Reasonable Society* (Austin: University of Texas Press, 1961).

Becker, Howard. *Through Values to Social Interpretation* (Durham, N.C.: Duke University Press, 1950).

Bierstedt, R. "Social Science and Social Values," *Bulletin of the American Association of University Professors*. XXXIV (Summer 1948).

CATTELL, R. B. "Ethics and the Social Science," *American Psychologist*. 3 (June 1948).

HARTUNG, FRANK. "Cultural Relativity and Moral Judgments," *Philosophy of Science*. 21 (April 1954).

JORDAN, ELIJAH. *The Good Life* (Chicago: University of Chicago Press, 1949).

KOLB, W. L. "Values, Positivism, and the Functional Theory of Religion: The Growth of a Dilemma," *Social Forces*. 31 (May 1953).

MILLS, C. WRIGHT. "The Professional Ideology of Social Pathologists," *American Journal of Sociology*. 49 (1943).

INDEX OF NAMES

INDEX OF SUBJECTS